A Glossary of Archival and Records Terminology

A|**F**|**S**
ARCHIVAL
FUNDAMENTALS
SERIES II

A Glossary of Archival and Records Terminology

RICHARD PEARCE-MOSES

Advisors
MARK GREENE
ROB SPINDLER
DIANE VOGT-O'CONNOR

Editorial Advisor
LAURIE BATY

CHICAGO

The Society of American Archivists
527 S. Wells Street, 5ᵗʰ Floor
Chicago, IL 60607 USA
312/922-0140   Fax 312/347-1452
www.archivists.org

Library of Congress Cataloging-in-Publication Data
Pearce-Moses, Richard.
  A glossary of archival and records terminology / Richard Pearce-Moses.
      p. cm. -- (Archival fundamentals series. II)
  Includes bibliographical references.
  ISBN 1-931666-14-8
  1. Archives--Terminology. 2. Records--Management--Terminology.
  I. Title. II. Series.

CD945.P43 2005
027'.0014--dc22

                                                    2005051613

Graphic design by Matt Dufek, dufekdesign@yahoo.com.
Fonts: Minion (text and footnotes); Meta (secondary text and captions).

A Glossary of Archival and Records Terminology is online at
www.archivists.org/glossary.

TABLE *of* CONTENTS

Preface to the
ARCHIVAL FUNDAMENTALS SERIES II

There was a time when individuals entering the archival profession could read a few texts, peruse some journals, attend a workshop and institute or two, and walk away with a sense that they grasped the field's knowledge and discipline. This was an inadequate perception, of course, but it was true that the publications—basic or advanced, practical or theoretical—were modest in number.

The archival world has changed considerably since these more quiet times. A rich monographic research literature is developing. Scholars from far outside the field are examining the "archive" and the "record." Archives, archivists, records, and records managers are in the daily news as cases appear testing government and corporate accountability, organizational and societal memory, and the nature of documentary evidence—all challenging basic archival work and knowledge.

The new edition of the Archival Fundamentals Series (AFS II) is intended to provide the basic foundation for modern archival practice and theory. The original preface (written by Mary Jo Pugh in her capacity as the series editor) to the first editions, which were published in the early to mid-1990s by the Society of American Archivists (SAA), argued that the seven volumes "have been conceived and written to be a foundation for modern archival theory and practice" and aimed at "archivists, general practitioners and specialists alike, who are per-forming a wide range of archival duties in all types of archival and manuscript repositories." It is hard to state the purpose of the new AFS editions better.

There are some differences, both subtle and obvious, in the new volumes. The new editions are more open-ended than earlier versions, extending back to the Basic Manual Series published a quarter-of-a-century ago by SAA, reflecting evolving viewpoints about archival theory and practice. Even more important a difference is the broader and deeper context of archival publishing AFS volumes reside in. Mary Jo Pugh, in her introduction of just a decade ago, noted that the AFS titles are companions to "more specialized manuals also available from SAA." Now, SAA has four other series (some just underway), including Archival Classics (featuring reprints or new collections of older publications with pivotal importance to the profession), Archival Readers (both collections of new and previously published essays intended to supplement the descriptions of foundational theory and practice of the AFS II volumes), International Archival Studies Readers (both collections of new and previously published essays intended to provide glimpses of archival work and knowledge outside of North America), and Archival Cases and Case Studies (examining archival work in a variety of institutional types and with a variety of media). Added to SAA's own publications is a vast sea of new titles pouring from the presses of other professional associations and trade, professional, and university publishers.

Both the earlier Basic Manual Series and the Archival Fundamentals Series provide benchmarks in the development of archival knowledge and work. One can trace changing ideas and practices about archival reference services by reading the 1977, 1992, and 2004 volumes dedicated to this subject in the respective SAA manual series. One also expects to find in this volume current standards and consensus about this aspect of archival work. One also expects now, of course, that some may disagree with aspects of the current presentation, and may point to the growing research and case study literature being generated by the archival profession.

Many people participated in the production of the various volumes constituting the Archival Fundamentals Series II. The profession owes its gratitude not only to the authors, but to various chairs and members of the SAA Publications Board; Miriam Meislik, Photo

Editor for the series; the SAA Executive Directors, Susan Fox and Nancy P. Beaumont; and especially to Teresa Brinati, SAA Director of Publishing, whose good humor, organization, and steady commitment to a quality product helped keep the publishing of these and other SAA volumes on track.

RICHARD J. COX
Publications Editor
Society of American Archivists

Acknowledgments

Made Possible With Support From

Arizona State Library, Archives and Public Records

National Historical Publications and Records Administration
Archival Research Fellowship Program
administered by the Massachusetts Historical Society

Mark Greene of the American Heritage Center at the University of Wyoming, Diane Vogt-O'Connor of the National Archives and Records Administration, and Rob Spindler of Arizona State University served as advisors, guided decisions about the work in general, and reviewed definitions. Over the years and during this project they taught me as much about what it means to be a professional as anything else. I am humbled by their knowledge, generosity, support, and friendship.

Laurie Baty served as a masterful editorial advisor. Her careful reading of the manuscript caught many problems that crept in between A and Z, including clarifying definitions, fixing awkward language, and catching typos. Mark Longley once again proved his skill as a careful, thoughtful, and patient editor. His knowledge of technical writing has made the language of the glossary much cleaner.

Diane Vogt-O'Connor was supported in her review of the definitions by Lew Bellardo, who co-authored the second edition, and by several others at the National Archives and Records Administration. I am grateful for the many comments during the review process sent by Leon Miller, Geoffrey Huth, Ken Thibodeau, Barry Cahill, John Gervais, Ala Rekrut, and Rebecca Remington.

I am grateful to the National Historical Publications and Records Commission, the staff of the Massachusetts Historical Society, and to those others involved in the archival research fellowships for the opportunity to spend some time thinking about the language of archives.

I would also like to give special thanks to two individuals for their support of this work. GladysAnn Wells, Director of the Arizona State Library and Archives, made it possible for me to undertake this project and provided additional support. She has been a mentor and helped me be a better professional. My partner, Frank Loulan, has been patient, encouraging, and his general, wonderful self when I have been more than a little consumed in words. He has helped make me a better person.

The Archival Lexicon

Words are, of course, the most powerful drug used by mankind.
    —Rudyard Kipling

Jargon—the specific use of certain terms—defines and distinguishes a profession. As the Bellardos noted in their preface to their 1992 glossary, "terminology serves to mark the current limits of professional concerns and responsibilities."[1] Since the publication of the Bellardos' glossary, the archival profession has experienced profound changes that warrant a reassessment of those limits.

Over the last ten years, academics and practitioners refined and rearticulated core archival concepts. Writings about appraisal introduced many new terms, including macro appraisal, functional analysis, and context analysis. Encoded archival description, a revolutionary change in a fundamental archival function, incorporated a number of technical terms such as DTD and XML into the archival lexicon, and elaborated concepts such as archival cataloging and finding aid.

Possibly the most significant impact on archival language and professional boundaries resulted from the challenges of electronic records. E-records forced archivists into collaborations with different disciplines. In response, archivists adopted terms from information technology, publishing, and knowledge management. They began to

---

1. Lewis J. Bellardo and Lynn Lady Bellardo, *A Glossary for Archivists, Manuscript Curators, and Records Managers* (Society of American Archivists, 1992), p. v.

grapple with born-digital documents and to become familiar with arcane aspects of technology used to record and authenticate electronic documents, such as ciphers, encryption keys, and encoding schemes. At the same time, other professions adopted—sometimes appropriated—archival terms. The very word that identifies the profession, archives, took on the meaning of offline storage and backup.

I believe that, at a fundamental level, the basic concepts of records and recordkeeping are not antiquated. They remain vital and important. However, the language of records is often tied to a paper realm, emphasizing physical qualities over functional characteristics. The challenge is to rearticulate the essential characteristics of those concepts in terms that make sense in a vastly different environment.

Samuel Johnson believed that one of the lexicographer's jobs was "to correct or proscribe . . . improprieties and absurdities." However, Johnson also believed that a dictionary should "register the language . . . ; not [to] teach men how they should think, but relate how they have hitherto expressed their thoughts."[2]

The Society of American Archivists' first glossary was founded on the "conviction that professionalism demands precision, which in turn implies standardization" and presented "the preferred term and meaning in each case."[3] The Bellardos continued that practice, noting that they "identified preferred terms and developed definitions reflecting the practices of leading archival institutions and professionals."[4]

While the first two editions were prescriptive, this glossary is descriptive. Rather than serving as an arbiter of correctness, it documents the different ways a term is used within and outside the profession. It is founded on the lexicographical principle of corpus linguistics. The definitions are not based on an ideal, theoretical model, but on how the words are used in the literature. While researching this glossary, I compiled a database containing more than 6,300 citations

---

2. Cited in Sidney Landau, *Dictionaries: The Art and Craft of Lexicography* – 2nd ed. (Cambridge University Press, 2001), p. 62.
3. "A Basic Glossary for Archivists, Manuscript Curators, and Records Managers," reprinted from *The American Archivist* 37:3 (July 1974), pp. 415–433. Citation, p. 415.
4. p. v.

from more than 500 sources.[5] Those sources included glossaries, monographs, and articles from the fields of archives, records management, libraries, preservation, bookbinding, computing, and law.

Many terms have meanings that differ between communities of interest or disciplines; 'record' has senses that are specific to cataloging, to computing, and to law. Even within the community of archivists, meanings vary. For example, some archivists carefully distinguish archives from personal papers, but others do not. Some of these differences are significant, others are slight. The variations underscore a lack of professional consensus. As a result, the glossary points out horizons of understanding, where key concepts are being reconsidered or established. A single definition for a term could easily confuse a reader who is confronted with a text that uses that term with a very different meaning.

Many words were charged with considerable discussion in the professional literature and were the subject of flame wars on Internet discussion groups. Even though the glossary was not intended to be prescriptive, reporting differing senses necessarily drew intellectual lines in the sand. Teasing meaning from polemics was a bit like walking on a mine field. I often heard in my head renowned archivists challenging me to prefer their particular point of view. It would have been a lot easier to ignore those voices if I did not have a great deal of respect for them.

A significant temptation that lexicographers face is a desire to normalize the language, to make it more rational. In its most innocent form, that temptation is a compulsion to tidy up those areas of ambiguity around the details of meaning, to correct the exception by making some irregularity in the language fit the mold. A darker side of normalization is for the lexicographer to intentionally interject bias into the work by preferring one definition over another, often in deference to a personal point of view.

---

5. The Bibliography is limited to those works cited in the Glossary. A more perfect glossary would have been based on a corpus that allowed a sophisticated analysis of a much larger and more diverse body of archival literature. Given the resources at hand, I built the corpus manually by reading many of those works and transcribing salient citations into a database. To complement that work, I also searched for citations from the Internet. Google was particularly useful to determine the more common form among variants because it reports the number of times the word or phrase appears in its database. For example, it reported 15,100 occurrences for archival science, but only 3,470 for archives science.

Hilary Jenkinson provides an excellent example of normalization when he synthesizes a definition of archives in his *Manual*.[6] Not satisfied with the definition in the *Oxford English Dictionary*, he constructs his own "by comparing in some well-known case documents which are obviously Archives with others which are obviously not."[7] However, another person in another situation could just as legitimately select different examples and wind up with a very different definition. For example, having begun my career some sixty years after Jenkinson published his *Manual* and having worked primarily with photographic archives and local history collections in the United States, I found Jenkinson's definition archaic, alien, and artificial. The foundation of Jenkinson's definition does not fit my experience, so from my perspective his logic falls apart.

The issue is not right or wrong, but rather language's irregular nature. Different people can impose or discern different orders on language. Language is ad hoc, not de jure. A word's meaning is derived from its use, not from a rational system. Answering Juliet's question, linguist Stephen Pinker observes

> What's in a name is that everyone in a language community tacitly agrees to use a particular sound to convey a particular idea. Although the word rose does not smell sweet or have thorns, we can use it to convey the idea of a rose because all of us have learned, at our mother's knee or in the playground, the same link between a noise and a thought.[8]

The difficulty is that individuals in the community have smelled roses with different colors. They may agree on the idea in general, but not in particular. This point was driven home for me when one particular sentence in a draft paper I was reading threw me into high dudgeon.

> With more and more information now created in electronic, rather than physical form, records may need to be re-defined for an electronic medium. . . .

With some incredulity I pondered, *Who* was going to redefine 'record'? The passive voice masks a presumption that the active voice would have underscored; if the authors rewrote the sentence in the

---

6. Hilary Jenkinson, *A Manual of Archive Administration* (Percy Lund, Humphries, 1966), p. 2 - 15.
7. p. 3.
8. *Words and Rules*, p. 2.

active voice, who would they expect to provide the new definition? There is no authority that establishes definitions for English words.

Language evolves. It is not constructed. My goal has been to document the former, and to avoid the presumption of the latter.

Language is largely transparent. Words surround us like air, and we are usually oblivious to them. Only when there is some disturbance do we take notice. Words are so familiar that most people would be hard-pressed to define them with any precision. While working on this project, I asked a group of well-respected archivists to come up with a definition for record by listing essential characteristics. They stumbled, some of which was a function of their being caught off guard. Before I began this project I could not clearly and succinctly describe the characteristics of a record, and I could not have answered the question well. Only by paying careful attention to the contexts in which the words were used could I begin to get sufficient perspective to perceive the nuances of meaning.

Professions use some words as shorthand. Jargon used within a professional context where it is understood is a handy shortcut. Using the language outside that community is often confusing. Unfortunately, people overly concerned with intellectual trendiness often adopt hot new jargon—buzzwords—without quite knowing what those words mean. Bruce Handy wondered about the use of the word 'postmodern'. Why would editors at *Elle* describe a ski parka as postmodern? To find out, he contacted several authors who had used the term in odd contexts. He concluded that 'postmodern' had become "culturespeak, short for Stuff That's Cool in 1988. It's the current version of groovy—except that using it makes you sound smart."[9]

Individuals with no desire to be trendy may similarly abuse language. Henry Fowler described cant as "insincere or parrotlike appeal to principles, religious, political, or scientific, that the speaker does not believe in or act upon, or does not understand."[10] Staff at the

---

9. "The Rise and Fall of a Great American Buzzword," *Spy* (April 1988).
10. H. W. Fowler, *Modern English Usage* – 2nd ed., revised and edited by Sir Ernest Gowers (Oxford University Press, 1965), p. 315.

National Endowment for the Humanities use the phrase 'magic words' instead of 'cant'. These magic words often appear in grant applications because applicants think grant reviewers want to hear them. Unfortunately, their use of the words makes it clear that they do not understand them. For example, an applicant may promise that finding aids will be in MARC format because they know that MARC has something to do with description and is a standard reviewers look for. Unfortunately, the sample finding aid attached to the application clearly has nothing to do with MARC.

In the archival community, buzzwords and magic words include 'evidence', 'digital object', 'resource', 'metadata', 'trustworthy', and the phrase 'authentic and reliable.' The more archivists work with other communities, the more they must take the time—and words—to fully explain these concepts. They must take the time to learn other communities' specialized language, and to express archival ideas and concerns in those terms.

The issue is not purity of language. Jargon, used within a professional context, is a handy shortcut because its meaning is clear and often carries nuances that allow for succinct expression. Buzzwords often point to important developments, and the meaning shifts as the thing it refers to evolves. However, people often use jargon as filler words, resulting in sloppy language that reflects sloppy thinking.

In the end, words are slippery. Meaning is elusive. Language is clear only when there is nothing to argue about. We are faced with a vicious circle. As our understanding of ideas changes, so do the meanings of the words we use to represent those ideas.

Writing the glossary has helped me understand and engage in the larger dialog of the archival profession. It forced me to think about the words more carefully and, in Frank Burke's terms, more theoretically about the profession.[11]

John Roberts summarized archivy in eleven words, "We save what is historically valuable—*there*; that is the theory."[12] Where Roberts

---

11. "Future Course of Archival Theory," *American Archivist* 49:3 (Summer 1986): 40–46.
12. "Archival Theory: Much Ado about Shelving," *American Archivist* 50:1 (Winter 1987): 66–74.

sees simplicity, I see confusion and complexity. Roberts sees reflection as so much useless navel gazing. I see many questions surrounding almost every word in his statement.

- The first question Roberts' statement raises is, Who is the 'we'? In context, it is clear that he is referring to archivists. In the age of electronic records, it will take more than archivists to preserve records. They must partner with information technologists and others, and those collaborations will blur the boundaries of who is an archivist.
- 'Save' raises the question of how the process of saving records has changed. Because the process of migrating records to avoid technological obsolescence often results in changes to the records, we must think about how records' reliability is affected.
- 'What' refers to the object of this process. Dynamic information systems, hyperdocuments, and virtual reality challenge our understanding of recordness.
- Roberts' final phrase 'historically valuable' side-steps any number of questions. What is valuable? To whom? For what purpose?

Roberts' statement becomes more complex when I consider not *what* the words mean, but the *why* underlying the words. How I understand those questions has an immediate, practical impact on how I do my job. I do not think the questions have answers, per se. Like words and definitions, the questions and how they are understood will change over time and in different situations.

Even though the language of archives and recordkeeping has evolved over the centuries, the fundamental function and essential characteristics of a record remain the same. Society has long needed a way to fix memory for future reference, and that need has not gone away. We must come to understand how people are using new forms of records. Archivists are, in my mind, uniquely qualified to consider how the characteristics of those new forms map to established characteristics and the significance of new ones.

In a paper environment, records were an unintended by-product of other activities; records just happened. At the University of Texas, Harry Ransom built his reputation by collecting the many drafts of authors' works; he saw those drafts as evidence of the creative process that gave a richer understanding of the final work. In the digital environment, records don't just happen. With word processing, many—if not most—of the drafts Ransom would have wanted are lost. Each time a document is opened, revised, then saved, the previous version disappears unless consciously preserved. Few database systems are designed to be able to roll back data so that it is possible to see the state of the data at any given point in the past; data is added, changed, and deleted, with no thought to preserving older data for future reference. The challenge of paper documents is an excess of irrelevant memory captured in piles of paper. The challenge of electronic records is incremental amnesia.

While the language and practice of recordkeeping has changed, the work of archivists and records professionals remains fundamentally the same. I believe—and this is not a novel concept—that the character of our profession must change. Archivists have often been seen as custodians of the past. We are seen as the keepers of old things. While we will remain the custodians of old records, we must change our emphasis from the preservation of culture as a thing of the past. We must become advocates for future users of current information by ensuring the transmission of culture. What of the present needs to be remembered for future users? I believe that our knowledge of what has enduring value and of how researchers use materials is our distinguishing expertise. It is that knowledge that can enable us to help records creators know when to commit intentional acts of memory, to know what to save. To do that, we must be able to speak clearly.

Some of the more animated discussions with my advisors revolved around words that I found personally interesting, but which are of limited value to the audience. Sometimes I thought a word, such as eschatacol, was fascinating precisely because it was arcane. Many times I found that the word—and its underlying meaning—captured a piece of the profession's history and provided context for and insight into current practice. JoAnne Yates' *Control Through Communication*[13] was a valuable source of terms from the nineteenth and early twentieth centuries. Those words, based in paper records, gave me significant insights into how people used paper records to solve problems in the past, and from that I gained a better understanding of parallel problems in the digital present. One reason I favored including those terms was that I saw modern parallels. *Ars dictaminis*, manuals of letter writing with established forms that could be used as boilerplate, persist today under other names, and some word processing programs come with canned text that are, in my mind, equivalent.

Ultimately, this particular glossary is a work of autobiography. The selection of words and their definitions reflects my own career and interests. While I sought to be as objective as possible, working with advisors, seeking others' opinions, and justifying definitions with citations from the literature, the work will ultimately be a reflection of me. Another person would have written another glossary.

---

13. (Johns Hopkins University Press, 1989).

Introduction

The first two editions of the glossary were, from their titles, "for archivists, manuscript curators, and records managers." This glossary targets a wider audience of anyone who needs to understand records because they work with them. It attempts to build a bridge between records, information technology, and business communities by interpreting archival concepts for people in other disciplines, while at the same time explaining those other disciplines to archivists and records professionals.

This glossary is based primarily on archival literature in the United States and Canada, in that order. In a few instances, terms, definitions, and citations from other English-speaking communities are included when relevant. This glossary includes terms that relate to the types of records that someone is likely to encounter when reading archival literature or when working with a fairly typical collection of records, and it emphasizes terms relating to electronic records. It also incorporates terms from the literature of preservation, law, and micrographics, as well as common form and genre terms from architectural and technical drawings, motion picture and video, photography, and sound recording. It includes some words that are no longer in common use, but which are useful when reading older literature; for example, Spindex. The glossary does not include many words specific to affiliated professions, such as rare books or printing.

In general, words with no archival connotation were excluded. While aisles are common in archives, any good dictionary will provide an adequate definition of the term. A few entries are common words or phrases which function as guide terms to illustrate the relationships between other terms. For example, box needs no definition but is included as a bucket term to group cross-references to related terms, such as Hollinger box, Bankers Box, and phase box. Similarly, the phrase 'preservation methods and techniques' is used to point to other entries scattered throughout the alphabet.

The glossary contains more than 2,000 defined entries and more than 600 lead-in terms, and nearly 700 citations from some 280 sources. Some 2,500 cross-references (not counting lead-in terms) in the syndetic structure illustrate relationships between terms.

Key to the Entries

heading, part of speech, variants, and definition

index, n. (**indexes, indices,** pl.) ~ 1. An ordered list of headings that points to relevant information in materials that are organized in a different order. – 2. Publishing · A portion of a book, usually located in the back, that provides an ordered list of subjects covered in the book, with pointers where those subjects are discussed. – 3. Printing · A typographical ornament in the shape of a fist with the index finger extended.

syndetic structure

RT: catalog, controlled vocabulary, general index, indexing

notes

An index[1] provides no explanation about the information it points to beyond its location. It is distinguished from a catalog, which provides additional information to help determine its relevance. An index may be created on cards, with separate cards for each entry to allow easy interfiling. It may also be on paper, or in a database or word processing file. – An index[2] usually uses page numbers for the pointers, but some works may use section numbers.

citations

†64 (*Burlington Agenda 2001, p. 295*): A superficial examination of a printed index would reveal that search engines available at this writing [2001] could retrieve many of its references from the full text of a work, but it is also clear that they could not build the web of relationships and analysis provided by a good back-of-the-book index, nor the navigational support provided by such an index.

Heading

Headings in the glossary are alphabetized in word-by-word order. An accented character is sorted after its unaccented equivalent, a digit is filed before a character, and internal punctuation (hyphen, slash, apostrophe) is treated as a space. All sort orders are imperfect, and the use of word-by-word order requires one to know how a term is written to be able to find it. Data base and database sort differently, as do email and e-mail. However, word-by-word order tends to place variant forms in reasonable proximity. The letter-by-letter sort traditionally used by dictionaries is disorienting to many people because they are more familiar with word-by-word order from other contexts; further, a letter-by-letter sort scatters variant forms throughout the alphabet. For example, A/V sorts after attribute and B reel sorts after break. If a multiword phrase is not found, look for it as a single phrase. Conversely, if a single word is not found, look for a compound form.

Headings are singular nouns, with some exceptions. Entries describing a class of material are entered under the plural form (corporate records). Some adjectival and verb forms are defined if there is a significant shift in meaning (write and writing).

Abbreviations and acronyms are almost always entered under the full form, with a reference under the short form (SAA points to Society of American Archivists). However, proper names formed from abbreviations are entered under their short form (the Association of Records Managers and Administrators is entered under the current form of its name, ARMA International). In a few cases where the short form is consistently used instead of full form, this convention is reversed (American Standard Code for Information Interchange points to ASCII).

Parts of Speech, Variants, and Definition

The definition begins with any variants followed by the part of speech, usually a noun, and then by any abbreviations, acronyms, or other forms for different parts of speech.

Definitions are in the same part of speech as the heading, and readers are left to infer definitions for other parts of speech. Other parts of speech or variant forms are explicitly defined if there is a significant shift in meaning. Definitions specific to a discipline or context are preceded by a qualifier in small caps. Definitions are intended to be terse so that they can be substituted for the heading in a sentence.

Syndetic Structure

References between terms are organized into a taxonomy by the following relationships between the entry in which they appear and headings for other entries.

DF	Distinguish from	A heading that is similar, and that is identical but often confused.
BT	Broader term	A heading for more general concept.
NT	Narrower term	A heading for a more specific concept.
RT	Related term	A heading that is closely associated.
Syn	Synonym	A heading with very nearly the same meaning.
See		A heading with fuller discussion of the entry.

Note that not all relationships pertain to all senses. When the association between senses and relationships is significant, the definition or notes provide clarification. References to entries that would sort in close proximity are, with a few exceptions, omitted.

Notes

Notes provide a gloss on the definitions, providing background and additional information. Superscripts in the notes relate a note to a specific definition. In the absence of a superscript, the note applies to all senses of the word.

Citations

In many cases, citations from the literature are included to give a more complete understanding of the heading. The citations are not intended to define the terms, but to give voice to diverse opinions underlying the concepts around the heading. Sometimes those voices may be contradictory. As such, the citations should not be interpreted to represent professional consensus.

Citations had to be succinct and salient. Some obvious and authoritative sources are missing from an entry because they did not contain an easily extracted citation.

The citations are usually exact quotes, including variant spellings, punctuation, and capitalization. In a few instances, wording was silently altered so that the quote would make sense out of context. For example, the phrase "as discussed above" might be omitted. Significant alterations are flagged using square brackets or an ellipsis. Bulleted lists have been run together. Similarly, paragraphs are run together, and a paragraph mark (¶) is inserted to indicate the new paragraph. Notes in the original text have been omitted, unless they are a substantive part of the citation.

Like notes, superscripts tie citations to specific definitions.

Each citation begins with a reference to its source. A dagger (†) precedes the source number in the Bibliography, followed by a short description of the source. The description is often formed from a familiar mnemonic that may save readers the need to consult the bibliography; for example, APPM for *Archives, Personal Papers, and Manuscripts,* or CFR for *Code of Federal Regulations.* If a work has no such mnemonic, the short citation is based on the name of the individual or organization responsible for the content or on the first few words of the title. The year of publication, when known, follows the short citation. Finally, any page number or section ends the reference.

URLs

Notes and citations occasionally contain links to resources on the web. Links were checked shortly before the glossary went to press. Active links are indicated as 'available.' Links to resources that are no longer active were not so marked. While links are notoriously unstable, resources are more persistent. If a URL is broken, a search on the web for key words in the note or citation or for the URL in the Internet Archives will often locate the resource.

Corrections and Revisions

After three years of work, I realized that this glossary would never be finished. Not only are new words and meanings being added to the language, as I continued reading I found other words and senses. I wanted more time to research obscure words and how meanings shifted in Canada, Great Britain, Australia, and other anglophone cultures. I wanted better tools to build the syndetic structure. I bemoaned the lack of illustrations. I wish I had known when beginning 'A' all that I had learned when I had finished 'Z.'

My greatest concern, however, is not what is missing, but that some definition or note I have written is just plain wrong. In his book on dictionaries, Sidney Landau noted, "Not the least value of lexicography is that one learns to be humble about one's own knowledge of the language."[14] I would extend his observation by noting that writing a professional glossary greatly adds to one's knowledge of the field. No one can know everything. Even a group of intelligent and diligent advisors has boundaries around their knowledge. Nor are any of us perfect. Editing and proofreading a glossary are exercises in somnambulism; after only a short while, the readers are mesmerized and wake to wonder when they stopped really reading and what they missed.

I offer this apology as an invitation. If you have comments on the glossary or its entries, believe a term or another sense for an existing

---

14. *Dictionaries: The Art and Craft of Lexicography* – 2nd ed. (Cambridge University Press, 2001), p. 115.

term needs to be added, or find errors in this work, please report them to the Society of American Archivists (glossary@archivists.org or www.archivists.org/glossary). Those comments and suggestions will be used to make the next edition better and more complete.

If you can supply an illustration that might be used for a term in the next edition, please send a photocopy or digital photograph to SAA (Attn: Glossary Project, 527 S. Wells Street, 5th Floor, Chicago, IL 60607). You will be contacted for camera-ready copy if it will be used in the next edition.

RICHARD PEARCE-MOSES
July 2005

A

A and B wind printing, n. ~ The orientation of the perforations on single-perforation film, such as 8 mm or 16 mm stock.

    Notes: When looking at single-perforation film stock, rolled counterclockwise, emulsion side out, the perforations of an A-wind print will be on the back side of the reel and the perforations of a B-wind print will be on the front side of the reel.

A reel, n. ~ The principal source of video or film, which is intermixed with footage from another camera (the B reel), to produce a finished program.

    RT: B reel, moving image

A/V ~ *see:* audiovisual

A4, n. ~ A metric paper size measuring 210 × 297 mm (8.27 × 11.69 inches).

AACR (also AACR2, AACR2r) ~ *see:* Anglo-American Cataloguing Rules

AASLH ~ *see:* American Association for State and Local History

AAT ~ *see:* Art and Architecture Thesaurus

abandoned property law (also **unclaimed property law**), n. ~ A statute describing specific procedures that allow an individual or organization to obtain clear, legal title to material that it holds but does not own.

    Notes: In the United States, federal statutes do not address abandoned property and are enacted state by state. Less than one half the states have such laws. For examples, see Arizona, Unclaimed Property in Museums (44-351ff); North Dakota, Museum or Historical Society Unclaimed Property (55-12); Maine, Property Deposited with Museums and Historical Societies (27 §601).

aberrant date, n. ~ DESCRIPTION · A date that falls outside the chronological sequence of the dates pertaining to the majority of the documents in the unit being described.

abstract, n. ~ 1. A concise summary of the key points of a larger work, often used to assist the reader in determining if that work is likely to be of use. – 2. ART · A genre of painting and other arts that originated in the 20th century, characterized by structures and patterns, rather than representational images and forms.

    RT: brief, extract, scope and contents note

ACA ~ *see:* Academy of Certified Archivists, Association of Canadian Archivists

academy file, n. ~ A series, often found in Congressional records, that includes applications for admission to a United States service academy, often with letters of recommendation from the member of Congress.

    Notes: Academies include the Military Academy (West Point), the Air Force Academy (Colorado Springs), the Naval Academy (Annapolis), the Merchant Marine Academy (King's Point), and the Coast Guard Academy (Groton).

Academy format, n. ~ MOVING IMAGES · An image with an aspect ratio of 1:1.33.

    BT: format

    RT: aspect ratio, moving image, widescreen

Academy of Certified Archivists, n. (**ACA**, abbr.) ~ A professional organization, founded in 1989, established to certify individuals who have met specific requirements for archival education, knowledge, and experience.

    RT: certified archivist

Notes: See http://www.certifiedarchivists.org/.

†7 *(Certified Archivists Website):* The Academy of Certified Archivists promotes fundamental standards of professional archival practice.

accelerated aging test, n. ~ A laboratory procedure that estimates a material's rate of deterioration, making it possible to predict its life expectancy.

RT: Arrhenius function, life expectancy, Preservation Environment Monitor

Notes: Many tests are based on the Arrhenius function, which predicts that materials age in a predictable manner relative to temperature. By determining how long it takes for materials in an environment with an elevated temperature to reach a predetermined level of deterioration (brittleness, fading, signal loss), it is possible to project how long it will take materials at normal storage conditions to reach that level of deterioration. Because the level of deterioration is set arbitrarily, the test has a subjective aspect that makes results open to dispute. For example, the test may accurately predict the time it will take film to reach a predicted level of brittleness, but some individuals would find the film to be sufficiently pliable to remain useful.

†248 *(Roberts and Etherington 1982):* Although sound in theory, accelerated aging tests are, at this time, of limited usefulness. The reason is that conditions of storage, which vary widely, have a considerable influence on the degree of permanence; also, it is difficult to verify empirically the accuracy of such tests except by experiments conducted over a number of years.

access, n. ~ 1. The ability to locate relevant information through the use of catalogs, indexes, finding aids, or other tools. – 2. The permission to locate and retrieve information for use (consultation or reference) within legally established restrictions of privacy, confidentiality, and security clearance. – 3. COMPUTING · The physical processes of retrieving information from storage media.

DF: accessibility

RT: authorization, classification, clearance, dark archives, description, Freedom of Information Act, light archives, read, restriction

Notes: 'Access' and 'accessibility' are frequently used synonymously, although 'accessibility' carries the connotation of providing access to individuals with disabilities that prevent normal use.

†48 *(CJS, Records §95):* Matters concerning the form of access to computerized records have been adjudicated. It has been held that an agency may require a person to inspect and copy hard copy printouts, and need not provide him with a computer diskette, and that copies of computer tapes themselves need not be supplied, but only copies of the records contained thereon. However, it has also been held that an agency must make computer tapes available for copying, and must provide information on computer tapes rather than in the form of hard copy, and must transfer information in a computer onto computer tapes.

†201 *(Nevada Glossary):* [access] To intercept, instruct, communicate with, store data in, retrieve from or otherwise make use of any resources of a computer, network or data.

access copy, n. ~ 1. A reproduction of a document created for use by patrons, protecting the original from wear or theft; a use copy. – 2. A digital object (typically a graphic) that has been scaled down from a high-quality original to a lower-quality, smaller version, to facilitate delivery over low-bandwidth networks.

Syn: use copy

Notes: Access copies[1] may be made in a variety of formats. Photocopying was often used to make inexpensive access copies of textual documents and, usually with limited success, photographs. Access copies are now likely to be digital scans of the original. – An access copy[2] is often derived from a high-resolution master scan. A master is useful for high-quality printing and reduces the chance that the original will need to be rescanned in the future, but it is typically very large. Creating an access copy that matches the lower resolution of video monitors significantly reduces the size of the file. Because these scans are often accessed through websites, the transmission time is reduced without apparent loss of quality.

access date, n. ~ 1. The date when records that have been closed or restricted become generally available for use by the public. – 2. A time stamp associated with a file indicating the last time the file was viewed. – 3. The portion of a bibliographic citation for a website indicating when the page, as cited, was known to be current.

BT: date

Notes: Access dates[1] are usually determined by a set period of time. – Access date[2] differs from the date the file was created and from the date the file was last updated; not all computer operating systems or databases track access date. – Access dates[3] document the version of a website used as the source; the frequency of change and disappearance of web pages makes the date particularly important.

access point, n. ~ 1. A category of headings in a catalog that serve a similar function. – 2. A name, term, phrase, or code used as a heading in a catalog, especially to group related information under that heading.

NT: nominal access point

RT: entry, heading, name-title reference

Notes: Examples of common access points within catalogs include author, title, and subject.

access policy, n. ~ Principles or procedures that control the conditions under which individuals have permission and ability to consult a repository's holdings.

BT: policy

access restriction ~ *see:* restriction

accessibility, n. ~ 1. The characteristic of being easily reached or used with a minimum of barriers. – 2. The ability to locate relevant information through the use of catalogs, indexes, finding aids, or other tools. – 3. The permission to locate and retrieve information for use (consultation or reference) within legally established restrictions of privacy, confidentiality, and security clearance; access[2].

DF: access

Notes: Accessibility[1] carries the connotation of providing access to individuals with disabilities that prevent normal use, especially under the terms of the Americans with Disabilities Act (Pub. L. 101-336, 42 USC 126). For example, closed captioning can make a television program accessible to individuals who have trouble understanding its sound. Other examples include providing at least one desk at a height appropriate for use by an individual in a wheelchair, and describing images on web pages with 'alternate text' so that visually impaired can understand the page. – Accessibility[2,3] is synonymous with access[1,2].

accession, n. ~ 1. Materials physically and legally transferred to a repository as a unit at a single time; an acquisition. – v. ~ 2. To take legal and physical custody of a group of records or other materials and to formally document their receipt. – 3. To document the transfer of records or materials in a register, database, or other log of the repository's holdings.

DF: acquisition

RT: accretion, accrual, deaccessioning, registration

Notes: The materials may be acquired by gift, bequest, purchase, transfer, retention schedule, or statute. An accession may be part of a larger, existing collection. An accession added to existing collections is sometimes called an accretion or an accrual.

'Accession' should be distinguished from 'acquisition'. As nouns, they are synonymous. However, the verb 'accession' goes far beyond the sense of 'acquire', connoting the initial steps of processing by establishing rudimentary physical and intellectual control over the materials by entering brief information about those materials in a register, database, or other log of the repository's holdings.

†220 *(Pederson 1987, p. 115):* Having made sure that new material has been legally transferred to your archives, the next, and vitally important, step is to gain control over it. This initial process is called *accessioning³* which records information about origins, creator, contents, format and extent in such a way that documents cannot become intermingled with other materials held by the archives. Accessioning provides the basic level of physical and intellectual control over incoming material.... ¶ Accessioning consists of a sequence of different activities. These include preliminary sorting of the accession, recording the essential identifying information about the material, and its creator in the accession register and providing suitable storage for the material.

accession number, n. ~ A number or code assigned to uniquely identify a group of records or materials acquired by a repository and used to link the materials to associated records.

Notes: Access numbers may consist of one or several parts. Some repositories use a two-part accession number, the first representing the year of the accession and the second part the number of the accessions in that year. For example, 2003:10 is the tenth accession in the year 2003. Museums often add a third part representing each item in the accession.

accession record, n. ~ 1. A form or log that summarizes standard information about the process of transferring materials to a repository. – 2. A case file containing all materials associated with the legal and physical transfer of records or other materials to a repository.

BT: record

Notes: An accession record¹ is typically created by the repository to capture in one place information that is often scattered in many different documents. The form is sometimes referred to as an accessions register. – An accession record² might include the deed of gift, a purchase agreement or receipt, or other proof of the transfer of ownership. It often includes supporting documentation, such as preliminary correspondence or information on rights and restrictions.

accessions list (also **accessions ledger, accessions log, accessions register**), n. ~ An official record of each group of records or other materials (an accession) received by a repository.

Notes: Entries in an accession register are usually ordered by date of receipt and may include a unique identifying number (the accession number), the source, and other information for the immediate physical control of the accession.

acclimation, n. ~ The process of allowing records or other materials to adapt to changes in temperature or humidity, especially when taken from cold storage for use by researchers at room temperature.

Syn: conditioning

RT: cold storage, staging

†*4 (National Archives of South Africa):* Items being removed from cold storage require time to acclimatize to regular room temperature. This can take hours, depending on the difference in temperature. Cold storage is not a practical solution for heavily consulted items.

accompanying material, n. ~ DESCRIPTION · Materials that are a physically distinct component, typically in a different form, of the item being described and intended to be used with that item.

RT: annex, attachment

Notes: Examples include liner notes accompanying a sound recording or a map in a pocket in a book's binding. When describing an oral history recording, the transcript is often treated as accompanying material rather than being described separately.

†*110 (NARA Senate Records, accompanying papers):* Petitions, affidavits, letters, and other papers that support or oppose claims for damages, pensions, or other forms of relief for which a private bill has been introduced, or papers relating to public bills.

†*252 (RAD 1990, accompanying papers):* Material issued with, and intended to be used with, the material being described.

account, n. ~ 1. A record of debits or credits, often issued periodically, that is arranged to show totals on a given date. – 2. A report describing events or the discharge of duty, especially one given to an someone in authority. – 3. An arrangement to facilitate the exchange of services or funds between a provider and a customer.

account book, n. ~ A journal, often in the form of a ledger, used to record transactions, especially financial transactions.

RT: cash book, daybook, ledger, shop book, waste book

accountability, n. ~ The ability to answer for, explain, or justify actions or decisions for which an individual, organization, or system is responsible.

RT: trustworthiness

†*164 (Lemieux 2001, p. 92):* Traditionally, archival thinking on the relationship between records and accountability has rested on a belief that the usual circumstances of records creation gives assurances of reliability and authenticity, and therefore of trustworthiness, a quality essential to giving of and holding to account.

†*180 (MacNeil 2000, p. 50):* The principle that underlies the concept of accountability . . . is linked to the conveying and evaluation of information. . . . For ongoing bodies, accountability required the development and refinement of procedures for carrying out actions and documenting them, 'to ensure that everything was done according to rule and in proper sequence, so that administrators could account . . . at any time precisely for anything that had been done. Effective institutional accountability has therefore depended on record-making, record-keeping and access to records, and it has influenced the procedures and timing of their creation, their form, their maintenance, their accessibility and their centralization. [Citing Parkinson.]

accretion, n. ~ 1. Materials added to an existing collection; an accrual. – 2. PRESERVATION · A deposit of foreign of matter; an accumulation.

Syn: accumulation

RT: accession, accrual, acquisition

Notes: Accretion[2] connotes a substance that increased over time, although it may no longer be growing.

accrual, n. ~ Materials added to an existing collection; an accretion.

Syn: addition

RT: accession, accretion, acquisition, open file

accumulation, n. ~ 1. The organic process by which a collection of records grows out of a routine process. – 2. PRESERVATION · A deposit of foreign matter; an accretion.

Syn: accretion

Notes: Accumulation[2] connotes a substance that increased over time, although it may no longer be growing.

accuracy, n. (**accurate**, adj.) ~ The degree of precision to which something is correct, truthful, and free of error or distortion, whether by omission or commission.

RT: alteration, completeness, error, fidelity, precision, reliability, veracity

†48 (CJS, Records §12): Under statutes which require that instruments filed for record shall be recorded at length in a book kept for that purpose it has been held that no particular method of recording is necessary, and as long as the method adopted is sufficient to give the instrument perpetuity and publicity and meets the requirements of accuracy and durability, there is compliance with the statute.

†104 (Goerler 1999, p. 316): Sometimes the historical accuracy of a documentary – its relationship to the historical evidence – may be in conflict with its commercial value as entertainment. . . . To rescue [a film about native life in Samoa] from financial disaster, the producers insisted on adding a prologue and retitling the film. Released as *The Love Life of a South Sea Siren*, Flaherty's revised documentary opened with scenes of chorus girls in grass skirts. Shortly thereafter, Flaherty fled Hollywood.

†139 (InterPARES2, p. 11): Accuracy refers to the truthfulness of the content of the record and can only be established through content analysis. With administrative and legal records, it is usually inferred on the basis of the degree of the records' reliability and is only verified when such degree is very low. The volatility of the digital medium, the ease of change, editing, and the difficulty of version control, all make it harder to presume accuracy on the traditional bases.

†221 (AIIM, Performance Guidelines 1992): Records produced within a short period after the event or activity occurs tend to be more readily acceptable as accurate than records produced long after the event or activity. However, a challenge to admissibility of a later-produced record can be overcome by a showing that the time lapse had no effect on the record's contents. For example, a computer printout of a statistical report produced annually in the regular course of business can be shown to accurately consolidate data compiled over the course of a year.

acetate ~ *see:* cellulose acetate

acid, n. ~ 1. A substance that reacts with an alkali to form a salt. – 2. A substance with a pH between 1.0 and 7.0. – **acid, acidic**, adj. ~ 3. The condition of having a high acid content.

RT: pH

Notes: Acid in materials generally results in a decreased life expectancy and brittleness.

†248 *(Roberts and Etherington 1982):* Acids, and particularly the inorganic acids (because of their corrosiveness and low volatility), are harmful to paper and bookbinding materials. Their presence weakens the holding power of the individual links of the cellulose chains of paper, causing brittleness; results in corrosive effects in some inks; and weakens the fibers of leather. The source of acids in archival materials may be intrinsic or extrinsic. They may be present in the materials used in the manufacture of paper, adhesives, leather, etc., and may be left in intentionally, e.g., alum-rosin sizing; they may be introduced during manufacture and not sufficiently removed, e.g., acids used in clearing and/or dyeing leather; or they may gain access during storage, e.g., sulfuric acid in paper or leather, resulting from the atmospheric pollutant, sulfur dioxide (SO_2).

acid-free paper, n. ~ Paper with a pH of 7.0 or greater when manufactured.

> *BT:* paper
>
> *RT:* alkaline-reserve paper
>
> *Notes:* Acid-free papers are distinguished from papers that contain a residue of the acids used to break up wood fibers during manufacture. The residual acid continues to attack the paper fibers, making the paper brittle over time. Archival papers are typically made from alpha cellulose, are lignin free, and often contain an alkaline buffer to counter any trace of acids used in processing or environmental acids.
>
> †248 *(Roberts and Etherington 1982):* [acid-free paper] In principle, papers which contain no free acid and have a pH value of 7.0 or greater. In practice, papermakers consider a paper having a pH value of 6.0 or greater to be acid free. Such papers may be produced from cotton fibers, rags, esparto, jute, chemical wood pulps, or virtually any other fiber, with special precautions being taken during manufacture to eliminate any active acid that might be present in the paper pulp. However free of acid the paper may be immediately after manufacture, the presence of residual chlorine from bleaching operations, aluminum sulfate (alum) from sizing, or sulfur dioxide in the atmosphere, may lead to the formation of hydrochloric or sulfuric acid unless the paper has been buffered with a substance capable of neutralizing acids.

acid migration (also called **acid transfer**), n. ~ The movement of acid from an acidic material to material of lesser or no acidity, either from direct contact or through exposure to acidic vapors in the surrounding environment.

> †248 *(Roberts and Etherington 1982):* [Acid migration] may occur either when the two materials are in contact with each other, or by vapor transfer from one material to nearby materials not actually in contact with it. Boards, endpapers, and protective tissues, as well as the paper covers of books and pamphlets, may contain acid and transfer it to otherwise low-acid or acid-free paper of the text.

acquisition, n. ~ Materials received by a repository as a unit; an accession[1].

> *DF:* accession
>
> *RT:* accretion, accrual, collection development, ingest
>
> *Notes:* As nouns, acquisition and accession are synonymous. However, the verb accession goes far beyond the sense of acquire, connoting the initial steps of processing by establishing rudimentary physical and intellectual control over the materials by entering brief information about those materials in a register, database, or other log of the repository's holdings.

†112 (Ham 1993, p. 2): The process of acquiring records from any source by transfer, donation, or purchase, or the body of records so acquired.

acquisition microfilm, n. ~ Microfilm copies of records acquired to supplement a repository's holdings.

    BT: microfilm

    Notes: Acquisition microfilm may be made by the repository from originals lent by an individual, organization, or other repository, or may be copies of existing film purchased from another source.

acquisition policy, n. ~ An official statement issued by an archives or manuscript repository identifying the kinds of materials it accepts and the conditions or terms that affect their acquisition. It serves as a basic document for the guidance of archival staff and organizations and persons interested in donating their records or papers.

    BT: policy

ACRL ~ *see:* Association of College and Research Libraries

Acrobat, n. ~ A suite of software programs that can convert documents from a variety of formats to the Portable Document Format (PDF), enabling them to be viewed, but not revised, with a very close approximation of the original formatting on many different computer systems.

    RT: Portable Document Format

    Notes: Acrobat is a registered trademark of Adobe Systems. The **Adobe Reader**, formerly called Acrobat Reader, is distributed at no cost and can be used to view documents in the Portable Document Format (PDF).

act, n. ~ 1. Something done intentionally; an accomplishment achieved, usually, over a period of time; an action[2]. – 2. Legislation that has been made law, especially a statute. – 3. CONGRESS · The engrossed version of a bill that has been passed by one chamber. – 4. DIPLOMATICS · A conscious exercise of will by an individual with an intent to create, maintain, modify, or extinguish a situation.

    Syn: action

    NT: compound act, mere act, simple act

    RT: bill

    †110 (NARA Senate Records): [act[3]] 1. As used by Congress, a bill that has been passed by one House and engrossed. – 2. As commonly used, a bill that has been passed by both Houses of Congress, enrolled, and either signed by the President or passed over his veto.

action, n. ~ 1. LAW · Any proceedings in court brought by an individual, or a corporate or a public entity, to seek judgment for the infringement of rights or laws. – 2. Something done intentionally; an accomplishment achieved, usually, over a period of time; an act[1].

    Syn: act

    NT: transaction

    †15 (AAT 2000): [actions (judicial events)] Use generally for any proceedings in court brought by one or more persons against another or others, or by the state against a person or persons, to enforce a private right, redress or prevent a private wrong, or to punish a public offense.

action copy, n. ~ The copy of a document sent to an agency, office, or individual with the appropriate authority to respond.

    DF: information copy

    BT: copy

Notes: An action copy is distinguished from an information copy, which is sent to an individual who is not expected to respond.

actionable information, n. ~ Data, often unrelated and dispersed, that has been assembled to facilitate decision making.

BT: information

RT: knowledge management

Notes: Knowledge management, in part, seeks to assemble information scattered throughout the organization's records and add value to that information by discovering patterns and meaning that would otherwise be overlooked. This newly discovered, actionable information, in principle, can serve as the basis for better decisions.

active records, n. ~ 1. Records that continue to be used with sufficient frequency to justify keeping them in the office of creation; current records. – 2. COMPUTING · Information stored on computer systems that can be readily accessed by the operating system or software without a need to reload media, undelete the information, or reconstruct it from other sources.

Syn: current records

RT: inactive records

Notes: The concept of active record[1] can be extended to records in electronic systems that are kept online. Using this analogy, records in nearline and offline storage could be considered inactive records.

acutance, n. ~ An objective measure of the distinctness of a line in an image.

DF: sharpness

RT: focus, resolution

Notes: Acutance is distinguished from sharpness, which is a subjective perception that includes factors such as contrast and focus.

added entry, n. ~ DESCRIPTION · A name, term, phrase, code, or other heading, other than the main entry, used as a secondary access point to locate a catalog record.

BT: entry

Notes: In MARC cataloging, added entries are entered in 6xx or 7xx fields.

addition, n. ~ 1. Materials added to an existing collection; an accretion[1]; an accrual. – 2. An amendment[1].

Syn: accrual

address, n. ~ 1. A formal communication delivered to an audience; a speech. – 2. The place where something is to be delivered. – 3. COMPUTING · The code indicating where information or a device can be located or is to be sent.

Notes: Examples of address[1] include the Gettysburg Address and a State of the Union address. – Examples of address[2] include street, postal, or email addresses. – Examples of address[3] include URLs, network addresses, or a location in memory.

addressee, n. ~ 1. The individual to whom something is to be delivered. – 2. DIPLOMATICS · The individual or organization to whom a record is directed.

RT: author, writer

†70 (Duranti 1998, p. 96): The addressee is the person to whom the document is directed within its intellectual form, and may or may not coincide with the person to whom the document is issued or delivered. For example, a letter of appointment of a professor is directed to the appointee, notwithstanding the fact that we may be examining the copy sent to the department concerned.

adequacy of documentation, n. ~ FEDERAL RECORDKEEPING · Practices to ensure that sufficient, reliable records are kept to provide information about the organization, functions, policies, decisions, procedures, and essential transactions and to capture information necessary to protect the legal and financial rights of the government and of organizations and persons directly affected by the agency's activities.

> *BT:* trustworthiness
>
> *RT:* completeness, documentation, documentation strategy, sufficiency
>
> †82 *(Federal Records Management Glossary 1989):* A standard of sufficiently and properly recording actions and/or decisions. Derives from the legal requirement that agency heads 'make and preserve records containing adequate and proper documentation of the organization, functions, policies, decisions, procedures, and essential transactions of the agency and designed to furnish the information necessary to protect the legal and financial rights of the Government and of persons directly affected by the agency's activities' (44 USC 3101).
>
> †281 *(USC, 44 USC 3101):* The head of each Federal agency shall make and preserve records containing adequate and proper documentation of the organization, functions, policies, decisions, procedures, and essential transactions of the agency and designed to furnish the information necessary to protect the legal and financial rights of the Government and of persons directly affected by the agency's activities.

administrative control, n. ~ The responsibility for management of materials in a repository's custody, including the documentation of actions taken on those materials.

> *RT:* intellectual control, physical control
>
> *Notes:* Administrative control is independent of the intellectual content of the records. The former includes accessioning materials into a records center, subsequent transfer to an archives, or disposal by destruction; managing rights and restrictions during access; and tracking use and preservation treatment of the materials.
>
> Administrative control is distinguished from physical and intellectual control. Administrative control emphasizes functions relating to the custody of a repository's holdings. For example, administrative control is concerned that a potential acquisition is subject to the appraisal process and that, if acquired, the acquisition process is properly followed. Should a collection be deaccessioned, administrative control would ensure that the process meets the legal and institutional requirements.

administrative history, n. ~ That portion of a finding aid or catalog record that provides context for the materials described by noting essential information about the organization that created or accumulated the materials.

> *RT:* archival description, biographical note, Encoded Archival Context
>
> *Notes:* **Agency history** is often used in governmental contexts. Typically such histories are not exhaustive but usually include only information that is relevant to the materials in the collection. They commonly include the full, legal name of the organization, as well as common short forms and earlier and later forms of the name; prominent dates, such as of charter, mergers, or acquisitions; function and mission; position within the hierarchy of a complex organization, including parents and subsidiaries; principal officers; and places of operation.

administrative metadata, n. ~ Data that is necessary to manage and use information resources and that is typically external to informational content of resources.

> *BT:* metadata

Notes: Administrative metadata often captures the context necessary to understand information resources, such as creation or acquisition of the data, rights management, and disposition.

†235 *(Puglia, Reed, and Rhodes 2004, p. 8):* Administrative metadata comprises both technical and preservation metadata, and is generally used for internal management of digital resources. Administrative metadata may include information about rights and reproduction or other access requirements, selection criteria or archiving policy for digital content, audit trails or logs created by a digital asset management system, persistent identifiers, methodology or documentation of the imaging process, or information about the source materials being scanned. In general, administrative metadata is informed by the local needs of the project or institution and is defined by project-specific workflows. Administrative metadata may also encompass repository-like information, such as billing information or contractual agreements for deposit of digitized resources into a repository.

administrative microfilming, n. ~ The conversion of paper records to microfilm for use while the records remain active.

RT: microfilm

Notes: Records may be microfilmed to create copies so that several people can access the records simultaneously or to save space.

administrative records (also **administrative support records**), n. ~ A document that has been preserved because it facilitates the operations and management of an agency, but which does not relate directly to programs that help the agency achieve its mission.

DF: program records

Syn: facilitative records, housekeeping records

BT: record

RT: administrative value

Notes: Administrative records are common to most organizations. Examples include routine correspondence or interoffice communications; records relating to human resources, equipment and supplies, and facilities; reference materials, routine activity reports, work assignments, appointment books, and telephone logs.

administrative regulation, n. ~ A rule, which has the force of law, issued by a government agency to interpret or implement a statute's provisions.

BT: regulation

administrative value, n. ~ The usefulness or significance of records to support ancillary operations and the routine management of an organization.

BT: value

RT: administrative records, operational value, primary value

Notes: Records having administrative value are generally considered useful or relevant to the execution of the activities that caused the record to be created and during an audit of those activities. Traditionally, archivists have seen administrative value as transient. For administrative records to be considered archival, they must also possess other values.

†215 *(O'Toole 1998, p. 284):* The ability of records to leave behind evidence for such matters as the proper calculation of Easter and 'all things necessary for the celebration of festal days' were examples of the administrative usefulness of records, one of the traditional justifications for archival programs, especially in organizational and institutional settings.

administratively controlled information, n. ~ Information that has been restricted from unauthorized disclosure for reasons other than national security.

> *BT:* restriction
>
> *Notes:* Records containing administratively controlled information often bear designations such as 'for official use only' or 'limited official use'. Several statutes provide for restricting records in certain circumstances on grounds of national security, privacy, protection of trade secrets, internal agency personnel matters, law enforcement, litigation, and other reasons.
>
> †244 *(OSHA, Records Management 1998, Ch. 9, pt. III):* Administratively controlled information is information which must not be released for public dissemination. This includes FOIA-exempt information, Privacy Act restricted information, and other information to which access is restricted such as individual medical records, trade secrets and other private or restricted company information.
>
> †244 *(OSHA, Records Management 1998, Ch. 2, pt. IV):* Public access to Government information is in the best interests of a free society. However, classified material (relating to the national defense or conduct of foreign policy) or administratively controlled information (relating to individuals – subject to the Privacy Act – or materials dealing with sensitive activities of the Agency whose disclosure would not be in the public interest) must be protected against disclosure.

admissibility, n. (**admissible,** adj.) ~ The quality of being permitted to serve as evidence in a trial, hearing, or other proceeding.

> *RT:* evidence
>
> *Notes:* Material admitted as evidence may be challenged as not authentic or as unreliable.
>
> †30 *(Black's 1999):* 'Admissibility' can best be thought of as a concept consisting of two quite different aspects: disclosure to the trier of fact and express or implied permission to use as 'evidence.' If we think of admissibility as a question of disclosure or nondisclosure, it us usually easy to say whether or not an item of evidence has been admitted. When we consider the question of permissible use, the concept seems much more complicated. In the first place, evidence may be 'admissible' for one purpose but not for another. . . . In the second place, questions of the permissible use of evidence do not arise only at the time of disclosure to the trier of fact. The court may have to consider admissibility in deciding whether to give the jury a limiting instruction, whether or not an opponent's rebuttal evidence is relevant, and whether or not counsel can argue to the jury that the evidence proves a particular point. [Citing 22 Charles Alan Wright & Kenneth W. Graham, Jr., *Federal Practice and Procedure* §5193, at 194 (1978).]
>
> †265 *(Skupsky and Montaña 1994, p. 61):* The key to establishing admissibility as business records is to integrate their creation and maintenance into the records management program prior to the initiation of any litigation. The controlled creation and retention of documents for business purposes is what makes them admissible business records, and it is the records management program which demonstrates controlled creation and retention.

Adobe Acrobat ~ *see:* Acrobat

Adobe Portable Document Format ~ *see:* Portable Document Format

Adobe Reader ~ *see:* Acrobat

ADP ~ *see:* automatic data processing

ADS, abbr. ~ Autographed document signed.

Notes: This abbreviation is often used in finding aids, catalog descriptions, and bibliographies.

aerial photograph, n. ~ A photograph made from the air.

BT: photograph

NT: oblique aerial, vertical aerial

RT: bird's-eye view, cityscape, perspective

Notes: 'Aerial photograph' often connotes images made from an aircraft or balloon to show natural features and built structures, especially those used for reconnaissance and mapping. Aerial photographs are frequently made when the sun is at a low angle so that shadows show relief. 'Aerial photograph' generally connotes a **vertical aerial**, in which the axis of the camera is pointing straight down. The phrase **oblique aerial** indicates that the camera is angled toward the horizon.

agency, n. ~ 1. A unit of government authorized by law to perform a specific function. – 2. A relationship, usually created by contract or by law, giving one party the authority to act or represent another party.

Notes: Agency names may use another word, such as department, office, bureau, or authority. Within federal and state governments, agencies typically are part of the executive branch.

agency history ~ *see:* administrative history

agency record, n. ~ 1. FEDERAL LAW · Records that are subject to the federal Freedom of Information Act (FOIA). – 2. Any record created or received by a federal agency.

BT: record

RT: Freedom of Information Act

Notes: FOIA does not allow or provide for access to all records. In particular, records not created or obtained by the agency in the course of business may not be covered by FOIA. For example, personal notes not shared with another may not be considered agency records.

†292 (US DOJ 1980): Since FOIA applies only to *agency* records, the mere fact that an item is a record does not automatically mean that it can be reached by a FOIA request. There has been an increasing amount of litigation over this issue of whether records are also agency records. ¶ The leading case on this question is *Forsham v. Harris*, 445 U.S. 169, 48 U.S.L.W. 4232 (Mar. 3, 1980), in which the Supreme Court held that records which had been generated by private grantees of the (then) Department of Health, Education and Welfare (HEW) working under a grant, and which had always remained in the grantees' possession, were not agency records despite the facts that HEW had a contract right to obtain copies of the records, and that it had used a report (which was an agency record) based on them in an agency deliberative process.

†292 (US DOJ 1980): Another aspect of 'agency records' is the concept of 'personal records'. In the leading case on this point, the court held that notes made by an agency employee could be his own and outside the FOIA concept of 'agency records' if they were made and kept purely voluntarily and 'not circulated to nor used by anyone other than the authors, and are discarded or retained at author's sole discretion for their own individual purposes in their own personal files.' *Porter County Chap., Etc. v. U.S.A.E.C.*, 380 F. Supp. 630, 633 (N.D. Ind. 1974).

agent, n. ~ 1. An individual who acts on behalf of another individual or an organization. – 2. Semi-autonomous software or hardware that uses information in a given environment to perform tasks for a user, typically according to the user's specifications.

aggregated records, n. ~ Records accumulated and organized into series and files that reflect the creator's activities.

> *BT:* record
> *RT:* original order

agreement, n. ~ 1. A mutual understanding, written or verbal, made by two or more parties regarding a matter of opinion or their rights and obligations toward each other. – 2. An instrument made to record the details of an understanding or arrangement.

AIC ~ *see:* American Institute for the Conservation of Historic and Artistic Works

AIIM ~ *see:* Association for Information and Image Management

ALA ~ *see:* American Library Association

Albertype, n. ~ 1. A tradename for a photomechanical process that is a variant of the collotype. – 2. A print made by this process.

> *BT:* collotype
> *RT:* photomechanical
> *Notes:* The collotype was used to make ink-on-paper prints from photographic negatives. It was commonly used to make postcards.
> †153 *(Jones 1911):* The first workable collotype process made known; invented by Josef Albert of Munich. . . . The process is said to give prints with fine halftones, but it requires considerable care and experience in manipulation, much depending on the printing.

album, n. ~ 1. A volume of blank pages, bound or loose leaf, used to collect photographs, documents, clippings, and the like. – 2. A long-playing phonograph record on a disk measuring ten to twelve inches in diameter, with a playing time of more than five minutes at 33⅓ revolutions per minute. – 3. A bound volume of envelopes used to hold several phonograph records.

> *Syn:* long-playing record
> *NT:* scrapbook
> *RT:* phonograph record
> *Notes:* Most items in albums[1] are, for practical purposes, flat. However, some albums may include relatively shallow objects, such as pressed flowers or campaign buttons.

albumen photograph, n. ~ An image created using a silver halide as the light-sensitive agent and egg whites (albumen) as the binder.

> *BT:* photograph
> *Notes:* Albumen photographs were introduced in the 1840s and were common by the 1850s. Albumen photographs can be on a glass base and were widely used to create lantern slides. Albumen photographic prints (a paper base) were the predominant print process through the 1890s when gelatin silver processes were introduced. Albumen photographs are monochromatic, but may be hand-colored.
> †153 *(Jones 1911):* [albumen process] Negatives: An old process invented by Niepce de St. Victor, in 1848. Glass was coated with albumen containing potassium iodide, and the film was sensitized by dipping in a nitrate of silver bath. Many modifications followed, but probably the most widely used was the one

published on May 21, 1855, by Mayall. ¶ At one time the albumen process was widely used for the production of positives or lantern slides. . . .

alienation, n. ~ 1. The possession of records by an individual or organization not legally entitled to their custody. – 2. Law · The transfer of ownership of property.

> *RT:* estray, removed archives, replevin

alkali, n. (**alkaline**, adj.) ~ 1. A substance that reacts with an acid to form a salt; a base. – 2. A substance with a pH between 7 and 14.

> *Syn:* base
> *RT:* buffer, pH

alkaline-reserve paper, n. ~ Paper containing a buffering agent to counteract any increase in acidity resulting from aging or interaction with the environment.

> *BT:* paper
> *RT:* acid-free paper, buffer
> *Notes:* Calcium or magnesium carbonate is often used as the buffering agent.
> †248 *(Roberts and Etherington 1982):* Papers which are to remain acid free for long periods of time, e.g., 500 years, should have approximately 3% precipitated carbonate by weight of paper.

alpha cellulose, n. ~ A form of long, durable plant fibers used to make high-quality paper products.

> *BT:* cellulose
> *Notes:* Alpha cellulose may be derived from wood, linen, cotton, and other plant materials.

alphabetic-subject filing system, n. ~ A system for ordering topical headings in strict alphabetical order, rather than classifying them on the basis of intellectual relationships.

> *BT:* filing system
> *Notes:* The arrangement is sometimes called **dictionary arrangement** or **dictionary order**.

alphanumeric, adj. ~ Belonging to a character set composed of letters and digits.

> *RT:* character set
> *Notes:* Punctuation marks are sometimes considered alphanumeric characters.

alphanumeric filing system (also **numeric-alphabetic filing system**), n. ~ A method for classifying materials for storage and access through use of letters and digits that represents a concept.

> *BT:* filing system
> *Notes:* Alphanumeric filing systems typically use indirect access, with users locating file headings through a hierarchical or alphabetical list that indicates the code used for filing or retrieval.
> †87 *(TSLA 1998):* Alphanumeric filing may use a combination of personal or business names and numbers, or more commonly, subject names and numbers. Once the alphabetic divisions or topic headings and appropriate subdivisions have been determined, number categories can be assigned. If larger quantities of records are to be stored within the system, smaller divisions within each letter of the alphabet can be used. A relative index lists the number codes assigned to each letter of the alphabet or to its divisions. The file worker refers to the index to determine the primary filing digit to be assigned to a file for a new correspondent or document.

ALS, abbr. ~ Autographed letter signed.

> *Notes:* Commonly used in finding aids, catalog descriptions, and bibliographies.

alteration, n. ~ A change to a document modifying the meaning or intent of its content.
  RT: accuracy, amendment, error, fixity, immutability, integrity, preservation
  †48 (CJS, Records §23): The record cannot be altered so as to show anything not in the instrument recorded at the time of the original record.
  †265 (Skupsky and Mantaña 1994, p. 124): Alteration of records is analogous to the destruction of records in that the original informational content of the records is obliterated and rendered unavailable for future use.

alternative title, n. ~ DESCRIPTION · A second title, typically separated from the first by the word 'or' or another conjunction; a subtitle.
  RT: title

ambient data ~ *see:* residual data

ambrotype, n. ~ A positive photograph on glass made using the wet-collodion process, often hand-tinted and mounted in a hinged case.
  BT: collodion photographs, photograph
  RT: cased photographs, tintype, wet collodion
  Notes: An ambrotype is an underexposed, underdeveloped, wet-collodion negative on glass that, when viewed with a dark background, appears as a positive image. The dark background is commonly a black varnish applied to the glass base but is sometimes a separate material behind the glass or the glass base itself may be dark. The same process using a black-varnished metal plate is known as a tintype.
  Ambrotypes were patented in 1854 by James Ambrose Cutting and were common through the 1870s. They largely supplanted daguerreotypes.

AMC File ~ *see:* Archives and Mixed Collections File

AMC format ~ *see:* MARC Format for Archival and Manuscripts Control

amendment, n. ~ 1. A change to a document by addition, deletion, or revision. – 2. A change to proposed legislation after it has been introduced.
  RT: alteration
  †48 (CJS, Records §24): It has been stated that the amendment of a record should be made not by erasures and interlineations on the record book but by drawing out the amendment in form and annexing it to the books where the original is recorded, so that the whole matter will appear.
  †110 (NARA Senate Records): [amendment] 1. A change made in proposed legislation after it has been formally introduced. An amendment may be proposed by the committee to which the bill was referred, or it may be proposed by a Member from the floor of either House when it is brought up for consideration. All amendments must be agreed to by a majority of the Members voting in the House where the amendment is proposed. – 2. A change in the Constitution. Such an amendment is usually proposed in the form of a joint resolution of Congress, which may originate in either House. If passed, it does not go to the President for his approval but is submitted directly to the States for ratification.

American Association for State and Local History, n. (**AASLH**, abbr.) ~ An association that supports organizations that preserve and interpret American history in states and communities, as well as the staff and volunteers who work in those organizations.
  Notes: Although principally an association of historical societies, AASLH is concerned with archives because these organizations typically hold archival collections. See http://www.aaslh.org/.

---

†9 (AASLH 2003): The American Association for State and Local History provides leadership, service, and support for its members, who preserve and interpret state and local history in order to make the past more meaningful in American Society.

American Institute for the Conservation of Historic and Artistic Works, n. (**AIC**, abbr.) ~ A national organization for professionals working in the field of preserving historical and artistic works.

Notes: Members include practicing conservators, conservation scientists, educators, administrators, collections care professionals, technicians, and students; archivists, curators, and other museum and library professionals; architects and art historians; and individuals from related disciplines. See http://aic.stanford.edu/.

American Library Association, n. (**ALA**, abbr.) ~ An organization that promotes the value of libraries and provides support for the professionals, staff, and volunteers who work in the field of librarianship.

RT: Rare Book and Manuscript Section

Notes: The mission of the ALA is 'to provide leadership for the development, promotion and improvement of library and information services and the profession of librarianship in order to enhance learning and ensure access to information for all. ALA is committed to focus its energy and resources in five key action areas: diversity, education and continuous learning, equity of access, intellectual freedom, and 21st century literacy.' Members work in academic, public, school, government, and special libraries. See http://www.ala.org/.

American National Standards Institute, n. (**ANSI**, abbr.) ~ A nongovernmental organization chartered to coordinate the development of standards within the United States and to harmonize national standards with those of the International Organization for Standardization (ISO).

Notes: See http://www.ansi.org/.

In this glossary, ANSI standards are entered under their full name, with a cross-reference from the code. For example, the International Standard Serial Number (ISSN) is found under that name, with a see reference from Z39.9.

†114 (Harrod 1978): The USA organization for issuing recommendations as to the production, distribution and consumption of goods and services. . . . From 1918, when it was founded, until 1966 it was known as the American Standards Association (ASA) and from then until October 1969 as the United States of America Standards Institute (USASI).

American Society for Testing and Materials ~ *see:* ASTM International

American Standard Code for Information Interchange ~ *see:* ASCII

Notes: Almost always abbreviated.

AMIA ~ *see:* Association of Moving Image Archivists

ammonia process, n. ~ A photographic process that produces images by exposing diazonium salts to ultraviolet light, then developing the image using ammonia fumes; diazo process.

Syn: diazo process

RT: microfilm

Notes: Typically used to make access copies of microfilm. The ammonia process is not considered suitable for archival microfilm due to its impermanent nature.

ammonium thiosulfate ~ *see:* fixer

analog, adj. ~ Continuously varying in correlation to a physical process.

> *DF:* digital
>
> *RT:* machine-readable
>
> *Notes:* Analog is typically distinguished from digital, which represents a process through a sequence of discrete measurements over time. Examples of analog formats include photographs and films made with light-sensitive media, NTSC and PAL video recordings, and phonograph records and older magnetic sound recordings on tape.

analysis, n. ~ 1. The process of identifying, reviewing, and abstracting the components of something. – 2. CATALOGING · The process of writing a separate, supplementary description (an in-analytic) for a part of a collection or item for which a more general description has been entered into the catalog or finding aid. – 3. CATALOGING · The process of assigning subject headings to materials described in a catalog; **subject analysis**. – 4. CLASSIFICATION · The process of subdividing a major subject category into its facets.

> *RT:* hierarchical description, in-analytic, level of description

analytical bibliography (also **critical bibliography**), n. ~ 1. The study of the physical characteristics of books and the process of bookmaking, especially with an eye to understanding how materials and production influence the text. – 2. A listing of works that indicates in precise details the name of the author, the exact title of the work, and publication details, and that emphasizes the material nature of the work, including the format, the pagination, typographical particulars, illustrations, and other characteristics, such as the kind of paper and binding.

> *Syn:* descriptive bibliography
>
> *BT:* bibliography
>
> †49 (Cox 1990, p. 262): Analytical (sometimes called critical) bibliography, and its related studies of historical, textual, and descriptive bibliography, is the 'study of books as material objects.' It is a specialty within library and humanistic spheres that studies the book and all its parts in the assumption that any individual book is a representation of the society in which it was produced and that analyzing aggregates of books will assist in understanding the means and circumstances of transmitting ideas and the general nature of past society.
>
> †242 (Reimer 1998): Analytical bibliography studies the processes of making books, especially the material modes of production, including the practices of [a] scriptorium or printing shop. One of the purposes of analytical bibliography is to understand how the processes of material production affect the nature and state of the text preserved in the book.

analytical entry, n. ~ CATALOGING · An entry in a catalog that describes a part of a larger work that is also described in the catalog.

> *Syn:* in-analytic
>
> *Notes:* In archival cataloging, analytical entries may be made for series or items within a collection. In bibliographic cataloging, analytical entries may be made for chapters of books, and special issues of or articles in periodicals.

analytical index, n. ~ A list of headings, organized into groups based on similar characteristics rather than in alphabetical order, that points to information relevant to the heading in materials organized in some other manner.

> *Syn:* classified index

BT: index

Notes: Analytical indexes are typically hierarchical, using general headings that are further subdivided by more specific headings.

analytical inventory, n. ~ A detailed description of a collection, often at the file or item level.

RT: calendar

ancient documents, n. ~ The principle that documents are in such condition and have been stored in such manner that their authenticity is not suspect.

BT: document

RT: authenticity

†84 *(Fed. R. Evid.):* Ancient documents or data compilation. Evidence that a document or data compilation, in any form, (A) is in such condition as to create no suspicion concerning its authenticity, (B) was in a place where it, if authentic, would likely be, and (C) has been in existence 20 years or more at the time it is offered.

Anglo-American Cataloguing Rules, n. (**AACR, AACR2, AACR2R,** abbr.) ~ A standard for creating catalogs of collections, especially library collections, including the consistent description of those materials and the formation and assignment of access points under which those descriptions are arranged.

RT: Archives, Personal Papers, and Manuscripts, cataloging, descriptive cataloging, descriptive standard, Subject Cataloging Manual: Subject Headings

Notes: The first edition of AACR, published in 1967, was based on *Rules for Descriptive Cataloging in the Library of Congress,* published in 1949. The second edition, AACR2, was published in 1978, and the third edition, AACR2R, in 1988. A revision of the third edition incorporating amendments approved since 1988 was released in 2002. *Archives, Personal Papers, and Manuscripts* is an amplification and interpretation of Chapter 4 of AACR that is designed to ensure that descriptions of archival materials can be integrated into bibliographic catalogs based on AACR.

Although used principally for describing published works, the rules can also be used to describe any materials, including maps, manuscripts, music, sound recordings, still and moving images, three-dimensional artifacts, and natural specimens. AACR provides rules for the title and statement of responsibility, edition, material (or type of publication) specific details, publication and distribution, physical description, series, notes, and standard numbers and terms of availability. It also includes rules for establishing the main entry and added entries, as well as the forms of those entries. AACR does not include rules for creating or assigning subject headings, which are covered by the *Subject Cataloging Manual.*

AACR is maintained by the Joint Steering Committee for Revision of Anglo-American Cataloguing Rules (see http://www.collectionscanada.ca/jsc/). The constituent organizations represented on the Joint Steering Committee include the American Library Association, the Australian Committee on Cataloguing, the British Library, the Canadian Committee on Cataloguing, CILIP (Chartered Institute of Library and Information Professionals), and the Library of Congress.

†11 *(AACR2, 0.1):* These rules are designed for use in the construction of catalogues and other lists in general libraries of all sizes. They are not specifically intended for specialist and archival libraries, but such libraries are recommended to use the rules as the basis of their cataloguing and to augment their provisions as necessary. The rules cover the description of, and the provision of access points for, all library materials commonly collected at the present time.

Ann Arbor Accords, n. ~ Principles and criteria used to develop a Standard Generalized Markup Language (SGML) document type definition (DTD) for archival and library finding aids, especially inventories and registers.

> *Notes:* The Ann Arbor Accords were developed in 1995 under a Bentley Library Research Fellowship by a team led by Daniel Pitti that included Steven DeRose, Jackie Dooley, Michael J. Fox, Steven Hensen, Kris Kiesling, Janice Ruth, Sharon Thibodeau, and Helena Zinkham. The thirteen accords are organized into Definitions and Parameters, General Principles, Structural Features, and Control and Maintenance.

annex, n. ~ 1. Something, usually a document, that is attached to a larger work as a supplement; an attachment. – 2. An addition to a building.

> *DF:* appendix
>
> *RT:* accompanying material, attachment
>
> *Notes:* An annex[1] is distinguished from an appendix by the fact that it is created independently of the larger document.
>
> †149 *(Jenkinson 1966, p. 7):* The distinction between what can and cannot be 'annexed' to a document is like all fine distinctions, difficult. Its particular difficulty may perhaps be illustrated by a *reductio ad absurdum*. Supposing for example that a Viceroy sends home to the Secretary of State in England an elephant with a suitable covering-note or label; or supposing, to take a more actual example, that the Government of a Colony presents to the First Commissioner of Works in London a two-hundred foot spar of Douglas Pine: the question may be imagined to arise: Is the spar 'annexed' to correspondence with the Government of British Columbia? Is the elephant attached to the label or the label to the elephant? ¶ The answer to those who would put this dilemma to us in the present connexion is that the Administration would be obliged in all such cases to solve the question of housing – to send the spar to Kew Gardens or the elephant to the Zoo – long before the label or letter comes into charge of the Archivist: the problem is an Administrative, not an Archive one.

annotation, n. ~ Information, especially explanatory notes or commentary, added to a completed document.

> *BT:* extrinsic element
>
> *RT:* gloss, marginalia
>
> *Notes:* In diplomatics, annotations include markings that relate to their handling or management, such as instructions, dates of hearing or readings, signs beside the text, cross-references, protocol number, classification code, date stamp. In documentary editing, annotations help explain texts, including information about variant editions and explanations of information once common knowledge but now unfamiliar to most readers. In rare books and archives, annotation usually refers to comments on the materials made by the collector.
>
> †17 *(InterPARES Authenticity, p. 6):* Annotations (additions made to a record after it has been created) . . . fall into three basic groups: 1) additions made to the record after its creation as part of its execution (e.g., the date and time of transmission added to an email record at the moment it is sent, or the indication of attachments added before it is transmitted); 2) additions made to the record in the course of handling the business matter in which the record participates (e.g., comments noted on the face of the record, or embedded in it, and dates of transmis-

---

BT: Broader Term • NT: Narrower Term • RT: Related Term • DF: Distinguish From

sion to other offices); 3) additions made to the record in the course of handling it for records management purposes (e.g., the classification code or file number assigned to the record, its draft and/or version number, cross references to other records, and an indication of scheduling actions).

†155 (Kline 1998, p. 211): Even while establishing the documentary texts that form the core of any edition, editors must consider the documents' need for editorial explanatory or informational annotation, glossaries and gazetteers, back-of-book records, and even the form of the index that provides the ultimate access to the contents of text and notes alike.

†167 (D Levy 2001, p. 92–93): Annotation is, of course, one of the most basic and important ways we have to tailor a document to particular circumstances of use. . . . We may write on a memo or a printed copy of an e-mail message, then fax the annotated copy to someone else. Or we may write in the margins of a book we're reading, or highlight the text with a colored marker.

annual report, n. ~ A summary of activities and a statement of accounts issued on a yearly basis by an organization, especially by a corporation for stockholders.

BT: report

RT: corporate report

anonymity, n. ~ 1. The right and ability to associate, receive information, and communicate without having to reveal one's identity. – 2. A lack of distinctiveness.

RT: privacy

†188 (McIntyre v. Ohio Elections Commission 1995): The decision in favor of anonymity[1] may be motivated by fear of economic or official retaliation, by concern about social ostracism, or merely by a desire to preserve as much of one's privacy as possible. . . . ¶ Anonymity is a shield from the tyranny of the majority. It thus exemplifies the purpose behind the Bill of Rights, and of the First Amendment in particular: to protect unpopular individuals from retaliation – and their ideas from suppression – at the hand of an intolerant society.

ANSI ~ see: American National Standards Institute

Notes: In this glossary, ANSI standards are entered under their full name, with a cross-reference from the code. For example, the International Standard Serial Number (ISSN) is found under that name, with a see reference from Z39.9.

anthronymy, n. ~ The study of personal names.

BT: onomastics

antiquarianism, n. ~ An interest in things that are old, especially because of their age rather than other qualities.

†6 (Abraham 1999): [Henry Adams'] 1910 report 'To American Teachers of History' . . . attempted to demonstrate that Darwinism, thermodynamics and modern scientific thought must influence the teaching of history as a scientific discipline. He argued that historians must rearrange their prevailing world-view or forever be consigned to antiquarianism.

aperture card, n. ~ A card, suitable for use in a data processing system, that is designed to hold one or more frames of microfilm.

RT: microfilm, microform

Notes: Aperture cards may have an area for printed information, as well as an area reserved for punching to encode information to facilitate automated storage and retrieval of the card.

API ~ *see:* application program interface

appendix, n. (**appendixes, appendices**, pl.) ~ Supplemental material that, due to its nature or limitations of space, is placed at the end of a work.

>   *DF:* annex, attachment

>   · *Notes:* An appendix is distinguished from an annex by the fact that the appendix is created as part of the document to which it belongs, rather than being added after the fact.

application, n. ~ 1. A request, usually submitted in written form. – 2. COMPUTING · A piece of software that performs a function; a computer program. – 3. The act of applying or superimposing.

>   *Syn:* computer program, program

>   *RT:* software

>   *Notes:* Applications² are often distinguished from the underlying operating system. The former are intended to support the work of the human users, while the latter supports the computer's internal processes. **Applets** are small applications that are designed to perform a specific function in a web browser to support client-side processing. – Application³ includes the physical, such as a coating on a surface, as well as the intangible, such as the practical use of a theoretical model.

application program interface (sometimes called **middleware**), n. (**API**, abbr.) ~ Software conventions that provide a link between one application and another piece of software.

>   *RT:* middleware

>   *Notes:* APIs are used primarily to support portability of applications across different operating systems. A single application makes calls to APIs customized to support that application on different platforms. However, APIs may also support interactions between an application and the system or between different applications.

APPM ~ *see:* Archives, Personal Papers, and Manuscripts

appraisal, n. ~ 1. The process of identifying materials offered to an archives that have sufficient value to be accessioned. – 2. The process of determining the length of time records should be retained, based on legal requirements and on their current and potential usefulness. – 3. The process of determining the market value of an item; monetary appraisal.

>   *DF:* evaluation, monetary appraisal

>   *NT:* content analysis, context analysis, documentation strategy, functional analysis, macro appraisal, use analysis

>   *RT:* collection development, fat file method, reappraisal, selection, valuation, value

>   *Notes:* In an archival context, appraisal¹ is the process of determining whether records and other materials have permanent (archival) value. Appraisal may be done at the collection, creator, series, file, or item level. Appraisal can take place prior to donation and prior to physical transfer, at or after accessioning. The basis of appraisal decisions may include a number of factors, including the records' provenance and content, their authenticity and reliability, their order and completeness, their condition and costs to preserve them, and their intrinsic value. Appraisal often takes place within a larger institutional collecting policy and mission statement.

Appraisal is distinguished from monetary appraisal, which estimates fair market value. Appraisal is distinguished from evaluation, which is typically used by records managers to indicate a preliminary assessment of value based on existing retention schedules.

†35 (Brichford 1977, p. 2): The archivists considering the records to be appraised will study their age, volume, and form, and will analyze their functional, evidential, and informational characteristics.

†70 (Duranti 1998, p. 177): The principle ·of provenance, as applied to appraisal, leads us to evaluate records on the basis of the importance of the creator's mandate and functions, and fosters the use of a hierarchical method, a 'top-down' approach, which has proved to be unsatisfactory because it excludes the 'powerless transactions,' which might throw light on the broader social context, from the permanent record of society.

†76 (Eastwood 2004, p. 40): This idea of Jenkinson's [that archivists ought not to be in the business of destroying records] has, as might be expected, almost universal condemnation by archivists who routinely conduct appraisal, often nowadays mandated in legislation where public records are concerned. It may seem that events have passed Jenkinson by, but, in fact, as several archivists inspired by postmodernist thinking have argued, when archivists decide what to save and what to destroy, they begin to be a factor in the determination of what archives are.

†112 (Ham 1993, p. 51): There are five analyses that make up the basic tools archivists need in their appraisal kits to identify and select records of enduring value. These are an analysis: of a record's functional characteristics – who made the record and for what purpose; of the information in the record to determine its significance and quality; of the record in the context of parallel or related documentary sources; of the potential uses that are likely to be made of the record and the physical, legal, and intellectual limitations on access; of the cost of preserving the record weighed against the benefit of retaining the information.

†223 (Personal communication, Mark Greene, 28 May 2004): The basis on which appraisal decisions should be made has been the subject of intense professional debate. Some archival theorists, notably Jenkinson, argue that such decisions should not be made by archivists at all, but only by records creators. In the United States, Schellenberg believed that appraisal was not only an appropriate archival function but an absolutely necessary one, in the face of increasing masses of documentation in the 20th century. U.S. archival theory and practice has been rooted in Schellenberg's philosophy and teaching.

aqueous deacidification ~ *see:* deacidification

Archaeological Resources Protection Act, n. (**ARPA,** abbr.) ~ A federal law, passed in 1979 (16 USC 1B, Pub. L. 96-95) 'to protect archaeological resources on public and Indian lands.'

architectural drawing, n. ~ A sketch, diagram, plan, or schematic used to design, construct, and document buildings and other structures.

BT: architectural records, drawing

NT: as-built drawing, measured drawing

RT: blueprint, brownline, computer-aided design, engineering drawing, technical drawing

Notes: The drawings may be used to indicate the overall appearance, inside or outside the structure, or they may be used to indicate precise measurements and

other details for construction. Drawings, especially those for construction purposes, may be issued as a set, with different sheets indicating different types of
construction (electrical, mechanical, plumbing). Schematic drawings were often
created on linen with ink, then reproduced by the blueprint process. These drawings are now often created using computer-aided design (CAD) tools.

'Architectural drawing' is commonly used to describe both originals and
reproductions, although some use the term to distinguish original drawings from
reproductions. '**Architectural reproductions**' is used as a generic term to describe
the broad class of copies made with many different processes.

architectural records, n. ~ Documents and materials that are created or assembled as
part of the design, construction, and documentation of buildings and similar
large structures, and that are preserved for their administrative, legal, fiscal, or
archival value.

> *DF:* engineering records
> *BT:* record
> *NT:* architectural drawing, architectural rendering, design drawing, elevation,
> oblique
> *Notes:* Architectural records include print and electronic formats, models, and
> other supporting records, such as contracts, specifications, and procurement
> records. The phrase 'architectural records' connotes records relating to buildings
> and similar, large built structures; they are generally distinguished from engineer-
> ing records, which connote records relating to smaller, fabricated materials, and
> records in which functionality takes precedence over aesthetics.

architectural rendering, n. ~ An illustration intended to suggest the appearance of a
building or other static structure when completed.

> *BT:* architectural records
> *RT:* drawing
> *Notes:* Renderings may be of an interior or exterior, and show volume and
> shadows, textures and colors, and surrounding environmental features, such as
> landscaping. They are often done in watercolor, pen-and-ink, or pastels. They are
> sometimes referred to as an artist's conception.

architectural reproductions ~ *see:* architectural drawing

architecture, n. ~ 1. The design of and specifications for how something is constructed, especially buildings and large, static structures. – 2. COMPUTING · The
design and specifications of hardware, software, or a combination of thereof, especially how those components interact.

archival, adj. ~ 1. Of or pertaining to archives. – 2. RECORDS · Having enduring value;
permanent. – 3. RECORDS MEDIA · Durable; lacking inherent vice; long-lived; see
archival quality. – 4. STORAGE CONDITIONS · Not causing degradation. – 5.
PROCEDURES · Following accepted standards that ensure maximum longevity. – 6.
COMPUTING · Information of long-term value that, because of its low use, is stored
on offline media and must be reloaded, or that is in a form that must be reconstructed before use.

> *RT:* archival quality
> *Notes:* The use of archival[2] to denote records whose content has been
> appraised as having enduring value is fairly standard. Some archivists prefer the
> phrase 'enduring value' to 'permanent' when describing archival records, but per-
> manence remains part of the vernacular understanding of the term.

†235 (Puglia, Reed, and Rhodes 2004, p. 61): The term 'archival'³ indicates the materials used to manufacture the CD-R (usually the dye layer where the data is recording, a protective gold layer to prevent pollutants from attacking the dye, or a physically durable top-coat to protect the surface of the disk) are reasonably stable and have good durability, but this will not guarantee the longevity of the media itself.

†262 (Sedona Principles 2003, p. 41): [archival⁶ data] Information that is not directly accessible to the user of a computer system but that the organization maintains for long-term storage and record-keeping purposes. Archival data may be written to removable media such as a CD, magneto-optical media, tape or other electronic storage device, or may be maintained on system hard drives in compressed formats.

archival administration ~ *see:* archives management

Archival Administration in the Electronic Information Age ~ *see:* Camp Pitt

archival agency ~ *see:* archives

Archival and Manuscripts Control Format (AMC) ~ *see:* MARC Format for Archival and Manuscripts Control

archival bond, n. ~ 1. PRINCIPALLY CANADIAN · The interrelationships between a record and other records resulting from the same activity. – 2. A grade of paper that is durable and has a long life expectancy.

RT: bond paper, context, durable paper, Permanence of Paper for Publications and Documents in Libraries and Archives, permanent paper

Notes: The archival bond¹ places a record in context and gives additional meaning to the record. It includes the relationships between records that relate to a specific transaction (such as an application, a resulting report, and the dispositive record that concludes the transaction), as well as the relationship between the records of preceding and subsequent transactions.

†140 (InterPARES Glossary 2002): [archival bond] The relationship that links each record, incrementally, to the previous and subsequent ones and to all those which participate in the same activity. It is originary (i.e., it comes into existence when a record is made or received and set aside), necessary (i.e., it exists for every record), and determined (i.e., it is characterized by the purpose of the record).

archival description, n. ~ 1. The process of analyzing, organizing, and recording details about the formal elements of a record or collection of records, such as creator, title, dates, extent, and contents, to facilitate the work's identification, management, and understanding. – 2. The product of such a process.

DF: bibliographic description

BT: description

RT: administrative history, biographical note, Encoded Archival Description, Manual of Archival Description, Rules for Archival Description, scope and contents note, series descriptive system

Notes: Archival description¹ is similar to the process of bibliographic description, and some standards for archival description are derived from bibliographic standards. A key difference is that, in the absence of a title page to serve as the chief source of information, archival description requires a significant amount of the content of the description to be supplied from the context of the materials being described, whereas the content of bibliographic description is transcribed directly from the material being described. Also, archival descriptions are intended to be updated if materials are added to the collection.

†227 *(Pitti 1999):* The distinction between what and for whom libraries and archives remember accounts form the major differences in archival and bibliographic description. A bibliographic description, such as that found in a MARC record, represents an individual published item, and thus is item-level. There is a one-to-one correspondence between the description and the item. The description is based on, and is derived from, the physical item. Archival description represents a fonds, a complex body of materials, frequently in more than one form or medium, sharing a common provenance. The description involves a complex hierarchical and progressive analysis. It begins by describing the whole, then proceeds to identify and describe sub-components of the whole, and sub-components of sub-components, and so on. Frequently, but by no means always, the description terminates with a description of individual items. The description emphasizes the intellectual structure and content of the material, rather than their physical characteristics.

archival integrity, n. ~ The principle that a body of records resulting from the same activity must be preserved as a group, without division, separation, or addition, to protect the evidential and informational value that can be discerned from its context.

RT: file integrity, integrity

Notes: The concept, articulated by Hilary Jenkinson, derives from the principles of provenance, which prevents records from different sources from being intermingled, and of original order, which ensures that the records reflect the manner in which they were used by their creator. The disposal of duplicate records within a collection is generally not considered a violation of archival integrity. If materials are relocated for preservation, restricted access, or security, archival integrity can be preserved by placing a separation sheet in the materials' original location.

†31 *(Boles and Greene 1996):* Faced with documents in quantities never before encountered in human history, many American archivists have a great deal of trouble believing that losing a few stray pieces of paper would truly matter. Indeed many American archivists might be willing to stand Jenkinson's dictum on its head, arguing that in nine cases out of ten weeding excess documents from a file may well make the inter-relationships clearer.

†286 *(ICA Dictionary 1988):* [archival integrity] A basic standard derived from the principle of provenance and the registry principle which requires that an archive/record group shall be preserved in its entirety without division, mutilation, alienation, unauthorized destruction or addition, except by accrual or replevin, in order to ensure its full evidential and informational value.

archival jurisdiction, n. ~ The limits of responsibility mandated to an archives by law.

Notes: Archival jurisdiction includes the agencies, organizations, and individuals creating or receiving records for which the archives is responsible, and the specific functions the archives is responsible for, including appraisal and scheduling, screening for restrictions, preservation, transfer, use, and disposal of records.

archival medium, n. (**archival media,** pl.) ~ The material that serves as the carrier of the content of a record and that, because of the manner in which it was made, has a very long life expectancy when properly stored and handled.

Notes: 'Archival medium' is not a technical concept that is appropriate for specifying media for creating permanent records, although it is often used informally to distinguish media appropriate for archival records from other media.

†*102 (ANSI/AIIM Glossary 1998, p. 5):* [archival medium] Recording material that can be expected to retain information forever, so that such information can be retrieved without significant loss when properly stored. However, there is no such material and it is not a term to be used in American National Standard material or system specifications.

archival nature, n. ~ The characteristics that are inherent in archival documents resulting from the circumstances of their creation, including naturalness, organic nature or interrelationship, impartiality, authenticity, and uniqueness.

RT: authenticity

Notes: While the origins of the concept lie in the United Kingdom and Europe, recent exponents have been Canadian. Some archivists believe that the term implies a universality and immutability of what archives inherently are that cannot be supported by evidence. **Naturalness** refers to the fact that the materials accumulate out of a routine process. The organic nature or **interrelationship** results from the materials' functional relationships to one another within and outside each given fonds. **Impartiality** describes records as a means for carrying out activities they document. **Authenticity** relates to records with their creator. **Uniqueness** describes the fact that each document is related to the others within and outside the fonds of which it is a part, and to the creator of the fonds by a special relationship, which makes it unique.

†*31 (Boles and Greene 1996, p. 302):* [Duranti] speaks of the 'nature' of archives as a fixed and immutable reality from which true archival theory derives. The nature of archives, however, is a human postulate, based on human assumptions and logically derived from those assumptions. These postulates may vary between individuals and societies and cannot be considered an observed fact or a testable hypothesis.

archival processing, n. ~ 1. The arrangement, description, and housing of archival materials for storage and use by patrons. – 2. PHOTOGRAPHY · Techniques for processing[2] photographs that are designed to produce very stable, long-lasting images.

RT: processing, residual hypo test

Notes: Archival processing[1] is frequently shortened to just 'processing'. – Archival processing[2] may include use of two fixing baths to remove all undeveloped silver and extended wash times. It may include toning images with gold, selenium, or sulfide to stabilize a pure metallic silver image. Archival processing may include a residual hypo test to ensure adequate washing.

archival quality, adj. ~ 1. RECORDS MEDIA · Resistant to deterioration or loss of quality, allowing for a long life expectancy when kept in controlled conditions. – 2. RECORDS STORAGE CONDITIONS · Not causing harm or reduced life expectancy.

RT: archival, permanence

Notes: ANSI/AIIM deprecates the use of 'archival' because it is a highly subjective term. Rather, they suggest using measures of 'life expectancy', which are based on empirical tests. While no materials meet the ideal definition of 'archival', many archivists use the term informally to refer to media that can preserve information, when properly stored, for more than a century. The use of 'archival' in commercial advertising to describe products suitable for materials and implying an infinite life span has made this use of the word nearly meaningless; some products so described would never be used by most archivists for such purposes.

Syn: Synonym · †: see Bibliography · *Superscript:* Definition number

When archivists need to specify media appropriate for records of enduring value or containers for the storage of such materials, they avoid the term 'archival' and use specific requirements such as 'lignin free' or 'acid free with a three percent calcium carbonate reserve.'

archival records, n. ~ Materials created or received by a person, family, or organization, public or private, in the conduct of their affairs that are preserved because of the enduring value contained in the information they contain or as evidence of the functions and responsibilities of their creator.

> *Syn:* permanent records
> *BT:* record
> *RT:* archives
> *Notes:* 'Archival records' connotes documents rather than artifacts or published materials, although collections of archival records may contain artifacts and books. Archival records may be in any format, including text on paper or in electronic formats, photographs, motion pictures, videos, sound recordings. The phrase archival records is sometimes used as an expanded form of archives to distinguish the holdings from the program.

archival science, n. ~ A systematic body of theory that supports the practice of appraising, acquiring, authenticating, preserving, and providing access to recorded materials.

> *Syn:* archival studies
> *RT:* archivy
> †73 *(Duranti and MacNeil 1996, p. 47):* Archival science, which emerged out of diplomatics in the nineteenth century, is a body of concepts and methods directed toward the study of records in terms of their documentary and functional relationships and the ways in which they are controlled and communicated.

archival software, n. ~ 1. Computer programs designed to facilitate the management of archives. – 2. Computer programs designed to extract noncurrent records from an online system and transfer them to offline or nearline storage.

archival storage conditions, n. ~ An environment suitable for the protection of materials from hazards such as theft, fire, flood, particulates, pests, or vandalism, and from extremes or fluctuations in temperature, relative humidity, or light.

> *RT:* staging area
> *Notes:* The phrase is used generally for areas with environmental controls specifically engineered for the protection of the materials, as distinguished from areas without environmental controls (attics, storage sheds) or with controls appropriate to other considerations (the comfort of office workers). No single standard defines an ideal archival environment, and different types of materials may require different conditions.

archival structure, n. ~ The administrative context and functionality of records, especially as reflected in the records' form and organization.

> *Notes:* Often expressed as the **principle of respect for archival structure**, which asserts the methodology that an archives' appraisal, arrangement, and description should reflect the organic nature of the records.

archival studies, n. ~ 1. A formal curriculum for teaching the theory and practice of archival science. – 2. The body of knowledge that supports the practice of appraising, acquiring, authenticating, preserving, and providing access to recorded materials; archival science.

Syn: archival science

RT: archivy

Notes: See http://www.archivists.org/prof-education/ed_guidelines.asp.

archival succession, n. ~ The transfer of legal responsibility for the management of archives as a result of changes in government or corporate structure.

archival teaching unit, n. ~ 1. A selection of facsimiles of documents, often in a variety of formats, with explanatory materials used to help teach research techniques based on archival materials. – 2. A selection of such documents relating to a specific topic intended for use in the classroom during study of that topic.

archival threshold, n. ~ 1. The point at which an archives takes physical custody of records. – 2. The point when records, especially those in an electronic recordkeeping system maintained by the agency of creation, are distinguished from active or semiactive records so that they may be preserved in accordance with an agreement with the archives.

Notes: The phrase is a metaphor based on the notion of an archives acquiring records by bringing them through a door (crossing the threshold).

archival value (also **permanent value, continuing value, enduring value,** and, mostly outside the United States, **indefinite value**), n. ~ The ongoing usefulness or significance of records, based on the administrative, legal, fiscal, evidential, or historical information they contain, justifying their continued preservation.

Syn: enduring value, historical value, permanent value

BT: value

RT: primary value, secondary value

Notes: In general, records with archival value are estimated to make up only three to five percent of an organization's records. In most organizations, the determination of which records are considered to have archival value is made by archivists.

archive, v. ~ 1. To transfer records from the individual or office of creation to a repository authorized to appraise, preserve, and provide access to those records. – 2. COMPUTING · To store data offline. – n. ~ 3. An archives.[1,2,3,5] – 4. COMPUTING · Data stored offline. – 5. COMPUTING · A backup. – 6. COMPUTING · An attribute in some file systems, typically used to indicate that a file has changed since it was backed up.

DF: archives, backup

NT: data archive

Notes: United States and Canadian archivists generally deprecate the use of 'archive' (without an s) as a noun to mean a collection of records ('archives'), but that form is common in other English-speaking countries. In information technology, the s-less form, 'archive', is commonly used as a verb and to describe collections of backup data.

A data archive[3] is sometimes distinguished from a backup (archive[5]), the former storing data in a form that is readily accessible by software applications and the latter storing data along with system files and applications in a format that supports restoration of part or all of a system after a disaster.

†181 *(Maher 1998, p. 254):* There are collateral tendencies to use the word 'archive' minus its North American requisite 's' and to 'verbify' the noun. ¶ In many cases, the nonprofessional appropriation of the term 'archives' appears to be part of an attempt by the scholar or database builder to lend panache or cachet and an air of respectability to what otherwise might be little more than a personal

hobby or collecting fetish. As archivists, should we simply welcome this popularization of the term 'archives' or should we be bothered by the prevalence of its frequent misuse? Perhaps we should look only on the positive side and see that the growing recognition of the value and importance of documentation that [David] Gracy sought. On the other hand, there is in the popularized use of 'archives' a rather significant threat to the basic goals of the archival profession. Call it paranoia, but I always have the sense that when we see 'archive' used as a verb, or the word 'archives' used in a bastardized way to describe what is clearly a singular, idiosyncratic, and synthetic gathering of documents, we are being confronted with a challenge to our position as professional archivists.

archive group, *see:* record group

archives (also **archive**), n. ~ 1. Materials created or received by a person, family, or organization, public or private, in the conduct of their affairs and preserved because of the enduring value contained in the information they contain or as evidence of the functions and responsibilities of their creator, especially those materials maintained using the principles of provenance, original order, and collective control; permanent records. – 2. The division within an organization responsible for maintaining the organization's records of enduring value. – 3. An organization that collects the records of individuals, families, or other organizations; a collecting archives. – 4. The professional discipline of administering such collections and organizations. – 5. The building (or portion thereof) housing archival collections. – 6. A published collection of scholarly papers, especially as a periodical.

DF: archive

BT: collection, repository

NT: business archives, collecting archives, corporate archives, dark archives, iconographic archives, institutional archives, joint archives, light archives, migrated archives, photographic archives, removed archives

RT: archival records, artificial collection, backup, fonds, manuscript repository, permanent records, total archives

Notes: In the vernacular, 'archives' is often used to refer to any collection of documents that are old or of historical interest, regardless of how they are organized; in this sense, the term is synonymous with permanent records. That use is reflected by archives[6], as used within the e-prints community and periodicals such as *The Archives of Internal Medicine*. Within the professional literature, archives are characterized by an organic nature, growing out of the process of creating and receiving records in the course of the routine activities of the creator (its provenance). In this sense, archivists have differentiated archives from artificial collections.

Many archivists, especially those in the United States who are influenced by the thinking of Theodore Schellenberg, follow an inclusive definition of archives, which encompasses a wide variety of documents and records. Schellenberg also distinguished between the primary and secondary value of the materials; only materials with secondary value, value beyond their original purpose, could be considered archival. For Schellenberg, archivists appraise records for transfer to the archives on the basis of their secondary, research, evidential, or informational value.

Other archivists follow the writing of Hilary Jenkinson, who argues that archives are 'documents which formed part of an official transaction and were preserved for official reference.' For Jenkinson, the records creator is responsible for determining which records should be transferred to the archives for preservation. Because Jenkinson emphasized that records are evidence of transactions, he did not recognize any collections of historical documents as archives, although he noted that collections of personal papers were of value to historians because they complemented archives.

'Manuscript repository' is sometimes used instead of archives³ to distinguish an organization that collects personal papers from an agency that collects the records of its parent organization.

Some United States archivists deprecate the use of the form 'archive' (without the final s) as a noun, but that form is common in other English-speaking countries. However, the noun 'archive' is commonly used to describe collections of backup data in information technology literature.

†27 (Berner 1983, p. 7): The fateful separation of the historical manuscripts tradition field from the public archives field began in 1910 at the AHA's Conference of Archivists, when the application of library principles was attacked as inapplicable to public archives. The differences that developed meant that the historical manuscripts tradition would remain linked to techniques of librarianship. Public archives, meanwhile, would develop along lines derived from European archival institutions where theory and practice had long been the object of scholarly discourse and refinement.

†51 (Cox 1994, p. 9): Archives are records with ongoing evidential value to the organization and society. Documents are all efforts to use data and information to capture knowledge. Records constitute transactional records within organizations.

†64 (Doyle 2001, p. 353): [Leonard] Rapport urged us to consider archives not as permanently valuable, but as *worthy of continued preservation* – a conceptual shift that justifies the reappraisal of current holdings and revision of the standards by which archivists appraised those records in the first place.

†119 (Henry 1998, p. 315): The value of archives is cultural and humanistic, not just bureaucratic. Archival programs that collect records or personal papers, which may contain electronic media, find the new definition of record [as evidence of a business transaction] bewildering. Personal papers may never show 'evidence' of 'business transactions,' but such archival sources provide a wealth of information needed for society's memory.

†120 (APPM2 1989, 1.0A): The preserved documentary records of any corporate body, governmental agency or office, or organization or group that are the direct result of administrative or organizational activity of the originating body and that are maintained according to their original provenance.

†123 (Hirtle 2000, p. 10): In the vernacular, the word archives has come to mean anything that is old or established. . . . A true archives is a contextually based organic body of evidence, not a collection of miscellaneous information. . . . The documents constituting a formal archives are further distinguished by the fact that they have to have been officially produced or received by an administrative body. Such documents become records. . . .

†149 (Jenkinson 1966, p. 11): A document which may be said to belong to the class of Archives is one which was drawn up or used in the course of an administrative or executive transaction (whether public or private) of which itself formed a part; and subsequently preserved in their own custody for their own informa-

tion by the person or persons responsible for that transaction and their legitimate successors. To this Definition we may add a corollary. Archives were not drawn up in the interest or for the information of Posterity.

†154 *(Kaplan 2000, p. 147):* The pervading view of archives as sites of historical truth is at best outdated, and at worst inherently dangerous. The archival record doesn't just happen; it is created by individuals and organizations, and used, in turn, to support their values and missions, all of which comprises a process that is certainly not politically and culturally neutral.

†167 *(D Levy 2001, p. 96):* In an informal and possibly unselfconscious way, we maintain a personal archive, a treasure chest of cherished artifacts and the memories they hold for us. The word 'archives' comes from the Latin *arca*, originally meaning a place to store things, a box or chest. (In English, we still find *ark* used in this way, in phrases like 'Noah's Ark' and 'the Ark of the Covenant.')

†174 *(Lubar 1999, p. 14):* We use an archives to remember things after they happen. But if we think of the records in archives as points of inscription, as sites of cultural production, we realize that they serve, if not to remember things before they happen, to remember things as they happen. Indeed, the process of 'archivization' *makes* things happen by allowing us to make sense of what is happening.

†181 *(Maher 1998, p. 255):* What is most troubling in these pseudo-repositories is their lack of the professional and theory-based application of the seven major archival responsibilities. That is, what defines the professional core of archival work is the systematic and theoretically based execution of seven highly interrelated responsibilities – securing clear authority for the program and collection, authenticating the validity of the evidence held, appraising, arranging, describing, preserving, and promoting use.

†191 *(Miller 1990, p. 20):* The documents in archival collections relate to each other in ways that transcend the information in each document. The archival whole is greater than the sum of its parts; the relationships are as important as the particulars.

Archives, Personal Papers, and Manuscripts, n. (**APPM,** abbr.) ~ A standard for developing a catalog of archival materials, principally at the collection level, with consistent descriptions and access points that can be integrated into bibliographic catalogs constructed using *Anglo-American Cataloguing Rules.*

RT: Anglo-American Cataloguing Rules, cataloging, descriptive standard

Notes: APPM was compiled by Steven L. Hensen. It was first published by the Library of Congress in 1983, and a second, revised edition was published by the Society of American Archivists in 1989.

†85 *(Feeney 1999, p. 207):* Revised and promoted as a standard in 1989 by the Society of American Archivists, APPM addresses inadequacies in standard library cataloging rules, developed for classification and description of published materials such as books rather than for unique materials such as archival documents and manuscripts.

†121 *(Henson 1993, p. 68):* The various rules laid down in APPM are either directly derived from their counterparts in AACR2 or are archival interpretations, expansions, and glosses of standard AACR2 rules – the last being particularly the case in the chapters on forming personal and corporate name headings.

archives administration ~ *see:* archives management

Archives and Mixed Collections File, n. (**AMC File,** abbr.) ~ A union catalog maintained by the Research Libraries Group (RLG) that contains catalog descriptions of literary and historical documents, public records, and other primary source materials in various formats.

> *Notes:* These catalog records include collections, portions of collections, and single items. The records can be searched by personal name, organization, subject, and format.

archives box (also **manuscript box**), n. ~ A container made from materials appropriate for the long-term storage of archival materials.

> *BT:* box
>
> *RT:* document box
>
> *Notes:* Archives boxes are usually the size of a document box, and the terms may be used interchangeably. However, archives box emphasizes that it is made from high-quality materials. Archives boxes are distinguished from records center boxes, the latter being made of inexpensive materials and used for nonpermanent records.

archives management (also **archives administration**), n. ~ The general oversight of a program to appraise, acquire, arrange and describe, preserve, authenticate, and provide access to permanently valuable records.

> *RT:* archivy
>
> *Notes:* Archives administration includes establishing the program's mission and goals, securing necessary resources to support those activities, and evaluating the program's performance. Archives management is distinguished from library, museum, and historical manuscripts traditions by the principles of provenance, original order, and collective control to preserve the materials' authenticity, context, and intellectual character.

archivist, n. ~ 1. An individual responsible for appraising, acquiring, arranging, describing, preserving, and providing access to records of enduring value, according to the principles of provenance, original order, and collective control to protect the materials' authenticity and context. – 2. An individual with responsibility for management and oversight of an archival repository or of records of enduring value.

> *RT:* curator, librarian, manuscript curator, records manager
>
> *Notes:* An archivist's work with records of enduring value may be at any stage in the records life cycle, from creation onward. In the United States, archivists are typically associated with collections of inactive records. However, the European tradition includes management of active records as well, which in the United States is often the responsibility of a separate records manager. In the United States, archivists may be called manuscript curators, especially if they are responsible for collecting and administering collections of historical records acquired from individuals, families, or other organizations.
>
> In some organizations, an archivist may be responsible for management of active, inactive, and archival records. In other organizations, an archivist may be responsible only for those records transferred to the archives. In a large repository, a practicing archivist may specialize in only one or a few archival functions noted above. A teaching archivist may not be currently responsible for collections but is familiar with the theory and practice of archival functions.
>
> †8 *(Adkins 1997, p. 9):* The archival profession in the United States began with the establishment of the National Archives in Washington, D.C., in 1934. Before

that, historians and librarians had shared a common concern for the preservation of archival records and manuscripts, but there were few individuals who called themselves archivists.

†13 *(Appraisal Methodology 2000):* Macro-appraisal asserts that archivists – not researchers or creators – are society's professional agents appointed by law to form its collective memory. By virtue of their appraisal decisions, archivists actively shape the documentary legacy of their own time.

†53 *(Craig and O'Toole 2000, p. 125):* Archivists have a dual personality. On the one hand they are cognizant of the utilitarian role of records in administration and the law. From this perspective they view the meaning of documents as largely fixed by explicit procedure, albeit procedure in a context. On the other hand, they are sensitive to the historical changes in records and the contingent circumstances in which they thrived. From this perspective archivists are uneasy about notions of fixed meanings and welcome the changing insights of historically based scholarship.

†108 *(Greene, et al., 2001):* Anyone who works as a keeper of stuff in a corporate environment cannot afford to worry too much about the fine distinctions between Record Manager, Librarian, Archivist and Document Control Manager. The key is to keep what the corporation needs. Need is difficult to define, but people in corporations know when you have something, or have organized something, in a way they find useful for the task at hand. If you keep stuff no one needs, it is quite likely your collection will be trashed, given away or simply die from lack of use.

†119 *(Henry 1998, p. 313):* Addressing the problems of volume and complexity of electronic records, some writers began formulating new ideas for dealing with such records. Influenced by the ideas of David Bearman, these writers called for a 'new paradigm' to deal with electronic records. They argued that archivists should change their focus, from the content of a record to its context; from the record itself to the function of the records; from an archival role in custodial preservation and access to a nonarchival role of intervening in the records creations process and managing the behavior of creators.

archivy, n. ~ The discipline of archives.

> *RT:* archival science, archival studies, archives management

area, n. ~ 1. CATALOGING · One of eight major sections in a catalog record defined in *Anglo-American Cataloguing Rules.*

> *RT:* descriptive element

> *Notes:* The eight areas are title; edition; material (or type of publication) specific details; publication, distribution, etc.; physical description; series; note; and standard number of terms of availability.

ARMA International (formerly **Association of Records Managers and Administrators**), n. ~ An organization of information management professionals, including records managers, archivists, corporate librarians, imaging specialists, legal professionals, knowledge managers, consultants, and educators.

> *Notes:* ARMA's mission is to 'provide education, research, and networking opportunities to information professionals, to enable them to use their skills and experience to leverage the value of records, information, and knowledge as corporate assets and as contributors to organizational success.' See http://www.arma.org/.

ARPA ~ *see:* Archaeological Resources Protection Act

arrangement, n. ~ 1. The process of organizing materials with respect to their prove-

nance and original order, to protect their context and to achieve physical or intellectual control over the materials. – 2. The organization and sequence of items
within a collection.

　DF: classification
　BT: processing
　RT: original order, provenance
　Notes: Archivist Oliver Wendell Holmes identified five levels of arrangement:
repository; collection or record group; series; folder; and item. Many archives
arrange records only to the folder level, although some archives arrange the items
within each folder. Arrangement is often combined with the process of rehousing
materials into archival containers and folders, and includes the labeling and shelving of materials. Though not widely practiced, arrangement can be employed in
an intellectual sense, without a corresponding physical ordering of material. For
example, five folders stored in four different boxes can be listed together in a finding aid as an ordered series without changing their storage location.

　Arrangement with respect to original order presumes such an order is discern-
able. Archivists are not required to preserve 'original chaos', and may arrange such
materials in a way that facilitates their use and management without violation of
any archival principle.

　Arrangement is distinguished from classification, which places materials in an
order established by someone other than the creator.

　†124 *(Holmes 1984, p. 162):* Archives are already arranged – supposedly, by the
agency of origin while it built them up day after day, year after year, as a systematic
record of its activities and as part of its operations. This arrangement the archivist is
expected to respect and maintain. Arrangement is built into archives; it is one of the
inherent characteristics of 'archives', differentiating them from nonarchival material.

　†191 *(Miller 1990, p. 7):* The process of organizing and managing historical
records by 1) identifying or bringing together sets of records derived from a common source which have common characteristics and a common file structure, and
2) identifying relationships among such sets of records and between records and
their creators.

arrearage ~ *see:* backlog

Arrhenius function, n. ~ A mathematical formula that can be used to predict the rate
　of deterioration of physical materials under given environmental conditions.

　RT: accelerated aging test, cold storage
　Notes: By knowing the rate at which materials change, it is possible to understand how those materials age and to predict the useful life of the materials. Note,
however, that the function is based on assumptions about usefulness. A prediction
on the longevity of paper based on brittleness indicates only the period of time it
will take to become brittle as defined. The information on the paper may continue
to be legible, and the paper itself will likely have some remaining integrity. Given
the inherent assumptions, some question the value of accelerated aging tests. See
Imaging materials – Test method for Arrhenius-type predictions (ISO 18924).

　†228 *(Pork 2000, p. 13–14):* The argument for the use of elevated temperatures
in artificial aging relies on the fact that in general a reaction proceeds faster at
higher temperatures, which makes it possible to observe its effects, in this case the
loss of paper strength, more quickly than at room temperature. Such artificial
aging experiments are sometimes called 'Arrhenius-tests'.

ars dictaminis, n. ~ 1. The art of composition and style of writing, especially letters. – 2. A manual, common in the middle ages, containing the standard form of common letters.

> *RT:* formulary
>
> †*70 (Duranti 1998, p. 137):* Since the early Middle Ages, the art of composition and style was the subject of regular instruction, which determined the development of a sort of documentary rhetoric, called *ars dictaminis* or *dictamen.*

ARSC ~ *see:* Association for Recorded Sound Collections

Art and Architecture Thesaurus, n. (**AAT**, abbr.) ~ A controlled vocabulary that includes terms useful for describing and indexing collections of fine art, architecture, decorative arts, archival materials, and material culture.

> *BT:* controlled vocabulary
>
> *RT:* authority file
>
> *Notes:* The AAT is published by the J. Paul Getty Trust and is available online at http://www.getty.edu/research/tools/vocabulary/aat/.

articles of incorporation, n. ~ A document describing the purposes and conditions of a joint enterprise, which may include the principal officers and the number and classes of shares.

> *Notes:* In the United States, articles of incorporation are typically filed with the secretary of state or territory in which the corporation's headquarters is located as part of the process of having the corporation legally recognized.

artifact (also **artefact**), n. ~ 1. A man-made, physical object. – 2. An anomaly in data that results from the methodology used to capture or analyze the data, or that was introduced or produced during a procedure.

> *DF:* specimen
>
> *BT:* material
>
> *RT:* noise, object, realia
>
> *Notes:* Artifact[1] is often used to distinguish man-made items from natural specimens. Even though documents and other two-dimensional materials are artifacts because of their physical nature, 'artifact' is often used to distinguish three-dimensional materials from two-dimensional materials. Artifacts may be preserved as records, documenting a design or function. For example, throughout the 19th century the United States Patent Office required models of inventions as part of the patent record. In addition, many archival record groups and manuscript collections contain artifacts among other more traditional visual and textual material, such as a campaign button filed with the flyer documenting the political rally at which it was acquired. – Examples of artifact[2] include specks in a digital image not in the original, but resulting from noise in the scanning process.

artifactual value, n. ~ The usefulness or significance of an object based on its physical or aesthetic characteristics, rather than its intellectual content.

> *BT:* value
>
> *RT:* intrinsic value
>
> *Notes:* An item may have artifactual value because it is a particularly good example of the class to which it belongs. For example, an albumen cabinet card photograph may be collected because it possesses many key characteristics of that form and is in excellent physical condition, although the subject of the photograph may be unknown. Artifactual value is a key component of intrinsic value.

artificial collection, n. ~ A collection of materials with different provenance assembled and organized to facilitate its management or use.

> *DF:* organic collection
> *BT:* collection
> *RT:* archives, collective record group, vertical file
> *Notes:* Artificial collections, as distinguished from organic collections, typically do not grow out of a single, specific function, and are often arranged for the convenience of description or retrieval rather than in an order originally established by the creator.
>
> †183 *(Manual for Small Archives 1999):* Many archives also house groups of material 'collected' for some reason, perhaps by a member of the community or organization, a previous archivist, or a local historian. For example, a member of the local historical society might have collected references to New Caledonia's railway construction, and in the process he might have removed individual letters, photographs, and maps from larger bodies of material, such as the records of a local construction company which helped build the train station or the papers of a citizen who worked on the railway. Once these items were removed from their original location, their provenance and original order were lost. The records then became an 'artificial collection' drawn together from diverse (and often unknown) sources.

as-built drawing, n. ~ Architectural drawings that reflect changes made during the construction process, recording differences between the original design and the completed structure.

> *BT:* architectural drawing, drawing
> *Notes:* As-built drawings are based on design drawings used during construction, where measured drawings are usually made long after construction is completed and no design drawings exist.

ASCII, n. ~ A standard, seven-bit character set for use by digital computers, which includes 96 displaying symbols (letters, digits, punctuation) and 32 control codes (line feed, newline, tab, etc.).

> *BT:* character set
> *Notes:* An acronym for the **American Standard Code for Information Interchange**. ASCII and its extensions are the most prevalent character set in computing. Standard ASCII, sometimes called **flat ASCII**, uses seven bits per byte, allowing for a total of 128 characters. The formal standard specification for ASCII can be found in ANSI X3.4 and ISO 646. Extended ASCII uses eight bits and can represent 256 characters. International, eight-bit extensions have been published in the ISO 8859 series.

aspect ratio, n. ~ The relationship between the height and width of a rectangle, typically expressed as a quotient.

> *RT:* Academy format, widescreen
> *Notes:* Aspect ratio is used to describe motion picture and television formats. In cinematography the standard Academy ratio is 1:1.33, with widescreen ratios typically ranging between 1:1.5 and 1:1.8, although the ratio may be as high as 1:2.5. The NTSC television standard uses a 4:3 aspect ratio; HDTV uses a 16:9 aspect ratio.

assemblage, n. ~ 1. Sculpture · A three-dimensional work of art made by combining different elements, especially found objects. – 2. Archaeology · Artifacts related as a group by level, activity, or site.

> *RT:* collage

assignment indexing, n. ~ The process of creating an ordered list of headings, using terms that may not be found in the text, with pointers to relevant portions in the material.

Syn: concept indexing

BT: indexing

RT: automatic indexing

Notes: Assignment indexing usually draws headings from a controlled vocabulary. Assignment indexing is distinguished from extraction indexing, typically done by a computer, which relies on the terms found in the document. At one point, assignment indexing was a manual process, requiring human judgment to link the headings to the concepts in the text. The process of assigning terms from a controlled vocabulary has been automated, with mixed success, by building rules of analysis that can assign headings on the basis of other, related terms in the text.

associated material, n. ~ DESCRIPTION · A reference in a description of an archival collection to materials that are intellectually a part of the collection but held by another repository.

associated records, n. ~ Documents preserved because they provide contextual information about artifacts, specimens, and other materials in museum collections or from anthropological excavations.

BT: record

Association for Information and Image Management, n. (**AIIM,** abbr.) ~ An international organization that supports consumers and suppliers of document and content technologies.

Notes: Founded as the National Microfilm Association in 1943, the association now describes itself as 'The Enterprise Content Management Association.' See http://www.aiim.org/.

Association for Recorded Sound Collections, n. (**ARSC,** abbr.) ~ An international organization of collectors, dealers, archivists, librarians, historians, musicians, producers, recording engineers, and others who are 'dedicated to research, study, publication, and information exchange surrounding all aspects of recordings and recorded sound.'

Notes: See http://www.arsc-audio.org/.

Association of Canadian Archivists, n. (**ACA,** abbr.) ~ A Canadian organization supporting professionals and others who work in archives and promoting the value of archives.

Notes: See http://archivists.ca/.

†16 *(Canadian Archivists Website):* Established in 1975 and incorporated in 1978, the Association of Canadian Archivists (ACA) evolved from the Archives Section of the Canadian Historical Association (CHA). Today, based in Ottawa and with hundreds of members across the world, the ACA has a four-fold focus: providing leadership for everyone engaged in the preservation of Canada's Documentary Heritage; encouraging awareness of archival activities and developments and the importance of archives to modern society; advocating the interests and needs of professional archivists before government and other regulatory agencies; communicating to further the understanding and cooperation amongst members of the Canadian archival system, and other information and culture based professions.

Association of College and Research Libraries, n. (**ACRL,** abbr.) ~ A national organization of academic and research libraries and librarians that seeks to "enhance the effectiveness of academic and research librarians to advance learning, teaching, and research in higher education."

> *Notes:* ACRL is a division of the American Library Association. See http://www.ala.org/ACRLTemplate.cfm.

Association of Moving Image Archivists, n. (**AMIA,** abbr.) ~ An organization that supports individuals working in archives of moving images in all formats.

> *Notes:* See http://www.amianet.org/.

Association of Records Managers and Administrators ~ *see:* ARMA International

associational value, n. ~ The usefulness or significance of materials based on its relationship to an individual, family, organization, place, or event.

> *BT:* value
> *Notes:* Associational value may be based on ownership, creation, or the subject matter of the material. It is a key component of intrinsic value.

ASTM International, n. ~ A not-for-profit organization that develops and publishes standards for research and development, product testing, quality systems, and commercial transactions.

> *Notes:* The society was founded in 1898 and was formerly known as the **American Society for Testing and Materials**. See http://www.astm.org.

atlas, n. ~ 1. A bound volume consisting primarily of maps, often with descriptive text and indexes. – 2. A large volume (approximately 26 × 34 inches) of plates or engravings of any subject.

> *BT:* cartographic record
> *RT:* map
> *Notes:* An atlas[1] may be issued independently or as part of another work.

attachment, n. ~ Something, usually a document, that is loosely bound or fastened to a document; an annex.

> *DF:* appendix
> *RT:* accompanying material, annex
> *Notes:* 'Attachment' often describes a file, sent as part of an email message, that is read using a program other than the email reader. Such an electronic attachment may be symbolized by a digital image representing a traditional paper fastener, the paper clip. For example, a word-processing document sent with an email. An attachment is distinguished from an appendix by the fact that it is created independently of the larger document.

attestation, n. ~ 1. A concluding portion of a document, especially a formal record, signed by witnesses and often containing language intended to strengthen the presumption that all statutory requirements have been met. – 2. The process of bearing witness, especially that a document being witnessed is authentic.

attribute, n. ~ A feature or characteristic; a property.

> *Notes:* 'Attribute' is often used to describe the nature of electronic data. For example, a data value's attributes may include its data type (numeric, character, or date), range of values, or length.

attribution, n. ~ 1. The process of suggesting the nature or identity of some feature not explicit in the object described, especially authorship. – **attribute,** v. ~ 2. To research and suggest such qualities.

Notes: In addition to authorship, provenance, date, place, or other quality may be attributed during description.

audio, adj. ~ 1. Sound, especially recorded sound. – n. ~ 2. The processes and materials used for the reception, recording, transmission, or reproduction of sound.

audio disc ~ *see:* phonograph record

audio recording ~ *see:* sound recording

audiotape (also **phonotape**), n. ~ Sound recordings on magnetic tape.

> *BT:* tape
> *RT:* Compact Cassette, open reel
> *Notes:* Common formats include open reel and cassette.

audiovisual, adj. (**A/V,** abbr.) ~ 1. Having sound and pictorial attributes, especially when combined. – n. ~ 2. The processes and materials used to capture, record, transmit, or reproduce sound or images.

> *RT:* visual materials
> *Notes:* 'Audiovisual' is often used in a general sense within archives to distinguish nontextual materials from written documents.
> †281 *(USC, 17 USC 101):* [audiovisual work] Works that consist of a series of related images which are intrinsically intended to be shown by the use of machines, or devices such as projectors, viewers, or electronic equipment, together with accompanying sounds, if any, regardless of the nature of the material objects, such as films or tapes, in which the works are embodied.

audit, n. ~ An independent review and examination of records and activities to test for compliance with established policies or standards, often with recommendations for changes in controls or procedures.

> *Notes:* Although principally associated with finances, audits may also review programs to ensure they are accomplishing their intended purpose. Sometimes called program reviews, evaluations, assessments, or inspections.

audit trail, n. ~ Information in records that tracks a transaction from beginning to end, making it possible to review whether it was done according to relevant policies and standards.

> *Notes:* An audit trail typically includes the time of transaction, the parties involved, and actions taken.
> †296 *(Cohasset):* Establishing the authenticity of an electronic forms transaction record for business and legal purposes requires the creation and maintenance of data that can be used to establish an audit trail. The information that is necessary to both the audit (business) and chain-of-custody (legal) processes includes, at a minimum, the following elements: who used the system; when they used it or instigated a transaction; what they did while using the system; and the results of the transaction. ¶ Properly implemented audit trails can establish that all pertinent information was captured at or near the time of the event, and that all procedures were followed to achieve an accurate and reliable result. In turn, this can add significant weight to establishing the authenticity of the electronic forms record for admissibility in evidence.

authentic copy, n. ~ A reproduction that has been officially certified, especially so that it may be admitted as evidence.

> *BT:* copy
> *RT:* authenticity

BT: Broader Term • *NT:* Narrower Term • *RT:* Related Term • *DF:* Distinguish From

authentication, n., ~ 1. The process of verifying that a thing is what it purports to be, that it is acceptable as genuine or original. – 2. COMPUTING · The process of establishing a user's identity. – **authenticate**, v. ~ 3. To verify that a thing is what it purports to be. – 4. COMPUTING · To establish an individual's identity.

> *DF:* authorization
>
> *RT:* authenticity, certification, indenture, validation
>
> *Notes:* Authentication[2] is often accomplished through a shared secret known to the individual and the system, such as a user id (or name) and password. If a shared secret is not available or the system might compromise that secret, digital signatures based on public key cryptography can be used to authenticate the identity of the individual who sends a signed message.

authenticity, n. ~ 1. The quality of being genuine, not a counterfeit, and free from tampering, and is typically inferred from internal and external evidence, including its physical characteristics, structure, content, and context. – **authentic**, adj. ~ 2. Perceived of as genuine, rather than as counterfeit or specious; bona fide.

> *NT:* trustworthiness
>
> *RT:* ancient documents, archival nature, authentic copy, authentication, counterfeit, diplomatics, genuine, reliability
>
> *Notes:* Authenticity is closely associated with the creator (or creators) of a record. First and foremost, an authentic record must have been created by the individual represented as the creator. The presence of a signature serves as a fundamental test for authenticity; the signature identifies the creator and establishes the relationship between the creator and the record.
>
> Authenticity can be verified by testing physical and formal characteristics of a record. The ink used to write a document must be contemporaneous with the document's purported date. The style and language of the document must be consistent with other, related documents that are accepted as authentic.
>
> Authenticity alone does not automatically imply that the content of a record is reliable.
>
> The authenticity of records and documents is usually presumed, rather than requiring affirmation. Federal rules of evidence stipulate that to be presumed authentic, records and documents must be created in the 'regular practice' of business and that there be no overt reason to suspect the trustworthiness of the record (*Uniform Rules of Evidence*, as approved July 1999).
>
> †25 *(Bearman and Trant 1998):* Judgments about authenticity are based on assessments of the origins, completeness and internal integrity of a document. They may also draw from the consistency and coherence that exists between a particular source and others in the same context or of the same type.
>
> †70 *(Duranti 1998, p. 45, n. 29):* In law, 'authentic' is defined as 'duly vested with all necessary formalities and legally attested.' An authentic document is called by the law 'authentic act' and is defined as 'an act which has been executed before a notary or public officer authorized to execute such functions, or which is testified by a public seal, or has been rendered public by the authority of a competent magistrate, or which is certified as being a copy of a public register.' [Citing *Black's Law Dictionary*, rev. IVth ed.]
>
> †70 *(Duranti 1998, p. 45–46):* Diplomatic authenticity does not coincide with legal authenticity, even if they both can lead to an attribution of historical authen-

ticity in a judicial dispute. ¶ Legally authentic documents are those which bear witness on their own because of the intervention, during or after their creation, of a representative of a public authority guaranteeing their genuineness. Diplomatically authentic documents are those which were written according to the practice of the time and place indicated in the text, and signed with the name(s) of the person(s) competent to create them. Historically authentic documents are those which attest to events that actually took place or to information that is true.

†76 (Eastwood 2004, p. 43): [Jenkinson] connected authenticity with continuous custody of archives by their creator and its legitimate successors. The argument is that the creating body has an interest in preserving its records free from any tampering that would affect their authenticity, of being what they seem to be.

†77 (Eastwood 1993, p. 243): In archival science, authenticity is the quality of archival documents to bear reliable testimony to the actions, procedures and processes which brought them into being.

†95 (Garner 2003, p. 75): Today the words [authentic and genuine] are interchangeable in most sentences, but a couple of distinctions do exist. First, 'authentic' is off-target when the sense is 'substantial'. . . . Second, 'authentic' is an awkward choice when the sense is 'sincere'. . . . The OED notes that late-18th-century theologians tried to differentiate the words, arguing that a book is 'authentic' if its content is accurate, and 'genuine' if it is correctly attributed to the writer. The point, weak as it was to begin with, has been preserved in some later usage guides.

†109 (Guercio 2001, p. 251): The authenticity of a record, or rather the recognition that it has not been subject to manipulation, forgery, or substitution, entails guarantees of the maintenance of records across time and space (that is, their preservation and transmission) in terms of the provenance and integrity of records previously created.

†175 (C Lynch 2000, p. 5, 6): Validating authenticity entails verifying claims that are associated with an object – in effect, verifying that an object is indeed what it claims to be, or what it is claimed to be (by external metadata). ¶ It is important to note that tests of authenticity deal only with specific claims (for example, 'did X author this document?') and not with open-ended inquiry ('Who wrote it?'). Validating the authenticity of an object is more limited than is an open-ended inquiry into its nature and provenance.

†266 (Smith 2000, p. vi): 'Authenticity' in recorded information connotes precise, yet disparate, things in different contexts and communities. . . . Beyond any definition of authenticity lie assumptions about the meaning and significance of content, fixity, consistency of reference, provenance, and context.

author, n. ~ The individual, group, or organization responsible for the content of a document.

RT: addressee, creator, director, writer

Notes: The role of the author is distinguished from other roles in the production of a document, such as editor, publisher, or translator.

†70 (Duranti 1998, p. 96): As to authorship, it may be worthwhile to restate that the author of the act is the person whose will produces the act. If this person is an abstract entity, like a university, its will coincides with the will of its representative(s) who act(s) in its name. The author of the document is the person having the authority and the capacity, that is, the competence to issue the document.

BT: Broader Term • NT: Narrower Term • RT: Related Term • DF: Distinguish From

authority control, n. ~ DESCRIPTION · The process of establishing the preferred form of a heading, such as proper name or subject, for use in a catalog, and ensuring that all catalog records use such headings.

>   RT: cataloging
>   Notes: The preferred form of a heading is typically defined by a standard. Once established, the form is usually recorded in an authority file for future reference, along with cross-references from other forms of the heading, to ensure consistency.

authority entry ~ see: authority record

authority file (also **authority list**), n. ~ A compilation of records that describe the preferred form of headings for use in a catalog, along with cross-references for other forms of headings.

>   NT: name authority file
>   RT: Art and Architecture Thesaurus, controlled vocabulary, Library of Congress Subject Headings, thesaurus, Union List of Artist Names
>   Notes: Authority files may be lists, card catalogs, databases, or printed publications.

authority list ~ see: authority file

authority record (also **authority entry**), n. ~ An entry in an authority file that contains information about the preferred form of a name or subject heading.

>   Notes: An authority record typically includes a list of cross-references of variant forms that point to the preferred form. The authority record may contain additional information to help ensure the heading is applied correctly. For example, entries for topic terms may include a scope note restricting its use to a specific meaning, or an entry for a personal name may include birth and death dates to distinguish the subject from other persons with that name.

authorization, n. ~ The right or permission granted to take an action or to access something.

>   DF: authentication
>   RT: access, security
>   Notes: In a records environment, authorization often pertains to classification and security clearance. It may also refer to particular uses of materials, such as permissions to reproduce materials. In a computing environment, authorization includes a similar right to view or write data but also includes having the permissions necessary to log in to a system, access portions of a network, or run a program.

autograph, n. (**auto**, abbr.) ~ 1. An individual's handwritten signature. – 2. A document written in the author's hand; a holograph. – 3. Materials bearing the author's signature. – v. ~ 4. To sign by hand. – adj. ~ 5. Handwritten.

automated (also **automatic**), adj. ~ Performed by mechanical or electronic means.

>   RT: digital, e-, machine-readable, office automation
>   Notes: Historically used within archives to indicate something mechanical, especially computerized, as in the name Committee on Automated Records and Techniques. Now largely supplanted in common use by 'digital', 'electronic', or 'e-'.

automated information system ~ see: information system

automated record ~ see: electronic record

automatic data processing, n. (**ADP**, abbr.) ~ The use of computers to analyze, organize, store, retrieve, and manipulate data, and to report the results of those operations, especially with a minimum of human intervention or assistance.

BT: data processing

†237 (Ralston 1976, p. 425): Automatic data processing (ADP) [is] closely analogous to EDP [electronic data processing], since it is intended to distinguish computer data processing from data processing where significant human assistance or intervention is required.

automatic indexing (also **computer-based indexing**, **machine indexing**), n. ~ The use of computers to enable concepts to be located within the material indexed.

BT: indexing

RT: assignment indexing, extraction indexing, full-text search, keyword and context index, keyword in context index, keyword out of context index

Notes: Early automatic indexing was largely limited to extraction indexing, relying on specific terms in the text to represent concepts. With increasing sophistication, computers were able to perform assignment indexing, allowing users to search using concepts in a controlled vocabulary using words that may not appear in the text. Both forms of automatic indexing created ordered lists of concepts that could be browsed, with pointers to the place where those concepts would appear in the text. Full-text search engines, such as those that index the web, create links between terms or phrases and the documents but generally do not produce a browsable list of headings.

B

B reel, n. ~ The source of video or film shot from a secondary camera, which is inter-mixed with footage from the principal camera (the A reel), to produce a finished program.

> *RT:* A reel, moving image

B wind printing ~ *see:* A and B wind printing

back-to-back shelving, n. ~ Two rows of shelving with their backs immediately adjacent to each other along their long axes.

> *BT:* shelving

backlog (also **arrearage**), n. ~ 1. Materials received by a repository, but not yet processed. – 2. Anything delayed while pending some action.

> *Notes:* 'Backlog' connotes materials that have been in a pending status for some time. 'Backlog' is often qualified to indicate the nature of work to be done; materials needing treatment might be described as a 'preservation backlog.'

backup, n. ~ 1. A copy of all or portions of software or data files on a system kept on storage media, such as tape or disk, or on a separate system so that the files can be restored if the original data is deleted or damaged. – 2. Equipment held in reserve that can be substituted in case equipment in regular use fails. – **back up**, v. ~ 3. To create such copies of data.

> *DF:* archive, data archive
>
> *RT:* archives, copy, restore, security copy
>
> *Notes:* In information technology, 'archive' is commonly used as a synonym for 'backup' and 'back up'.
>
> †262 *(Sedona Principles 2003, p. 11):* An effective document retention policy, combined with a preservation approach triggered by the reasonable anticipation of litigation, would establish the principal source of discovery material, thus reducing the need to routinely access backup tapes or hard drives. Under such a policy, backup tapes and hard drives would not be governed by an inaccurate characterization of them as retention systems, but rather by a proper understanding of their role in providing for system reconstruction in the event of loss of functionality. [Note:] Unlike archival systems, which contemplate restoring data, in part or whole, to an existing, active system to be used along with other active data, backup systems are designed to completely restore active systems that have been lost or corrupted as the result of some disaster. Therefore, while data stored in offline archives may often be restored to the active system and searched, searching backup files often requires either taking active data off the system or 'cloning' the system. Both alternatives involve significant disruptions and expense.

balance sheet, n. ~ A document showing the financial position of an organization at a moment in time, including assets, liabilities, and equity.

Bankers Box, n. ~ A trade name of cardboard drawer files and storage boxes.

> *BT:* box
>
> *Notes:* Bankers Box is a trademark of Fellowes, Inc. but is sometimes used to describe any box made of heavy-duty corrugated cardboard that is roughly the height and width of a file folder and the length of a file cabinet drawer (approximately 24 inches).

bar code, n. ~ A pattern of vertical lines used to encode data on a nonelectronic medium that can be read by an optical scanner and converted to machine-readable language.

> *RT:* scanner

> *Notes:* The Universal Product Code (UPC) is a common form of bar code printed on many items sold in stores, allowing those items to be scanned by automated registers at checkout. Books frequently have a similar bar code that enable machines to read the ISBN. Many bar codes are a single row of lines. Some bar codes are formed from several adjacent rows of lines, each row encoding different data.

barrier sheet, n. ~ A piece of paper or other substance placed between different types of materials to prevent contamination resulting from direct contact.

> *RT:* interleaving, slip sheet

> *Notes:* Barrier sheets are commonly inserted during printing or binding to prevent the transfer of ink from a plate or illustration; it may be loose, sewn into the binding, or tipped in. During archival processing[1], barrier sheets are often inserted in albums to protect acid migration from pages to materials on a facing page.

BASCS ~ *see:* business activity structure classification system

base, n. ~ 1. A support on which something is applied or built; a carrier; a substrate. – 2. An alkali.

> *Syn:* alkali

> *Notes:* For paper documents, paper is the base that supports the ink, graphite, or other material that forms the words or images of the content. Photographs may use paper, transparent or opaque plastic, ceramic, glass, metal, cloth, or other materials as a base to support the light-sensitive chemicals that form the image. Magnetic media used for audio or digital recordings often use a polyester base.

batch, n. ~ 1. A group of materials distinguished from similar materials by some characteristic, such as time of manufacture, receipt, or activity. – 2. A group of materials treated as a unit separate from a larger body of materials. – 3. Computing · A group of jobs, data, or programs treated as a unit for computer processing. – v. ~ 4. To group materials together.

> *DF:* series

> *Notes:* Different batches[1] of a commodity, such as film or paper, may vary slightly due to fluctuations in the manufacturing process. Manufacturers may mark batches with identifying numbers and may also indicate the nature of variations from a standard. For example, some color photographic films indicate how each batch diverges from a neutral color balance so that photographers can use filters to correct for that variation. – Batch[2] is distinguished from 'series'; the former generally connotes that the items are identical and does not imply an internal order.

batch processing, n. ~ 1. A method of processing a computer program and its data without user intervention. – 2. A method of entering and sorting transactions to ensure that a master file is updated or queried in a specific order.

bay, n. ~ A unit of shelving, single or double sided, consisting of horizontal shelves between standards, uprights, or upright frames.

> *Syn:* compartment, section

> *RT:* shelving

bcc, abbr. ~ Blind carbon copy.

bench memo, n. ~ 1. A brief submitted by a lawyer to a trial judge. – 2. A document prepared by a law clerk for an appellate court judge that summarizes the facts of a case, the relevant procedural history, the issues, and the parties' arguments on each point.

Notes: A bench memo may also supply the judge with the law clerk's recommended ruling and with copies of key cases and key portions of the record.

benchmark, n. ~ A standard or reference against which something or some process can be measured or compared.

RT: color bars, gray scale, precision, standard, step wedge

bequest, n. ~ A gift of property made through a will.

Berne Convention for the Protection of Literary and Artistic Works, n. ~ An international treaty providing that copyright for a work created by a citizen of a signatory nation will be respected by other signatory nations.

RT: copyright

Notes: Commonly referred to as the Berne Convention, the treaty was drawn up in Berne in 1886 and now administered by the World Intellectual Property Organization. The United States became a signatory nation in 1989, modifying several of its laws to comply with the treaty's terms. See http://www.wipo.int/treaties/ip/berne/index.html.

best evidence, n. ~ The legal principle that an original is superior to a copy.

Notes: If the original is available, a copy generally will not be allowed as evidence in a trial. The requirement is detailed in the *Federal Rules of Evidence* 1001–1004, and similar rules enacted by states. The rules allow the admission of copies, notes, or testimony under certain circumstances.

best practices, n. ~ Procedures and guidelines that are widely accepted because experience and research has demonstrated that they are optimal and efficient means to produce a desired result.

RT: de facto standard, standard

Notes: Best practices are not necessarily formal standards, but they may be considered ad hoc or de facto standards.

†148 (NetLingo 2002, p. 59): [best practices] A business management term for optimal tactics and strategies. Best practices do not guarantee success; rather, they describe those tactics and strategies used in successful companies.

bibliographic description, n. ~ 1. A document that analyzes and structures details about the formal elements of the materials, such as creator, title, dates, extent, and contents, to facilitate the identification, management, and understanding of the work. – 2. The process of creating such a record.

DF: archival description

BT: description

RT: bibliography, cataloging

Notes: Bibliographic descriptions[1] act as surrogates for the things described and are typically assembled into catalogs or bibliographies. Although the term's etymology is tied to the concept of 'book', it is commonly used to refer to the process of creating similar catalogs or lists for other published and nonpublished formats, such as documents, photographs, and moving images, especially when the list contains several formats. Bibliographic description emphasizes the transcription of information found in the materials being described, although the bibliographer or cataloger may supply some explanatory notes.

†223 (Personal communication, Steve Hensen, 17 March 2003): APPM went to some lengths drawing a distinction between bibliographic and archival descrip-

tion; to wit: the former relies more on formal presentation of elements and the subsequent transcription of those elements, the latter more on interpolation and supplying of descriptive data.

bibliographic utility, n. ~ An organization that maintains a database of bibliographic descriptions for use by organizations and individuals for purposes of access, cataloging, circulation, and management.

NT: OCLC Online Computer Library Center, Research Libraries Group, Research Libraries Information Network

RT: cataloging

Notes: These utilities grew out of cooperative cataloging projects in libraries, allowing one library to catalog a book and other libraries to use that record in their catalog. The utilities were able to exploit the information in the database to provide interlibrary loan services to member libraries and to provide subscribers the ability to search for works across many libraries' holdings. One factor motivating archives' use of the MARC format was to enable descriptions of archival collections to be entered, searched, and retrieved in these utilities alongside related materials from other repositories. Two prominent utilities are OCLC and RLIN.

bibliography, n. ~ A list of books or other materials, that details each entry's formal elements, such as creator, title, date, and extent, and sometimes includes annotations that describe the content or place the work in context.

NT: analytical bibliography, descriptive bibliography, discography, filmography, textual bibliography

RT: bibliographic description, catalog, checklist

big bucket, n. ~ The application of appraisal criteria to related groups of information, usually based on function, to establish a uniform retention period.

Notes: The big bucket approach deemphasizes the importance of series. The concept of big buckets is part of the National Archives and Records Administration's *Strategic Directions: Flexible Scheduling* (January 2004).

bill, n. ~ 1. A statement of monies owed for goods or services. – 2. A document proposing new law or changes to existing law for consideration by members of a legislative body.

NT: engrossed copy, enrolled bill

RT: act

bill file, n. ~ A case file containing materials relating to legislation.

Notes: The file may include copies of bills, reports, staff memos, correspondence, secondary informational material, committee prints, and printed hearings and transcripts of executive session hearings. Bill files often form a series in Congressional or legislative papers.

binder, n. ~ 1. A device used to hold loose documents together; a notebook. – 2. A fastener used to hold loose sheets together. – 3. A bookbinder. – 4. A substance used to hold disparate components together in a solid or to give even consistency to a liquid.

Notes: Examples of binder[4] include gelatin or collodion used to bind the metallic silver that forms a photographic image to the base, or the substance that holds the magnetized metal particles in an audio tape to a base.

binding, n. ~ 1. The cover of a book or pamphlet, and the means for securing its contents. – 2. The process of securing the leaves or groups of pages (signatures) between covers to form a book.

NT: stationery binding

biographical note, n. ~ That part of a catalog record or finding aid that places the materials in context by providing basic information about the materials' creator or author.

RT: administrative history, archival description

Notes: For individuals, the biographical note may include date and place of birth, full and variant forms of the name, occupations, significant accomplishments, places of residence and work, family members, and date and place of death.

bird's-eye view, n. ~ 1. An image that depicts its subject from above. – 2. A genre of print that shows the buildings and streets of a city or town from an oblique, aerial perspective.

BT: perspective

RT: aerial photograph, cityscape, scene, worm's-eye view

Notes: In a bird's-eye view, the horizon is often placed high in or outside of the frame to emphasize the area below and minimize the sky. – Bird's-eye view[2] prints of a city or town are not generally drawn to scale, but they show major features in perspective.

bit, n. ~ 1. A b(inary dig)it. – 2. The smallest unit of information in a binary system.

RT: byte, character set

Notes: A string of bits can be used to represent a number using only zeros and ones (base two). A fixed number of bits treated as a unit can be used to represent a digit, character, or punctuation mark. Standard ASCII uses seven bits per byte, allowing for a total of 128 characters; extended ASCII uses eight bits and can represent 256 characters. The relationship with the binary number and the character it represents is arbitrary. In ASCII, the character A is represented by the bits 1000001; in EBCDIC, A is represented by 11000001.

bit depth, n. ~ The number of bits used to form a pixel in a graphics array.

RT: pixel depth

bit loss, n. ~ The corruption of the lowest level of information digital data in transmission or during storage.

Notes: Bit loss indicates that information at the smallest level has changed or become erratic. Within character data, the change of a single bit may be significant; changing the middle bit in A (1000001) to alters it to I (1001001). Such a change in a binary executable file may make it impossible for the program to run or to authenticate a bitstream using a digital signature. However, such a change in an image or sound file may result in only a minor amount of noise.

bitmap, n. ~ 1. A raster graphic formed by an array of bits, each bit representing the corresponding pixel's value (light or dark). – 2. A raster image formed by an array of bytes, each byte (or bytes) representing the corresponding pixel's color; a **pixmap**.

RT: pixel, raster graphic

Notes: A bitmap[1] is necessarily a bitonal image as a bit can represent only two values. – A bitmap[2] that represents shades of gray or color requiring more than one bit per pixel is sometimes called a pixmap. In Microsoft Windows conventions, a file name for a bitmap[2] has the extension .bmp.

bitstream, n. ~ 1. A sequence of binary information transmitted, stored, or received as a unit without regard for internal organization or grouping. – 2. The flow of data over a network.

black and white, adj. ~ 1. Having neutral tones; the absence of color. – 2. Monochrome.

> *RT:* black-and-white photograph, monochrome
>
> *Notes:* Typically used to describe photographic, film, and video processes that render scenes by representing the brightness of objects as white, black, and intermediate tones. In common parlance, the phrase is used to describe any image that fails to capture natural color, although the image may have a distinct, single tone. In its strictest sense, 'black and white' is limited to those images that represent brightness in shades of gray, as distinguished from monochrome processes. For example, cyanotypes are monochromatic, but because of their distinctive blue shade are not accurately described as 'black and white.'

black-and-white photograph, n. ~ 1. A photographic image in which all colors are reproduced in varying shades of a neutral tone, especially one made using a gelatin silver process. – 2. VERNACULAR · A monochromatic photographic image.

> *RT:* black and white, gelatin silver photograph
>
> *Notes:* The vast majority of modern, monochromatic photographs are made using the gelatin silver process. These photographs usually have a very neutral tone. Other processes, especially 19th-century processes, used to make monochromatic images include albumen, collodion, platinum, and palladium, which may have a pronounced warm tone, or cyanotypes, which have a pronounced blue tone. 'Black and white' is sometimes used to when 'monochromatic' is the more accurate term.

black box, n. ~ A conceptual model used to simplify the representation of a process by indicating only the inputs and outputs of a device without regard to its internal functions or mechanisms.

> *Notes:* In archives, the term usually refers to Frank Boles' and Julia Marks Young's article, "Exploring the Black Box: The Appraisal of University Administrative Records," *American Archivist* 48 (Spring 1985), p. 121–140. The authors argue that for too long the actual process of making archival appraisal decisions (what factors are considered, how much weight they are given, etc.) was implicitly viewed as an impenetrable mystery. Boles and Young defined specific elements that should go into making an appraisal, and argued that these could be refined to a mathematical model.
>
> In object-oriented programming, an object is an example of a black box. The object's methods that return a property or transform an input are designed to reveal as little as possible about its internal code.

blanching, n. ~ CONSERVATION · The appearance of a milky substance after the application of a solvent.

> *DF:* bloom
>
> *Notes:* Blanching is distinguished from bloom[3], a change in the appearance of a surface caused by moisture.

blip code (also **blip**), n. ~ A mark recorded on roll microfilm outside the image area that can be used to count frames automatically.

> *Syn:* sensing mark
>
> *RT:* microfilm

BLOB, n. (**B(inary) L(arge) Ob(ject)**, abbr.) ~ A digital object treated as a unit for purposes of storage in a database management system.

Notes: Typically the database software functions solely as a storage mechanism for a BLOB, which is transferred to another application for use. BLOBs are frequently audio or image files.

block, n. ~ 1. RECORDS MANAGEMENT · A group of files within a series bounded by cutoff points that are treated as a unit for disposition purposes. – 2. COMPUTING · A series of contiguous data elements broken into standard units for processing; a physical record.

RT: physical record

Notes: Blocks[1] are often determined by dates. For example, correspondence may be broken into blocks by fiscal year.

blocking, n. ~ 1. The use of a machine to make a mark by pressing a die, plate, or frame against a surface. – 2. CONSERVATION · The condition in which materials, especially photographic film and magnetic tape, adhere to adjacent materials or to itself, if in a reel or layers, usually as the result of poor storage conditions.

DF: ferrotyping

Notes: Blocking[1] is distinguished from stamping, the latter being done by hand. – Blocking[2] is distinguished from ferrotyping, where materials of different types adhere, such as a framed photographic print being ferrotyped to the glass.

bloom, n. ~ 1. The appearance of mold or fungus on an object. – 2. A powdery residue that is shed from magnetic tape coating. – 3. A change in the appearance of a surface caused by moisture, often from the atmosphere.

DF: blanching

Notes: Bloom[3] is distinguished from blanching, which is the appearance of a milky substance after the application of a solvent.

blow-up ~ *see:* enlargement

blueline, n. ~ 1. A proof copy of a printed work made directly from the negatives that will be used to create the printing plates. – 2. A reproduction of an architectural or engineering drawing made with blue lines on a neutral background.

RT: copy

Notes: Originally bluelines[1,2] were made using the diazo process and appeared as a blue-and-white positive. The term has been generalized to a variety of processes that produce bluelines on a neutral background. – Bluelines[1] are a final check to verify camera work, folding, or trimming. – Bluelines[2] are a positive image, maintaining the same polarity as the original drawing, as distinguished from blueprints, which are negatives.

blueprint, n. ~ 1. A print made using the Prussian blue (ferroprussiate) process; a cyanotype. – 2. A reproduction of an architectural drawing, especially one made using the blueprint process.

BT: print

RT: architectural drawing, cyanotype

Notes: In general, 'blueprint' is used for architectural drawings, while cyanotype is used to describe continuous-tone photographic prints, even though the process is the same. It is not uncommon for 'blueprint' to be used generically to refer to any architectural drawings, regardless of process.

blur, n. ~ The loss of sharpness in a photographic image resulting from motion of the subject or the camera during exposure.

RT: focus

Notes: Blur may be a flaw or a desired effect. Photographers may use blur to suggest motion, especially in a pan shot where the camera tracks a moving subject to show the subject as relatively sharp against a blurred background. Blur is distinguished from poor focus, the latter being a lack of sharpness resulting from the lens' point of greatest clarity being in front of or behind the subject.

body of the entry, n. ~ CATALOGING · That portion of a catalog record that describes the material in terms of its title, edition, material (or type of publication) specific details, and imprint (production, distribution, etc.).

    BT: descriptive element

bond, n. ~ 1. A written obligation to indemnify for a loss suffered or for the failure to perform in some specified manner. – 2. A certificate of debt.

bond paper, n. ~ A strong, high-quality paper, especially paper made from spruce fibers or cotton.

    BT: paper

    RT: archival bond

    Notes: The name derives from papers, used to make legal records (bonds), that would not deteriorate significantly over time.

booklet, n. ~ A short, nonserial printed work, often with a paper cover.

    DF: leaflet

    Syn: brochure, pamphlet

    RT: publication

    Notes: A booklet is distinguished from a leaflet, a single sheet that has been folded.

Boolean logic, n. ~ A branch of mathematics that that operates on the truth value of a condition to determine relationships between propositions.

    Notes: Boolean operators include if, then, and, or, not, and except. Boolean logic is used heavily in computer programming to form sets and for the conditional flow of operations. It is also commonly used to improve the accuracy of searches in automated catalogs, databases, and search engines.

bootleg, n. ~ 1. Something made or distributed illegally. – 2. An unauthorized reproduction, especially of a motion picture or sound recording.

    DF: counterfeit

    RT: piracy

    Notes: A bootleg[2] is distinguished from a counterfeit, the latter being represented as authentic.

born analog, n. ~ Information that was created in a nondigital format and subsequently digitized.

    DF: born digital

    Notes: A handwritten document that has been scanned would be described as born analog.

born digital, adj. ~ Information created in electronic format.

    DF: born analog

    RT: digital document

    Notes: Born-digital information is distinguished from digitized, the latter describing a document created on paper that has been scanned (and possibly transformed into character data using OCR). A document created using a word processor may be described as born digital.

box, n. ~ A rigid container, usually with square or rectangular sides, typically used to store nonliquid materials.

> *BT:* container
>
> *NT:* archives box, Bankers Box, box file, document box, document case, flip-top box, Paige Box, pamphlet box, phase box, records center box, Solander box, transfer file
>
> *Notes:* Boxes often have a lid, which may be detachable or hinged, to provide access to the inside.

box file, n. ~ A container designed to hold flat, loose documents and to be stored vertically on a shelf, like a book.

> *Syn:* letter box
>
> *BT:* box
>
> *RT:* flat file
>
> *Notes:* Box files often contain dividers for organizing the documents and a spring clip to keep the contents from slumping. The effect was not unlike a book, with the back of the box visible on a shelf similar to a book binding and the top hinged to open like the front cover of a book. Box files were common in the 19th and early 20th centuries.

bracket, n. ~ 1. An L-shaped bookend or brace. – 2. The typographic characters [ ], < >, and { }. – v. ~ 3. To surround. – 4. To create a short sequence of photographs, each with slightly different exposure.

> *Notes:* Brackets[2] are frequently described as square ([ ]), angle (< >), and curly ({ }) brackets. Curly brackets are also called braces. – Photographers will often bracket[4] a shot if they are uncertain of the proper exposure or if the light conditions are extreme. The multiple versions provide some insurance that at least one exposure will create a useful negative.

break ~ *see:* file break

brief, n. ~ 1. A short summary of a document; an abstract. – 2. A summary of the facts of a law suit, especially with reference to relevant law, submitted to the court or other body hearing the case.

> *RT:* abstract

brightness, n. ~ 1. The degree to which an object reflects or transmits light. – 2. A measure of the amount of light in a space.

> *RT:* contrast
>
> *Notes:* Brightness[1] is the opposite of darkness. It is typically used to emphasize the presence of light. – Brightness[2] is often measured in lux or foot candles.

brittle, adj. ~ Fragile from a loss of flexibility, causing the material to break or crack, rather than bend or fold.

broadcast date, n. ~ DESCRIPTION · A date when a sound recording or moving image program was broadcast on radio or television.

> *BT:* date

broader term, n. (**BT**, abbr.) ~ A cross-reference pointing to a more general concept in a hierarchy.

> *BT:* cross-reference
>
> *RT:* Guidelines for the Construction, Format, and Management of Monolingual Thesauri, upward reference
>
> *Notes:* Broader terms are part of the syndetic structure used in a thesaurus, especially one constructed using the ANSI Z39.19 standard, *Guidelines for the*

Construction, Format, and Management of Monolingual Thesauri. Broader terms are reciprocal to narrower terms. For example, an entry for 'bed', 'chair', or 'chest' may each include a broader-term reference 'furniture'. 'Furniture' would include a narrower-term reference for each of those terms.

broadsheet ~ *see:* broadside

broadside (also **broadsheet**), n. ~ A single sheet with information printed on one side that is intended to be posted, publicly distributed, or sold.

> *DF:* poster

> *Notes:* Occasionally a broadside may be formed from a number of sheets assembled edge-to-edge to create a larger whole.

> †278 *(LCGTM 1995, p. 506):* [Broadsides] provide information, commentary, proclamation, or other announcement or advertisement. Primarily posted but also distributed by hand. They are usually less pictorial than posters and have more extensive text than signs.

brochure, n. ~ 1. A short printed work, sometimes a leaflet, providing general information about an organization or service. – 2. A printed work of only a few leaves with a stitched or stapled binding; a pamphlet.

> *Syn:* booklet

> *RT:* leaflet, pamphlet, publication

> *Notes:* Web pages that have general information about an organization, rather than rich content, are often called a glass brochure.

bronzing, n. ~ 1. CONSERVATION · The result of deterioration exhibited by some gelatin silver photographic prints, characterized by the blacks turning to a shiny brown, typically as the result of poor processing. – 2. In printing, the use of metallic inks.

> *RT:* silver mirroring, tarnish

brownline, n. ~ 1. A photographic process using light-sensitive iron salts producing brown lines on a neutral background, commonly used to reproduce architectural drawings. – 2. A print with brown lines on a neutral background.

> *RT:* architectural drawing, brownprint, Vandyke process

> *Notes:* 'Brownline' and 'brownprint' are frequently used synonymously to refer to the same process. A negative is made of a drawing, producing a brownprint; the brownprint is then reprinted to make a positive (brownline). A variety of other processes have been used to make prints described as brownlines and brownprints, although the Vandyke process is one the earliest. Manufactured since the 1890s, this process was frequently found on medium or lightweight paper as the print was often used as an intermediary to create negatives or positives of damaged original drawings.

brownprint, n. ~ 1. A reproduction process, commonly used for architectural drawings, that produces white lines on a brown background. – 2. A print, especially of an architectural drawing, with neutral lines on a brown background.

> *BT:* print

> *RT:* brownline

browse, v. ~ 1. To review in a casual manner. – 2. To scan a list or document. – 3. To download and view information from the World Wide Web through the use of a browser.

> *RT:* search

> *Notes:* Browsing[1] connotes a process that is random and opportunistic, suggesting the sense of stumbling onto something desirable by serendipity. However,

browsing² may be systematic. It can be distinguished from searching by the fact that browsing is the process of discovery through a careful review of information in hopes of spotting something interesting because it triggers an association. Searching, on the other hand is a process of inquiry that is based on specific, known concepts or terms.

†277 *(Delpi Group 2002, p. 6–7):* Browsing is dynamic, interactive and iterative. ... Browsing is an iterative process. Repeating the process refines your focus while broadening your knowledge. Accessing relevant information and interrelated ideas and concepts supports a fundamental change in your activity – from simply searching, to finding and discovering.

BT ~ *see:* broader term

bucket ~ *see:* big bucket

buckle, n. ~ A deformation in a flat surface making it warped or twisted.

>*RT:* channeling, cockle, pack
>
>*Notes:* In reels of tape or film, buckling may appear as irregular waves in the tape pack.

Buckley Amendment ~ *see:* Family Educational Rights and Privacy Act

buffer, n. ~ 1. A substance that can neutralize acids; an alkali. – 2. A means or mechanism that can transform an irregular flow to a regular rate, especially in data transmission. – 3. A means or mechanism for reducing shock or impact. – 4. A technique in geographic information systems that can indicate a region around a data point to show a an area of influence or interaction.

>*RT:* alkali, alkaline-reserve paper, calcium carbonate reserve, pH
>
>*Notes:* A buffer¹ made from calcium carbonate or magnesium carbonate is often added to paper to compensate for residual manufacturing acids or from acidic environmental contaminants.

bulk dates, n. ~ DESCRIPTION · The earliest and latest dates of the majority of materials being described.

>*BT:* date
>
>*RT:* inclusive dates
>
>*Notes:* Bulk dates indicate the chronological or period strength of a collection, especially when the inclusive dates may be misleading.

bulk eraser, n. ~ A device used to rapidly remove recorded information from magnetic media without having to touch the surface; a degausser.

>*RT:* degaussing
>
>*Notes:* Neutralizing magnetic fields in recording media effectively destroys the patterns that make up the recording, with the result that it is impossible to read the information by conventional means. Degaussing also minimizes distortion and the noise level when reusing tape.

bulk reduction microfilming ~ *see:* disposal microfilming

bundle, n. ~ A group of individual documents, normally tied together by string, linen tape, or the like.

bureaucracy, n. ~ 1. The administrative structure of a corporate body or government that divides work into hierarchical units and subunits. – 2. The nonelected officials of a government.

>*RT:* red tape
>
>†46 *(Cook 1993, p. 31):* The classic mono-hierarchical theory of bureaucracy elucidated by Max Weber, in which each subordinate unit is responsible to one

superior unit, has long been a thing of the past. Parallel structures, task forces and project teams, joined across organizations by broken-line horizontal linkages, exercising consensus management and collegial relationships, now compete openly for power with the traditional, vertical, solid-line hierarchical authorities, and these new 'structures' all create and often maintain records.

†180 (MacNeil 2000, p. 51): The most pervasive characteristic of bureaucracy is the existence of a system of control based on rational rules, that is, rules meant to design and regulate the entire organization on the basis of technical knowledge and with the aim of achieving maximum efficiency.

business activity structure classification system, n. (**BASCS**, abbr.) ~ A classification system developed and designed at the National Archives of Canada that looks at functions in terms of policies, practices, and initiatives.

BT: classification

RT: system

Notes: The abbreviation is pronounced like 'basis'.

business archives, n. ~ Records created or received by a commercial enterprise in the course of operations and preserved for their enduring value.

BT: archives

NT: corporate archives

RT: business records

Notes: Business archives may be created by any size commercial activity, ranging from a sole proprietorship to a multinational corporation.

business continuation and disaster recovery, n. ~ The procedures necessary to resume operations after an atypical disruption of routine activities.

RT: disaster plan, dispersal, emergency-operating records, essential records

Notes: Disasters can be either natural or human in origin, including earthquakes, fire, sabotage, or war. Government business continuation and disaster recovery plans generally emphasize protecting the lives, health, safety, rights, and entitlements of citizens and businesses.

business exception rule, n. ~ A provision in the hearsay rule allowing for the admission of business records.

RT: business records, evidence, hearsay rule

Notes: The exception is in the Federal Rules of Evidence 802 §6. State rules of evidence generally have an equivalent rule.

business needs, n. ~ Operational requirements that must be met in order for an organization to fulfill its functions.

†61 (DIRKS 2001): The methodology for designing and implementing recordkeeping systems . . . helps organisations (i) identify what records they should make and keep to satisfy their business needs, accountability requirements and community expectations; (ii) develop and implement strategies to meet these purposes; and (iii) regularly review the effectiveness of these strategies.

business process, n. ~ Related activities, sequential or parallel, that have been systematically implemented to produce a specific service or product.

RT: systematic management

business process reengineering, n. ~ Redesigning the way activities in an organization (business processes) are carried out to improve efficiency and reduce costs.

RT: change management

Notes: Business process reengineering is often undertaken when paper-based recordkeeping systems are automated. Rather than merely recreating existing forms and procedures, they are analyzed and streamlined for greater efficiency.

†157 (New Words 1997): The idea of business process re-engineering was invented in 1990 by two Americans, James Champy and Michael Hammer, and it was pioneered in practice by a number of US firms. The redesign process seeks to determine how information flows through a business and how it is processed, to search out unnecessary or duplicated operations, and to improve decision-making and the responsiveness and accuracy of the steps involved.

business records, n. ~ Documents and other materials created or received by a commercial enterprise in the course of operations and preserved for future use.

BT: record

NT: corporate records

RT: business archives, business exception rule, family papers, organizational records

Notes: An organization may have many business records[1] that fall under the general definition of a record[2] but that are not covered by the more specific definition of business records established by the Federal Rules of Evidence (cited below; most states have similar rules). The distinction is significant in the context of litigation. All materials that fall under the more general understanding of business records are subject to discovery, but only those records that are the result of regularly conducted activity fall under the hearsay exemption of the Federal Rules of Evidence and are admissible in court as evidence.

†84 (Fed. R. Evid., 804 §6): Records of regularly conducted activity. A memorandum, report, record, or data compilation, in any form, of acts, events, conditions, opinions, or diagnoses, made at or near the time by, or from information transmitted by, a person with knowledge, if kept in the course of a regularly conducted business activity, and if it was the regular practice of that business activity to make the memorandum, report, record or data compilation, all as shown by the testimony of the custodian or other qualified witness, or by certification that complies with Rule 902 (11), Rule 902 (12), or a statute permitting certification, unless the source of information or the method or circumstances of preparation indicate lack of trustworthiness. The term 'business' as used in this paragraph includes business, institution, association, profession, occupation, and calling of every kind, whether or not conducted for profit.

†265 (Skupsky and Mantaña 1994, p. 23–24): Business records are hearsay. 'Hearsay' is normally inadmissible in evidence, but records which meet the definition of business records are admissible notwithstanding that they are hearsay. . . . From a judicial standpoint, a record or data compilation must have four qualities in order to qualify as a business record: It must be made at or near the time of the event that it records; It must be made by or from information transmitted by a person with knowledge of the event; It must be made in the course of a regularly conducted business activity; It must have been the regular practice of that business activity to make a document or data compilation.

byte, n. ~ A sequence of bits used to represent a control character, an alphanumeric, or punctuation mark.

RT: bit

Notes: Standard ASCII bytes are seven bits long, allowing for 128 characters. Extended or high-order ASCII bytes are eight bits long, allowing for 256 characters.

Syn: Synonym • †: see Bibliography • *Superscript:* Definition number

C

c. ~ *see:* circa, copyright

> *Notes:* A common convention, especially in cataloging, is to use 'c' (without a period) to mean copyright and 'c.' (with a period) to mean circa.

CA ~ *see:* certified archivist

ca. ~ *see:* circa

cabinet card, n. ~ A photographic print mounted on cardboard approximately 4½ × 6¼ inches.

> *BT:* card-mounted photographs, photograph

> *Notes:* Introduced in the 1860s, cabinet cards superseded the carte-de-visite. The format was common until about 1900. Early cabinet cards typically used albumen prints, although a variety of other process were used for later cards. The photograph is usually smaller than the card, leaving approximately a half inch at the bottom, where the name of the photographer or studio was printed.

CAD ~ *see:* computer-aided design

cadastral map, n. ~ A map showing boundaries of subdivisions of land for purposes of describing and recording ownership as a basis for taxation.

> *NT:* map

cadastre, n. ~ A record of real property, with its value, compiled for tax purposes.

CAE ~ *see:* computer-aided engineering

calcium carbonate reserve, n. ~ An alkali (calcium carbonate) added to paper during manufacture to serve as a buffer against acidic residues of the manufacturing process or environmental acids.

> *RT:* buffer

calendar, n. ~ 1. A document organized chronologically, especially those in tabular form, indicating the day of week, date, and month. – 2. A finding aid that is a chronological listing of documents in a collection, which may be comprehensive or selective, and which may include details about the writer, recipient, date, place, summary of content, type of document, and page or leaf count; a chronological inventory.

> *Syn:* chronological inventory

> *BT:* finding aid

> *RT:* analytical inventory, inventory

> *Notes:* Though common through the first half of the 20th century, the production of calendars² by archives has become increasingly rare.

> †27 *(Berner 1983, p. 6):* It was assumed that historians were the main users and that they were best served by chronological and subject arrangements. Historians themselves thought so. The descriptive practice of calendaring responded to this felt need among historians and was a goal in most manuscript repositories before 1940.

calendering, n. ~ The process of giving paper a hard, smooth surface during manufacture.

> *Notes:* The surface of calendered paper is formed during manufacture by rolling the paper between smooth cylinders under pressure. Paper with a minimum of calendering has an antique finish. When highly calendered, it has a glossy finish.

†114 (Harrod 1978, calendered paper): [Calendered paper is] given a smooth surface by rolling, when newly-made, between smooth cylinders under pressure. Paper which receives a minimum of calendering emerges as an antique. With more calendering it acquires a machine finish, then an English finish, and it finally becomes a super-calendered, glossy sheet.

call number, n. ~ A unique combination of letters and numbers used to identify an item and to facilitate storage and retrieval.

Syn: reference code

Notes: 'Call number' is used more commonly in libraries than in archives. A call number frequently consists of a class and a shelf number. (Shelf numbers are also called cutter numbers, book numbers, or author numbers.) For example, the call number TR 15 .P43 consists of the Library of Congress classification for photographic collections (TR 15) and a shelf number (.P43) to give the work a unique number.

call slip, n. ~ A form used to request materials be retrieved from storage for use, typically in a reading room; a request slip, a research request slip, a reference slip.

Syn: request slip

camera microfilm, n. ~ The first generation of film used to photograph documents and subsequently used to produce copies.

BT: microfilm

RT: printing dupe

Notes: Camera microfilm is typically used to produce a second generation copy used as a 'printing dupe' or 'printing master', which is used to make additional, third-generation copies. Archival microfilm is made with a silver halide emulsion on a polyester base.

CAMiLEON, n. ~ An acronym for Creative Archiving at Michigan and Leeds: Emulating the Old on the New, a research project "investigating the viability of emulation as a preservation strategy that maintains the intellectual content, structure, and 'look and feel' of software-dependent complex digital objects."

Notes: See http://www.si.umich.edu/CAMILEON.

Camp Pitt, n. ~ A series of institutes designed to assist government records professionals in developing programs to deal with electronic records.

Notes: Cosponsored by the National Association of Government Archives and Records Administrators and the University of Pittsburgh. Formally titled the **Archival Administration in the Electronic Information Age: An Advanced Institute for Government Archivists,** the programs were held from 1989 to 1994 and again in 1996 and 1997.

can, n. ~ 1. A short cylindrical metal or plastic container. – 2. CINEMATOGRAPHY, PHOTOGRAPHY · Such a container used to store film, roughly the height and width of the film plus any reel.

BT: container

Canadian-United States Task Force on Archival Description, n. (**CUSTARD,** abbr.) ~ A project, funded by the National Endowment for the Humanities and the Gladys Kriebel Delmas Foundation, that attempted to reconcile *Archives, Personal Papers, and Manuscripts* (APPM), the Canadian *Rules for Archival Description* (RAD), and the *General International Standard Archival Description* (ISAD(G)) to create a set of descriptive rules that can be used with EAD and MARC 21.

RT: Describing Archives: A Content Standard

Notes: The Society of American Archivists published the United States team's implementation of the proposed rules as *Describing Archives: A Content Standard* in 2004.

caption, n. ~ 1. A short description accompanying an illustration. – 2. Moving images · Text, usually at the bottom of the frame, that reproduces dialog and may describe other sound effects; a subtitle; a closed caption. – 3. Records · Information on a folder, file guide, or drawer.

DF: closed captioning

RT: subtitle

captured archives ~ *see:* removed archives

CAR ~ *see:* computer-aided retrieval

carbon copy, n. (**cc**, abbr.) ~ A copy of a document made at the same time as the original through the use of paper coated with a pigment (originally carbon) that is transferred to another sheet from the pressure of a pen or typewriter.

BT: copy

Notes: It is possible to make several copies simultaneously by adding more layers of carbon paper and regular paper. The quality of subsequent copies is reduced because the pressure is more diffuse, making the impression less sharp. Carbon paper was invented by Ralph Wedgewood in the 1800s in England, and was available in the United States by the 1820s. Because the copying technique did not work well with the quill pens of the time, carbon copies did not become common until the introduction of the typewriter.

†*300 (Yates 1989, p. 45):* Carbon paper soon replaced the letter press for making routine file copies, while various sorts of duplicators provided, for the first time, rapid and inexpensive methods of mass reproduction.

carbon ink, n. ~ A very stable ink made from a mixture of fine carbon particles carried in a vehicle of glue or a gum.

card catalog, n. ~ Descriptions of materials, with each entry on a separate card (or cards), systematically arranged to facilitate access.

BT: catalog

RT: cataloging

Notes: In a card catalog, copies of the card(s) describing the material may be filed under different headings, with separate entries for creator, title, or subject. Headings may be grouped by the type of access point, forming an author catalog, a title catalog, or a subject catalog. A catalog in which all headings are grouped in a single alphabetical sequence is described as a dictionary catalog. A card catalog may be distinguished from a card index by the amount of description. A catalog typically has enough information to help patrons assess whether the material is likely to be useful.

The use of separate cards for each item facilitated the interfiling of new or corrected entries, and the removal of obsolete entries.

Online catalogs continue to be called 'card catalogs', although such use is becoming less common.

card index, n. ~ References or short citations to materials, with each item described separately on a card (or cards), and arranged to facilitate access.

BT: index

Notes: A card index may be distinguished from a catalog by the amount of description. An index may indicate only the location of potentially relevant material, and the usefulness of the material references can be determined only by direct examination of the material. The use of separate cards for each item facilitated the interfiling of new or corrected entries and the removal of obsolete entries.

card-mounted photographs, n. ~ A general class of photographic prints attached to a standard-sized sheet of cardboard.

BT: photograph

NT: cabinet card, carte-de-visite

RT: stereograph

Notes: In addition to cabinet cards and cartes-de-visite, less common sizes include boudoir (8½ × 5½ inches, introduced in the 1890s), imperial (10 × 7 inches, introduced in the 1890s), promenade (7 or 7½ × 4 inches, introduced ca. 1874), and Victoria (5 × 3½ inches, introduced in the 1870s).

carrier, n. ~ A mechanism by which information is transported over distance or time.

RT: medium

Notes: For manuscripts or printed documents, the carrier consists of a base and the medium, typically paper and ink. For photographs, the carrier includes the base, commonly paper, film, glass, or metal; the substance that forms the image, such as silver or dye; and any binder, such as gelatin or albumen. For digital information the carrier may be physical, such as a disk or a tape with a magnetic or optical layer, or a signal convede by radio frequency or electrical current.

CART ~ *see:* Committee on Automated Records and Techniques

carte-de-visite, n. (**cartes-de-visite**, pl.; **CDV**, abbr.) ~ A photographic print mounted on cardboard approximately 4½ × 2 inches.

BT: card-mounted photographs

Notes: Patented by Parisian photographer André-Adolphe-Eugène Disdéri in 1854. The format added a photograph to a visiting card. Cartes remained popular through the early 1880s, when they were superseded by the larger cabinet card. On later cartes, the print is slightly smaller than the card, leaving room for the name of the photographer or studio at the bottom of the card.

cartographic record, n. ~ Materials that use images, numbers, or relief to represent physical or cultural features of the earth or celestial body (or portion thereof).

NT: atlas, chart, globe, map, profile

RT: geographic information system, section

Notes: Cartographic records may include maps, atlases, charts, globes, and geographic information systems. They commonly represent physical features (land masses, bodies of water, elevations, weather, and coordinates) but may also represent human, animal, plant distributions (population centers or distributions, political and cultural boundaries, migrations). Maps incorporate a degree of analysis or abstraction; a photograph of a land mass is not in itself a map, but the addition of information identifying features to the photograph may make it a map.

cartography, n. ~ The science of making maps and other abstract representations of the earth, heavenly bodies, or portions thereof.

RT: cartouche, compass rose, projection, scale, technical drawing

†*115 (Harvey 2000, p. 65):* Ptolemy systematized cartography by insisting that maps be drawn to scale and that they be oriented to the north. He was the first to offer a projection by which a spherical earth could be rendered on a flat surface.

cartouche, n. ~ 1. A decoration, often in the shape of an oval, a box, or a scroll, used to enclose or highlight information within a larger work. – 2. CARTOGRAPHY ·

Such a decoration used to set off information that identifies the map, map maker, publisher, date, and other details.

> *RT:* cartography

cartridge, n. ~ 1. A container used to store and facilitate access to a roll of tape or film on a single core. – 2. A removable data disk.

> *DF:* cassette

> *Notes:* Cartridges are principally used in readers, projectors, recorders, or computer drives to avoid users having to manually thread the media through the drive mechanism. Cartridges may be constructed so that the media is on a continuous loop. Cartridges have a single core, distinguishing them from cassettes, which have two cores.

cartulary (also **chartulary**), n. ~ 1. A collection of charters, title deeds, grants of privileges, and other documents, especially copies in bound volumes, belonging to a person, family, or corporate body. – 2. The keeper of an archives.

> *Notes:* The term is medieval in origin and has not had common usage in the United States.

Cascading Style Sheet, n. (**CSS**, abbr.) ~ An extension of Hypertext Markup Language (HTML) that governs the appearance of a document.

> *RT:* format, Hypertext Markup Language

> *Notes:* CSS version 1 became a World Wide Web Consortium (W3C) Recommendation in 1996. CSS2 became a W3C Recommendation in 1998. Although CSS can be used with extensible markup language (XML), it is generally used with HTML documents; Extensible Stylesheet Language (XSL) is superseding CSS for formatting XML documents.

case file, n. ~ A collection of documents (a file) relating to a particular investigation or in support of some administrative action.

> *DF:* dossier

> *Syn:* transactional file

> *RT:* subject file

> *Notes:* Case files are sometimes referred to as a **project file** or, in Canada, a **transactional file**. Also called dossiers, although that term has a more general sense of file. Case files are often found in the context of social services agencies (public and private), and in Congressional papers. Examples include criminal investigations, patient records, and tenure files. The types of documents in each file in a series of case files tends to capture the same categories of information about each case.

cased photographs, n. ~ A class of photographs common in the mid-19th century mounted in a shallow, hinged box.

> *BT:* photograph

> *RT:* ambrotype, daguerreotype, union case

> *Notes:* Typically used for daguerreotypes and ambrotypes, although it is not uncommon to find later photographic processes put in cases that had formerly held earlier types of photographs. The case provided protection for fragile processes. The cases were often made of wood with a tooled leather, paper, or cloth cover, or from an early molded composite (see union case).

cash book (also **cash journal**), n. ~ A volume used to record all money spent or received.

RT: account book, daybook, ledger

†*55 (Densmore 2000, p. 81):* Cash books were kept by businesses in which it was important to know the amount of money on hand at any given time or in partnerships in which it was necessary to keep a record of the total assets of the firm.

cassette, n. ~ A container holding a roll of tape or film stored on two cores.

DF: cartridge

RT: Compact Cassette

Notes: Cassettes have been used for sound, video, and microfilm. The Compact Cassette, introduced in 1964 and still in use for audio recording, is a common example of a cassette. A cassette is distinguished from a cartridge, the latter having one hub instead of two.

catalog (also **catalogue**), n. ~ 1. A collection of systematically arranged descriptions of materials. – 2. A listing of items with descriptions. – 3. A publication produced in conjunction with an exhibit that lists the materials exhibited and that may have text that relates to the subject of the exhibit. – v. ~ 4. See **cataloging**.

NT: card catalog, catalogue raisonné, dictionary catalog, divided catalog, National Union Catalog, National Union Catalog of Manuscript Collections, online public access catalog, union catalog

RT: bibliography, cataloging, finding aid, index, intellectual control

Notes: Catalogs[1] may be in a variety of formats, including bound volumes, cards, microform, or online databases.

catalog record, n. ~ An entry[1] describing a work within a catalog, especially in an automated catalog.

BT: record

cataloging, v. ~ 1. The process of providing access to materials by creating formal descriptions to represent the materials and then organizing those descriptions through headings that will connect user queries with relevant materials. – 2. The process of providing such access, plus additional work to prepare the materials for use, such as labeling, marking, and maintenance of authority files.

NT: descriptive cataloging

RT: Anglo-American Cataloguing Rules, Archives, Personal Papers, and Manuscripts, authority control, bibliographic description, bibliographic utility, card catalog, catalog, description

Notes: The United States data content standard for cataloging archival collections is *Archives, Personal Papers, and Manuscripts*. The equivalent Canadian standard is *Rules for Archival Description*. The standard for bibliographic materials in English-speaking countries is *Anglo-American Cataloguing Rules*.

†*120 (APPM2 1989, p. 4):* The process of archival cataloging consists predominantly of *interpreting, extrapolating,* or *extracting* information from the material and its context. . . . By contrast, a bibliographic approach is characterized by item oriented cataloging to provide a description, usually of a published item, as a physical entity. The cataloging process consists predominantly of *transcribing* information that appears on or with the item.

catalogue raisonné, n. (**catalogues raisonnés**, pl.) ~ A publication that describes all the works of an artist, including photographers and occasionally architects, or less commonly, a school of artists or art movement.

BT: catalog

cc ~ *see:* carbon copy

CCITT (Comité Consultatif International Téléphonique et Télégraphique, abbr.) ~ *see:* International Telecommunication Union

CD (also CD-ROM, CD-R, CD-RW, CD-I, VCD, CD-V, and other variations) ~ *see:* Compact Disc

CDV ~ *see:* carte-de-visite

Cedars Project, n. ~ A research project that investigated strategic, methodological, and practical issues for digital preservation.

> *Notes:* The project, a collaboration between the universities of Leeds, Oxford, and Cambridge, began in 1998 and ended in 2002. See http://www.leeds.ac.uk/cedars/documents/Metadata/cedars.html.

cel (also **cell**), n. ~ A sheet of clear plastic on which figures are drawn and subsequently photographed in sequence with other cels to create an animated film.

> *Notes:* A cel often contains only a portion of a scene and is photographed with other cels and a separate background to form a complete image. The images on a sequence of cels represent the portion of a scene that appears to move when viewed against the static background.

celluloid, n. ~ 1. An early thermoplastic made from cellulose nitrate and camphor used to produce film and objects. – 2. SLANG · Motion picture film.

> *RT:* motion picture
>
> *Notes:* Celluloid was often used to make film and other commercial products, such as containers and brushes. The term was originally a trademark of the Celluloid Manufacturing Company. – Celluloid[2] is derived from the use of cellulose nitrate for early motion pictures and has been generalized to refer to motion picture films regardless of the material from which it is made.

cellulose, n. ~ 1. A long-chain polymer ($C_6H_{10}O_5$) commonly found in plants and used in making paper, lacquers, synthetic fibers, and explosives. – 2. PHOTOGRAPHY · A family of plastics used as the base in still and moving image films.

> *NT:* alpha cellulose, cellulose acetate, cellulose nitrate

cellulose acetate, n. ~ An extruded plastic made from hydrolyzed cellulose, usually wood pulp or cotton, dissolved in acetone.

> *BT:* cellulose
>
> *RT:* safety film, vinegar syndrome
>
> *Notes:* Variant forms of cellulose acetate include **cellulose diacetate** and **cellulose triacetate**. Cellulose diacetate was commonly used as the base of photographic and motion picture films beginning in the early 20th century. It was replaced by cellulose triacetate in the mid-20th century. Use of cellulose triacetate as a film base was largely, but not entirely, superseded by polyester beginning in the 1950s. Clear sheets of cellulose triacetate are used as protective sleeves for photographs. Deterioration of cellulose acetate films often results in a condition called vinegar syndrome.
>
> †163 *(Leggio, et al. 2000):* Cellulose acetate is the generic term used to describe a variety of acetylated cellulose polymers, including cellulose diacetate, cellulose triacetate and the mixed esters of cellulose acetate propionate and cellulose acetate butyrate.

cellulose diacetate ~ *see:* cellulose acetate

cellulose nitrate (also **nitrate**, **nitrocellulose**), n. ~ An extruded plastic made from

cellulose, usually from wood pulp or cotton, mixed with nitric and sulfuric acids.
BT: cellulose
Notes: Cellulose nitrate was commonly used as the base of photographic and motion picture film from the late 19th century through the early 20th century. It is highly flammable and in advance stages of deterioration can combust spontaneously.

cellulose triacetate ~ *see:* cellulose acetate

CENSA ~ *see:* Collaborative Electronic Notebook Systems Association

census, n. ~ A count of all members of a population that may also capture information about specific qualities of the members, such as age, gender, ethnicity, occupation, and living conditions.
RT: sampling
Notes: A census may be of human or other populations, such as animals or plants. A census is distinguished from sampling, which obtains information about a portion of the population that is generalized to the whole. In the United States an official census, taken every ten years as required by the Constitution, is used to apportion seats in Congress and has been used to gather a wide range of information about citizens and other residents.

central records (also **central files, centralized files**), n. ~ 1. The files of several organizational units consolidated in one location. – 2. The files of several individuals consolidated into a common filing system.
Notes: In central records[1], each unit's files are usually kept separate from those of other units. – For central records[1,2], the files are usually organized according to a filing plan, with each file typically having a file code indicating a classification under which it is filed.
†*300 (Yates 1989, p. 62):* Most books on vertical filing systems advocated centralized filing departments that handled all of the firm's files. They saw filing as a function activity, like accounting or sales, that would benefit from specialization and systematization. Moreover, they felt that efficiently managed centralized filing could give departments throughout the facility faster service than decentralized filing could.

central registry, n. ~ 1. Information compiled to serve as a master source for public or official reference. – 2. PRINCIPALLY EUROPEAN AND CANADIAN · See central records.
Notes: Examples of a central registry[1] include firearms, missing child, and sex offender registers.

centralized files ~ *see:* central records

certificate, n. ~ An official document attesting to the truth of a fact, qualification, or promise.
RT: certification
Notes: Certificates of fact include birth and death certificates. Certificates of qualification include those issued by professional associations.

certificate authority (also **certification authority**), n. ~ A trusted third party that supports authentication infrastructures by registering individuals and organizations, and then issuing them an X.509 digital certificate attesting to their identity.
RT: digital certificate, public key infrastructure
Notes: A certificate authority issues public and private keys in the form of digital certificates for message encryption and decryption. By issuing, managing, and validating these certificates, a certificate authority guarantees the authenticity of the user.

certification, n. (**certify**, v.) ~ 1. The formal process of asserting that a fact or process meets a standard. – 2. The process of issuing an official document (a certificate) attesting to the truth of a fact, the quality of a process, or the authenticity of a record. – 3. The process by which individuals can demonstrate that they have mastered an organization's requirements for professional practice. – **certified**, adj. ~ 4. Judged as authentic or as conforming to a standard.

RT: authentication, certificate, validation, verification

Notes: The term derives from the Latin *certus* (sure, determined, resolved, certain). Frequently used in the context of certified copies so that the copies can be accepted as equivalent to the original. Also used to attest that a process is trustworthy.

certified archivist, n. (**CA**, abbr.) ~ An individual who has met the Academy of Certified Archivists' requirements for education, experience, and knowledge.

RT: Academy of Certified Archivists

Notes: In addition to a master's degree and a year of experience, certified archivists must pass an exam that covers 1) selection, 2) arrangement and description, 3) reference service and access, 4) preservation and protection, 5) outreach, advocacy, and promotion of documentary collections and archival repositories, 6) managing archival programs, and 7) professional, legal, and ethical responsibilities. Certified archivists must maintain their certification by submitting evidence of ongoing continuing education, experience, and professional participation.

certified copy, n. ~ A duplicate that has been verified as an accurate reproduction of the original by an authorized official, typically the individual responsible for creating or maintaining the original.

BT: copy

certified records manager, n. (**CRM**, abbr.) ~ A professional records or information manager who has experience in active and inactive records systems, and in related disciplines such as archives, computerization, micrographics, and optical disk technology, and who has been certified by the Institute of Certified Records Managers as meeting both educational and work experience requirements by passing required examinations.

RT: Institute of Certified Records Managers

certify ~ *see:* certification

CFR, abbr. ~ [United States] *Code of Federal Regulations.*

chad, n. ~ 1. The waste material created when holes are punched out of a paper medium, especially punched cards; chaff, computer confetti, and keypunch droppings. – 2. Perforated strips on the sides of continuous paper, removed after printing, that allow the paper to be feed through a printer on sprocket wheels; selvage, perf.

†239 *(New Hacker's Dictionary 1994):* One correspondent believes [the term] derives from the Chadless keypunch (named for its inventor), which cut little U-shaped tabs in the card to make a hole when the tab folded back, rather than punching out a circle/rectangle; it was clear that if the Chadless keypunch didn't make them, then the stuff that other keypunches made had to be 'chad'.

chain index, n. ~ An index that uses hierarchical headings that reflect a faceted classification scheme.

BT: index

RT: faceted classification

Notes: The technique of chain indexing was developed by Ranganathan.

†159 (Lancaster 1998, p. 54): [Chain indexing includes] each step of the hierarchical chain from the most specific to the most general. Thus, an item represented by the class number AbCfHYqZh would generate the following index entries: Nineteenth century, Germany, Manufacture, Woolen goods, Clothing (AbCfHYqZh); Germany, Manufacture, Woolen goods, Clothing (AbCfHYq); Manufacture, Woolen goods, Clothing (AbCfH); Woolen goods, Clothing (AbCf); Clothing (Ab).

chain of custody, n. ~ 1. RECORDS · The succession of offices or persons who have held materials from the moment they were created. – 2. LAW · The succession of officers or individuals who have held real evidence from the moment it is obtained until presented in court.

RT: custodial history, custody

Notes: In both senses, the ability to demonstrate an unbroken chain of custody is an important test of the authenticity of records or evidence.

†24 (Bastian 2001, p. 96): Custody, both the legal and physical ownership of records, has long been recognized as a fundamental principle of archival management. . . . Hilary Jenkinson based the sanctity of evidence on the ability to prove continuous custody. T. R. Schellenberg, while rejecting 'continuous custody' as unworkable for the National Archives of the United States, still considered that having custody of the records that crossed the threshold of the Archives was essential to protecting their integrity.

chalking ~ *see:* powdering

chancery, n. ~ 1. An office of public records; an archives. – 2. LAW · A court of equity.

change management, n. ~ Planned, systematic alterations to established missions, objectives, policies, tasks, or procedures within an organization.

RT: business process reengineering

Notes: Change management typically refers to an intentional process undertaken by management in response to internal needs. However, it may also include strategies for responding to external events. It often includes tracking of historical data to plan future changes, a structured procedure for communicating the status of changes to all stakeholders, and a systematic recording of actions taken.

changeover cue, n. ~ A small mark made in the frame of a motion picture, usually in the upper right-hand corner, signaling the projectionist to be prepared to change to another projector with the next reel.

RT: cue mark, moving image

Notes: Changeover cues can often be seen in video recordings of older motion pictures.

channel, n. ~ 1. BROADCASTING · A circuit or portion of a frequency spectrum set aside for carrying information. – 2. A portion of a signal that carries information in parallel with other portions, which are assembled to make a whole. – 3. A path of communication between people; for example, official channels, proper channels. – 4. A trench, tube, or path directing the passage of materials.

Notes: Examples of channel[1] include television and radio channels. – An example of channel[2] is stereo, which uses a left and right channel that are combined to give a sense of acoustic space. – Microfilm jackets have channels[4] to hold strips of microfilm.

channeling, n. ~ CONSERVATION · Irregular veins (channels[4]) in photographic negatives formed by the separation of the emulsion from the base.

RT: buckle

Notes: Channeling is characteristic of cellulose diacetate films. Over time the base shrinks, although the emulsion does not. As a result, the stress causes the emulsion to buckle and separate.

character, n. ~ 1. A letter, digit, or other symbol that can be arranged in groups to represent information. – 2. The whole of features, traits, and attributes that distinguish something. – 3. COMPUTING · The combination of bits treated as a unit in computing; a byte. – 4. DRAMA · A role played by an individual in a dramatic performance, including plays, radio and television programs, and films.

character set, n. ~ The letters, symbols, numbers, and special codes allowed within an environment, which may be constrained by hardware, software, or an established standard.

NT: ASCII, control character, EBCDIC, Information Technology – 8-bit Single-byte Coded Graphic Character Sets, Unicode

RT: alphanumeric, bit, code

Notes: Two prominent key character sets include ASCII and EBCDIC. Seven-bit ASCII has a number of extended, eight-bit character sets; the first 128 characters are the same in all sets, but the second half of the set contains characters appropriate to different languages.

chargeout, n. ~ 1. A record of materials removed from storage for use. – 2. The process of removing materials for use.

RT: circulation record

Notes: A chargeout makes it possible to track the individual to whom materials were given or where the materials have been moved, allowing them to be found if needed. The process can also be used as a record of who has used a file in the past. Forms documenting the chargeout are sometimes called out cards, reference retrieval slips, or pull strips.

chart, n. ~ 1. A diagram or table intended to communicate information visually. – 2. A map used for navigation by air or sea, for weather data, or for archaeological site data listed by stratigraphy. – 3. An outline map with special information.

BT: cartographic record, map

RT: scale

Notes: Example of charts[1] include graphs, programming flow charts, and organizational charts.

charter, n. ~ 1. A document, issued by a government, that grants rights, liberties, or powers to its citizens. – 2. A government act or filing establishing a business, especially articles of incorporation. – 3. A document outlining the mission, principles, and procedures of an organization. – 4. HISTORICAL · A record documenting title to land obtained by livery of seisin.

Notes: A charter[1] is distinguished from a constitution in that the former is granted by the sovereign, while the latter is established by the people themselves. Both are the fundamental law of the land.

chartulary ~ *see:* cartulary

checklist, n. ~ 1. An itemized account, especially for inventory control. – 2. Short descriptions of actions to be taken, procedures to be followed, or things to be remembered. – 3. A brief catalog of items in an exhibit.

RT: bibliography, inventory, list

Notes: Checklists vary in the amount of detail given about the items, but the term connotes only a brief description.

checksum, n. ~ A mathematical value used in a simple error-detection method to verify data.

> *RT:* error detection and correction code
> *Notes:* A checksum is calculated from the data using a known formula that returns a single-digit value and is stored with the data. At any point the checksum can be recalculated to see if the value has changed. The final digit in a universal product code (UPC) is a checksum calculated from the two five-digit parts. The checksum is calculated during scanning, and if the calculated checksum does not match the checksum printed in the bar code, the scan is incorrect. The use of a parity bit is a very simple checksum.

chemical wood pulp, n. ~ A paper pulp made from coniferous and deciduous trees by cooking the wood with an alkaline solution to neutralize naturally occurring acids and to remove lignin.

> *BT:* paper, pulp
> *RT:* mechanical wood pulp
> *Notes:* Paper made from chemical wood pulp lasts longer than mechanical wood pulp paper because it has longer fibers and is therefore stronger. It is shorter-lived than most high alpha-cellulose paper such as rag paper.

chief source of information, n. ~ CATALOGING · The prescribed source of data identifying an object being described.

> *DF:* key informant
> *Notes:* Cataloging rules prescribe a hierarchy of typical sources of information, the chief source of information being the first available in the hierarchy. For books, the title page is preferred as the chief source of information over a cover title. For archival collections, the finding aid typically serves as the chief source of information.

chip, n. ~ 1. IMAGING · A microform that contains both microimages and coded identification. – 2. SOUND RECORDINGS · A defect in a cylinder of disc recording resulting from a piece that is missing from an edge. – 3. CONSERVATION · Mechanical damage to a document, such as a small piece broken off a glass plate or brittle board. – 4. COMPUTING · An integrated circuit on a piece of semiconductive material.

> *Notes:* Chip^2 should be distinguished from a gouge or dig, which is a defect in the recording surface.

chirograph, n. ~ 1. A handwritten document. – 2. A record that has been torn or cut into two pieces, often with writing across the division, each piece serving to authenticate the other; an indenture.

> *Syn:* indenture

chlorobromide photograph, n. ~ Photographic prints, negatives, and transparencies made using an emulsion containing a combination of two light-sensitive salts, silver chloride and silver bromide.

> *BT:* photograph
> *Notes:* The ratio of silver chloride to silver bromide determines the sensitivity of the emulsion to light. Chlorobromide photographs are typically developed, rather than printed out, and have a warm-toned image.

choropleth map, n. ~ A map that uses shades or colors to indicate some attribute of given regions on a map.

DF: isopleth map

BT: map

Notes: Choropleth maps are often used for political districts (counties, wards, census tracts), with a different color used to indicate the data value for the area. For example, a map of voting precincts might be colored red or blue to indicate which party won an election. A map of census tracts might use shades of a color to indicate population density. A choropleth map differs from an isolpeth map in that in the latter the regions are defined by some quality other than the data itself.

chron file (also **chrono file**) ~ *see:* chronological file

chronological date, n. ~ A moment in time, especially a day.

BT: date

RT: topical date

Notes: As used by the University of British Columbia and United States Department of Defense project, *Preservation of the Integrity of Electronic Records*, chronological date is used to distinguish a point in time from topical date (location).

chronological file (also **chron file, chrono file, continuity file, day file**), n. ~ A file containing materials ordered by date or other time sequence.

RT: reading file, time stamp

Notes: A chronological file circulated for reference is often called a **reading file**.

chronological inventory, n. ~ A listing of materials in a collection organized by date, which may be comprehensive or selective, and which may include details about the writer, recipient, date, place, summary of content, type of document, and page or leaf count; a calendar².

Syn: calendar

BT: inventory

chronology, n. ~ 1. The sequence of events over time. – 2. The science of computing time and of assigning events to their dates. – 3. A document that describes events or other information in their order of occurrence.

CIDOC ~ *see:* Comité international pour la documentation du Conseil international des musées

CIM ~ *see:* computer input microfilm

CIMI, n. ~ A consortium of cultural heritage institutions and organizations that encourages the use of standards in museums.

Notes: Founded in 1990 as the **Consortium for the Computer Interchange of Museum Information**. The organization concluded operations in December 2003.

cinching, n. ~ The condition of film or tape being wound too tight on a reel, often resulting in longitudinal scratches (cinch marks).

RT: pack

ciné mode, n. ~ 1. The arrangement of images on roll film with frames (portrait or landscape) oriented vertically, parallel to the long axis of the film; synonymous with motion picture mode. – 2. The arrangement of images on microfiche with frames filling the rows in a column before preceding to the next column.

DF: comic mode, horizontal mode

Syn: vertical mode

cinefilm ~ *see:* motion picture

cinematography, n. ~ The art and science of making motion pictures.

   RT: motion picture, movie

cipher (also **cypher**), n. ~ 1. A technique to convert information (plaintext) into a form that is unintelligible (ciphertext) without knowing the rules (algorithm) to convert it back to its original form. – 2. A message that is so encoded; synonymous with ciphertext. – 3. A key that is used to convert the plaintext to ciphertext. – 4. A design of interlacing initials; also cypher monogram.

   Notes: Cipher[4] monograms frequently appear on the backs of 19th-century cartes-de-visite and cabinet cards.

ciphertext, n. ~ Encrypted information that cannot be read without the knowledge of the rules to convert it back into its original form (plaintext).

   RT: cryptanalysis, cryptography, plaintext

circa, adj. (**c.**, **ca.**, abbr.) ~ DATES · Approximately; about.

   Notes: The abbreviation 'ca.' is often used to avoid confusion with the use of 'c' (often without a period) for copyright.

circular letter, n. ~ Correspondence intended to be distributed widely throughout an organization or group to disseminate information in a thorough and consistent manner.

   †*300 (Yates 1989, p. 66):* Orders or circular letters, issued (in printed form) by the U.S. Army beginning in 1813, allowed a military commander to announce a change in the chain of command, to give orders, or to establish procedures for all or some of the men under his command. Another influence on widely disseminated announcements, suggested by the use of the term *circular* or *circular letter* for such documents, is the advertising circular, a form of external communication.

circulation record, n. ~ 1. Documentation of who has used materials. – 2. LIBRARIES · A log of books or other materials a patron has checked out, which can also be used to indicate all books checked out from a library. – 3. A document that records the movement of something such as blood, books, drugs, immigrants, money, or water from one place to another.

   RT: chargeout

Cirkut panorama ~ *see:* panorama

CITRA ~ *see:* Conférence internationale de la Table Ronde des Archives

cityscape, n. ~ 1. A scene of an urban areas. – 2. A genre of art in which the urban environment is the principal subject.

   RT: aerial photograph, bird's-eye view, landscape, scene, seascape

   Notes: Cityscapes are urban equivalents of landscapes and include street scenes and skylines. For images made from above, looking down on an urban scene, see aerial photograph and bird's-eye view.

civil register, n. ~ 1. A record of births, marriages, deaths, and other major events in citizens' lives. – 2. A record of cases tried in a civil court.

   RT: vital statistics

   Notes: Separate civil registers[1] may be kept for different events. For example, births, deaths, and marriages may each be recorded in their own register.

clamshell case, n. ~ A box with the lid and base, each having three sides and sharing a fourth side that serves as a hinge.

   RT: document case, Solander box

   Notes: The dimensions of the bottom of the box are slightly smaller than the lid, and the sides of the top and bottom are roughly the same height. When closed, the sides of the bottom nest inside the sides of the top.

class, n. ~ 1. A group of things sharing common characteristics; members of a set. – 2. The highest or root element in a hierarchy. – 3. Records · A division within a file plan. – 4. Computing · In object-oriented programming, a group of objects that are derived from the same template and that share common structure and behavior.

> *BT:* classification
>
> *RT:* object, series

class code, n. ~ 1. Letters, numbers, or other symbols used to represent a division within a file plan or classification scheme.

> *BT:* classification
>
> *Notes:* Class codes are often formed from several parts, each part reflecting a division within a classification scheme. For example, administrative files may be represented by the class code ADM.

classification, n. (**classify**, v.) ~ 1. The organization of materials into categories according to a scheme that identifies, distinguishes, and relates the categories. – 2. The process of assigning materials a code or heading indicating a category to which it belongs; see code. – 3. The process of assigning restrictions to materials, limiting access to specific individuals, especially for purposes of national security; security classification.

> *DF:* arrangement
>
> *NT:* business activity structure classification system, class, class code, coded classification, faceted classification, functional classification, security classification, subject classification, synthetic classification
>
> *RT:* access, code, controlled vocabulary, decimal filing system, declassification, taxonomy
>
> *Notes:* Classification may involve physically arranging the materials or use of a class code to index and retrieve documents stored in a different order. For electronic documents, classification may involve assigning a class code used to index and retrieve the document. In some schemes, documents may be assigned to more than one class. – Classification² in libraries refers to the process of assigning a Dewey, Library of Congress, or other code to indicate where a book is to be shelved.

classification scheme (also **classification plan**), n. ~ A diagram or chart that describes standard categories used to organize materials with similar characteristics.

> *RT:* mnemonic filing system, ontology, taxonomy
>
> *Notes:* Classification schemes are often hierarchical in nature and frequently associating codes with each class. Typically used in an office of origin to file active records or in archives as a finding aid. Libraries commonly use either the Library of Congress Classification System or the Dewey Decimal Classification to organize their books. These bibliographic standards have only limited use in archives, which maintain the records in their original order.

classified, adj. ~ 1. Accessible only by permission, especially as regards national security. – 2. Restricted from general disclosure. – 3. Organized into groups, each group containing like materials.

> *RT:* clearance, closed, confidential, restriction, sensitive

classified filing, n. ~ A hierarchical method of organizing materials first by major concepts, then by related, subsidiary topics.

BT: Broader Term · *NT:* Narrower Term · *RT:* Related Term · *DF:* Distinguish From

Syn: encyclopedic arrangement

Notes: Materials organized by location often use classified filing to group materials first by state, then by city, and finally by a specific entry, such as a name. Classified filing may be used for organizing files or entries in a document.

classified index, n. ~ A list of headings, organized into groups based on similar characteristics rather than in alphabetical order, that points to information relevant to the heading in materials organized in some other manner.

Syn: analytical index

BT: index

Notes: Classified indexes are typically hierarchical, using general headings that are further subdivided by more specific headings.

cleaning, n. ~ 1. The process of removing dirt, smudges, stains, or other foreign material from an object. – 2. The process of redacting confidential, private, or restricted information.

Syn: redaction

Notes: Light cleaning[1] to remove surface dirt is often considered a routine part of processing. Extensive cleaning of accretions or stains, especially treatments that involve washing or bleaching, requires the services of a trained conservator.

clearance, n. ~ 1. Authorization necessary for access to classified information. – 2. Permission to take an action. – 3. The distance between two objects reserved for passage or some other function.

RT: access, classified

click-wrap license, n. ~ COMPUTING · An agreement granting conditions and terms of use, displayed during program installation or initiation, and acknowledged and agreed to by clicking a button.

BT: license

RT: copyright, shrink-wrap license

Notes: Failure or refusal to accept the conditions in a click-wrap license usually prevents the user from installing or accessing the program. The phrase is a derivation of shrink-wrap license, where the physical act of breaking a seal or the cellophane on the package indicates consent to the conditions and terms.

clip, n. ~ 1. A short segment taken from a moving image program. – 2. An item cut from a newspaper or magazine; see clipping. – 3. A fastener used to hold several sheets together.

Syn: clipping

RT: excerpt, moving image

Notes: Paper clips and binder clips are examples of clips[3].

clipping, n. ~ 1. An article or photograph cut from a newspaper or magazine; a news clipping. – 2. A distortion of sound when a recording is played at a volume exceeding the capacity of the amplifier. – 3. The loss of the beginning or end of audio signals due to the operation of sound-activated equipment starting late or ending early.

Syn: clip, news clipping

close-up, n. ~ 1. A photograph or motion picture image made with the camera near the subject. – 2. A portrait that shows only the face.

Notes: Two photographs made with lenses of different focal lengths may show the same area of the subject, but the overall effect may be quite different. Close-ups tend to exaggerate variations in the surface of a subject; a close-up of a face will make the nose appear larger because the nose is significantly closer to the camera than the ears. Images made with longer focal length lenses tend to 'flatten' the subject because the distances between the camera and the different parts of the subject are more nearly the same.

closed, adj. ~ 1. Restricted access; unavailable. – 2. COMPUTING · Proprietary; see discussion at open[2-5].

> *RT:* classified, open, restriction

closed captioning, n. ~ A transcription of a television program audio track encoded in the signal that allows hearing-impaired viewers to read dialog as subtitles or on a special decoder.

> *DF:* caption, subtitle

> *Notes:* The transcription generally captures only spoken language, but may use symbols or description to indicate other sounds necessary to understand the program. For example, the sound of a car off-camera driving away may be described as 'car leaving.' The closed-caption signal is encoded on line 21 of an National Television Systems Committee (NTSC) signal. Closed captioning is limited to video programs. It is distinguished from subtitles, which are captions in movies, and captioning in other settings, such as opera or theatrical productions.

closed file, n. ~ 1. A file containing records generated by a process that has been completed and to which additional information is not likely to be added; a cut-off file. – 2. A file to which access is not allowed.

> *RT:* restriction

> *Notes:* A closed file[2] carries the connotation that no one may see the file until the conditions causing the file to be closed have expired or have been removed. Files with limited access are sometimes referred to as restricted or classified.

closed index, n. ~ An index to which additional entries will not be made.

> *BT:* index

cockle, n. ~ A planar distortion in flat materials, especially paper or vellum, that is characterized by puckering, waves, or rippling.

> *RT:* buckle

> *Notes:* May be caused by uneven drying, by stretched paper shrinking while drying, or by excessive heat and moisture.

code, n. ~ 1. A set of characters, numbers, and other symbols used to represent a concept in a short, standard manner. – 2. Ciphers and other systems used to disguise the meaning of information. – 3. COMPUTING · A set of symbols used to communicate information; a character set. – 4. LAW · An official statement of law that is complete and systematically arranged. – v. ~ 5. RECORDS MANAGEMENT · To classify a record or file by assigning a set of characters, numbers, or symbols representing the series to which it belongs. – 6. COMPUTING · To write a program or macro containing instructions to perform operations on a computer.

> *Syn:* file code

> *RT:* character set, classification, cryptography, law, program

codebook ~ *see:* data dictionary

coded classification, n. ~ A technique to use a sequence of characters and digits (codes) as headings in a hierarchical filing scheme.

> *BT:* classification

> *Notes:* Coded classification is an example of classified filing that uses codes rather than words and phrases.

codex, n. ~ A document, especially an old manuscript, made from two or more flat pieces that have been hinged to open like the leaves of a modern book.

> *Notes:* The hinged binding of a codex distinguishes it from a scroll. The leaves of a codex may be made of any material, including metal, wood, ivory, or more commonly paper, papyrus, or vellum. The term is derived from early versions of the Christian Bible.

codicil, n. ~ 1. An informal document, usually attached to a will, giving instructions as to the disposition of assets. – 2. An addition to a document.

codicology, n. ~ The study of manuscripts, especially their physical nature.

cold storage, n. ~ 1. A technique for extending the life expectancy of materials by keeping them at a temperature below room temperature, thereby reducing the rate of deterioration. – 2. An area where materials can be kept at below normal room temperature.

> *RT:* acclimation, Arrhenius function, conditioning
>
> *Notes:* In general, cold begins at 65°F (18°C) and continues down to 0°F (18°C). Sometimes cool storage (65°F to 40°F, 18°C to 5°C) is distinguished from cold storage (40°F to 0°F, 18°C to 5°C). Because deterioration caused by chemical reactions is directly related to temperature (see Arrhenius function), keeping materials at a lower temperature can significantly slow the effects of aging. A number of standards include precise definitions of cold, based on the materials to be stored. See, for example, *Storage: Paper Records* (NISO TR01), *Storage: Photographic Film* (ANSI/PIMA IT9.11/ISO 5466), and *Storage: Optical Disc Media* (ANSI/PIMA IT9.25).
>
> Cold storage is frequently used to stabilize large quantities of materials. Cold storage is particularly effective for color and nitrate photographs and motion pictures. In cool storage, materials can be paged directly to a reading room without acclimatization. In cold storage, materials may be kept at freezing temperatures and must go through a staging process to bring them up to temperature where they can be used safely.

Collaborative Electronic Notebook Systems Association, n. (**CENSA**, abbr.) ~ A group representing a variety of industries that facilitates the automated management, collaboration, and recordkeeping of research and development data.

> *Notes:* See http://www.censa.org/.
>
> †1 *(CENSA):* Our mission: To drive creation, convergence, effective usage, and continuous improvement of automation technologies and methodologies that facilitate scientific discovery, product development and collaboration among technical and business professionals.

collage, n. ~ 1. A technique of assembling different materials onto a flat surface. – 2. A work produced using this technique.

> *DF:* composite, montage, photomontage
>
> *RT:* assemblage
>
> *Notes:* Materials used may include photographs, paper, printed materials, and fabric. A work that has sufficient depth to be considered three-dimensional is described as an assemblage. If the materials form a unified image, the work is described as a montage. A photograph that combines images from many negatives onto a single sheet of paper is called a photomontage. An image composed of small, regular pieces of glass, tile, or other durable material is called a mosaic.

collecting archives, n. ~ A repository that collects materials from individuals, families, and organizations other than the parent organization.

> *Syn:* manuscript repository
> *BT:* archives
> *RT:* institutional archives
> *Notes:* The scope of collecting archives is usually defined by a collections or acquisition policy.

collection, n. ~ 1. A group of materials with some unifying characteristic. – 2. Materials assembled by a person, organization, or repository from a variety of sources; an artificial collection. – **collections,** pl. ~ 3. The holdings of a repository.

> *Syn:* holdings
> *NT:* archives, artificial collection
> *RT:* fonds, manuscript collection, manuscript group, personal papers, record group
> *Notes:* Collection¹ is synonymous with record group if provenance is the unifying characteristic.
>
> †120 *(APPM2 1989, 1.0A):* [Collection¹] A body of archival material formed by or around a person, family group, corporate body, or subject either from a common source as a natural product of activity or function, or gathered purposefully and artificially without regard to original provenance. [May contain manuscripts, documents] correspondence, memoranda, photographs, maps, drawings, near-print materials, pamphlets, periodical tear-sheets, broadsides, newspaper clippings, motion picture films, computer files, etc.
>
> †152 *(Johnston and Robinson 2002):* The archival community has not traditionally used the term 'collection' to label the aggregates of material they typically describe. Archivists make the distinction between an archival fonds, where the items are of known provenance and their arrangement reflects their original working order as the records of an organisation or individual, and an 'artificial collection,' where the items are associated but lack the coherence of a fonds. The archivist recognises the fonds as the set of items that have been created and accumulated by an identifiable individual body (or bodies). However, it should be emphasised that both these classes of aggregates (the fonds and the artificial collection) are 'collections' in the more general sense in which the term is used here. Within an archival fonds, an item can be fully understood only within the context of its relationship with other items and aggregates in the fonds, and descriptive practice reflects this.

collection development, n. ~ The function within an archives or other repository that establishes policies and procedures used to select materials that the repository will acquire, typically identifying the scope of creators, subjects, formats, and other characteristics that influence the selection process.

> *RT:* acquisition, appraisal
> *Notes:* Collection development originated as a library term but has been commonly employed by archives, and to a lesser extent by museums, since the 1980s. When used to refer to the policy resulting from the function, some archives use the synonymous term acquisition policy or scope of collections statement.
>
> †257 *(Sauer 2001, p. 308):* Written collection development policies are advocated as a way to ensure that collections have coherent and well-defined focus,

while cooperative collecting practices are seen as a way to ensure that related materials are not scattered among far-flung repositories and that repositories' scarce resources are not needlessly squandered on unnecessary competitiveness for collections.

collective description, n. ~ A technique of cataloging related items as a unified whole in a single record.

> *BT:* description
>
> *Notes:* Collective description is distinguished from item-level description, which attempts to describe materials individually. Given the size of archival collections, item-level description is impractical except for the most important materials. Collective description proceeds from the general to the specific, starting with the collection as a whole, then describing groups and subgroups, series and subseries, and sometimes folders within the collection.

collective record group, n. ~ An artificial collection of records assembled from a number of relatively small or short-lived agencies that have an administrative or functional relationship.

> *BT:* record group
>
> *RT:* artificial collection
>
> *Notes:* Within a collective record group, each agency's records are usually segregated as a subgroup or series.
>
> *†124 (Holmes 1984, p. 167):* The records of small though essentially independent satellite agencies were often included with the records of major agencies to which they were related. Many smaller *fonds*, such as the records of claims commissions or arbitration boards, were grouped together in what became known as 'collective record groups,' of which a number were established. There would otherwise be thousands of *fonds*.

collective title, n. ~ CATALOGING · A formal title proper that is an inclusive title for an item containing two or more parts.

> *RT:* title

collective work, n. ~ COPYRIGHT · A work, such as a periodical issue, anthology, or encyclopedia, in which a number of contributions, constituting separate and independent works in themselves, are assembled into a collective whole (17 USC 101).

> *RT:* compilation, copyright
>
> *†281 (USC, 17 USC 101):* A collective work is a work, such as a periodical issue, anthology, or encyclopedia, in which a number of contributions, constituting separate and independent works in themselves, are assembled into a collective whole.

collector, n. ~ An individual, or group of individuals, responsible for acquiring materials.

collodio-chloride photograph, n. ~ A photographic print that uses collodion as the emulsion and silver chloride as the light-sensitive salt.

> *BT:* collodion photographs
>
> *Notes:* Collodio-chloride prints may be either developed out or printed out. The process was common from the mid-1880s through the 1910s.

collodion photographs, n. ~ Photographic prints, negatives, and transparencies that use collodion (cellulose nitrate dissolved in ether) as the emulsion that holds the light-sensitive salts to the base.

> *NT:* ambrotype, collodio-chloride photograph, tintype, wet collodion

collotype, n. ~ A photomechanical process that uses ink to produce prints from a reticulated gelatin matrix; a gelatin print[2].

Syn: gelatin print
BT: print
NT: Albertype
RT: photomechanical

Notes: Collotypes have a reticulated pattern of light and dark that approximate the continuous tones of a photograph.

†153 *(Jones 1911):* [collotype] A process known also as phototype, and in slight variations, as Albertype, Artotype, etc. It is based on the principle that if a film of bichromated gelatin is exposed to light under a negative, and the unaltered bichromate is washed out, the film will have a similar property to that possessed by a lithographic stone of attracting ink in some parts and absorbing water in others, the water repelling the ink.

†196 *(Nadeau 1990, v. 1, p. 73):* This planographic process was invented by Alphonse Poitevin in 1855 and can be considered the first process of photolithography.

colon classification ~ *see:* faceted classification

color, n. ~ 1. A property of an object that is determined by the wavelengths of light it reflects or transmits, giving it the appearance of red, blue, green, yellow, or their combinations. – 2. Chroma; hue. – adj. ~ 3. Having more than one color; not black and white. – 4. Reproducing the hues of the subjects depicted.

RT: monochrome

Notes: Color[1] is distinguished from saturation (the intensity of the color) and luminance (the brightness of the color). – Color[3] is often used to distinguish materials that are not monochromatic or black and white. For example, a two-color print uses two different colors of ink on a base that may be a third color.

color balance, n. ~ 1. The overall color of an image, especially as regards deviation from the accurate reproduction of tones. – 2. The ability of photographic materials to reproduce colors accurately.

Notes: Images with an inaccurate color balance[1] have a general cast, often subtle but sometimes quiet pronounced. For example, as color photographs age, their color balance may shift from neutral to a distinct hue due to the relative instability of the dyes. In some processes, yellow dyes often fade more rapidly than other dyes, and images may take on a magenta cast over time. In other cases, a layer becomes uniformly stained, giving the image a yellow cast. – Color balance[2] may be distorted by using materials designed for use with the wrong type of light source. For example, color film intended to be used outdoors will appear yellow if exposed under incandescent lights or green if exposed under fluorescent light.

color bars, n. ~ A standard signal used as a benchmark to test the color balance of video equipment.

RT: benchmark

color correction, n. ~ The process of adjusting the hues and tones of an image so that it accurately reproduces those of the original subject.

Notes: Color correction is used in photography, including digital photography, motion pictures, video, and other media that reproduce images directly from nature. Variations in film, processing, lighting, and other conditions may cause colors in an image to be overly blue, yellow, or some other color. Adding blue to an image with an overall yellow cast can eliminate that color imbalance.

color management, n. ~ The process of ensuring that hues and tones are translated between imaging systems as accurately as possible.

Notes: Different color management systems have different capacities for reproducing the entire range of colors that the human eye can see. Printed images have a smaller range of tones than images viewed by transmitted light. Similarly, different computer monitors may display the same file with very different colors due to variations in hardware design and age. Color management systems attempt to minimize differences by calibrating equipment and processes to standard colors to control the appearance of color.

COM, n. ~ 1. A communications port on a computer, especially the serial port on a personal computer. – 2. A top-level domain for Internet hosts in the United States intended for use by commercial sites. – 3. A file extension used by Microsoft DOS, Windows, and compatible software to indicate an executable file.

DF: component object model, computer output microfilm

combination printing, n. ~ PHOTOGRAPHY · A technique of creating a photographic print with a single, unified image from several different negatives.

DF: photomontage

RT: composite, multiple exposure, photograph

Notes: At its simplest, combination printing may be little more than the use of two separate negatives made of the landscape and the sky that are printed together. This technique was used to compensate for orthochromatic negatives that could not properly record the sky and scenery in a single exposure. At the other extreme, combination printing is frequently associated with the Pictorialist photographers of the 19th century. O. G. Rejlander and H. P. Robinson were two well-known practitioners. One of the best known examples is Rejlander's *The Two Ways of Life*, described below. A print made using this technique may be described as a combination print or a composite print.

†203 *(Newhall 1982, p. 74):* [Describing Rejlander's use of combination printing to create *The Two Ways of Life*.] He would have needed a huge studio and many models to take this picture with a single negative. Instead, he enlisted the services of a troupe of strolling players and photographed them in groups at scales appropriate to the distance at which they were to appear from the spectator. On other negatives he photographed models of the stage. He made thirty negatives in all, which he masked so they would fit together like a picture puzzle. Then, painstakingly masking a sheet of sensitized paper to match each negative in turn, he printed them one after the other in the appropriate positions.

comic mode, n. ~ 1. The arrangement of images on roll film with frames (portrait or landscape) oriented horizontally, perpendicular to the long axis of the film; horizontal mode. – 2. The arrangement of images on microfiche with frames filling the columns in a row before preceding to the next row.

DF: ciné mode, vertical mode

Syn: horizontal mode

Comité Consultatif International Téléphonique et Télégraphique ~ *see:* International Telecommunication Union

Comité international pour la documentation du Conseil international des musées
(also **International Committee for Documentation of the International Council
of Museums**), n. (**CIDOC**, abbr.) ~ A committee of the International Council of
Museums (ICOM) that focuses on the documentation of museum collections and
that promotes collaboration among curators, librarians and information specialists interested in documentation, registration, collections management, and computerization.

Notes: See http://www.willpowerinfo.myby.co.uk/cidoc/.

common records schedule ~ *see:* general records schedule

commonplace book, n. ~ A personal anthology of aphorisms, short passages from literature, poems, and other notes transcribed into a blank volume to serve the
memory or reference of the compiler.

Syn: memorandum book

Notes: Increasingly rare in the United States after the first quarter of the 20th
century.

communication, n. ~ 1. An expression of ideas or information through speech, text,
or symbolic behavior. – 2. The process of exchanging such ideas. – **communications**, pl. ~ 3. A division within an organization that serves as the official public
contact, especially with news media; public relations. – 4. A division within an
organization responsible for managing technology used to send and receive messages, such as telephones.

Compact Cassette, n. ~ A standard format for magnetic audiotape measuring just
under $4 \times 2\frac{1}{2}$ inches, with the tape measuring 0.15 inch on two hubs.

RT: audiotape, cassette

Notes: The Compact Cassette was introduced in 1962 by Philips and quickly
became a de facto standard. Although used principally for audio recordings, the
Compact Cassette was used by some early personal computers for data storage.
Standard lengths are 60, 90, and 120 minutes.

compact disc, n. (**CD, CD-ROM, CD-I, VCD, CD-V**, abbr.) ~ A 120mm (4.7 inch)
digital optical disk, commonly used for sound recordings and computer data, that
stores approximately 600 MB of data in a spiral track.

DF: phonograph record

BT: optical disk

NT: Photo CD

RT: High Sierra

Notes: The original CD format was introduced in 1983 by Sony and Philips as
a medium for recorded sound. Variations of the format are now used to store
other types of data. Other formats include CD-ROM (CD Read Only Memory)
for computer data, CD-I (CD Interactive) that allowed interactive multimedia to
be played on a television, VCD (Video CD) for video recorded in MPEG-1, CD-V
(CD Video) for uncompressed video, and Photo CD.

The original CD format was read-only. Later versions allowed write-once and
read-write capabilities. Writable versions include CD-R, CD+R, and CD-RW.

Although the spelling 'disk' is common in the United States, the format is
spelled 'disc.'

compact shelving (also **compact storage, mobile shelving, mobile aisle shelving,
movable shelving**), n. ~ Shelving designed so that rows can be moved next to each
other, with no intervening aisle, to provide dense storage.

BT: Broader Term • NT: Narrower Term • RT: Related Term • DF: Distinguish From

BT: shelving

Notes: By moving rows together, it is possible to eliminate aisles. An aisle can be created between two any rows as needed. Generally rows are parallel to each other, although they may be on a central pivot. Depending on the system, compact shelving may be moved using a manual crank or an electric motor.

compartment, n. ~ A unit of shelving, single- or double-sided, consisting of horizontal shelves between standards, uprights, or upright frames.

Syn: bay, section

RT: shelving

compass rose, n. ~ A circular design on a map to indicate north and other points of the compass.

RT: cartography

compatibility, n. ~ 1. The ability of components to work together properly. – 2. COMPUTING · The ability of different pieces of hardware, software, and data to work together.

Notes: Compatibility[1] applies to many technologies found in archives. Microfilm must match the readers, sound recordings must match playback machines, and slides and motion pictures must match projectors.

Compatibility[2] is necessary for hardware and software to function properly. An operating system designed for one computer architecture may not run on another architecture. Microsoft Windows 2000, written to run on modern Intel-based personal computers, does not function on a Macintosh computer and does not run on an early Intel-based personal computer (PC). Different programs must be compatible to function properly. A program written for the Windows 2000 operating system may not run on a PC running Windows 3.1 unless it is specifically written to be backwards compatible (designed to work with previous versions). Data and software must be compatible if the program is to be able to manipulate the data properly. A word processing file written in Corel WordPerfect cannot be read directly by Microsoft Word without a conversion filter. A file written by a different versions of the same software may not be compatible unless the different versions use the same format or the software is backward compatible. Word 2000 may not be able to read an older file created with Word 5.

competence, n. ~ 1. Having the basic qualifications to perform a function. – 2. DIPLOMATICS · The mandate and authority given to an office or person to accomplish something.

RT: function, mandate

Notes: Competence is not necessarily tied to responsibility. If a competent individual acts as an agent for another person, the person represented may be responsible for any action taken. For example, an archivist in a large repository may have competence to negotiate deeds of gift, but the responsibility for those deeds may lie with the repository's director.

†70 (Duranti 1998, p. 90, n. 10): Function[1] and competence are a different order of the same thing. Function is the whole of the activities aimed to one purpose, considered abstractly. Competence is the authority and capacity of carrying out a determined sphere of activities within one function, attributed to a given office or an individual. . . . While a function is always abstract, a competence must be attached to a juridical person.

compilation, n. ~ A work assembled from a variety of material taken from various sources to create a new work; an anthology.

 RT: collective work

 Notes: A compilation may also include new material, especially material that serves as an introduction, that provides a bridge between or commentary on the material from other sources, or that closes the work. Often used to describe motion pictures and sound recordings.

 †281 (USC): Copyright · A work formed by the collection and assembling of preexisting materials or of data that are selected, coordinated, or arranged in such a way that the resulting work as a whole constitutes an original work of authorship. The term 'compilation' includes collective works.

compiler, n. ~ 1. An individual who assembles materials from various sources and organizes it for publication. – 2. Computing · A program that translates high-level programming code into machine code that serves as instructions for a computer.

 Notes: A compiler² may create code that is executable (object code), or it may generate low-level code (assembly language), which must then be made executable by an assembler.

completeness, n. ~ 1. The property of having every necessary step concluded with nothing wanting. – 2. The property of having all physical and intellectual components required by the process or laws regulating the system that created the record. – **complete**, adj. ~ 3. Having every necessary step concluded with nothing wanting. – 4. Having all physical and intellectual components required by the process or laws regulating the system that created the record.

 RT: accuracy, adequacy of documentation, integrity, reliability, sufficiency

 Notes: In the context of records, completeness has the connotation of ensuring that all required information is included when the record is created. It is distinguished from sufficiency, which considers whether enough information has been captured; a form may be complete but insufficient. Completeness is distinguished from integrity, which relates to the potential of loss or degradation of information after it has been created.

complex entry, n. ~ A heading used in an index or catalog that has been subdivided, typically to group related headings in a classified index or catalog.

 BT: heading

 RT: entry

 Notes: Complex entries may be formed by inverting a natural language phrase ('government archives' entered as 'archives, government') or by adding a subheading ('archives – government – 20th century').

complimentary clause, n. ~ Diplomatics · A statement of respect included in the final clauses.

 Notes: Common English examples include 'yours truly' and 'sincerely.'

component object model, n. (**COM**, abbr.) ~ An open standard that defines digital objects with interfaces that allow other software to access their features, especially for use in cross-platform, client/server environments.

 DF: COM, computer output microfilm

 Notes: Developed and promoted by Microsoft, COM has been extended to include the Distributed Component Object Model (DCOM) and COM+ standards. Distinguish from computer output microfilm and technology-related senses that are also abbreviated COM.

composite, n. ~ 1. A video signal that combines color and luminance information into a single signal for recording and broadcast and that is decoded when viewed. – 2. Motion picture film containing both the picture and matching sound; a married print. – 3. PHOTOGRAPHY · A photographic print with a single, unified image from several different negatives. – 4. PHOTOGRAPHY, ANTHROPOLOGY · A single portrait made from photographs of many people. – 5. CONSERVATION · A complex material in which several components combine to produce characteristics and properties that are not found in the individual components (ceramics, glass, plastics).

> *DF:* collage, photomontage

> *RT:* combination printing, montage, video

> *Notes:* Composite[3,4] is distinguished from 'collage', which are prints assembled from pieces of other prints. – A composite[3] photograph may be made using the technique of combination printing. – Composite[4] describes a technique used in the late 19th century. In some instances, these photographs were purported to have anthropological value by revealing a generic 'type' of the class of people photographed, often a race or ethnic group, but sometimes a family.

compound act, n. ~ DIPLOMATICS · Something that is done on behalf of another physical or juridical person, or among several persons, and that involves a number of steps in execution.

> *BT:* act

compound document, n. ~ COMPUTING · A digital document that includes a variety of formats, each of which is processed differently.

> *RT:* digital document, document, Open Document Architecture

> *Notes:* A compound document may include text, raster or vector graphics, audio files, spreadsheets, and other formats. A compound document may be fixed or dynamic, and may either store the components internally or draw them from external data sources. Web pages are often compound documents, as they include text and images. Sometimes called a **multisensory document**.

comprehensive records schedule (also **comprehensive records plan**) ~ *see:* general records schedule

compression, n. ~ COMPUTING · A process that reduces the amount of space necessary for data to be stored or transmitted.

> *RT:* JPEG, lossless, lossy

> *Notes:* 'Compression' is often used to describe the process of compacting and extracting the information, although the term can be used to distinguish the first phase from the second phase, which is called decompression. The digital image formats JPEG and GIF both use compression to minimize file size.

> Compression may be described as lossless and lossy. Lossless compression ensures that the uncompressed version is identical to the original; no information has been lost. Lossy compression results in some difference between the original and an uncompressed version. In general, lossy compression may produce a smaller file size. The GIF file format incorporates a compression algorithm that is lossless for images that contain fewer than 256 colors; images with more colors are reproduced with a limited palette. The JPEG format can, in theory, be configured to have varying degrees of loss, including a lossless option.

compulsory rights (also **compulsory license, mandatory rights**), n. ~ COPYRIGHT · A permission granted by law allowing the use of protected materials without explicit permission of the owner of copyright, but requiring the user to pay a specified fee to the copyright owner.

RT: copyright

Notes: In the United States, compulsory rights have governed the mechanical reproduction of music, cable television systems, noncommercial broadcasts, and jukeboxes.

computer, n. ~ 1. An electronic device that accepts data as input, which is then analyzed or manipulated according to specific instructions, with the resulting data stored for future use, output in human-readable form, or used as input to another process or to control another device. ~ 2. One who counts or adds numbers.

RT: computer system, legacy system

Notes: Computers[1] are often categorized in terms of their processing power. '**Mainframe**' (in slang, 'big iron') refers to large computers, especially older systems that relied on batch or centralized processing. They continue to be used for applications that require many individuals to work simultaneously with a large amount of shared data, such as a large corporate accounting system. Because 'mainframe' describes older systems, the term '**supercomputer**' was introduced to describe a new class of very powerful computers, especially very fast or massively-parallel architectures. '**Minicomputer**' was used to describe smaller systems, especially those with all components contained in a single cabinet. The term has generally fallen out of use. '**Microcomputer**' and '**personal computer**' (PC) are near synonyms that refer to small systems that rely on a single-chip central processing unit (CPU). '**Workstation**' connotes a very powerful microcomputer designed for use by an individual for processor-intensive applications but is often used to mean any personal computer. Given the increase of speed and capacity of hardware, the distinctions between these categories of computers are significantly blurred by the fact that many modern laptops are more powerful than early mainframes. Modern computers are digital, using binary code and programmed using software. Some early computers did not use binary code, and analog computers were programmed by physical wiring.

Computer[2] is now largely obsolete, though the profession was not uncommon through the mid-20th century. Computers might have been involved in producing large tables of numbers from formulas.

computer-aided design, n. (**CAD,** abbr.) ~ Software that is used to create precision drawings in two or three dimensions and that often incorporates details about the physical and performance characteristics of the objects represented.

RT: architectural drawing

Notes: CAD software is commonly used by architects and engineers. It is often capable of analyzing the characteristics of the materials represented in the design to check tolerances, loads, capacities, and the like.

computer-aided engineering, n. (**CAE,** abbr.) ~ A broad term that encompasses most uses of computers in design, planning, manufacturing, and testing.

computer-aided retrieval (also **computer-assisted retrieval,** n. (**CAR,** abbr.) ~ The use of computers to aid access to information on physical media, especially microfilm.

Notes: Computer-aided retrieval typically includes an index and sometimes a brief description of the material that can be searched. When relevant material is identified, the system may automatically load microfilm or offline-storage media containing the materials, then locate it within its container and display it.

computer-based indexing ~ *see:* automatic indexing

Computer Graphics Metafile, n. ~ A standard (ISO/IEC 8632) specifying a mechanism to store and transfer picture description information between systems.

†*134 (ISO/IEC 8632, 1999):* ISO/IEC 8632 provides a file format suitable for the storage and retrieval of picture description information. The file format consists of an ordered set of elements that may be used to describe pictures in a way that is compatible between systems of different architectures, compatible with devices of differing capabilities and design, and meaningful to application constituencies. This picture description includes the capability for describing static images.

computer input microfilm, n. (**CIM**, abbr.) ~ 1. The process of using hardware and software to transform data on microforms to machine-readable code. – 2. A microform used as the source of data to be transformed for computer input.

   BT: microfilm

computer output microfilm, n. (**COM**, abbr.) ~ Microfilm containing information that has been generated or stored by a computer and that has been written directly to film without the use of an intermediary paper printout.

   DF: COM, component object model

   BT: imaging, microfilm

   Notes: Distinguish from component object model and other technology-related senses that are often abbreviated COM.

computer program, n. ~ A sequence of instructions given to a computer to perform a specific task or produce a desired outcome; a program[5].

   Syn: application, program

   RT: software

   Notes: Modern programs are typically written in a high-level language such as Basic, C, Java, or Pascal, which reflect the steps necessary to accomplish the task. That high-level language is then translated into executable code by an assembler or compiler.

computer system, n. ~ A collection of related hardware, software, or both that work together for a common purpose or are regarded as a whole.

   BT: system

   RT: computer

   Notes: Human users play an integral role in some computer systems. For example, a human may be asked to make a decision based on results in the middle of a process, authorize the next process, or transform data manually.

concealment, n. ~ 1. LAW · The failure to disclose something, either passively, by not declaring what is known about the thing, or actively, by hiding the thing or hindering its discovery. – 2. IMAGING · The use of interpolation to supply an approximation of missing or questionable data in an image.

   Notes: An example of concealment[2] is a process that fills in information between scan lines in a television picture to produce a smoother image.

concept indexing, n. ~ The process of creating an ordered list of headings, using terms that may not be found in the text, with pointers to relevant portions in the material.

   Syn: assignment indexing

   BT: indexing

   Notes: Concept indexing draws headings from a controlled vocabulary, rather than relying on the terms found in the material that is indexed. Concept indexing is distinguished from extraction indexing, typically done by a computer, which relies exclusively on the terms found in the document. At one point, concept indexing was a manual process, requiring human judgment to link the headings to the ideas in the text. The process of assigning terms from a controlled vocabulary has been automated, with mixed success, by building rules of analysis that can assign headings on the basis of related terms in the text.

concordance, n. ~ 1. A list of terms used in a body of work, with pointers to the location of those terms. – 2. ARCHIVES · A finding aid that lists previous and current reference numbers of records that have been renumbered or relocated.

Notes: A concordance[1] may be abridged to exclude common words or may be exhaustive to include every word. Concordances often contain every variation of a word, rather than combining them under a general form. – A concordance[2] is also called a **conversion list**.

concurrent resolution, n. ~ A formal expression of an opinion or decision by one chamber of a legislature and agreed to by the other.

BT: resolution

Notes: A concurrent resolution does not have the force of law, as distinguished from a joint resolution, which does carry the force of law and is subject to veto.

conditioning, n. ~ 1. The process of preparing materials for storage or use by placing them in a special environment; staging. – 2. PAPER MANUFACTURING · A process during paper making in which moisture is added or removed to match the environment of print rooms. – 3. MOTION PICTURES · Coating film stock with a lubricant during cleaning.

Syn: acclimation, staging

RT: cold storage, reconditioning

Notes: Conditioning[1] is typically used to describe steps necessary to place materials in cold storage or to make them available for use in the reading room. When materials are conditioned for cold storage, they may have moisture removed to prevent the formation of ice. When removing from cold storage, conditioning ensures that the materials are at a suitable temperature and moisture content to avoid problems of condensation or brittleness.

Conférence internationale de la Table Ronde des Archives (also **International Conference of the Round Table on Archives**, n. (**CITRA**, abbr.) ~ The annual meeting of heads of national archival institutions, of the heads of national professional associations, and of the chairs of ICA sections and committees.

RT: International Council on Archives

Notes: See http://www.ica.org/citra/.

†137 (CITRA): [CITRA] membership is that of the Delegates Meeting. It is held in between quadrennial international congresses and allows members holding important responsibilities within the profession to meet every year to debate their views, update their knowledge and share experiences on subjects of common interest.

confidential, adj. ~ 1. Kept secret within an authorized group. – 2. Not to be disclosed.

RT: classified, disclosure-free extract, privacy, public, sensitive

Notes: Confidential information may require restrictions on access to protect the rights of the parties involved.

†10 (AJS, Records §29): Access to a document in the possession of a public official may properly be denied, in some instances, on the grounds that the information was received in confidence. But a person who sends a communication to a
public officer relative to the public business cannot make his communication private and confidential simply by labeling it as such. The law determines its character – not the will of the sender.

configuration, n. ~ 1. The manner in which parts are assembled into a whole. – 2.
Computing · The manner in which various pieces of hardware and software are
connected to allow them to work together.

conservation, n. ~ 1. The repair or stabilization of materials through chemical or
physical treatment to ensure that they survive in their original form as long as possible. – 2. The profession devoted to the preservation of cultural property for the
future through examination, documentation, treatment, and preventive care, supported by research and education.

    DF: preservation, restoration

    Notes: Conservation[1] counters existing damage, as distinguished from preser-
vation[2], which attempts to prevent damage. Conservation does not always eliminate evidence of damage; restoration includes techniques to return materials to
their original appearances (which may include fabrication of missing pieces). –
However, conservation[2] is often used to include preservation[1] activities.

conservation laboratory (also **preservation laboratory**), n. ~ A facility with specialized equipment to support the treatment or repair of materials through the use of
chemical or physical treatments.

    Notes: Conservation laboratories often have microscopes and other devices to
inspect materials, tables and sinks to hold large, flat items, and fume hoods to prevent the spread of toxic gases.

conservator, n. ~ A professional whose primary occupation is the practice of conservation and who, through specialized education, knowledge, training, and experience, formulates and implements all the activities of conservation in accordance
with an ethical code such as the *AIC Code of Ethics and Guidelines for Practice* (AIC
Definitions).

    Notes: The AIC also defines a number of related jobs, including

    Conservation Administrator, a professional with substantial knowledge of
conservation who is responsible for the administrative aspects and implementation of conservation activities in accordance with an ethical code such as the *AIC
Code of Ethics and Guidelines for Practice.*

    Conservation Educator, a professional with substantial knowledge and expe-
rience in the theory and techniques of conservation whose primary occupation is
to teach the principles, methodology, and/or technical aspects of the profession in
accordance with an ethical code such as the *AIC Code of Ethics and Guidelines for
Practice.*

    Conservation Scientist, a professional scientist whose primary focus is the
application of specialized knowledge and skills to support the activities of conservation in accordance with an ethical code such as the *AIC Code of Ethics and
Guidelines for Practice.*

    Conservation Technician, an individual who is trained and experienced in
specific conservation treatment activities and who works in conjunction with or

under the supervision of a conservator. A conservation technician may also be trained and experienced in specific preventive care activities.

Collections Care Specialist, an individual who is trained and experienced in specific preventive care activities and who works in conjunction with or under the supervision of a conservator.

Consortium for the Computer Interchange of Museum Information ~ *see:* CIMI

Conspectus, n. ~ A project begun in 1980 by the Research Libraries Group to evaluate and compare the relative strengths of the subjects held in library collections to facilitate coordinated collection by member libraries.

constituent correspondence, n. ~ Letters received by elected officials from individuals in their districts, often expressing the authors' opinions on matters of public policy or seeking assistance in interactions with the government.

construction drawing ~ *see:* architectural drawing, engineering drawing

constructive notice, n. ~ The communication of information in a manner that, by law, cannot be controverted or disputed because a party had the opportunity and obligation to be aware of it.

    RT: evidence, public record

    Notes: The intent of constructive notice is to give individuals an opportunity to protect their interests, to ensure that they are familiar with the details of an action, and to give all parties an opportunity to support or oppose the matter at issue. In the United States, many records are kept in a public office to provide constructive notice. Examples include, records of real property; births, marriages, and deaths (vital records); judicial decisions; minutes of public meetings. Many of these records are held by the office of a city or town clerk, a county recorder, or the secretary of state.

    †10 *(AJS, Records §102):* The doctrine of constructive notice rests on the idea that all persons may learn and actually know that of which the law gives notice and implies knowledge. The notice imparted by the due and proper record of an instrument, although called a constructive notice, is just as effectual for the protection of the rights of the parties as an actual notice by word of mouth, or otherwise.

contact copy, n. ~ A photographic reproduction made by holding the copy and original together during exposure.

    BT: copy

    NT: contact print

    Notes: A generic term used when the copies may be in a variety of formats, such as print, negative, or transparency. Commonly used in photographic reproduction, including micrographics, where the original and copy are held together with glass.

contact paper, n. ~ A slow-speed photographic paper intended to be exposed while emulsion-to-emulsion with the negative.

    BT: paper

    Notes: Contact paper is distinguished from enlarging paper, which is faster and does not require as intense a light source. Contact paper may be printed out or developed out. Azo is an example of contact paper.

contact print, n. ~ A photographic print made while the paper is held emulsion-to-emulsion with the negative.

    BT: contact copy

contact sheet, n. ~ A standard size sheet of photographic paper (typically 8 × 10 inches) used to make a contact print of all images on a roll of photographic film.

Notes: A contact sheet for 2¼″ film typically has twelve images. A contact sheet for 35 mm film typically holds 35 images (seven rows of five images).

container, n. ~ A package or housing used to hold materials; a receptacle.

NT: box, can, folder, portfolio, slipcase, tub file

Notes: Container carries the connotation that the contents can be separated, especially when the materials are in use. A slipcase for a book or a document box is a container. The shell for the tape in a videocassette may be called a housing, but it is not a container.

container list, n. ~ The part of a finding aid that indicates the range of materials in each box (or other container) in a collection.

DF: folder list

Notes: A container list may include the title of the series and a description of the first and last items in the container, omitting descriptions of materials between, or it may merely list the series in each box. A container list may contain shelf locations. A container list is distinguished from a folder list, which includes a description of each folder in the container.

contamination, n. ~ 1. The condition of having undesirable, foreign material added in. – 2. The process of adding unwanted material.

Notes: Most often refers to the introduction of chemicals or other physical materials, but may also indicate the corruption of a digital or analog signal with noise.

content, n. ~ The intellectual substance of a document, including text, data, symbols, numerals, images, and sound.

BT: record

RT: context, structure

Notes: Along with context and structure, content is one of the three fundamental aspects of a record.

content analysis, n. ~ 1. A methodology to appraise records by considering the significance of the informational value and the quality of information contained in the records. – 2. CATALOGING · The process of examining a work to determine its subjects, especially for purposes of writing an abstract or assigning access points.

BT: appraisal

Notes: Content analysis assesses quality in terms of the time span, the completeness, and the level of detail of the information contained in records.

†112 *(Ham 1993, p. 64):* Content analysis: The archivist must evaluate the significance of the subjects or topics documented in the records and then determine how well the information in the records document those subjects or topics.

content date, n. ~ CATALOGING · The time period of the intellectual content or subject of the unit being described, often expressed as a date range.

DF: creation date

Syn: coverage date

BT: date

Notes: A content date is distinguished from the creation date, the latter referring to when the materials were made. A contemporary collection of materials about to the Korean War would have a content date in the 20th century and a creation date in the 21st.

content management, n. ~ Techniques to set policies and supervise the creation, organization, access, and use of large quantities of information, especially in different formats and applications throughout an organization.

> *BT:* management
>
> *RT:* document management, information system, knowledge management, records management
>
> *Notes:* Content management is often used to describe the management of websites, but in other instances refers to the management of all information across the whole of an enterprise.
>
> †69 *(Duhon 2003, p. 10):* Enterprise content management (ECM) is the technologies, tools, and methods used to capture, manage, store, preserve and deliver content across an enterprise. At the most basic level, ECM tools and strategies allow the management of an organization's unstructured information, wherever that information exists. ECM is a process that takes your content throughout its lifecycle – from the creation of an idea scribbled on a sheet of paper to the management of the multiple working documents to flesh out that idea to the archival and ultimate disposition of the policy that had its genesis in that flash of inspiration.

content standard, n. ~ A set of formal rules that specify the content, order, and syntax of information to promote consistency.

> *DF:* data structure standard
>
> *BT:* standard
>
> *Notes:* A content standard goes beyond identifying the general type of information and indicates how to select between different, equivalent representations of the information and the manner the information is to be structured. For example, a content standard for a field called 'name' might indicate whether an individual's common or full name should be used and whether the name should be inverted. For example, Lewis Carroll might be entered as Dodgson, Charles Lutwidge. *Anglo-American Cataloguing Rules* (AACR) and *Archives, Personal Papers, and Manuscripts* (APPM) are examples of content standards.
>
> †89 *(Fox and Wilkerson 1998, p. 27):* Data content standards govern the order, syntax, and form in which the data values are entered. For example, if Paul Joseph Smith is the authorized name in the authority file, the data content standard might specify that the last name be entered first, as in Smith, Paul Joseph.
>
> †287 *(Weber 1989, p. 509):* Standards for data contents and data construction provide guidelines for the content of the data structures. . . . Many data content standards are guidelines, namely 'rules for activities that should be applied as consistently as possible but which, by their nature, will not necessarily produce identical results even when followed.'

contents note, n. ~ CATALOGING · A concise summary of the sections of a work.

> *RT:* scope and contents note
>
> *Notes:* In bibliographic cataloging, a contents note often reproduces the titles of chapters in a book. In USMARC format, it is recorded in field 505.

context, n. ~ 1. The organizational, functional, and operational circumstances surrounding materials' creation, receipt, storage, or use, and its relationship to other materials. – 2. The circumstances that a user may bring to a document that influences that user's understanding of the document.

> *RT:* archival bond, content, Encoded Archival Context, original order, provenance, structure

Notes: Along with content and structure, context is one of the three fundamental aspects of a record.

context analysis, n. ~ A methodology for assessing the value of records in light of other sources of the same or similar information.

> *BT:* appraisal
>
> *Notes:* Context analysis considers whether information in the records is unique, is in a preferred form, is of superior quality, is scarce, or is in some form that enhances the importance or usefulness of the records.

contingent records, n. ~ Records whose disposition is not based on a fixed period of time, but on some future event that will take place on a date unknown.

> *BT:* record
>
> *RT:* retention period

continuation, n. ~ 1. A supplement to an existing work. – 2. An additional part or issue in a run of serials, series, or monographs.

continuing value, n. ~ The enduring usefulness or significance of records, based on the administrative, legal, fiscal, evidential, or historical information they contain, justifying their ongoing preservation.

> *Syn:* enduring value
>
> *BT:* value
>
> *RT:* historical value, permanent value
>
> *Notes:* Many archivists prefer to describe archival records as having continuing value or enduring value, rather than permanent value. The phrase 'continuing value' emphasizes the perceived value of the records when they are appraised, recognizing that a future archivist may reappraise the records and dispose of them. The phrases are often used interchangeably.

continuity, n. ~ Moving images · The process of ensuring that details in different takes match in the context of the program.

> *Notes:* Continuity ensures that time within a program is perceived as realistic, not the actual time required to make the program. For example, some scenes may be shot several times or be shot in an order different from that in the program. Continuity records details necessary to give a sense of a seamless flow. For example, if a scene filmed over a day takes only a few minutes, a clock visible in the scene must appear to represent narrative time, not actual time.

continuity file ~ *see:* chronological file

continuous forms, n. ~ Forms printed on fanfold paper.

> *RT:* fanfold
>
> *Notes:* Each form is usually on a separate sheet, defined by the folds. Perforations along the fold facilitate bursting. The paper is usually intended for use in a computer, and may have holes along the edges to facilitate transport past a print mechanism using a tractor feeder.

continuous-tone image, n. ~ A graphic made by a process that can reproduce a smooth gradation of tones or colors without the use of a halftone screen.

> *Notes:* Continuous-tone images are distinguished from those made using a line process with one or a few colors of ink. Examples of continuous-tone images include photographic prints, negatives, and transparencies.

continuum ~ *see:* life continuum, records continuum

contract, n. ~ 1. A legally binding agreement between two parties. – 2. – An enforceable promise made by a party to a transaction. – 3. A document that records the terms and conditions of a legally binding agreement.

contrast, n. ~ The relative difference between the lightest and darkest areas of an image.

> *RT:* brightness

> *Notes:* High-contrast images have a significant difference between the highlights and shadows, often having very few midtones. Low-contrast images have relatively less difference between the highlights and shadows, often lacking a pure white or pure black. Contrast is sometimes expressed as a ratio of the lightest and darkest areas of an image, as measured by a densitometer.

contributor, n. ~ An individual or organization with secondary responsibility for the creation of a collaborative work or a collection.

> *Notes:* Contributors may supply separate parts of a larger work; for example, several authors may contribute essays to an anthology. A contributor may also serve a specific role for a work as a whole, such as an editor, translator, producer, or director.

control character, n. ~ A computer code within a character set typically used to direct operations rather than for informational content.

> *BT:* character set

> *Notes:* In ASCII, characters between 0 and 31, and character 127 are reserved as control characters. Common control characters within documents include tab, carriage return, and newline. Other control characters used to control transmission of data include Start of Text, End of Text, and End of Transmission. Control characters used to indicate data records and fields include the file, group, record, and unit separators.

controlled vocabulary, n. ~ A limited set of terms and phrases used as headings in indexes and as access points in catalogs.

> *NT:* Art and Architecture Thesaurus, Library of Congress Subject Headings

> *RT:* authority file, classification, descriptor, index, index term, thesaurus, Thesaurus for Geographic Names, Thesaurus for Graphic Materials, vocabulary

> *Notes:* Terms in a controlled vocabulary are selected so that only one term represents a concept, allowing all material relating to that concept to be retrieved using that term even if the term does not appear in the text. The term used for indexing purposes is the preferred term. The vocabulary may also include cross-references from nonpreferred terms to preferred terms.

> †75 *(Durrance 1993, p. 41):* Without a controlled vocabulary, one cannot ensure the retrievability of the records sought and *only* those records.... [It is] the totality of all the identified access points, the preferred terms and the linkages established among preferred and variant terms within a particular [authority] file.

convenience file (also **crutch file**), n. ~ A file containing duplicates of records kept near the point of use for ease of reference.

> *BT:* file

> *RT:* office file, personal file

> *Notes:* Because convenience files contain duplicates of the record copy, preserved elsewhere, they are often considered nonrecords. The documents in a convenience file are often called **convenience copies**.

†*271 (Texas A&M Procedures 2002):* Care must be taken by records management coordinators and University executives in determining if duplicate records are convenience copies or if two or more copies of the same information or records series are to be considered an official record copy. It is possible for the same information or records series to be present in two or more units of the University and be the official record copy in each unit if it serves a different function in each of the units.

convention, n. ~ 1. A generally accepted custom arising from practice rather than law. – 2. A formal standard that will produce similar but not identical results. – 3. An agreement or compact between groups, especially nations, that is less formal than a treaty.

    BT: standard

    Notes: A convention[2] is more specific than a guideline, but not as precise as a technical standard. Conventions produce more consistent results than guidelines but less than technical standards.

conventional records, n. ~ 1. Textual records. – 2. Records that are human-readable.

    BT: record

    Notes: Conventional records[1] distinguishes written documents from other formats, such as audio or pictorial records. – Conventional records[2] distinguishes traditional, four-corner documents from other formats, such as audio recordings and electronic records.

conversion, n. ~ 1. A process of changing something's form or function. – 2. COMPUTING · To move data to a different format, especially data from an obsolete format to a current format; migration.

    NT: persistent object preservation

    RT: migration

    Notes: Conversion[1] includes scanning paper documents to create digital images or rekeying paper text into a computer. – Conversion[2] is more than copying files. It involves a change in media internal structure, such as from diskette to tape, from one version of an application to a later version, or from one application to another.

conversion list ~ *see:* concordance

coordinate indexing system, n. ~ A set of rules to provide access to materials by assigning separate headings for each concept, which are then related (coordinated) during a search to retrieve materials based on the relationship among those headings.

    BT: indexing

copy, n. ~ 1. Something that is nearly identical to something else; a facsimile; a reproduction. – 2. A duplicate made from an original. – 3. Text, especially a document that is to be set in type or used in a news story. – v. ~ 4. To make a reproduction; to duplicate.

    DF: duplicate

    Syn: dubbing, reproduction

    NT: action copy, authentic copy, carbon copy, certified copy, contact copy, engrossed copy, figured copy, file copy, imitative copy, information copy, microcopy, photocopy, preservation copy, preservation photocopy, reference copy, security copy, simple copy, true copy, use copy

RT: backup, blueline, counterfeit, direct image film, disclosure-free extract, dubbing, duplicate, duplicate original, edition, electrostatic process, facsimile, fair copy, forgery, generation, hard copy, letterpress copybook, original, record copy, reformat, replica, reprographics, soft copy, text, transcript, version

Notes: A copy[1] can vary significantly in its fidelity to the original. In some instances, it may be sufficient for a copy to capture only the intellectual content of the record without regard to formatting (see fair copy). Or it may be an exacting facsimile of the original. Because there is always some loss of quality when making a copy, originals have greater authenticity than copies. Hence originals are preferred over copies for evidence (see best evidence). The value of the information is not increased by repetition. However, the presence of many copies of a record may serve as a check on the trustworthiness of a record; the presence of multiple, identical copies suggests that the record has not be altered. Similarly, publication has been used as a means to preserve records by distributing copies among many owners and many locations to increase the odds that at least one copy will survive if others are lost or damaged. – Copy[1,2] and duplicate[1] are often synonyms. However, 'copy' connotes a something reproduced from an original; for example, a Xerox copy. 'Duplicate' connotes a version that may be considered an original; for example, duplicate prints made from the same negative. – A copy[1,2] made with the intent to deceive is often described as a forgery or a counterfeit. A copy or similar work made by the creator of the original is often described as a replica or version.

†281 (USC, 17 USC 101): 'Copies' are material objects, other than phonorecords, in which a work is fixed by any method now known or later developed, and from which the work can be perceived, reproduced, or otherwise communicated, either directly or with the aid of a machine or device. The term 'copies' includes the material object, other than a phonorecord, in which the work is first fixed.

copy of record ~ *see:* record copy

copy status ~ *see:* generation

Copyflo, n. ~ A tradename for a high-speed duplicating process developed by Xerox, principally used to create print copies of roll microfilm.

RT: microfilm

Notes: The Copyflo process was introduced in 1955.

Copyleft ~ *see:* General Public License

copyright, n. (**c.**, abbr.) ~ A property right that protects the interests of authors or other creators of works in tangible media (or the individual or organization to whom copyright has been assigned) by giving them the ability to control the reproduction, publication, adaptation, exhibition, or performance of their works.

BT: intellectual property

RT: Berne Convention for the Protection of Literary and Artistic Works, click-wrap license, collective work, compulsory rights, cultural property rights, derivative work, digital rights management, Eldred v. Ashcroft, fair use, first sale doctrine, General Public License, joint work, literary works, mechanical rights, moral rights, performance rights, Visual Artists Rights Act

Notes: In the United States, copyright is provided for by the Constitution (Article I, Section 8) and is codified by the Copyright Act of 1976, 17 USC 101–1332. Internationally, copyright is defined by the Berne Convention, which the United States joined in 1989.

Copyright protects the owner's interests in the intellectual property (content), rather than in the physical property that serves as a container for the content. For example, an archives may own a collection of papers, but the author retains copyright.

As property, copyright can be transferred or inherited, hence the owner of a work's copyright may not be the work's creator. Those works may be in a wide range of media, including literary works; musical works, including any accompanying words; dramatic works, including any accompanying music; pantomimes and choreographic works; pictorial, graphic, and sculptural works; motion pictures and other audiovisual works; sound recordings; and architectural works. Copyright does not protect any idea, procedure, process, system, method of operation, concept, principle, or discovery in such works; it only protects their tangible manifestation.

†47 (US CBO 2004, p. 1): Copyright grants to creators exclusive rights over their original works. After a copyright expires, the creative work enters the public domain and may be used freely. Copyright law is thus characterized by the balance [it] seeks to achieve between private incentives to engage in creative activity and the social benefits deriving from the widespread use of creative works.

core, n. ~ A cylinder on which film or tape is wound to form a spool.

Syn: hub

Notes: The core may have a flange, in which case the whole is called a reel. The core and material it holds may be contained within a cassette, cartridge, or magazine.

corporate archives, n. ~ 1. Documents and other materials created or received by a group of people (a company, an organization) in the course of operations and preserved for their enduring value. – 2. The division within an organization responsible for such materials.

BT: archives, business archives

RT: corporate records

Notes: 'Corporate archives' connotes the records of a corporation, a legally recognized entity. However, the term may also be used to describe the records of informal groups.

corporate body, n. ~ CATALOGING · An organization or group of individuals with an established name that acts as a single entity.

Notes: Examples include associations, business firms, churches, conferences, governments, government agencies, institutions, nonprofit organizations, and religious bodies.

corporate memory, n. ~ The information in records and in individuals' personal knowledge that provide an understanding of an organization's or group's history and culture, especially the stories that explain the reasons behind certain decisions or procedures.

Syn: institutional memory

†300 (Yates 1989, p. 62): Vertical filing systems organized by intended use rather than by origin and chronology allowed companies to create an accessible corporate memory to supplement or supercede individual memories.

corporate records, n. ~ Documents and other materials created or received by an incorporated commercial enterprise in the course of operations and preserved for future use.

BT: business records, record

RT: corporate archives

corporate report, n. ~ A summary of activities and a statement of accounts issued by a corporation for stockholders, usually on an annual basis.

   BT: report
   RT: annual report

   †171 *(Linard and Sverdloff 1997, p. 96):* Early on, corporate reports were rather meager communiqués, intended for company internal distribution only. They tended to consist of little more than a letter to stockholders signed by the Chief Executive Officer, a balance sheet, and an auditor's statement. Several events at the end of the nineteenth and beginning of the twentieth centuries conspired favorably to transform such reports into a company's most important marketing and public relations piece.

correspondence, n. ~ 1. Written communication, especially those sent by courier or post; letters. – 2. The process of communicating in writing.

   NT: general correspondence file, in letter
   RT: letter, mail, out letter

   Notes: Correspondence[1] is distinguished from other documents by the fact that it is typically addressed to a specific individual or group, and is intended to be delivered by a third party. Examples include letters[2], email, postcards, and telegrams.

correspondence management, n. ~ The application of records management principles to written communications.

   Notes: In Canada, 'correspondence management' is known as 'treatment of correspondence'.

corroboration, n. ~ The explicit mention of the means used to validate a record.

COSHRC ~ *see:* Council of State Historical Records Coordinators

cost-avoidance justification, n. ~ A technique to demonstrate the benefits of some action by comparing the money saved by taking the action against money that would be spent by not taking the action.

   RT: strategic information management

cost-benefit analysis, n. ~ A methodology to evaluate different actions, methods, or strategies by estimating the ratio of all expenses to benefits, both tangible and intangible, inherent in each option.

   RT: strategic information management

   Notes: Cost analysis is more than the purchase price of the thing being evaluated. It includes the fully burdened cost that includes indirect costs over the expected life. For example, the fully burdened cost of an electronic recordkeeping system may include maintenance contracts or support, staff training, and time necessary to ensure that the system conforms to appropriate recordkeeping requirements. Similarly, benefit analysis considers more than immediate direct savings by monetizing intangible benefits. For electronic recordkeeping systems, direct savings may include salary savings over the life of the project as a result of increased efficiency, as well as increased functionality and improved customer satisfaction.

   For example, a comparison of storing paper records off site versus scanning those records will need to address the reduced costs of storing records in less-expensive space, the added costs of retrieving the records, and the intangible costs of the delay in retrieving the records. A scanning project would consider the reduced costs of storing records in the office, the intangible benefits of rapid retrieval, and the future costs of migrating records to overcome obsolescence.

Council of State Historical Records Coordinators, n. (**COSHRC**, abbr.) ~ A United States organization made up of representatives from state historical records advisory boards that works to ensure the nation's documentary heritage is preserved and accessible.

Notes: See http://www.coshrc.org/.

†*37 (Burke 2000, p. 38):* The State [SHRAB] Coordinators realized in later years that when they acted in the capacity dictated by the NHPRC mandate, they crossed organizational lines between the mission of NAGARA and that of SAA and AASLH. Their charge was to chair boards in each state and thereby work with archivists, historians, records managers, librarians, elected and appointed government officials, and other professionals. . . . For practical purposes, in 1989, the coordinators formed themselves into a group called the Council of State Historical Records Coordinators, or COSHRC.

count, n. ~ An expression of the quantity of materials, including the nature of the unit used to measure that quantity.

NT: piece count

RT: dimension, extent

Notes: Examples of counts include 32 items, 52 boxes.

counterfeit, n. ~ An item that is falsely represented as the thing it imitates; an unauthorized copy presented as an authentic original; a forgery.

DF: bootleg, replica

RT: authenticity, copy, forgery

Notes: 'Counterfeit' includes casts of a sculpture not authorized by the artist.

counterseal, n. ~ A mark impressed into the back of an object (typically wax or metal) to give added validity or authenticity to the principal seal on the front of the object.

cover, n. ~ 1. Something that conceals or protects something else. – 2. The outer boards or sheets attached to a bound document. – 3. A sheet attached to the front of a document. – 4. An envelope; first day cover. – 5. The performance of a musical work written by another.

cover paper (also **cover stock**), n. ~ A generic term for heavy paper stock, often used as the outer sheets of a brochure or pamphlet.

BT: paper

Notes: Cover paper is typically available in a range of colors and may have a textured finish.

coverage date, n. ~ The time period of the subjects covered in materials, often expressed as a range of dates.

Syn: content date

Notes: The coverage date is independent of the date the materials were created. The coverage dates for a history of the United States Civil War written in 1990 might be 1850–1870.

cradle, n. ~ A support used to hold fragile materials.

Notes: Cradles are often used to support books during use or display.

crayon enlargement, n. ~ A photographic print, typically a portrait, in which the image has been reinforced with pastels or an airbrush.

BT: enlargement

Notes: Crayon enlargements are typically made using a bromide print. The photographic image may be underexposed and serve as a guide for a final work that looks more like a drawing. The final image may be monochromatic or may use colored crayons to give the sense of a color photograph. Common in the first part of the 20th century.

crazing, n. ~ A fine, irregular pattern of cracks in the surface of hard or dry materials, such as varnish, a ceramic glaze, albumen, or paint.

Notes: Crazing typically does not reveal the underlying support.

crease, n. ~ A deformation in a surface made by a sharp fold.

creating office (also **creating agency**) ~ *see:* office of origin

creator, n. ~ The individual, group, or organization that is responsible for something's production, accumulation, or formation.

RT: author, entity of origin, provenance

Notes: More-specific terms may be used for creators of some works in certain formats, such as author, photographer, cinematographer, or sculptor. An individual who interprets the work of a creator is often described as a performer.

credibility, n. ~ The quality of being accepted as believable or trustworthy.

BT: trustworthiness

crescent, n. ~ A small crease formed around a point of stress in a surface.

Notes: In photographic images, the physical deformation may be accompanied by a change in the image density.

critical apparatus, n. ~ Information captured in notes and marginalia that indicate variations in source documents that form the basis of a definitive edition of a text that no longer exists in the original version.

RT: definitive edition, textual criticism

critical bibliography ~ *see:* analytical bibliography

critical edition, n. ~ A text that has been published with an editor's extensive annotations, commenting on variations between different versions of the text (manuscripts, drafts, editions), and that provides an understanding of the text based on other sources.

RT: documentary publication

CRM ~ *see:* certified records manager

cross-reference, n. ~ An entry in a list, index, or catalog that points to other headings.

NT: broader term, downward reference, narrower term, related term, see also reference, see reference, upward reference

RT: reference, syndetic relationships, thesaurus

Notes: Cross-references may establish a preferred heading among equivalent headings. For example, a cross-reference from one form of an individual's name to another (Mark Twain, see Samuel Langhorn Clemens). A cross-reference may indicate more general or more specific headings (cats, see pets; cats, see Siamese cats).

crosswalk, n. ~ 1. The relationships between the elements of two or more data structures. – 2. A chart or diagram that indicates the correspondence between two systems.

Notes: A crosswalk between MARC format and Dublin Core would indicate that a title is entered in MARC field 245 and tagged Title in Dublin Core.

crutch file ~ *see:* convenience file

cryptanalysis, n. ~ The process of decoding encoded text (ciphertext) into its original form (plaintext).

RT: ciphertext, plaintext

cryptography (also **cryptology**), n. ~ The process of making information secure for storage or transmission by transforming it into a form (ciphertext) that is unintelligible without the knowledge to decipher the encrypted form back into its original form (plaintext).

   NT: public key cryptography

   RT: ciphertext, code, dual-key encryption, encryption, plaintext, symmetric-key encryption

cryptology ~ *see:* cryptography

CSS ~ *see:* Cascading Style Sheet

cubic foot, n. ~ 1. A volume of space that is approximately 12 × 12 × 12 inches. – 2. RECORDS · A measure used to indicate the quantity of materials, commonly used to describe the size of large collections.

   RT: linear foot

   Notes: Because the surface of a standard file folder (10 × 12 inches) is roughly a square foot, a linear foot of files is roughly a cubic foot. A records center box, which measures approximately 10 × 12 × 16 inches, is generally counted as a cubic foot, even though it is slightly larger.

cue mark, n. ~ A mark made in a frame of a motion picture that is used to signal an upcoming event, such as the end of a reel.

   RT: changeover cue, moving image

   Notes: Cue marks are often a circle and frequently appear in the upper right corner of the frame. They can often be seen in video recordings of older motion pictures.

culling, n. ~ The process of pulling and disposing of unwanted materials.

   Syn: purging, stripping, weeding

   Notes: Duplicates are commonly culled for disposal. Weeding and culling connote item-level separation, where purging, stripping, and screening connote removal of materials at the folder level or higher.

cultural property rights, n. ~ The concept that a society, especially that of indigenous peoples, has the authority to control the use of its traditional heritage.

   BT: intellectual property

   RT: copyright

   Notes: Cultural property rights are roughly analogous to copyright, but the rights are held by a community rather than an individual and the property protected was received by transmission through generations rather than being consciously created. Cultural property rights have not been generally established or codified by statute in the United States, although the Native American Graves Preservation and Repatriation Act (NAGPRA) may be seen as recognizing those rights. Other countries, notably Australia, have begun to codify cultural property rights.

   †*216 (Our Culture, Our Future 1998): Report on Australian Indigenous Cultural and Intellectual Property Rights.* 'Indigenous Cultural and Intellectual Property' refers to Indigenous Peoples' rights to their heritage. Heritage comprises all objects, sites and knowledge, the nature or use of which has been transmitted or continues to be transmitted from generation to generation, and which is regarded as pertaining to a particular Indigenous group or its Territory. Heritage includes: Literary, Performing and Artistic Works (including songs, music, dances, stories, ceremonies, symbols, languages and designs); Scientific, agricultural, technical and ecological knowledge (including cultigens, medicines and the phenotypes of flora

and fauna); All items of movable cultural property; Human remains and tissues; Immovable cultural property (including sacred and historically significant sites and burial grounds); Documentation of Indigenous Peoples' heritage in archives, film, photographs, videotape or audiotape and all forms of media. The heritage of an Indigenous people is a living one and includes objects, knowledge and literary and artistic works which may be created in the future based on that heritage.

cumulative index, n. ~ An index that combines entries from previous indexes to provide integrated access to a larger body of material.

> *BT:* index
>
> *Notes:* An example of a cumulative index is an annual index to monthly reports that integrates separate, monthly indexes produced for each report.

curator, n. ~ 1. An individual responsible for oversight of a collection or an exhibition. – 2. The administrative head of a museum or collection.

> *NT:* manuscript curator
>
> *RT:* archivist
>
> *Notes:* Often carries the connotation, especially in museums and galleries, of an individual who selects items based on artistic merit or connoisseurship.
>
> †258 (Schwartz 1995, p. 56): Yet when archivists focus on a single photograph, they are quickly denounced as 'curators,' suggesting somehow that single photographs are less deserving of individual attention than are single written documents. The pejorative tone attached to the term 'curator' usually derives from the erroneous assumption that a photo-archivist is motivated by the same concerns as the curator, namely artistic merit or connoisseurship. . . . The curator, with a mandate to collect for aesthetic reasons, isolates the photographs from the context of creation and offers them up for, what Svetlana Alpers calls, 'attentive looking' and thereby transforms documents into art.

current records, n. ~ Records that continue to be used with sufficient frequency to justify keeping them in the office of creation; active records.

> *Syn:* active records
>
> *BT:* record
>
> *Notes:* The frequency of use that makes records current is subjective. The distinction between active and inactive records attempts to relate the costs of storing records in the office against the costs of retrieving them from off-site storage. If records continue to be active, the cost of frequent retrieval from off-site storage will negate any savings in office storage.

cursive, n. ~ Handwriting that uses connected letters.

> *BT:* handwriting
>
> *RT:* disjoined hand, printing, write

CUSTARD ~ *see:* Canadian-United States Task Force on Archival Description

custodial history, n. ~ 1. RECORDS · The succession of offices, families, or persons who held materials from the moment they were created. – 2. LAW · The succession of officers or individuals who held real evidence from the moment it is obtained until presented in court. – 3. DESCRIPTION · An <admininfo> subelement in Encoded Archival Description (EAD) used for information about the chain of ownership of the materials being described before they reached the immediate source of acquisition.

> *RT:* chain of custody, provenance

Notes: Custodial history[3] can be used to describe both physical possession and intellectual ownership and to provide details of changes of ownership or custody that are significant in terms of authority, integrity, and interpretation.

custodian, n. ~ The individual or organization having possession of and responsibility for the care and control of material.

Notes: Custodians may not own the materials in their possession. The function of custodianship may be assigned to individuals with other job titles, including archivist, files custodian, records custodian, or records management clerk. In some instances, a custodian may have legal custody without physical custody.

custody, n. ~ Care and control, especially for security and preservation; guardianship.

NT: legal custody

RT: chain of custody, noncustodial records, physical custody, postcustodial theory of archives

Notes: Custody does not necessarily imply legal title to the materials.

cutoff, n. ~ 1. A point where a record series can be broken into a regular segment that can be disposed of as a block. – v. ~ 2. To isolate a portion of a series into regular segments, for purposes of disposal.

Syn: file break

Notes: A cutoff interval is often based on a recurring date, such as end of month or fiscal year, or an event, such as contract payoff. The disposition of records within a series may be determined by the cutoff date, rather than the date of creation or receipt, allowing a group of records created or received over a period of time to be disposed of in one action.

cutting, n. ~ BRITISH · An article or photograph cut from a newspaper or magazine; a news clipping.

Syn: news clipping

cyanotype, n. ~ 1. A photographic process that uses Prussian blue for the image to produce a positive print from a negative. – 2. A print made by the process.

BT: photograph

RT: blueprint

Notes: Cyanotype is identical to the blueprint process, but the former is typically used to describe continuous-tone photographic prints, while the latter is used to describe reproductions of line drawings. The Pellet or blueline process produces a positive image from a positive image. Typically on paper but sometimes on cloth or another support. The process was invented by Sir John Herschel in 1840 and remains in use today.

cylinder, n. ~ 1. A regular shape with a circular base and with sides at right angles to the base. – 2. AUDIO · A sound recording format. – 3. COMPUTING · In a multiplatter hard drive, the set of tracks on all platters sharing the same distance from the hub.

Notes: The cylinder[2] format was invented by Thomas Edison in 1877–1878. It could hold between two and four minutes of sound. In addition to its use for commercial entertainment, the Dictaphone Company used the format in early machines for dictation and transcription.

D

DACS ~ *see:* Describing Archives: A Content Standard

daguerreotype, n. ~ A photograph made on a silver-coated copper plate and developed using fumes of mercury.

    BT: photograph

    RT: cased photographs

    Notes: Invented by Louis Jacques Mandé Daguerre in the late 1830s and announced publicly in 1839, daguerreotypes were the first practical photographic process. They remained common until the popularization of the ambrotype in 1854. The surface is highly reflective. The image appears as a positive when viewed while reflecting a dark background and as a negative when reflecting a light background. The image is monochromatic, although color may have been added by hand. Unless special camera optics were used, the image is laterally reversed. The surface is fragile and may be tarnished. To protect the image, a daguerreotype is almost always mounted under glass with a paper seal around the edge; most daguerreotypes are mounted in a hinged case.

DAO ~ *see:* digital archival object

dark archives, n. ~ A collection of materials preserved for future use but with no current access.

    BT: archives

    RT: access, light archives

    Notes: 'Dark archives' is principally associated with collections of online serial publications and databases that are held by an organization other than the publisher. These materials are kept in escrow for future use in case they are no longer available from the publisher.

DAT ~ *see:* digital audio tape

data, sing. or pl. n. (**datum**, sing.) ~ Facts, ideas, or discrete pieces of information, especially when in the form originally collected and unanalyzed.

    RT: information, macro data

    Notes: Traditionally a plural noun, data – rather than datum – is now commonly used with a singular verb.

    Data often is used to refer to information in its most atomized form, as numbers or facts that have not been synthesized or interpreted, such as the initial readings from a gauge or obtained from a survey. In this sense, data is used as the basis of information, the latter distinguished by recognized patterns or meaning in the data. The phrase 'raw data' may be used to distinguish the original data from subsequently 'refined data'.

    Data is independent of any medium in which it is captured. Data is intangible until it has been recorded in some medium. Even when captured in a document or other form, the content is distinct from the carrier.

data architecture, n. ~ An overall description of information elements and their relationships, especially in regards to their use to support broad functions, goals, objectives, or strategies.

    RT: information architecture

†132 (GAO 2002, p. 75): The framework for organizing and defining the inter-relationships of data in support of an organization's missions, functions, goals, objectives, and strategies. Data architectures provide the basis for the incremental, ordered design and development of systems or subject databases based on successively more detailed levels of data modeling.

data base ~ *see:* database

data compression ~ *see:* compression

data content standard ~ *see:* content standard

data dictionary (also **codebook, data directory**), n. ~ Documentation of the names of entities used in a software application or database, including in each entry its definition (size and type), where and how it is used, and its relationship to other data.

Notes: Named entities can include variables, data objects, functions, types, procedures, files, directories, or devices.

†57 (Dictionary of Computing 1996, p. 122): Developed in the late 1960s the purpose of such a dictionary was originally simply to assist in the maintenance of large-scale data-processing systems. The idea was further developed in the 1970s with the advent of special-purpose software systems to maintain such dictionaries. . . . ¶ The term data dictionary is sometimes used misleadingly by software vendors to refer to the alphabetical listings of names automatically produced when database schema and data manipulation coding is being processed and compiled. . . .

data directory ~ *see:* data dictionary

data element, n. ~ A unit of information as defined within an information system, typically corresponding to a field in a database record or printed form.

RT: field

Notes: A data element may include subelements (or subfields) and may simultaneously be a part of a larger data element. For example, a field in a MARC record consists of a number of elements, including a tag, indicators, and the contents, which may be divided into subfields. The field itself may be considered an element of the MARC record.

data entry, n. ~ The process of inputting information into a computer.

RT: digitization

Notes: Implies the activity of people transferring data from a form to a computer by keyboard, either directly or – now obsolete – through cards or tape. Typically not used to describe the process of populating databases or other applications through digitization or optical character recognition (OCR).

data field ~ *see:* field

data file (also **datafile**), n. ~ A collection of information for use on a computer that is treated as a unit for storage.

RT: file, machine-readable

Notes: Some applications may store one or many files within a larger file or in a database. For example, a file compression utility may pack several files into what the operating system sees as a single file; the operating system may not be able to access the compressed files until they are extracted. A records management application or document management application may store files within a database, providing users controlled access to those files through the application rather than through the operating system.

data mining, n. ~ The process of identifying previously unknown patterns by analyzing relationships in large amounts of data assembled from different applications.

Syn: Synonym • *†:* see Bibliography • *Superscript:* Definition number

RT: data warehouse

†57 *(Dictionary of Computing 1996, p. 125):* The nontrivial explication or extraction of information from data, in which the information is implicit and previously unknown; an example is identification of the pattern of use of a credit card to detect possible fraud. The data is normally accessed from one or more databases, so the technique is also known as knowledge discovery in databases (KDD). It involves a number of different methods from artificial intelligence such as neural networks and machine induction, together with statistical methods such as cluster analysis and data summarization.

data model, n. ~ An abstraction of a transaction, event, or situation expressed in terms of information about its physical or conceptual entities and their relationships.

BT: model

Notes: Data models are often used in the development of a data or system architecture. The entity-relationship model and the relational model are two widely used modeling techniques.

data object, n. ~ A collection of information treated as a logical entity.

RT: digital object, object

Notes: 'Data object' connotes information in electronic form. A complex document, such as a suite of HTML files, including images and style sheets, may be considered a single data object.

data processing, n. ~ The analysis, organization, storage, retrieval, and manipulation of data, especially through the use of computers.

Syn: information processing

NT: automatic data processing, electronic data processing

Notes: 'Data processing', now largely obsolete, is associated with the use of computers in a batch environment. It often connotes large, commercial applications for payroll or stock control.

†237 *(Ralston 1976, p. 425):* Data processing is a widely used term with a variety of meanings and interpretations ranging from one that makes it almost coextensive with all of computing . . . to much narrower connotations in the general area of computer applications to business and administrative problems. ¶ In a broad sense, data processing may be said to be what computers *do.* In this context it should be compared to *information processing,* which some prefer to data processing because 'information' does not carry to connotation of 'number'.

data protection, n. ~ The legal protection of personal information that organizations hold in electronic format.

RT: privacy

Notes: Although the United States has legislation controlling the use of personal data by the government, it does not have laws controlling the use of personal information collected by organizations or individuals. For more information on relevant laws in Europe, see Directive 97/66/EC of the European Parliament and the Council of the European Union, 15 December 1997, 'concerning the processing of personal data and the protection of privacy in the telecommunications sector.' The European laws may affect multinational corporations doing business there.

†57 *(Dictionary of Computing 1996, p. 126):* The aim of the legislation is to control the immense potential for misuse of information that arises when personal data is stored in computers. . . . To combat the fear of misuse of data, gov-

ernments have introduced legislation that, among other things, makes the following requirements of organizations that maintain personal records on computers: to declare and/or register the use for which the data is stored; to provide the data subject with a right of access to data concerning himself or herself on their computer; to maintain a prescribed minimum level of electronic and physical security in their computer installation; not to transmit personal data to any organization that does not have similar controls over misuse of data.

data record, n. ~ Computing · A collection of related fields treated as a unit, such as a row in a relational database table; a record.

    RT: logical record, record

    Notes: A data record, as a unit of information, may not have the attributes of an archival record. For example, a data record may be frequently updated, so that its contents would not be considered fixed. A data record may not have sufficient content, context, or structure to be considered complete or have meaning apart from other data records.

    A logical record is a data record that is stored in a different format from that in which it is presented.

data set (also **dataset**), n. ~ A collection of related information, especially information formatted for analysis by a computer.

    Notes: Often used synonymously with data file and database. The data is often related by being a sequence of information about a recurring event or conditions; for example, a collection of humidity and temperature readings at different points in a region taken at regular intervals over a period of time. The data may be related by some characteristic of the thing recorded, such as student records. The term implies that the information has been structured to facilitate analysis.

data strip, n. ~ A long, narrow area on a card, typically coated with a magnetic media, used to encode digital information that can be read by a special reader.

    Notes: For example, most credit cards and debit cards have a data strip on the back that allows a computer to read the card number.

data structure, n. ~ The manner in which information is organized into interrelated components.

    Notes: Common data structures include lists, trees, arrays, records, and tables.

data structure standard, n. ~ A formal guideline specifying the elements into which information is to be organized.

    DF: content standard, data value standard

    BT: standard

    RT: MARC

    Notes: By establishing a set of elements to be included, a data structure standard also excludes other types of information. EAD and MARC format are examples of data structure standards.

data type (also **datatype**), n. ~ A classification of a string of bits that indicates the characteristics of the encoded information and governs its representation.

    Notes: On a primitive level, common data types include integer, real, double precision, and string. Complex data types include array, file, image, and binary large objects (BLOB). Data types are established within a specific context; applications and operating systems may define different data types.

data value, n. ~ The information assigned to a data element in a record, field, or variable.

data value standard, n. ~ An established list of normalized terms used as data elements to ensure consistency.

>*DF:* data structure standard
>
>*BT:* standard
>
>*Notes:* Examples of data value standards include thesauri, controlled vocabularies, and authority files. Data value standards often include lead-in terms that are not authorized for use but point to an accepted term to be used instead.

data warehouse, n. ~ Information collected from a variety of sources that is analyzed to discover trends and correlations that may not be apparent when the data is isolated in the original, separate systems.

>*RT:* data mining, executive information system
>
>†236 *(Quass 2000):* Bill Inmon, the recognized father of the data warehousing concept, defines a data warehouse as a subject-orientated, integrated, time variant, non-volatile collection of data in support of management's decision-making process. Another data warehousing pioneer, Richard Hackathorn, describes the data warehouse as a single image of the business reality [citing Lambert]. ¶ Data warehouses are becoming an increasingly popular tool for the management of data. The most fundamental reason for this is, firstly, that executives need rapid, easy access to data for planning and control. Secondly, data have historically been stored in disparate systems, in multiple locations, which made a complete view of organizational data almost impossible [citing Laudon & Laudon].

database (also **data base**), n. ~ 1. Computing · Information that is accessed and updated through software (a database management system) that has been organized, structured, and stored so that it can be manipulated and extracted for various purposes. – 2. Colloquialism · Any collection of information, automated or not, without regard to how it is accessed or stored.

>*NT:* relational database
>
>*RT:* information system
>
>*Notes:* Database[1] connotes computer-based information that is typically atomized into fields, records, and tables. Databases may be designed to conform with data structure standards and best practices to facilitate the interchange of information. Information may be entered into a database in accordance with data content standards or data value standards to increase consistency and quality.

database management system, n. (**DBMS**, abbr.) ~ Software that allows information to be captured, organized, and stored, so that the information can be analyzed, reorganized, and reported in many different ways.

>*RT:* system
>
>*Notes:* A DBMS includes facilities to define data structures and their data elements, and a programming language to manipulate and display the information. Some DBMSes include the ability to log transactions and to roll back changes.

date, n. ~ A particular point in time, especially a specific day.

>*NT:* access date, broadcast date, bulk dates, chronological date, content date, inclusive dates, production date, release date, topical date
>
>*Notes:* Date may refer to a month or year; for example, a letter dated May 1939. More specific references to a particular hour, minute, or second are typically referred to as time.

date range ~ *see:* inclusive dates

BT: Broader Term • *NT:* Narrower Term • *RT:* Related Term • *DF:* Distinguish From

datum ~ *see:* data

day file ~ *see:* chronological file

daybook, n. ~ A bookkeeping record, typically a bound volume, detailing each day's receipts and expenditures in order of their occurrence.

   DF: shop book, waste book

   RT: account book, cash book, journal, ledger, original entry

   †55 *(Densmore 2000, p. 79):* Two books were required: a book of original entry called a 'day book' in which transactions were entered in chronological order, and a 'ledger' in which transactions were entered under individual accounts as debits ('Dr.') and credits ('Cr.'). The terms 'waste book', 'daybook', and 'journal' were sometimes used interchangeably. A waste book is simply the rough form of a daybook; 'journal' usually refers to the book used in double entry bookkeeping to separate transactions into debits and credits.

DBMS ~ *see:* database management system

DC ~ *see:* Dublin Core

de facto standard, n. ~ A consistent manner of doing something that has been established by practice.

   BT: standard

   RT: best practices

   Notes: De facto standards often result from one method or product dominating the market place. For example, Microsoft Windows may be considered the de facto standard for operating systems in the United States.

de jure standard, n. ~ A consistent manner of doing something established by a deliberate process.

   BT: standard

   Notes: De jure standards are often established by professional organizations, industry groups, a government body, or other group. The development process often involves negotiations between parties with different interests in the standard.

deaccessioning, n. ~ The process by which an archives, museum, or library permanently removes accessioned materials from its holdings.

   RT: accession, reappraisal, withdrawal

   Notes: Materials may be deaccessioned because the repository has changed its collections policy and the material is no longer within its scope. Materials may be deaccessioned because they have been reappraised and found to be no longer suitable for continuing preservation. Materials that are badly decomposed and beyond repair may be deaccessioned. Deaccessioned material may be offered back to its donor, offered to another institution, or destroyed. Also called **permanent withdrawal**.

deacidification, n. ~ A preservation technique intended to increase the longevity of paper documents by raising the pH to at least 7.0, and often including the deposit of an alkaline buffer.

   RT: mass deacidification

   Notes: **Aqueous deacidification** uses water as the solvent carrier of the alkaline agent. **Nonaqueous deacidification** uses organic solvents as the solvent carrier. **Vapor phase deacidification** involves the interleaving of documents and the pages of volumes with treated sheets that emit an alkaline vapor; now rarely used because it reportedly produces toxic vapors and does not leave an alkaline reserve.

Mass deacidification refers to one of various techniques designed to treat large numbers of documents at one time with either gaseous or liquid agents.

decimal filing system, n. ~ A technique to classify materials using numbers to represent concepts and any subdivisions.

> *BT:* filing system
>
> *RT:* classification
>
> *Notes:* In a decimal filing system, related concepts are often grouped in units of ten, and subdivided as necessary for greater specificity. Major categories are typically integer values; secondary and tertiary headings are separated using subsequent decimal points. For example, 50 through 59 might be used for major classes of policies. Policies for fringe benefits might be coded 55, and the maternity leave policy might be coded 55.2.

decision support system, n. ~ An information system that supports management-level decisions through a combination of data and analytical models.

> *BT:* information system
>
> *RT:* management information system, online analytical processing, system
>
> *†236 (Quass 2000):* A shortcoming of the original DSS systems was that they were developed by different business units, resulting in disagreement between users on data definitions. Thus, no organisational view on data existed. These different data definitions also lead to inconsistent reports that cannot be used by management for decision making. In turn, the inconsistent reports cause users not to trust reports and organisational data. These problems were aggravated by the fact that data that went into the DSS systems were sometimes 'dirty' or inaccurate as there was no 'scrubbing' or cleansing process to ensure accurate data, presented in a uniform format. Lastly, data were shared reluctantly in business-unit-centric systems, and the data were not integrated, requiring complicated bridges to share data [citing Moss & Adelman 1999a]. The shortcomings of DSS systems became profound as the users of these systems changed from administrators at a tactical level to analysts and managers at the strategic level.

declassification, n. ~ The process of making materials that have been restricted for reasons of national security accessible to individuals without security clearance.

> *RT:* classification, downgrade, security classification

decoding, n. ~ To decipher an encrypted message.

> *RT:* encryption

decomposition vent, n. ~ An opening in a storage chamber that allows gases that result from deterioration to escape.

> *Notes:* The National Fire Protection Association standard NFPA 40 specifies requirements for decomposition vents where nitrate film is stored.

deed, n. ~ A document that details an agreement relating to the transfer of ownership of property, especially real property, from one individual to another.

> *RT:* title
>
> *Notes:* A deed is an instrument, as distinguished from title[3], which is a right. Title is sometimes used synonymously with deed, but deed is usually used only in the narrower sense of the instrument.

deed of gift, n. ~ An agreement transferring title to property without an exchange of monetary compensation.

> *Notes:* Deeds of gift may be for real, personal, or intellectual property. In archives, deeds of gift frequently take the form of a contract establishing condi-

tions governing the transfer of title to documents and specifying any restrictions on access and use.

†64 *(Doyle 2001, p. 358):* Statements that . . . allow for deaccessioning should be included in the deed of gift. As [Gerald] Ham notes, 'donor agreements cannot become the dead hand of the past; they must contain some option for reappraisal and deaccessioning.'

deep web (also **invisible web**), n. ~ Information, usually in databases, that is not directly accessible through a hyperlink and that cannot be indexed by most search engines.

Notes: Deep web content is often accessed through a form on a web page. A search engine may find the form, but cannot retrieve results because the form requires a search term.

†211 *(Olsen 2004):* [Yahoo!] introduced its Content Acquisition Program designed to index the billions of documents contained in public databases but that are commonly inaccessible to search engines, or what's called the invisible or deep Web.

definitive edition, n. ~ An authoritative version of a work, usually issued after the creator's death, that establishes among variants the form the editor believes to represent the author's intentions.

BT: edition

RT: critical apparatus, variorum edition

Notes: A definitive edition typically includes critical apparatus to document the variations in the work and to support the editor's choice among those versions.

degaussing, n. ~ The process of removing information from magnetic media by neutralizing the magnetic signal that encodes the information.

RT: bulk eraser

dehumidification, n. ~ 1. The process of removing moisture from air. – 2. The process of drying objects that have absorbed moisture from the air.

delamination, n. ~ The separation of layers that compose an item.

Notes: Compact discs, video discs, photographic film, and magnetic tape are made up of several layers that are held together by mechanical or chemical means. Delaminating occurs when the binding mechanism fails and the layers separate.

deletion, n. ~ 1. The process of removing or eliminating information, especially the process of marking information to be removed during editing. – 2. Computing · The process of removing the link between the directory and the data, allowing the space used by the data to be overwritten.

DF: erase

RT: disposition

Notes: Deletion[2] does not necessarily make data unreadable. The original information may remain intact and, if not overwritten, could be recovered using special software tools. Some software applications make it possible to undelete information and delay overwriting deleted information as long as possible to maximize the possibility of recovering deleted information. Deletion is distinguished from erasing, in which data is made unreadable by overwriting the areas containing the information.

†262 *(Sedona Principles 2003, p. 41):* Deletion is the process whereby data is removed from active files and other data storage structures on computers and rendered inaccessible except using special data recovery tools designed to recover

deleted data. Deletion occurs in several levels on modern computer systems: (a) File level deletion: Deletion on the file level renders the file inaccessible to the operating system and normal application programs and marks the space occupied by the file's directory entry and contents as free space, available to reuse for data storage. (b) Record level deletion: Deletion on the record level occurs when a data structure, like a database table, contains multiple records; deletion at this level renders the record inaccessible to the database management system (DBMS) and usually marks the space occupied by the record as available for reuse by the DBMS, although in some cases the space is never reused until the database is compacted. Record level deletion is also characteristic of many e-mail systems. (c) Byte level deletion: Deletion at the byte level occurs when text or other information is deleted from the file content (such as the deletion of text from a word processing file); such deletion may render the deleted data inaccessible to the application intended to be used in processing the file, but may not actually remove the data from the file's content until a process such as compaction or rewriting of the file causes the deleted data to be overwritten.

delimited ASCII sequential files, n. ~ COMPUTING · A format for data output in which information is written as a continuous stream, with fields separated by special characters.

Notes: The format is often used when fields are variable in length. A common format is comma-separated values (CSV); each field in a record is separated by a comma, with text fields enclosed with single or double quotation marks, brackets, or braces so that internal commas are not confused with delimiters; each record is delimited by a new line.

densitometer, n. ~ PHOTOGRAPHY · A device that measures light reflected from the surface of a print or transmitted through a transparency or negative.

RT: gray scale, step wedge

Notes: Densitometers can be used to check the exposure and development of photographic materials by measuring the image of a gray scale to plot a characteristic curve.

densitometric method (silver), n. ~ A procedure to test for residual thiosulfate (fixer) in silver halide photographs.

BT: residual hypo test

RT: methylene-blue test

Notes: The test uses a chemical that combines with thiosulfate to produce a yellow stain, which is then measured by a densitometer to determine the concentration of thiosulfate.

density, n. ~ 1. The relative difference between the lightest and darkest part of an image, as measured by a densitometer. – 2. PHOTOGRAPHY · The relative amount of the material that forms the image. – 3. COMPUTING · The relative amount of information that can be stored in a given area of a storage medium.

Notes: In photography, areas of high density typically appear dark or opaque, whether in a negative or positive image. Areas of low density are light or transparent.

deposit, v. ~ To transfer records or other materials to a repository without transfer of title. – n. ~ Materials placed in a repository by such action.

DF: donation, gift

Notes: A deposit does not necessarily imply a future intention to transfer title.

deposition, n. ~ 1. Out-of-court testimony given under oath and transcribed for use in discovery or in court. – 2. The process of taking such testimony.

depository, n. ~ A library designated to receive all or selected government publications in order to provide the public access throughout the jurisdiction.

> *BT:* repository
>
> *Notes:* In the United States, the federal and many state governments operate depository libraries.

depth indexing, n. ~ A process of providing access to detailed information contained within documents.

> *BT:* indexing
>
> *Notes:* Depth indexing is distinguished from general indexing, which provides access to the broad subjects treated by a document as a whole. For example, general indexing may create entries for the author, recipient, and possibly a few subjects of a letter; depth indexing might provide access to every name mentioned in the letter. The level of detail that is indexed is described as the **specificity of indexing**.

depth of description (also **fullness of description**), n. ~ The level of detail about the contents of a collection in a finding aid or catalog record.

> *RT:* description, level of description
>
> *Notes:* Depth of description is sometimes expressed in terms of hierarchy. For example, collections may be described at the level of record group or collection, series, subseries, folder, or item.

derivative work, n. ~ LAW · A work that is the result of adapting, arranging, translating or transforming an existing intellectual work protected by copyright.

> *RT:* copyright
>
> *Notes:* Examples of derivative works include extracts, anthologies, abridgments, adaptations, translations, revisions, compilations, and arrangements of a musical work. 'Derivative work' is defined in copyright law (17 USC 101, below).
>
> †281 (USC, 17 USC 101): A work based upon one or more preexisting works, such as a translation, musical arrangement, dramatization, fictionalization, motion picture version, sound recording, art reproduction, abridgment, condensation, or any other form in which a work may be recast, transformed, or adapted. A work consisting of editorial revisions, annotations, elaborations, or other modifications which, as a whole, represent an original work of authorship, is a 'derivative work'.

Describing Archives: A Content Standard, n. (**DACS**, abbr.) ~ A standard for creating access tools for all forms of archival materials, including their archival creators and the forms of creator names.

> *RT:* Canadian-United States Task Force on Archival Description, descriptive standard
>
> *Notes:* While DACS can be used with any type of descriptive output, its examples illustrate its application to MARC 21 and Encoded Archival Description (EAD). DACS is intended to supersede *Archives, Personal Papers, and Manuscripts.* The standard is based on generally accepted archival principles, listed here but with extensive commentary in the standard.
>
> 1. Records in archives possess unique characteristics.
> 2. Respect des fonds is the basis of archival arrangement and description.
> 3. Arrangement involves the identification of groupings within the material.
> 4. Description reflects arrangement.

5. Description applies to all archival materials regardless of form or medium.
6. The principles of archival description apply equally to records created by corporate bodies and by individuals or families.
7. Archival descriptions may be presented in a variety of outputs and with varying levels of detail.
8. The creators of archival materials, as well as the materials themselves, must be described.
9. DACS is the United States implementation of rules proposed by the Canadian-United States Task Force on Archival Description.

†56 (DACS, p. 3): Introduction to Describing Archival Materials. ¶ Part I of this standard contains rules to ensure the creation of consistent, appropriate, and self-explanatory descriptions of archival material. The rules may be used for describing archival and manuscript material at all levels of description, regardless of form or medium, and may also be applied to the description of intentionally assembled collections, and to discrete items.

†56 (DACS, p. 83): Introduction to Describing Creators. ¶ It is insufficient for the archivist simply to include the name of the creator in the title of the description of the materials. Additional information is required regarding the persons, families, and corporate bodies responsible for the creation, assembly, accumulation, custody, and/or maintenance and use of the archival material being described. Part II describes the information that is required to establish this context.

†56 (DACS, p. 113): Introduction for Form of Names. ¶ Part III of this standard provides information about creating standardized forms for the names of persons, families, or corporate bodies associated with archival materials as the creators, custodians, or subjects of the records.

description, n. ~ 1. The process of creating a finding aid or other access tools that allow individuals to browse a surrogate of the collection to facilitate access and that improve security by creating a record of the collection and by minimizing the amount of handling of the original materials. – 2. RECORDS MANAGEMENT · A written account of the physical characteristics, informational content, and functional purpose of a records series or system.

BT: processing

NT: archival description, bibliographic description, collective description, hierarchical description, multilevel description

RT: access, cataloging, depth of description, descriptive element, level of description, Paris Principles

†68 (Duff and Johnson 2001, p. 43): In the 1980s and early 1990s, the Society of American Archivists' *Archives, Personal Papers, and Manuscripts* and the Canadian *Rules for Archival Description (RAD)* codified archival practice and established the elements needed to represent a *fonds* or collection. The primary purpose of creating descriptive tools is to help users locate relevant material.

†71 (Duranti 1993, p. 52): In the 1930s in Europe, description began to be seen as a means for making the user independent of the archivists specialized knowledge, and to be aimed primarily at compiling 'instruments of research' for the user, not the archivist. Moreover, the description activity acquired a non-evaluative character as a consequence of the recognition that its products, in order to be useful for every kind of research, had to serve none in particular.

†178 (MacNeil 1995, p. 30): Metadata systems capture and communicate information about transactions and the context in which they occur within an electronic record system. . . . Description, on the other hand, captures and communicates knowledge about the broad administrative and documentary contexts of records creation within an organization as a whole as one moves further away from the original circumstances of creation. Its purpose is to preserve, perpetuate, and authenticate meaning over time so that it is available and comprehensible to all users – present and potential.

descriptive bibliography, n. ~ 1. The study of the physical characteristics of books and the process of bookmaking, especially with an eye to understanding how materials and production influence the text. – 2. A listing of works that indicates in precise details the name of the author, the exact title of the work, and publication details, and that emphasizes the material nature of the work, including the format, the pagination, typographical particulars, illustrations, and other characteristics, such as the kind of paper and binding.

Syn: analytical bibliography

BT: bibliography

descriptive cataloging, n. ~ That portion of the cataloging process that is concerned with the choice and form of the main entry, the title and statement of responsibility, edition, material (or type of publication) specific details, publication and distribution, physical description, series, notes, and standard numbers and terms of availability.

BT: cataloging

RT: Anglo-American Cataloguing Rules

Notes: Descriptive cataloging is distinguished from subject cataloging, which determines appropriate headings for access to the contents of the work described.

descriptive element, n. ~ Cataloging · A word, phrase, or group of characters representing a distinct unit of information that forms part of an area of formal description.

NT: body of the entry, extent, general material designation, other title information, parallel title, scope and contents note, statement of responsibility, supplied title, technical access requirements note, title

RT: area, description

descriptive metadata, n. ~ Information that refers to the intellectual content of material and aids discovery of such materials.

BT: metadata

Notes: Descriptive metadata allows users to locate, distinguish, and select materials on the basis of the material's subjects or 'aboutness.' It is distinguished from information about the form of the material, or its administration.

†235 (Puglia, Reed, and Rhodes 2004, p. 7): Descriptive metadata refers to information that supports discovery and identification of a resource (the who, what, when and where of a resource). It describes the content of the resource, associates various access points, and describes how the resource is related to other resources intellectually or within a hierarchy. In addition to bibliographic information, it may also describe physical attributes of the resource such as media type, dimension, and condition.

descriptive record, n. ~ CATALOGING · An accurate representation of a unit of archival material created by the process of capturing, collating, analyzing, and organizing information that serves to identify the material and explain the context and records system(s) that produced it.

descriptive standard, n. ~ A collection of rules, practices, and guidelines that codify the kinds and structure of information used to represent materials in a finding aid, catalog, or bibliography.

BT: standard

RT: Anglo-American Cataloguing Rules, Archives, Personal Papers, and Manuscripts, Describing Archives: A Content Standard, Encoded Archival Description, General International Standard for Archival Description, Manual of Archival Description , MARC, Rules for Archival Description

descriptive unit, n. ~ DESCRIPTION · A document or aggregation of documents in any physical form, treated as an entity and forming the basis of a single description.

descriptor, n. ~ A word, phrase, or code used as a heading in an index or catalog.

Syn: index term

RT: controlled vocabulary

Notes: Descriptors are frequently taken from a controlled vocabulary to ensure that the same term is used consistently for the same concept.

desiccant, n. ~ A substance used to remove moisture from the atmosphere or from materials.

desiderata, n. ~ A list of materials, especially books, that a repository seeks to acquire, especially published works.

†115 *(Harvey 2000, p. 6):* Morris and his successor, Nathaniel Holmes Morison, carefully compiled massive desiderata – or wish lists – of books for the library. Publishing these lists in bound form, they sent them out to booksellers, bibliophiles, and librarians all over America and Europe in what surely must have been one of the greatest literary scavenger hunts in history.

Design Criteria for Electronic Records Management Software Applications, n. ~ A standard (DOD 5015.2) issued by the Assistant Secretary of Defense for Command, Control, Communications and Intelligence (Department of Defense).

RT: records management application

Notes: The standard sets forth mandatory and optional baseline functional requirements for records management application software. The standard is available at http://jitc.fhu.disa.mil/recmgt/.

design drawing, n. ~ An illustration of an object, chiefly through lines, that is intended to give sufficient information to allow the thing illustrated to be completed.

BT: architectural records, drawing, engineering records

Notes: Design drawings are generally more detailed than sketches.

destruction, n. ~ A disposal process that results in the obliteration of records.

RT: disposal, disposition, maceration, pulping, shredding

Notes: At a minimum, destruction may be no more complicated than placing materials in the trash for transfer to a landfill. In other instances, the manner of destruction is appropriate to the sensitivity of the information contained in the materials and may involve shredding, maceration, or incineration. For electronic records, simple destruction may be accomplished by deleting the record, which merely removes the pointer from an index without overwriting the data. For sensitive information in electronic format, the media may be overwritten numerous time or physically destroyed to make it impossible to recover the data.

destruction schedule ~ *see:* retention schedule

destruction suspension, n. ~ An order to halt routine, scheduled destruction of records that may be relevant to pending or current litigation, audit, or investigation.

 Notes: An individual or corporation is expected to prevent the destruction of records if it is reasonable to expect a lawsuit, audit, or investigation, even if no official notice of such an event has been served.

diacetate ~ *see:* cellulose acetate

diary, n. ~ 1. A document, usually bound, containing a personal record of the author's experiences, attitudes, and observations. – 2. A blank book, usually lined and often dated, to be used to create such a record.

 RT: journal

diazo film, n. ~ A photographic film with an emulsion of diazonium salts that is exposed using ultraviolet light and developed with ammonia.

 RT: microfilm

 Notes: Diazo film is typically used to create duplicates of microfilm. The copy has the same polarity as the original; the image may be blue or black. The process is not permanent and is unsuitable for preservation copies.

diazo process, n. ~ A photographic process that produces images by exposing diazonium salts to ultraviolet light, then developing the image using ammonia fumes.

 Syn: ammonia process

 Notes: Typically used to make access copies of microfilm. The diazo process is not considered suitable for archival microfilm due to its impermanent nature.

dictamen ~ *see:* ars dictaminis

dictionary catalog, n. ~ A catalog in which all entries and references are sorted into a single alphabetical sequence.

 DF: divided catalog

 BT: catalog

 Notes: A dictionary catalog in a library might interfile entries for name, title, subject, and other headings.

diffusion transfer process, n. ~ A photographic process in which a print or transparency is developed while in contact with the negative, the image-forming material migrating from the negative through a thin layer of liquid.

 Notes: Developed in 1939 as a means to create rapid copies of documents. The process was later adapted for instant print cameras, such as Polaroid. Black-and-white images typically use silver halide as the image-forming material. Color photographs use dyes. The negative is typically disposed of after development, although Polaroid did make products (Type 51 and Type 105) that could produce a print and a negative that could be fixed and preserved.

digest, n. ~ 1. An abridged version of a work. – 2. LAW · A collection of summaries of court cases that are arranged by subject and subdivided by jurisdiction and court.

digital, adj. ~ Representing information through a sequence of discrete units, especially binary code.

 DF: analog

 RT: automated, e-, electronic, machine-readable

 Notes: 'Digital' is distinguished from 'analog', the latter representing information as a continuous signal. Often used as a synonym of automated, computerized, electronic, or the prefix e-. 'Digital' and 'electronic' are often used synonymously, although 'electronic' may include analog as well as digital formats.

digital archival object, n. (**DAO**, abbr.) ~ DESCRIPTION · An empty linking element in Encoded Archival Description (EAD) that uses the attributes ENTITYREF or XLINK to connect the finding aid information to electronic representations of the described materials.

Notes: Digital archival objects include graphic images, audio or video clips, images of text pages, and electronic transcriptions of text. The objects can be selected examples, or digital surrogates of all the materials in an archival collection or series.

digital assets management system, n. ~ Software to support the acquisition, description, tracking, discovery, retrieval, searching, and distribution of collections of digital objects.

RT: system

digital audio tape, n. (**DAT**, abbr.) ~ A magnetic tape format that uses a helical scan to record binary information on tape that is housed in a cassette.

BT: tape

Notes: DAT was originally developed to make sound recordings but has been adapted to store computer data.

digital certificate, n. ~ A file issued by a certificate authority that binds an individual or organization to a public key so that the identity of the individual or organization can be authenticated.

RT: certificate authority, electronic signature, public key infrastructure

†138 (RFC 2828, 2000): A certificate document in the form of a digital data object (a data object used by a computer) to which is appended a computed digital signature value that depends on the data object. ¶ [Deprecated] ISDs SHOULD NOT use this term to refer to a signed CRL [certificate revocation list] or CKL [compromised key list]. Although the recommended definition can be interpreted to include those items, the security community does not use the term with those meanings.

digital document, n. ~ 1. Information created on nonelectronic media, typically text or images on paper or film, and converted to an electronic format that can be stored and manipulated by a computer. – 2. Digital information that has been compiled and formatted for a specific purpose, that includes content and structure, and that may include context.

BT: document

RT: born digital, compound document

Notes: Digital documents that were created by converting documents originally in analog media are often described as born analog or reborn original. Digital documents originally created in electronic form are described as born digital.

†138 (RFC 2828, 2000): An electronic data object that represents information originally written in a non-electronic, non-magnetic medium (usually ink on paper) or is an analogue of a document of that type.

digital entity, n. ~ A bitstream that represents knowledge through the use of attributes and their relationships.

RT: digital object

Notes: Digital entities are highly abstract representations of concepts. They may be considered to embody more than information because the entity indicates how the data elements that form the information (attributes) relate to one another and how the information as a whole relates to a larger information environment. Digital entities are often used to represent digital objects in models, and some software packages automatically map entities to object-oriented maps.

†194 *(Moore 2003):* Digital entities are 'images of reality,' made of: data, the bit (zeros and ones) put on a storage system; information, the semantics used to assign semantic meaning to the data; knowledge, the structural relationships described by a data model. ¶ Every digital entity requires information and knowledge to correctly interpret and display.

digital government, n. ~ The use of information technology, especially the Internet, to improve government services for and interactions with citizens (G2C), business and industry (G2B), and different divisions of government (G2G) by simplifying processes and by integrating and eliminating redundant systems.

Syn: e-government

digital library, n. ~ 1. A collection of information resources in electronic format. – 2. A service that uses information technology to provide services similar to traditional libraries, including selection and acquisition, cataloging, reference, and preservation, to provide access to information in electronic format.

BT: library

Notes: 'Digital library' carries the connotation of information made accessible to a general audience over the Internet.

†166 *(D Levy 2000):* As many observers have pointed out, the term 'digital library' means different things to different people. For librarians, the word 'library' conjures up an institution that manages one or more collections. For computer scientists, the institutional aspect plays a minor role, if any. Instead, this group is more likely to focus on the collections themselves – digital collections – and on the enabling technologies through which these collections are built and searched.

digital object, n. ~ A unit of information that includes properties (attributes or characteristics of the object) and may also include methods (means of performing operations on the object).

RT: data object, digital entity, Digital Object Identifier, entity, object

Notes: The concept of digital object comes from object-oriented programming. Objects typically include properties and methods. Objects may belong to classes and inherit properties and methods from a parent class. Similarly, an object may have child objects that inherit its properties and methods.

Digital objects are an abstraction that can refer to any type of information. The object may be simple or complex, ranging from values used in databases to graphics and sounds. An object called *name* may include properties such as title, first name, and last name, as well as methods for returning the value of the name in natural language or inverted order. An object called *graphic* may include properties that define an image, such as dimensions, color scale, and encoding scheme and might include methods that make that image data available at different resolutions.

Objects are not necessarily self-contained. For example, a graphics object may require an external piece of software to render the image.

In addition to the data that makes up the fundamental content, the object often includes metadata that describes the resource in a manner that supports administration, access, or preservation.

†59 (CDL Metadata 2001, p. 2): Something (e.g., an image, an audio recording, a text document) that has been digitally encoded and integrated with metadata to support discovery, use, and storage of those objects. ¶ It should be noted that there is an important distinction between *digital objects* (e.g., an encoded text document or a digitized image) and the *digital collections* (e.g., the Online Archive of California) to which they belong. The distinction between digital objects and digital collections is analogous to the distinction between a collection of works by Arthur Conan Doyle and a particular copy of the *Hound of the Baskervilles.* Continuing the analogy, this document would describe standards for the description, structure and content of the digital *Hound.* This document, however, would be silent on how to represent the fact that *A Study in Scarlet* was also part of the collection.

†139 (InterPARES2, p. 3): Clifford Lynch, director of the Coalition for Networked Information, describes experiential digital objects as objects whose essence goes beyond the bits that constitute the object to incorporate the behavior of the rendering system, or at least the interaction between the object and the rendering system.

Digital Object Identifier, n. (**DOI,** abbr.) ~ A standard string of characters used to distinguish and identify intellectual property in an electronic environment over an extended period of time.

> *RT:* digital object
>
> *Notes:* The DOI System is an implementation of the Handle System, which is a distributed computer system that stores names, or handles, of digital items and that can quickly resolve those names into the information necessary to locate and access the items. See *Syntax for the Digital Object Identifier* (ANSI/NISO Z39.84), http://www.niso.org/standards/resources/Z39-84-2000.pdf.

digital photograph, n. ~ 1. An image produced using a digital camera and stored as an electronic file. – 2. An image originally produced using a digital camera and rendered for viewing as a virtual image or on film or paper; also called digital print.

> *BT:* photograph
>
> *RT:* scanning, scanning
>
> *Notes:* Traditionally photographs have been defined as an image made using light to trigger a chemical reaction that forms the image. Digital photographs blur that definition because the original camera image is made by a photoelectric effect and prints made using most computer printers (ink jet, laser printers) are mechanical rather than photochemical. The use of 'photograph', rather than 'print', to describe these images results from the use of a camera and their mechanical fidelity of detail to the original.

digital record ~ *see:* electronic record

digital rights management, n. ~ A system that identifies intellectual property rights relevant to particular works in digital formats and that can provide individuals with access to those works on the basis of permissions to the individuals.

> *BT:* rights management
>
> *RT:* copyright, intellectual property
>
> *Notes:* Primarily associated with copyright, digital rights management can also

be used for privacy, confidentiality, and performance rights. Digital rights management systems are intended to promote automated distribution of materials while protecting those materials from unauthorized copying or access.

†36 *(Briston 2003, p. 14)*: Copyright law delineates a bundle of exclusive rights that could conceivably be expressed in a DRM system. The extent of these rights, however, is limited by several exceptions, and it is harder to program in exceptions. One such exception is the fair use exception Section 107. This example calls for a judge to balance four factors, and no one factor definitively weighs for or against fair use. DRM systems are designed for precision, not for balancing, with the default configuration intended to minimize or prevent perfect copying. Thus, the system usually bars activities that would otherwise be legal.

digital signature, n. ~ A code, generally created using a public key infrastructure (PKI) associated with a digital object that can verify the object has not been altered and, in some contexts, may be used to authenticate the identity of the sender.

> *BT:* electronic signature
>
> *RT:* message digest
>
> *Notes:* A digital signature is typically a message digest that is derived from the digital object being signed and encoded with a public key. The recipient can use the message digest to ensure that the object has not been altered and can use the matching private key to ensure the identity of the sender. See American Bar Association, Information Security Committee, *Digital Signature Guidelines* at http://www.abanet.org/scitech/ec/isc/digital_signature.html.

†60 *(ABA, p. 3)*: From the information security point of view, 'Digital signature' means the result of applying to specific information certain specific technical processes described below. The historical legal concept of 'signature' is broader. It recognizes any mark made with the intention of authenticating the marked document. [Note: See, e.g., U.C.C. §1-201(39) (1992).] In a digital setting, today's broad legal concept of 'signature' may well include markings as diverse as digitized images of paper signatures, typed notations such as '/s/ John Smith,' or even addressing notations, such as electronic mail origination headers.

†289 *(Webopedia website)*: A digital code that can be attached to an electronically transmitted message that uniquely identifies the sender. Like a written signature, the purpose of a digital signature is to guarantee that the individual sending the message really is who he or she claims to be. Digital signatures are especially important for electronic commerce and are a key component of most authentication schemes. To be effective, digital signatures must be unforgeable. There are a number of different encryption techniques to guarantee this level of security.

digital watermark, n. ~ A pattern of bits, hidden in a digital file, that can be used to provide protection of intellectual property rights.

> *RT:* watermark
>
> *Notes:* A digital watermark is designed to be imperceptible in ordinary use; they are invisible in images and inaudible in sound recordings. At most, they appear as slight noise in the signal. They are designed so that they cannot be identified or manipulated without special software.

†58 *(Digimarc 2003, p. 3)*: One of the most promising technologies to help protect digitized copyrighted content, in conjunction with legal remedies, is digital watermarking. Digital watermarks are digital data embedded within the content,

where the digital data can be read by machines but is not noticeable by people viewing or listening to the content. Digital watermarks provide a critical and economically feasible content identification and security layer that enables copyright holders to protect and track distribution and use of their content.

digitization, n. (**digitize**, v.; **digitized**, adj.) ~ The process of transforming analog material into binary electronic (digital) form, especially for storage and use in a computer.

   NT: scanning

   RT: data entry, electronic imaging

   Notes: 'Digitized' is used to distinguish materials that have been transformed from the media in which they were created from materials that are born digital. Digitization is distinguished from 'data entry', which is the process of typing textual records, often in forms designed to facilitate the process, into a computer system.

   Digitization may start with information that is in electronic or physical form; for example, magnetic audio tape or phonograph discs. Digitization of textual documents typically produces an image of the words, which must be transformed to character data through a process of optical character recognition (OCR). In some instances, the OCR process may preserve text and page formatting.

   Digitalization is sometimes used as a synonym for digitization, however the term properly refers to the administration of the medicine digitalis.

dimension, n. ~ 1. Often pl. · The extent of an object, especially its height, width, depth, or volume. – 2. Computing · A specification for the size of an array or variable.

   RT: count, extent

diplomatics, n. ~ The study of the creation, form, and transmission of records, and their relationship to the facts represented in them and to their creator, in order to identify, evaluate, and communicate their nature and authenticity.

   NT: general diplomatics, special diplomatics

   RT: authenticity, reliability, trustworthiness

   Notes: The first major work on diplomatics is Jean Mabillon's *De Re Diplomatica* (1681; supplement, 1704). Diplomatics is primarily concerned with the process of determining whether a document is authentic or a forgery through a detailed examination of internal and external characteristics.

   †70 *(Duranti 1998, p. 177):* Diplomatics gives importance to the broad context of creation by emphasizing the significance of the juridical system (that is, the social body plus the system of rules which constitute the context of the records), the persons creating the records, and the concepts of function, competence, and responsibility; but never distances itself from the reality of the records.

   †77 *(Eastwood 1993, p. 242):* The historian uses diplomatics as a tool of interpretation, but the archivist uses it for its value for understanding the universal characteristics of the archival document.

   †219 *(Park 2001, p. 271):* Archival science derives its construction of authenticity through the management of aggregates of records with reference to their functional, procedural, and documentary contexts from the principles of diplomatics. Diplomatics, a parent discipline to archival science and legal theory that was developed to authenticate medieval documents, examines the genesis and form of individual documents. The diplomatic understanding of authenticity is that a document is authentic when it is what it claims to be.

direct access, n. ~ 1. A means to retrieve information without the need for an intermediary finding aid or index. – 2. COMPUTING · The ability to enter or extract information from the equipment or media that stores data through physical access, as opposed to remote access via a network. – 3. COMPUTING · The ability to enter or retrieve data from storage media by means of an address, rather than by sequential access to all preceding data; also called random access.

DF: remote access

RT: indirect access, random access, sequential access

direct duplication, n. ~ A copying process that does not require an intermediary.

RT: intermediate, internegative, interpositive

Notes: 'Direct duplication' is distinguished from processes that require an intermediary copy, such as an interpositive or internegative.

direct entry, n. ~ DESCRIPTION · The natural language order of a name or phrase used as a heading.

BT: heading

Notes: Direct entry is distinguished from inverted entry. For example, AACR2 uses direct entry for corporate names formed from personal names. While a heading for Fred Harvey, the man, would be inverted (Harvey, Fred), the company he founded would be entered as Fred Harvey Company.

direct image film, n. ~ A photographic film that, with normal processing, has the same polarity as the original.

RT: copy

Notes: Direct image film is often used to create duplicates of negatives without need for an intermediate interpositive or reversal processing.

direct positive, n. ~ Photographs exposed in the camera that, when developed, have the same polarity as the original subject.

RT: lateral reversal, negative-positive process, reversal film

Notes: Commonly used to describe 19th-century processes that were unique originals made without a negative, including daguerreotypes, tintypes, and ambrotypes. Images made on opaque supports were laterally reversed, unless a reversing lens was used. Sometimes used synonymously with direct image film.

direct read after write, n. (**DRAW**, abbr.) ~ An error-detection technique used in writing to mass storage devices in which the data is read and verified immediately after it is written.

†57 *(Dictionary of Computing 1996, p. 154):* This term is sometimes erroneously used in an optical-storage context simply to imply that written information is immediately ready for reading, without an intermediate processing operation as would be required for photographic recording.

directive, n. ~ Orders, regulations, bulletins, and similar materials issued as a written order.

director, n. ~ 1. The individual responsible for the overall artistic aspects of a production in the performing arts, including supervision of the actors and crew. – 2. A title often given to the chief administrator of an organization or unit.

RT: author

Notes: A director's[1] authority may be limited by a production company.

directory, n. ~ 1. A list of personal or corporate names with information on how to contact them, such as an address, phone number, or email address. – 2. COMPUTING · An index of files in a data storage system. – 3. COMPUTING · A description of the characteristics and contents of a file.

Notes: A MARC record includes an example directory[3], which indicates the order and start of the data of each field within the record.

disaster, n. ~ A sudden, unexpected event that causes sufficient loss or damage to disrupt routine operations of an individual or organization.

Notes: Disasters may be natural, including fire, flood, or infestation, or may be man-made, including theft, malicious destruction, or error.

disaster plan (also **disaster mitigation planning**), n. ~ Policies, procedures, and information that direct the appropriate actions to recover from and mitigate the impact of an unexpected interruption of operations, whether natural or man-made.

NT: salvage plan

RT: business continuation and disaster recovery

Notes: Disaster plans typically include a variety of directions for different scenarios. Disaster planning includes anticipatory activities done to mitigate the impact of disaster, such as maintaining lists of employee home phone numbers, names and phone numbers of recovery services, and off-site storage of vital records and data backups. Disaster planning also includes information about what to do should a disaster actually take place, such as establishing an order of staff responsible for coordinating activities, prioritizing materials for treatment, and noting when staff should be contacted.

disaster recovery ~ *see:* business continuation and disaster recovery

disc ~ *see:* disk

Notes: The spelling 'disc' is more common in non-US, English-speaking countries. 'Disc' is preferred for the name of some standard formats, including Compact Disc and LaserDisc.

disclosure-free extract, n. ~ A copy of a record made available for public use that redacts information in accordance with provisions of open records or privacy laws.

Syn: public use file

RT: confidential, copy, privacy, redaction

discography, n. ~ A list of selected sound recordings, typically noting titles, composers, performers, and catalog numbers.

BT: bibliography

Notes: Although discography implies one particular format of phonograph records, the word is used to describe lists that include other formats, such as cylinder recordings, wire recordings, audio tape, and compact discs. Discographies are often a survey of recordings of a composer's works or of performances by an artist or group of artists.

discovery, n. ~ 1. LAW · The process that compels a party in a lawsuit to disclose evidence and information relevant to the case. – 2. ACCESS · The process of searching for and identifying potentially relevant materials.

RT: production, relevant

Notes: For discovery[1], see "Depositions and Discovery," *Federal Rules of Civil Procedure*, part V (2003).

†117 *(Hazard and Taruffo 1993, p. 115):* Discovery has broad scope. According to Federal Rule 26, which is the model in most procedural codes, inquiry may be made into 'any matter, not privileged, that is relevant to the subject matter of the action.' Thus, discovery may be had of facts incidentally relevant to the issues in the

pleadings even if the facts do not directly prove or disprove the facts in question.

†*265 (Skupsky and Mantaña 1994, p. 87):* The objectives of the pretrial discovery are to enhance the truth-seeking process, to enable attorneys to better prepare and evaluate cases, to eliminate surprises, and to insure that judgments rest on the merits and not upon the skillful maneuvering of counsel.

discrete item, n. ~ DESCRIPTION · An individual item that is not part of a provenancial collection (a fonds).

> *RT:* item

disinfection, n. ~ The removal of germs and microorganisms.

> *RT:* fumigation

disinfestation, n. ~ The removal of small pests, such as rodents or insects.

> *RT:* fumigation

disjoined hand, n. ~ Handwriting in which the letters are not connected; printing[2].

> *Syn:* printing
> *RT:* cursive

disk (also **disc**), n. ~ 1. A very short cylinder; a platter. – 2. COMPUTING · A computer device used to store and retrieve data, especially the disk itself apart from any associated hardware. – 3. SOUND RECORDINGS · A phonograph record.

> *Notes:* The spelling 'disc' is used in some formats and tradenames, including LaserDisc and Compact Disc. Computer disks include hard drives (hard disks), floppy disks, optical disks, and compact discs.

disk drive, n. ~ 1. A device, including housing, drive, controller, and read-write heads, used to store computer data on a disk.

> *Notes:* The drive may have an integral disk, such as a hard drive, or may mount interchangeable disks, such as CD-ROM or floppy disk drives.

diskette ~ *see:* floppy disk

Disneyfication, n. ~ The process of increasing the marketability of a story by removing or downplaying distasteful or potentially controversial facts from the historical record to make the story as unobjectionable to as wide an audience as possible.

> *RT:* edutainment, infotainment

> †*181 (Maher 1998, p. 259):* Lost in a Disneyfied World: Archivists and Society in Late-Twentieth-Century America. ¶ Archivists understand the past as complex, multifaceted, and fractal. They know it conflicts with the present and offers both intellectually and spiritually enriching perspectives on life. In the other world, we see well-funded, slick, and often superficial presentations of the past that generally reflect a single harmonious, monolithic, and monocultural image, free from disturbing incidents or experiences that might engender the question of 'why.' ¶ The social appropriation of the past for commercial and political use is a complex phenomenon. One the one hand, it bolsters public interest in history and would seem beneficial to archives. On the other hand, much of the mass market appeal of history seems to operate on a more superficial and sinister level. There is a strong primary emphasis on the emotive appeal of the past; nostalgia and 'event experiences' are very much in contrast to documentary-based examinations of the past where the evidence can be removed and reexamined.

dispersal, n. ~ A technique to protect records by placing copies in different locations.

> *RT:* business continuation and disaster recovery

> *Notes:* Dispersal of paper records is typically limited to essential (vital) records

due to the costs associated with their duplication. Dispersal of electronic records often includes, in addition to the records themselves, application and system software necessary to access the records.

display case, n. ~ A cabinet with a transparent top or sides, typically made from glass or Plexiglas, that protects materials while on exhibit.

> *Syn:* exhibition case, show case

disposable record ~ *see:* temporary record

disposal, n. ~ The transfer of records, especially noncurrent records, to their final state, either destruction or transfer to an archives.

> *RT:* destruction, disposition, transfer
>
> *Notes:* Disposal is not synonymous with destruction. The manner and timing of disposal is typically described on a retention schedule.

disposal date (also **disposition date**), n. ~ A point in time specified in a records schedule when records should be destroyed or transferred to an archives.

> *Notes:* Disposal dates based on the date a record was created are often designed to batch records for disposal; for example, 'destroy one year after the end of the fiscal year in which the records were created.' Disposal dates may often be triggered by an event associated with the record; for example, disposal of contracts is often timed from the date the contract is completed.

disposal list, n. ~ A document listing records that are no longer being created and granting one-time authorization for their destruction or transfer to an archives for permanent retention.

> *Notes:* Disposal lists are often created for offices that have not had a records retention program in place and hold many obsolete records that do not need to be listed on a records schedule for future disposal.

disposal microfilming (also called **bulk-reduction microfilming, space-saving microfilming, substitution microfilming**), n. ~ The duplication of documents on microfilm, allowing the originals to be destroyed to save space.

> *RT:* microfilm

disposal schedule ~ *see:* retention schedule

disposition (also **final disposition**), n. ~ 1. Materials' final destruction or transfer to an archives as determined by their appraisal. – 2. DIPLOMATICS · That portion of a record that expresses the will or judgment of the author.

> *RT:* deletion, destruction, disposal, retirement, select and dispose
>
> *Notes:* Records may be transferred to archives in their entirety, or in part by sampling or selection.
>
> †70 *(Duranti 1998, p. 147):* The core of the text is the disposition[2], that is, the expression of the will or judgment of the author. Here, the fact or act is expressly enunciated, usually by means of a verb able to communicate the nature of the action and the function of the document, such as 'authorize,' 'promulgate,' 'decree,' 'certify,' 'agree,' 'request,' etc.

disposition authority, n. ~ Formal permission granting an agency the right to destroy materials or to transfer them to the archives.

> *Notes:* Disposition authority may be granted on a one-time basis through a disposal list or on a routine basis through a records schedule.

disposition date ~ *see:* disposal date

disposition instructions, n. ~ Specific directions regarding the manner in which records are to be disposed.

Notes: Disposition instructions may include procedures for screening records before transfer to the archives or specific instructions on how records are to be destroyed.

disposition program ~ *see:* records management program

disposition schedule ~ *see:* retention schedule

disposition standard ~ *see:* retention period

dispositive record, n. ~ A record that specifies an action to be taken.

　　BT: record

　　†99 (Gilliland-Swetland 2000b): Some records are created for legal purposes such as effecting an action (known as 'dispositive records') or proving that an act of action took place (known as 'probative records'), while other records, such as working papers and correspondence may merely provide supporting documentation of actions in which an organisation or individual was involved.

distortion, n. ~ An alteration in a signal carrying information resulting in a loss of fidelity or reproduction.

　　NT: flutter

　　Notes: Distortion in sound recordings include clipping, wow, and flutter. In optical systems, such as cameras, enlargers, or projectors, distortion includes pincushion and barrel distortion.

distributed system, n. ~ Computing · A group of computers that have been linked in a manner that allows them to function together to perform a task.

　　BT: system

　　Notes: A distributed system may be used to create a unified view of data drawn from data sets on different systems, or to distribute data from a single source to many systems for faster processing.

distributor, n. ~ 1. A wholesaler who provides materials to retailers. – 2. Cataloging · An agent or agency that has exclusive or shared marketing rights for an item. – 3. Motion pictures · An organization that arranges for motion pictures to be shown in theaters, often taking responsibility for advertising the movie.

　　RT: publisher

ditto ~ *see:* spirit process

diversity, n. ~ Variations within a group resulting from differences among members of that group.

　　Notes: The diversity of a group is often assessed in reference to another, larger population. As examples, Does an elected body reflect the population it represents? or Does the student body of a school reflect the larger community? Differences in patterns of diversity between a group and a larger population may reflect prejudice, bias, or some other factor. Many organizations have diversity efforts to ensure that underrepresented classes feel welcome and to increase membership of those classes, so that the organization more accurately reflects the larger population.

　　†229 (SAA 1999): The Society of American Archivists is committed to integrating diversity concerns and perspectives into all aspects of its activities and into the fabric of the profession as a whole. SAA is also committed to the goal of a Society membership that reflects the broad diversity of American society. SAA believes that these commitments are essential to the effective pursuit of the archival mission "to ensure the identification, preservation, and use of the nation's historical record."

divided catalog, n. ~ A catalog in which similar types of entries are grouped into different sections.

> *DF:* dictionary catalog
> *BT:* catalog
> *Notes:* Divided catalogs often have separate sections for authors, titles, and subjects. Another common arrangement separates name and title entries, which includes all proper names and titles of works, from subject entries. Entries in each section are generally in alphabetical order, although the section for subjects may be classified. Divided catalogs are distinguished from dictionary catalogs, in which all entries are organized in a single alphabetical sequence.

DMA ~ *see:* document management application

docket, n. ~ 1. A schedule of cases to be heard before a court. – 2. A record maintained by the court containing a note of all the proceedings and filings in a court case; a judicial record.

> *Notes:* A docket is usually maintained by the clerk of the court and may include notes regarding actions taken in the cases.

docudrama, n. ~ A television program or movie of historical events recreated through the use of props and actors, rather than original images.

> *RT:* documentary, edutainment, infotainment, mockumentary
> *Notes:* Docudrama often connotes melodrama.

document, n. ~ 1. Any written or printed work; a writing. – 2. Information or data fixed in some media. – 3. Information or data fixed in some media, but which is not part of the official record; a nonrecord. – 4. A written or printed work of a legal or official nature that may be used as evidence or proof; a record[1].

> *Syn:* writing
> *BT:* material
> *NT:* ancient documents, digital document, dynamic document, formatted document, manuscript, photograph, publication
> *RT:* compound document, four-corners document, miscellaneous documents, papers, record, text
> *Notes:* Document[1] is traditionally considered to mean text fixed on paper. However, document[2] includes all media and formats. Photographs, drawings, sound recordings, and videos, as well as word processing files, spreadsheets, web pages, and database reports, are now generally considered to be documents.
>
> Like records, documents are traditionally understood to have content, context, and structure. However, the nature of those attributes may change in electronic documents. Electronic formats can present information in complex layers that are three-dimensional or have a nonlinear structure. The phrase 'four-corners document' is sometimes used to distinguish an electronic document that can be printed on paper without loss of information from more complex, three dimensional documents. Similarly, some electronic document content is not fixed, but may change over time; for example, a word processing document that pulls data from a constantly changing database. These documents are described as dynamic documents to distinguish them from traditional, fixed documents
>
> In some contexts, document[3] refers to an item that is not a record[2,3], such as drafts, duplicates of record copies, and materials not directly relating to business activities. In this sense, documents are not usually included on retention schedules and can be disposed of without authorization.

However, in other contexts, document[4] is used synonymously with record[2,3]. In this sense, 'record' connotes an official document, especially the final version of one created in the routine course of business with the specific purpose of keeping information for later use as evidence or proof of the thing to which it refers.

In some instances, there are clear distinctions between a document and a record. For example, in civil litigation in the United States all documents held by an organization are discoverable. However, those documents are admissible as evidence only if they fall within the definition of business record in the Federal Rules of Evidence (or state equivalent).

Document[1] is often used interchangeably with 'publication', although this use has the sense of many identical copies in distribution. This use is common in state and federal depository libraries that collect government documents.

A document's content may reflect formula and conventions in its structure, including formal rules of representation, literary style, and specialized language that reflect the author's political, professional, or social cultures. A document's physical characteristics may also follow conventions relating to the medium, organization of internal elements, and presentation of the information.

†42 *(Clanchy 1993, p. 294):* Documents did not immediately inspire trust. As with other innovations in technology, there was a long and complex period of evolution, particularly in the twelfth century in England, before methods of production were developed which proved acceptable both to traditionalists and to experts in literacy. There was no straight and simple line of progress from memory to written record. People had to be persuaded – and it was difficult to do – that documentary proof was a sufficient improvement on existing methods to merit the extra expense and mastery of novel techniques which it demanded.

†44 *(Cook 2001, p. 25):* Documents, individually and collectively, are all a form of narration, postmodernists assert, that go well beyond being mere evidence of transactions and facts. Documents are shaped to reinforce narrative consistency and conceptual harmony for the author, thereby enhancing position, ego, and power, all the while conforming to acceptable organization norms, rhetorical discourse patterns, and societal expectations.

†46 *(Cook 1993, p. 30):* In so-called 'smart' documents, such as those in relational databases and geographical information systems or in hypertext formats, data in various forms are combined electronically to produce a virtual 'document' on the monitor or at the printer. This 'document' can change from day to day as the attribute 'feeder' data on which it depends is continually altered.

†70 *(Duranti 1998, p. 41):* Any written document in the diplomatic sense contains information transmitted or described by means of rules of representation, which are themselves evidence of the intent to convey information: formulas, bureaucratic or literary style, specialized language, interview technique, and so on. These rules, which we call form, reflect political, legal, administrative, and economic structures, culture, habit, myths, and constitute an integral part of the written document, because they formulate or condition the ideas or fact which we take to be the content of the documents. The form of a document is of course both physical and intellectual.

†167 *(D Levy 2001, p. 23):* What are documents? They are, quite simply, talking things. They are bits of the material world – clay, stone, animal skin, plant fiber, sand – that we've imbued with the ability to speak.

†262 (Sedona Principles 2003, p. 30): The best approach to understanding what is a document is to examine what information is readily available to the computer user in the ordinary course of business. If the employee can view the information, it should be treated as the equivalent of a paper 'document.' Data that can be readily compiled into information, whether presented on the screen or printed on paper, is also a 'document' under Rule 34. [Note: Fed. R. Civ. P.] However, data used by a computer system but hidden and never revealed to the user in the ordinary course of business should not be presumptively treated as a 'document.' Nor should data that is not accessible except through forensic means, such as deleted or residual data.

document box, n. ~ A container that holds folders containing paper documents vertically and that measures roughly 10 inches high, 12 or 15 inches wide, and 6 or 3 inches deep, and that usually has an integral top hinged at the upper back.

Syn: flip-top box
BT: box
RT: archives box
Notes: Sometimes called a **Hollinger box**. Document boxes are typically made from cardboard. They are often neutral gray and lined on the inside with white, acid-neutral paper. Boxes made from lignin-free cardboard are often tan and unlined. They may have a string, handle, or hole on one end to facilitate removal from a shelf. Document boxes made from high-quality materials suitable for long-term storage of archival materials are often called archives boxes.

document case, n. ~ A shallow container that is used to store documents in a flat position and that has an integral top that is hinged on a bottom side.

BT: box
RT: clamshell case, Solander box
Notes: Document boxes are commonly three inches high. They may be made of cardboard or from a more rigid material such as wood or fiberboard.

document interchange, n. ~ COMPUTING · The use of a standard to allow the content and format of documents to be transferred among different systems.

RT: Electronic Data Interchange, Portable Document Format, processable document, Standard Generalized Markup Language
Notes: Documents may be transmitted in a revisable form that allows them to be read and edited on different systems, or they may be transmitted in a final form that permits reading but not alteration. Standard Generalized Markup Language (SGML) is an example of a document interchange standard that can be used to create and share revisable documents. A commercial word processing format may also support document interchange through the use of a proprietary standard, such as WordPerfect. Adobe PDF is an example of a final form document interchange format.

document management, n. ~ Techniques that ensure that recorded information, regardless of format, is properly distributed, used, stored, retrieved, protected, and preserved according to established policies and procedures.

BT: management
RT: content management, information system, knowledge management, records management
Notes: Often used in the context of electronic document management systems,

which coordinate different individual workflows to facilitate the production, modification, and management of publications.

document management application, n. (**DMA**, abbr.) ~ Software and data storage that ensures documents are secure and accessible and that typically controls and tracks access and changes to a document, especially in a collaborative environment.

DF: document retrieval system, records management application

RT: electronic document management system, electronic information system, version control

Notes: Unlike records management applications (RMAs), most DMAs do not have the ability to schedule documents for retention.

document retrieval system, n. ~ Software that is used to store, index, and retrieve the full text of documents.

DF: document management application

RT: system

Notes: The system may be used to store documents that have been scanned from paper or documents that are born digital. A document retrieval system is distinguished from a document management application by its inability to control the creation, use, or disposition of the documents it contains.

document type ~ *see:* form

document type definition, n. (**DTD**, abbr.) ~ A set of rules that specify the structure of a document and the tags used to define that structure and that can be used to validate whether a document is well formed.

RT: Standard Generalized Markup Language

Notes: Originally specified in the SGML standard, DTDs are also specified in XML. A DTD may be included in a document header, or it may be a separate (external) resource referenced in the document header. A **document type declaration** is a statement in an XML document that names the particular document type definition used.

†*126 (Hunter, et al. 2000, p. 331):* DTD refers only to the *definition* of a document type – not the DOCTYPE declaration that associates a DTD with an XML document instance.

documentary, n. ~ A narrative work, usually an audiovisual format, about contemporary or historical facts in a manner that purports to be objective.

RT: docudrama, moving image

Notes: Most commonly associated with moving image works, documentaries can be in any format, including still photography, sound recordings, and texts. Often used as an adjective with a specific format; for example, documentary photograph, documentary film.

Popularized in the 1930s by filmmaker John Grierson, sometimes called the father of the documentary. Images and sound used in the documentary may be original to the period or may be recreations contrived for the camera and audio recorder. Because the narrative, which strings together different pieces of the story, is ultimately the creation of the documentarist, documentaries are often considered to be more an interpretation of the past than history. This lack of objectivity distinguishes it from journalism.

†*104 (Goerler 1999, p. 317):* According to Boorstein [in *The Image: A Guide to Pseudo-Events in America*], the documentary is a 'pseudo-event,' and not simply a facsimile of the event itself. A pseudo-event is planned rather than spontaneous;

functions primarily for the purpose of being reported or reproduced; has an ambiguous relationship to reality in that the image rather than the event becomes the object of study; and is usually intended to be a self-fulfilling prophecy; i.e., constructed to provide a consistent interpretation.

documentary editing, n. ~ The selection, description, and critical annotation of original documents for publication.

RT: documentary publication, editor, historical editing

Notes: The publication of historical documents was motivated, in part, by a desire to ensure their preservation through the distribution of many copies. The production of documentary editions also was intended to make works of prominent writers and historical figures more accessible, growing in part out of a 19th-century romantic belief in the inspirational nature of these documents.

†50 *(Cox 1997):* It is generally the past half century that would be recognized as the height of documentary editing as a systematic, professionalized, and effective pastime. Clearly, the late nineteenth century movement called scientific history, with its emphasis on the careful use of documentary sources akin to the running of experiments in scientific laboratories, had much to do with the development of more rigorous standards for documentary editing.

†63 *(Burlington Agenda 2001, p. 295):* Formal documentary editing contextualizes documents, which is to say, it orients or situates documents among other historically and intellectually related documents.

†155 *(Kline 1998, p. 271):* ['Documentary editing'] became current in the later 1970s to describe the process of creating reading texts intended to capture the substance and quality of the source texts so that the editorial texts would have substantially the same evidentiary value as their sources.

documentary form, n. ~ DIPLOMATICS · Rules that structure a document's extrinsic and intrinsic elements in order to communicate its content, its administrative and documentary context, and its authority.

Notes: The phrase 'documentary form' is sometimes used to indicate information that has been recorded by writing or tangible process. It is also used in the sense of 'documentary'.

documentation, n. ~ 1. Materials created or collected to provide facts for reference, especially when created to substantiate decisions, actions, or events. – 2. Citations, including footnotes, endnotes, bibliographies, and similar devices, that indicate an author's sources. – 3. COMPUTING · Instructions, specifications, and other descriptive information relating to the installation and use of hardware, software, systems, or files.

RT: adequacy of documentation

Notes: Documentation may be in any format, including text, photographs, moving images, or sound.

†185 *(McCrank 2002, p. 42):* To cover all formats the term documentation[2] was preferred over the older use of bibliography not only to enlarge the idea of embracing archives as wells as libraries, but because documentation included everything, the physical and the metaphysical, whereas information seemed to pertain more to the latter.

documentation planning, n. ~ A proactive technique to ensure that an institution's functions, programs, or activities are adequately documented through a holistic process of institutional analysis, leading to the deliberate selection of appropriate records.

Notes: Documentation planning focuses on an archives working to document its parent institution, as distinguished from documentation strategy, which is a collaborative effort among several archives to document a topic or region.

†158 *(Krizack 1994, p. xiv):* A documentation plan is formulated in two stages, analysis and selection. The first stage consists of three tiers of analysis: 1. an institutional analysis, 2. a comparison of the institution with others of the same type, and 3. an analysis of the relationship of the institutions to the larger system of which it is a part. . . . The selection stage consists of making decisions about what to document at three levels: 1. the function, 2. the activity or project, and 3. the record series.

documentation strategy, n. ~ A methodology that guides selection and assures retention of adequate information about a specific geographic area, a topic, a process, or an event that has been dispersed throughout society.

BT: appraisal

RT: adequacy of documentation

Notes: Documentation strategies are typically undertaken by collaborating records creators, archives, and users. A key element is the analysis of the subject to be documented; how that subject is documented in existing records, and information about the subject that is lacking in those records; and the development of a plan to capture adequate documentation of that subject, including the creation of records, if necessary.

†49 *(Cox 1990, p. 20):* The term 'documentation strategy' was coined and initially defined at a session of the 1984 Society of American Archivists meeting that included papers presented by Helen W. Samuels, Larry J. Hackman, and Patricia Aronnson. The origins of the concept date from the early and mid-1970s efforts by some archivists to grapple with documenting social movements, minority issues, popular concerns, and other topics that were not well-represented in most archival and historical records repositories.

†255 *(Samuels 1986, p. 116):* A documentation strategy consists of four activities: 1. choosing and defining the topic to be documented, 2. selecting the advisors and establishing the site for the strategy, 3. structuring the inquiry and examining the form and substance of the available documentation, and 4. selecting and placing the documentation.

†255 *(Samuels 1986, p. 109):* A modern, complex, information-rich society requires that archivists reexamine their role as selectors. The changing structure of modern institutions and the use of sophisticated technologies have altered the nature of records, and only a small portion of the vast documentation can be kept. Archivists are challenged to select a lasting record, but they lack techniques to support this decision-making. Documentation strategies are proposed to respond to these problems.

DOD 5015.2 ~ *see:* Design Criteria for Electronic Records Management Software Applications

DOI ~ *see:* Digital Object Identifier

donation, n. ~ Material for which legal title is transferred from one party to another without compensation.

DF: deposit

Syn: gift

Syn: Synonym • †: see Bibliography • *Superscript:* Definition number

donor, n. ~ An individual or organization who gives property or money to another without reciprocal compensation.

> *Notes:* In many instances, individuals who donate collections are not the provenance of the collection.

donor restriction, n. ~ A limitation placed on access to or use of materials that has been stipulated by the individual or organization that donated the materials.

> *BT:* restriction

> *Notes:* Donor restrictions may require that the collection, or portions of the collection, be closed for a period of time or that a specific credit line be used if materials from the collection are exhibited or published.

dossier, n. ~ A group of documents assembled to provide information about a specific topic.

> *DF:* case file

> *RT:* file

> *Notes:* 'Dossier' connotes information purposefully collected from various sources, as opposed to documents in an organic collection resulting from routine activities. In some instances, 'dossier' may be used interchangeably with file[1] in the sense of a case file. It is not equivalent to a file folder or other container; a dossier may be housed in several folders or other containers.

double fold ~ *see:* folding endurance

double lookup index, n. ~ 1. An index that points to another index, requiring users to check two sources to locate the information they seek. – 2. COMPUTING · The simultaneous use of two indexes for greater precision in locating data.

> *BT:* index

> *Notes:* An example of a double lookup index[1] includes a classified index, which requires users to first consult a list of classes to determine the class (often a number) under which relevant information is indexed. The Domain Name System (DNS) is another example of a double lookup. Computers connected to the Internet are addressed using an Internet protocol (IP) address. Because numerical addresses are not mnemonic and because the IP address may change frequently, users are typically given a Uniform Resource Locator (URL), such as http://www.archivists.org/. Applications submit the URL to a DNS server, which returns the IP address necessary to connect to the desired machine. – An example of a double lookup index[2] includes the use of a column and row headings to specify a cell.

double shelving, n. ~ The practice of placing boxes two deep on a shelf.

> *RT:* shelving

downgrade, n. ~ The process of reducing restrictions on access to a lower security classification.

> *RT:* declassification

> *Notes:* 'Downgrade' implies that the material continues to have some restrictions on access. The removal of all restrictions is described as declassification.

download, v. ~ 1. COMPUTING · To transfer information from a server on a network to a local machine. – n. ~ 2. COMPUTING · A copy of a file on a local machine that has been copied from a server through a network connection.

> *RT:* upload

downward reference, n. ~ A cross-reference from a general to a more specific topic; a direction to a narrower term.

Syn: narrower term

BT: cross-reference

RT: upward reference

Notes: Downward references are part of the syndetic structure used in a thesaurus. Downward references are reciprocal to upward references. For example, an entry for furniture may include downward references to bed, chair, and chest. Entries for each of those terms would include furniture as upward references.

draft, n. ~ 1. A version of a text or image, especially a preliminary version to be further revised. – 2. A document ordering a second party to transfer a specified amount of money to an individual named in the document.

DF: note

RT: transmission

Notes: Draft[1] is nearly synonymous with text[1,2], although draft has the connotation that the work is not the final version. However, it is not uncommon to hear a finished document described as the final draft.

DRAW ~ *see:* direct read after write

drawing, n. ~ 1. An image using lines and shades to convey the appearance of an object. – 2. A schematic showing the components and structure of an object or idea.

BT: image, picture

NT: architectural drawing, as-built drawing, design drawing, elevation, engineering drawing, measured drawing, oblique, technical drawing

RT: architectural rendering, projection, scale, visual materials

Notes: Drawing[1] connotes a work done by hand, often in pencil, ink, or crayon, that emphasizes an abstraction of an object's contours to show its general form. However, that connotation is not defining; 'drawing' may refer to works done with the assistance of or by a computer program. A drawing may have shading, but generally does not have color. – A drawing[2] uses shapes to represent ideas, with position and lines indicating the relationships among those ideas; for example, an architectural drawing or a flowchart.

dressing, n. ~ The process of creating finished leather from rough-tanned hides or crust leather.

dropout, n. ~ The loss of an electronic signal due to a defect in the media.

dry mount, n. ~ The process of attaching a flat object, such as a drawing, text, or photograph, to surface without the use of liquid adhesives.

RT: mount, wet mount

Notes: A common dry mount technique is to place a thin sheet of tissue covered with a heat-activated adhesive between the object and the support, then place the sandwich under the platen of a heated press. Another technique involves a thin layer of adhesive between two layers of silicon release paper; one sheet is removed, and the object to be mounted placed on the adhesive, then the second sheet is removed leaving the adhesive on the object without any tissue.

dry silver process, n. ~ A photographic process that uses silver halides as the light sensitive material but uses heat rather than chemicals to develop the image.

Notes: Some dry processes rely on a heat-activated developer incorporated into the emulsion.

DSpace, n. ~ A specialized content management system that allows different communities to use the web to capture, distribute, and preserve digital works and to provide access to those works through metadata.

RT: institutional repository

Notes: DSpace, short for Durable Space, was developed at MIT as an institutional repository. DSpace builds portals for specific communities, allowing a community to set policies for the content and access to the works within the repository. This emphasis enables the portal to reflect a community's practices and terminology. DSpace allows any type of digital object to be submitted but promises that only a limited set of formats will remain renderable; nonsupported objects will be preserved as a bitstream, placing the responsibility for maintaining the usefulness of the file on the creator. See http://www.dspace.org/.

†176 (C Lynch 2003, http://dspace.org/what/faq.html): DSpace identifies two levels of digital preservation: bit preservation, and functional preservation. Bit preservation ensures that a file remains exactly the same over time – not a single bit is changed – while the physical media evolve around it. Functional preservation goes further: the file does change over time so that the material continues to be immediately usable in the same way it was originally while the digital formats (and the physical media) evolve over time. Some file formats can be functionally preserved using straightforward format migration (e.g. TIFF images or XML documents). Other formats are proprietary, or for other reasons are much harder to preserve functionally

DTD ~ *see:* document type definition

dual-key encryption, n. ~ A technique of using two separate keys for encrypting and decoding information.

DF: symmetric-key encryption

RT: cryptography

dubbing, n. ~ 1. The process of creating a duplicate (dub). – 2. Substituting a new soundtrack in a film, often lip-synched dialog in another language.

Syn: copy

RT: copy, duplicate

Notes: Generally used to describe the process of copying audiotapes.

Dublin Core, n. (**DC**, abbr.) ~ A standard (ISO 15836, ANSI Z39.85) that defines metadata elements used to describe and provide access to online materials.

BT: metadata

Notes: Dublin Core is often used to provide a common bridge between different metadata schemes, although some projects use Dublin Core as their native descriptive metadata. Originally intended to describe online resources, DC is often used to describe offline, nondigitized materials or digital surrogates of those materials.

The data elements of **unqualified Dublin Core** include title, creator, subject, description, publisher, contributor, date, type, format, identifier, source, language, relation, coverage, and rights. In **qualified Dublin Core**, elements may be refined for greater specificity.

DC is maintained by the Dublin Core Metadata Initiative. See http:// dublincore.org/.

†65 (Dublin Core 1995): [Dublin Core Metadata Initiative] An organization dedicated to promoting the widespread adoption of interoperable metadata standards and developing specialized metadata vocabularies for describing resources that enable more intelligent information discovery systems. ¶ The original workshop for the Initiative was held in Dublin, Ohio in 1995. Hence the term 'Dublin Core' in the name of the Initiative.

BT: Broader Term • NT: Narrower Term • RT: Related Term • DF: Distinguish From

dumb terminal, n. ~ A computer peripheral designed for input/output that has no ability to process information independent of the computer to which it is attached.

    BT: terminal

dummy, n. ~ 1. A card or block placed where an object should be stored in a sequence that indicates another location where the object is actually stored. – 2. Publishing · A mockup of a page created by pasteup or computer that is used to show the final design. – 3. Publishing · A mockup of a book, cover, and dust jacket created to show the final design.

    Notes: A dummy[1] may be filed in place of an original that must be stored elsewhere because of size or preservation concerns.

duplex-numeric filing system, n. ~ A technique to classify numbers by assigning groups of numbers that represent a hierarchy of concepts.

    BT: filing system

    Notes: The major classes and subdivisions may be separated by a dash, decimal, space, or other punctuation. For example, Policies 5, Fringe Benefits 5-1, Maternity Leave 5-1-3.

duplicate, n. (**dup**, **dupe**, abbr.) ~ 1. One of a number of copies of an object made at the same time from the same master. – 2. The process of making such copies.

    DF: copy

    RT: copy, dubbing, original

    Notes: Duplicate[1] and copy[1,2] are often synonyms. 'Duplicate' connotes versions that may be considered an original; for example, duplicate prints made from the same negative. 'Copy' connotes something reproduced from an original; for example, a photocopy.

duplicate original, n. ~ A copy that has all the essential aspects of the original, including signatures.

    RT: copy, original

    Notes: A duplicate original of a letter may be created and sent by different routes to increase the likelihood that at least one original copy arrives to the addressee.

duplicating master, n. ~ A copy of a microfilm or motion picture, often made from a camera original, that is used to produce copies for access or distribution.

    RT: microfilm

    Notes: Use of a duplicating master to produce access copies reduces the number of times the camera original needs to be touched, reducing risk to the original.

durability, n. ~ The ability of a material to resist wear and degradation over time while maintaining its original properties.

    Notes: For paper, film, and other media with a flexible base, durability may be measured in terms of strength and pliability.

    †215 (*O'Toole 1998, p. 272*): Here were the oral and literate side by side, but writing has some advantages. In written form, information achieved a stability and durability it would not have so long as it remained only in the mind or in spoken words. What is more, writing was in itself coming to be recognized as an effective way for gathering and sharing information: some people would now learn things only from books, Bede realized.

durable paper, n. ~ Permanent paper, especially one treated to resist heavy use.

    BT: paper

    RT: archival bond, permanent paper

Syn: Synonym · †: see Bibliography · *Superscript:* Definition number

dust jacket, n. ~ A lightweight cover for a book, typically a single sheet the same height as the book, that wraps around the fore-edges of the cover and held in place by friction rather than being attached.

Notes: Commonly made from paper and used to protect the cover of hard-bound books.

dye transfer process, n. ~ A photomechanical process to make prints from photographs by creating a gelatin relief matrix that is used to transfer dye to an emulsion on paper.

RT: imbibition process, photomechanical, print

Notes: The depth of the matrix is relative to the density of the image, with areas of greater density able to transfer a greater amount of dye. A single matrix produces a monochrome print, although separation negatives can be used to create several matrices, each of which is printed in registration using a different dye to produce a full-color image.

dynamic document, n. ~ 1. A document that includes content taken from external sources that changes as those external sources change. – 2. A document, especially a web page, that changes content through periodic transactions between the client and server.

BT: document

Notes: A dynamic document[1] may also include information that remains consistent each time it is viewed. For example, a report written in a word processor may include a graph that draws information from an external spreadsheet. Each time the report is opened, it updates the graph based on the most current information in the spreadsheet.

In other instances, a dynamic document is little more than a template. For example, a web page may use different graphics and include different text based on a variety of factors. As a result, the web page may be different every time it is viewed.

Because the content of dynamic documents changes as the information in external sources changes, it lacks fixity and cannot be relied on as a source of historical information. If the information in a dynamic document needs to be preserved, it must be written to a nondynamic format to create a record of the information.

A dynamic document[2] on the web may use client-pull, server-push, or other techniques to trigger content updates.

dynamic website, n. ~ A website that can use a single URL to generate a webpage with content that changes based on a number of factors.

DF: static website

BT: website

Notes: Dynamic websites connote more than a simple scheme to display a variety of graphics mixed with the same text. A dynamic website is usually driven by a database so that current content is always up-to-date or so that content is customized to the individual viewing the page; for example, a portal.

E

e-, prefix ~ An abbreviation for 'electronic'; see various headings beginning with the word electronic.

    RT: automated, digital, electronic

    Notes: The addition of 'e-' to a word to indicate a computerized variant of the concept is the modern equivalent of the use of the word 'automated' in the 1960s and 1970s.

e-government, n. ~ The use of information technology, especially the Internet, to improve government services for and interactions with citizens (G2C), business and industry (G2B), and different divisions of government (G2G) by simplifying processes and by integrating and eliminating redundant systems.

    Syn: digital government

    Notes: E-government is analogous to e-commerce. In principle, it goes beyond providing a web interface to manual processes by ensuring that back-office operations are reengineered to improve efficiency and reduce costs. Improved services to citizens include the ability to interact with agencies outside normal office hours and away from physical offices, increased access to information through improved search facilities and online documents, and new means of citizen participation in the democratic process. While services to citizens are typically provided through the web, services to business and other government agencies are often part of an automated process performed by computers without manual intervention. For example, a procurement process may be fully automated, working within established business rules.

EAC ~ *see:* Encoded Archival Context

EAD ~ *see:* Encoded Archival Description

EBCDIC, n. ~ An eight-bit binary code used to represent characters in IBM computers.

    BT: character set

    Notes: An acronym for **Extended Binary Coded Decimal Interchange Code**. Because the binary representation of characters differs from that used by ASCII, the order of characters is different. EBCDIC defines 258 characters, where standard ASCII defines only 128. IBM no longer uses EBCDIC in most of its machines.

ECURE, n. ~ An annual conference held at Arizona State University in Tempe, Arizona, beginning in 1999 that seeks to bring diverse stakeholders in academic records together to better understand electronic recordkeeping challenges and to discover solutions.

    Notes: An acronym for **Electronic College and University Records Events**.

edge curl (also **lipping**), n. ~ A distortion in the base of film or tape that causes an outer edge to be larger than the center.

edge fluting, n. ~ A wave-shaped deformation along the edges of a flat surface.

    Notes: Edge fluting may appear on the edge of cut sheets or rolls. It may be caused by an expansion of the edge of the material, which is exposed to greater variations in temperature and humidity than the center. It may also be caused by physical deformation, sometimes caused by the material rubbing against the flange of the reel or being pulled unevenly through a transport mechanism.

edge-notched card (also **edge-punched cards**), n. ~ A card with holes around the edges that can be punched out to code the information on the card for retrieval.

> *Notes:* Edge-notched cards have some information written in the body. The holes at the edge are associated with a specific attribute about the subject to be coded for retrieval. A hole is cut out (notched) if the card is to be retrieved for that piece of information. When a thin rod is inserted through the hole associated with an attribute, cards with that hole notched out are not picked up by the rod. Several rods may be inserted to retrieve cards based on more than one attribute.

> For example, cards may be created for each member of a group. An individual's name is written on the card, and possibly other information. Appropriate holes assigned for age and ethnicity are notched. Inserting rods into the holes for a specific age and a specific ethnicity will allow cards that have been notched for both that age and ethnicity to fall out of the cards that are not notched and remain on the rods.

EDI ~ *see:* Electronic Data Interchange

edit, n. ~ 1. The process of revising a work, especially for final publication or release. – 2. The act of holding back or modifying ideas expressed to make them appropriate to a particular audience.

> *Notes:* Editing generally refers to the effort of someone other than the author, the latter being said to revise a draft. In the context of audio and moving image materials, editing emphasizes selecting and assembling pieces, which may have been created in one order, into the final order that may eliminate much of the original material.

edit status, n. ~ The degree to which a preproduction copy of audio or moving image materials has been prepared for final release.

> *Notes:* Edit status is generally one of three states: unedited, partially edited, and edited.

edited master, n. ~ The final copy of a recorded production[1] that is ready for broadcast or duplication.

> *BT:* master

> *Notes:* An edited master video includes test bars, slate, and tone.

edition, n. ~ 1. All copies of a work that are produced at the same time using the same process, with the result that each copy is essentially identical. – 2. A particular instance of a serial work; a version.

> *DF:* issue, printing

> *NT:* definitive edition, impression

> *RT:* copy, version, work

> *Notes:* An edition[1] may be released over time in several printings. The copies in an edition may show some variation between printings. In early printing, production and proofreading processes sometimes overlapped. As errors were found, the type was corrected; however, earlier impressions that included the error may have already been used.

> Edition[2] is roughly synonymous with 'version'; for example, the first edition of a book, or the 6:30 P.M. edition of a broadcast news program. In this sense, different editions may have different content or physical characteristics.

edition statement, n. ~ CATALOGING · A word or phrase describing the particular version of a work.

> *Notes:* In Encoded Archival Description, an edition statement is an optional subelement that includes information about the edition of the finding aid. In bibli-

---

BT: Broader Term · *NT:* Narrower Term · *RT:* Related Term · *DF:* Distinguish From

ographic cataloging, an edition statement refers to the work described and may include statements of responsibility, and parallel and additional edition statements.

editor, n. ~ 1. One who prepares another person's work for publication by checking that spelling, punctuation, grammar, and style are correct and internally consistent, and who may also give the author feedback on content that needs clarification or reworking. – 2. One who oversees the creation of a work containing portions contributed by several individuals, and who may also provide an introduction or commentary on those contributions. – 3. NEWSPAPERS · One who serves as the representative of a newspaper's publisher or owner and who has responsibility for establishing policies for content and for the daily operations of the organization's reporting activities. – 4. MOVING IMAGES · One who evaluates, selects, and assembles the scenes of a moving image to create a final work that has narrative value and continuity.

> *RT:* documentary editing

EDMS ~ *see:* electronic document management system

EDP ~ *see:* electronic data processing

edutainment, n. ~ Works designed to simultaneously educate and entertain through amusing content that also includes factual information on a subject.

> *RT:* Disneyfication, docudrama, infotainment
>
> *Notes:* Often used to describe television programs or interactive multimedia.
>
> †181 *(Maher 1998, p. 261):* If it is fair to say that archivists are in the business of the past, we can also be said to have a legitimate concern about how others utilize and exploit the past. We appreciate the entertainment value of the past, but we care more about the educational value of the past. And we understand that the greatest educational value comes from archives not as a source for images of the past but as the font of evidence. Where we particularly should be taking issue with the mass media use of the past is when it is used for escapism from the present. Indeed, we have a special responsibility to note when slick edu-tainment presentations are built upon narrow selections of the past in order to paper over the moral ambiguities and cruelties of the past which we know are often well reflected in our archives.
>
> †251 *(DigiCULT 2003, p. 19):* Play is a fundamental human activity and an important way to learn. Cultural institutions do not take sufficient advantage of games to expand awareness and knowledge of collections through 'edutainment' packages and other strategies.

Eldred v. Ashcroft, n. ~ A lawsuit filed by Eric Eldred and others that challenged the constitutionality of the Copyright Term Extension Act (Pub. L. 105–298, §102(b) and (d)), which extended the length of copyright.

> *RT:* copyright
>
> *Notes:* The Copyright Term Extension Act was made law in 1998. The United States Supreme Court decided against Eldred (No. 01-618, 15 January 2003).
>
> †254 *(SAA, Copyright):* In 1998 Congress passed the Copyright Term Extension Act increasing the duration of copyright from life of the author plus fifty years to life of the author plus seventy years. The effect was to stop for twenty years the addition of any published work to the public domain. As Roy Rosenzweig noted in a recent article in the *Journal of American History*, '[f]or historians, copyright protection has redlined ... much twentieth-century history....' In response, a group of publishers and preservationists filed suit challenging the

constitutionality of copyright term extension. The suit, *Eldred v. Ashcroft*, argues that 'perpetual copyright on the installment plan' is in direct violation of the constitutional stipulation that the monopoly rights granted by copyright be for a limited term. The suit has lost in the Federal Appeals court, and recently the plaintiffs asked the Supreme Court to rule on the issue. ¶ A coalition of information organizations, including the Society of American Archivists, the Association of Research Libraries, the American Library Association, the Digital Futures Coalition, and others have filed an amicus brief with the Court asking that they hear the case. The brief notes the irreparable harm done to historians and institutions that exploit the public domain when copyright term is excessive.

electronic, adj. ~ Utilizing devices that operate using electrical charge.

    RT: digital, e-, machine-readable

    Notes: Electronic and digital are often used synonymously, although electronic includes analog as well as digital formats. NTSC and PALS video, and AM and FM radio are examples of analog electronic formats. HDTV is a digital video format, and XM is a digital radio format.

Electronic Data Interchange, n. (**EDI**, abbr.) ~ A standard (ANSI X12 and EDI-FACT) for the use of computers to conduct the automated exchange of business information between trading partners.

    RT: document interchange

    Notes: An EDI message typically contains a header and trailer, and a number of business facts, known as data elements, that typically appear on a form used when executing a transaction. EDI messages are generally used to exchange information between applications, not free-form messages between human agents. The format of the message is established by the trading partners, usually in compliance with the ANSI X12 or EDIFACT standards.

electronic data processing, n. (**EDP**, abbr.) ~ The use of computers to analyze, organize, store, retrieve, and manipulate data, and to report the results of those operations.

    BT: data processing

    Notes: Essentially a synonym for data processing, the longer form distinguishes computerized processing from manual methods.

electronic document management system, n. (**EDMS**, abbr.) ~ A software application that uses automated techniques to ensure that information stored in digital formats is properly distributed, used, stored, retrieved, protected, and preserved according to established policies and procedures.

    RT: document management application, system

electronic imaging, n. ~ Various technologies used to store, retrieve, and manipulate pictures using a computer or video system.

    BT: imaging

    NT: scanning

    RT: digitization

    Notes: Electronic imaging frequently connotes an electronic document management application. Most contemporary electronic imaging formats are digital, but some early electronic imaging technology used analog video media.

electronic information system, n. ~ An automated system that facilitates the access to and management of information and records in a computer system.

    DF: records management application

RT: document management application, system

Notes: 'Electronic information system' connotes a system that is dedicated to a specific business process and is tailored to manage information relating to that process. Such a system may not have records management functionality.

electronic mail (**email, e-mail**), n. ~ 1. An asynchronous message, especially one following the RFC 2822 or MIME standards, including a header, body, and – optionally – attachments, sent via a computer network held in online accounts to be read or downloaded by the recipients. – 2. A system for transmitting email.

RT: mail, Multipurpose Internet Messaging Extensions, PROFS case

Notes: Email is not real-time communication, although delivery time is often minimal. Unlike instant messaging, the sender and recipients do not need simultaneous connections to send or receive email. The header includes information that enables the messages to be delivered and additional metadata to identify, classify, and contextualize the message. The body is often plain or formatted text; it may contain embedded graphics or sound, although not all email readers can properly parse anything beyond plain ASCII. Attachments may be in any format, such as word processing documents, spreadsheets, or media files.

An email system requires an application, sometimes called a mail user agent (MUA), client, or reader, that incorporates a simple text editor used to compose messages and to send and receive messages. The system also requires a mail transport agent (MTA) to store and forward messages. An email system may be implemented on a closed network using proprietary software to exchange messages. However, an email system typically formats messages using the RFC 2822 or MIME standards when the messages are to be exchanged with another system. Email systems commonly transmit messages using the simple mail transport protocol (SMTP). Many MUAs and MTAs are based on the POP3 or IMAP standards to allow interoperability between different systems.

See http://www.faqs.org/rfcs/rfc2822.html and 36 CFR 1234.

electronic record (also **digital record; automated record**, largely obsolete), n. ~ Data or information that has been captured and fixed for storage and manipulation in an automated system and that requires the use of the system to render it intelligible by a person.

BT: record

RT: machine-readable

Notes: 'Electronic records' can encompass both analog and digital information formats, although the term principally connotes information stored in digital computer systems. 'Electronic records' most often refers to records created in electronic format (born digital) but is sometimes used to describe scans of records in other formats (**reborn digital** or **born analog**). Electronic records are often analogous to paper records; email to letters, word processing files to reports and other documents. Electronic records often have more complex forms, such as databases and geographic information systems.

†17 *(InterPARES Authenticity, p. 7):* Strictly speaking, it is not possible to preserve an electronic record. It is always necessary to retrieve from storage the binary digits that make up the record and process them through some software for delivery or presentation.

†70 *(Duranti 1998, p. 167):* Electronic records are not *always* copies, because a copy is by definition a reproduction of an original, a draft or another copy (the

first copy made being always a reproduction of a document in a different status of transmission); therefore, electronic records having a different status of transmission must be created for copies to exist. It is more appropriate to say that electronic records are all made as drafts and received as originals, in consideration of the fact that the records received contain elements automatically added by the system which are not included in the documents sent, and which make them complete and effective.

†73 (Duranti and MacNeil 1996, p. 49): Diplomatic examination shows that an electronic record, just like every traditional record, is comprised of medium (the physical carrier of the message), form (the rules of representation that allow for the communication of the message), persons (the entities acting by means of the record), action (the exercise of will that originates the record as a means of creating, maintaining, changing, or extinguishing situations), context (the juridical-administrative framework in which the action takes place), archival bond (the relationship that links each record to the previous and subsequent one and to all those which participate in the same activity), and content (the message that the record is intended to convey). However, with electronic records, those components are not inextricably joined one to the other, as in traditional records : they, and their parts, exist separately, and can be managed separately, unless they are consciously tied together for the purpose of ensuring the creation of reliable records and the preservation of authentic records.

†231 (Digital Preservation Testbed 2003, p. 13): Digital records are not simply the 21st century equivalent of traditional paper records. They have other properties, characteristics and applications. However, both digital and paper records must meet the same legal requirements. In practice, this requires a different approach. ¶ Digital records are not tangible objects like a book or a magazine, but a combination of hardware, software and computer files. This combination is necessary to be able to use the documents or examine them. In the context of Testbed we looked specifically at text documents, databases, email messages and spreadsheets. Multimedia documents, digital video and sound can also be digital records, but these remained outside the scope of this study. ¶ An important difference compared to paper records is the greater loss of information that can occur even while the records are being used, or afterwards when the records are being maintained. After all, hard discs and computers are replaced regularly and there are few barriers to destroying computer files. A single click on the 'delete' button and a record disappears without leaving a trace.

†275 (Suderman 2001): Records in the electronic environment have unique characteristics . . . durability; lifespan; maintenance; ease of editing, copying, erasure, and reformatting (manipulability); ease of manipulation, including the difficulty of tracing manipulation; need for supporting documentation to describe the contents, arrangement, codes, and technical characteristics; need for specialized personnel for the processing and maintenance of the records, introducing a new player in the normal clique of archivist, creator, and user. [Referencing Harold Naugler.]

electronic recordkeeping system, n. ~ A computer application that can collect, organize, and categorize records to facilitate their management, preservation, retrieval, use, and disposition.

RT: records management application, system

Notes: 'Electronic recordkeeping system' includes applications that manage the records of a single workflow process or that can receive electronic records created in external systems.

electronic seal, n. ~ A technique to demonstrate that the content of an electronic document has not been altered or, in some cases, read.

> *BT:* seal
>
> *Notes:* Electronic seals serve similar functions to physical seals. A seal[2,3] bearing a distinctive mark associated with an individual or office gives the document authenticity. A seal[4] on a closed container can prevent unauthorized access, and an unbroken seal on container indicates that no one has had opportunity to alter the thing sealed.
>
> Electronic seals perform similar functions of demonstrating the authenticity of the sender, the unchanged nature of the content, and – in some instances – to protect the content from unauthorized access. Electronic seals usually involve the use of digital signatures, especially public key infrastructure.

electronic signature, n. ~ A digital mark, code, or other symbol that identifies an individual and that indicates responsibility for or consent to the content of the material to which it is affixed.

> *BT:* extrinsic element, signature
>
> *NT:* digital signature
>
> *RT:* digital certificate
>
> *Notes:* Electronic signatures range from simple to highly complex and secure. They may be nothing more than a name typed in ASCII characters at the end of the body of a document. They may also be computer code using encryption keys to demonstrate that the message has not be altered and to authenticate the identity of the signer.

Electronic Signatures in Global and National Commerce Act, n. (**ESIGN**, abbr.) ~ A federal law giving an electronic signature the same legal status as one that is written by hand.

> *Notes:* Pub. L. 106-229, 114 Stat. 464 (2000), codified at 15 U.S.C. §7001 et seq.
>
> †*79 (NTIA 2003):* Congress passed ESIGN in June 2000 to facilitate the use of electronic documents and signatures in domestic interstate and international commercial transactions. The Act was designed to promote the use of electronic signatures in commercial transactions involving both businesses and consumers and to ensure that the electronic documents and signatures resulting from these transactions are given the same legal validity and enforceability as written documents and signatures.

electrophotography, n. ~ A process that forms images using the photoelectric properties of sensitive substances.

> *RT:* photograph
>
> *Notes:* Electrophotography includes electrostatic (xerographic), dielectric paper, electroplastic, and persistent internal polarization processes. It has been used for microfilm that can be updated, allowing new images to be added after creation or existing images to be overwritten with new images.
>
> The dielectric paper process uses paper coated with a photoconductive pigment in a binder resin. The electro-plastic process uses a plastic film coated with a photoconductive layer; exposure to light causes a stress in the plastic and, when heated, the plastic deforms to reveal the image.

electrostatic process (also **electrostatography**), n. ~ A technique for making reproductions, often called photocopies, by using charged pigments to create an image of the original on paper or film.

RT: copy, photocopy, print, reproduction, thermography

Notes: The electrostatic process uses the photoelectric properties of certain metals. An image of the original is projected onto a light-sensitive substance, creating a charge relative to the light and dark portions of the original. The charge on the surface attracts or repels toner, a charged pigment, that duplicates the original. In a direct positive, the image is formed directly on paper or film. In an indirect process, the image is formed on a metallic drum that is then transferred to paper or film.

Sometimes called **xerography**, derived from the tradename Xerox.

element of description ~ see: descriptive element

elevation, n. ~ An orthographic drawing of the vertical surfaces of a built structure rendered from a vantage point perpendicular to the structure.

BT: architectural records, drawing

RT: oblique, perspective

Notes: An elevation may be of the front, side, or back of a building or may be of an interior wall. An elevation gives no sense of recession into three dimensions.

ELF ~ see: eliminate legal-size files

eliminate legal-size files, n. (ELF, abbr.) ~ RECORDS MANAGEMENT · An initiative of ARMA to promote the use of letter sized paper instead of legal size paper in order to minimize costs associated with creating and filing the larger documents.

Notes: Sometimes **end legal-sized files, folders, or forms**.

†241 (BC Ministry of Forests 1997): The goal of government-wide ELF program is to reduce administrative costs by eliminating legal-size paper in favor of letter-size paper. Letter-size records: reduce costs by eliminating the need to purchase file supplies and equipment to accommodate multiple paper sizes; reduce inefficiencies associated with files containing multi-size documents (e.g., it is often difficult to find letter-size records inter-filed with legal-size records); reduce accommodation costs by reducing the amount of floor space required to store records; reduce paper consumption; reduce mailing costs (letter-size paper is 21% smaller and 24% lighter than legal-size paper) between different systems.

email ~ see: electronic mail

emboss, v. ~ The process of creating a raised design on a surface.

RT: stamp

Notes: The design created by embossing is called an embossment. Blind embossing does not use color, and the design is the same color as the background. Embossing may incorporate ink, foil, or other color to further distinguish the raised design from the background, but the term alone – without the modifier 'blind' – does not connote such color.

emergency destruction, n. ~ The immediate destruction of records under extraordinary circumstances, as provided by law or regulation.

Notes: Emergency destruction may take place in time of war to prevent sensitive information from being captured by a foreign power or to record the effective, premature destruction of records as the result of a disaster.

emergency-operating records, n. ~ Records necessary for an organization to resume basic, emergency operations immediately after a disaster.

BT: record

RT: business continuation and disaster recovery, essential records, vital records

Notes: Vital records[2], also called essential records, include emergency operating records and rights-and-interests records. Emergency records are typically stored in paper format to avoid machine and power dependence, and describe responsibilities, including delegation of authority and line of succession. Examples include the records necessary to mobilize and protect manpower and resources, and to ensure health, safety, and order. Government agencies may also include records relating to the mobilization of the military, civil defense, and public heath. Rights-and-interests records include those records necessary after initial recovery to protect the assets and rights of the organization, its employees, and others. Rights-and-interests records may include payroll, leave and insurance records, titles and deeds to real property, contracts, and other similar data.

emulation, n. ~ The use of one system to reproduce the functions and results of another system.

†132 *(GAO 2002, p. 45):* A proposed approach to the problem of software and hardware dependence is emulation, which aims to preserve the original software environment in which records were created. Emulation mimics the functionality of older software (generally operating systems) and hardware. . . . This technique seeks to recreate a digital document's original functionality, look, and feel by reproducing, on current computer systems, the behavior of the older system on which the document was created.

emulsion, n. ~ 1. A suspension of a liquid in another liquid without being dissolved. – 2. Photography · The material that contains the light-sensitive substance and binds it to the support.

RT: gelatin emulsion

Notes: Chemically speaking, a photographic emulsion is not an emulsion because it is not a liquid. It is a colloidal suspension.

encapsulation, n. ~ 1. Conservation · The process of placing a document between two sheets of plastic (usually polyester), which are sealed at the edges, in order to provide support and to protect it from handling and from the atmosphere. – 2. Computing · The combination of several digital objects into a single unit that preserves the association of those objects.

RT: lamination, silking

Notes: Encapsulation[1] does nothing to protect against the continued chemical deterioration of the document within the enclosure, and the creation of a microclimate may accelerate its deterioration. However, the technique provides significant support and protection for fragile documents. Unlike heat lamination, the document is not permanently fixed to the enclosure and can be easily removed.

Encapsulation[2] may be used, for example, to combine an electronic record, metadata, and a viewer to render the record.

enclosure, n. ~ A container used to store materials.

Notes: Examples of enclosures include sleeves, boxes, canisters.

Encoded Archival Context, n. (**EAC,** abbr.) ~ A standard to mark up (encode) information relating to the circumstances of record creation and use, including the identification, characteristics, and interrelationships of the organizations, persons, and families who created, used, or were the subject of the records.

RT: administrative history, context, markup, Toronto Tenets

Notes: EAC is defined in a document type definition (DTD) that is compatible with both Standard Generalized Markup Language (SGML) or extensible markup language (XML). It is intended to extend and complement Encoded Archival Description (EAD).

†226 (Pitti 2003): The description of individuals, families, and organizations that create records is an essential component of the preservation of the documentary evidence of human activity. Identifying record creating entities; recording the names or designations used by and for them; and describing their essential functions, activities, and characteristics, and the dates and places they were active is an essential component of the management of archival records. Creator description facilitates both access to and interpretation of records.

Encoded Archival Description, n. (**EAD,** abbr.) ~ A standard used to mark up (encode) finding aids that reflects the hierarchical nature of archival collections and that provides a structure for describing the whole of a collection, as well as its components.

RT: archival description, descriptive standard, finding aid, markup, Standard Generalized Markup Language

Notes: EAD is defined as a document type definition (DTD) that is compatible with both Standard Generalized Markup Language (SGML) and extensible markup language (XML). See the related standards *Encoded Archival Description: Application Guidelines,* ver. 1.0 (Society of American Archivists, 1999); and *Encoded Archival Description: Tag Library,* ver. 2002 (Society of American Archivists, 2003);

†85 (Feeney 1999, p. 207–208): [EAD] is intended to provide repositories with a means of establishing an effective, accessible, and stable presence for their holdings information. EAD accommodates variations in the length and content of finding aids within and among repositories, and preserves in electronic form the complex, hierarchically structured descriptive information found in archival repositories and registers, while also enabling the documents to be navigated and searched in ways that their printed counterparts cannot.

encryption, n. ~ The process of rendering plaintext unintelligible by converting it to ciphertext that can be read only by those with the knowledge to decode the plaintext from the ciphertext.

RT: cryptography, decoding, key

encyclopedic arrangement, n. ~ A hierarchical method of organizing materials first by major concepts, then by related, subsidiary topics.

Syn: classified filing

Notes: Materials organized by location often use encyclopedic arrangement, grouping materials first by state, then by city, and finally by a specific entry, such as a name. Encyclopedic arrangement may be used for organizing files or entries in a document.

end legal-sized files ~ *see:* eliminate legal-size files

endorsement (also **indorsement**), n. ~ 1. A signature on the back of a document, especially a check or other negotiable instrument. – 2. The signature itself. – 3. Official or personal approval or recommendation.

Notes: An endorsement may include additional notes, such as a qualification that limits the liability to subsequent parties if the instrument is invalid or a restriction that places limits on the use of the instrument.

enduring value, n. ~ The continuing usefulness or significance of records, based on the administrative, legal, fiscal, evidential, or historical information they contain, justifying their ongoing preservation.

> *Syn:* archival value, continuing value
> *BT:* value
> *RT:* permanent value
> *Notes:* Many archivists prefer to describe archival records as having 'enduring value' or 'continuing value', rather than 'permanent value'. 'Enduring value' emphasizes the perceived value of the records when they are appraised, recognizing that a future archivist may reappraise the records and dispose of them. The phrases are often used interchangeably.

energiatype, n. ~ A photographic process using iron salts on paper; a ferrotype.

> *Syn:* ferrotype

engineering drawing, n. ~ A schematic representation of a building, object, or component made according to precise conventions and intended to aid in the construction or fabrication of the thing depicted.

> *BT:* drawing
> *RT:* architectural drawing, technical drawing
> *Notes:* Engineering drawings are frequently used to describe public works projects, such as bridges, highways, and dams.

engineering records, n. ~ Drawings and supporting documents intended to aid in the construction or fabrication of a building, object, or component.

> *DF:* architectural records
> *BT:* record
> *NT:* design drawing
> *Notes:* 'Engineering records' connotes subjects other than buildings, the latter described as 'architectural records'. However, engineering records may include subjects that relate to a building, such as drawings of a mechanical system. Engineering records are distinguished from architectural records, the former emphasizing functionality over aesthetics.

engraving, n. ~ 1. A design incised into a surface of an object. – 2. A print made from an engraved plate. – 3. A sound recording made using a cutting stylus to make an analog signal as the groove is cut.

> *DF:* etching
> *BT:* intaglio
> *RT:* print
> *Notes:* An engraving[2] is made by scoring a design into a plate. The plate is then inked, and the surface wiped, leaving ink in the incised design. The engraved plate is then pressed against paper to force the paper into the ink. Sometimes 'engraving' is used to describe all prints, including prints made using other processes.

engrossed copy, n. ~ The final version of a document in its prescribed form, especially a bill passed by one chamber of a legislature.

> *BT:* bill, copy
> *RT:* enrolled bill, fair copy
> *†110 (NARA Senate Records):* The engrossed copy of a bill that has passed both Houses together with its engrossed amendments is the official working copy from which an enrolled bill is prepared.

enlargement, n. ~ A reproduction larger than the original; a **blow-up**.

> *NT:* crayon enlargement
>
> *Notes:* Commonly used to describe photographic prints larger than a standard size print. Although 3 × 5 or 4 × 6 inch prints made from 35 mm negatives are technically enlargements, the term is typically used to describe prints that are 5 × 7 inches or larger.

enlargement ratio ~ *see:* magnification

enlarger-printer, n. ~ An optical device for producing enlargements, incorporating processing facilities for the rapid production of hard copy, usually under conditions of room lighting.

> *DF:* reader-printer
>
> *Notes:* An enlarger-printer is typically designed for making large-scale prints (17 × 22 inches or larger). It is not intended for use as a reader.

enrolled bill, n. ~ A bill passed by both chambers of a legislature and signed by the presiding officers.

> *BT:* bill
>
> *RT:* engrossed copy
>
> †110 (NARA Senate Records): [An enrolled bill is] printed on paper (formerly copied by a clerk in a fair, round hand on parchment) and is signed first by the Speaker of the House and second by the President of the Senate. On the back is an attestation by the Clerk of the House or the Secretary of the Senate, as the case may be, indicating the House of origin. The enrolled bill is presented to the President for his approval or disapproval.

enterprise architecture, n. ~ A method to relate an organization's goals and objectives to a technology system that integrates all of the organization's data and business processes.

> *NT:* technical reference model
>
> *RT:* information architecture
>
> †132 (GAO 2002, p. 75): An enterprise architecture . . . describes an agency in both 1) logical terms, such as the interrelated business processes and business rules, information needs and flows, and work locations and users; and 2) technical terms, such as hardware, software, data, communications, and security attributes and standards. An enterprise architecture provides these perspectives both for the current environment and for the target environment, as well as a transition plan for sequencing from the current to the target environment.

enterprise content management ~ *see:* content management

entitling, n. ~ DIPLOMATICS · The name, title, capacity, and address of the physical juridical person issuing a document, or of which the author of the document is an agent.

entity, n. ~ 1. A thing. – 2. SYSTEMS MODELING · A member of a set that has defined characteristics.

> *RT:* digital object
>
> *Notes:* An entity[1] may be tangible or intangible, animate or inanimate, or corporate or individual. – Entity[2] refers generally to all objects or agents of the system being analyzed. Characteristics are equivalent to the concept of digital object properties. However, entities do not share the digital objects notion of class and methods.
>
> †56 (DACS): (entities[1]) The corporate bodies, persons, or families associated in

some way with the creation, accumulation, maintenance, and/or use of archival materials.

entity of origin, n. ~ The corporate body, administrative unit, family, or individual that creates, receives, or accumulates a body of records, personal papers, or objects.

    RT: creator, office of origin, provenance

entrance interview ~ *see:* reference interview

entry, n. ~ 1. A reference to an item in a list, register, or catalog. – 2. A heading used to organize information. – 3. CATALOGING · The word or phrase under which the description of a work is organized in a list, register, or catalog.

    NT: added entry, main entry, subject entry, title entry

    RT: access point, complex entry, heading, inverted entry, name-title reference, open entry

entry word, n. ~ The first word in a heading, other than an article, under which a heading is sorted.

    Notes: The Cat in the Hat is sorted under the entry word 'cat'. However, if an article is integral to the phrase, it may serve as the entry word; for example, *El Paso City Directory* would be arranged under 'el'.

envelope, n. ~ 1. An enclosure for a flat or folded document, especially one used for sending mail. – 2. A digital entity used for sending electronic mail or messages, consisting of a header for addressing and defining the contents of a message and a body for containing a message.

    Notes: An envelope[1] is typically made of paper, folded and glued so that one side remains open to allow a flat document to be inserted, possibly after being folded, and with a flap that allows the envelope to be sealed. Standard size envelopes include letter (approximately 4 × 6 inches, 10 × 15 cm) and legal or C10 (approximately 4 × 9 inches, 10 × 23 cm).

environmental control, n. ~ The process of creating and maintaining storage or display conditions appropriate to protect materials from adverse effects of temperature, humidity, air quality, light, and biological infestation, as well as human risks associated with housekeeping procedures, security, and fire and water damage.

    RT: microenvironment

ephemera, pl. n. (**ephemeron**, sing.) ~ Materials, usually printed documents, created for a specific, limited purpose, and generally designed to be discarded after use.

    Notes: Examples of ephemera include advertisements, tickets, brochures, and receipts. A repository may collect ephemera as examples or specimens. Individuals often collect ephemera as mementos or souvenirs because of their association with some person, event, or subject; personal collections of ephemera are often kept in scrapbooks.

ephemeral value, n. ~ Useful or significant for a limited period of time.

    BT: value

    RT: transitory record

    Notes: Records of ephemeral value, such as transitory records, are often scheduled to be destroyed after use.

epigraph, n. ~ 1. A quotation used as an opening of a book, chapter, or section of a document, typically to set a tone or introduce a theme. – 2. An inscription, especially on a monument or building.

    †264 (Sickinger 1999, p. 232): One of the characteristic features of ancient Athenian democracy was its habit of displaying certain types of state documents

on stone stelai – large rectangular slabs of marble. . . . Epigraphists who spend their time studying inscriptions have traditionally assumed that these stone documents were copies of other, original records housed in archival collections. . . . One difficulty with this traditional view is the failure of Athenian sources to acknowledge the existence of archival originals.

episode, n. ~ MOVING IMAGES · An individual program that is part of a larger series or serial.

> *RT:* moving image, part
>
> *Notes:* The episode title, with the series or serial title, forms an integral part of the title proper in the catalog record of a moving image or sound recording work.

EPrints, n. ~ 1. Copies of drafts (preprints) and final versions (postprints) of articles published in refereed journals that are freely accessible online. – 2. Software that supports the acquisition and storage of articles for online access.

> *RT:* Open Archives Initiative, preprint
>
> *Notes:* The EPrints initiative (see http://www.eprints.org/) had its origins at the University of Southampton in the United Kingdom. It encourages authors to make the products of their research rapidly and easily accessible in order to maximize and accelerate the impact of that research, in hopes of greater outcomes in productivity, progress, and rewards. Although not required to be considered an EPrints archives, the project encourages the use of open archives initiative (OAI) protocols to make the materials widely accessible.

equivalence relation, n. ~ The association between terms that, for indexing purposes, are treated as the same concept.

> *BT:* reference
>
> *RT:* related term
>
> *Notes:* In thesaurus construction, preferred and nonpreferred (lead-in) terms are associated using 'use' and 'use for'. One term is established as the preferred term, and equivalent terms point to that term. The terms may not be exactly synonymous, but the preferred term is used to bring closely related concepts together for improved access.

erase, v. ~ 1. To remove by making invisible, especially by rubbing or wiping. – 2. COMPUTING · To make information irretrievable by overwriting it. – 3. AUDIO-VIDEO · To neutralize the magnetic field from magnetic tape, removing any existing signal.

> *DF:* deletion
>
> *Notes:* Erasure[1] is not always perfectly invisible; the original markings may not be entirely removed or may leave a physical indentation. The intent is to create a space that is sufficiently clean for new information to be written. Erasure[1,2] both are clearly distinguished from deletion. In the case of written document, deleted information is clearly marked but may remain legible. In the case of computer files, deletion implies that pointers to the files are removed from the directory, but the data remains untouched on the media; erasure requires a further effort to ensure that the data is made unreadable.

error, n. ~ 1. A mistake. – 2. A deviation from what is correct or specified by standard. – 3. STATISTICS · The difference between an observed or calculated value and the theoretical correct value, especially resulting from variations in measurement. – 4. COMPUTING · A failure of software or hardware that produces an incorrect result or a failure in the system. – 4. LAW · A mistake in a court's opinion, judgment, or order.

> *RT:* accuracy, alteration, precision

BT: Broader Term · *NT:* Narrower Term · *RT:* Related Term · *DF:* Distinguish From

Notes: Error[1] includes poor judgment in a decision or the belief that something false is true or the converse. – Error[2,3] is generally relative. The degree to which something deviates from a standard or theoretical value is measured in terms of its accuracy. The ability of a system to measure the difference depends on the precision of the system.

†48 (*CJS, Records §21*): Defects or errors in public records may be corrected in order to make them conform to the facts. However, amendments are subject to the rights of third persons. ¶ Those having authority to do so may correct a record in order to make it conform to the truth. . . . In fact, it has been held that it is the duty of the recording officer to correct mistakes and to supply omissions in records whenever he discovers them from data in his office. ¶ Changes in a public record may be made only by or under official authority.

error detection and correction code, n. ~ A short sequence of characters associated with a message that makes it possible to determine if the message has been corrupted and, if necessary, repaired.

RT: checksum

Notes: Error detection may be implemented without error correction. A hash value is an example of an error detection code. Recalculating the hash value can provide assurance that the original message has not changed. Error correcting codes include enough information to enable the original message to be reconstituted; Reed-Solomon is an example of an error correcting code method.

eschatocol, n. ~ DIPLOMATICS · The final section of a document, which may include a formulaic sentence of appreciation, and the attestation of those responsible for the document (the author, the writer, or the countersigner, and any witnesses to the enactment or the subscription).

BT: intrinsic element

Notes: Example of formulaic appreciation include 'sincerely', 'your humble servant', or 'yours truly'. The attestation is the most essential part of the eschatocol.

ESIGN ~ *see:* Electronic Signatures in Global and National Commerce Act

essential records, n. ~ Emergency-operating records immediately necessary to begin recovery of operations after a disaster, and rights-and-interests records necessary to protect the assets, obligations, and resources of the organization, as well as its employees and customers or citizens; vital records[2].

DF: vital records

BT: record

NT: rights-and-interests records

RT: business continuation and disaster recovery, emergency-operating records, important records, security copy

Notes: Essential records typically document delegation of authority and line of succession, and include legal documents and contracts, financial records, and other rights-and-interests records.

estray, n. ~ A document not in the possession of the authorized custodian, especially government records in private hands.

RT: alienation, removed archives

estray record, n. ~ A register giving public notice of valuable, tame animals, either lost or found wandering and presumed escaped from their owners, allowing the owners to reclaim the animals.

BT: record

etching, n. ~ 1. A process to remove selected portions from a surface to create a design. – 2. A print made from an etched plate using such a process.

> *DF:* engraving
>
> *BT:* intaglio
>
> *RT:* print
>
> *Notes:* Etchings are typically made using a corrosive chemical or electrolysis. They are distinguished from engravings by the fact that the latter are created using a tool to cut into the surface.

ethylene oxide, n. ~ A biocide used as a fumigant to kill mold and to sterilize materials.

> †118 *(Hengemihle, Weberg, and Shahani 1995):* Over the past several decades, ethylene oxide gained such wide acceptance in the library and archival preservation world, that in spite of the risks its usage presents, it has not been easy to replace with another fumigant. . . . A little over ten years ago, several public and private repositories routinely fumigated materials that were even remotely suspected of mold or insect infestation. For example, the U.S. National Archives subjected all incoming records to ethylene oxide fumigation as a precautionary measure for several decades. Now we know that ethylene oxide can be deadly not just for mold and insects, but also for us if it is not used within accepted limits.

evaluation, n. ~ The process of assessing the value of records, especially as regards their destruction.

> *DF:* appraisal
>
> *RT:* valuation, value
>
> *Notes:* Evaluation is typically used by records managers to indicate a preliminary assessment of value based on existing retention schedules. It is distinguished from appraisal, which is typically used by archivists to describe their assessment of the value of records, especially as regards a determination of whether records should be transferred to the archives for permanent preservation.

evidence, n. ~ 1. Something that is used to support an understanding or argument. – 2. LAW · A record, an object, testimony, or other material that is used to prove or disprove a fact.

> *RT:* admissibility, business exception rule, constructive notice, hearsay rule
>
> *Notes:* In order for a record to be accepted as credible evidence, it is necessary to demonstrate that the record is authentic and reliable, that it is not fraudulent, and that its content is sufficient and accurate. The Federal Rules of Evidence (and similar state rules) distinguish documents and records; while both are subject to discovery, only business records are admissible as evidence under the business exception rule to the hearsay rule.
>
> †167 *(D Levy 2001, p. 16):* The receipt is meant to function as 'proof of purchase,' as evidence that an exchange of money for goods actually took place. Coming into being at the very time and place the food was prepared and the goods were delivered, the receipt serves as witness to these facts.
>
> †180 *(MacNeil 2000, p. 40):* The Latin word *evidence* means 'that which is manifest of in plain sight.' In its metaphoric sense, evidence is that which brings the invisible (that is, a past event) back into plain sight.

evidential value, n. ~ 1. The quality of records that provides information about the origins, functions, and activities of their creator. – 2. LAW · The importance or usefulness of something to prove or disprove a fact.

BT: value

Notes: Evidential value[1] relates to the process of creation rather than the content (informational value) of the records.

†62 *(Dollar 1991, p. 45):* A growing number of archivists are now urging that archival appraisal return to basics and pay more attention to the documentation of program accountability, which suggests that the informational value of information application systems may be eclipsed by their evidential value.

†259 *(Schellenberg 1984, p. 58):* The secondary value of records can be ascertained most easily if they are considered in relation to two kinds of matters: 1) the evidence they contain of the organization and functions of the Government body that produced them, and 2) the information they contain on persons, corporate bodies, things, problems, conditions, and the like, with which the Government body dealt. ¶ The value that attaches to records because of the evidence they contain of organization and function will be called 'evidential values.' By this term I do not refer to the value that inhere in public records because of any special quality of merit they have a documentary evidence. I do not refer, in the sense of English archivists Sir Hilary Jenkinson, to the sanctity of the evidence in archives that is derived from 'unbroken custody,' or from the way they came into the hands of the archivist. I refer rather, and quite arbitrarily, to the value that depends on the character and importance of the matter evidenced, i.e., the origin and the substantive programs of the agency that produced the records. The quality of the evidence *per se* is thus not the issue here, but the character of the matter evidenced.

exceptional sampling, n. ~ A technique of selecting a subset based on unusual or important qualities.

BT: sampling

Notes: Examples of criteria used for exceptional sampling include controversial subjects, notorious or famous individuals, and 'firsts.' Although not statistically valid, exceptional sampling can frequently capture materials commonly requested by patrons.

excerpt, n. ~ A portion of a larger work reproduced without change to the content.

RT: clip

Notes: An excerpt is often a distinct part of the larger work, such as a chapter of a textual document or a scene or sequence in a moving image. In moving images, an excerpt is generally longer than a clip.

executive communications, n. ~ 1. Letters, speeches, or other messages sent from the office of a high-ranking official in an organization. – 2. RECORDS · Letters, reports, or other messages from the Executive Branch of government sent to Congress and recorded as House documents.

Notes: Executive communications[2] include presidential messages, as well as annual and special reports from executive agencies.

executive information system, n. ~ A user interface to complex data designed to assist senior managers by summarizing, integrating, and analyzing current information so that they can quickly and effectively monitor operations and trends.

RT: data warehouse, system

Notes: Executive information systems often, but not always, use online analytical processes (OLAP) built on top of a data warehouse.

†212 *(MIT Urban Studies and Planning 1996, http://yerkes.mit.edu/NARC/ Technology/Data%20Analysis/executiveinfosys.html):* Whereas the traditional focus

of Management Information Systems (MIS) has been on the storage and processing of large amounts of information, the focus of EIS is on the retrieval of specific
information about the daily operational status of the organization's activities.
Whereas the purpose of an EIS is the monitoring and scanning of the environment
to give executives rapid exposure to changes in the environment, the purpose of
Decision Support Systems (DSS) is to support ad hoc decisions as well as routine
analysis. And while the core of DSS is extensive modeling and analysis capabilities,
the core of EIS is status information about the organization's performance. Expert
Systems use artificial intelligence to go beyond basic decision support.

executive procedure, n. ~ Diplomatics · A set of processes for conducting regular
affairs of business according to rules established by an external authority.
> *BT:* procedure

executive session, n. ~ A meeting of the members of a board or governing body and
invited guests that is closed to the public and the press and may also be closed to
staff and guests.
> *BT:* hearing
>
> *Notes:* If testimony is taken, an executive session may be called an executive
> hearing. Most governments in the United States are controlled by open meeting
> laws that regulate the conditions under which an executive session may be called
> and any business that may be conducted at such a meeting.

executive support system, n. ~ A software application that provides a high-level user
interface to complex data, summarizing and analyzing current information about
operations and trends.
> *BT:* information system
>
> *RT:* system
>
> *Notes:* Executive support systems include tools that support analysis of and
> interaction with complex data and that facilitate communication among senior
> management to assist decision making.

exemplary sampling, n. ~ A technique of selecting a limited number of typical items
to represent the a larger group.
> *BT:* sampling
>
> *Notes:* Taking all the files of one regional office to suggest how other regional
> offices operate is an example of exemplary sampling.

exemplification, n. ~ Diplomatics · Copies made directly from the original and
signed by the author of the original.

exhibition (also **exhibit**), n. ~ 1. An organized display of materials. – 2. A public
demonstration of skills.
> *Notes:* An exhibition[1] generally includes materials such as artworks, docu-
> ments, or objects that have been selected and ordered so that their interaction
> demonstrates an idea or theme for cultural or educational purposes. The selection
> of materials for an exhibit is sometimes called curation, and the individual
> responsible a curator.

exhibition case, n. ~ A cabinet with a transparent top or sides, typically made from
glass or Plexiglas, that protects materials while on exhibit.
> *Syn:* display case, show case

existing light, n. ~ Photography · Illumination not supplied by the photographer;
available light.

Notes: 'Existing light' includes natural light from the sun, moon, or sky, and also includes room light that was not supplied specifically for the act of making the photograph. It is distinguished from 'artificial light', which a photographer supplies by using flash or lamps. Existing light photography implies low light levels that require special techniques to capture the image without supplemental light.

exit interview, n. ~ A formal conversation between a reference archivist and a patron that is designed to evaluate the success of the research visit and the effectiveness of the reference service offered to the research.

RT: reference interview

Notes: An exit interview is the final part of the reference interview, which begins with an entrance or orientation interview and follows the use of materials.

expense-reduction justification, n. ~ A technique to justify new equipment or procedures by demonstrating that existing costs will decrease.

experiential system, n. ~ A software system that accurately renders the characteristic sensations a user would experience when interacting with the original of the thing rendered.

BT: system

Notes: Coined by Clifford Lynch.

†175 (C Lynch 2000, p. 37): In meatspace, we cheerfully extend the notion of authenticity to much more than objects – in fact, we explicitly apply it to the experiential sphere, speaking of an 'authentic' performance of a baroque concerto or an 'authentic' Hawaiian luau. To the extent that we can make the extension and expansion of the use of authenticity as a characteristic precise within the framework and terminology of this paper, these statements seem to parallel statements about integrity of what in the digital environment could be viewed as experiential works, or performance.

expert system, n. ~ A class of artificial intelligence program used in problem solving through the use of a specialized collection of facts and rules of inference.

RT: system

Notes: An expert system is created by interviewing many experts in a field to determine rules of thumb that guide their decision-making process. Those rules are organized into a formal heuristic system. Those rules often do not make either-or decisions but use fuzzy logic. Expert systems generally perform well in a very specific area of knowledge.

explanatory reference record, n. ~ DESCRIPTION · A truncated or otherwise stylized or exemplary form combined with other information that serves a) to inform the user of a convention that applies generally or to a defined category of headings and b) to provide guidance in searching for such headings.

exploitation film, n. ~ Motion pictures, typically made with low budgets, low production values, and an eye to quick profits, about a subject that is often sensational, prurient, or violent.

†151 (Johnson 1999): Exploitation cinema arose as an alternative to Hollywood cinema. While the major studios were forced to follow the Motion Picture Production Code, the exploiteers could film virtually anything they wanted, as long as they wrapped their productions in a cloak of moralizing. These movies typically began with scrolling text that warned the audiences about a social problem (drug addiction, prostitution, venereal disease, etc.). Or they began with a lec-

turer who warned the audience about the dangers of the vices depicted in the film. This framing method is one of the hallmarks of exploitation cinema. It could be used to justify showing almost anything on film – drug parties, skinny dipping, opium dens, etc. – as long as the exploiteers also feigned disgust and claimed a higher purpose.

exposition, n. ~ DIPLOMATICS · The beginning of the substance of the text that provides background to the circumstances that cause the document to be written.

> *BT:* intrinsic element

> *†70 (Duranti 1998, p. 146):* The substance of the text is usually introduced by the exposition, that is the narration of the concrete and immediate circumstances generating the act and/or document. In documents resulting from procedures, whether public or private, the exposition may include the memory of the various procedural phases, or be entirely constituted by the mention of one or more of them.

exposure, n. ~ 1. Coming into contact with something. – 2. PHOTOGRAPHY · The intensity and duration of light or other radiant energy to make a photographic image. – 3. PHOTOGRAPHY · The image produced by the action of light on photosensitive material; a shot. – 4. PUBLIC RELATIONS · Visibility in the public media.

> *RT:* shot, underexposure

expunge, v. ~ 1. To erase or destroy completely. – 2. To remove a person's criminal conviction from the court records.

> *†48 (CJS, Records (§28)):* Where an instrument not entitled to be recorded is recorded, it should be expunged or erased from the record, and appropriate proceedings may be maintained to secure its cancellation.

Extended Binary Coded Decimal Interchange Code ~ *see:* EBCDIC

> *Notes:* Almost always abbreviated.

extended-term storage, n. ~ Storage conditions with relative humidity, temperature, and other controls that will ensure that information will remain intact and useful for 500 years.

> *RT:* life expectancy

> *Notes:* The specific conditions will vary with the materials.

Extensible Hypertext Markup Language, n. (**XHTML**, abbr.) ~ A revision of the Hypertext Markup Language standard HTML 4.0 that conforms with the Extensible Markup Language standard XML 1.0.

> *RT:* Hypertext Markup Language, markup

> *Notes:* XHTML defines codes to format and provide limited structure to hypertext or hypermedia documents, especially for the web.

> *†127 (W3C HTML):* With a wealth of features, XHTML 1.0 is a reformulation of HTML 4.01 in XML, and combines the strength of HTML 4 with the power of XML. ¶ XHTML 1.0 is the first major change to HTML since HTML 4.0 was released in 1997. It brings the rigor of XML to Web pages and is the keystone in W3C's work to create standards that provide richer Web pages on an ever increasing range of browser platforms including cell phones, televisions, cars, wallet sized wireless communicators, kiosks, and desktops. ¶ XHTML 1.0 is the first step and the HTML Working Group is busy on the next. XHTML 1.0 reformulates HTML as an XML application. This makes it easier to process and easier to maintain. XHTML 1.0 borrows elements and attributes from W3C's earlier work on HTML 4, and can be interpreted by existing browsers, by following a few simple guidelines.

Extensible Markup Language, n. (**XML**, abbr.) ~ A standard to promote sharing information over the Internet by specifying ways to describe the information's semantic structure and to validate that the structure is well formed.

BT: Standard Generalized Markup Language

RT: Hypertext Markup Language, markup, simple object access protocol

Notes: XML is described as extensible because it is a metalanguage that allows the creation of tags to be used for semantic markup. The greatest value of XML can be realized through common vocabularies of tags, so that applications can use those vocabularies to understand documents from different sources.

†64 *(Doyle 2001, p. 3):* XML documents are containers for information. Within the primary container may be information and more containers, which themselves may contain information and more containers. These named containers form neatly hierarchical structures, creating an incredibly flexible and remarkably powerful framework for storing and exchanging information of all kinds, from memos to database tables to poetry to program structures to invoices. XML documents may also include or reference sets of rules describing their structures, which applications may use to validate that documents conform to those rules.

Extensible Stylesheet Language, n. (**XSL**, abbr.) ~ A standard to indicate how an Extensible Markup Language (XML) document is to be formatted for user display.

Notes: XSL is defined by the World Wide Web Consortium (W3C). XSL differs from Cascading Style Sheets (CSS) in two main areas. XSL cannot be used with Hypertext Markup Language (HTML) documents, and XSL has the ability to use Extensible Stylesheet Language Transforms (XSLT) to change an XML document to another XML document with a different structure.

Extensible Stylesheet Language Transforms, n. (**XSLT**, abbr.) ~ A metalanguage that describes rules to convert an XML document with one set of tags to a different XML document with different tags, effectively changing the structure of the document.

Notes: XSLT is part of the Extensible Stylesheet Language (XSL) standard. It is commonly used to transform documents created or stored in XML to XHTML for display using different devices, ranging from computer monitors to PDAs to telephones.

extent, n. ~ CATALOGING · An description of the physical quantity of the material described.

BT: descriptive element

RT: count, dimension

Notes: In descriptive cataloging, extent is the first element of the physical description area and includes the number and the specific material designation of the material being described, and other details depending on format.

extract, n. ~ A portion taken from a larger item.

RT: abstract

extraction indexing, n. ~ A technique using words and phrases found in text, rather than a controlled vocabulary, to provide the headings used in an index.

BT: indexing

RT: automatic indexing

extranet, n. ~ A technology that gives authorized outsiders access to all or part of an organization's restricted resources on its network.

RT: Internet, intranet

Notes: Extranets often allow access over the Internet, using firewalls or virtual private network (VPN) software to block unauthorized access.

extrinsic element, n. ~ The physical and formal characteristics that constitute a document's material nature and appearance, independent of its intellectual content.

NT: annotation, electronic signature, medium, script, seal, special sign, time stamp

RT: intrinsic element, physical form

Notes: Extrinsic elements include medium, script[1], language, special signs, seals, and annotations.

†17 (InterPARES Authenticity, p. 5): Extrinsic elements refer to specific, perceivable features of the record that are instrumental in communicating and achieving the purpose for which it was created. For electronic records, these include: overall presentation features (e.g., textual, graphic, image, sound, or some combination of these); specific presentation features (e.g., special layouts, hyperlinks, colors, sample rate or sound files); electronic signatures and electronic seals (e.g., digital signatures); digital time stamps; other special signs (e.g., digital watermarks, an organization's crest or personal logo).

eye-readable, adj. ~ 1. Capable of being recognized and understood without mechanical assistance. – 2. MICROGRAPHICS · Able to be read without magnification.

Syn: human-readable

Notes: Microfilm is generally not considered eye-readable[1] because it requires magnification. However, some people consider it ultimately eye-readable because the necessary equipment is uncomplicated and common. Digital and analog records, including computer tapes and disks, phonograph records, and cassette tapes, are not considered eye-readable because all require special equipment to transform the encoded information into a form that is meaningful to people. – Eye-readable[2] characters are common used to label microfilm so that it is possible to rapidly identify film without having to load it in a reader. It may be created by filming targets with text significantly larger than that in the documents being filmed.

F

faceted classification, n. ~ A system for organizing materials into categories based on a systematic combination of mutually exclusive and collectively exhaustive characteristics of the materials (facets) and displaying the characteristics in a manner that shows their relationships.

BT: classification

RT: chain index, synthetic classification

†298 *(Wynar and Taylor, 1992, p. 321):* A faceted structure relieves a classification scheme from the procrustean bed of rigid hierarchical and excessively enumerative subdivision that resulted in the fixed 'pigeonholes' for subjects that happened to be known or were foreseen when a system was designed but often left no room for future developments and made no provision for the expression of complex relationships and their subsequent retrieval.

†298 *(Wynar and Taylor, 1992, p. 320):* A faceted classification differs from a traditional one in that it does not assign fixed slots to subjects in sequence, but uses clearly defined, mutually exclusive, and collectively exhaustive aspects, properties, or characteristics of a class or specific subject. Such aspects, properties, or characteristics are called facets of a class or subject, a term introduced into classification theory and given this new meaning by the Indian librarian and classificationist S. R. Ranganathan and first used in his Colon Classification in the early 1930s. Although the term was then new to classification, the idea was not (as Ranganathan freely admitted). It had its roots in Dewey's device of place (location) as using a standard number (e.g., the United States always being 73) appended to any subject number by means of digits 09, a device now known as a facet indicator.

facilitative records, n. ~ A document that has been preserved because it supports (facilitates) the operations and management of an agency, but which does not relate directly to programs that help the agency achieve its mission.

Syn: administrative records, housekeeping records

BT: record

Notes: More commonly called administrative support records or housekeeping records. These records are common to most organizations. Examples include routine correspondence or interoffice communications; records relating to human resources, equipment and supplies, and facilities; reference materials, routine activity reports, work assignments, appointment books, and telephone logs.

facsimile, n. ~ 1. A reproduction that simulates the appearance of the original as closely as possible. – 2. A system that enables a document to be reproduced remotely by transmitting its image, usually over a telephone line. – 3. Usually **fax** · The reproduction of a document so transmitted.

DF: figured copy

RT: copy, replica, reprint, reproduction

Notes: A facsimile[1] attempts to reproduce the visual and tactile qualities of the original. – Facsimiles[2] were originally analog devices that used paper documents as the original and copy. They now use digital technologies, and the original document, the copy, or both may be electronic and viewed on a computer rather than printed.

fair copy, n. ~ A version of a document that reproduces the text exactly, though not necessarily the formatting, and incorporates any changes made in the source.

 RT: copy, engrossed copy

 †*217 (Quaker Life 2003):* Rough minutes are usually signed at the end of the meeting, giving the clerk authority to sign the fair copy as correct next time. Rough minutes may then be destroyed, but if only one fair copy exists, you should retain rough minutes until permanent deposit of the fair minute book.

fair market value, n. ~ The amount a willing buyer would pay a willing seller in an unregulated market.

 BT: value

 RT: monetary appraisal

fair use, n. ~ A provision in copyright law that allows the limited use of copyright materials without permission of the copyright holder for noncommercial teaching, research, scholarship, or news reporting purposes.

 RT: copyright

 †*131 (LC Fair Use 1999):* Examples of activities that courts have regarded as fair use: "quotation of excerpts in a review or criticism for purposes of illustration or comment; quotation of short passages in a scholarly or technical work, for illustration or clarification of the author's observations; use in a parody of some of the content of the work parodied; summary of an address or article, with brief quotations, in a news report; reproduction by a library of a portion of a work to replace part of a damaged copy; reproduction by a teacher or student of a small part of a work to illustrate a lesson; reproduction of a work in legislative or judicial proceedings or reports; incidental and fortuitous reproduction, in a newsreel or broadcast, of a work located in the scene of an event being reported."

 †*281 (USC, 17 USC 107):* Notwithstanding the provisions of sections [17 USCS Sects. 106, 106A], the fair use of a copyrighted work, including such use by reproduction in copies or phonorecords or by any other means specified by that section, for purposes such as criticism, comment, news reporting, teaching (including multiple copies for classroom use), scholarship, or research, is not an infringement of copyright. In determining whether the use made of a work in any particular case is a fair use the factors to be considered shall include: 1. the purpose and character of the use, including whether such use is of a commercial nature or is for nonprofit educational purposes; 2. the nature of the copyrighted work; 3. the amount and substantiality of the portion used in relation to the copyrighted work as a whole; and 4. the effect of the use upon the potential market for or value of the copyrighted work.

fake, n. ~ 1. Something not authentic or genuine. – adj. ~ 2. Inauthentic – 3. Artificial

 Syn: forgery

 RT: fraud, replica, reproduction

 Notes: 'Forgery' and 'fake' are near synonyms and are often used interchangeably. 'Forgery' connotes an intent to deceive. Something made in imitation of an original or a style may be called a fake but may also be called a reproduction to emphasize that the item is not original.

false hit (also **false drop**), n. ~ In information retrieval systems, entries retrieved that are not pertinent to the search.

 RT: hit

Family Educational Rights and Privacy Act, n. (**FERPA**, abbr.) ~ A law (20 USC 1232g) protecting student and parent rights to access their own student records kept by the school, and restricting access to those records by others without the permission of the student or parents.

  Notes: The amendment allows directory information to be made public without permission, including the student name, address, telephone listing, date and place of birth, major field of study, participation in officially recognized activities and sports, weight and height of members of athletic teams, dates of attendance, degrees and awards received, and the most recent previous educational agency or institution attended by the student. Commonly referred to as the **Buckley Amendment**, in reference to the name of the bill's sponsor.

family papers, n. ~ Records created or collected by a group of individuals who are closely related by ancestry and relating to their personal and private affairs.

  RT: business records, manuscript collection, personal papers

  Notes: Family papers may span generations or may pertain only to an immediate family group. Papers that are predominantly associated with a single individual are often described as personal papers, even if they contain materials from other family members. Family papers, especially those created before the mid-20th century, often contain considerable content relating to the business affairs of family members, although the records are not generally characterized as business records.

fanfold, n. ~ A continuous sheet of paper that is folded in a regular, alternating fashion.

  BT: paper

  RT: continuous forms, printout

  Notes: Fanfold is usually perforated at the folds so that it can be separated into standard-sized sheets. It is usually intended for use in a computer printer; it often has holes along the edges to allow a tractor feeder to move it past a print mechanism. Fanfold has become less common with the introduction of laser and inkjet printers, which use precut sheets.

FAQ ~ *see:* frequently asked questions

fascicle, n. ~ A group of pages, usually in a temporary paper cover, that are part of a larger work and that are issued in installments intended to be bound together.

  DF: part

  Notes: Fascicles are often incomplete works because they do not correspond to the intellectual sections of the larger work.

fat file method, n. ~ A technique for appraising individual case files based on the notion that those relatively larger than others in the series have greater value.

  RT: appraisal, sampling, systematic sampling

  Notes: The use of size to select certain files for preservation is an example of systematic sampling. The fat file method assumes that the greater the number of documents, the increased activity associated with a case, suggesting the case was of greater importance when it was current.

  †34 *(Bradsher 1988, p. 109):* The 'fat file' hypothesis put forth in the Massachusetts Supreme Court cases appraisal . . . suggested that the likelihood of case files having archival value increased with their size. [Citing Michael Stephen Hindus, Theodore M. Hammett, and Barbara M. Hobson, *The Files of the Massachusetts Supreme Court, 1859–1959: An Analysis and a Plan for Action; A Report of the Massachusetts Judicial Records Committee of the Supreme Court, Boston, 1979* (G. K. Hall, 1980).]

†*45 (Cook 1991):* As exceptional, unusual, or controversial cases almost by definition generate more correspondence than their routine counterparts, such files will be thick and thus easily identifiable even in vast series to be pulled for archival retention. Of course, not all thick files necessarily follow this pattern: it may be that someone was routinely repaying a loan in monthly payments over thirty years (thus generating a fat file of 360 receipts). The archivist will have to assess the reasons for the thickness of particular files in series where they occur to ensure that such files are indeed exceptional.

fax ~ *see:* facsimile

FDC, abbr. ~ First day cover; an envelope or card with a stamp that has been postmarked on the day the stamp was first sold.

feature, n. ~ 1. A motion picture that is of substantial length, generally running an hour or more. – 2. A news story, in any media, in which human interest is more important than immediacy.

> *RT:* news film, short

> *Notes:* Feature¹ length films are distinguished from shorts, films that run from a few minutes to half an hour. No standard definition sets time limits for either features or shorts.

Federal Records Act, n. ~ A series of laws, currently codified in 44 USC 21, 23, 25, 27, 29, 31 and 33 that sets forth the records management policies and practices of federal agencies in the federal government, and establishing the National Archives and Records Administration as possessing the responsibility for preserving records of permanent historical value to the United States.

> *RT:* Records Disposal Act of 1943

> *Notes:* Prior legislation from the late 1930s and 1940s is usually also swept up in the catch-all phrase 'Federal Records Act', including most prominently the material in currently codified Chapter 33, which was originally enacted as part of the Disposal of Records Act of 1943.

> †*281 (USC, 44 USC 31 §3101):* The head of each Federal agency shall make and preserve records containing adequate and proper documentation of the organization, functions, policies, decisions, procedures, and essential transactions of the agency and designed to furnish the information necessary to protect the legal and financial rights of the Government and of persons directly affected by the agency's activities

Fedora, n. ~ Software used for managing a library of digital objects.

> *RT:* institutional repository

> *Notes:* An acronym for **Flexible Extensible Digital Object Repository Architecture.** See http://www.fedora.info/.

FERPA ~ *see:* Family Educational Rights and Privacy Act

ferrotype, n. ~ 1. A direct-positive photograph made using the wet-collodion process, using a base of iron coated with black varnish; a tintype. – 2. RARE · A photographic process using iron salts on paper; an energiatype.

> *Syn:* energiatype, tintype

> *RT:* wet collodion

ferrotyping, n. ~ 1. PHOTOGRAPHY · A process to produce a high gloss on gelatin silver photographic prints by drying the print with its emulsion in contact with a polished plate. – 2. PRESERVATION · A condition where the emulsion of a gelatin silver photographic print becomes bound to an enclosure with a polished surface (usually the glass in a frame), typically the result of a fluctuating, humid environment.

  DF: blocking

  RT: glossy

fiche ~ *see:* microfiche

fidelity, n. ~ Accuracy of reproduction.

  RT: accuracy

  Notes: 'Fidelity' may be used to describe news accounts that provide a correct, complete, and factual account of events. 'High fidelity' is a relative term commonly used in the consumer market to describe sound recordings and equipment that have a minimum of noise and the ability to reproduce sound with quality similar to the original.

field, n. ~ COMPUTING · A storage area that is designated to hold a particular type of information and that, in some contexts, may be subdivided into smaller fields.

  NT: fixed-length field, variable-length field, variable-occurrence field

  RT: data element

  Notes: A field may be used to hold a string of characters, a numeric value, or a digital object. Fields may be fixed in length, truncating data longer than that length and padding unused space if the value is less than that length. Or, they may be variable length. Fields may be as small as a bit, a byte holding seven or eight binary fields, though this practice is now uncommon. Fields may be in header, computer instruction, or record. A record consists of one or more fields. For example, a MARC record includes fixed fields that facilitate machine processing, and textual fields for main entry, title, imprint, extent, different kinds of notes, and access points that are both human-readable and used for processing.

field book, n. ~ 1. Volumes containing notes made while working at a site (in the field) to make a record of observations and discoveries. – 2. Land records made by surveyors as an official record of property ownership.

  Notes: Field books were traditionally handwritten notes and sketches made in blank volumes. Field books for scientific surveys may describe general conditions of the site, measurements, description of procedures and methods, and sketches.

field recording, n. ~ A permanent copy of sounds or images made outside a controlled, studio environment, typically with portable equipment.

  Notes: Field recordings may be on tape, film, or other media. They are often made by oral historians, ethnomusicologists, or linguists.

field tag, *see:* tag

figured copy, n. ~ A copy of a document that accurately reproduces the handwriting and form of the original.

  DF: facsimile

  BT: copy

file, n. ~ 1. A group of documents related by use or topic, typically housed in a folder (or a group of folders for a large file). – 2. PLURAL (files) · The whole of a collection of records. – 3. COMPUTING · Collections of data stored for use by a computer; see data file. – v. ~ 4. To store documents in an organized collection for safekeeping and future reference. – 5. To present a document to the clerk of a court or recorder so that it can be entered into the official record. – 6. To initiate a lawsuit.

  NT: convenience file, suspense file

RT: data file, dossier, filing system, filing unit, recordation

Notes: File[1] in the singular generally refers to related documents that are kept together in one or a few folders. In the plural, it typically indicates a larger collection of all or part of an organization's records.

†48 (CJS, Records §24): [file[5]] There is a well defined distinction between filing an instrument, and offering it for record or causing it to be recorded. The term 'recorded' signifies copied or transcribed into a permanent book, while the term 'filing' signifies merely delivery to the proper official.

†109 (Guercio 2001, p. 248–249): Every record is, therefore, an element in an ensemble of other records, or better, of recordkeeping structures, functional aggregations constructed by the creator in the course and for the conduct of its activity and, thus, set in a specific juridical/administrative and documentary/ archival context, in the form of *files*,[1,2] that is, of records related to the same affair or matter, or of *records series*, that is types of records which are homogeneous in form (for example, the series of minutes, of decisions, of circulars, or of ledgers).

†237 (Ralston 1976, p. 561): The term file[3] must have been one of the first to be used in commercial data processing terminology. Even before the advent of computers a deck of punch cards was often called a 'card file,' a term also applied to the cabinet in which the cards were stored. In the very early days of computers, any collection of data or programs was identified as a file.

file break, n. ~ A point where a record series is broken into regular intervals so that portions can be stored or destroyed as a block.

Syn: cutoff

Notes: A file break is often based on a recurring date, such as end of month or fiscal year, or an event, such as contract payoff.

file cabinet, n. ~ A piece of furniture with drawers designed to hold folders containing documents.

NT: flat filing, lateral file, pigeonhole, vertical file

Notes: File cabinets come in a variety of configurations. 'File cabinet' generally connotes a vertical file, in which drawers open from the narrow side. File cabinets that open from the long side are generally called lateral files, although that term includes other types of filing equipment.

file classification scheme ~ *see:* classification scheme

file code (also **file designation**), n. ~ A short sequence of letters or numbers used to indicate a file classification; code[1].

Syn: code

file copy, n. ~ 1. Record copy. – 2. A copy of outgoing correspondence kept in a suspense file.

Syn: record copy

BT: copy

Notes: File copy[1] is often preceded by the adjective 'official' to clearly distinguish it from other copies in files.

file cover ~ *see:* folder

file designation ~ *see:* file code

file group ~ *see:* series

file guide, n. ~ Something used to indicate major divisions within a group of files.

Notes: File guides are often made from card stock with a tab that extends above the height of the folders for visibility.

file integrity, n. ~ 1. RECORDS · The quality of being accurate, complete, and in original order. – 2. COMPUTING · The quality of being free of corruption, especially as a result of broken links between segments, of errors resulting from read or write operations, or of malicious tampering.

> *RT:* archival integrity

file maintenance, n. ~ The process of keeping files current by adding, changing, or deleting information. – 2. The process of inspecting files for the purposes of replacing worn files folders, mending torn documents, removing duplicate copies, locating possible misfiles, and ensuring proper sequence of contents.

file management (also **files management**), n. ~ Oversight of the administration of activities relating to the creation, use, maintenance, and disposal of files, including design and review of classification systems, equipment, and procedures, in order to ensure that the operations are efficient and economical.

> *†112 (Ham 1993, p. 33):* Appropriate file structure can segregate records of long-term value from those of transitory use and thus facilitate appraisal and other archival processes. As a result of carefully considered file design and maintenance, the archivist can accession records with most of the weeding or purging already completed.

file name (also **filename**), n. ~ COMPUTING · A series of characters used to identify a data file in a system.

> *BT:* name
>
> *Notes:* The form of file names is generally governed by the operating system. For example, some early operating systems limited file names to eight characters, followed by a period and a three-letter file extension.

file plan, n. ~ A classification scheme describing different types of files, how they are identified, where they should be stored, how they should be indexed for retrieval.

> *RT:* filing system
>
> *Notes:* Sometimes called a filing system. A file plan is usually identified by the type of code used to classify the files, such as alphabetical, numerical, alphanumerical, or decimal.

file server, n. ~ A computer configured to store and provide access to files for clients connected by a network.

> *Notes:* File servers are typically customized with high-speed disk drives and broadband network connections. They are often used for central storage of data, making it easy to back up many users' data. As a result, they often include tape or other backup systems. Client systems are often configured to make it appear that the file server is a local drive.

file station, n. ~ A location where current files are kept for convenient access.

file structure, n. ~ 1. The manner in which data and other objects are organized within a file. – 2. The manner in which files are organized in a system. – 3. COMPUTING · The format of fields within a data record.

> *Notes:* File structure[1] differs significantly between file types. File structures may define the positions of elements in a file, especially with fixed-length data elements. Another structure commonly used with variable-length data elements incorporates a header that points to the location of elements within the body of the file. – File structure[2] is often used to describe the organization of pages on a website.

File Transfer Protocol, n. (**FTP**, abbr.) ~ A standard (RFC 959) establishing rules for copying files from one system to another.

Syn: Synonym · *†:* see Bibliography · *Superscript:* Definition number

Notes: The FTP protocol negotiates the exchange of data between the systems and manages any differences in data structures on the systems. For example, FTP can move plain-ASCII text from a seven-bit to an eight-bit system without altering the content.

†86 *(FTP 1994, http://www.w3.org/Protocols/rfc959/1_Introduction.html):* The objectives of FTP are 1) to promote sharing of files (computer programs and/or data), 2) to encourage indirect or implicit (via programs) use of remote computers, 3) to shield a user from variations in file storage systems among hosts, and 4) to transfer data reliably and efficiently. FTP, though usable directly by a user at a terminal, is designed mainly for use by programs.

file type, n. ~ 1. A category of files based on content; a genre. – 2. A category of files based on physical or formal characteristics; a format.

Notes: File types[1] include correspondence, case files, reading files, tickler files, and others. – File types[2] is primarily used in connection with computer files; the MIME standard defines different file types, including text/html, text/plain, text/css, multipart/form-data, application/pdf, and many others.

files custodian ~ *see:* custodian

filing feature, n. ~ An element of an item that may be used to classify the item within a filing system.

Notes: Classification for a series may be based on the filing feature most commonly used to request items belonging to that series. For example, filing features commonly found on correspondence include the name of the correspondent, the name of the addressee, a date, and a subject. Depending on the office, the series may be organized by any one of these filing features. Accounting records may be organized under a filing feature such as a purchase order number or account number.

filing system, n. ~ Policies and procedures directing how files should be stored and indexed in order to ensure their retrieval, use, and disposition.

NT: alphabetic-subject filing system, alphanumeric filing system, decimal filing system, duplex-numeric filing system , mnemonic filing system , numeric filing system , subject-numeric filing system

RT: file, file plan, recordkeeping system, system

Notes: Sometimes called a recordkeeping system. Filing systems often include a records inventory, a retention schedule, and a file plan.

†265 *(Skupsky and Mantaña 1994, p. 151–152):* In *Alliance to End Repression v. Rochford* [75 FRD 441, 447 (N.D.Ill. 1977)], the court rejected an objection to discovery requests on the grounds that production of the information would be unduly burdensome because the materials were not in an organized filing system. ¶ The court further concluded that: 'To allow a defendant whose business generates massive records to frustrate discovery by creating an inadequate filing system, and then claiming undue burden, would defeat the purpose of discovery rules.

filing unit (also **file unit**), n. ~ 1. A group of related documents treated as a single item for purposes of classification, storage, and retrieval. – 2. A number or word within a heading used to sort the headings.

RT: dossier, file, folder

Notes: A filing unit[1] is not necessarily the same as a physical item. While a single folder containing all related documents is the most common example of a filing unit, a large file spanning several folders is also considered a single filing unit.

– Filing unit[2] identifies the parts of a heading for word-by-word arrangement. For example, the title *The Cat in the Hat* is filed under C, because an article in the first position is not considered a filing unit. The name Saint Theresa is filed before Saints of Old based on the first filing unit; in letter-by-letter arrangement, the order would be reversed.

†124 *(Holmes 1984, p. 173):* Although filing units within series may be single documents or single documents within enclosures or annexes, they are more likely to be assemblages of documents relating to some transaction, person, case, or subject, depending upon the filing policy or system used by the agency.

film, n. ~ 1. A thin coating or covering. – 2. A thin, flexible sheet, especially of plastic. – 3. PHOTOGRAPHY, MOTION PICTURES · A thin sheet of plastic, in a sheet or roll, coated with light-sensitive emulsion to be exposed in a camera. – 4. MOTION PICTURES · A motion picture production; a movie. – 5. MOTION PICTURES · The discipline of making motion pictures.

DF: plate

NT: print film, roll film, sheet film

RT: microfilm, motion picture, movie, photograph

Notes: Film[2] generally refers to unexposed materials. After the film has been developed, it is often called a negative, transparency, or slide. – Film[3] is often used as a short form for microfilm.

film footage, n. ~ 1. Motion picture or video stock of a scene or sequence. – 2. An unspecified quantity of motion picture or video stock.

RT: linear foot

Notes: 'Film footage' connotes a part of a larger whole and emphasizes the physical material rather than the intellectual content. The phrase is derived from the fact that motion picture film is commonly measured in feet.

film jacket ~ *see:* microfilm jacket

film still ~ *see:* movie still

filmography, n. ~ A list of motion pictures.

BT: bibliography

Notes: Filmographies are to motion pictures what bibliographies are to print publications. They may be topical, relating to a specific director, actor, or other subject. They may be complete or selective. They may be annotated, so that they are equivalent to an analytical bibliography[2].

filmstrip, n. ~ A short length of film containing images intended to be viewed individually.

Notes: Filmstrips are often on 35 mm film. They are roughly equivalent to a slide show, with the images kept on a continuous roll of film rather than mounted individually. The images may be photographs, drawings, or text. Some filmstrips have accompanying audio distributed on phonograph records or cassettes; the sound is synchronized with the filmstrip by the use of an audible tone to indicate the film is to be manually advanced, or in later systems by an inaudible tone that the projector senses to automatically advance the filmstrip.

final clauses, n. ~ DIPLOMATICS · Formulaic statements at the end of the document intended to ensure its proper execution.

BT: intrinsic element

†70 *(Duranti 1998, p. 147–148):* The text of most documents contains after or within the disposition several formulae, the object of which is to ensure the execu-

tion of the act, to avoid its violation, to guarantee its validity, to preserve the rights of third parties, to attest the execution of the required formalities, and to indicate the means employed to give the document probative value. These formulae constitute the final clauses, which can be divided into groups as follows: ¶ Clauses of injunction: those expressing the obligation of all those concerned to conform to the will of the authority. ¶ Clauses of prohibition: those expressing the prohibition to violate the enactment or oppose it. ¶ Clauses of derogation: those expressing the obligation to respect the enactment, notwithstanding other orders or decisions contrary to it, opposition, appeals or previous dispositions. ¶ Clauses of exception: those expressing situations, conditions or persons which would constitute an exception to the enactment. ¶ Clauses of obligation: those expressing the obligation of the parties to respect the act, for themselves and for their successors or descendants. ¶ Clauses of renunciation: those expressing a threat of punishment should the enactment be violated. They comprise two categories: 1) spiritual sanctions, comprising threats of malediction or anathema; 2) penal sanctions, comprising the mention of specific penal consequences. ¶ Promissory clauses: those expressing the promise of a prize, usually of a spiritual nature, for those who respect the enactment. ¶ Clauses of corroboration: those enunciating the means used to validate the document and guarantee its authenticity. The wording changes according to the time and place, but these clauses are usually formulaic and fixed. Examples are, 'I have hereunto set my Hand and Seal of Office', 'Signed and Sealed', 'Witness our Trustworthy and Beloved . . . ', etc.

final disposition ~ *see:* disposition

finding aid, n. ~ 1. A tool that facilitates discovery of information within a collection of records. – 2. A description of records that gives the repository physical and intellectual control over the materials and that assists users to gain access to and understand the materials.

> *NT:* calendar, guide, inventory, register, scope and contents note, special list
> *RT:* catalog, Encoded Archival Description, intellectual control
> *Notes:* Finding aid[1] includes a wide range of formats, including card indexes, calendars, guides, inventories, shelf and container lists, and registers. – Finding aid[2] is a single document that places the materials in context by consolidating information about the collection, such as acquisition and processing; provenance, including administrative history or biographical note; scope of the collection, including size, subjects, media; organization and arrangement; and an inventory of the series and the folders.

fire detection system, n. ~ Temperature, smoke, and other sensors installed in a building to monitor the environment for early stages of fire, to trigger an alarm, and sometimes to trigger a fire extinguishing system.

fire extinguishing system, n. ~ A technology installed in a building to suppress a fire after its ignition.

> *Notes:* Fire extinguishing systems use many different techniques. Water sprinklers may be wet or dry pipe and may trigger all sprinklers or only those sprinklers directly over the fire. Gas systems suffocate a fire by replacing available oxygen in the room with Halon, carbon dioxide, or other gas. Misting systems create a dense fog.

firmware, n. ~ A computer program that has been embedded in a circuit or stored in a chip.

> *RT:* hardware, read-only memory, software

first sale doctrine, n. ~ COPYRIGHT · A limit on a copyright owner's interests beyond the initial sale of a particular copy of a protected work.

> *RT:* copyright
>
> *Notes:* While the owner of copyright has exclusive rights to control the distribution of a protected work, the owner of a legally acquired copy may, with some restrictions, sell or otherwise dispose of that copy without regard to the copyright owner. The doctrine does not allow for the rental, lease, or lending of a sound recording or computer program for commercial advantage. See 17 USC 109(a).

fiscal value, n. ~ The usefulness or significance of records containing financial information that is necessary to conduct current or future business or that serves as evidence of financial transactions.

> *BT:* value
>
> *RT:* primary value

fixed-length field, n. ~ COMPUTING · An area in a file or record with a specific number of bytes reserved to hold data.

> *DF:* variable-length field
>
> *BT:* field
>
> *Notes:* Data that is smaller than the allocated space is usually padded to fill unused space. Data that is larger than the field is truncated. Fixed-length fields are distinguished from variable-length fields.

fixed media, n. ~ COMPUTING · Mass storage in which the material that holds data is a permanent part of the device.

> *DF:* removable media
>
> *Notes:* Fixed media devices are distinguished from those in which the data is stored on a cartridge, disk, or other material that is removable and interchangeable. Hard drives are typically fixed media, with platters sealed inside the drive chassis. Floppy disk and CD-ROM drives are examples of removable media.

fixer, n. ~ A chemical used to remove unexposed light-sensitive salts from photographic materials, making the image stable when exposed to light.

> *RT:* methylene-blue test
>
> *Notes:* Fixer, often called **hypo**, is commonly made from **sodium thiosulfate** or **ammonium thiosulfate**. Residual fixer can cause photographs to fade or become stained.

fixity, n. (**fixed**, adj.) ~ The quality of being stable and resisting change.

> *RT:* alteration, immutability, integrity, stability
>
> *Notes:* Documents preserve memory because they fix information on a stable medium. The information may fade with time, or it may be may erased and overwritten, but barring external action the information remains unchanged over time.
>
> †139 (*InterPARES2, p. 3*): The special challenges for making and keeping reliable records and preserving authentic records, the most salient characteristic of which is the lack of a stable form and content (that is, of fixity), as is the case with experiential, interactive and dynamic records.
>
> †281 (*USC, 17 USC 101*): COPYRIGHT · A work is 'fixed' in a tangible medium of expression when its embodiment in a copy or phonorecord, by or under the authority of the author, is sufficiently permanent or stable to permit it to be perceived, reproduced, or otherwise communicated for a period of more than transitory duration. A work consisting of sounds, images, or both, that are being

transmitted, is 'fixed' for purposes of this title if a fixation of the work is being made simultaneously with its transmission.

fl., abbr. ~ Floruit; the period when an individual was active.

> *Notes:* 'Floruit' is the third person, singular, indicative of the Latin *florere*, to flourish. It is often used in a heading for an individual when the birth and death dates are not known.

flaking, n. ~ A process of deterioration resulting in the loss of small, flat pieces from a surface.

> *RT:* peeling

> *Notes:* Flaking may be observed on older magnetic media in which the oxide coating is separating from the base. It may also be seen in art papers and coated cloth. Flaking is sometimes used synonymously with peeling, although it is generally used to describe a condition that is more localized than peeling.

flange, n. ~ The edge of a reel that protrudes from the hub.

> *RT:* hub, reel

> *Notes:* Reels commonly have flanges on both sides. They are designed to prevent film or tape from falling off the hub.

flat file, n. ~ 1. Container or shelf used to store documents and planar materials in a horizontal position, parallel to the shelf. – 2. Containers designed to hold documents unfolded. – 3. Computing · A file containing data that has no structure or markup. – 4. Computing · A data structure that is nonhierarchical, having one record per row; a table.

> *RT:* box file, formatted document, relational database

> *Notes:* Flat file[3] is often used to describe a formatted document that has been stripped of all internal codes that affect the appearance of the content, such as a word processing file or web page saved as plain text. – A flat file[4] may have fixed-length fields or delimited data.

> †300 *(Yates 1989, p. 31–32):* Flat filing[2], which emerged in the second half of the nineteenth century, was a more satisfactory interim storage technology [than pigeonholes] that increased efficiency of retrieval as well as capacity. The various types of flat files, in which documents were stored flat rather than folded, eliminated abstracting, reduced retrieval problems, and allowed unlimited expansion. Forms of flat files ranged from bound volumes, simple imitations of the bound press book used for copies of outgoing correspondence, to rearrangable cabinet flat files, harbingers of the vertical filing systems that were to revolutionize storage and retrieval of documents.

flat filing, n. ~ 1. A technique to store documents horizontally. – 2. A technique to store documents unfolded.

> *Syn:* horizontal filing

> *BT:* file cabinet

> *RT:* pigeonhole

> *Notes:* Flat filing[1] is distinguished from vertical filing, in which documents are stored on edge as in a filing cabinet. – Flat filing[2] is distinguished from the use of pigeonholes or cabinets in which documents are folded before being stored.

flatbed camera (also **flat-bed camera**), n. ~ Equipment for production of microfilm that consists of a table to hold the original, an upright to support the film unit (camera) overhead, lights extending above and to the side of the table, and a control unit.

> *Syn:* planetary camera

BT: microfilm camera

RT: microfilm

Notes: When filming with a flatbed camera, both the film and document are stationary during exposure.

flatbed scanner (also **flat-bed scanner**), n. ~ Equipment used to create digital images of documents that are placed on a stationary platen.

BT: scanner

Notes: Most flatbed scanners use reflected light during scanning, but some have the ability to scan using transmitted light to scan transparencies. Flatbed scanners lack the speed of rotary scanners but do not strain the original as much.

flattening, n. ~ 1. A conservation treatment to remove curls, creases, or cockles from a document to return it to its original, flat condition. – 2. COMPUTING · The process of removing information about the structure or formatting of a file, especially transforming hierarchical data into a linear sequence of elements.

Notes: Flattening[1] generally involves relaxing the document by introducing moisture through humidification. Documents may be flatted under weights or using a suction table. – Flattening[2] implies that the data is stored in plain (seven bit) ASCII without embedded formatting codes.

Flexible Extensible Digital Object Repository Architecture ~ *see:* Fedora

flexible scheduling, n. ~ A technique to apply disposition instructions to different types of information or categories of records.

Notes: The technique's flexibility is derived from the ability to assign retention periods to groups of records other than series. The concept is described in the National Archives and Records Administration's *Strategic Directions: Flexible Scheduling* (January 2004).

flip-top box, n. ~ A container that holds folders of documents vertically and that measures roughly 10 inches high, 12 or 15 inches wide, and 6 or 3 inches deep, and that usually has an integral top hinged at the upper back.

Syn: document box

BT: box

Notes: Document boxes are typically made from cardboard. They are often neutral gray and lined on the inside with white, acid-neutral paper. Boxes made from lignin-free cardboard are often tan and unlined. They may have a string, handle, or hole on one end to facilitate removal from a shelf.

float, n. ~ A technique to mount items so that all edges are visible through the opening in the overmat.

floor load, n. ~ The amount of weight a structure's floors can bear, including the dead weight and the live load.

Notes: Buildings for storing records must have particularly strong floor loads because of the weight of the records.

floor-space ratio, n. ~ A ratio of the cubic volume to the square area of storage space.

Notes: When calculated using floor space in square feet and volume in cubic feet, a standard, four-drawer file cabinet has a floor-space ratio of 1:4.3. A five-drawer cabinet has a ratio of 1:5.3. The larger cabinet has a 23% more efficient use of floor space.

floppy disk (also **diskette**), n. ~ A circular sheet of polyester (the disk) coated with magnetic oxide and housed in a thin, square plastic jacket that is used as a removable data storage medium.

RT: magnetic disk

Notes: The disk rotates within the jacket. An opening in the jacket provides the read-write heads access to the disk. Standard sizes include 8 inches, 5¼ inches, and 3½ inches. The larger sizes use a flexible jacket and the disk is exposed through an access slot. The smallest size has a rigid plastic case with a metal shutter to protect the disk and is sometimes called a flexi-disk.

A flippy is a single-sided 5¼-inch disk that has been altered so that data can be stored on both sides. The disk must be turned over (flipped) to use the second side.

Floptical, n. ~ Removable disk that stores data on magnetic media using heads guided by a separate optical track.

Notes: A trademark of Insite Peripherals, which developed the format. Floptical disks were the same size as a 3½-inch floppy disk, and most Floptical drives could read a standard floppy. Because the heads used a more precise optical track for positioning, a Floptical drive could store more information in the same amount of space. Flopticals could store 21 MB of data without sacrificing access time. The product, introduced in 1989, was never widely adopted.

flow camera, n. ~ Equipment designed to reproduce large quantities of documents on microfilm.

Syn: rotary camera

RT: microfilm

Notes: Flow cameras film documents while they are being transported through the device. The film is also in motion during filming, and optics ensure that the image of the document is stationary relative to the film. The width of the original is limited by the camera, but the length of the original is, theoretically, limited only by the length of the film.

fluting, n. ~ 1. Parallel furrows used as decoration. – 2. CONSERVATION · A wave-shaped deformation at the edge of flat surface.

Notes: Fluting² may appear on the edge of film wound on reels or pages of books if the outer edges are exposed to a humid environment, allowing them to take on more moisture and swell, while the inner portions remain dry and the original size.

flutter, n. ~ A distortion in the reproduction of a moving image or sound recording, usually resulting from a rapid, repetitive variation in the speed of a playback device.

BT: distortion

RT: wow

focus, n. ~ 1. The sharpness of an image created by an optical system. – 2. The plane where an optical system causes light rays parallel to the system's axis to converge. – 3. A concentration. – v. ~ 4. To adjust an optical system so that the image is sharp.

RT: acutance, blur, sharpness, soft focus

Notes: Focus¹ is perceived in terms of sharp, distinct lines and high contrast. Focus is relative to the optical system; distortion in the system may degrade focus.

fog, n. ~ PHOTOGRAPHY · A defect in an image characterized by increased density not a part of the image.

Notes: Fog may be caused by stray light hitting the sensitive surface before development; for example, a light leak in a camera. Fog may also result from the use of improperly stored or outdated materials, or from poor processing chemicals. Fog tends to reduce image contrast.

FOIA ~ *see:* Freedom of Information Act

folder, n. ~ 1. A sheet of cardboard or heavy paper stock that is used as a loose cover to keep documents and other flat materials together, especially for purposes of filing; a **file cover**. – 2. A printed leaflet in which the text does not cross the folds. – 3. COMPUTING · A directory structure that organizes files into groups; a directory or subdirectory.

> BT: container
>
> RT: filing unit, leaflet
>
> *Notes:* Folders[1] usually have tabs where a title can be written. Tabs commonly run a fifth, a third, a half, or the full length of the folder, and may be staggered.

folder list, n. ~ That part of a completed finding aid or a rudimentary finding aid that lists the folder titles in a collection.

> DF: container list
>
> *Notes:* A folder list makes it possible to browse the contents of the collection without having to physically access the materials. Some folder lists may also include information about the series and about the span dates of the contents in each folder.

folding endurance, n. ~ A test of the strength and durability of a planar material, usually paper.

> †248 *(Roberts and Etherington 1982):* The number of folds which a specimen (usually paper) will withstand before failure, under controlled conditions in a specified instrument. In the usual test, a specimen is subjected repeatedly to double folds through a wide angle while under tension. Folding endurance is a very important indication of the durability of archival papers. A decline in folding endurance is the most sensitive indicator of aging and deterioration of paper.

foliation, n. ~ 1. The number of leaves in a book or manuscript. – 2. The numbers placed on leaves in a book or manuscript, generally used to indicate order.

> RT: pagination

folio, n. ~ 1. A single leaf in a book or a manuscript. – 2. A number assigned to a leaf, typically to represent order. – 3. A book size made from sheets[2] folded in half. – 4. A bill of accounts, especially for guests in a hotel. – 5. ACCOUNTING · Two facing pages used to record information about a single account. – 6. LAW (ARCHAIC) · A number of words used as a measure in legal documents; in the United States, 100 words, in England, 72 or 90 words.

follow-up file, n. ~ A group of documents filed chronologically under some future date when they require attention or action.

> *Syn:* pending file, suspense file, tickler file

follow-up interview ~ *see:* reference interview

fonds, n. ~ The entire body of records of an organization, family, or individual that have been created and accumulated as the result of an organic process reflecting the functions of the creator.

> RT: archives, collection, manuscript collection, manuscript group, provenance, record group
>
> †46 *(Cook 1993, p. 33):* The fonds, therefore, should be viewed primarily as 'an intellectual construct.' The fonds is not so much a physical entity in archives as it is the conceptual summary of descriptions of physical entities at the series level or lower, and descriptions of the administrative, historical and functional character of the records creator(s) – as well as descriptions of the records-creating processes

(metadata). The fonds is thus the conceptual 'whole' that reflects an organic process in which a records creator produces or accumulates series of records which themselves exhibit a natural unity based on shared function, activity, form or use. It is at the heart of this process or relationship linking the creator to the records that the essence of *respect des fonds* can be found and must be protected.

†116 (Hayworth 1993, p. 56): The Canadian preference for the French term *fonds* to define the records of one creator originated with *Towards Archival Descriptive Standards*, which purposefully chose it in order 'to avoid certain terminological confusion which has grown around the terms 'record group,' 'manuscript group,' 'collections,' and so on, in North American practices.

†149 (Jenkinson 1966, p. 101): The *fonds* is the chief Archive Unit in the Continental system and the basis of all rules of arrangement. The most important of all principles of Archive Management is named from it *le respect pour les fonds*. . . . A *fonds* is an organic whole and that any Administration, or one or more of its *fonctionnaires*, can create a *fonds d'archives* provided that these include *résolutions* or *procès-verbaux*; the inclusion of archives of such a type making it *autonome*. Roughly speaking, we may take it that they would make the qualities of a *fonds d'archives* depend on its including those which, when the administration which created it was active, constituted the final authority for executive action. For our purposes we may do better perhaps to represent this quality in terms of Administration rather than terms of documents, the forms of which are not necessarily constant. *Fonds* we may render, for lack of a better translation, *Archive Group*, and define this as the Archives resulting from the work of an Administration which was an organic whole, complete in itself, capable of dealing independently, without any added or external authority, with every side of any business which could normally be presented to it. This, it may be said, is to make the *Archive Group* a division much wider, much less strictly defined that the *Fonds*.

font, n. ~ A collection of type or electronic character forms that share a particular design.

Notes: Traditionally, font is used to describe a set of type of the same style, size, and weight. Font is now commonly used to mean what was historically called a family of type, all the variants of a particular style of type. Common examples of fonts (or families) include Bodoni, Century, Helvetica, and Times New Roman.

foolscap, n. ~ A sheet of paper approximately 13 × 16 inches, usually folded to 8 × 13 inches, and used for writing or printing.

RT: legal size

†41 (Ciardi 1980, p. 136): A sheet of paper 13 × 16 inches, folding to 8 × 13, now called legal size, to distinguish it from letter size or common typewriter paper, which is 8½ × 11 inches. Surviving documents on such paper show that it was watermarked with the belled cap of a court jester, a 'fool's cap,' and that watermark (still in use as part of the tradition of papermaking) is an evident source of the term. But this paper was originally imported from Italy, and is attested in XVIII as Genoa foolscap. In It. such a sheet was called *un foglio capo*, a chief (large) sheet. If *foglio* is given an English plural as *foglios capo*, the resultant form is very close to foolscap, whereby one must conclude that the term derives from both the watermark and the Italian name.

footage ~ *see:* film footage

---

for official use only ~ *see:* administratively controlled information

forensic document examination, n. ~ Scientific study of a document to determine its characteristics and to answer questions of evidence, especially authenticity or authorship.

    Notes: Examination emphasizes physical aspects of the document and its production, including handwriting or printing, paper, and inks.

forgery, n. ~ Something that is represented as something it is not; something not authentic or genuine.

    DF: replica

    Syn: fake

    RT: copy, counterfeit, fraud

    Notes: 'Forgery' and 'fake' are near synonyms and are often used interchangeably. However, 'forgery' connotes an intent to deceive.

form, n. ~ 1. A printed document with clearly defined areas left blank that are to be completed later. – 2. The materials and structure of an item; format[1]. – 3. The overall appearance, configuration, or shape, independent of its intellectual content; a **document type**. – 4. A model[1] or pattern; something that gives shape; a mold[2,3]. – 5. A style or convention for expressing ideas in a literary work or document; documentary form, including extrinsic and intrinsic elements. – 6. TYPOGRAPHY · Type, spacers, and other materials assembled in a chase for printing.

    Syn: format

    NT: intellectual form, physical form

    RT: transmission form

    Notes: Form[2] is synonymous with format[1], although this equivalence is a fairly recent shift in the language. Form is often used to distinguish between versions of an item in different media; for example, a document may be described as being in its original form, a microform, or a duplicate form.

    †*70 (Duranti 1998, p. 134):* Diplomatics defines form[4] as the complex of the rules of representation used to convey a message, that is, as the characteristics of a document which can be separated from the determination of the particular subjects, or places it concerns. Documentary form is both physical and intellectual.

    †*140 (InterPARES Glossary 2002):* Documentary form[4]: The rules of representation according to which the content of a record, its administrative and documentary context, and its authority are communicated. The two types of documentary form are extrinsic elements and intrinsic elements.

    †*167 (D Levy 2001, p. 69):* The birth of the form[2] nicely illustrates how documents were streamlined and tailored in the service of ever greater efficiency. . . . [Workers' documentation of their activities] could be standardized and speeded up by printing forms, sheets of paper whose printed material indicated exactly what information was needed to be filled in, and where. This meant the worker had less to write; the familiarity of a standard layout also increased his speed. This standardization also facilitated reading and summarizing as the report traveled up the hierarchy.

    †*247 (Robek, et al. 1996, p. 338):* Business forms[5] serve as the primary means of communicating information in a methodical, standardized, and repetitive way. A well-designed form constitutes the equivalent of a flowchart which describes and standardizes a process. The form serves as a catalyst in providing information in

an organized fashion so that it is possible to determine if a task has been completed or to reach a decision about the course of action.

format, n. ~ 1. A standard size or configuration; form[2]. – 2. Motion pictures · The aspect ratio of a film. – 3. Computing · A structure used for the interchange, storage, or display of data. – 4. The layout of a document. – 5. Publishing · The appearance of a book, especially the number of times a printed sheet has been folded to make a book. – v. ~ 6. Computing · To prepare a disk for storing data. – 7. Computing · To apply a particular design to a document.

> *Syn:* form
>
> *NT:* academy format, letter box, split screen, widescreen
>
> *RT:* Cascading Style Sheet, landscape orientation, portrait orientation, reformat, structure
>
> *Notes:* Format[1] is synonymous with form[2] and the use of this sense is a fairly recent shift in the language. Format is commonly used to describe certain standard sizes of photographs, including cartes-de-visite, cabinet cards, stereographs, and many numerical designation for film sizes, and this sense appears in *The Focal Encyclopedia of Photography* (1965). *AACR2* (1976) and *AACR2R* (1988) use format to mean "a particular physical presentation of an item," but the term does not appear in *AACR* (1967, 1970). – Examples of format[3] include the USMARC format, HTML, and XML, along with proprietary formats such as Adobe PDF or Microsoft Word. – Examples of format[5] include folios, quartos, and octavos. – Examples of format[7] include the use of Cascading Style Sheets (CSS) to apply style to a Hypertext Markup Language (HTML) document.
>
> †136 *(ICP Encyclopedia 1984, p. 209):* The dimensions of standard negative, print, and transparency sizes are called formats. In general, the nominal dimensions of the picture area (e.g., 2¼ inches square) are used for roll, cassette, and cartridge films, while the actual outer dimensions of the material are used for sheet films and print papers.

format migration, n. ~ 1. The process of copying data from one type of storage material to another to ensure continued access to the information as the data structure becomes obsolete; media migration. – 2. The process of converting a data from an obsolete structure to a new structure to counter software obsolescence.

> *BT:* migration
>
> *Notes:* Format migration[1] makes no change to the bitstreams within the files copied. Examples might include moving files from a floppy disk to a CD-ROM. Moving a bitstream usually does not alter the file content. – Format migration[2] may involve changes in the internal structure of a data file to keep pace with changing application versions, such as migration from Word 95 to Word 2000. Or, it may involve a more radical change in structure, such as changes from one application to another, such as Word to WordPerfect. Making changes in a data structure places the original at risk, as the new structure may not accurately capture the form and function of the original.

formatted document, n. ~ Computing · A document that includes instructions to control how its content is displayed.

> *BT:* document
>
> *RT:* flat file
>
> *Notes:* Formatted documents are generally laid out to enhance their human readability by adding structure, such as headings, indentation, font variations, and

other devices that transform plain (unformatted) text so that they have an appearance similar to published works.

forms management, n. ~ The systematic analysis, design, production, control, maintenance, and use of forms[1] to provide improved quality, increased efficiency, and reduced costs.

> *BT:* management
>
> *Notes:* Forms management includes forms control, which establishes routines for the design, production, storage, and use of forms, as well as revision and discontinuation of obsolete forms.

formula, n. ~ Standard or prescribed language used in official documents or ceremonies that define or declare a general fact, rule, or principle.

> †70 (Duranti 1998, p. 137): Theorists established [the rules of *ars dictaminis*, the art of composition and style], which were meant to direct the composition, style and rhythm of every type of public document, private contract, and business and family correspondence. The various treatises which result used to be accompanied by collections of models and examples, or of copies of actual documents, assembled for the purpose of showing the application of the doctrine. Those volumes, regularly used by public officers, notaries and all those who needed to communicate in writing, were called *formularia*.

formulary, n. ~ A compilation of standard or prescribed language (formula) that serve as models for common documents.

> *RT:* ars dictaminis
>
> *Notes:* A formulary may include language for oaths, declarations, contracts, or writs.

four-corners document, n. ~ VERNACULAR · Writing, graphics, or other information that can be reasonably displayed on a two-dimensional surface.

> *RT:* document
>
> *Notes:* 'Four-corners document' is used to distinguish information formats that cannot be easily or meaningfully reduced to a sheet or sheets, such as paper or film. A motion picture is not considered a four-corners document; while it may be on a single – if very long – sheet, the sense of motion is not meaningfully recreated without special equipment. Three-dimensional visualizations in a geographic information system and dynamic, interactive systems are other examples of information that cannot be captured in a four-corners document.

foxing, n. ~ Small, irregular, brown blemishes on paper.

> †248 (Roberts and Etherington 1982): Stains, specks, spots and blotches in paper. The cause or causes of foxing, which usually occurs in machine-made paper of the late 18th and the 19th centuries, are not completely understood, but in all likelihood, it is fungoid in nature. ¶ Two significant differences between foxed and clean areas of a paper are the higher proportion of acid and iron in the former, although there does not seem to be any clear and definitive relationship between iron and foxing. Insofar as the acid is involved, it is not clear whether this is produced chemically or as a byproduct of the life function of the organisms present.

frame, n. ~ 1. PHOTOGRAPHY, MOTION PICTURES · An image on a roll of film representing a single exposure. – 2. PHOTOGRAPHY, MOTION PICTURES, VIDEO · The edges of an image. – 3. COMPUTING · The information visible on a display at one time. – 4. COMPUTING · A technique in HTML to divide a browser window into different panes, each containing a different document. – 5. COMPUTING, TELECOMMUNICATIONS · Data transmitted as a unit over a network with header and trailer fields that 'frame' the data and include information about how the data is to be moved across the network. – v. ~ 6. PHOTOGRAPHY, MOTION PICTURES · To compose an image by selecting what will fall within its borders.

frame enlargement, n. ~ A photographic print made from a single frame of a motion picture.

> *RT:* movie still
>
> *Notes:* Frame enlargements are generally of poorer quality than movie stills.

framing (also **inlaying, window repair**), n. ~ CONSERVATION · The process of reinforcing damaged edges of a sheet of paper with repair paper or other material from which the central part covering the text has been removed.

frass, n. ~ Debris or excrement left by insects or insect larvae.

fraud, n. ~ An act of deliberate deception, especially to induce someone to act against his or her best interests.

> *RT:* fake, forgery
>
> †10 *(AJS, Records §102):* Fraud may be predicated on false representation or concealments, though the truth could have been ascertained by an examination of public records.
>
> †48 *(CJS, 37 CJS §2):* While it is true that there is a distinction between fraud and forgery, and forgery contains some elements that are not included in fraud, forgeries are a species of fraud. In essence, the crime of forgery involves the making, altering, or completing of an instrument by someone other than the ostensible maker or drawer or an agent of the ostensible maker or drawer.

Freedom of Information Act, n. (**FOIA**, abbr.) ~ A law that describes an individual's rights to access information held by a government agency, as well as the agency's legal authority to refuse access to such information.

> *RT:* access, agency record, open records law, sunshine law
>
> *Notes:* The federal Freedom of Information Act is codified at 5 USC §552. Most states have similar laws, though the names may vary, including open records law and sunshine law. The laws are not uniform among states. The laws are intended to allow citizens to know what agencies are doing so that the agencies can be held accountable.
>
> †10 *(AJS, Records §32):* The federal Freedom of Information Act [in 5 USC §552] requires that each agency, in accordance with published rules, shall make available for public inspection and copying final opinions, including concurring and dissenting opinions, as well as orders, made in the adjudication of cases; those statements of policy and interpretations which have been adopted by the agency and are not published in the Federal Register; and administrative staff manuals and instructions staff that affect a member of the public; unless the materials are promptly published and copies offered for sale. . . . The Act further provides that, to the extent required to prevent a clearly unwarranted invasion of personal privacy, an agency may delete identifying details. . . . [The Act specifically excludes defense or foreign policy secrets, trade secrets and confidential commercial or financial information, intragovernmental communications, personnel and medical files, and investigatory files.]

freeze, v. ~ To suspend the scheduled destruction of records because of special circumstances, such as litigation, investigation, audit, or merger.

RT: frozen records, hold order

Notes: Records are typically frozen if they are potentially relevant to impending or current litigation, regardless of whether a subpoena or hold order has been issued.

freeze drying (also **lyophilization**), n. ~ A treatment to dry water-soaked materials by freezing the materials and placing them in a vacuum to remove the ice through sublimation.

Notes: Techniques vary by the use of heat and the degree of vacuum. Freeze drying often connotes a hard vacuum and the use of heat. **Vacuum drying** connotes a lower vacuum and no heat.

frequently asked questions, n. (**FAQ**, abbr.) ~ A document containing answers to common questions and problems.

†157 *(New Words 1997):* Online discussion groups, particularly Usenet ones, have developed FAQs to minimize repetitive discussion about queries which are continually raised, particularly by newcomers; it is a point of Usenet netiquette to consult the FAQ before posting a question.

friable, adj. ~ Easily broken apart into powder or small pieces.

front end, n. ~ 1. COMPUTING · A user interface, especially an application separate from the system with which it interacts. – 2. COMPUTING · A system designed to process data before being submitted to another system. – 3. COMPUTING · A specialized computer that performs input and output functions in a large system.

frozen records, n. ~ Records that are scheduled for routine destruction but are preserved because they may be needed as evidence in litigation, investigation, audit, merger, or other special circumstance.

BT: record

RT: freeze, hold order

FTP ~ *see:* File Transfer Protocol

fugitive, adj. ~ Fleeting; ephemeral.

Notes: When used of documents or records, fugitive connotes materials that are not held by the designated archives or library charged with their preservation[3].

full-text search, n. ~ COMPUTING · A technique to provide access to electronic materials by indexing every word in every item.

BT: search

RT: automatic indexing, keyword

Notes: Full-text searching is distinguished from manual indexing, which searches headings assigned to each document. Early full-text searching was limited, especially in its ability to distinguish different senses of a word; a search for glass might find documents relating to Philip Glass, window glass, and glass ice. More sophisticated search engines could use several terms, with Boolean logic and adjacency rules, to help narrow false hits. Modern search engines seen on the web use a variety of similar techniques to rank documents in terms of likely relevancy.

fullness ~ *see:* depth of description

fumigation, n. ~ A conservation treatment to disinfest or disinfect materials through the use of a vacuum or toxic gas.

RT: disinfection, disinfestation

function, n. ~ 1. The activities of an organization or individual performed to accomplish some mandate or mission. – 2. COMPUTING · Software code that performs a specific task, usually accepting one or more data values as input and, based on a manipulation of the input values, returning a single output value.

DF: procedure

RT: competence, functional analysis

†70 (Duranti 1998, p. 90, n. 10): Function[1] and competence are a different order of the same thing. Function is the whole of the activities aimed to one purpose, considered abstractly. Competence is the authority and capacity of carrying out a determined sphere of activities within one function, attributed to a given office or an individual. . . . While a function is always abstract, a competence must be attached to a juridical person.

functional analysis, n. ~ A technique that sets priorities for appraising and processing materials of an office based on the relative importance of the functions the office performs in an organization.

BT: appraisal

RT: function

†106 (Greene 1998b, p. 6): Functional analysis . . . argues that records be appraised only after the functions of an institution are defined and understood. Record appraisal then becomes a matter of identifying or creating records which best document the institution's functions. Because it is institutionally based, functional analysis implicitly shuns any prioritization among similar institutions, and suggests that there is a universal and objective set of records which comprise 'adequate' documentation of each and every example of a particular type of institution.

functional classification, n. ~ 1. A system for organizing materials on the basis of activity or program (function). – 2. The process of placing materials into such a system.

BT: classification

functional pertinence, n. ~ The activity or program (function) to which records relate.

RT: pertinence

functional provenance, n. ~ The origin of a group of materials as determined by the activities that produce the materials (the function), rather than organizational unit.

Notes: Functional provenance allows for intellectual control of multiprovenance series that result from administrative or political change. The concept ensures that, with a transfer of functions from one authority to another, relevant records or copies thereof are transferred to ensure administrative continuity.

Functional Requirements for Evidence in Recordkeeping ~ see: University of Pittsburgh Electronic Records Project

G

Gantt chart, n. ~ A graph using horizontal bars to represent tasks to be performed, with the order of the bars indicating the sequence and the length of the bars the time necessary to complete the task.

†*300 (Yates 1989, p. 88)*: Perhaps the best-known application of graphic analysis to scheduling is the Gantt chart. Henry Laurence Gantt was an early follower of Frederick Taylor . . . and a major proponent of scientific management. . . . Developed in 1917 to aid in the war effort, the widely praised Gantt chart focused on progress toward scheduled goals, rather than on actual quantities.

gateway, n. ~ 1. COMPUTING · A user interface to a complex information system; a portal. – 2. COMPUTING · Hardware or software used to pass information between networks.

gauge, n. ~ 1. A device used to measure the size, condition, or some other characteristic of material or machinery. – 2. MOTION PICTURES · The width of film stock as measured in millimeters.

gelatin emulsion, n. ~ PHOTOGRAPHY · A layer in film or prints of light-sensitive salts in a colloid of natural protein.

RT: emulsion

Notes: Gelatin emulsions began to be used in the 1880s, replacing collodion and albumen as common binders for holding the light-sensitive salts to a base, usually glass or paper.

gelatin print, n. ~ 1. A photographic print that uses gelatin as the binder. – 2. A photomechanical process that uses ink to produce prints from a reticulated gelatin matrix; collotype.

Syn: collotype

gelatin silver photograph (also **silver gelatin photograph**), n. ~ A photographic print, negative, or transparency with an image formed from metallic silver in a gelatin emulsion on a base of paper, plastic film, glass, or other material.

BT: photograph

RT: black-and-white photograph

Notes: The metallic silver is formed from silver halides (silver chloride, silver bromide, and silver iodide). Different processes use different combinations of silver halides. A gelatin silver photograph usually has a neutral black-and-white tone unless it is chemically altered (toning) or color is added after it is developed. Gelatin silver became the dominant photographic process after the 1890s and remains the dominant black-and-white photographic process.

genealogy, n. ~ 1. The study of ancestry. – 2. A list or diagram detailing a family tree.

general correspondence file, n. ~ Written communications, especially those sent by courier or post, organized as a series rather than interfiled with records relating to a specific subject.

BT: correspondence

Notes: General correspondence may be filed by subject, date, or correspondent.

general diplomatics, n. ~ The study of records that identifies their generic characteristics, independent of their manner of creation, the nature of the individual or organization that created them, or the social system in which they were created.

BT: diplomatics

†70 (Duranti 1998, p. 31): The application of [general diplomatics] to infinite individual cases constitutes the function of diplomatic criticism, that is of special diplomatics. Theory (general diplomatics) and criticism (special diplomatics) influence each other. The latter, analyzing specific situations, uses the former; the former guides and controls and is nourished by the latter.

general index, n. ~ An ordered list of subjects that appear in a variety of sources or collections, with pointers to where those subjects may be found within the materials.

RT: index, union catalog

Notes: A general index provides integrated access to the whole of a repository's holdings, rather than requiring a patron to look at separate indexes for each collection.

General International Standard for Archival Description, n. (**ISAD(G)**, abbr.) ~ A standard published by the International Council on Archives that establishes general rules for the description of archival materials, regardless of format, to promote consistent and sufficient descriptions, and to facilitate exchange and integration of those descriptions.

RT: descriptive standard

Notes: ISAD(G) was first published in 1994 and revised in 1999.

†144 (ISAD(G) 2000, p. 7): I.5 This set of general rules for archival description is part of a process that will a. ensure the creation of consistent, appropriate, and self explanatory descriptions; b. facilitate the retrieval and exchange of information about archival material; c. enable the sharing of authority data; and d. make possible the integration of descriptions from different locations into a unified information system. ¶ I.6 The rules accomplish these purposes by identifying and defining twenty-six (26) elements that may be combined to constitute the description of an archival entity. The structure and content of the information in each of these elements should be formulated in accordance with applicable national rules. As *general* rules, these are intended to be broadly applicable to descriptions of archives regardless of the nature or extent of the unit of description. However, the standard does not define output formats, or the ways in which these elements are presented, for example, in inventories, catalogues, lists, etc.

general material designation, n. (**GMD**, abbr.) ~ CATALOGING · A broad category of the material being described that, optionally, is included in the title of a cataloging record.

BT: descriptive element

RT: specific material designation

Notes: Anglo-American Cataloguing Rules (1.1C) specifies the following categories for use as a general material designator: art original, art reproduction, braille, chart, computer file, diorama, filmstrip, flash card, game, globe, kit, manuscript, map, microform, microscope slide, model, motion picture, music, picture, realia, slide, sound recording, technical drawing, text, toy, transparency, and videorecording.

General Public License, n. (**GPL**, abbr.) ~ A model agreement, developed by the Free Software Foundation, that establishes terms under which individuals may sell, copy, or modify a product, while protecting the creator's interests.

RT: copyright, open, open source software

Notes: Sometimes referred to as **Copyleft**. The GPL is typically issued with software, allowing programmers to use the software for free. The standard GPL includes a requirement that any modifications to the code must also be made freely available.

†193 *(Moody 1997, p. 4):* Linus [Torvalds] also adopted the standard GNU licensing scheme called Copyleft. The general public license, or GPL, allows users to sell, copy, and change Copylefted programs – which can also be copyrighted – but you must pass along the same freedom to sell or copy your modifications and change them further. You must also make the source code of your modifications freely available.

†268 *(Soderberg 2002):* 'Copyleft uses copyright law, but flips it over to serve the opposite purpose instead of a means of privatizing software, it becomes a means of keeping software free' [citing Stallman].

general record group, n. ~ An aggregation of the records from an agency executive office and from other units that pertain to matters that affect the entire organization.

BT: record group

Notes: A general record group may include administrative, fiscal, personnel, and similar records.

general records schedule (also **common records schedule**, **comprehensive records schedule**, **general schedule**), n. ~ A list of records series commonly found in many divisions within an organization, indicating their respective retention periods and other instructions for the disposition of those records.

BT: retention schedule

Notes: General records schedules are often used for administrative records.

generation (also **copy status**), n. ~ 1. A class characterized by the number of reproduction cycles between a copy and the original. – 2. Something that reflects a significant development from a previous version.

RT: copy

Notes: Generation[1] does not consider the number of reproductions made from the same source. Rather, it describes the number of times a new source is made from a copy. A print made directly from a negative is described as a first-generation copy. A reproduction from that print is a second-generation copy, and so forth. – Generation[2] is often used to describe major evolutions in technology.

generation loss, n. ~ A degradation of quality resulting from imperfect reproduction techniques.

RT: noise

Notes: Generation loss may include the introduction of noise and a loss of acuity. The quality of successive generations[1] generally deteriorates when using an analog process. Although digital reproduction is, in theory, capable of producing successive generations without loss of quality, in practice the copying process may introduce errors.

genre, n. ~ A distinctive type of literary or artistic materials, usually characterized by style or function rather than subject, physical characteristics, or form[2].

DF: subject

RT: record type

Notes: Typical examples of genres include correspondence and contracts. The subject matter and form of a genre may be quite varied. For example, a contract may relate to work done for hire, the loan of materials, or purchase of materials. Those contracts may be take the form of personalized letters or boilerplate documents and may be preprinted forms or holographs.

genuine, adj. ~ Authentic; original; bona fide; not counterfeit or fake.

> *RT:* authenticity, original
>
> †95 *(Garner 2003, p. 75):* Today the words [authentic and genuine] are interchangeable in most sentences, but a couple of distinctions do exist. First, 'authentic' is off-target when the sense is 'substantial'. . . . Second, 'authentic' is an awkward choice when the sense is 'sincere'. . . . The *OED* notes that late-18th-century theologians tried to differentiate the words, arguing that a book is 'authentic' if its content is accurate, and 'genuine' if it is correctly attributed to the writer. The point, weak as it was to begin with, has been preserved in some later usage guides.

geographic information system, n. (**GIS**, abbr.) ~ A combination of hardware, software, and rules that supports complex analysis of geospatial and temporal information and that often uses static or dynamic maps for reports.

> *BT:* information system
>
> *RT:* cartographic record, system

GIF, n. (abbr. for **Graphic Interchange Format**) ~ A proprietary standard for digital representations of images.

> *Notes:* GIF was developed by CompuServe in the 1980s. Its palette is limited to 256 colors, but which 256 colors may vary from image to image. The image uses lossless compression to minimize file size.

gift, n. ~ Material, including title, that is transferred, without compensation, from one party to another.

> *DF:* deposit
>
> *Syn:* donation

GILS ~ *see:* global information locator service

GIS ~ *see:* geographic information system

glass plate negative, n. ~ A photographic image that uses glass as a base and in which the image polarity reversed from the original.

> *Notes:* From 1851 through the 1870s, glass plate negatives generally used collodion as the binder to hold the light-sensitive salts to the glass base. After that, gelatin was used as the binder.

glassine, n. ~ A supercalendared, semitransparent paper.

> *BT:* paper
>
> *Notes:* Glassine is often used to make envelopes to store photographic negatives. Its hygroscopic properties make it inappropriate for archival use.
>
> †103 *(UNESCO A/V Glossary 2001):* Glassine paper is a supercalendered, smooth, dense, transparent or semi-transparent paper manufacturer primarily from wood pulps, which have been beaten to secure a high degree of hydration of the stock. It is grease resistant, and has a high resistance to the passage of air and many essential oil vapors used as food flavoring and, when waxed, lacquered, or laminated, is practically impervious to the transmission of moisture vapors.

global information locator service (also **government information locator service**), n. (**GILS**, abbr.) ~ An open standard used to describe and promote access to information and services.

> †101 *(GILS.net, FAQ (http://www.gils.net/faq.html)):* GILS specifies how information sources are described through locator records on network servers. Yet, no

one expects networks to be the only way to reach all audiences. We all depend on information providers and intermediaries to add essential value. They compile, edit, translate, and present information in appropriate media. Sometimes, a printed book or newsletter is the best media for helping people find information. A telephone referral service or face-to-face contact is best in yet other situations.

globe, n. ~ A graphic representation of features of the Earth or another celestial body made on a sphere.

> *BT:* cartographic record
> *RT:* map, scale
> *Notes:* Globes usually have a smooth surface but may use relief to represent altitude.

gloss, n. ~ 1. A note explaining a difficult or obscure word or phrase, especially such a note made between lines or in the margin of a document. – 2. An interpretation.

> *RT:* annotation, marginalia

glossy, adj. ~ 1. Having a hard, shiny surface. – n. ~ 2. A photograph with a hard, shiny surface, especially one used for publicity.

> *RT:* ferrotyping, matte

GMD ~ *see:* general material designation

GMGPC ~ *see:* Thesaurus for Graphic Materials

go list, n. ~ A list of words or phrases to be searched for in a text for inclusion in an automated index.

> *RT:* stop list
> *Notes:* A go list is the opposite of a stop list. Now generally obsolete in an age of full-text searching.

government document (also **government publication**), n. ~ A publication issued under the imprint of a government agency.

> *Notes:* When used as a single lexical unit, 'government document' connotes, especially in libraries, a work broadly distributed, traditionally in print, because of its educational value or public interest. When the phrase is formed from two distinct lexical units, it may refer to any document created or held by a governmental entity.

government information locator service ~ *see:* global information locator service

Government Paperwork Elimination Act, n. (**GPEA**, abbr.) ~ A federal law (44 USC 3504 (a)(1)(B)(vi)) that allows the Office of Management and Budget to establish procedures for the acquisition and use of information technology for electronic submission, maintenance, or disclosure of information, in lieu of paper, and for the use and acceptance of electronic signatures.

> †105 *(NOAA GPEA 2003):* Although confusing to many people, the Government Paperwork Elimination Act (GPEA) and the Paperwork Reduction Act (PRA) are not synonymous. The focus of the PRA is to limit the information the Federal government collects from the public in any form. The focus of the GPEA is to promote the doing of business electronically, with the public and otherwise.

GPEA ~ *see:* Government Paperwork Elimination Act

GPL ~ *see:* General Public License

grain, n. ~ 1. A pattern or structure in materials caused by the alignment of component fibers or particles. – 2. A design embossed on a surface to imitate a natural pattern. – 3. PHOTOGRAPHY · The relative coarseness of an image that results from the size of silver particles in the emulsion.

RT: granularity

Notes: Grain[3] is usually invisible to the naked eye. It becomes more visible as a negative is enlarged; prints made from small negatives are generally grainer than prints of the same size from a larger negative. Grain is generally more pronounced in high-speed emulsions.

granularity, n. ~ 1. PHOTOGRAPHY · An objective measure of variation in density caused by the size of particulate silver or dyes that give the appearance of grain[3]. – 2. The degree to which data is broken up into its most elemental components.

RT: grain

graphic, n. ~ 1. An image; an illustration; a picture. – 2. A symbolic representation of something. – 3. CATALOGING · A still, two-dimensional representation intended to be viewed by reflected light.

RT: image, picture, visual materials

Notes: A graphic may be two-dimensional, such as a print, or three-dimensional, such as a hologram. It may be a component in a larger work, or an independent work. – Graphic[1] is not necessarily representational; it may be colors and shapes that do not attempt to depict the appearance, abstract or precise, of any real-world object or scene. – Graphic[2] may be used to describe something that is a pictorial representation of the world, or an abstract representation of ideas through the positioning of shapes, lines, words, or other visual devices.

†103 *(UNESCO A/V Glossary 2001):* [Graphic[3]] A two-dimensional representation whether opaque (e.g., art original and reproductions, flash cards, photographs, technical drawings) or intended to be viewed, or projected without motion, by means of an optical device (e.g., film strips, stereographs, slides).

Graphic Interchange Format ~ *see:* GIF

graphic records, n. ~ A broad class of records that are primarily images, as distinguished from textual records.

BT: record

RT: photograph

Notes: Graphic records may include architectural, engineering, or artistic works, and may be drawings, designs, photographs, sketches, or other media.

gray card ~ *see:* neutral test card

gray scale, n. ~ A standard target consisting of discrete tones progressing from black to white that is used to calibrate exposure and color balance in photographs.

RT: benchmark, densitometer, step wedge

Notes: A gray scale is opaque, as distinguished from a step wedge, which is transparent.

great register, n. ~ 1. A list of individuals registered to vote in a particular year. – 2. A list of individuals registered for classes at an educational institution.

Notes: Great registers[1] sometimes included other information about the individual, including birth date, naturalization date, address, or occupation.

grey literature, n. ~ Reports and other materials printed for distribution outside commercial publishing channels.

RT: publication, quasi-publication, report

Notes: 'Grey literature' connotes publications with limited distribution and with subject matter of a professional, often academic, nature. The phrase is not generally used to describe fanzines, underground publications, family newsletters, or similar materials.

BT: Broader Term · *NT:* Narrower Term · *RT:* Related Term · *DF:* Distinguish From

†*293 (NY Acad of Medicine Library 2002):* In general, grey literature publications are non-conventional, fugitive, and sometimes ephemeral publications. They may include, but are not limited to the following types of materials: reports (pre-prints, preliminary progress and advanced reports, technical reports, statistical reports, memoranda, state-of-the art reports, market research reports, etc.), theses, conference proceedings, technical specifications and standards, non-commercial translations, bibliographies, technical and commercial documentation, and official documents not published commercially (primarily government reports and documents) [citing Alberani, 1990].

guide, n. ~ A broad description of the holdings at one or more archives, typically at the collection level.

BT: finding aid

NT: summary guide

Notes: A guide covering several repositories' holdings is often called a **repository guide** or a **interrepository guide**. A guide that describes collections relating to a specific subject is often called a **subject guide** or a **thematic guide**.

guideline, n. ~ Recommendations suggesting, but not requiring, practices that produce similar, but not identical, results.

BT: standard

Guidelines for the Construction, Format, and Management of Monolingual Thesauri, n. ~ A standard (ANSI Z39.19-1993) for systematically creating and maintaining a controlled vocabulary, including rules for formulating headings and relationships among the terms.

RT: broader term, narrower term, related term, thesaurus, use reference, used for reference

†*111 (Z39.19):* [This standard] provides guidelines for constructing monolingual thesauri: formulating the descriptors, establishing relationships among terms, and effectively presenting the information in print and on a screen. It also includes thesaurus maintenance procedures and recommended features of thesaurus management systems.

gum print, n. ~ A photograph, usually on paper, made using the gum bichromate process.

BT: photograph, pigment print

Notes: The emulsion is made from sensitized gum arabic mixed with a pigment. The gum bichromate process is monochromatic, but the image may be in many different colors. Separation negatives can be overprinted to produce a color image.

Gum prints are popular with many photographers because the image can be easily manipulated. The process was widely used for fine art photographs from the 1880s through the 1920s and continues to be used today.

H

halftone, n. ~ 1. A photomechanical process used to print a continuous tone, monochromatic image using one color of ink. – 2. A print made using such a process.

   RT: photomechanical, print

   Notes: A halftone gives the illusion of many shades of a tone by representing different densities using dots of different sizes. A dark area would be made up of many large dots, which may bleed into each other to form a solid. A light area has a few small dots, or no dots at all, allowing the light-colored base to reflect light. Color images may be printed in halftone by separating the original into its four component colors (cyan, magenta, yellow, and black) and combining each as a separate halftone.

hand-coloring, n. ~ PHOTOGRAPHY, PRINTS · The manual application of color to an image.

   Notes: Hand coloring may be used to give the appearance of natural color, or may be used for artistic effect.

handwriting, n. ~ 1. Text inscribed manually, typically using a pen or pencil. – 2. The characteristic manner in which an individual forms characters by hand.

   NT: cursive, disjoined hand

   Notes: Handwriting[1] may be in a disjoined hand, in which the characters are not connected; printing is an example of a disjoined hand. Or, it may be cursive, in which the characters are connected.

hard copy, n. ~ 1. A document made using paper or other durable media that is in human-readable form. – 2. COMPUTING · A **printout**.

   DF: soft copy

   Syn: printout

   RT: copy, output

   Notes: Hard copy[1] is distinguished from data on an ephemeral medium, such as a text on a computer screen. It generally implies a human-readable format, as distinguished from machine-readable format such as a floppy disk, but may be used to include microfilm. – Hard copy[2] connotes paper.

hard drive (also **hard disk**), n. ~ COMPUTING · A magnetic storage device designed to provide rapid access to large quantities of data.

   RT: magnetic disk

   Notes: A hard drive is typically made up of one or more disks mounted on a core and spinning in unison. Separate heads for each side of each disk read and write data on the magnetic coating of the disks. A hard drive usually has fixed disks, but the disks may be removable from the drive.

hardware, n. ~ Physical, mechanical, and electrical components of a system, especially a computer.

   RT: firmware, software

hardware dependent, adj. ~ Requiring a specific type of equipment to operate.

   Syn: machine dependent

   RT: open system, software dependent

Notes: 'Hardware dependent' is commonly used to describe software that can used only in conjunction with a specific type of equipment, such as a specific processor. It can also be used to describe film or audio media that require specific recording and playback equipment.

hardware independent, adj. ~ Able to operate on many different types of equipment.

Syn: machine independent

Notes: Hardware independence does not imply the ability to run on all equipment. Hardware-independent software may require an intermediary program or translation to enable it to run on different platforms; for example, a program written in C must be compiled using different tools to run on different computers.

harvester (also **spider**), n. ~ A software application designed to download pages from the Internet.

Notes: A harvester generally follows links on pages that it downloads, capturing the pages those links point to. A harvester often follows rules that limit its operations to a specific server or domain, the number of links to follow, and the kinds of files to download.

hashing, n. ~ 1. COMPUTING · A technique to provide rapid access to items in a table, especially tables in which entries are made in an unpredictable fashion. – 2. COMPUTING · A technique to transform a string of characters into a unique, fixed-length code (a hash).

Notes: Hashing[1,2] uses a hash function, such as MD5 or SHA, to calculate a hash value. – Hashing[2] is a significant component of public key infrastructure (PKI) and digital signatures.

header, n. ~ 1. Information that appears at the top of each page of a document; a running head. – 2. COMPUTING · Structured information that appears at the beginning of a data object and that provides information about the structure of data in the object body. – 3. COMPUTING · Information at the beginning of a packet that indicates the destination and is used to control how the packet is routed over the network.

Notes: A header[1] may contain the title or author of the work and a page number. With the exception of the page number, information in the header is usually the same within a section of a document, or throughout the document; a work may use different headers on odd and even number pages. – A header[2] is logically separate from the data it describes.

heading, n. ~ 1. A word or phrase set apart from subsequent text that serves as a title or summary. – 2. CATALOGING · A word or phrase that appears at the beginning of an entry in a catalog or bibliography that is used to organize entries.

NT: complex entry, direct entry, inverted entry

RT: access point, entry, subheading

Health Insurance Portability and Accountability Act, n. (**HIPAA**, abbr.) ~ The Health Insurance Portability and Accountability Act of 1996 (Pub. L. 104-191).

†279 *(LC Thomas, http://thomas.loc.gov/cgi-bin/bdquery/z?d104:HR03103:|TOM:/ bss/d104query.html|):* [From the act:] To amend the Internal Revenue Code of 1986 to improve portability and continuity of health insurance coverage in the group and individual markets, to combat waste, fraud, and abuse in health insurance and health care delivery, to promote the use of medical savings accounts, to improve access to long-term care services and coverage, to simplify the administration of health insurance, and for other purposes.

Syn: Synonym • †: see Bibliography • *Superscript:* Definition number

hearing, n. ~ 1. A meeting, usually formal and often before an official, at which parties may voice opinions or give testimony. – 2. A meeting before a judge to determine matters of fact or law, usually held in public and often with witnesses giving testimony. – 3. A meeting at which members of a legislative body receive testimony and ask questions regarding potential legislation or an investigation.

NT: executive session, public hearing

hearsay rule, n. ~ Provisions in the Federal Rules of Evidence (801–807) that disallow testimony by a witness that is based on what another person has said, rather than on the witness's personal knowledge.

RT: business exception rule, evidence

Notes: Most state courts have similar provisions in their rules of evidence. The rule allows 28 exceptions. Business records, written recollections, and other documents may be allowed as evidence under these exceptions.

†30 (Black's 1999, p. 726): The chief reasons for the rule are that out-of-court statements amounting to hearsay are not made under oath and are not subject to cross-examination.

hectograph, n. ~ A 19th-century process for duplicating documents using aniline dyes.

hierarchical database, n. ~ A database management system that is built on a model of one-to-many relationships between parent and child entities.

Notes: In a hierarchical database, any parent can have many children. Any child can also be a parent with many children, but a child can have only one parent.

hierarchical description, n. ~ A technique of writing a finding aid by describing the collection from general to specific, starting with the whole, then proceeding to the components (series, subseries, folders, and items).

BT: description

RT: analysis, level of description, multilevel description, series descriptive system

Notes: Hierarchical description does not necessarily include every level; item-level description is uncommon. See level of description.

hierarchical storage management, n. ~ A mass storage device that automatically moves data from expensive, rapid-access online media to less-expensive, nearline storage based on the frequency of use of the data.

RT: nearline storage, offline storage, online storage

Notes: Hierarchical storage management systems generally keep frequently used data on high-speed hard drives. As the frequency of access decreases, typically with age, data may be moved to compressed formats on hard drives, then to optical disks, and ultimately to tape. Moving data to slower media saves significantly on storage costs.

hierarchical system, n. ~ A classification scheme that includes headings that may be subdivided as necessary for greater granularity.

Notes: A hierarchical system can keep related subjects together rather than dispersing them throughout the alphabet. For example, a hierarchy of pets, subdivided into cats and dogs, would group Persian, Siamese, and tabby cats separately from golden retriever, greyhound, and poodle dogs.

High Sierra, n. ~ A vernacular name for the standard (ISO 9660) for storing data on a Compact Disc.

RT: compact disc

†157 (New Words 1997): The name is derived from that of an ad hoc group of CD-ROM researchers and developers which named itself the High Sierra Group

following a meeting at the High Sierra Hotel at Lake Tahoe, California. . . . A modified version of the High Sierra format was accepted by the [International Organization for Standardization] as the international standard ISO 9660 in 1988.

highlight, n. ~ PHOTOGRAPHY · The most luminous area of an image.

> *RT:* shadow
>
> *Notes:* In a negative, a highlight is an area of greatest density.
>
> *†136 (ICP Encyclopedia 1984, p. 247):* The brightest areas of a subject or an image are called the highlights. An area may be light because of the color of the subject matter, such as pale skin or light-colored clothing, or it may be inherently bright, as with lamps or fire. . . . When films and prints are properly exposed and processed, highlights will show detail and traces of color or tone; they will not be glaring, blank white areas.

HIPAA ~ *see:* Health Insurance Portability and Accountability Act

historiated, adj. ~ Adorned with scenes, plants, animals, or birds.

> *RT:* illumination, versal
>
> *Notes:* Typically used to describe a capital letter at the beginning a section of text, or the capitals of columns.

historic, adj. ~ Noteworthy among past events or old things.

> *Notes:* Distinguish from **historical**, an adjective used to describe events or things of the past. 'Historic' connotes significance, 'historical' implies nothing more than age.
>
> *†88 (Fowler 1965, p. 247):* The ordinary adjective of history is historical; historic means memorable, or assured of a place in history, now in common use as an epithet for buildings worthy of preservation for their beauty of interest; historical should not be substituted for it in that sense.

historical manuscripts tradition, n. ~ Techniques of curating historical manuscripts and records based on principles of librarianship that emphasize items rather than collections.

> *RT:* manuscript curator
>
> *†27 (Berner 1983, p. 1–2):* This historical manuscripts tradition, in relation to both collecting and intellectual control, was dominant from the eighteenth century until about 1960. In the twentieth century before 1960 practices were added from the public archives field from time to time. By 1960 the nature of collecting itself had changed from a concentration on papers of remote vintage to an emphasis on those of recent origin. The latter had many characteristics of public archives, because of their comparable extent, structure, and depth of documentation. ¶ The historical manuscripts tradition is rooted in librarianship. Because manuscripts were generally brought under some form of library administration, it is understandable that library techniques would be applied to them. . . . Because of their rarity (unique handwritten items) and their separation from related papers, the collected materials were handled as discrete items.
>
> *†27 (Berner 1983, p. 7):* The fateful separation of the historical manuscripts tradition field from the public archives field began in 1910 at the AHA's Conference of Archivists, when the application of library principles was attacked as inapplicable to public archives. The differences that developed meant that the historical manuscripts tradition would remain linked to techniques of librarianship. Public archives, meanwhile, would develop along lines derived from

European archival institutions where theory and practice had long been the object of scholarly discourse and refinement.

historical society, n. ~ An organization that seeks to preserve and promote interest in the history of a region, a period, or a subject.

> *RT:* repository
>
> *Notes:* Historical societies are typically focused on a state or a community. They often have collections of artifacts, books, and records, and may include a museum. Some state historical societies, such as Minnesota, are quasi-governmental institutions, organized as a private corporation but maintaining the official state archives.
>
> †154 (Kaplan 2000, p. 134): The historical society movement in America originated in 1791 when Jeremy Belknap and seven others met to organize the Massachusetts Historical Society in Boston [citing Louis Leonard Tucker.] ... The historical society had become, by [the 1890s], almost obligatory for groups seeking to establish and present to the larger culture a cohesive identity.

historical value, n. ~ 1. The usefulness or significance of records for understanding the past. – 2. The importance or usefulness of records that justifies their continued preservation because of the enduring administrative, legal, fiscal, or evidential information they contain; archival value.

> *Syn:* archival value
>
> *BT:* value
>
> *RT:* continuing value

hit, n. ~ COMPUTING · 1. An entity that matches the criteria of a search. – 2. COMPUTING · A request for a file from a web server.

> *RT:* false hit
>
> *Notes:* A hit[1] is commonly a member of a set of results. For example, a search for an author in a catalog may return separate hits for each title by the author. – A hit[2] involves only one file; because a complete web page typically contains many files for text and images, a count of hits is not equivalent to a count of pages.

hold order, n. ~ A communication directing the halt of scheduled destruction of any records that are potentially relevant to litigation, investigation, or audit.

> *RT:* freeze, frozen records
>
> *Notes:* Records subject to a hold order are said to be frozen. Records are typically frozen if they are potentially relevant to impending or current litigation, regardless of whether a hold order or subpoena has been issued.

holding area, n. ~ An area used for the temporary storage of materials.

> *Notes:* Records are often kept in a holding area when first accessioned so that they can be inspected and treated, if necessary, for pests or mold. Records may also be kept in a holding area for transfer to the archives after they have been removed from office space.

holdings, n. ~ The whole of a repository's collections.

> *Syn:* collection

holdings maintenance, n. ~ PRESERVATION · Activities to stabilize materials for long-term storage by placing materials in appropriate housings and environments.

> *Notes:* Holdings maintenance includes ensuring materials are in containers, that the documents are supported within containers, and that fragile documents have individual enclosures for additional protection. It also includes all aspects of the storage environment, including temperature, humidity, and shelving.

†93 *(Garlick 1992)*: A holdings maintenance program is responsive to the institutional reality that existing records may be housed inadequately or inappropriately; that they are found in an assortment of containers, wrappers, envelopes, and folders; that they are bundled, tied, pinned, and fastened together; that too many may be wedged in one place or too few allowed to slump and curl; that their format and size requirements may not be addressed; that the mechanics of good housing may not have been followed; and that enclosures used to provide additional protection may have caused damage. Most often, incoming records are housed in modern office-quality folders and boxes that meet short-term rather than long-term retention requirements. ¶ With these points in mind, a holdings maintenance program has three major procedural objectives: to place documents into a good primary housing (a container that fully encloses them, supports them, and protects them from the environment); within the container, to group documents into folders for additional protection and support and to enhance safe access; to place documents that are severely damaged or vulnerable into individual enclosures. ¶ Also defined in a holdings maintenance program are the four functional, design, and compositional features of the housing supplies – the containers, folders, and sleeves – used during the course of work: housings and enclosures must perform their assigned function; they must be as simple and straightforward to use as possible to facilitate easy and safe access to the documents; they must not contain any structural features that will physically damage or jeopardize the documents; they must be made of stable materials that will not contribute to the deterioration of the documents in the present or the future.

Hollerith card (also **IBM card, punched card**), n. ~ A card that records data or machine instructions through a pattern of perforations.

Notes: Standard cards are 7⅜ inches by 3¼ inches and contain 12 rows of 80 columns. Some cards had 90 columns.

†237 *(Ralston 1976, p. 610)*: Herman Hollerith (b. Buffalo, NY, 1860; d. Washington, D.C., 1929) was the inventor of punched-card data processing and found of a firm that evolved to become IBM. For the quarter-century from 1890 to World War I, he had a virtual monopoly on punched-card data processing. He held the foundation patents on the field (U.S. patents 395 781 – 395 783) and nearly 50 other United States and foreign patents on basic techniques and equipment.

Hollinger box ~ *see:* document box

†223 *(Personal communication, Bill Hollinger, 1 October 2003)*: The term Hollinger box is just a generic name archivists have given to this particular style of box.

hologram, n. ~ A three-dimensional image that reproduces on a two-dimensional surface an object's appearance, as well as the perception of parallax and depth perspective.

Notes: Holograms are made by the process of **holography**, which exposes the objects and the recording material to a split beam of coherent light, typically from a laser. Although the process does not include a camera, it is generally considered to be a photographic process. When the image is viewed, an object behind another is covered or revealed as the view point changes side to side (parallax). The relative distance between objects changes as the viewpoint moves closer or farther to the image (depth perspective).

holograph, n. ~ 1. Handwriting. – 2. An original document entirely in the handwriting of its author.

> *Syn:* manuscript

home page, n. ~ A web page intended to be the primary or root point of entry to a website or to a collection of web pages that comprise a document.

> *RT:* web page

> *Notes:* A home page is frequently named index, default, or home, and may have a file extension of .htm, .html, .asp, .cfm, or .jsp. A home page is frequently published as the logical entrance to a site or document and contains introductory matter and links to the rest of the site or document.

honeycombing, n. ~ A technique of leaving open spaces in storage shelving to allow for additions to existing collections.

> *RT:* shelving

horizontal filing, n. ~ A technique to store documents horizontally.

> *Syn:* flat filing

> *Notes:* Horizontal filing is distinguished from vertical filing, in which documents are stored on edge as in a filing cabinet.

horizontal mode, n. ~ 1. The arrangement of images on roll film with frames (portrait or landscape) oriented horizontally, perpendicular to the long axis of the film; comic mode. – 2. The arrangement of images on microfiche with frames filling the columns in a row before preceding to the next row.

> *DF:* ciné mode, vertical mode

> *Syn:* comic mode

house organ, n. ~ A periodical issued by an organization for its employees.

> †*300 (Yates 1989, p. 17):* One of the tools that they used in humanizing the workplace was a new form of internal communication, in the in-house magazine or shop paper. Its function was described in a 1918 article. 'Many shops have outgrown the one-man stage. No longer can the head of the organization interpret his policies personally to the workmen. But a factory house organ, whether it be a single typewritten sheet or a 24-page magazine, offers an opportunity to bind personal interest closer in the small shop and keep management from becoming mechanical in the large plant.' [Citing *Factory*].

housekeeping records, n. ~ Records that facilitate the operations and management of an agency, but which do not relate directly to programs that help the agency achieve its mission.

> *Syn:* administrative records, facilitative records

> *BT:* record

> *Notes:* Housekeeping records are common to most organizations. Examples include routine correspondence or interoffice communications; records relating to human resources, equipment and supplies, and facilities; reference materials, routine activity reports, work assignments, appointment books, and telephone logs.

HTML ~ *see:* Hypertext Markup Language

hub, n. ~ 1. A cylinder on which film or tape is wound to form a spool. – 2. Computing · Hardware that serves as a central connection in a network, allowing several attached devices to access the network.

> *Syn:* core

> *RT:* flange, open reel, pancake, reel

Notes: A hub[1] may have a flange, in which case the whole is called a reel. The hub and the material it holds may be contained within a cassette, cartridge, or magazine.

human-readable, adj. ~ Capable of being recognized and understood without mechanical assistance.

> *Syn:* eye-readable
>
> *Notes:* Microfilm is generally not considered eye-readable because it requires magnification, although it is certainly human-readable after magnification. Digital and analog records, including computer tapes and disks, phonograph disks, and cassette tapes, are not considered human-readable because all require special equipment to transform the encoded information into a form that is meaningful to people.

humidification, n. ~ 1. The process of adding moisture to the atmosphere. – 2. CONSERVATION · A treatment to restore pliability and flatten documents by placing them in a chamber where they absorb moisture from the air.

humidity, n. ~ The amount of absolute moisture in the air.

> *RT:* relative humidity

hydrophilic, adj. ~ Having an affinity for moisture.

> *RT:* hygroscopic

hygrometer, n. ~ An instrument to measure the amount of moisture in the air.

> *RT:* psychrometer, thermohygrometer

hygroscopic, adj. ~ 1. Easily dissolved in water. – 2. Easily absorbing moisture from the air.

> *RT:* hydrophilic

hygrothermograph, n. ~ A device for recording atmospheric humidity and temperature over time.

> *RT:* thermohygrometer
>
> *Notes:* Older models of hygrothermographs used pens to leave a trace on paper that a clockwork advanced. Modern instruments record the information in digital form to be downloaded to a computer for analysis and preservation.

hyper-, prefix ~ COMPUTING · A qualifier indicating a nonlinear, multidimensional organization that allows numerous paths through the structure.

> *RT:* hypermedia, hypertext
>
> †157 *(New Words 1997):* The two key terms in this field, hypermedia and hypertext, were both introduced in the mid sixties. Hypermedia is a method of structuring information in a mixture of media (text, video, graphics) in such a way that related items of information are connected together by links or threads called hyperlinks; hypertext is machine-readable text that forms an interconnected structure in a similar way. . . . The term hypermedia is frequently treated as a synonym for the related term multimedia; however, multimedia presentations can be linear and non-interactive, whereas hypermedia ones necessitate decisions by the user to select one route through the presentation over another.

hypermedia, n. ~ A hypertext system that links information in many different formats, including text, still and moving images, and audio.

> *RT:* hyper-, multimedia

hypertext, n. ~ A document with a nonlinear, multidimensional structure with links between parts, allowing the document to be read in many different sequences.

> *RT:* hyper-

Notes: The term was coined by Ted H. Nelson in 1965.

†*167 (D Levy 2001, p. 110):* All the current talk about hypertext as a medium that will liberate the reader from the tyranny of the author is pure hype.

†*167 (D Levy 2001, p. 149):* It was Ted Nelson who first coined the term 'hypertext.' Nelson and Douglas Englebart are considered to be the fathers of *computer-based* hypertext, the ability to link fragments of text together via computer, allowing the reader to follow a link from one piece of text to another. (The more recent term 'hypermedia' is a further generalization of hypertext, in which not only text but other media types, such as static graphics, animation, and sound, are linked together.)

†*167 (D Levy 2001, p. 110):* Vannevar Bush is generally credited with coming up with the idea of hypertext (but not its name); his Memex system – envisioned in a paper published in 1945 but never implemented – stored text fragments on microfiche. Yet the notion of non-linear Webs of text is an ancient one – surely as old as annotation – and other hypertext-like designs precede Bush's in the twentieth century.

Hypertext Markup Language, n. (**HTML**, abbr.) ~ COMPUTING · A standard defining codes to format hypertext or hypermedia documents, especially for the web.

RT: Cascading Style Sheet, Extensible Hypertext Markup Language, Extensible Markup Language, markup

Notes: HTML was first developed by Tim Berners-Lee in 1990. Version 2.0 (RFC 1866) was released in 1994, version 3.2 was released in 1996, and version 4.0 was released in 1997 and revised in 1998. Version 4.01, a subversion of version 4.0 was released in 1999. HTML is being superseded by Extensible Hypertext Markup Language (XHTML). HTML and XHTML are maintained and developed by the World Wide Web Consortium (W3C). See http://www.w3.org/MarkUp/.

hypo ~ *see:* fixer

I

IASA ~ *see:* International Association of Sound and Audiovisual Archives
IASSIST ~ *see:* International Association of Social Science Information Service and Technology
IBM card ~ *see:* Hollerith card
ICA ~ *see:* International Council on Archives
iconographic archives, n. ~ Pictorial works collected and preserved because of the information they contain or because of their enduring value.

> *BT:* archives
>
> *Notes:* 'Iconographic archives' is often used to distinguish such collections from textual archives. Iconographic archives may include images in many different formats, including prints, paintings, drawings, and photographs.

iconography, n. ~ 1. A discipline of art history that identifies, describes, classifies, and interprets imagery used to represent subjects in visual arts. – 2. Symbols, emblems, or images commonly used to represent a subject.

> *RT:* visual literacy, visual materials

ICR ~ *see:* intelligent character recognition
ICRM ~ *see:* Institute of Certified Records Managers
identity management, n. ~ 1. Administrative tools used to distinguish and recognize individuals within a system. – 2. COMPUTING · Software controls that identify users and that restrict resources users can access and actions they can take within the system.

> *Notes:* Identity management[1] in a nontechnical environment can be based on birth certificates, passports, or driver's licenses. – Identity management[2] on a single system may be as simple as manually assigned user IDs and passwords. To promote e-commerce, global, interoperable standards for identity management are being proposed by several organizations and corporations.
>
> †129 (RSA Security 2003): When it comes to conducting business online, an organization can only use identities that are trusted. That's where the real value of identity management lies. An effective identity management solution establishes trust in an organization's online environment. Who users are (Authentication) and what users can do (Access management) are tightly coupled and rooted in the ability to manage (Administration) the full life cycle of a digital identity from creation and maintenance to termination, as well as enforcement of organizational access policies. Similarly, the identifiers carried by a transaction (authentication) and the associated security requirements and permissions are critical to enabling automated ebusiness. These components are absolutely critical to the success of an organization's identity management solution.

IFLA ~ *see:* International Federation of Library Associations and Institutions
illumination, n. ~ 1. Hand-decorated, ornamental letters, border designs, and pictures in manuscripts or books, usually in colors and with gold or silver leaf. – 2. The process of decorating a manuscript or book.

> *RT:* historiated, versal

illustrative sampling, n. ~ A method of appraisal that selects a portion of records for preservation from a larger series based on the selector's judgment, which may be informed by specific criteria.

BT: sampling

Notes: Illustrative sampling is neither systematic nor random.

IM ~ *see:* instant messaging

image, n. ~ 1. A representation of the appearance of something or someone; a picture. – 2. PHOTOGRAPHY, REPROGRAPHICS · The content of a graphic that captures the appearance of something within its borders. – 3. COMPUTING · An exact, logical copy of data held in another media.

NT: drawing

RT: graphic, moving image, photograph, picture, print, video, visual materials

Notes: Image[1] may be tangible, like a drawing, or ephemeral, like a mental image suggested by a textual description.

†130 *(Images in Time 2003, p. 166):* All images[1] constitute a record, irrespective of the value we may attach to the information they contain. The unique property of photographic records reside in their ability to capture a moment in time and to highlight the inevitable passing of time.

imaging, n. ~ The process of copying documents by reproducing their appearance through photography, micrographics, or scanning.

NT: computer output microfilm, electronic imaging

RT: reprographics

Notes: Imaging, by itself, makes no attempt to make any text in the document machine-readable, although a system may use optical character recognition to convert imaged text to such form. Imaging, especially scanning, is often used to copy paper documents into a document management system that provides the ability to access the images.

imbibition process, n. ~ A photomechanical process to make prints from photographs by creating a gelatin relief matrix that is used to transfer dye to an emulsion on paper.

RT: dye transfer process, print

Notes: The dye transfer process is one of the best known examples of the imbibition process. The imbibition process can be used to make color images by creating separation negatives, which are then used to create different matrices. Each matrix is used to print a different color ink, which combine to form a full color image.

imitative copy, n. ~ A reproduction that captures the content and appearance of the original, but which can be clearly distinguished from the original.

BT: copy

RT: simple copy

immutability, n. ~ The quality of being unchanging.

RT: alteration, fixity, integrity, preservation

Notes: The content of a document is fixed in that it is stable and resists change, but it may not be immutable. Words may be erased or added. 'Immutability' connotes a significantly greater resistance to change, such that any change is clearly evident. In information technology, immutability is accomplished by creating a process to demonstrate that the record has not been altered.

†210 *(OCLC/RLG Preservation Metadata 2001, p. 4):* Digital objects are not

immutable therefore, the change history of the object must be maintained over time to ensure its authenticity and integrity.

impact printer, n. ~ A technology to print characters or graphics by using a hard surface to strike a ribbon containing a pigment or dye against the printing surface.

> *BT:* printer
>
> *Notes:* Typewriters are examples of impact printers, but the phrase is generally used to describe computer printers that use similar technology. The device may form characters from a pattern of dots created using small pins (dot matrix) or by using a mechanism that contains fully formed characters (for example, a daisy wheel).

impartiality ~ *see:* archival nature

import, n. ~ The process of incorporating data from an external source into an application.

> *Notes:* Transferring data from one source to another may be merely copying. 'Import' connotes a transformation of the data in order to integrate it with existing data or by changing it to a useful form.
>
> †157 *(New Words 1997):* This word came into use in the mid eighties. Like export, it usually now implies the movement of data into an application, most frequently data which is in another format and which has to be translated by the receiving application. So a user may add new records to a database by importing them from a source file which may be text or may be in the format of another database; a desktop-publishing system may import text and graphic files in a variety of formats and convert them to its internal representation.

important records, n. ~ Records that are of significant importance for continued operation after a disaster.

> *BT:* record
>
> *RT:* essential records, vital records
>
> *Notes:* The loss of important records is not as ruinous as the loss of essential or vital records. They can be reconstructed, but only after considerable time and cost.

imprescriptibility, n. ~ Not capable of having ownership transferred as the result of continuous possession over a statutory period of time.

> *Notes:* As it pertains to public records, imprescriptability means that records remain permanently subject to replevin because they are inalienable public property.

impression, n. ~ 1. A design or mark made by pressing something into a surface. – 2. PUBLISHING · All copies of a document, book, or pamphlet printed at one time. – 3. GRAPHICS · A specific print distinguished from other prints made from the same source.

> *BT:* edition
>
> *RT:* print, printing, reprint
>
> *Notes:* Impression³ is distinguished from printing, the latter suggesting all copies of the work or for printed images in general.

in-analytic, n. ~ An entry in a catalog that describes a part of a larger work that is also described in the catalog.

> *Syn:* analytical entry
>
> *RT:* analysis
>
> *Notes:* In archival cataloging, an in-analytic may be made for series or items within a collection. In bibliographic cataloging, analytical entries may be made for chapters of books, special issues of or articles in periodicals.

in-house archives ~ *see:* institutional archives

in letter, n. ~ A record series composed of correspondence received.
> *BT:* correspondence
> *RT:* out letter

inactive records, n. ~ Records that are no longer used in the day-to-day course of business, but which may be preserved and occasionally used for legal, historical, or operational purposes.
> *Syn:* noncurrent records
> *BT:* record
> *RT:* active records, semicurrent records
> *Notes:* Inactive records are often stored out of the office of creation in a records center or on offline media. They may either be destroyed when their frequency of use falls so low that they have lost all value or they may be transferred to an archival repository for permanent retention.

inalienability, n. ~ A prohibition against the transfer or assignment of title.
> *RT:* inviolability
> *Notes:* As regards public records, inalienability prevents such materials from being given, surrendered, or transferred to anybody except those the law allows to possess them.

incipit, n. ~ The opening phrase of an early manuscript or book or of one of its sections.
> *Notes:* An incipit often includes the title and the name of the author of the work and sometimes details of its production. In the absence of a title, the incipit may be used to identify the work.

inclusive dates (also **span dates**), n. ~ Description · The dates of the oldest and most recent items in a collection, series, or folder.
> *BT:* date
> *RT:* bulk dates

incremental backup, n. ~ A backup containing only those files in a set, often the entire contents of a disk or system, that have changed since the last incremental backup.
> *Notes:* Restoring files using incremental backups begins with the most recent backup of the full set, then each incremental backup in the order created.

indefinite value ~ *see:* archival value

indenture, n. ~ 1. A formal agreement between two or more parties, usually a written document with a serrated edge; a chirograph. – 2. A contract binding an individual to work for another for a period of time.
> *Syn:* chirograph
> *RT:* authentication
> *Notes:* An indenture¹ traditionally was cut with a serrated edge to reduce the possibility of forgery. Indentures are distinguished from a deed poll, which have a smooth edge.

independent agency, n. ~ An agency of the executive branch of the government that is not under the direction of an executive department.
> *Notes:* The head of an independent agency is not a member of the President's Cabinet. The National Archives and Records Administration is an independent agency.

index, n. (**indexes, indices,** pl.) ~ 1. An ordered list of headings that points to relevant information in materials that are organized in a different order. – 2. Publishing ·

A portion of a book, usually located in the back, that provides an ordered list of subjects covered in the book, with page numbers or other reference to where those subjects are discussed. – 3. A scale or reference used as a measure. – 4. PRINTING · A typographical ornament in the shape of a fist with the index finger extended.

NT: analytical index, card index, chain index, classified index, closed index, cumulative index, double lookup index, keyword and context index, keyword in context index, keyword out of context index, line code index, line code index, open index, permuted index, phonetic index, rotated index

RT: catalog, controlled vocabulary, general index, indexing

Notes: Generally, an index[1] provides no explanation about the information it points to beyond its location. It is distinguished from a catalog, which provides additional information to help determine relevance. An index may be created on cards, with separate cards for each entry to allow interfiling. It may also be on paper or in a database or word processing file. – An index[2] usually uses page numbers for the pointers, but some works may use section numbers. – Examples of index[3] include quality index and time-weighted preservation index.

†63 *(Burlington Agenda 2001, p. 295):* A superficial examination of a printed index would reveal that search engines available at this writing [2001] could retrieve many of its references from the full text of a work, but it is also clear that they could not build the web of relationships and analysis provided by a good back-of-the-book index, nor the navigational support provided by such an index.

index term, n. ~ A word, phrase, or code used as a heading in an index or catalog.

Syn: descriptor

RT: controlled vocabulary

Notes: Index terms are frequently taken from a controlled vocabulary to ensure that the same term is used consistently for the same concept.

index vocabulary (also **index language**), n. ~ The complete set of terms or phrases used in an index.

RT: lead-in vocabulary

indexing, n. ~ The process of creating an ordered list of concepts, expressed as terms or phrases, with pointers to the place in indexed material where those concepts appear.

NT: assignment indexing, automatic indexing, concept indexing, coordinate indexing system, depth indexing, extraction indexing, postcoordinate indexing, precoordinate indexing

RT: index, self-indexing files, specificity of indexing

indictment, n. ~ 1. A formal, written accusation of a crime. – 2. The process of making such an accusation.

Notes: In the United States, indictments are made by a grand jury.

indirect access, n. ~ A technique to retrieve information that requires an intermediary finding aid or index.

RT: direct access

Notes: Indirect access systems typically classify materials using a code; they are often hierarchical. To locate a file, a user must consult an index of filing plan to look up the code under which relevant material is filed.

info-, prefix ~ Information.

Notes: Often used as a prefix to other words, such as infotainment, infomercial, infodump, infoglut, infobahn, and infonaut.

†157 (New Words 1997): Info has been a colloquial abbreviation of information for most of this century, but it was only with the increasing influence of information technology and the vogue for snappy combining forms that compounds began to appear.

informatics, n. ~ 1. The study of the computational, social, cognitive structure, and the properties of information, especially as regards the use of technology to organize, store, retrieve, and disseminate information. – 2. Computer applications, especially the use of structured databases used to store and extrapolate research.

RT: information science

†185 (McCrank 2002, p. 50): The term with its classical etymology had been coined simultaneously in more than one place and in more than one language. Before long 'informatics' evolved into a generic term in American English for computer applications in any field and was widely adopted in Biomedicine without regard for its origins.

†290 (Ediburgh University Informatics): Informatics studies the representation, processing, and communication of information in natural and artificial systems. It has computational, cognitive and social aspects. The central notion is the transformation of information – whether by computation or communication, whether by organisms or artifacts. ¶ Understanding informational phenomena – such as computation, cognition, and communication – enables technological advances. In turn, technological progress prompts scientific enquiry. The science of information and the engineering of information systems develop hand-in-hand. Informatics is the emerging discipline that combines the two.

information, n. ~ 1. A collection of data, ideas, thoughts, or memories. – 2. The meaningful portion of a signal, as distinguished from noise. – 3. Law · Formal criminal charges against an individual made by a prosecutor without a grand jury.

NT: actionable information

RT: data, record

Notes: Information[1] and data are near synonyms. Whereas data connotes facts or ideas in their most atomized form, information refers to more complex concepts made up of multiple data elements. Information may take many forms, including words, sounds, images, and formulas.

Information, like data, is independent of any medium in which it is captured as content. Information is intangible until it has been recorded in some medium. Recorded information may be captured in databases, spreadsheets, documents, sound recordings, or motion pictures. Even when captured in a document or other form, the information remains distinct from the medium.

†26 (Bergeron 2002, p. 9): Data are numerical quantities or other attributes derived from observation, experiment, or calculation. ¶ Information is a collection of data and associated explanations, interpretations, and other textual material concerning a particular object, event, or process. ¶ Metadata is data about information. Metadata includes descriptive summaries and high-level categorization of data and information. ¶ Knowledge is information that is organized, synthesized, or summarized to enhance comprehension, awareness, or understanding. That is, knowledge is a combination of data and an awareness of the context in which the data can be successfully applied. Although the concept of knowledge is roughly equivalent to that of metadata, unlike data, information, or metadata,

knowledge implies a human – rather than a computer – host. ¶ Understanding is the possession of a clear and complete idea of the nature, significance, or explanation of something. It is a personal, internal power to render experience intelligible by assimilation of knowledge under broad concepts. Like knowledge, understanding is currently limited to *homo sapiens*.

†26 *(Bergeron 2002, p. 9)*: *Data* are numerical quantities or other attributes derived from observation, experiment, or calculation. *Information* is a collection of data and associated explanations, interpretations, and other textual material concerning a particular object, event, or process. *Metadata* is data about data. Metadata includes descriptive summaries and high-level categorization of data and information. *Knowledge* is information that is organized, synthesized, or summarized to enhance comprehension, awareness, or understanding. That is, knowledge is a combination and an awareness of the context in which the data can be successfully applied. Although the concept of data is roughly equivalent to metadata, unlike data, information, or metadata, knowledge implies a human – rather than computer – host. *Understanding* is the possession of a clear and complete idea of the nature, significance, or explanation of something. It is a personal, internal power to render experience intelligible by assimilation of knowledge under broad concepts.

†33 *(Bouissac 1998, p. 311)*: [information] A theory of information was first formulated in 1948 by Claude Shannon and Warren Weaver as a theory of communication to study the receiving, conserving, processing, and transmitting of signals. The notion of information, however, goes back to Ludwig Boltzmann (1896), who stated that the increase in information about a certain system is related to a reduction in the number of states of the system and therefore to an entropy decrease. This concept was later generalized by Léon Brillouin (1956), who defined information as negative entropy or negentropy.

†57 *(Dictionary of Computing 1996, p. 240)*: Information must be distinguished from any medium capable of carrying it. A physical medium (such as a magnetic disk) may carry a logical medium (data, such as binary or text symbols). The information content of any physical objects, or logical data, cannot be measured or discussed until it is known what range of possibilities existed before and after they were received. The information lies in the reduction in uncertainty resulting from the receipt of the objects or the data, and not in the size of complexity of the objects or data themselves. Questions of the form, function, and semantic import of data are only relevant to information inasmuch as they contribute to the reduction of uncertainty. If an identical memorandum is received twice, it does not convey twice the information that its first occurrence conveyed: the second occurrence conveys no information at all, unless, by prior agreement, the number of occurrences is itself to be regarded as significant.

†237 *(Ralston 1976, p. 658)*: Information systems accept (as inputs), store (in files or a data base), and display (as outputs) strings of symbols that are grouped in various ways (digits, alphabetical characters, special symbols). Users of the information systems attribute some value or meaning to the string of symbols. Sometimes a distinction is made between the mechanistic representation of the symbols, which is called data, and the meaning attributed to the symbols, which is called information. A given output datum, under this definition, can result in different information to different users.

information architecture, n. ~ The structure and interrelationship of information, especially with an eye toward using business rules, observed user behaviors, and effective interface design to facilitate access to the information.

> *RT:* data architecture, enterprise architecture, network architecture
>
> *Notes:* Information architecture is frequently used in the context of websites. It covers how the underlying information is organized and how users gain access to that information.
>
> *†236 (Quass 2000):* Information architecture can be seen as four interrelated architectural views, namely information architecture, business architecture, application architecture and technology architecture [citing Finnerman]. This view is based on the Zachman framework. An architectural approach provides operational definitions as a part of its common business terminology and therefore facilitates common business rules enforcement mechanisms [citing Finnerman]. Business architecture provides a start for business process redefinition and improvement, as it requires defined business process models.

information copy, n. ~ A copy of a record distributed to make recipients aware of the content, but not directing the recipient to take any action on the matter.

> *DF:* action copy
>
> *BT:* copy
>
> *RT:* reference copy
>
> *Notes:* Information copies are often considered to be nonrecords, having only ephemeral value. Because information copies are duplicates of the record copy, some retention schedules allow them to be disposed of at any time without authorization.

Information Documentation – Records Management, n. ~ An international standard (ISO 15489) that establishes principles to ensure that adequate records are created, captured, and managed, including guidelines for their implementation.

Information Interchange Format ~ *see:* MARC

information management, n. ~ 1. Principles and techniques to process, store, retrieve, manipulate, and control access to information so that users can find information they need.

> *BT:* management
>
> *Notes:* Information management is distinguished from documentation, which is the process of gathering and recording information. The results of documentation are subject to information management.

information processing, n. ~ The analysis, organization, storage, retrieval, and manipulation of data, especially through the use of computers.

> *Syn:* data processing
>
> *Notes:* Information processing is often used instead of data processing to emphasize that the information is conceptual rather than numerical.

information resource management, n. (**IRM,** abbr.) ~ Principles and techniques to oversee and administer the creation, use, access, and preservation of information in an organization, founded on the belief that information is an asset comparable to financial, human, and physical resources.

> *Notes:* Information resource management emphasizes maximizing the value of information assets through the efficient, effective control of those assets.

information retrieval, n. ~ A process that mediates between large quantities of information and users by retrieving a selected subset from the information that most nearly matches the user's request.

BT: Broader Term • NT: Narrower Term • RT: Related Term • DF: Distinguish From

Notes: 'Information retrieval' generally connotes an automated system. The system may provide users with a citation, a document, or a passage within a document.

Information Retrieval Application Service Definition and Protocol Specification for Open Systems Interconnection, n. ~ An international standard (Z39.50, ISO 23950) for passing search queries and results between complex information systems.

information science, n. ~ The study of the theory and practice of creating, acquiring, processing, managing, retrieving, and disseminating information, especially the use of computers to facilitate these processes.

RT: informatics

†57 *(Dictionary of Computing 1996, p. 241):* The term was coined in the aftermath of the spread of computers and the corresponding revolution in information-handling techniques. Information science therefore inevitably pays substantial attention to, but is not confined to, what can be achieved with computers.

information system, n. ~ An organized set of procedures and techniques designed to store, retrieve, manipulate, analyze, and display information.

NT: decision support system, executive support system, geographic information system, management information system, transaction processing system

RT: content management, database, document management, knowledge management, system

Notes: 'Information system' usually connotes the use of computers. If automated, 'information system' also refers to the hardware and software. Automated information systems are generally distinguished from real-time control systems, message-switching systems, and software engineering environments.

information technology, n. ~ The use of hardware and software, especially digital computers, to capture, process, store, and disseminate complex data in many forms, including audio, images, and text.

†18 *(20th Century Words 1999, p. 347):* Originally US; the abbreviation IT is not recorded before 1982.

Information Technology – 8-bit Single-byte Coded Graphic Character Sets, n. ~ A standard (ISO/IEC 8859) that defines eight-bit graphic character sets.

BT: character set

Notes: The standard is divided into several parts, each defining a different character set with graphic characters appropriate to different languages, including Latin, West European, East European, South European, North European, Cyrillic, Arabic, Greek, Hebrew, Turkish, and Nordic. The standard includes several Latin character sets for different languages that use variants of the Roman alphabet. The standard defines only 191 printing characters in each set; unspecified characters are reserved for control characters.

Information Technology – Open Systems Interconnection – The Directory: Public-key and Attribute Certificate Frameworks, n. ~ A standard (X.509) published by the International Telecommunication Union that allows e-commerce transactions and communications to be secured as rigorously as needed – from consumer transactions with limited risk, to mission-critical business-to-business transactions.

RT: public key infrastructure

†146 *(ITU 2000):* X.509 is viewed throughout the Information Technology (IT) industry as the definitive reference for designing applications related to Public Key Infrastructures (PKI). The elements defined within X.509 are widely

utilized – from securing the connection between a browser and a server on the Web to providing digital signatures that enable electronic transactions to be conducted with the same confidence as in a traditional paper-based system.

informational value (also **reference value** and **research value**), n. ~ The usefulness or significance of materials based on their content, independent of any intrinsic or evidential[1] value.

BT: value

RT: secondary value

Notes: Census records have informational value to genealogists long after those records' evidential value as an enumeration of the population for the federal government has passed.

†8 *(Adkins 1997, p. 20):* In a corporate environment it is much more important to appraise records for their informational value than for their evidential value. My experience at Kraft and Ford shows that executives and employees tend to request bits and pieces of information from our records, not records that provide evidence of how business has been conducted over the years.

†62 *(Dollar 1991, p. 45):* A growing number of archivists are now urging that archival appraisal return to basics and pay more attention to the documentation of program accountability, which suggests that the informational value of information application systems may be eclipsed by their evidential value.

†259 *(Schellenberg 1984, p. 58):* The secondary value of records can be ascertained most easily if they are considered in relation to two kinds of matters: 1) the evidence they contain of the organization and functions of the Government body that produced them, and 2) the information they contain on persons, corporate bodies, things, problems, conditions, and the like, with which the Government body dealt.... ¶ The values that attach to records because of the information they contain will be referred to as 'informational values.' The information may relate, in a general way, either to persons, or things, or phenomena. The term 'persons' may include either individuals or corporate bodies. The term 'things' may include places, buildings, physical objects, and material things. The term 'phenomena' relates to what happens to either persons or things – to conditions, problems, activities, programs, events, episodes, and the like. ¶ It should be emphasized that the distinction between evidential and informational values is made solely for purposes of discussion. The two types of values are not mutually exclusive.

infotainment, n. ~ Programming based on factual information, or historical or current affairs, in a manner intended to be entertaining.

RT: Disneyfication, docudrama, edutainment

Notes: Infotainment is intended to make subjects often perceived of as dry or academic more accessibly by making the presentation more lively. Infotainment is often delivered through television or interactive media.

†157 *(New Words 1997, p. 156):* Infotainment is the presentation of information as entertainment on television and through multimedia; the word is sometimes applied pejoratively to news bulletins which overemphasize entertainment at the expense of information.

infrared photography, n. ~ A technique of recording the portion of the light spectrum between roughly 700 and 900 nanometers, which is not normally visible to the human eye.

Notes: Infrared light is just below the red portion of the spectrum, at the opposite end of the visible spectrum from ultraviolet. Infrared photography commonly captures between 700 and 900 nanometers, but specialized materials may record as low as 1200 nanometers. Depending on the techniques and materials, infrared photography may include a portion of the visible light spectrum.

Infrared photographs may represent the amount of radiation in a single color, with variations in shades representing the intensity of the radiation. Infrared photographs may also be made with color materials, using different visible colors to represent different portions of the spectrum; for example, blue might represent infrared, with green and red representing the visible spectrum.

infringement, n. ~ LAW · A violation of intellectual property protected by a patent, copyright, or trademark.

   RT: intellectual property, piracy

ingest, n. ~ In the Open Archival Information System (OAIS) model, processes related to receiving information from an external source and preparing it for storage.

   RT: acquisition, Open Archival Information System

inherent vice (also **inherent fault**), n. ~ The tendency of material to deteriorate due to the essential instability of the components or interaction among components.

   Notes: Nitrate film and highly acidic paper suffer inherent vice because they are chemically unstable. An object made of metal and leather suffers inherent vice because the leather causes the metal to corrode.

initial interview ~ *see:* reference interview

injunction, n. ~ An order issued by a court directing a party to take or to refrain from some action.

inkjet printer (also **ink jet**), n. ~ A nonimpact computer output device that forms characters and graphics by spraying tiny drops of ink from a matrix of small nozzles onto paper or another media.

   BT: printer

   Notes: Inkjet technology can be used for black-and-white or color printouts.

inner title (also **intertitle, interior title**), n. ~ Text displayed on the screen of motion pictures as a title between scenes, to provide continuity or to show dialog.

   RT: subtitle, title

   Notes: Inner titles were common in silent films.

input, n. ~ 1. An opinion, viewpoint, or other information. – 2. COMPUTING · Data received from some external source. – 3. COMPUTING · The process of entering data or a program into a computer system.

   RT: output

input device, n. ~ Hardware that is used to enter data or programs into a computer.

   Notes: Examples of input devices include keyboards, optical character recognition (OCR) scanners, bar code readers, or telemetry equipment.

input records, n. ~ 1. Paper documents containing information to be entered into an electronic recordkeeping system. – 2. Files containing data (records) used to update another computer file, especially a master file.

   BT: record

   RT: master file

inspection (right of), n. ~ 1. An individual's right to view public records, especially those that have been filed for public notice. – 2. The right of an archival or records management program to review the records of organizations under its jurisdiction to ensure that the recordkeeping practices are appropriate.

†10 (AJS, Records §14): The right of inspection[1] is subject to reasonable rules and regulations as to when, where, and how the inspection may be made, in order to guard against loss or destruction of records, and to avoid unreasonable disruption of the functioning of the office in which they are maintained.

inst, abbr. ~ The current month.

Notes: The abbreviation for 'instant' was commonly used in 19th-century letters to mean 'in the same month.' For example, an individual replying to a letter sent the same month might write, 'In your letter of the 12th inst.' The abbreviations **ult** (*ultimo*) was used for 'the previous month', and **prox** (*proximo*) was used for 'the next month.' *Garner's Modern American Usage* describes the abbreviations as 'commercialese.'

instant messaging, n. (**IM**, abbr.) ~ 1. A private, synchronous exchange of messages between parties over a computer network. – 2. A system for allowing instant message sessions.

Notes: Instant messaging (IM) requires users to subscribe to an IM service and run service-specific software. Because of competing standards, the parties must use the same service and application to be able to participate in instant messaging sessions.

Instant messaging allows users to chat in real time. Unlike email, both parties must be simultaneously connected to allow messages to be exchanged. Although most IM services are restricted to plain text, some allow users to send attachments. Unlike email, many IM services are similar to phone calls in that they create no record that documents the content of the communication. However, some IM systems are designed to record the content.

Institute of Certified Records Managers, n. (**ICRM**, abbr.) ~ A professional organization founded in 1975 that allows records managers to demonstrate that they meet specific criteria of experience and capability established by their peers.

RT: certified records manager

Notes: See http://www.icrm.org/.

†135 (ICRM website 2003, http://www.icrm.org/intro.html): The primary objective of the ICRM is to develop and administer the program for professional certification of records managers, including certification examinations and a certification maintenance program. The ICRM serves as the official certifying body for both the Association of Records Managers and Administrators, International, (ARMA International) and the Nuclear Information Records Management Association (NIRMA).

institutional archives (also **in-house archives**), n. ~ A repository that holds records created or received by its parent institution.

BT: archives

RT: collecting archives

institutional memory, n. ~ The information held in employees' personal recollections and experiences that provides an understanding of the history and culture of an organization, especially the stories that explain the reasons behind certain decisions or procedures.

Syn: corporate memory

Notes: Records may be considered a part of institutional memory, but the term generally connotes informal, unrecorded knowledge.

institutional repository, n. ~ Software and associated rules used to capture, structure, provide access to, and preserve digital materials produced by an organization or community.

RT: DSpace, Fedora

Notes: Institutional repositories have their origin in academic environments and were intended to enable scholarly communities to share information in a variety of formats, including e-prints, data sets, electronic theses and dissertations, image collections, and courseware. DSpace and Fedora are two technologies designed to implement institutional repositories.

†176 *(C Lynch 2003):* In the fall of 2002, something extraordinary occurred in the continuing networked information revolution, shifting the dynamic among individually driven innovation, institutional progress, and the evolution of disciplinary scholarly practices. The development of institutional repositories emerged as a new strategy that allows universities to apply serious, systematic leverage to accelerate changes taking place in scholarship and scholarly communication, both moving beyond their historic relatively passive role of supporting established publishers in modernizing scholarly publishing through the licensing of digital content, and also scaling up beyond ad-hoc alliances, partnerships, and support arrangements with a few select faculty pioneers exploring more transformative new uses of the digital medium.

instrument, n. ~ A legal document, such as a contract, deed, or promissory note, that establishes, secures, modifies, or terminates rights, duties, entitlements, or liabilities.

instrument of gift ~ *see:* deed of gift

intaglio, n. ~ A technique of carving or cutting a design into a surface.

DF: relief image

NT: engraving, etching

intangible property ~ *see:* intellectual property

integrated pest management, n. (**IPM**, abbr.) ~ Techniques to combat insects and other vermin through a combination of biological, cultural, physical, and chemical tools that minimize health and environmental risks, and costs.

†39 *(Center for IPM, http://cipm.ncsu.edu/history.html):* The history of integrated pest management (IPM) traces its first real beginnings to the late 1960s, where a number of factors came together to initiate a search for better methods of pest control than simple reliance on prophylactic pesticide use. These factors included not only the well known litany of pesticide misuse problems (resistance and non-target effects), but also the rapid development of technologies enabling more sophisticated approaches, primarily due to rapid advances in communication and computing, with the allied new sciences of operations research, systems analysis, and modeling. ¶ Although much of the initial push for IPM came from California researchers in sympathetic response to Rachael Carson's *Silent Spring*, national acceptance of IPM as a philosophy and technology can be traced to 1970 to the first symposium of agricultural scientists brought together to discuss IPM in a conference held at North Carolina State University, which was jointly funded by the Rockefeller Foundation, NSF, and USDA/CSRS.

integrity, n. ~ The quality of being whole and unaltered through loss, tampering, or corruption.

RT: alteration, archival integrity, completeness, fixity, immutability

Notes: Integrity is a relative concept that assesses whether the essential nature of a record has changed. As a record ages, its ink may fade or bits of the paper may be chipped from edge without any significant loss of integrity. Contrawise, loss of a page from a record, especially one bearing authorizing signatures, has a significant impact on the record's integrity.

In the context of records, integrity relates to the potential loss of physical or intellectual elements after a record has been created. It is distinguished from completeness, which refers to the presence of all required physical and intellectual elements when the record is created.

†23 *(InterPARES2, 2003, p. 3):* The integrity of a record refers to its wholeness and soundness: a record has integrity when it is complete and uncorrupted in all its essential respects. This does not mean that the record must be precisely the same as it was when first created for its integrity to exist and be demonstrated. When we refer to an electronic record, we consider it essentially complete and uncorrupted if the message that it is meant to communicate in order to achieve its purpose is unaltered. This implies that its physical integrity, such as the proper number of bit strings, may be compromised, provided that the articulation of the content and any required elements of form remain the same. The integrity of a record may be demonstrated by evidence found on the face of the record, in metadata related to the record, or in one or more of its various contexts.

†103 *(UNESCO A/V Glossary 2001):* [archival integrity] A basic standard derived from the principle of provenance and the registry principle which requires that an archive/record group shall be preserved in its entirety without division, mutilation, alienation, unauthorized destruction or addition, except by accrual or replevin, in order to ensure its full evidential and informational value.

†175 *(C Lynch 2000, p. 5):* When we say that a digital object has 'integrity,' we mean that it has not been corrupted over time or in transit; in other words, that we have in hand the same set of sequences of bits that came into existence when the object was created.

intellectual control, n. ~ The creation of tools such as catalogs, finding aids, or other guides that enable researchers to locate relevant materials relevant to their interests.

RT: administrative control, catalog, finding aid, physical control, process control

Notes: Intellectual control includes exploiting access tools developed by the creator of the materials and, typically, received with the collection. However, these tools must be integrated into the repository's other tools.

intellectual form, n. ~ DIPLOMATICS · The sum of a record's formal attributes that represent and communicate the elements of the action in which the record is involved and of its immediate context, both documentary and administrative.

BT: form

RT: intrinsic element

†70 *(Duranti 1998, p. 134):* The term *physical form* refers to the external make-up of the document, while the term *intellectual form* refers to its internal articulation. Therefore the element of the former are defined by diplomatists as external or *extrinsic*, while the elements of the latter are defined as internal or *intrinsic*.

intellectual property (also **intangible property**), n. ~ 1. A group of intangible rights that protect creative works, including copyright, trademarks, patents, publicity rights, performance rights, rights against unfair competition. – 2. The title to such rights in a tangible or intangible work.

　　NT: copyright, cultural property rights, moral rights, patent, performance rights, publicity rights, trademark, Visual Artists Rights Act

　　RT: digital rights management, infringement, rights management

　　Notes: Intellectual rights may be divided into industrial rights, which include patents, trademarks, industrial designs, and geographical indications, and copyright and related rights, which include the rights of reproduction, adaptation, distribution, exhibition, and performance, and moral rights.

　　†218 *(Parezo 1999, p. 284–285):* Some, but by no means all, native peoples feel that in certain cases the knowledge recorded in field interviews is proprietary and can endanger users who are not ritualistically prepared to access it. [Note:] This is an emerging ethical issue, often listed under intellectual property rights and privacy rights. . . .

intelligent character recognition, n. (**ICR**, abbr.) ~ A technique of converting images of text, especially handwriting, into machine-readable data that uses patterns to match characters, then improves accuracy through an analysis of the characters in context.

　　RT: optical character recognition

　　Notes: ICR typically checks words against a dictionary. Some implementations of ICR may display unrecognized forms for manual correction.

interactive media, n. ~ A technology designed to present content that varies in response to a user input.

　　RT: system

interface, n. ~ 1. A place where two things come together. – 2. The design or specifications for two systems to function together.

　　Notes: An interface may be between different technologies or between a human and technology. An RS-232 serial port defines an interface between different types of hardware, such as a computer and a modem or a mouse. A web browser serves as an interface between a human user and a complex information system.

interfile, n. ~ To place an item in its proper place within an existing body of materials.

　　RT: refile

interior title ~ *see:* inner title

interleaving, n. ~ 1. Sheets of paper, usually tissue, inserted between the pages of a book or album, especially between illustrative plates and text. – 2. Blank sheets bound in a work that are intended for taking notes. – 3. The process of inserting such sheets. – 4. Video · In NTSC, a blend of two video fields to create a single frame, each field contributing every other scan line.

　　RT: barrier sheet

　　Notes: A single sheet of interleaving is an **interleaf**. Interleaving[1,2] is often inserted during printing and binding between the front of printed, illustrative plates and adjacent pages to prevent transfer of inks. The sheets may be bound in, tipped to the plate, or loose. Interleaving made from high-quality paper, often with an alkaline reserve, may be placed in a scrapbook or photo album to prevent contamination between materials on facing pages.

intermediate, n. ~ A copy of a master, usually the camera original, specifically created for and used in the process of creating other copies.

> *NT:* printing dupe
> *RT:* direct duplication, internegative, interpositive
> *Notes:* Examples of intermediates include submasters, duplicating masters, printing dupes, internegatives, and interpositives.

International Association of Social Science Information Service and Technology, n. (**IASSIST**, abbr.) ~ An international organization of professionals working with information technology and data services to support research and teaching in the social sciences. Its members work in a variety of settings, including data archives, statistical agencies, research centers, libraries, academic departments, government departments, and nonprofit organizations.

> *Notes:* See http://www.iassistdata.org/.

International Association of Sound and Audiovisual Archives, n. (**IASA**, abbr.) ~ A professional organization of individual and institutional members that promotes cooperation among sound and audiovisual archives.

> *Notes:* See http://www.iasa-web.org/.

International Committee for Documentation of the International Council of Museums ~ *see:* Comité international pour la documentation du Conseil international des musées

International Conference of the Round Table on Archives ~ *see:* Conférence internationale de la Table Ronde des Archives

International Council on Archives (**Le Conseil international des Archives**), n. (**ICA**, abbr.) ~ An international organization of state, public, and private archives and individual archivists that promotes the preservation of the archival heritage in all countries and provides opportunities to share knowledge of archival and records management practices.

> *RT:* Conférence internationale de la Table Ronde des Archives
> *Notes:* See http://www.ica.org/.
> †128 (ICA): The International Council on Archives (ICA) is a decentralized organisation governed by a General Assembly and administered by an Executive Committee. Its branches provide archivists with a regional forum in all parts of the world (except North America); its sections bring together archivists and archival institutions interested in particular areas of professional interest; its committees and working groups are engaging the contribution of experts to the solution of specific problems. The ICA Secretariat serves the administrative needs of the organisation and maintains relations between members and cooperation with related bodies and other international organizations. ¶ ICA is the professional organisation for the world archival community, dedicated to promoting the preservation, development, and use of the world's archival heritage. It brings together national archive administrations, professional associations of archivists, regional and local archives and archives of other organizations as well as individual archivists. ICA has more than 1,500 members in over 170 countries and territories, making it truly international. It is a non-governmental organisation, which means that it maintains an independence from the political process and that its members include public and private archive institutions and individuals. ICA works closely with inter-governmental organizations such as UNESCO and the Council of Europe. It also has strong links with other non-governmental organizations.

International Federation of Library Associations and Institutions, n. (**IFLA**, abbr.)
~ An international organization that promotes the library and information professions.

> *Notes:* See http://www.ifla.org/.

> †*195 (IFLA 2004):* IFLA (The International Federation of Library Associations
and Institutions) is the leading international body representing the interests of
library and information services and their users. It is the global voice of the library
and information profession. ¶ Founded in Edinburgh, Scotland, in 1927 at an
international conference, we celebrated our 75th birthday at our conference in
Glasgow, Scotland in August 2002. We now have over 1700 Members in more than
150 countries around the world. IFLA was registered in the Netherlands in 1971.
The Royal Library, the national library of the Netherlands, in The Hague, gener-
ously provides the facilities for our headquarters. ¶ IFLA is an independent, international, non-governmental, not-for-profit organization. Our aims are to: promote
high standards of provision and delivery of library and information services;
encourage widespread understanding of the value of good library & information
services; represent the interests of our members throughout the world.

International Organization for Standardization, n. (**ISO**, abbr.) ~ A membership
organization that works with national standards organizations from more than
140 countries to promote and coordinate the development of international standards.

> *Notes:* See http://www.iso.org/.

> †*182 (UN ACCIS 1990, http://www.iso.org/iso/en/aboutiso/introduction/
index.html):* ISO is a network of the national standards institutes of 147 countries,
on the basis of one member per country, with a Central Secretariat in Geneva,
Switzerland, that coordinates the system. ¶ ISO is a non-governmental organization: its members are not, as is the case in the United Nations system, delegations
of national governments. Nevertheless, ISO occupies a special position between
the public and private sectors. This is because, on the one hand, many of its member institutes are part of the governmental structure of their countries, or are
mandated by their government. On the other hand, other members have their
roots uniquely in the private sector, having been set up by national partnerships of
industry associations. ¶ Therefore, ISO is able to act as a bridging organization in
which a consensus can be reached on solutions that meet both the requirements of
business and the broader needs of society, such as the needs of stakeholder groups
like consumers and users.

International Research on Permanent Authentic Records in Electronic Systems, n.
(**InterPARES**, abbr.) ~ A research project with members from several countries
that is investigating the problems of the authenticity, reliability, and accuracy of
electronic records throughout their life cycle.

> *Notes:* InterPARES 1 began in 1999 and concluded in 2001; reports are avail-
able on the project website. InterPARES 2 began in 2002 and will run through
2006. See http://www.interpares.org/.

> †*139 (InterPARES2, p. 5):* Thus the proposed research project, hereinafter
called InterPARES 2, aims at developing a theoretical understanding of the records
generated by interactive, dynamic, and experiential systems, of their process of
creation, and of their present and potential use in the artistic, scientific and government sectors. On the basis of this understanding, the project will formulate

methodologies for ensuring that the records created using these systems can be trusted as to their content (that is, are reliable and accurate) and as records (that is, are authentic) while used by the creator; for selecting those that have to be kept for legal, administrative, social or cultural reasons after they are no longer needed by the creator; for preserving them in authentic form over the long term; and for analyzing and evaluating advanced technologies for the implementation of these methodologies in a way that respects cultural diversity and pluralism.

†141 (*InterPARES website 2002, http://www.interpares.org/index.htm*): The InterPARES (International Research on Permanent Authentic Records in Electronic Systems) Project is a major international research initiative in which archival scholars, computer engineering scholars, national archival institutions and private industry representatives are collaborating to develop the theoretical and methodological knowledge required for the long-term preservation of the authenticity of records created in electronic systems. The InterPARES Project is based in the School of Library, Archival and Information Studies at the University of British Columbia. ¶ The first phase of the project, InterPARES 1, began in 1999 and was concluded in 2001. It focused on the preservation of the authenticity of records that are no longer needed by the creating body to fulfill its own mission or purposes. This phase has produced conceptual requirements for authenticity, models of the processes of selection and preservation of authentic electronic records, a glossary, and other reports.

International Standard Book Numbering, n. (**ISBN**, abbr.) ~ A standard (ISO 2108) ten-digit number used to uniquely identify books.

Notes: An ISBN is commonly printed with a bar code to facilitate scanning. ISBNs are scheduled to become thirteen digits after 2005. See http://www.isbn.org/.

International Standard for Archival Authority Records: Corporate, Personal, Families, n. (**ISAAR (CPF)**, abbr.) ~ A standard published by the International Council on Archives to establish controls for the creation and use of access points in archival descriptions and to identify the kinds of information that should used to describe a corporate body, person, or family.

Notes: Originally published in 1996, a second edition was published in 2004. Available online at http://www.ica.org/biblio/ISAAR2EN.pdf.

International Standard for Archival Description (General) ~ *see:* General International Standard for Archival Description

International Standard Recording Code, n. (**ISRC**, abbr.) ~ A standard (ISO 3901) number used to uniquely identify sound recordings and music videos.

Notes: The International Federation of the Phonographic Industry (IFPA) is the ISO-appointed international registration authority for ISRC. See http://www.ifpi.org/isrc/.

International Standard Serial Number, n. (**ISSN**, abbr.) ~ A standard (Z39.9, ISO 3297) eight-digit number used to uniquely identify serial publications, including electronic serials.

RT: key title

Notes: See http://www.issn.org:8080/pub/.

International Standards Organization ~ *see:* International Organization for Standardization

International Telecommunication Union (also **Comité Consultatif International Téléphonique et Télégraphique**), n. (**ITU, CCITT**, abbr.) ~ An international organization that includes governments and private industry and that works to coordinate the interoperation of telecommunication networks and to advance communications technology.

   Notes: See http://www.itu.int/.

   †289 *(Webopedia website):* The ITU was founded in 1865 and became a United Nations agency in 1947. It is responsible for adopting international treaties, regulations and standards governing telecommunications. The standardization functions were formerly performed by a group within the ITU called CCITT, but after a 1992 reorganization the CCITT no longer exists as a separate body.

internegative, n. ~ A negative, made from a transparency, that is used to make prints or copies.

   RT: direct duplication, intermediate

   Notes: Internegative is sometimes used to describe copy negatives made from prints.

Internet (often **net**), n. ~ 1. An international telecommunications network that uses the TCP/IP protocol to connect smaller computer networks. – **internet** (uncapitalized), n. ~ 2. A connection of networks, possibly by means of the Internet.

   RT: extranet, intranet, World Wide Web

   Notes: The Internet[1] is not synonymous with the World Wide Web. The latter is a service that is provided using the Internet. The Internet can be used for a variety of other services, including file transfer, telnet, email, and instant messaging. The Internet grew out of Department of Defense research to develop a robust communications system that could withstand significant damage to the physical network, especially damage caused by a nuclear war. That original network was called ARPAnet.

   †157 *(New Words 1997):* The abbreviated term internet, uncapitalized, began to be used in the early seventies; it was a shorthand term for the communications circuits and their controlling software which linked together the separate computer networks comprising the US military ARPANET system. By the early eighties, the number of linkages had grown greatly to include many universities and other research bodies; by then the word had gained an initial capital letter, referring to the set of computer systems connected in this way as a single unique entity.

   †173 *(Long 2004):* Effective with this sentence, Wired News will no longer capitalize the "I" in internet. ¶ At the same time, Web becomes web and Net becomes net. . . . the decision wasn't made lightly. Style changes are rarely capricious, since change plays havoc with the editor's sacred cow, consistency. ¶ A change in our house style was necessary to put into perspective what the internet is: another medium for delivering and receiving information. That it transformed human communication is beyond dispute. But no more so than moveable type did in its day. Or the radio. Or television.

interoperability, n. ~ Computing · The ability of different systems to use and exchange information through a shared format.

   Notes: Interoperability implies that the information does not need to be transformed during exchange; the different systems can use the data in its native format. Standards facilitate interoperability; for example, a web page marked up in

Hypertext Markup Language (HTML) can be read on different browsers.

Interoperability is often a relative term. In the example of web pages, different browsers may render the code with subtle – and sometimes not so subtle – differences. A browser on one person's computer may display the text in 10-point Times Roman, another browser on another person's computer may display the text in 12-point Helvetica, and a third browser on another person's computer may read the text out loud.

†231 *(Digital Preservation Testbed 2003, p. 31):* Interoperability in the technical sense tackles the problem of digital obsolescence by reducing the dependency of files and records on a particular combination of hardware and software. Interoperability means that a file can be transferred from one platform to another and can then still be reproduced in the same or a similar way. In its simplest implementation two forms are possible: dependency on the application, but not on the operating system; independency of both the operating system and the application.

InterPARES ~ *see:* International Research on Permanent Authentic Records in Electronic Systems

interpositive, n. ~ A photograph, usually on film, with normal polarity that is created during a two-step process to duplicate negatives.

RT: direct duplication, intermediate

Notes: Interpositives are typically made using negative film; a negative of a negative produces a positive image. The interpositive is then used to make another negative. Interpositives are frequently used to make printing masters from original camera film or to reproduce still negatives that are deteriorating. Interpositives can be either color or monochrome.

interrelationship ~ *see:* archival nature

interrepository guide ~ *see:* guide

interrogatory, n. ~ A question submitted in writing to an opposing party in a lawsuit.

Notes: Interrogatories take place as part of discovery. They are answered under oath and may be used as evidence at trial.

intertitle ~ *see:* inner title

intranet, n. ~ A computer network that is restricted to users within a specific organization, especially network services intended for disseminating information within the organization through the use of web technology.

RT: extranet, Internet

Notes: An intranet is distinguished from the Internet, in that it is not generally accessible to the public. 'Intranet' sometimes includes closed networks that allow limited access to some users outside the organization, but such a system is often called an extranet.

intrinsic element, n. ~ 1. An internal component of a document's contents. – 2. The elements of a record that convey a its action and immediate context.

NT: eschatocol, exposition, final clauses, protocol, text, title

RT: extrinsic element, intellectual form

†17 *(InterPARES Authenticity, p. 5):* Intrinsic elements are the discursive parts of the record that communicate the action in which the record participates and the immediate context. They fall into three groups: 1) elements that convey aspects of the record's juridical and administrative context (e.g., the name of the author, addressee, the date); 2) elements that communicate the action itself (e.g., the indication and description of the action or matter); 3) elements that convey

aspects of the record's documentary context and its means of validation (e.g., the name of the writer, the attestation, the corroboration).

intrinsic value, n. ~ The usefulness or significance of an item derived from its physical or associational qualities, inherent in its original form and generally independent of its content, that are integral to its material nature and would be lost in reproduction.

BT: value

RT: artifactual value

Notes: Intrinsic value may include an item's form, layout, materials, or process. It may also be based on an item's direct relationship to a significant person, activity, event, organization, or place. Intrinsic value is independent of informational or evidential value. A record may have great intrinsic value without significant informational or evidential value; records with significant informational or evidential value may have little intrinsic value. The process of copying a document may sufficiently capture its informational or evidential value but fail to preserve some aspects of the material nature of the original – its intrinsic value – that merit preservation. Hence, documents with significant intrinsic value are often preserved in their original form.

For example, a document written by a famous individual, such as a signature on a scrap of paper, may tell us little about the person. However, the document may have intrinsic value if it is the only surviving specimen of a document written by the individual. The document may have intrinsic value if it is made using a process of historical interest, such as inks made from flowers.

†143 *(NARA Intrinsic Value 1982, abridged):* All record materials having intrinsic value possess one or more of the following specific qualities or characteristics. These qualities or characteristics relate to the physical nature of the records, their prospective uses, and the information they contain. ¶ 1. Physical form that may be the subject for study if the records provide meaningful documentation or significant examples of the form. – 2. Aesthetic or artistic quality. – 3. Unique or curious physical features. – 4. Age that provides a quality of uniqueness. – 5. Value for use in exhibits. – 6. Questionable authenticity, date, author, or other characteristic that is significant and ascertainable by physical examination. – 7. General and substantial public interest because of direct association with famous or historically significant people, places, things, issues, or events. – 8. Significance as documentation of the establishment or continuing legal basis of an agency or institution. – 9. Significance as documentation of the formulation of policy at the highest executive levels when the policy has significance and broad effect throughout or beyond the agency or institution.

†189 *(McRanor 1996, p. 402):* In 1979, the concept [of intrinsic value] took on a more central role upon its invocation by the National Archives and Records Service, following the demand of the General Services Agency that the institution microfilm all its records and destroy the originals.

inventory, n. ~ 1. A list of things. – 2. DESCRIPTION · A finding aid that includes, at a minimum, a list of the series in a collection. – 3. RECORDS MANAGEMENT · The process of surveying the records in an office, typically at the series level.

BT: finding aid

NT: chronological inventory

RT: calendar, checklist, preliminary inventory

Notes: Inventory[2]: A **summary inventory**, also called a **series inventory** or a **title inventory**, includes only terse descriptions of the materials. A summary inventory may be made for materials with very technical form or contents, which would require extensive description to adequately capture the nuance difference. They are also made for collections of homogenous materials, in which details would be redundant.

†85 (Feeney 1999, p. 208): Inventories[1] differ among repositories, but most include an introduction or abstract; a history or biography of the collection's originating agency or individuals; a scope note detailing the size, contents, media, and arrangement of the collection; descriptions of the series subdivisions within the collection; container-level (box or folder) listings of the materials in each series; and an index or list of subject headings used to describe the collection.

inverted entry, n. ~ A heading with the natural order of words transposed so that it is sorted under a word that normally appears at the end.

BT: heading

RT: entry

Notes: Inverted headings are commonly used for personal names; for example, 'Jones, Lisa'. Inverted headings were often used in subject catalogs to collocate related concepts; for example, 'archives', 'archives, audiovisual', 'archives, motion picture', 'archives, photographic', and so forth.

inviolability, n. ~ The quality of being safe from violation; not broken, infringed, or impaired; secure.

RT: inalienability

invisible web ~ *see:* deep web

invocation, n. ~ DIPLOMATICS · A reference to the deity as the authority of an act or as a supplication.

†70 (Duranti 1998, p. 143): The *invocation*, that is, the mention of God, in whose name each action had to be done, was present in both public and private documents in the medieval period. It can still be found in documents issued by religious bodies, but more and more rarely. . . . It is possible to say that modern and contemporary documents contain an invocation whenever they present a claim that that the act therein is done in the name of the people, the king, the republic, the law, or similar entity.

IPM ~ *see:* integrated pest management

IRM ~ *see:* information resource management

iron-gall ink, n. ~ An indelible ink used for writing and drawing.

RT: Japan ink

Notes: Iron-gall inks came into widespread use by the 9th century; by the 11th century, they had largely replaced carbon inks as a writing medium. Iron-gall inks are acidic and can cause the underlying paper to deteriorate. They are black when fresh, but the acidic reaction with paper can turn the ink brown over time.

†81 (Iron Gall Ink website, http://www.knaw.nl/ecpa/ink/html/ink.html): Iron gall ink is primarily made from tannin (most often extracted from galls), vitriol (iron sulfate), gum, and water. Because iron gall ink is indelible, it was the ink of choice for documentation from the late Middle Ages to the middle of the twentieth century. Iron gall ink was also easily made; the ingredients were inexpensive

and readily available. Good quality iron gall ink was also stable in light. It was very popular with artists as a drawing ink, used with quill, reed pen or brush. The coloring strength of iron gall ink was high and it had, depending on its manufacture, a deep blue-black, velvety tone.

ISAAR (CPF) ~ *see:* International Standard for Archival Authority Records: Corporate, Personal, Families

ISAD(G) ~ *see:* General International Standard for Archival Description

ISBN ~ *see:* International Standard Book Numbering

ISO ~ *see:* International Organization for Standardization

ISO 646 ~ *see:* ASCII

ISO 2108 ~ *see:* International Standard Book Numbering

ISO 3297 ~ *see:* International Standard Serial Number

ISO 3901 ~ *see:* International Standard Recording Code

ISO 5466 ~ *see:* cold storage

ISO 7498 ~ *see:* Open Systems Interconnection Reference Model

ISO 8613 ~ *see:* Open Document Architecture

ISO/IEC 8632 ~ *see:* Computer Graphics Metafile

ISO 8859 ~ *see:* Information Technology – 8-bit Single-byte Coded Graphic Character Sets

ISO 8879 ~ *see:* Standard Generalized Markup Language

ISO 9660 ~ *see:* High Sierra

ISO 9706 ~ *see:* Permanence of Paper for Publications and Documents in Libraries and Archives

ISO/IEC 10646 ~ *see:* Unicode

ISO/IEC 10918 ~ *see:* Joint Photographic Experts Group, JPEG

ISO 12234-2 ~ *see:* Tagged Image File Format

ISO/IEC 13250 ~ *see:* topic map

ISO 14523 ~ *see:* Photographic Activity Test

ISO 15489 ~ *see:* Information Documentation – Records Management

ISO 15836 ~ *see:* Dublin Core

ISO 18917 ~ *see:* methylene-blue test

ISO 18924 ~ *see:* Arrhenius function

ISO 23950 ~ *see:* Information Retrieval Application Service Definition and Protocol Specification for Open Systems Interconnection

isoperm, n. ~ A combination of relative humidities and temperatures that produce equivalent effects on the permanence of materials.

> *Notes:* An isoperm forms a continuous line when plotted on a graph with axes for relative humidities and temperature.

> †261 (*Sebera 1994*): The isoperm method arises from one idea: the rate of deterioration of hygroscopic materials such as paper is influenced by the temperature and percent relative humidity of its surrounding environment. The isoperm method combines and quantifies the preservation effects of the two environmental factors, temperature and percent relative humidity, and presents the results in a readily comprehensible and usable graphical form. ¶ What is at first sometimes confusing but is essential to an understanding of isoperms is that relative rather than absolute rates of deterioration (and paper permanence) are employed. That is, if r1 and r2 are the (absolute) rates of deterioration of a specific paper under two

sets of temperature and relative humidity conditions we shall not deal with r1 and r2 individually but only with their ratio r2/r1 which measures the relative change in the deterioration rate resulting from the change in environmental conditions.

isopleth map, n. ~ A map that uses lines or colors to indicate areas with similar regional aspects.

>   *DF:* choropleth map
>
>   *BT:* map
>
>   *Notes:* Isopleth maps simplify information about a region by showing areas with continuous distribution. Isopleth maps may use lines to show areas where elevation, temperature, rainfall, or some other quality is the same; values between lines can be interpolated. Isopleths may also use color to show regions where some quality is the same; for example, a map that use shades from red to blue to indicate temperature ranges. An isopleth differs from a choropleth because the lines or regions are determined by the data rather than conforming to a predefined area, such as a political subdivision.

ISRC ~ *see:* International Standard Recording Code

ISSN ~ *see:* International Standard Serial Number

issue, n. ~ 1. All the copies of a periodical or serial distributed on a specific date. – 2. The number of identical prints or maps made from a plate.

>   *DF:* edition, reprint
>
>   *RT:* serial

IT9.11 ~ *see:* cold storage

IT9.17 ~ *see:* methylene-blue test

IT9.25 ~ *see:* cold storage

item, n. ~ A thing that can be distinguished from a group and that is complete in itself.

>   *Syn:* piece
>
>   *RT:* discrete item, object
>
>   *Notes:* An item may consist of several pieces[2] but is treated as a whole. For example, a letter may have several physically discrete pages but is treated as an item because of its content. A decision about the boundaries of an item is sometimes ambiguous; a photograph album may be considered an item, and the individual photographs within the album may also be considered items. Items are generally considered to be the smallest archival unit.

ITU ~ *see:* International Telecommunication Union

J

jacketed microfilm, n. ~ Microfilm that has been cut into short strips and placed in a plastic sleeve (a microfilm jacket) to give roll film a format similar to microfiche.

 BT: microfilm

 RT: microfilm jacket, microfilm strip

Japan ink, n. ~ A type of iron-gall ink that consists of almost completely oxidized iron tannate with large proportions of gum.

 RT: iron-gall ink

 Notes: Japan ink creates a glossy, black line.

joint archives, n. ~ 1. An archives containing the records of two or more organizations, especially governmental bodies, that are kept together to preserve their archival integrity. – 2. A repository that manages the archives of other organizations.

 BT: archives

Joint Photographic Experts Group, n. ~ A work group established by the International Organization for Standardization and the International Electrotechnical Commission that has developed the JPEG standard (ISO/IEC 10918) for a compressed graphic file format.

 RT: JPEG

 Notes: See http://www.jpeg.org/.

joint resolution, n. ~ Law · A formal expression of the opinion of a legislative body that has the weight of law and is subject to executive veto.

 BT: resolution

 Notes: A joint resolution is passed by both chambers. The term is used to refer to both the resolution as introduced, whether passed or not, and to versions that have been passed and signed into law.

joint work, n. ~ Copyright · A work prepared by two or more authors with the intention that their contributions be merged into inseparable or interdependent parts of a unitary whole (17 USC 101).

 RT: copyright

journal, n. ~ 1. An impartial record of an organization's events, proceedings, and actions. – 2. A personal account of events in the individual's life. – 3. Accounting · In double-entry bookkeeping, a record containing original entries of daily transactions, as distinguished from a ledger. – 3. Publishing · A periodical, especially one of a scholarly nature or published for a professional group.

 RT: daybook, diary, ledger, magazine, waste book

 Notes: Journal[1] connotes entries made for each day business occurred; for many organizations, no entries would be made on weekends. The Constitution requires the House of Representatives to keep a journal of floor proceedings. The journal records actions taken but unlike *The Congressional Record* it does not contain the substance of discussion. – Journal[2] also connotes daily entries. Some people distinguish journals from diaries, the former containing terse entries about events and the latter also including observations and opinions of a reflective nature.

journal of notarial acts ~ *see:* notarial record

JPEG (also **jpg**), n. ~ A standard (ISO/IEC 10918) that specifies a digital graphic file format that can reproduce a large color space and that can compress the data to minimize the file size.

    RT: compression, Joint Photographic Experts Group

    Notes: In principle, the JPEG file format can produce either lossy or lossless compression. The more a file is compressed, the greater the loss of image quality. However, most implementations of JPEG do not implement lossless compression. The format is commonly used for photographs.

JSTOR, n. ~ An organization that seeks to collect, provide access to, and preserve scholarly journals for use by the scholarly community and to assist scholarly organizations and publishers to transition to electronic formats for those journals.

    Notes: See http://www.jstor.org/.

judgment, n. ~ Law · The decision of a court on the rights and obligations of parties to a suit.

juridical person, n. ~ Diplomatics · An entity, constituted either by a collection or succession of natural or physical persons, that can take part in legal actions.

    RT: person

    †70 *(Duranti 1998, p. 42):* The term 'juridical person' is used in the sense of an entity having the capacity of the potential to act legally and constituted either by a collection or succession of physical persons or a collection of properties. Examples of juridical persons are states, agencies, corporations, associations, committees, partnerships, ethnic and religious groups, positions to which individuals are nominated, appointed, or hired, character groups (women, fathers, children, deceased persons), the estates of bankrupt or deceased persons, counties, and so on. . . . In English, the United States, and English-speaking Canada, there is a legal distinction between 'natural' and 'artificial' persons which is close to the distinction between physical and juridical persons, but the jurists in those countries do not agree on a definition of the two terms.

juridical system, n. ~ Diplomatics · A organization of individuals that is based on a system of positive law, beliefs, mores, and values.

    RT: system

    †70 *(Duranti 1998, p. 43, n. 22):* The term 'juridical' is broader than the term 'legal.' It refers to the nature of abstract legal concepts. Thus, a 'juridical transaction' is a transaction legally supposed or conceived of, to some extent irrespective of its actual existence, even if it contemplates incidents and circumstances not recognized by the law.

    †70 *(Duranti 1998, p. 125–126):* Within [a juridical system], however much the governing principle changes over time and from place to place, human endeavors always present an *organizational*, an *instrumental*, and an *executive* or a *constitutive* nature.

jurisdiction, n. ~ 1. A region, especially one defined by political boundaries, over which an authority may exercise its power. – 2. The authority of a power over persons and their activities within a region. – 3. The authority of a court to issue a decree or to decide a case.

justification, n. ~ 1. Cataloging · The requirement that access points assigned to a catalog record are referenced in the description. – 2. Printing · The addition of space between words or characters in a line of type to create even margins.

RT: literary warrant

†120 *(APPM2 1989, 2.0B):* Generally, determine access points for the material being cataloged from its chief source of information. When statements appearing in the chief source are ambiguous or insufficient, use information appearing outside the material and the chief source for determining access points. However, all access points should be justified[1] in the catalog record.

K

key, n. ~ 1. A list of symbols or abbreviations used in a map or other work. – 2. CRYPTOGRAPHY · A sequence of characters that is used to convert plaintext to ciphertext or ciphertext to plaintext.

> *NT:* symmetric-key encryption
>
> *RT:* encryption

key informant, n. ~ The principal source of information for oral histories or ethnographies.

> *DF:* chief source of information
>
> *Notes:* A key informant is selected on the basis of the interviewer's qualitative assessment that the informant has particular knowledge of and position in a community. Use of a key informant distinguishes this type of research from random sampling.

key title, n. ~ A uniform title assigned to periodicals and linked to a specific International Standard Serial Number (ISSN) that combines a publication's title with any necessary qualifiers to distinguish it from other publications with the same title.

> *RT:* International Standard Serial Number, title
>
> †*145 (ISSN):* If the title of the publication changes in any significant way, a new ISSN must be assigned in order to correspond to this new form of title and avoid any confusion. A serial publication whose title is modified several times in the course of its existence will be assigned each time a new ISSN, thus allowing precise identification of each form of the title: in fact it is then considered that they are different publications even if there is a logical link between them.

keyword, n. ~ 1. One of a small set of words used to characterize the content of a document for use in retrieval systems. – 2. In KWIC and KWOC indexes, words in a title or document that serve as access points. – 3. COMPUTING · Reserved words in a programming language that has a functional meaning for the compiler or interpreter and that cannot be used for the names of variables, functions, or other entities.

> *RT:* full-text search
>
> *Notes:* Keywords[1] are often taken from the title, abstract, or sometimes the full text of the work. In other cases, keywords are taken from a controlled vocabulary. – Keywords[2] include any word in the title that is not in a list of common words of limited value for retrieval (a stop list).

keyword and context index, n. (**KWAC**, abbr.) ~ An ordered list that sorts each entry under all nontrivial words in the title.

> *BT:* index, search
>
> *RT:* automatic indexing
>
> *Notes:* A KWAC is formatted so that the keyword appears as a heading, and is then followed by the full titles of all works containing that keyword. A KWAC repeats the keyword in the title; a KWOC replaces the keyword with a symbol. Long titles may be truncated.

keyword in context index, n. (**KWIC**, abbr.) ~ An ordered list that sorts each entry under all nontrivial words in the title.

> *BT:* index, search

RT: automatic indexing, permuted index

Notes: A KWIC is formatted so that the keyword is in the center of the page, with words preceding and following the keyword on either side. Long titles may be truncated. A KWIC index is limited to terms in the title.

keyword out of context index, n. (**KWOC**, abbr.) ~ An ordered list that sorts each entry under all nontrivial words in the title.

BT: index, search

RT: automatic indexing

Notes: A KWOC is formatted with the keyword as a heading, followed by all the titles containing that keyword. A KWOC replaces the keyword with a symbol, such as an asterisk; a KWAC repeats the keyword in the title. Long titles may be truncated. A KWOC index may sort titles under keywords in the title or from headings assigned to the title by an indexer.

kinescope, n. (**kine**, abbr.) ~ 1. A recording of a television program on film by focusing the camera on a monitor. – 2. A television picture tube.

RT: television

Notes: Kinescopes[1] were used to make records of live television programs before videotape recording was practical. They were in common use in the late 1940s, and were replaced in the 1950s by videotape. Kinescopes were used to transfer programming from the studio where the program was recorded to other stations for rebroadcast.

knowledge management, n. ~ The administration and oversight of an organization's intellectual capital by managing information and its use in order to maximize its value.

BT: management

RT: actionable information, content management, document management, information system

†256 (Santosus and Surmacz 2001): Not all information is valuable. Therefore, it's up to individual companies to determine what information qualifies as intellectual and knowledge-based assets. In general, however, intellectual and knowledge-based assets fall into one of two categories: explicit or tacit. Included among the former are assets such as patents, trademarks, business plans, marketing research and customer lists. As a general rule of thumb, explicit knowledge consists of anything that can be documented, archived and codified, often with the help of IT. Much harder to grasp is the concept of tacit knowledge, or the know-how contained in people's heads. The challenge inherent with tacit knowledge is figuring out how to recognize, generate, share and manage it. While IT in the form of e-mail, groupware, instant messaging and related technologies can help facilitate the dissemination of tacit knowledge, identifying tacit knowledge in the first place is a major hurdle for most organizations.

kraft paper, n. ~ A strong paper made from wood pulp by a modified sulfate process.

BT: paper

Notes: Normally brown, kraft paper can be bleached to tan or white. Commonly used to make grocery bags and for counter rolls.

KWAC ~ *see:* keyword and context index

KWIC ~ *see:* keyword in context index

KWOC ~ *see:* keyword out of context index

L

l'ordre primitif ~ *see:* original order

label, n. ~ 1. A short description used as an identifier. – 2. A tag, piece of paper, or other material with identifying information attached to the thing identified. – 3. COMPUTING · In a program, code at the beginning of a statement used to refer to that statement. – 4. COMPUTING · Identifying information at the head of a tape.

> *RT:* tag

> *Notes:* A label[2] may be made from a variety of materials, including paper, plastic, leather, and cloth. The label is usually planar. It may be affixed to the item with adhesive or with a string.

lacquer disk, n. ~ A glass, metal, or fiber disk coated with acetate or cellulose nitrate (lacquer) used to make instantaneous sound recordings.

> *Notes:* The pattern of sound vibrations is cut in a spiral groove in the lacquer. A lacquer disk could be used to create a master for pressed recordings. Before the introduction of magnetic tape, lacquer disks were a common means of recording sound.

lamination, n. ~ 1. A process of fusing layers of materials into a composite. – 2. Applying a thin plastic coating to a planar document to give it additional strength and protect it from the environment.

> *RT:* encapsulation, silking

> *Notes:* Silking is an example of lamination[1], although the process generally uses an adhesive that makes it relatively easy to separate the silk. – Lamination[2] connotes use of a thermoplastic film that is applied to the document using heat and pressure, or a sheet of plastic attached with an adhesive through the use of a solvent. If the document is not deacidified before lamination, it will continue to deteriorate through inherent vice. Lamination[2] is generally not considered appropriate for archival preservation because the plastic may interact with the document over time and because the film is difficult to remove. Lamination differs from encapsulation because the latter does not attach the protective film to the document and is reversible.

LAN ~ *see:* local area network

land grant, n. ~ The transfer of ownership of public land to an organization, individual, or subordinate government.

> *RT:* patent

> *Notes:* A **land patent** is a record that documents such a transfer of public land to an individual.

landscape, n. ~ 1. An outdoor scene. – 2. A genre of art in which the natural, outdoor environment is the principal subject, using natural features as the basis of the composition. – 3. A metaphorical terrain that gives an understanding of the relationships among different aspects of an idea or activity.

> *RT:* cityscape, scene, seascape

> *Notes:* A landscape[1] may refer to either the scene itself or to an artwork that depicts such a scene. – Landscapes[2] may be made in many media, including oils, watercolors, sketches, and photographs. – Landscape[3] is an extension of the natural environment to the world of ideas; for example, the social landscape, the political landscape.

†206 *(Cosmopolis 2000):* A lot of American 19th-century artists considered that the essence of the origin of their country was reflected in the landscape. With nature as the starting point, they developed their own artistic current which distanced itself from the European tradition by making nature their primary source of inspiration and by representing nature as the promised land whereas in Europe man's relationship with nature and not nature itself was at the center of attention. Americans were not interested in the landscape marked by man's presence but they regarded nature as a virgin territory, a landscape that had not been sullied by human kind, in which the hand of God, its creator, could be seen. They combined this religious feeling for nature with the idea of national identity.

landscape orientation (also **landscape mode**), n. ~ A layout that is wider than it is high.

    RT: format, portrait orientation

lantern slide (also **stereopticon slide**), n. ~ A transparent image on glass, approximately 3½ × 4 inches, that is intended to be viewed by projection.

    BT: photograph

    RT: magic lantern, slide, stereopticon

    Notes: Lantern slides may have images that are hand-painted, printed, or photographed.

laser printer, n. ~ A nonimpact printer that uses a dry ink powder (toner) to form characters and patterns on paper or plastic film.

    BT: printer

    Notes: Most laser printers use technology similar to an electrostatic copier but use a modulated laser to create an electrostatic image of a document on a rotating cylinder. The charged portions of the cylinder attract charged particles of toner. When a sheet of paper is passed over the surface of the drum, the toner is transferred to the paper. Finally, the toner is fused to the paper using heat. 'Laser printer' is sometimes used to describe page printers that use light-emitting diodes (LED) or a liquid crystal display (LCD) as the light source.

LaserDisc, n. ~ A read-only optical disk that records a video program in either NTSC or PAL format.

    BT: optical disk

    RT: video, videodisc

    Notes: A registered trademark of the Pioneer Electronic Corporation.

lateral cut recording, n. ~ A technique of recording sound on an analog disc by cutting the signal into the sides of the groove, causing the pickup stylus to move from side to side.

    RT: vertical cut recording

    Notes: The technique was invented by Emile Berliner in 1887.

lateral file (also **side-open cabinets**), n. ~ Furniture used to hold folders containing documents and designed to provide access from the long side.

    DF: vertical file

    BT: file cabinet

    Notes: Lateral files may have a cover to protect files on stationary shelves or may use drawers that pull out.

lateral reversal, n. ~ An image that is reversed left to right; a mirror reflection.

    RT: direct positive

Notes: Some direct-positive images, such as daguerreotypes and tintypes, are laterally reversed unless made using a reversing lens.

law, n. ~ 1. The whole of statutes, administrative regulations, judicial precedents, and legal principles that define socially accepted limits and obligations on human behavior. – 2. A statute.

> *Syn:* statute
>
> *NT:* slip law
>
> *RT:* code, regulation
>
> *Notes:* Laws² passed by legislative bodies are distinguished from regulations, which are made by an agency. Before an agency can make regulations, it must be given authority to do so by a legislative body.

LCSH ~ *see:* Library of Congress Subject Headings

LCTGM ~ *see:* Thesaurus for Graphic Materials

lead-in vocabulary, n. ~ The terms included in a controlled vocabulary that are not used as headings, but which point to preferred headings.

> *RT:* index vocabulary
>
> *Notes:* Terms in the lead-in vocabulary are synonymous or closely related to terms in the index vocabulary. Filing all entries under one heading ensures related entries are grouped together, rather than scattered among several headings. For example, ferrotype and tintype describe the same process; in a controlled vocabulary, one would be made the preferred heading under which entries are filed, and a cross-reference would be made from the lead-in heading to the preferred heading.

leader, n. ~ AUDIO-VIDEO · A blank section at the beginning of a film or tape.

> *DF:* trailer
>
> *Notes:* A leader is used to thread the film or tape through a camera, projector, recorder, or other equipment. It also protects the first part of the recorded information.

leaf, n. ~ A sheet of paper or parchment.

> *RT:* page
>
> *Notes:* A leaf is part of a document, book, pamphlet, or similar work; either or both sides of the leaf may be blank. A leaf is composed of two pages, one on either side. A sheet folded in half has two leaves, or four pages, and is called a folio. A sheet folded in half twice has four leafs, or eight pages, and is called a quarto. Leafs are numbered individually, with the front and back distinguished as recto (front) and verso (back).

leafcasting, n. ~ CONSERVATION · A technique to replace missing parts of paper with freshly cast paper.

> *Notes:* The damaged leaf is supported on a screen. Water containing pulp in suspension is pulled through the screen, filling up the missing area.
>
> †248 *(Roberts and Etherington 1982):* For certain kinds of materials, particularly those of large format, e.g., newspapers and maps, leafcasting is a much more efficient and economical method of repair than the traditional manual methods. Its use can also strengthen the entire leaf, as leafcasting not only fills in the holes but also fills cracks, joins fragments, repairs margins and may also be used to provide linings. In contrast to hand repairs, these procedures have the additional advantage of requiring little or no use of adhesives.

leaflet, n. ~ A single printed sheet, which may be folded.

DF: booklet

RT: brochure, folder, pamphlet, publication

Notes: For short, nonserial, bound works of more than one sheet, see booklet or pamphlet.

ledger, n. ~ A document containing a record of debits, credits, and other financial transactions, typically organized into separate accounts.

    RT: account book, cash book, daybook, journal, shop book, waste book

    Notes: Originally bound volumes, ledgers may not be kept in an electronic format. In double-entry bookkeeping, a ledger is a record of final entry.

legacy system, n. ~ COMPUTING · Software or hardware that was built using methods that are outdated or obsolete.

    RT: computer, system

    Notes: 'Legacy system' connotes a system that is large and monolithic, and that is difficult to modify because the software is written in a programming language that is no longer common. It is maintained because the costs of converting to a new system do not justify the benefits to an organization. As a legacy system becomes older, the costs of maintenance will likely be greater than the value of the information it contains or greater than the costs of upgrading the system. In the former case, the information is effectively destroyed when the system is decommissioned.

legal cap ~ *see:* legal size

legal custody, n. ~ The ownership and the responsibility for creating policy governing access to materials, regardless of their physical location.

    BT: custody

    RT: physical custody

legal size (also **legal cap**), n. ~ In the United States, a standard paper size measuring 8½ × 14 inches. – adj. ~ 2. Being 8½ × 14 inches. – 3. Able to hold something 8½ × 14 inches.

    RT: foolscap

    Notes: A piece of foolscap folded in half is roughly the size of legal size paper.

legal value, n. ~ The usefulness or significance of records to document and protect the rights and interests of an individual or organization, to provide for defense in litigation, to demonstrate compliance with laws and regulations, or to meet other legal needs.

    BT: value

    RT: primary value

letter, n. ~ 1. A character in the alphabet. – 2. A written communication, especially one sent by courier or post; correspondence. – **letters**, pl. ~ 3. Knowledge, especially of literary culture; *belles lettres.*

    RT: correspondence, mail, memorandum

letter box, n. ~ 1. A container for receipt of delivered mail or outgoing mail; a mailbox. – 2. A container for storing correspondence; a box file. – 3. MOVING IMAGES · An aspect ratio of 24:13.

    Syn: box file

    BT: format

letter-by-letter arrangement, n. ~ A sorting technique that orders entries based on each character in a heading without regard for spaces or punctuation.

    DF: word-by-word arrangement

Notes: Letter-by-letter arrangement is distinguished from word-by-word arrangement, the latter sorting spaces and punctuation between words before other characters.

letter-by-letter	*word-by-word*
access copy	access copy
accessibility	access restriction
accession	accessibility
access restriction	accession

letter size, n. ~ 1. A standard paper size, 8½ × 11 inches. – adj. ~ 2. Designed for documents that are 8½ × 11 inches.

letterbook, n. ~ A volume containing copies of outgoing correspondence, usually in chronological order.

    RT: letterpress, letterpress copybook

    Notes: The volume may be made of blank, lined paper and contain drafts or fair copies, or it may be made up of loose copies that were bound.

letterhead, n. ~ 1. Stationery with information about an individual or organization printed at the top, and sometimes the side or bottom. – 2. Printed information at the top of stationery.

    Notes: Business stationery commonly has a letterhead[2] that contains the name, address, and phone and fax numbers. It often contains a logo and names of officers.

letterpress, n. ~ 1. A printing technique using raised type that is inked and then pressed into paper or other material. – 2. Material printed using this technique.

    RT: letterbook, print

    Notes: Distinguish works made using the letterpress process from copies in a letterpress copybook, which are made using a transfer process.

letterpress copybook (also **press copy**), n. ~ A volume containing reproductions of correspondence, made directly from the originals using a transfer process.

    RT: copy, letterbook

    Notes: Distinguish copies made using a transfer process and bound in a letterpress book from ink-on-paper works made using a letterpress[1].

    †*300 (Yates 1989, p. 26–28):* The first mechanical method of copying to gain widespread use in American business was press copying, first patented by James Watt in 1780 but not widely adopted in business until much later. As the technology came into common use, a screw-powered letter press was used in conjunction with a press book, a bound volume of blank, tissue paper pages. A letter freshly written in special copying ink was placed on a dampened page while the rest of the pages were protected by oilcloths. The book was then closed and the mechanical press screwed down tightly. The pressure and moisture caused an impression of the letter to be retained on the underside of the tissue sheet. This impression could then be read through the top of the thin paper. ¶ These letter presses were used by some individuals and businessmen in the first half of the nineteenth century, but they only came into general use in the second half of the century. ¶ A letter press reduced the labor cost, both by decreasing copying time and by allowing an office boy to do the copying once performed by a more expensive clerk. As the same time, it eliminated the danger of miscopying. Copies were now facsimiles of the letter sent, down to the signature.

level of description, n. ~ 1. The amount of detail or number of elements in a formal description of a work. – 2. The amount of detail in a collection included in a finding aid or catalog record, as determined by the number of hierarchical levels.

    RT: analysis, depth of description, description, hierarchical description

    Notes: The level of description[1] may be terse or exhaustive. In some instances, description of a collection may be limited to its provenance and title; in other cases, it may include notes and other information. – In a finding aid or catalog record, the level of description[2] typically begins with the collection as a whole, and it may include details about subordinate divisions, such as series, subseries, folders, or items.

    †120 (APPM2 1989, p. 5): There may be several appropriate levels of description for any given body of archival material. These levels normally correspond to natural divisions based on provenance or physical form. The principle corresponds with the bibliographic concept of *analysis*, 'the process of preparing a bibliographic record that describes a part or parts of an item for which a comprehensive entry has been made' [citing AACR2 §13.1A].

levels of arrangement, n. ~ The hierarchical, intellectual, and physical divisions used in archives management, including repository, record group, fonds, collection, subgroups, series, subseries, file, and item.

    †124 (Holmes 1984, p. 164): In all archival depositories there can be distinguished, usually, at least five levels of arrangement: 1. *Arrangement at the depository level* – the depository's complete holdings into a few major divisions on the broadest common denominator possible and the physical placement of holdings of each such major division to best advantage in the building's stack areas . . . usually reflected in parallel administrative units. . . . 2. *Arrangement at the record group and subgroup levels* – the breakdown of an administrative division or branch . . . into record groups and the physical placement of these in some logical pattern in stack areas. . . . 3. *Arrangement at the series level* – the breakdown of record groups into natural series and the physical placement of each series in relation to other series in some logical pattern. 4. *Arrangement at the filing unit level* – the breakdown of series into its filing unit components. . . . 5. *Arrangement at the document level* – the checking and arranging, within each filing unit, of the individual documents, enclosures and annexes, and individual pieces of paper that together comprise the filing unit.

liability, n. ~ Being legally responsible or accountable.

librarian, n. ~ An individual responsible for acquiring, providing access to, and managing collections of published materials.

    RT: archivist

    Notes: While the title connotes work with published materials, many rare books and special collections librarians also work with unpublished materials that range from handwritten inscriptions in books to collections of personal papers.

    †108 (Greene, et al., 2001): Anyone who works as a keeper of stuff in a corporate environment cannot afford to worry too much about the fine distinctions between Record Manager, Librarian, Archivist and Document Control Manager. The key is to keep what the corporation needs. Need is difficult to define, but people in corporations know when you have something, or have organized something, in a way they find useful for the task at hand. If you keep stuff no one needs, it is quite likely your collection will be trashed, given away or simply die from lack of use.

    †115 (Harvey 2000, p. 113): If it were up to me, I would abolish the word entirely and turn back to the lexicological wisdom of the ancients, who saw librar-

ians not as feeble sorters and shelvers but as heroic guardians. In Assyrian, Babylonian, and Egyptian cultures alike, those who toiled at the shelves were often bestowed with a proud, even soldierly, title: Keeper of the Books.

†181 *(Maher 1998, p. 262–263):* Librarianship is an information profession wherein data are valued as independent entities, separate from the context that created them. By contrast, archivists must focus on unique documents created often as the accident rather than the object of an action. We are not information professionals like librarians – we are evidence professionals.

library, n. ~ 1. A collection of published materials, including books, magazines, sound and video recordings, and other formats. – 2. A building used to house such a collection. – 3. COMPUTING · Commonly used subroutines or functions collected for use in different programs.

> *BT:* repository
> *NT:* digital library
> *Notes:* A library[3] often contains static code that is incorporated into a program during compilation or loaded from a dynamic linking library (DLL).

Library of Congress Subject Headings, n. (**LCSH**, abbr.) ~ A controlled vocabulary typically used to provide topical access points for catalog records.

> *BT:* controlled vocabulary
> *RT:* authority file, Subject Cataloging Manual: Subject Headings
> *Notes:* LCSH is published by the Library of Congress. The Library stresses that the subject headings reflect its collections, rather than serving as a general tool for all collections. However, the breadth of the Library's collections, and consequentially LCSH, has made it useful to many libraries and archives. LCSH is intended to be used in conjunction with the Subject Cataloging Manual, which provides instructions for establishing precoordinated subheadings for greater specificity.

license, n. ~ 1. Permission or right granted to an individual or organization to enter into a transaction, business, or occupation, or to take an action. – 2. A document that serves as evidence of such permission or right.

> *NT:* click-wrap license, shrink-wrap license
> *RT:* permit

life continuum, n. ~ The unified pattern of a record's life, comprised of four interrelated stages: creation or receipt; classification; scheduling and its implementations, including maintenance in the creating office, an active storage area or records center, or an archives; and use (primary or secondary).

> *RT:* records continuum

life cycle, n. ~ RECORDS · The distinct phases of a record's existence, from creation to final disposition.

> *NT:* records creation, records maintenance and use
> *RT:* records continuum
> *Notes:* Different models identify different stages. All models include creation or receipt, use, and disposition. Some models distinguish between active and inactive use, and between destruction and archival preservation.

> †20 *(Bantin 1998):* The life cycle model for managing records, as articulated by Theodore Schellenberg and others, has been the prominent model for North American archivists and records managers since at least the 1960s. . . . This model portrays the life of a record as going through various stages or periods, much like

a living organism. In stage one, the record is created, presumably for a legitimate reason and according to certain standards. In the second stage, the record goes through an active period when it has maximum primary value and is used or referred to frequently by the creating office and others involved in decision making. During this time the record is stored on-site in the active or current files of the creating office. At the end of stage two the record may be reviewed and determined to have no further value, at which point it is destroyed, or the record can enter stage three, where it is relegated to a semi-active status, which means it still has value, but is not needed for day-to-day decision making. Because the record need not be consulted regularly, it is often stored in a off-site storage center. At the end of stage three, another review occurs, at which point a determination is made to destroy or send the record to stage four, which is reserved for inactive records with long-term, indefinite, archival value. This small percentage of records (normally estimated at approximately five per cent of the total documentation) is sent to an archival repository, where specific activities are undertaken to preserve and describe the records. ¶ The life cycle model not only describes what will happen to a record, it also defines who will manage the record during each stage. During the creation and active periods, the record creators have primary responsibility for managing the record, although records managers may well be involved to various degrees. In the semi-active stage, it is the records manager who takes center stage and assumes major responsibility for managing the records. Finally, in the inactive stage, the archivist takes the lead in preserving, describing, and providing access to the archival record.

life cycle tracking, n. ~ The control of records from creation through disposition.

Notes: Life cycle tracking involves the identification, description, and scheduling of records from their creation. It includes creating prompts or reports to initiate microfilming, transfer to a records center or archives, vital records protective actions, and destruction. Tracking may also include monitoring actions performed on records after transfer to a records center or archives.

life expectancy, n. ~ The length of time that an item is expected to remain intact and useful when kept in a typical office environment (70°F, 21°C and 50% RH).

RT: accelerated aging test, extended-term storage

†234 *(Puglia 2000):* Life Expectancy (LE) is a term that describes the stability of imaging materials. The standard has always been "archival." But when computer folks say archival, they are talking about something that is usable in 2 months. When librarians say archival, they mean forever. Life expectancy is a new term that accommodates both ends of this continuum. The definition of Life Expectancy is the length of time that information is predicted to be acceptable in a system of 21 degrees Celsius, and 50% relative humidity, standard office environment.

light archives, n. ~ A collection of materials that is accessible to the public without restrictions.

BT: archives

RT: access, dark archives

Notes: Light archives is generally distinguished from dark archives, the latter being materials that are being preserved for future use but without current access.

lignin, n. ~ A complex polymer that makes cell walls in plants strong and rigid.

Notes: Lignin left in papers made from wood pulp leads to chemical degradation. Most lignin can be removed from pulps during manufacturing.

line code index, n. ~ A pattern of transparent and opaque bars between frames on a roll of microfilm that can indicate the general location of a particular document.
> *BT:* index, index
> *RT:* microfilm

linear foot, n. ~ 1. A measure of shelf space necessary to store documents. – 2. A measure of motion picture stock; film footage.
> *RT:* cubic foot, film footage
> *Notes:* A linear foot measures twelve inches for documents stored on edge, or twelve inches high for documents stored horizontally. For letter size documents, it is slightly less than a cubic foot. The number of leaves within a linear foot varies with the thickness of the material.

linen, n. ~ 1. Cloth made from the straw of flax plants. – 2. ARCHITECTURE · Fine, thin, cotton or linen cloth, sized with starch, that is used for drawings.

lipping ~ *see:* edge curl

list, n. ~ A written series of discrete items.
> *RT:* checklist
> *Notes:* A list may be ordered or random. The items in a list may be of any nature, and the list may contain different types of items.

literary manuscripts, n. ~ Drafts, notes, worksheets, manuscripts, proofs, and other materials commonly associated with the production of creative works, including fiction, poetry, plays, still or motion pictures, and other works.
> *BT:* manuscript

literary warrant, n. ~ 1. A justification or authorization found in text. – 2. A written requirement.
> *DF:* warrant
> *RT:* justification
> *Notes:* This glossary, for example, uses more than 6,000 citations from professional literature as literary warrant[1] for its definitions.
> †67 *(Duff 1998, p. 91):* The University of Pittsburgh Electronic Recordkeeping Project suggested that requirements for electronic recordkeeping should derive from authoritative sources, such as the law, customs, standards, and professional best practices accepted by society and codified in the literature of different professions concerned with records and recordkeeping rather than developed in isolation. . . . These statements, or 'literary warrant'[2] as the project named them, delineate the requirements for capturing, maintaining, and using records over time.

literary works, n. ~ COPYRIGHT · Works, other than audiovisual works, expressed in words, numbers, or other verbal or numerical symbols or indicia, regardless of the nature of the material objects, such as books, periodicals, manuscripts, phonorecords, film, tapes, disks, or cards, in which they are embodied (17 USC 101).
> *RT:* copyright

lithography, n. ~ A planographic printing process in which the image areas accept a greasy ink and wet, nonimage areas resist the ink.
> *RT:* print
> *Notes:* Lithography was invented in Munich by Aloys Senefelder in 1798. A greasy substance is used to create the design on a flat, porous surface. The surface is then moistened with water. When a greasy ink is applied, the water-soaked areas resist the ink, and the greasy image areas accept the ink. The design is then trans-

ferred to paper in a press. The original printing surfaces were made from limestone. Offset lithography using flexible metal plates is a modern variation of the process.

loan, n. ~ The temporary transfer of materials from one party to another.

> *Notes:* Archives may borrow or lend materials from individuals or other organizations for the purposes of exhibition, consultation, or reproduction.

local area network, n. (**LAN**, abbr.) ~ A collection of computers, printers, storage devices, and other devices connected to allow resource sharing.

> *Notes:* LANs are typically installed and maintained within a single organization and normally at a single location. A network covering geographically dispersed sites may be described as a metropolitan area network or a wide area network (WAN). Local area networks may be configured using star, token ring, or other topologies. They may use different networking protocols, such as TCP/IP or IPX/SPX. A LAN may be connected to the Internet, allowing computers and other devices to access – or be accessed via – the Internet.

local records, n. ~ Public records created or received by a county, city, town, district, or other governmental entity smaller than a state.

> *BT:* record
> *RT:* public record

location index (allso **location register**), n. ~ A finding aid used to record the place where materials are stored.

> *Notes:* Many archives do not include the storage location of materials in finding aids used by the general public. Restricting this information adds one more layer of security. When a patron requests materials, reference staff use a location index to determine where the material is stored so that it can be pulled.

LOCKSS ~ *see:* Lots of Copies Keep Stuff Safe

locus sigilli, n. (**l.s.**, abbr.) ~ The place where a document is to have a seal affixed.

> *Notes:* The abbreviation l.s. often appears on certificates, indicating where the notary public's seal should be placed. It does not stand for 'legal signature.' It may also be used in a fair copy to·indicate the presence of a seal in the original.

logical, adj. ~ The conceptual representation (of a thing) apart from its physical implementation; virtual.

> *Syn:* virtual
> *Notes:* 'Logical' is used to describe the conceptual model of something, as opposed to its physical implementation. For example, a logical file structure may have branches that appear to be contiguous, when in fact they are stored in separate locations on a disk.

logical design, n. ~ COMPUTING · Specifications for the flow of data within a computer system independent of the underlying hardware.

logical record, n. ~ A collection of related data elements treated as a conceptual unit, independent of how or where the information is stored.

> *DF:* physical record
> *RT:* data record
> *Notes:* A logical record is defined by a particular data structure in an application, independent of the physical characteristics and constraints of the storage medium.

lone arranger, n. ~ An individual who is the sole staff of an archives.

long-playing record, n. (**LP**, abbr.) ~ A sound recording on an analog disk measuring ten to twelve inches in diameter, with a playing time of more than five minutes at 33⅓ revolutions per minute.

Syn: album
BT: phonograph record

lossless, adj. ~ Undegraded; retaining all information.

RT: compression

Notes: Lossless is used to describe digital compression techniques in which no information is lost; an object is identical before and after being compressed and restored.

lossy, n. ~ Degraded by a loss of information.

RT: compression

Notes: Lossy is used to describe digital compression techniques in which information is lost; an object is altered after being compressed and restored. Lossy compression sacrifices fidelity for size; fidelity and compressed file size are inversely proportional. The technique may be used in instances where the loss of information is not noticeable or significant. MPEG and JPEG are lossy compression algorithms.

Lots of Copies Keep Stuff Safe, n. (**LOCKSS,** abbr.) ~ A project designed to preserve copies of electronic publications by ensuring that multiple copies are stored at different organizations.

Notes: See http://lockss.stanford.edu/.

†172 (LOCKSS): For centuries libraries and publishers have had stable roles: publishers produced information; libraries kept it safe for reader access. There is no fundamental reason for the online environment to force institutions to abandon these roles. ¶ The LOCKSS model capitalizes on the traditional roles of libraries and publishers. LOCKSS creates low-cost, persistent digital 'caches' of authoritative versions of http-delivered content. The LOCKSS software enables institutions to locally collect, store, preserve, and archive authorized content thus safeguarding their community's access to that content. The LOCKSS model enforces the publisher's access control systems and, for many publishers, does no harm to their business models. ¶ Accuracy and completeness of LOCKSS caches are assured through a peer-to-peer polling and reputation system (operated through LCAP, LOCKSS' communication protocol), which is both robust and secure. LOCKSS replicas cooperate to detect and repair preservation failures. LOCKSS is designed to run on inexpensive hardware and to require almost no technical administration. The software has been under development since 1999 and is distributed as open source.

LP ~ *see:* long-playing record

ls ~ *see:* locus sigilli

lyophilization ~ *see:* freeze drying

M

maceration, n. ~ A technique of destroying paper documents by soaking them in water and grinding them into pulp; pulping.

    Syn: pulping

    RT: destruction

machine dependent, adj. ~ Computing · Requiring a specific type of hardware to operate.

    Syn: hardware dependent

    Notes: 'Machine dependent' is commonly used to describe software that can run only on a specific type of hardware, such as a specific processor. It can also be used to describe film or audio media that requires specific recording and playback equipment.

machine independent, adj. ~ Able to operate on many different types of equipment.

    Syn: hardware independent

    Notes: Machine independent does not imply the ability to run on all equipment. Machine independent software may require an intermediary program or translation to enable it to run on different platforms; for example, a program written in C must be compiled using different tools to run on different computers.

machine indexing ~ *see:* automatic indexing

machine-readable, adj. ~ In a medium or format that requires a mechanical device to make it intelligible to humans.

    RT: analog, automated, data file, digital, electronic, electronic record

    Notes: 'Machine-readable' is commonly used to refer to digital computer data files, which may be stored on magnetic media or punch cards. However, phonograph records, audio cassettes, and LaserDiscs are examples of analog machine-readable formats.

macro appraisal, n. ~ A theory of appraisal that assesses the value of records based on the role of the record creators, placing priority on why the records were created (function), where they were created (structure), and how they were created, rather than content (informational value).

    BT: appraisal

    †13 *(Appraisal Methodology 2000):* Essentially, macro-appraisal shifts the primary focus of appraisal from the record – including any research characteristics or values it may contain – to the functional context in which the record is created. The main appraisal questions for the archivist are no longer what has been recorded, where it is, and what research value it has. Instead, the archivist uses knowledge gained by a functional analysis of an institution, including an analysis of the interaction of function and structure, of organizational culture, of records-keeping systems, and of citizen-client involvement with the institution or function.

    †44 *(Cook 2001, p. 30):* The macro-appraisal model developed first to appraise the records of the Government of Canada, for example, finds sanction for archival appraisal value of determining what to keep and what to destroy, not in the dictates of the state, as traditionally, nor in following the latest trends of historical research, as more recently, but in trying to reflect society's values through a functional analysis of the interaction of citizen with the state.

†*156 (Klopfer 2001, p. 124):* Based on empirical research, macro-appraisal is intended to result in an archives that documents processes and functions. If functional analysis reveals gaps or overrepresentation in what is documented, then steps can be taken, including, for the former, the collection of oral documents.

macro data, n. ~ Information that has been aggregated or summarized from more detailed information.

> *RT:* data

MAD ~ *see:* Manual of Archival Description

magazine, n. ~ 1. A publication, often illustrated, containing essays, articles, short stories, poems, or other short works, issued periodically and directed to a popular audience. – 2. A container designed to supply material to a machine.

> *RT:* journal, serial
>
> *Notes:* A magazine[1] may contain articles on many different topics or may be focused on a specific subject. – A magazine[2] is often used to hold film so that it can be loaded in a camera.

magic lantern, n. ~ A device using a light and lens to project images on glass onto a surface for viewing by an audience.

> *Syn:* stereopticon
>
> *RT:* lantern slide
>
> *Notes:* Magic lanterns were developed in the mid-17th century.

magnetic disk, n. ~ COMPUTING · A circular platter coated with a substance that can be used to record data.

> *RT:* floppy disk, hard drive
>
> *Notes:* A magnetic disk is written and read in a disk drive.

magnetic media, n. ~ Materials in various formats that use a magnetic signal to store information.

> *Notes:* 'Magnetic media' includes audio and video tape, floppy disks, and hard drives. The signal may be either analog or digital. The media may use iron oxide, chromium dioxide, or other material to store the signal.

magnetic tape, n. ~ A thin strip (tape) of material coated with a substance capable of recording magnetic signals.

> *BT:* tape
>
> *Notes:* Videotape, audiotape, and computer data tape are examples of magnetic tape. Magnetic tape may be analog or digital. It may be stored on a hub or a reel or housed in a cartridge or cassette.

magnetic wire recording, n. ~ A sound recording made on a thin strand of metal.

> *Notes:* Magnetic wire recording was patented by Danish inventor Valdemar Poulsen in 1900 utilizing stainless steel wire. Wire recordings were replaced by magnetic tape.

magneto-optical media, n. ~ A recording technique that uses polarized light to read the magnetic field used to store digital data.

> *Notes:* Magneto-optical media are usually glass or plastic disks.

magnification (also **enlargement ratio, reproduction ratio**), n. ~ 1. An apparent increase in size of an item when viewed through an optical system. – 2. The linear ratio of the size of an image compared to the original.

> *RT:* reduction ratio
>
> *Notes:* If a line in an original is 1 inch, it would be 8 inches long in a reproduction with an 8× magnification.

mail, n. ~ 1. Items sent using a postal service. – 2. A postal service.

   RT: correspondence, electronic mail, letter

   Notes: Mail[1] includes letters, postcards, newspapers, magazines, and small packages.

main entry, n. ~ 1. Description · The principal access point in a catalog record. – 2. Description · A complete bibliographic description, including the heading used as the principal access point, presented in the form by which the item is to be identified and cited.

   BT: entry

   Notes: The main entry[1] is usually the name of the individual chiefly responsible for the intellectual or artistic content of a work, a corporate entity, or the title of the work. See "Choice of Access Points" (chapter 12) in *Anglo-American Cataloguing Rules* for details. If the main entry is a name, it is recorded in MARC fields 100, 110, 111, or 130; if it is a title, it is recorded in field 245. – A main entry[2] may include added entries.

mainframe computer ~ *see:* computer

management, n. ~ 1. The administration, organization, supervision, and oversight of the conduct of a business or activity. – 2. The individual or group responsible for those functions in an organization.

   NT: content management, document management, forms management, information management, knowledge management, records management, strategic information management

   Notes: Management focuses on the implementation of policy, rather than its development. Management is often applied to specific activities and record types, such as directives management, forms management, mail management, and reports management.

management information system, n. (**MIS**, abbr.) ~ A set of procedures, usually automated, designed to give information on current operations in an organization in a form tailored to the needs of managers.

   BT: information system

   RT: decision support system, system

   Notes: The information provided by an MIS may be strategic, tactical, or operational.

   †57 *(Dictionary of Computing 1996, p. 293):* The early concept of an MIS, commonplace in the 1960s and early 1970s, was that systems analysts would determine the information requirements of individual managers in an organization, and would design systems to supply that information routinely and/or on demand.

mandate, n. ~ 1. The authority invested by law in an agency to perform a specific function. – 2. An official directive issued by an authority. – 3. An order issued by an appellate court directing a lower court to take a specific action. – 4. An order issued by a court directing an officer to enforce a court order.

   RT: competence

mandatory rights ~ *see:* compulsory rights

manifest, n. ~ A list of the passengers or cargo carried on a ship, plane, or other vehicle.

   Notes: A manifest may also include notes about contents or commodity, consignee, and other information for use at terminals or customhouses.

Manual of Archival Description, n. (**MAD**, abbr.) ~ A British guideline for describing archival collections written by Michael Cook and Margaret Proctor.

>   *RT:* archival description, descriptive standard
>
>   *Notes:* A third edition was published by Gower in 2000.
>
>   †116 *(Hayworth 1993, p. 58):* MAD is intended to be a standard for the production of finding aids; it has rejected the bibliographic model as a standard for archival description. . . . MAD's focus on more rigorous models for output reflects perhaps the British archival tradition, where more emphasis has been placed on classification schemes and custodianship than on description.

manuscript, n. (**ms**, abbr.) ~ 1. A handwritten document. – 2. An unpublished document. – 3. An author's draft of a book, article, or other work submitted for publication.

>   *DF:* typescript
>
>   *Syn:* holograph
>
>   *BT:* document
>
>   *NT:* literary manuscripts
>
>   *RT:* papers, personal papers
>
>   *Notes:* Other abbreviations include **mss** for manuscripts (plural) and **MsS** for manuscript signed. – Manuscript¹ is principally text or musical notation on paper, but may be supplemented by drawings. Typewritten documents are generally classified as manuscripts but are more accurately described as typescripts.
>
>   †120 *(APPM2 1989, 1.0A):* Any text in handwriting or typescript (including printed forms completed by hand or typewriter) which may or may not be part of a collection of such texts. Examples of manuscripts are letters, diaries, ledgers, minutes, speeches, marked or corrected galley or page proofs, manuscript books, and legal papers.

manuscript box ~ *see:* archives box

manuscript collection, n. ~ A collection of personal or family papers.

>   *RT:* collection, family papers, fonds, papers
>
>   *Notes:* Although manuscript literally means handwritten, 'manuscript collection' is often used to include collections of mixed media in which unpublished materials predominate. They may also include typescripts, photographs, diaries, scrapbooks, news clippings, and printed works.
>
>   †294 *(National Library of Australia):* Although the literal meaning of manuscript is 'handwritten,' the Library's manuscript collections cover all kinds of unpublished written records and many contain published and pictorial records as well. The kinds of records are extremely diverse: letters, diaries, notebooks, speeches, lectures, drafts of books and articles, research or reference files, cutting books, photographs, drawings, minute books, agenda papers, logbooks, financial records, maps and plans.

manuscript curator, n. ~ An individual responsible for appraising, acquiring, arranging, describing, preserving, and providing access to a collection of original documents; an archivist.

>   *BT:* curator
>
>   *RT:* archivist, historical manuscripts tradition
>
>   *Notes:* The use of 'archivist' to describe a manuscript curator is common in the United States. Some archives use the phrase to distinguish responsibilities for dif-

ferent types of materials. For example, a manuscript curator is responsible for collections of textual documents, while a photograph curator is responsible for collections of photographs. 'Manuscript curator' is also used by some to distinguish individuals responsible for assembled or acquired collections, or for collections unconnected to the archives' parent organization. 'Manuscript curator' is sometimes related to the historical manuscripts tradition, which relied on techniques of curating materials based on principles of librarianship that emphasized item-level control rather than collection-level control.

manuscript group, n. ~ A collection of materials that share the same provenance.

　　RT: collection, fonds, record group, series

　　Notes: Manuscript group is equivalent to record group, but applied to collections of personal or family papers, or nonofficial records.

manuscript repository, n. ~ An institution that collects historically valuable records of individuals, families, and organizations from sources other than the organization that operates the institution.

　　Syn: collecting archives

　　RT: archives

map, n. ~ 1. A graphic representation of features of the Earth or another celestial body. – 2. A representation of the relationships among things.

　　BT: cadastral map, cartographic record

　　NT: chart, choropleth map, isopleth map, plan, plat

　　RT: atlas, globe, scale

　　Notes: A map^1 is typically flat, as opposed to a globe, which is round. Some maps use relief to represent altitude. Maps are typically drawn to scale using a projection technique, such as an azimuthal, a Mercator, or a cylindrical projection. Maps commonly include political boundaries, rounds, and geological features. Maps are commonly associated with surface features but also include climatic, hydrological, weather, and astronomical maps. – Map^2 is a metaphorical extension of map^1; the former often uses images, lines, and other graphics to show how ideas or activities are related in time or space.

　　†192 *(Monmonier 1996, p. xi):* All maps distort reality. All mapmakers use generalization and symbolization to highlight critical information and to suppress detail of lower priority. All cartography seeks to portray the complex, three-dimensional world on a flat sheet of paper or on a television or video screen. In short, the author warns, all maps must tell white lies. [Citing H. J. de Blij]

MARC (also **USMARC, MARC 21**), n. ~ A data communications format that specifies a data structure for bibliographic description, authority, classification, community information, and holdings data.

　　BT: metadata

　　RT: data structure standard, descriptive standard, MARC Format for Archival and Manuscripts Control

　　Notes: An acronym for MAchine Readable Cataloging. MARC is a United States implementation of the *Information Interchange Format* (ANSI Z39.2). Other countries implemented that standard with minor variations. The variations included UKMARC, and CanMARC. Efforts to harmonize the variations to create a single standard are reflected by the use of the name MARC 21. See http://lcweb.loc.gov/marc/.

†170 (MARC 21): The Library of Congress and the National Library of Canada are pleased to announce that the harmonized USMARC and CAN/MARC formats will be published in a single edition in early 1999 under a new name: MARC 21. The name both points to the future as we move into the 21st century and suggests the international character of the format, which is appropriate and important given its expanding worldwide use. ¶ MARC 21 is not a new format. From 1994-1997 the USMARC and CAN/MARC user communities worked to eliminate all remaining differences in their two already-similar formats. Compatibility had been a feature of the development processes for both formats for many years. In 1997 and early 1998, updates to the formats were issued that made the format specifications identical. MARC 21, a continuation of both USMARC and CAN/MARC, publishes the formats in one edition under a new name.

MARC AMC format ~ *see:* MARC Format for Archival and Manuscripts Control

MARC Format for Archival and Manuscripts Control, n. ~ A standard data communications format that specifies a data structure for description of records (archives and manuscripts).

RT: MARC

Notes: Also **Archival and Manuscripts Control Format (AMC), USMARC Format for Archival and Manuscripts Control, AMC format,** and **MARC AMC format.**

†253 (Russell and Hutchinson 2000): In recent years, the archival community has given much attention to the idea of adapting standard bibliographic cataloging processes in order to describe the kinds of materials often held by archives and other depositories. This adaptation has become increasingly common in recent years, as the special MARC AMC format was eliminated in favor of a single bibliographic format for MARC records that describes all formats of materials and the underlying and unifying principles that can be used to describe both published and unpublished materials. The introduction of Encoded Archival Description as an electronic standard for displaying finding aids on the World Wide Web has not diminished the importance of bibliographic cataloging, especially in institutions with collections including archives, published material, and other formats.

marginalia (also **marginal notes**), n. ~ Notes made in the margin of a document.

RT: annotation, gloss

marking, n. ~ The process of affixing an identifying number to an item, either directly or through the use of a tag or label.

RT: stamping

markup, n. ~ 1. PUBLISHING · The process of editing copy[3] for printing, including making corrections and adding instructions to a typesetter for layout. – 2. COMPUTING · The process of adding codes to a digital document to give semantic structure to the content.

RT: Encoded Archival Context, Encoded Archival Description, Extensible Hypertext Markup Language, Extensible Markup Language, Hypertext Markup Language, Standard Generalized Markup Language, Text Encoding Initiative

Notes: Encoded Archival Description (EAD) is a markup[2] language used to distinguish the parts of a finding aid in order to facilitate automated manipulation of the content.

MAS ~ *see:* master of archival studies

mass deacidification, n. ~ Techniques to neutralize acid and leave an alkaline reserve in large quantities of paper materials.

RT: deacidification

†113 *(Harris and Shahani 1994):* Over the past two decades, the Library of Congress has been at the forefront of the development of deacidification processes that can be applied en masse to large collections. In its search for an ideal mass deacidification process, the Library invented and further developed the diethyl zinc (DEZ) gaseous process and also brought about key improvements in solvent-based, liquid phase processes. In the conservation science community, gaseous processes have traditionally been deemed to have a significant edge over liquid phase, solvent-based processes, mainly because they preclude any possibility of adverse effects on inks, dyes and colored pigments in manuscripts, color plates and book covers due to bleeding or softening of inks.

master, n. ~ An item from which duplicates are to be made.

NT: edited master, protection master

master file, n. ~ A complete and accurate collection of long-lived data that is periodically updated and used for queries.

RT: input records

Notes: Master files were typically used in batch, rather than interactive, systems. Transactions were collected in a separate file, which was then used to update the master on a periodic basis.

master negative (also **master film, camera film**), n. ~ Film used to create positive intermediaries or distribution copies.

Notes: The master negative is usually the film that was originally exposed in the camera.

master of archival studies, n. (**MAS,** abbr.) ~ A graduate degree program designed for preappointment education of future archivists.

Notes: See http://www.archivists.org/prof-education/edd-arched.asp.

Master Record of Manuscript Collections, n. (**MRMC,** abbr.) ~ An early computer application to assist in the production and indexing of finding aids for manuscript collections at the Library of Congress.

†122 *(Hickerson 1981, p. 24):* MRMC II, developed and used by the LC Manuscripts Division, is an expanded version of the MRMC system designed for administrative control. After modifying the system several times since its creation in 1967, the staff decided in 1973 that major changes were desirable. Enhancements made possible the production of catalog cards and a cumulative index to the Division's holdings, thus providing access as well as administrative control. These modifications were based on the LC MARC II format (record structure, content, and coding) and were intended to be compatible with the MARC format for manuscripts.

†184 *(LC Mss 1997):* The Master Record of Manuscript Collections serves as the basic guide to the division's collections. It consists of Master Record I, a brief checklist of all collections in the division's custody, and Master Record II, a more comprehensive catalog containing summary descriptions of collections and an index to the names and key terms cited in these descriptions. Neither Master Record I nor II has been published, but copies are available in reading rooms throughout the Library. In addition, Master Record II may be accessed through the Library's online catalog which is available on-site and through the Internet.

Syn: Synonym • †: see Bibliography • *Superscript:* Definition number

mat, n. ~ 1. A sheet of cardboard or other materials used in mounting flat items for storage or framing. – 2. A simple frame made from cardboard or other material.

> *NT:* sink mat
>
> *RT:* mount
>
> *Notes:* A mat[1] commonly has a solid back, on which the item is mounted, and a front with a window cut to allow the item to be viewed. – Mat[2] refers to the sheet placed in front of the item; it is distinguished from the mount, which is the backing board to which the item is attached.

material, n. ~ 1. The substance of which something is made. – 2. A thing; a resource[1,3]. – 3. An object having physical or intellectual substance.

> *NT:* artifact, document, record, specimen
>
> *RT:* object, resource
>
> *Notes:* This glossary uses 'material' as an encompassing, generic term to describe the broad variety of items that an archives might collect, regardless of medium, format, or type. It is used to avoid connotations carried by terms such as record, document, or object. In this sense, materials may be tangible (of matter) or virtual (electronic) and may be used to describe a group of individual items. In the context of digital information, 'material' is roughly synonymous with 'resource'.

matrix, n. ~ 1. A mold, especially one made by impression. – 2. A metal master used to press phonograph records. – 3. An array of elements.

> *Notes:* In printing, matrix[1] generally means the thing that holds the ink to be transferred to the printed surface. For example, a matrix used to make a dye transfer print or Woodburytype is a shallow, three-dimensional relief formed in hardened gelatin. – A matrix[2] can be used as a stamper to produce pressings or as a mother to produce a stamper.

matte (also **mat**), n. ~ 1. A dull, nonreflecting finish, principally used to describe the surface of photographic prints. – 2. MOTION PICTURES · A mask used to block a portion of the film during shooting, allowing another scene to be printed in composite to create a final image.

> *RT:* glossy
>
> *Notes:* The use of a matte[2] for special effects was a very common before the introduction of computer generated imagery (CGI).

measured drawing, n. ~ An architectural drawing, made to scale, of a building or structure.

> *BT:* architectural drawing, drawing
>
> *Notes:* Measured drawings are not used to guide construction but are created to document an existing building or structure.

mechanical rights, n. ~ The rights of creators to royalties when others record and distribute their works.

> *DF:* performance rights
>
> *RT:* copyright
>
> †83 (*Fed. Reg., 66:47 (9 March 2001), p. 14099.*): The copyright laws of the United States grant certain rights to copyright owners for the protection of their works of authorship. Among these rights is the right to make, and to authorize others to make, a reproduction of the copyrighted work, and the right to distribute, and to authorize others to distribute, the copyrighted work. Both the reproduction right and the distribution right granted to a copyright owner inhere in all works of authorship and are, for the most part, exclusive rights. However, for

copyright holders of nondramatic musical works, the exclusivity of the reproduction right and distribution right are limited by the compulsory license of section 115 of the Copyright Act. Often referred to as the 'mechanical license,' section 115 grants third parties a nonexclusive license to make and distribute phonorecords of nondramatic musical works. The license can be invoked once a nondramatic musical work embodied in a phonorecord is distributed 'to the public in the United States under the authority of the copyright owner.' 17 U.S.C. 115(a)(1). Unless and until such an act occurs, the copyright owner's rights in the musical work remain exclusive, and the compulsory license does not apply. Once it does occur, the license permits anyone to make and distribute phonorecords of the musical work provided, of course, that they comply with all of the royalty and accounting requirements of section 115. It is important to note that the mechanical license only permits the making and distribution of phonorecords of a musical work, and does not permit the use of a sound recording created by someone else. The compulsory licensee must either assemble his own musicians, singers, recording engineers and equipment, or obtain permission from the copyright owner to use a preexisting sound recording. One who obtains permission to use another's sound recording is eligible to use the compulsory license for the musical composition that is performed on the sound recording. The mechanical license was the first compulsory license in U.S. copyright law, having its origin in the 1909 Copyright Act. It operated successfully for many years, and it continued under the 1976 Copyright Act with only some technical modifications. However, in 1995, Congress passed the Digital Performance Right in Sound Recordings Act ('Digital Performance Act'), Public Law 104-39, 109 Stat. 336, which amended sections 114 and 115 of the Copyright Act to take account of technological changes which were beginning to enable digital transmission of sound recordings. With respect to section 115, the Act expanded the scope of the mechanical license to include the right to distribute, or authorize the distribution of, a phonorecord by means of a digital transmission which constitutes a 'digital phonorecord delivery.'

mechanical wood pulp, n. ~ A paper pulp made by physically grinding wood without separating the cellulose fibers from impurities such as lignin.

> *BT:* paper, pulp
> *RT:* chemical wood pulp
> *Notes:* Paper made from mechanical wood pulp has relatively low strength, discolors fairly rapidly upon exposure to air and light, and has very little permanence. It does, however, possess good bulk, opacity, and compressibility. Life expectancy is relatively low for wood pulp paper – about 100 years – depending upon storage, handling, acidity of inks or pigments used upon the paper, and sizing.

media, n. ~ 1. Plural of medium. – 2. The mass communications industry and profession as a whole, including newspapers, television, and radio.

> *RT:* medium

media migration, n. ~ The process of converting data from one type of storage material to another to ensure continued access to the information as the material becomes obsolete or degrades over time.

> *BT:* migration
> *Notes:* Media migration does not alter the bitstream. Examples of media migration include copying files from 5¼ floppy disks to 3½ floppy discs to CD to DVD.

medium, n. (**media**, pl.) ~ 1. The physical material that serves as the carrier for information. – 2. ART · The materials and technique used to create a work. – 3. PAINTING · The liquid in which pigment is suspended.

BT: extrinsic element

RT: carrier, media

Notes: Medium[1] refers to the thing that bears the information, as distinguished from the base[1]. For example, in printing, the ink is the medium and the paper is the base. In videotape, the magnetic material that holds the signal is the media, and the polyester film is the base. – Medium[2] is frequently used when describing artworks; for example, oil on canvas or mixed media. – An example of medium[3] is linseed oil, which is used in oil paint.

†17 (InterPARES Authenticity, p. 6): [There is a question as to whether] medium – that is, the physical carrier on which a record is stored – is a part of the record itself or as a part of its technological context. For diplomatists examining medieval documents, the medium is an essential component of a record because the examination of the physical carrier on which the document is inscribed is one of the most obvious proofs of its authenticity. In the translation of diplomatic concepts into the modern, paper-based, recordkeeping environments, the medium has continued to be treated as a part of the record itself, mainly because the medium and the message are inextricably linked. ¶ The question was whether, in an electronic recordkeeping environment, the medium should continue to be treated as an essential part of the record itself given that 1) the medium and the message are no longer inextricably linked; 2) what is inscribed on or affixed to the medium is not a record as such (or words, or pictures), but a bitstream; and 3) the choice of a medium by those creating or maintaining the record is often arbitrary and carries no particular significance.

†26 (Bergeron 2002, p. 59 ff): The medium is the physical material, whether in the form of a disk or a tape, used to store computer data. The material, whether it is a thin layer of iron oxide sprayed on a paper, plastic, or a metal base, or whether it is a thin sheet of aluminum foil sandwiched between disks of plastic, or whether it is a paper card punched full of holes, imparts certain characteristics to the media. [Characteristics include compatibility, speed, capacity, data density, cost, volatility, durability, and stability.]

Melinex, trademark ~ A polyester film manufactured by DuPont.

BT: polyester

memex, n. ~ A massive store of human knowledge that serves as an extension of human memory, envisioned by Vannevar Bush in 1945.

Notes: Some consider Bush's description of memex to be the first conception of hypertext.

†38 (Bush 1945): Consider a future device for individual use, which is a sort of mechanized private file and library. It needs a name, and, to coin one at random, 'memex' will do. A memex is a device in which an individual stores all his books, records, and communications, and which is mechanized so that it may be consulted with exceeding speed and flexibility. It is an enlarged intimate supplement to his memory. ¶ It consists of a desk, and while it can presumably be operated from a distance, it is primarily the piece of furniture at which he works. On the top are slanting translucent screens, on which material can be projected for conven-

ient reading. There is a keyboard, and sets of buttons and levers. Otherwise it looks like an ordinary desk.

memorandum (frequently **memo**), n. (**memorandums, memoranda, memos,** pl.) ~ 1. A textual communication used principally in business that lacks the formal salutation and complimentary ending of a letter. – 2. A short note made as a personal reminder. – 3. An informal document detailing the terms of a contract or transaction; a memorial[3].

> *RT:* letter

> †*167 (D Levy 2001, p. 70–71):* The memo[1], too, was a product of the search for speed, efficiency, and standardization. It arose most directly from the letter. Letters as a form of personal correspondence had of course existed for many centuries. They were already used in commerce, mainly for external communication. The conventions of letter writing were well established. These included the date of writing, a formal salutation ('Dear . . . ') as well as a formal closing ('Your most . . .') . . . As the letter was increasingly used for internal communication, within and across departments, the new business experts, masters of efficiency, argued for a much simplified format. Typing time could be saved if the company printed up letterheads with fields such as *To, From,* and *Subject,* and if openings and closings were stripped down to a bare minimum. . . . ¶ . . . The 'Subject' field had a double purpose. It of course gave the recipient a quick way to determine what the memo was about. But it was equally important as a resource for a new class of workers, the file clerk. It helped the clerk determine where in the vertical files to store the memo.

memorandum book, n. ~ A personal anthology of aphorisms, short passages from literature, poems, and other notes transcribed into a blank volume to serve the memory or reference of the compiler.

> *Syn:* commonplace book

memorial, n. ~ 1. A commemorative item, especially a monument honoring an individual or individuals who have died. – 2. A written statement of facts accompanying a petition. – 3. An informal document detailing the terms of a contract or transaction; a memorandum[3]. – 4. A formal document issued by a legislative body expressing an opinion or requesting another body outside its jurisdiction to take some action.

> *RT:* petition

> †*243 (NARA/SRA, Current Recordkeeping Practices 2001):* Generally speaking, in the late 18th and 19th centuries a petition, unlike a memorial, included a prayer (e.g., petition of John Smith praying that his claim be granted). Memorials also express opposition to ('remonstrate against') some pending action. In modern usage, there is no apparent difference between a memorial and a petition, and petition has become the commonly accepted generic term. A similar document transmitted to Congress by a legislative body such as a State legislature takes the form of a resolution and is sometimes termed a memorial.

memorial record, n. ~ 1. A book containing information about a person after their death. – 2. A book provided at funeral or memorial services for guests to sign.

> *BT:* record

memory, n. ~ 1. The knowledge of events, people, places, and other things of the past. – 2. An individual's knowledge of the past. – 3. A specific recollection of something in the past. – 4. COMPUTING · The portion of a computer used to store information.

Syn: Synonym • †: see Bibliography • *Superscript:* Definition number

Notes: Memory⁴ connotes a computer's internal storage that is directly accessible by the operating system (RAM or ROM), as opposed to hard drives or other data stores.

†255 (Samuels 1986): Who controls the past, controls the future: who controls the present, controls the past. . . . The mutability of the past is the central tenet of Ingsoc. Past events, it is argued, have no objective existence, but survive only in written records and in human memories. The past is whatever the records and the memories agree upon. And since the Party is in full control of all records, and in equally full control of the minds of its members, it follows that the past is whatever they Party chooses to make it. [Quoting George Orwell, *1984.*]

mend, n. ~ A minor rehabilitation to an item not that does not require any material to be replaced.

    RT: repair, restoration

    Notes: Mending requires less than repairing.

mere act, n. ~ Diplomatics · An act that is neither directed toward, nor capable of, changing the relationships between two or more physical or juridical persons.

    BT: act

message digest, n. ~ 1. Computing · A unique numerical value derived from a data stream, typically through a one-way hash function, that can be used to test the integrity of the data stream. – 2. A collection of email messages sent to a distribution list over a period of time and combined into a single email message for distribution.

    RT: digital signature

    Notes: A message digest¹ can be generated using the MD5, secure hash algorithm (SHA), or other algorithms. If a message digest is calculated on a data stream and compared to an earlier message digest, it is possible to determine if there has been even a minor alteration in the content of the data stream. Message digests are key components of digital signatures.

message handling system, n. (**MHS,** abbr.) ~ A part of the International Telecommunications Union X.400 standard that specifies functions for the user agents and message transfer system used in the exchange of email.

metadata, n. ~ A characterization or description documenting the identification, management, nature, use, or location of information resources (data).

    NT: administrative metadata, descriptive metadata, Dublin Core, MARC, preservation metadata, structural metadata

    Notes: Metadata is commonly defined as "data about data." Metadata is frequently used to locate or manage information resources by abstracting or classifying those resources or by capturing information not inherent in the resource. Typically metadata is organized into distinct categories and relies on conventions to establish the values for each category. For example, administrative metadata may include the date and source of acquisition, disposal date, and disposal method. Descriptive metadata may include information about the content and form of the materials. Preservation metadata may record activities to protect or extend the life of the resource, such as reformatting. Structural metadata may indicate the interrelationships between discrete information resources, such as page numbers.

    In terms of archives, MARC format and EAD are standards for structuring descriptive metadata about collections. Dublin Core is a standard for structuring metadata that is intended for describing web resources.

In terms of information technology, metadata includes the documentation of data architecture, properties, and methods necessary to store, retrieve, and use the data in a meaningful manner. To the extent that data is a record, it may also include administrative, descriptive, preservation, and structural information.

†26 *(Bergeron 2002, p. 9):* Metadata includes descriptive summaries and high-level categorization of data and information. *Knowledge* is information that is organized, synthesized, or summarized to enhance comprehension, awareness, or understanding. That is, knowledge is a combination and an awareness of the context in which the data can be successfully applied. Although the concept of data is roughly equivalent to metadata, unlike data, information, or metadata, knowledge implies a human – rather than computer – host.

†92 *(Future 1999):* Having heard someone once define information science as 'librarianship practiced by men,' Mr. Gorman concluded by defining metadata as 'cataloging practiced by ill-informed men.'

†175 *(C Lynch 2000, p. 34):* We have an object and a collection of assertions about it. The assertions may be internal, as in a claim of authorship or date and place of publication on the title page of a book, or external, represented in metadata that accompany the object, perhaps provided by third parties. We want to ask questions about the integrity of the object: Has the object been changed since its creation, and, if so, has this altered the fundamental essence of the object? (This can include asking these questions about accompanying assertions, either embedded in the object or embodied in accompanying metadata).

†223 *(Personal communication, Ken Thibodeau, 19 May 2003):* Metadata used to have a perfectly nice meaning in engineering, and information technologists' appropriation of the term 'ontology' was payback for librarians' corruption of 'metadata'.

†235 *(Puglia, Reed, and Rhodes 2004, p. 6):* Metadata makes possible several key functions – the identification, management, access, use, and preservation of a digital resource – and is therefore directly associated with most of the steps in a digital imaging project workflow: file naming, capture, processing, quality control, production tracking, search and retrieval design, storage, and long-term management.

metadata encoding and transmission standard, n. (**METS**, abbr.) ~ An Extensible Markup Language (XML) schema used to package digital objects, along with descriptive, administrative, and structural metadata.

†190 *(METS 2003):* Maintaining a library of digital objects of necessity requires maintaining metadata about those objects. The metadata necessary for successful management and use of digital objects is both more extensive than and different from the metadata used for managing collections of printed works and other physical materials. While a library may record descriptive metadata regarding a book in its collection, the book will not dissolve into a series of unconnected pages if the library fails to record structural metadata regarding the book's organization, nor will scholars be unable to evaluate the book's worth if the library fails to note that the book was produced using a Ryobi offset press. The same cannot be said for a digital version of the same book. Without structural metadata, the page image or text files comprising the digital work are of little use, and without technical metadata regarding the digitization process, scholars may be unsure of how accurate a reflection of the original the digital version provides. For internal management purposes, a library must have access to appropriate technical metadata in order to periodically refresh and migrate the data, ensuring the durability of valuable

resources. ❡ The Making of America II project (MOA2) attempted to address these issues in part by providing an encoding format for descriptive, administrative, and structural metadata for textual and image-based works. METS, a Digital Library Federation initiative, attempts to build upon the work of MOA2 and provide an XML document format for encoding metadata necessary for both management of digital library objects within a repository and exchange of such objects between repositories (or between repositories and their users). Depending on its use, a METS document could be used in the role of Submission Information Package (SIP), Archival Information Package (AIP), or Dissemination Information Package (DIP) within the Open Archival Information System (OAIS) Reference Model.

methylene-blue test, n. ~ A standard (ISO 18917, ANSI IT9.17) for determining the amount of residual thiosulfate ions that remains in gelatin silver film after processing.

BT: residual hypo test

RT: densitometric method (silver), fixer, microfilm inspection

Notes: The standard is used to assess the relative permanence of film by determining how much thiosulfate (hypo or fixer) remains in the film.

METS ~ *see:* metadata encoding and transmission standard

mezzotint, n. ~ 1. An intaglio process to make prints in which the image midtones and highlights are drawn on a dark background. – 2. A print made using this process.

Notes: A mezzotint plate is usually copper or steel. It is prepared by using a rocker to give it a uniformly roughened surface that accepts ink. A burnisher or other tool is used to create the design by smoothing the surface so that it accepts less ink. The mezzotint was introduced in the 17th century.

MHS ~ *see:* message handling system

microcard ~ *see:* micro-opaque

microclimate, ~ n. ~ The physical conditions, especially temperature, humidity, pollution, and air movement, within an enclosed space.

DF: microenvironment

Notes: Microclimates are distinguished from microenvironments, the latter describing physical conditions within an enclosure, such as a polyester sleeve or storage box.

microcomputer ~ *see:* computer

microcopy (also **microimage**), n. ~ 1. A copy that has been reduced during reproduction to a size that requires magnification to be read. – 2. An image on microfilm.

BT: copy, microfilm

microenvironment, n. ~ The physical conditions within a storage enclosure, especially as regards the interaction of trapped, still air immediately surrounding an object.

DF: microclimate

RT: environmental control

Notes: In the context of preservation, 'microenvironment' connotes the environment within an enclosure holding an item, such as a polyester sleeve, a CD jewel case, or a paper envelope. While such an enclosure can provide a barrier against external conditions, it can accelerate deterioration of the item by trapping undesirable chemicals in the item. For example, a polyester sleeve can capture and concentrate gases from a decomposing nitrate negative. Microenvironments are distinguished from microclimates, the latter describing physical conditions within an enclosed space that is significantly larger, such as a display case.

microfiche (also **fiche**), n. ~ A sheet of transparent film with microimages arranged in rows and columns, usually with an area for an eye-readable description at the top.

    BT: microfilm

    RT: step-and-repeat camera

    Notes: Two standard sizes of microfiche are 105 × 148 mm (about 4 × 6 inches) and 75 × 125 mm (about 3 × 5 inches). Microfiche may be printed from strips of microfilm or may be created using a step-and-repeat camera.

microfilm, n. ~ 1. Transparent film containing highly reduced copies of documents. – 2. High-resolution, low-grain film used make such copies.

    BT: microform

    NT: acquisition microfilm, camera microfilm, computer input microfilm, computer output microfilm, jacketed microfilm, microcopy, microfiche, preservation microfilm, serialized microform, unitized microform

    RT: administrative microfilming, ammonia process, aperture card, blip code, Copyflo, diazo film, disposal microfilming, duplicating master, film, flatbed camera, flow camera, line code index, micrographics, planetary camera, reader-printer, rotary camera, security microfilming, step-and-repeat camera

    Notes: Microfilm[1] may be in rolls, sheets (microfiche), strips (usually in jackets), or chips (usually in aperture cards). Standard widths of roll film include 35 mm and 16 mm. Microfilm may use gelatin silver, diazo, or vesicular processes to form the images.

microfilm camera, n. ~ A camera specifically designed to produce microfilm.

    NT: flatbed camera, planetary camera, rotary camera, step-and-repeat camera

microfilm inspection, n. ~ 1. A quality control test performed on microfilm after production to determine if it meets standards for archival processing[2], completeness, targeting, and other factors. – 2. Periodic examination of microfilm in storage to monitor its condition and check for deterioration or damage.

    RT: methylene-blue test

microfilm jacket (also **film jacket**), n. ~ A thin plastic sleeve with separate channels to house short strips of microfilm and with a space reserved for a header.

    RT: jacketed microfilm

    Notes: Microfilm jackets are used to hold strips of microfilm cut from rolls so that the materials filmed can be unitized and be filed like microfiche.

microfilm strip, n. ~ A short piece of microfilm cut from a roll so that it can be inserted in a jacket.

    RT: jacketed microfilm

    Notes: Inserting microfilm strips in a jacket gives roll film the convenience of microfiche.

microform, n. ~ A general term used for any medium, transparent or opaque, that holds highly reduced reproductions.

    NT: microfilm, micro-opaque, serialized microform, unitized microform

    RT: aperture card

microform publication, n. ~ A serial or monograph distributed on microform.

    BT: publication

microform reader, n. ~ Equipment that enlarges microfilm images so that they can be easily viewed.

    DF: reader

RT: reader-printer

Notes: A microform reader may be designed to work with only film or with fiche or jacketed film, or it may be able to read from different formats. A microform reader-printer incorporates a mechanism to make copies, typically on paper.

micrographics, n. ~ The process and techniques of creating microforms.

RT: microfilm, microphotography, print film, reprographics

Notes: Micrographics includes the preparation of materials, the camera work to make the reproductions, the development and testing of film, and indexing and retrieval systems.

microimage ~ *see:* microcopy

micro-opaque (also **microcard**, **microprint**), n. ~ A nontransparent base with highly reduced reproductions arranged in rows and columns.

BT: microform

Notes: A micro-opaque may be made by a photographic or a printing process.

microphotography, n. ~ The use of photographic processes and techniques to create highly reduced images.

RT: micrographics, photograph, photomicrography

Notes: Microphotography is distinguished from photomicrography, the processes and techniques of creating greatly enlarged photographs of things normally too small to be seen with the unaided eye.

microprint ~ *see:* micro-opaque

middle digit filing, n. ~ A filing system that uses a tripartite number, using the middle part for the initial sort, the first part of the number for the second sort, and the third part for the final sort.

Notes: A file code 123-45-678 would be filed 45, 123, 678.

†247 (Robek, et al. 1996, p. 124): The important advantage of middle-digit filing in comparison to straight numeric filing is its almost perfect distribution of folders throughout the entire system. This makes it possible to place responsibility for accuracy in filing on the clerk assigned to a specific section. It also eliminates the queuing or congestion that occurs with straight numeric arrangements, which tend to concentrate file activity in the most recent or higher sequential order.

middle gray ~ *see:* neutral test card

middleware, n. ~ Software that mediates the exchange of information between two applications or between an application and a network.

RT: application program interface

Notes: Sometimes called an application programming interface.

migrated archives, n. ~ 1. The archives of a country that have moved from the country where they were originally accumulated; removed archives. – 2. Older computer files that have been moved to a new medium or software format.

Syn: removed archives

BT: archives

migration, n. ~ The process of moving data from one information system or storage medium to another to ensure continued access to the information as the system or medium becomes obsolete or degrades over time.

NT: format migration, media migration

RT: conversion, reformat

Notes: Copying information onto the same format storage media without any alteration is generally referred to as refreshing.

†262 (Sedona Principles 2003, p. 4): In a perfect world, electronic records that continue to be needed for business purposes or litigation are converted for use in successor systems and all other data is discarded. In reality, though, such migrations are rarely flawless.

MII, n. ~ An analog videotape format introduced by Panasonic in 1986 with a helical scan and two longitudinal audio tracks.

    RT: video

    Notes: Pronounced M2.

mildew, n. ~ A fungus that obtains its food from the organic substance on which it grows and that generally has the appearance of a gray or white powder.

    Notes: Mildew produces citric, gluconic, oxalic, or other organic acids, which can damage paper, leather, cloth, and similar materials. They may create colored stains that are difficult to remove.

MIME ~ *see:* Multipurpose Internet Messaging Extensions

mimeograph, n. ~ A process to create multiple copies using an inked stencil.

    RT: stencil process

    Notes: Originally a tradename of the A. B. Dick company, now considered a generic term. The mimeograph process forces ink through a stencil, as distinguished from a spirit process, which transfers a small layer of pigment from a master.

minicomputer ~ *see:* computer

Minnesota method, n. ~ An strategy for appraising materials that combines aspects of collection analysis, documentation strategy, appraisal, and functional analysis.

    Notes: See Mark A. Greene and Todd J. Daniels-Howell, "Documentation with 'An Attitude': A Pragmatist's Guide to the Selection and Acquisition of Modern Business Records" in James M. O'Toole, ed., *The Records of American Business* (Society of American Archivists, 1997).

    †150 (Jimerson 1998): The 'Minnesota Method' [Mark A. Greene and Todd J. Daniels-Howell] developed is based on the assumption that 'all archival appraisal is local and subjective', but that, through careful analysis of both records creators and the records themselves, archivists can establish appraisal and selection criteria that are 'rational and efficient relative to a specific repository's goals and resources'. The strategy they propose includes: defining a collecting area; analyzing existing collections; determining the documentary universe, including relevant government records, printed and other sources; prioritizing industrial sectors, individual businesses, geographic regions, and time periods from which records will be sought; defining functions performed by businesses and the collecting levels needed to document major functions; connecting documentary levels to priority tiers; and updating this process every three to seven years. They outline priority factors used in making these decisions, documentation levels, and decision points to refine the priority levels. This Minnesota Method combines features of archival approaches to collection analysis, documentation strategy, appraisal, and functional analysis.

minutes, n. ~ A record containing notes of actions taken and comments made at a meeting.

    DF: proceedings

mirroring ~ *see:* silver mirroring

MIS ~ *see:* management information system

miscellaneous documents, n. ~ CONGRESS · A series of documents from nongovernmental sources that were printed by the United States House of Representatives.

   RT: document

   †110 (NARA Senate Records): Petitions, memorials, communications from non-governmental sources, special reports, reports from independent agencies, and other miscellaneous items that were ordered printed by the House. These were numbered in each Congress in the following manner H. Misc. Doc. 23, 53d Cong., 1st sess. In 1895 this series was consolidated with the Executive Document series, and the resulting series became known simply as House Documents.

mitigation ~ *see:* disaster plan

mixed media, n. ~ Works of art that combine different materials.

   RT: multimedia

   Notes: Collages are often examples of mixed media, combining photographs, text, objects, and painting. Mixed media is distinguished from multimedia, which combines different presentation formats, such as sculpture and music.

mnemonic filing system, n. ~ A system to classify files using codes that are reminiscent of the category they represent.

   BT: filing system

   RT: classification scheme

   Notes: Examples of codes used in a mnemonic filing system include ADM for administrative files, FIN for financial files, and PER for personnel files. The codes are usually arranged alphabetically.

mobile shelving ~ *see:* compact shelving

mockumentary, n. ~ A parody in the form of a documentary.

   RT: docudrama

   Notes: Often used to describe movies made by Christopher Guest, including *This is Spinal Tap* and *A Mighty Wind*.

mockup, n. ~ 1. GRAPHICS · A prototype of a page design used for proofreading and as instructions to a typesetter. – 2. A model used for demonstration, testing, or analysis.

model, n. ~ 1. A three-dimensional representation of an idea or object. – 2. A simplified representation of something, especially a diagram.

   NT: data model

   Notes: Model[1] includes prototypes, which may suggest the general appearance and parts or may be functional; for example, a patent model. Model implies something that is smaller than the thing it represents; for example, a model railroad. – Model[2] may represent a process or concept. For example, the waterfall model describes a method for software development, and IDEF can be used to describe data models.

model shot, n. ~ PHOTOGRAPHY, MOTION PICTURES · The use of miniatures, shot to appear full-scale, in lieu of location shots or real objects.

   Notes: Model shots are commonly used for special effects. For example, on the program "Star Trek," exterior shots of the star ship *Enterprise* were filmed using model shots.

mold, n. ~ 1. A fungus that grows on organic matter. – 2. A container that gives shape to liquid materials. – 3. A wooden frame with a wire screen used in making paper.

monetary appraisal, n. ~ The process of determining a fair market value for materials.

   DF: appraisal

Syn: valuation

RT: fair market value

monetary value, n. ~ The estimated amount of money that an item would bring if offered for sale.

BT: value

Notes: Monetary value is commonly used for tax deductions when materials are donated.

monochrome, adj. ~ 1. Having a single color. – **monochromatic**, adj. ~ 2. PHOTOGRAPHY · Being sensitive to only one color in the spectrum.

RT: black and white, color, orthochromatic, panchromatic

Notes: A monochrome[1] image may have many shades of the same color. For example, a cyanotype is a monochrome image with many shades of Prussian blue. Although the phrase 'black and white' is commonly used to mean monochrome, it is properly limited to items with neutral shades of gray. – Early photographic emulsions were monochromatic[2] because they were sensitive only to blue light.

monograph, n. ~ 1. A published work limited to a single topic. – 2. DESCRIPTION · A nonserial publication.

monophonic (also **mono**, **monaural**), adj. ~ Having a single audio channel.

Notes: A monophonic recording or broadcast reproduces sound from a single source, although it may combine signals from several microphones. 'Monophonic' is distinguished from 'stereophonic' (two channels) and 'quadraphonic' (four channels).

montage, n. ~ 1. The technique of combining existing images to form a larger, unified picture. – 2. A work created using such a technique. – 3. MOTION PICTURES · A shot formed by superimposing two separate shots.

DF: collage

NT: photomontage

RT: composite

Notes: Montage[1,2] is distinguished from collage, which combines elements but does not form a unified picture.

moral rights, n. ~ The legal right of creators to have their works attributed to them and to protect the integrity of their works.

BT: intellectual property

RT: copyright, Visual Artists Rights Act

Notes: In the United States, moral rights are defined in the Visual Artists Rights Act (17 USC 106A). The federal law is restricted to certain still photographs, paintings, drawings, prints, and sculptures that are signed and consecutively numbered by the author and that are unique or limited to editions of 200 or less. Outside the United States and in some states, moral rights may cover the rights of creators of other formats, including written works.

†250 (Rosenblatt 1998): The term 'moral rights' is a translation of the French term *droit moral*, and refers not to 'morals' as advocated by the religious right, but rather to the ability of authors to control the eventual fate of their works. An author is said to have the "moral right" to control her work. The concept of moral rights thus relies on the connection between an author and her creation. Moral rights protect the personal and reputational, rather than purely monetary, value of a work to its creator. . . . ¶ In the U.S., moral rights are primarily protected by VARA. Before

VARA was passed, courts and commentators struggled to find moral rights in the "derivative work" provision of the Copyright Act, the laws of defamation, the rights of privacy and publicity, the doctrine of misappropriation, and especially the Lanham Act, which deals with trademarks and unfair competition. Authors may seek moral rights protection from state moral rights laws and art preservation statutes in California and New York, whose provisions resemble those of VARA. Authors whose works are not covered by VARA and the state statutes may also seek moral rights-type protection from various other sources of law.

†281 (USC, 17 USC 106A): The author of a work of visual art shall have the right to claim authorship of that work, and to prevent the use of his or her name as the author of any work of visual art which he or she did not create; shall have the right to prevent the use of his or her name as the author of the work of visual art in the event of a distortion, mutilation, or other modification of the work which would be prejudicial to his or her honor or reputation; and subject to the limitations set forth in section 113(d), shall have the right to prevent any intentional distortion, mutilation, or other modification of that work which would be prejudicial to his or her honor or reputation, and any intentional distortion, mutilation, or modification of that work is a violation of that right, and to prevent any destruction of a work of recognized stature, and any intentional or grossly negligent destruction of that work is a violation of that right.

MoReq ~ *see:* Requirements for the Management of Electronic Records

mosaic panorama ~ *see:* panorama

mother, n. ~ An intermediate master used to create stampers in the mass-production of disk recordings.

  Notes: The process is used in the mass production of analog phonograph records and of digital CDs and DVDs.

motion, n. ~ 1. A request made to a court for a ruling or order. – 2. A proposal made according to formal parliamentary procedure.

motion picture (also **movie, moving picture, picture show, cinefilm**), n. ~ A sequence of images that, when viewed in rapid succession, gives the appearance of movement.

  DF: picture, video

  Syn: movie

  BT: moving image

  NT: news film, newsreel

  RT: celluloid, cinematography, film, visual materials

  Notes: 'Motion picture' connotes the use of film, as distinguished from 'video', which uses magnetic tape. 'Motion picture' is sometimes used as a generic term synonymous with 'moving image'.

  †281 (USC, 17 USC 101): Copyright · 'Motion pictures' are audiovisual works consisting of a series of related images which, when shown in succession, impart an impression of motion, together with accompanying sounds, if any.

mount, n. ~ 1. An item used as a support. – 2. The process of placing an item on such a support. – 3. The process of placing the items of an exhibit for display.

  RT: dry mount, mat, wet mount

  Notes: A mount may be a frame, stand, or board used to display or protect an item. A mount is secondary to the item mounted. Flat works, such as drawings or photographs, may be attached to a cardboard mount using glue, dry mount tissue, or hinges. Slides made with 35 mm film are typically placed in 2 × 2 inch cardboard mounts that surround the image.

movie (also **motion picture, moving picture,** and **cinefilm**), n. ~ A sequence of images that, when viewed in rapid succession, gives the appearance of movement.

> *DF:* video
> *Syn:* motion picture
> *BT:* moving image
> *RT:* cinematography, film
> *Notes:* 'Movie' connotes the use of film, as distinguished from video, which uses magnetic tape.

movie still (also **film still, still picture**), n. ~ Photographs made during the production of a motion picture, showing the actors and sets.

> *BT:* photograph
> *RT:* frame enlargement
> *Notes:* Movie stills appear to be scenes from the production; they do not show the equipment and supporting staff that are not visible in the final production. They are commonly used for publicity. A photograph made from a frame of the motion picture itself is called a frame enlargement. Movie stills are generally of much higher quality than frame enlargements.

moving image, n. ~ A generic term for a visual work that has the appearance of movement.

> *NT:* motion picture, movie, screenplay, video
> *RT:* A reel, academy format, B reel, changeover cue, clip, cue mark, documentary, episode, image, outtake, rough cut, rushes, scene, screening, sequence, shot, split screen, time lapse photography, trailer, visual materials, work print
> *Notes:* 'Moving image' includes motion pictures, video, and flip books.

moving picture ~ *see:* motion picture

MRMC (also **MRMC I, MRMC II**) ~ *see:* Master Record of Manuscript Collections

ms ~ *see:* manuscript

> *Notes:* **Mss** is an abbreviation for manuscripts (plural). **MsS** is an abbreviation for manuscript signed.

MS23 ~ *see:* quality index

multilevel description, n. ~ DESCRIPTION · A finding aid or other access tool that consists of separate, interrelated descriptions of the whole and its parts, reflecting the hierarchy of the materials being described.

> *BT:* description
> *RT:* hierarchical description
> *Notes:* Multilevel description proceeds from the general to the specific. Each level contains information relevant only to that level. Descriptions of a subordinate part does not repeat information in a description of its parent, with the exception of information necessary to link the part to its parent.
> †*144 (ISAD(G) 2000, p. 12):* If the fonds as a whole is being described, it should be represented in one description. If description of the parts is required, they may be described separately. The sum total of all descriptions thus obtained, linked in a hierarchy represents the fonds and those parts for which descriptions were made. For the purposes of these rules, this technique of description is called multilevel description. [Abridged.]

multimedia, n. ~ A work that combines different formats into an integrated whole.

   RT: hypermedia, mixed media

   Notes: Multimedia commonly refers to works that combine sound, images, and text. However, the term is more encompassing, and can include works that combine sculpture and music, or music and light. Multimedia should be distinguished from mixed media, which are works that combine different materials, such as photography and paint.

   †269 *(Spingarn-Koff 2000):* Multimedia isn't confined to computers, [Randall] Packer said, but has its roots in Wagner's 19th century operas. ¶ Wagner's concept of the 'Gesamtkunstwerk,' or Total Artwork, envisioned a synthesis of the arts which is now found in the latest digital environments, Packer said. ¶ 'There's a lineage of scientists and artists who envisioned the integration of media and artistic form,' Packer said. 'Virtual reality didn't come from nowhere.'

multiple exposure, n. ~ 1. An image consisting of several separate exposures recorded in a single photograph. – 2. The technique of creating such an image.

   RT: combination printing

   Notes: Multiple exposures may be intentional or accidental. If the shutter in a camera is tripped more than once without advancing the film, the different exposures are superimposed. A similar effect can be done on photographic paper in the darkroom, sometimes called **multiple printing**. Multiple exposures can also be made by leaving the shutter open while a strobe is fired in succession. Multiple exposures are distinguished from combination printing, in which several negatives are used to print separate parts of a larger, unified image.

Multipurpose Internet Messaging Extensions, n. (**MIME**, abbr.) ~ A standard (RFC 2045) that allows complex data formats to be sent as the content of email.

   RT: electronic mail

   Notes: The email standard RFC 822 says little about the content of message bodies. The MIME provides specifications for textual message bodies in character sets other than US-ASCII, an extensible set of different formats for nontextual message bodies, multipart message bodies, and textual header information in character sets other than US-ASCII. See http://www.faqs.org/rfcs/rfc2045.html.

multisensory documents ~ *see:* compound document

municipal records, n. ~ The records of a town, city, or other local government body.

   BT: record

   †49 *(Cox 1990, p. 76):* The records of the larger American municipalities pose greater problems for the archival profession than that of most local governments due to their size, greater complexity in government, and broader sense of independence.

muniment, n. ~ A deed, charter, or similar document that documents the rights or privileges of a person, family, or organization.

   Notes: Munimuents are kept for use as evidence to defend title or other property rights in land, possessions, or inheritances.

muster roll, n. ~ 1. A list of troops present on the review of troops (day of muster), noting their condition. – 2. A shipmaster's list of all crew on a ship that includes their names, ages, and nationality and that is used in war to determine a ship's neutrality.

Mylar, trademark ~ A polyester film manufactured by DuPont.

   BT: polyester

N

n.d., abbr. ~ No date.

n.p., abbr. ~ No place.

> *Syn:* s.l.
>
> *Notes:* Typically used in bibliographic citations to indicate that the place of publication is not known.

NAANICA ~ *see:* North American Archival Network of the International Council of Archives

NAF ~ *see:* name authority file

NAGARA ~ *see:* National Association of Government Archives and Records Administrators

NAGPRA ~ *see:* Native American Graves Protection and Repatriation Act

name, n. ~ The word or phrase by which an individual, family, organization, or thing is known.

> *NT:* file name, personal name, variant name
>
> †14 *(NARA ARC glossary):* The preferred name may include surname, forename, family name, birth and death dates, letters, initials, abbreviations, phrases, or numbers used in place of a name, or some combination of those elements. You can find other names by which the person is known, including nicknames, pen names, or transliterations in Variant Names.

name authority file, n. (**NAF**, abbr.) ~ A compilation of authority records that describe the preferred forms of names used as headings in a catalog, along with cross-references from variant forms of the name.

> *BT:* authority file
>
> *Notes:* A name authority file often includes a few key facts about the entry to help ensure that the name being checked matches the entity represented by the authority record. For example, a heading for John Smith might note a middle name, birth and death dates, and other details to distinguish one John Smith from another. The authority record might include notes about his works, his nationality, or his occupation to ensure that the heading is applied correctly.

name-title reference, n. ~ DESCRIPTION · A heading formed by combining the name of an individual or organization and the title of a work.

> *BT:* reference
>
> *RT:* access point, entry
>
> *Notes:* Name-title references are often used as topical access points for works that discuss other works. For example, a book of critical essays on Shakespeare's *Hamlet* might have a name-title reference for that work.

NARA ~ *see:* National Archives and Records Administration

narrative record, n. ~ Information in fixed form (a record) that documents some aspect of individual or organizational activities, but which does not relate to specific transactions.

> *BT:* record
>
> *RT:* report

Notes: Because narrative records do not grow out of a routine process, they often have an ad hoc form. Narrative records may include reports, work diaries, and personal notes.

†73 *(Duranti and MacNeil 1996, p. 53):* [A] large portion of electronic records has a narrative function, that is, it does not relate to business activity other than by being the expression of the way in which individuals set themselves to work and go through the informal motions of carrying out activities and decision making. . . . Supporting and narrative records are records whose existence is not required by the juridical system, but that are generated by their author for his or her convenience and by choice.

narrower term, n. (**NT**, abbr.) ~ A cross-reference pointing from a general to a more specific topic.

Syn: downward reference

BT: cross-reference

RT: Guidelines for the Construction, Format, and Management of Monolingual Thesauri

Notes: Narrower terms are part of the syndetic structure used in a thesaurus, especially one constructed using the ANSI Z39.19 standard, *Guidelines for the Construction, Format, and Management of Monolingual Thesauri.* Narrower terms are reciprocal to broader terms. For example, an entry for 'furniture' may include references to the narrower terms 'bed', 'chair', and 'chest'. Entries for each of those terms would include references to 'furniture' as a broader term.

NARS (National Archives and Records Service) ~ *see:* National Archives and Records Administration.

NASARA (National Association of State Archives and Records Administrators) ~ *see:* National Association of Government Archives and Records Administrators.

NASCIO ~ *see:* National Association of State Chief Information Officers

NASIRE (National Association of State Information Resource Executives) ~ *see:* National Association of State Chief Information Officers.

NASIS (National Association of State Information Systems) ~ *see:* National Association of State Chief Information Officers.

National Archives and Records Administration, n. (**NARA**, abbr.) ~ An independent federal agency possessing primary responsibility for managing the records of all three branches of the United States federal government, for providing guidance to federal agencies on records management policies and practices, for authorizing the disposition of federal records, for storing federal records, and for preserving records of permanent historical value to the United States in both federal archives and presidential libraries.

RT: National Historical Publications and Records Commission, Presidential Records Act

Notes: Established in 1934 as the National Archives, the agency was renamed the **National Archives and Records Service (NARS)** when it was made part of the General Services Administration (1949–1984). The new name reflected expanded responsibility for current records as well as archives, which was clarified by the Federal Records Act of 1950. The National Archives again attained independence as an agency in October 1984 (effective April 1, 1985), when it became known as the National Archives and Records Administration (NARA).

†198 (NARA website, http://www.archives.gov/about_us/vision_mission_values.
html): Our Vision. The National Archives is not a dusty hoard of ancient history. It
is a public trust on which our democracy depends. It enables people to inspect for
themselves the record of what government has done. It enables officials and agencies to review their actions and helps citizens hold them accountable. It ensures
continuing access to essential evidence that documents: the rights of American
citizens; the actions of federal officials; the national experience. ¶ To be effective,
we at NARA must do the following: determine what evidence is essential for such
documentation; ensure that government creates such evidence; make it easy for
users to access that evidence regardless of where it is, where they are, for as long as
needed; find technologies, techniques, and partners worldwide that can help
improve service and hold down cost; help staff members continuously expand
their capability to make the changes necessary to realize the vision.

National Archives and Records Service ~ *see:* National Archives and Records
Administration

National Association of Government Archives and Records Administrators, n.
(**NAGARA**, abbr.) ~ An organization of professionals working in local, state, and
federal archives.

    Notes: Formerly **National Association of State Archives and Records
Administrators (NASARA)**. See http://www.nagara.org/.

    †199 (NAGARA website): The National Association of Government Archives
and Records Administrators is a professional organization dedicated to the effective use and management of government information and publicly recognizing
their efforts and accomplishments.

National Association of State Archives and Records Administrators ~ *see:* National
Association of Government Archives and Records Administrators

National Association of State Chief Information Officers, n. (**NASCIO**, abbr.) ~
National Association of State Chief Information Officers.

    Notes: When founded, the organization was known as the **National Association
of State Information Systems (NASIS)**. In 1989 the association realigned its
membership and changed its name to the **National Association of State
Information Resource Executives (NASIRE)** (https://www.nascio.org/aboutNascio/
index.cfm). At its 2001 midyear meeting, the name was changed to the National
Association of State Chief Information Officers. See https://www.nascio.org/.

    †197 (NASCIO website): NASCIO represents state chief information officers
and information resource executives and managers from the 50 states, six U. S. territories, and the District of Columbia. State members are senior officials from any
of the three branches of state government who have executive-level and statewide
responsibility for information resource management. Representatives from federal, municipal, and international governments and state officials who are
involved in information resource management but do not have chief responsibility for that function participate in the organization as associate members. Private-
sector firms and non-profit organizations may join as corporate members. ¶
NASCIO's mission is to foster government excellence through quality business
practices, information management, and technology policy. NASCIO's vision is
government in which the public trust is fully served through the efficient and
effective use of technology.

National Association of State Information Systems ~ *see:* National Association of State Chief Information Officers

National Forum on Archival Continuing Education, n. (**NFACE**, abbr.) ~ A national meeting sponsored by the Council of State Historical Records Coordinators (COSHRC), in partnership with the American Association State and Local History (AASLH) to assess the status of and plan for the future of archival education in the United States.

†204 (NFACE 2002): The National Forum on Archival Continuing Education (NFACE), held April 27–29, 2000, in Decatur, Georgia, was a response to a profession-wide call for attention to continuing education. The Forum's 120 participants included representatives from more than 45 organizations that currently provide continuing education to those caring for historical records or whose constituents are potential consumers of such services. Forty-three State Coordinators were among the participants. ¶ The goals of the Forum were to: inform the organizations about what educational services and information resources were already available; encourage collaboration and coordination among providers in developing offerings that addressed gaps in existing educational opportunities; improve accessibility to information resources about best practices in the care of historical records that support these educational efforts; and develop an action agenda for archival continuing education in the next decade. This agenda will be shared with federal funding agencies, resource allocators, and key stakeholders in archival continuing education.

National Historical Publications and Records Commission, n. (**NHPRC**, abbr.) ~ The division of the National Archives and Records Administration (NARA) that makes grants to nonfederal institutions to help those institutions preserve and make accessible records of historical value through grants to archival institutions, manuscript repositories, and publications in multiple formats.

RT: National Archives and Records Administration, State Historical Records Advisory Board

Notes: Originally the **National Historical Publications Commission (NHPC)**, which was founded in 1934 at the same time at the National Archives. The Commission was expanded in 1974 to include records and renamed the National Historical Publications and Records Commission. See http://www.archives.gov/grants/index.html.

†205 (NHPRC Strategic Plan 1997): The Archivist of the United States chairs the Commission and makes grants on its recommendation. The other fourteen members of the Commission represent the President (two appointees), the U.S. Senate and House of Representatives, the Federal judiciary, the Departments of State and Defense, the Librarian of Congress, and six national, professional associations of archivists and historians.

National Historical Publications Commission ~ *see:* National Historical Publications and Records Commission

National Information Standards Organization, n. (**NISO**, abbr.) ~ An organization accredited by the American National Standards Institute (ANSI) to identify, develop, maintain, and publish technical standards relating to information management.

Notes: See http://www.niso.org/.

†2 (NISO 2003): NISO standards apply both traditional and new technologies to the full range of information-related needs, including retrieval, re-purposing,

storage, metadata, and preservation. ❡ Founded in 1939, incorporated as a not-for-profit education association in 1983, and assuming its current name the following year, NISO draws its support from the communities it serves. The leaders of over 70 organizations in the fields of publishing, libraries, IT and media serve as its voting members. Hundreds of experts and practitioners serve on NISO committees and as officers of the association.

National Information Systems Task Force, n. (**NISTF,** abbr.) ~ A committee of the Society of American Archivists (1977–1983) that investigated systems for sharing information about the holdings of archives and manuscript repositories.

†288 *(Weber 1990, p. 124):* With SAA Council's approval, NISTF disbanded itself in 1983 and was succeeded by the Committee on Archival Information Exchange (CAIE). CAIE's responsibilities include maintaining the data element dictionary and the MARC AMC format.

†288 *(Weber 1990, p. 120):* In 1977, the Society of American Archivists (SAA), appointed the National Information Systems Task Force (NISTF) to examine the issues surrounding its decision about which national information system (automated or not) to support. The two most likely candidates were NUCMC and the NHPRC's National Guide Project. NISTF extricated itself from these highly political questions by focusing its energies on creating the 'preconditions' for archival information exchange.

National Television Systems Committee, n. (**NTSC,** abbr.) ~ An organization created in 1953 by the Federal Communications Commission (FCC) to establish a standard for video broadcasts in the United States.

RT: video

Notes: The analog NTSC standard is being replaced by the digital HDTV standard.

†207 *(NTSC):* NTSC video is transmitted in an analog format using a 4-by-3 nearly square aspect ratio and providing 525 horizontal lines of maximum resolution (although only DVD comes close to using all the lines). . . . NTSC video is an interlaced format that creates two separate fields, one every sixtieth of a second, and combines them to form one complete video frame thirty times per second. The horizontal scan rate of NTSC video is 15,750 Hz (it draws 15,750 horizontal lines each second). Each field (one half of a frame) consists of all the odd lines or all the even lines in an image. The even and odd lines essentially blend together to form complete images.

National Union Catalog, n. (**NUC,** abbr.) ~ A series of volumes that contain reproductions of catalog records describing works published before 1956 and held by libraries in the United States.

BT: catalog

National Union Catalog of Manuscript Collections, n. (**NUCMC,** abbr.) ~ 1. A collection of descriptions of manuscript collections, archives, and oral history materials held by eligible archival and manuscript repositories throughout the United States and its territories. – 2. The program within the Library of Congress that oversees production of the catalog and supports access to the database.

BT: catalog

Notes: Commonly pronounced nuck-muck. Originally issued as printed volumes starting in 1961, NUCMC began entering descriptions into the Research

Libraries Group (RLG) database in 1986. Many of those records are duplicated in the OCLC National Union Catalog. The print series was discontinued after volume 29 in 1993. NUCMC currently functions as a "virtual" catalog, providing free searching at its website of cataloging in the RLIN and OCLC databases describing archivally controlled materials. See http://www.loc.gov/coll/nucmc/nucmc.html.

†208 (NUCMC 2002): The National Union Catalog of Manuscript Collections (NUCMC) is a free-of-charge cooperative cataloging program operated by the Library of Congress. On the basis of cataloging data supplied by eligible repositories, NUCMC catalogers create MARC (Machine Readable Cataloging) bibliographic records in the RLG (Research Libraries Group) data base, a national-level database, describe collections held by participants, and establish pertinent name and subject authority headings. Descriptions and locations of the material are then available to researchers throughout the United States and around the world.

Native American Graves Protection and Repatriation Act, n. (**NAGPRA**, abbr.) ~ A federal law, passed in 1990 (Pub. L. 101-602, 25 USC 32), which provides for the return of certain sacred and ceremonial objects held by museums and other repositories to the Native American peoples from which they were originally acquired.

natural language, n. ~ Verbal communication in a form normally spoken or written by people.

RT: programming language

Notes: Natural language is distinguished from artificial languages, such as programming languages, that are designed to write computer applications, to query a database, or otherwise interact with a machine. Natural language processors use rules of syntax and semantics to parse ordinary language into a form that a machine understands. Natural language order is used to distinguish headings in a sequence used in normal communication from headings that are inverted to place the principal term first for sorting.

natural language query, n. ~ A request submitted to an online database that is not parsed into artificial, machine-based semantics and syntax.

†63 (Burlington Agenda 2001, p. 299): Researchers in natural language processing of text have observed that what makes text retrieval so difficult is the large volume of real-world knowledge not included in the text, but which is necessary to understand it.

naturalness ~ see: archival nature

nearline, adj. ~ COMPUTING · Not immediately or directly accessible by a system.

RT: offline, online

Notes: Nearline storage is distinguished from offline storage, which requires the media to be mounted manually.

nearline storage, n. ~ 1. A technique to provide automated access to data from media that must be mounted before being read. – 2. The device or media where such data is kept.

RT: hierarchical storage management, offline storage, online storage

Notes: A contraction of 'near online storage'. Examples of nearline storage include tape and disk libraries. Nearline storage is slower than online storage, which uses media that are permanently mounted on the system.

near-print document (also **processed document, quasi-published document**), n. ~ A booklike document that is not commercially published and that has limited distribution.

> *Syn:* quasi-publication
>
> *RT:* publication
>
> *Notes:* A near-print document may be bound, have a title page, table of contents, and index. However, it is typically distributed by the author rather than an established publisher. Copies of near-print documents may be made by carbon copy, mimeograph, or photocopy.

negative, n. ~ PHOTOGRAPHY · A photographic image, usually on transparent film or glass, with reversed tones.

> *BT:* photograph
>
> *RT:* polarity, positive
>
> *Notes:* In a negative, highlights appear dark and shadows appear light. In color negatives, a color is represented by its complement; color negatives often have an overall orange cast.

negative-positive process, n. ~ Techniques used to create a positive image through use of an intermediary negative.

> *RT:* direct positive
>
> *Notes:* The negative-positive process is distinguished from the direct-positive process, in which a positive image is created without the use of an intermediary negative.

network, n. ~ 1. A collection of individuals or objects, and their interconnections, seen as a whole. – 2. COMPUTING · The equipment and materials used to connect servers and terminals.

> *Notes:* A network[2] may be configured as a ring, bus, star, or tree topology. Networks vary in size and may be described as a local area network (LAN) or a wide area network (WAN). The Internet is a network of networks.

network architecture, n. ~ COMPUTING · The specifications of a network, including topology, information encoding, transmission, and error detection and correction.

> *RT:* information architecture, Open Systems Interconnection Reference Model
>
> *Notes:* The Open Systems Interconnection Reference Model (OSI) is a network architecture defined by ISO standards. The Systems Network Architecture (SNA) is supported by IBM.

neutral test card (also **gray card**), n. ~ A standard target used to calibrate photographic exposures.

> *Notes:* A neutral test card reflects 18% of the light striking it, roughly halfway between the least (2–5%) and greatest (95–98%) possible. The value[4] is commonly called **middle gray**. The gray has a neutral tone so that it can be used to determine color balance.

news clipping, n. ~ An article or photograph cut from a newspaper or magazine; a clipping[1].

> *Syn:* clipping, cutting

news film, n. ~ 1. Nonfiction television programming that reports on current events, as distinguished from a feature. – 2. Nonfiction motion picture footage of important or current events shown in theaters before the feature program; a newsreel.

> *BT:* motion picture
>
> *RT:* feature

newsreel, n. ~ Short, nonfiction motion pictures on current or important events, shown in theaters before the feature film.

    BT: motion picture

    Notes: Newsreels were introduced by the French in the 1890s. They were common in the United States from the 1910s through the 1950s.

NFACE ~ *see:* National Forum on Archival Continuing Education

NHPC ~ *see:* National Historical Publications and Records Commission abbr. ~ National Historical Publications Commission.

NHPRC ~ *see:* National Historical Publications and Records Commission

NISO ~ *see:* National Information Standards Organization

NISTF ~ *see:* National Information Systems Task Force

nitrate ~ *see:* cellulose nitrate

nitrocellulose ~ *see:* cellulose nitrate

noise, n. ~ 1. Unwanted or extraneous information that degrades the reproduction of an original. – 2. Undesirable sounds in an environment.

    RT: artifact, generation loss

    Notes: Noise[1] in a video signal may appear as specks in the image that were not in the original but introduced during transmission or reproduction. In sound recordings or broadcasts, noise is perceived as static. In computer networks, noise may cause bit loss and result in corrupted data.

nominal access point, n. ~ A heading in a catalog (access point) that is a personal, family, or corporate name.

    BT: access point

nonaqueous deacidification ~ *see:* deacidification

nonbook materials, n. ~ Items that are not books, periodicals, or pamphlets; nonprint materials[1].

    RT: nonprint materials

    Notes: 'Nonbook materials' is found in *Anglo-American Cataloguing Rules* (1967), which includes separate sections for manuscripts; maps; motion pictures and film strips; music; phonorecords; pictures, designs, and other two-dimensional representations. The division between book and nonbook materials does not appear in AACR2 (1978).

noncurrent records, n. ~ Records that are no longer used in the day-to-day course of business, but which are preserved and occasionally used for legal, historical, or operational purposes.

    Syn: inactive records

    BT: record

    Notes: Noncurrent records are often stored out of the office of creation in a records center or on offline media. Either they may be destroyed when their frequency of use falls so low that they have lost all value or they may be transferred to an archival repository for permanent retention.

noncustodial records, n. ~ Archival records, usually in electronic format, that are held by the agency of origin, rather than being transferred to the archives.

    RT: custody, postcustodial theory of archives

    Notes: A noncustodial agreement may be made between an archives and the office of origin if the records require special software or hardware to read the records.

    †223 (*Personal communication, Terry Cook, posting on Aus-Archivists, 19*

November 1996.): To Australians, it is important to note that the National Archives of Canada has not adopted a non-custodial or distributed custody approach in toto, but neither has it rejected such an approach. . . . While the normal practice of the NA is to acquire electronic records into our custody, some specified categories of electronic records will be 'left out' under the control of their creators, and indeed perhaps left there for a very long time. Ultimately, however, if the agency goes defunct, or no longer operates the system, or maintains records in it for any sort of operational use, the NA would assume custody.

nonofficial papers, n. ~ Materials made or received by an individual at work, but not pertaining to the conduct of business; personal papers.

RT: nonrecords, personal papers

Notes: Some archives collect nonofficial papers that complement the official records of the organization. For example, a university archives might collect the personal papers of students and faculty to capture a more complete record of campus life.

nonprint materials, n. ~ 1. Items that are not books, periodicals, or pamphlets; non-book materials. – 2. Audiovisual materials.

RT: nonbook materials, nontextual records, special records, visual materials

nonrecords, n. ~ 1. Materials not considered to fall within the definition of an official record. – 2. Copies, duplicates, or publications that are kept for purposes of personal reference or convenience. – 3. Materials that do not appear on a records retention schedule and that may be destroyed without authorization.

RT: nonofficial papers, record

Notes: Used primarily in records management to indicate materials that may be destroyed without authorization. – Nonrecord[3] presumes that all records are scheduled, although in practice schedules may be out-of-date and fail to describe all records held by an organization. As such, the mere fact that materials are not on a schedule is not dispositive of their being a nonrecord.

nonrepudiation, n. ~ DIGITAL SIGNATURES · The ability to demonstrate the integrity and origin of electronically signed data and to assert that the means to authenticate the data cannot be refuted.

†186 *(McCullagh and Caelli 2000):* There is a definitional distinction between the legal use of the term 'non-repudiation' and its crypto-technical use. In the legal sense an alleged signatory to a document is always able to repudiate a signature that has been attributed to him or her. The basis for a repudiation of a traditional signature may include: The signature is a forgery; The signature is not a forgery, but was obtained via unconscionable conduct by a party to a transaction, fraud instigated by a third party, undue influence exerted by a third party. ¶ There appears to be a movement within the electronic commerce environment to take away these fundamental rights that exist within common law jurisdictions. The general rule of evidence is that if a person denies a particular signature then it falls upon the relying party to prove that the signature is truly that of the person denying it. It should be understood that the term 'deny' and the term 'repudiate' are synonymous and this position is supported by standard dictionary definitions. ¶ Furthermore, the common law trust mechanism established to overcome a false claim of non-repudiation is witnessing. Witnessing simply occurs at the time the signature is being affixed. That is, by having an independent adult witness the

signing of a document reduces the ability of the signatory to successfully deny the signature as a forgery at a later date. It is always open for the signatory to deny the signature on other grounds such as those enumerated above. [Citations omitted.]

nontextual records, n. ~ Records in audiovisual, pictorial, and sound formats.

> BT: record

> RT: nonprint materials, special records, textual records, visual materials

> Notes: 'Nontextual records' is used generically to include records formats that are not principally words on paper, such as maps, photographs, motion pictures and video, sound recordings, and the like. In some repositories, electronic records are treated as a third major category of records.

North American Archival Network of the International Council of Archives, n. (**NAANICA**, abbr.) ~ A branch of the International Council of Archives that serves as a clearinghouse for ICA information, encourages members to respond to ICA requests for input, promotes awareness of ICA in North America, and represents North America in the ICA governing structure.

> Notes: See http://www.ica.org/body.php?pbodycode=NAANICA&plangue=eng.

notarial archives, n. ~ Records of all contracts executed before a notary at civil law.

> Notes: Records in notarial archives typically relate to the transfer of property, but also include wills, marriage contracts, building contracts, powers of attorney, and individual declarations.

> †202 (New Orleans Notarial Archives): Founded in 1867 when it gathered in the records of colonial and ante bellum notaries, the New Orleans Notarial Archives relates closely to those European and Western Hemisphere repositories that share Louisiana's heritage of civil law. The world's civil law notarial collections derive from a Roman law-based system that elevates the notary to a prominent place in society as the draftsman, guarantor, and finally, archivist of contracts in the private sector. In New Orleans, nearly every property transaction that has occurred since the founding of the city was recorded by, or found its way to, a notary's office.

notarial record (also **journal of notarial acts**), n. ~ 1. A register, usually kept in a bound volume, that lists the date, time, and type of each official act. – 2. A document drafted or paraphrased by a civil law notary, filed into public record, and housed in a notarial archives.

> BT: record

> Notes: The notarial record[1] typically includes the instrument presented to the notary, the signature of each person whose signature is notarized, the information used to verify the parties' identities, and any fee charged. – A notarial record[2] has a different meaning in Louisiana, which has a civil law, rather than common law, tradition.

> †80 (ICA Notarial Records, p. 1): 'Notaries meet a need which is as old as the organisation of society itself. By conferring the authority of society on individual actions relating to persons or property, they ensure to each of these actions its proper place in the world.' [citing Jean Favier] Those authoritative legal deeds which touch the lives of individuals and of organisations, and are indispensable to both, were already being preserved as far back as the 12th century. Notarial records[2] are an extraordinarily rich source of information for all aspects of history, and nowadays are amongst the materials most consulted by researchers.

> †223 (Personal communication, Ann Wakefield, 6 October 2004): An authentic notarial act is a document of one to many pages in length that is executed by a civil

law notary according to a protocol. The document is housed and protected in an archives, sometimes at the notary's office and sometimes in a government office, and made accessible to the general public. (The New Orleans Notarial Archives is an example of a notarial archives. It is the only one in the United States.)

notch code, n. ~ PHOTOGRAPHY · An pattern of shallow indentations cut in the edge of sheet film and used to identify the type of film and which side is light-sensitive.

> *RT:* sheet film
>
> *Notes:* The pattern used to create a notch code may include a combination of one or more shapes that are square, round, triangular, or scooped. Notch codes are not unique; the same pattern may be used by different manufacturers for different films, and the same manufacturer may recycle a code. The code is also used to help photographers correctly load film into holders in the dark. When holding film with the notch code in the upper right corner, the emulsion is on the upper (facing) side.

note, n. ~ 1. A short, written document, often informal and used as an aid to memory. – 2. A short piece of correspondence. – 3. An annotation or comment in a document, often handwritten marginalia or a gloss. – 4. A written promise for one party to pay another a specified sum. – 5. LAW · A short essay, often written by a law student for a law review, relating to a particular set of cases or a general area of the law. – **notes**, pl. ~ 6. A terse record of the contents of a conversation or meeting made for future reference. – 7. A short summary or abstract.

> *DF:* draft
>
> *NT:* numbering note, physical restriction note
>
> *RT:* reference
>
> *Notes:* A note^5 is made between two parties and is distinguished from a draft^2, which is among three parties.

NT ~ *see:* narrower term

NTSC ~ *see:* National Television Systems Committee

NUC ~ *see:* National Union Catalog

NUCMC ~ *see:* National Union Catalog of Manuscript Collections

numbering note, n. ~ DESCRIPTION · A note explaining the numeric or alphanumeric scheme used in the materials being described.

> *BT:* note
>
> *Notes:* A numbering note may indicate gaps or changes in numbers or alphanumeric codes used to identify materials. For example, a numbering note may indicate that a code consists of a series, subseries, file, and date.

numeric-alphabetic filing system ~ *see:* alphanumeric filing system

numeric filing system, n. ~ 1. A system for organizing records through the use of numbers that appear on the materials. – 2. A system to classify materials using numbers as headings.

> *BT:* filing system
>
> *Notes:* A numeric filing system^1 is commonly used for purchase orders, checks, and other records that have a unique number assigned to each document. – A numeric filing system^2 uses an index or file plan to associate concepts with specific numbers, which are then applied to the materials being filed.

O

OAI ~ *see:* Open Archives Initiative

OAIS ~ *see:* Open Archival Information System

OASIS ~ *see:* Organization for the Advancement of Structured Information Standards

oath, n. ~ 1. A solemn pledge that binds an individual to perform a specific act. – 2. A solemn, formal promise to speak the truth.

Notes: An oath is often accompanied by swearing to god, to a loved one, or a thing as witness to the faithfulness and truthfulness of the promise. Oaths of office sometimes replace 'swear' with 'affirm'.

object, n. ~ 1. An item that is tangible, especially one with significant depth relative to its height and width; an artifact or specimen. – 2. COMPUTING · A collection of data with defined boundaries that is treated as a single entity; a resource; a digital object. – 3 COMPUTING · An instantiation of a class or entity that forms a component of a system.

RT: artifact, class, data object, digital object, item, material, realia, replica, resource, specimen

Notes: Object[1] connotes something that has substantial height, width, and depth. While documents have three dimensions and fall under the broadest sense of 'object', they are often distinguished from objects because of their flat, nearly two-dimensional nature. In museums, 'object' connotes something manmade and is synonymous with 'artifact'. – Object[2] is used generically to cover a variety of things, object referring to graphics and data files that can be inserted into a larger container using object linking and embedding (OLE) techniques. – Object[3] is derived from object-oriented programming. An object is a particular occurrence (instantiation) of a class template. The object contains data in structures defined by the template. The object responds to messages based on internal procedures (methods), either by changing its internal data values or by returning some value based on existing data. Smalltalk and C++ are examples of object-oriented programming languages.

oblique, adj. ~ 1. Slanting; sloping. – 2. Not parallel or perpendicular. – n. ~ 3. ARCHITECTURE, TECHNICAL DRAWING · A drawing that shows two sides of a building.

BT: architectural records, drawing

RT: elevation, oblique view, perspective

Notes: In an oblique[3], two dimensions form a plane parallel to the plane of view, and the third dimension is at a 45 degree angle. As a result, oblique drawings do not have a vanishing point; parallel lines in the original remain parallel in the drawing. Obliques are distinguished from elevations, which show only one side of the building or object. **Oblique perspective** describes a drawing or image that shows the subject from the side, but which has perspective; parallel lines in the original converge to a vanishing point in the drawing.

oblique aerial, n. ~ A photograph made from the air, with the camera at an angle to the horizon.

DF: oblique view

BT: aerial photograph

RT: vertical aerial

Notes: A low oblique does not show the horizon, while a high oblique includes the horizon. 'Oblique aerial' should be distinguished from 'oblique view', a non-photographic image.

oblique light, n. ~ 1. Illumination from an angle to review the relief of a surface; raking light. – 2. OPTICS · A technique of illuminating a microscope specimen from the side, rather than by transmitted light.

Syn: raking light

Notes: Oblique light[1] is not necessarily at as extreme an angle as raking light.

oblique view, n. ~ 1. An image of an object made from an angle. – 2. An aerial image of a land surface made from an angle.

DF: oblique aerial

RT: oblique

Notes: Oblique view[1] includes drawings, paintings, maps, and computer models. Although 'oblique view' is sometimes used to describe photographs, 'oblique aerial' connotes photographs.

obverse, n. ~ The front, top, or surface of a coin, medal, seal, or printed currency that bears the head or the principal design.

RT: recto

OCLC Online Computer Library Center (usually **OCLC**), n. ~ A nonprofit cooperative of libraries, archives, and other cultural institutions that share information about their holdings in an online union catalog and that offers other services to member organizations.

BT: bibliographic utility

Notes: Originally, OCLC stood for the Ohio College Library Center. The name was changed in 1981. See http://www.oclc.org/.

†3 *(OCLC 2004):* Founded in 1967, OCLC Online Computer Library Center is a nonprofit, membership, computer library service and research organization dedicated to the public purposes of furthering access to the world's information and reducing information costs. More than 45,000 libraries in 84 countries and territories around the world use OCLC services to locate, acquire, catalog, lend and preserve library materials. ¶ Researchers, students, faculty, scholars, professional librarians and other information seekers use OCLC services to obtain bibliographic, abstract and full-text information when and where they need it. ¶ OCLC and its member libraries cooperatively produce and maintain WorldCat – the OCLC Online Union Catalog.

OCR ~ *see:* optical character recognition

ODA ~ *see:* Open Document Architecture

off gassing ~ *see:* outgassing

off-site storage, n. ~ Facilities for housing materials away from where they are used; remote storage.

Syn: remote storage

Notes: Off-site storage may be used to house inactive records, reducing the costs of storing records in expensive office areas by moving them to less expensive warehouse facilities. Off-site storage may also be used to keep copies of vital (essential) records to increase the chances that at least one copy will survive a disaster.

Syn: Synonym · †: see Bibliography · *Superscript:* Definition number

office, n. ~ 1. A room where business is conducted. – 2. A position of responsibility. – 3. Part of a government agency, usually below a department.

    Notes: Office[2] often connotes a public position to which an individual is appointed or elected; for example, the office of the attorney general.

office automation, n. ~ The use of computers to assist in business tasks.

    RT: automated

    Notes: 'Office automation' typically includes administrative, management, and clerical duties, as opposed to manufacturing or design. Typical office automation applications support word processing and desktop publishing, filing, email, data management, accounting, and decision support systems.

office document architecture ~ *see:* Open Document Architecture

office file, n. ~ A file containing business records kept in an individual's office for convenient access.

    RT: convenience file, personal file

    Notes: Office files relate to the individual's work activities. They are distinguished from personal papers, which may kept by the individual at work, but which do not relate to work. A document kept in an office file is sometimes called an office copy.

office of origin (also **creating office, originating office**), n. ~ The corporate body or administrative unit in which a group of records is created or received, and accumulated during the course of business.

    RT: entity of origin, provenance

office of record, n. ~ The organization or administrative unit that is officially designated for the maintenance, preservation, and disposition of record copies.

    Notes: The office of record is not always the office of origin.

official copy ~ *see:* record copy

official files, n. ~ Files containing records, as distinguished from other materials, held by an organization.

    RT: official record, record copy

    Notes: 'Official files' carries the connotation that the contents are the complete, final, and authorized record copies, excluding drafts, convenience files, personal papers, and other nonrecords. An item contained within an official file is sometimes called an official record or record copy.

official record, n. ~ 1. A record created by, received by, sanctioned by, or proceeding from an individual acting within their designated capacity. – 2. A complete, final, and authorized copy of a record, especially the copy bearing an original signature or seal.

    BT: record

    RT: official files, record copy

    Notes: Official record[2] is sometimes used to distinguish records from drafts, convenience files, personal papers, and other nonrecords.

offline, adj. ~ COMPUTING · Not connected to a system.

    RT: nearline, online

    Notes: Something offline requires manual intervention to bring it online. 'Offline' is distinguished from 'nearline', the latter not requiring manual intervention to make it accessible to the system.

offline storage, n. ~ Techniques to store data on media that must be manually loaded before being accessible to the system.

RT: hierarchical storage management, nearline storage, online storage

Notes: Offline storage is frequently used to store older, inactive data that is seldom accessed. It may be stored on tape or disk.

offprint, n. ~ A single article printed separately from the journal in which it originally appeared; a reprint[2].

RT: reprint

Notes: An offprint typically is produced from the same plates used to print the journal, hence it has the same formatting as the version in the journal, including the same page numbering. Authors are frequently given a small number of offprints.

OLAP ~ *see:* online analytical processing

online, adj. ~ COMPUTING · Connected to a system and available for use.

RT: nearline, offline

online analytical processing, n. (**OLAP**, abbr.) ~ Techniques using decision support software that allow a user to analyze information that has been summarized into multidimensional views and hierarchies.

RT: decision support system

†280 (OLAP 1994): E. F. Codd, father of the relational database, and his associates have produced a white paper listing the 12 rules for OLAP (on-line analytical processing) systems. The list is fundamentally a formula for a successful information system, whether you call it an EIS, a DSS, or a business information system. ¶ 1. Multidimensional conceptual view. This supports EIS 'slice-and-dice' operations and is usually required in financial modeling. – 2. Transparency. OLAP systems should be part of an open system that supports heterogeneous data sources. Furthermore, the end user should not have to be concerned about the details of data access or conversions. – 3. Accessibility. The OLAP should present the user with a single logical schema of the data. – 4. Consistent reporting performance. Performance should not degrade as the number of dimensions in the model increases. – 5. Client/server architecture. Requirement for open, modular systems. – 6. Generic dimensionality. Not limited to 3-D and not biased toward any particular dimension. A function applied to one dimension should also be able to be applied to another. – 7. Dynamic sparse-matrix handling. Related both to the idea of nulls in relational databases and to the notion of compressing large files, a sparse matrix is one in which not every cell contains data. OLAP systems should accommodate varying storage and data-handling options. – 8. Multiuser support. OLAP systems, like EISes, need to support multiple concurrent users, including their individual views or slices of a common database. – 9. Unrestricted cross-dimensional operations. Similar to rule 6; all dimensions are created equal, and operations across data dimensions do not restrict relationships between cells. – 10. Intuitive data manipulation. Ideally, users shouldn't have to use menus or perform complex multiple-step operations when an intuitive drag-and-drop action will do. – 11. Flexible reporting. Save a tree. Users should be able to print just what they need, and any changes to the underlying financial model should be automatically reflected in reports. – 12. Unlimited dimensional and aggregation levels. A serious tool should support at least 15, and preferably 20, dimensions.

online public access catalog, n. (**OPAC**, abbr.) ~ A computerized database that allows patrons to search descriptions of materials in a repository's holdings.

BT: catalog

Notes: 'OPAC' connotes a system that conforms to bibliographic standards such as *Anglo-American Cataloguing Rules* and MARC format. OPACs often include many other library functions, such as acquisition and circulation.

online storage, n. ~ Techniques for storing and retrieving data on media that is mounted and directly accessible to the system.

RT: hierarchical storage management, nearline storage, offline storage

Notes: 'Online storage' connotes facilities such as hard drives used principally for data storage, rather than system memory used as cache or firmware used to load the operating system.

onomastics, n. ~ 1. The study of names, including their origins, form, meaning, and use. – **onomastic**, n. ~ 2. A handwritten signature in a different hand from that used in the body of a manuscript or on a typed or printed document.

NT: anthronymy, toponymy

Notes: Onomastics includes place names (toponymy) and personal names (anthronymy).

ontology, n. ~ 1. PHILOSOPHY · The study of the nature of existence. – 2. COMPUTING · The study of concepts and their relationships in an information system.

RT: classification scheme, taxonomy

†223 *(Personal communication, Ken Thibodeau, 22 October 2003):* As used in [computer science] circles, an ontology² is a family tree of taxonomies. Whereas a taxonomy orders members of a single taxon, an ontology specifies relationships among taxa whose respective members, absent the ontology, might not be seen as having any relationship.

OPAC ~ *see:* online public access catalog

open, adj. ~ 1. Available and accessible; without restrictions; not closed. – 2. COMPUTING · Proprietary, but available to other developers. – 3. COMPUTING · Vendor neutral. – 4. COMPUTING · Published under terms of the General Public License or a similar agreement. – 5. COMPUTING · Collaboratively developed, especially by volunteers. – 6. Maintained by and available from a government or standards organization.

RT: closed, General Public License, open architecture, Open Archival Information System, Open Archives Initiative, Open Document Architecture, Open Source Initiative, open source software, open standard, open system

Notes: Open¹ is the opposite of closed, restricted, or classified. – Within computing, open²⁻⁵ has many meanings that vary with context and use. In general, it is used as an antonym of closed, which refers to proprietary software and hardware that is a black box to all but the developer. A closed system has defined inputs and outputs, but without additional information about the system it is impossible to make that system do anything else. An open system exposes its internal workings, allowing others to understand how the system works. In principle, others can then interact with, modify, or add to the system. In practice, licensing agreements may restrict what can be done with an open system. For example, it may be permissible to build components that connect to an open hardware system, but not to reproduce the system itself.

†260 *(Schmelzer 2003):* The word 'open' has no commonly accepted meaning in the phrase 'open standard.' For many organizations, 'open' means that they aren't the only organization that supports the advancement and development of a

given technology. However, this is an all-too-broad definition that puts Microsoft's .NET in the same camp as Java – since there are millions of developers for each of those platforms. For others, a standard is open only if a vendor-neutral third-party organization (or even governmental body) creates and manages it. However, this definition is too strict in that it excludes the term 'open source' from its meaning. Finally, many organizations consider a standard to be 'open' if the specification has merely been published for review.

open access publication, n. ~ A scholarly work distributed online that is freely accessible, has no restrictions on reproduction or distribution, and has been deposited in an online repository.

> *RT:* publication

> †*29 (Bethesda Statement 2003):* An Open Access Publication is one that meets the following two conditions: – 1. The author(s) and copyright holder(s) grant(s) to all users a free, irrevocable, worldwide, perpetual right of access to, and a license to copy, use, distribute, transmit and display the work publicly and to make and distribute derivative works, in any digital medium for any responsible purpose, subject to proper attribution of authorship, as well as the right to make small numbers of printed copies for their personal use. – 2. A complete version of the work and all supplemental materials, including a copy of the permission as stated above, in a suitable standard electronic format is deposited immediately upon initial publication in at least one online repository that is supported by an academic institution, scholarly society, government agency, or other well-established organization that seeks to enable open access, unrestricted distribution, interoperability, and long-term archiving (for the biomedical sciences, PubMed Central is such a repository).

open architecture, n. ~ COMPUTING · System specifications for hardware or software that are publicly available, allowing anyone to develop components that work with the system.

> *RT:* open, open source software

> *Notes:* Open architecture is often not developed through a collaborative process, like open source software. The design process may be closed, but publishing the system details permits easier interaction with other systems.

Open Archival Information System, n. (**OAIS**, abbr.) ~ A high-level model that describes the components and processes necessary for a digital archives, including six distinct functional areas: ingest, archival storage, data management, administration, preservation planning, and access.

> *RT:* ingest, open, system

> *Notes:* The standard is not intended for use as an implementation model. The model was developed under the auspices of NASA's Consultative Committee for Space Data Systems (http://www.ccsds.org/). See http://www.ccsds.org/documents/650x0b1.pdf.

> †*210 (OCLC/RLG Preservation Metadata 2001, p. 8):* The [OAIS] model establishes terminology and concepts relevant to digital archiving, identifies the key components and processes endemic to most digital archiving activity, and proposes an information model for digital objects and their associated metadata. The reference model does not specify an implementation, and is therefore neutral on digital object types or technological issues – for example, the model can be applied at a broad level to archives handling digital image files, 'born-digital' objects, or

even physical objects, and no assumptions are imposed concerning the specific implementation of the preservation strategy for example, migration or emulation.

Open Archives Forum, n. ~ A group of organizations collaborating on the implementation of the Open Archives Initiative in a European context.

> *RT:* Open Archives Initiative
>
> *Notes:* See http://www.oaforum.org.

Open Archives Initiative, n. (**OAI**, abbr.) ~ An organization that has developed interoperability standards to facilitate the efficient dissemination of online content, especially EPrints.

> *RT:* EPrints, open, Open Archives Forum
>
> *Notes:* OAI has published the **Protocol for Metadata Harvesting (OAI-PMH)**. The protocol defines an application-independent interoperability framework based on metadata harvesting. The framework is used by data providers, who expose metadata about information held in a repository, and by service providers, who use that metadata to build value-added services. See http://www.openarchives.org/.
>
> †213 *(OAI website, FAQ):* The OAI technical framework is intentionally simple with the intent of providing a low barrier for participants. Protocols such as Z39.50 have more complete functionality; for example, they deal with session management and results sets and allow the specification of predicates that filter the records returned. However, this functionality comes at an increase in difficulty of implementation and cost. The OAI technical framework is not intended to replace other approaches but to provide an easy-to-implement and easy-to-deploy alternative for different constituencies or different purposes than those addressed by existing interoperability solutions.

open collection (also **open fonds**, **open record group**), n. ~ 1. A collection to which items may be subsequently added. – 2. A collection that has no restrictions on access.

Open Document Architecture (formerly **Office Document Architecture**), n. (**ODA**, abbr.) ~ A standard (ISO 8613) designed to facilitate the exchange of office documents such as reports, letters, and memorandums.

> *RT:* compound document, open, processable document
>
> *Notes:* The standard supports compound documents. It supports character, raster, picture content, and other formats. The standard allows documents to be exchanged in a format that allows them to be modified or to be viewed in a read-only mode.

open entry, n. ~ DESCRIPTION · An entry in a catalog or index representing a group of materials to which items may be added.

> *RT:* entry
>
> *Notes:* Before computer databases and word processing were common, open entries reserved blank space for information to be added later.

open file, n. ~ 1. A file to which items continue to be added. – 2. A file without access restrictions.

> *RT:* accrual

open index, n. ~ An ordered list of headings to which headings may be added.

> *BT:* index

Notes: Before computer databases and word processing became common, open indexes were typically in card format. Separate cards were created for each heading so that they could be interfiled.

open records law, n. ~ A statute that guarantees the public has access to information held by governments.

RT: Freedom of Information Act, sunshine law

Notes: The types of materials that fall under the scope of open records laws are often much more encompassing than what may be considered a formal record. Open records laws generally provide access to any information in a governmental agency, provided that the information is not excluded on the basis of privacy, confidentiality, security, or a need to protect specific government activities or resources, such as procurement, investigation, or archaeological sites.

†161 *(Laws on Openness):* Laws on access to government meetings and records are often called 'Sunshine' laws or 'Freedom of Information Acts.' In Iowa, such laws more typically are referred to as 'the open meetings law,' which is Iowa Code Chapter 21, and 'the open records law,' which is Iowa Code Chapter 22. The intent of Chapter 21 is made clear in its opening lines: "This chapter seeks to assure . . . that the basis and rationale of government decisions, as well as those decisions themselves, are easily accessible to the people. Ambiguity in the construction or application of this chapter should be resolved in favor of openness."

open reel (also **reel-to-reel**), n. ~ A continuous ribbon of film or tape on a single hub with flanges, not contained in a cartridge.

RT: audiotape, hub

open shelf filing, n. ~ Techniques to store files directly on shelves without the need for boxes.

BT: shelving

Notes: Open shelf filing units have closed ends and dividers on the shelves to support the files. Open shelf filing units are distinguished from file cabinets, which store the files in closed drawers. Open shelf filing units are distinguished from warehouse shelving, which is designed to store records in boxes.

Open Source Initiative, n. (**OSI,** abbr.) ~ A nonprofit organization that promotes the use and development of open source software in the commercial environment.

RT: open

Notes: See http://www.opensource.org/.

†214 *(OSI website):* Open Source Initiative (OSI) is a non-profit corporation dedicated to managing and promoting the Open Source Definition for the good of the community, specifically through the OSI Certified Open Source Software certification mark and program.

open source software, n. ~ Computer code that is developed and refined through public collaboration and distributed without charge but with the requirement that modifications must be distributed at no charge to promote further development.

RT: General Public License, open, open architecture

Notes: Open source software is often distributed under terms of the General Public License to ensure collaboration.

†214 *(OSI website):* The basic idea behind open source is very simple: When programmers can read, redistribute, and modify the source code for a piece of software, the software evolves. People improve it, people adapt it, people fix bugs.

And this can happen at a speed that, if one is used to the slow pace of conventional software development, seems astonishing. ¶ We in the open source community have learned that this rapid evolutionary process produces better software than the traditional closed model, in which only a very few programmers can see the source and everybody else must blindly use an opaque block of bits.

†246 (Rivlin 2003, p. 154): Linux . . . was created by coders abiding by the open source credo: Do what you wish to improve a product, charge for it if you like, but share the underlying source code you added.

open standard, n. ~ 1. A set of formal, published specifications that enables independently created systems that conform with those specifications to work together. – 2. Formal, published specifications developed by more than one organization. – 3. A vendor-neutral standard maintained by a government or standards organization.

RT: open

open system, n. ~ A collection of hardware or software that can interact with independently developed components or systems.

RT: hardware dependent, open, software dependent, system

Open Systems Interconnection Reference Model, n. (**OSI**, abbr.) ~ A standard (ISO 7498) that describes a common basis for coordinating standards development for systems interconnection and allowing existing standards to be coordinated with the overall reference model.

RT: network architecture

Notes: The model includes the physical layer, the data link layer, the network layer, the transport layer, the session layer, the presentation layer, and the application layer. The model is not an implementation standard.

operating system, n. (**OS**, abbr.) ~ Software that controls the basic functions of a computer and its components, including memory, hardware, system utilities, applications, and network connections.

RT: system

Notes: On most computers, the operating system is initially loaded from disk using a firmware boot program. Some small, embedded operating systems may be stored and run entirely in firmware. Examples of operating systems include CMS, DOS, Linux, Mac OS X, Unix, VMS, and Windows.

operational records, n. ~ 1. Records that relate to the substantive activities an organization undertakes to accomplish its mission or mandate; program records. – 2. Information documenting the performance and use (operation) of a piece of equipment

Syn: program records

BT: record

operational value, n. ~ 1. The usefulness or significance of records to support ancillary operations and management of an organization. – 2. PRINCIPALLY CANADIAN · The usefulness or significance of records related to the mandate, role, or mission of an organization by documenting the duties, responsibilities, functions, activities, and services performed.

BT: value

RT: administrative value, program records

Notes: Operational value[1] is generally considered to be limited to that period in which the documented activities occur and ending with any audit of those activities.

BT: Broader Term · NT: Narrower Term · RT: Related Term · DF: Distinguish From

optical character recognition, n. (**OCR**, abbr.) ~ 1. The process of transforming images of characters in a document to the equivalent ASCII code for those characters. – adj. ~ 2. TYPOGRAPHY · Designed to be read using such techniques.

> *RT:* intelligent character recognition

optical disk, n. ~ A platter used to store large quantities of data that can be read using light.

> *NT:* compact disc, LaserDisc, write once read many
>
> *RT:* videodisc
>
> *Notes:* Data may be stored as an analog or digital signal. Most optical systems use a laser to read the data. Optical disks that are mass produced, such as commercial LaserDiscs and compact discs, may be recorded mechanically by stamping. Some optical disk formats record data using laser light, including write-once read-many (WORM) and writable compact disc formats.

optical scanner ~ *see:* scanner

oral history, n. ~ 1. An interview that records an individual's personal recollections of the past and historical events. – 2. The audio or video recordings, transcripts, and other materials that capture and are associated with such an interview.

> †*156 (Klopfer 2001, p. 112):* Documents described as oral histories range from personal reminiscences to structured interviews to recordings of contemporary thoughts or events saved for posterity. The arrangement of oral histories also range from raw tapes to edited tapes, translations, transcripts, re-wordings, syntheses and interpretations.

order, n. ~ 1. A meaningful sequence. – 2. A written or oral command to take or refrain from some action. – 3. A written or oral request for materials or services.

> *Notes:* Order² includes injunctions, directives, and commands. – Order³ includes, for example, purchase orders given to a supplier for goods or food orders given to staff in a restaurant.

ordinance, n. ~ A law or regulation, especially of municipal government.

organic collection, n. ~ A body of records that grows as the result of the routine activities of its creator.

> *DF:* artificial collection

organization, n. ~ 1. A corporate body. – 2. The coordination and relationships between items; arrangement.

> *Notes:* This glossary uses organization¹ generically to denote a wide range of corporate bodies, such as companies, agencies, and their internal units; legislatures and other governmental bodies; nongovernmental agencies, whether formally structured or a loose affiliation of people, such as the Red Cross or clubs, respectively.

Organization for the Advancement of Structured Information Standards (formerly known as **SGML Open**), n. (**OASIS**, abbr.) ~ A not-for-profit, global consortium that promotes the development and adoption of standards for electronic commerce.

> *Notes:* See http://www.oasis-open.org/.
>
> †*209 (OASIS website, /who):* OASIS produces worldwide standards for security, Web services, XML conformance, business transactions, electronic publishing, topic maps and interoperability within and between marketplaces. ¶ The OASIS Network includes UDDI, CGM Open, LegalXML and PKI. ¶ OASIS was founded in 1993 under the name SGML Open as a consortium of vendors and users devoted to developing guidelines for interoperability among products that sup-

port the Standard Generalized Markup Language (SGML). OASIS changed its name in 1998 to reflect an expanded scope of technical work, including the Extensible Markup Language (XML) and other related standards.

organizational records, n. ~ 1. The records of a corporate body. – 2. The records of a nonprofit organization, as distinguished from commercial business records.

    BT: record

    RT: business records

orientation interview ~ *see:* reference interview

original, n. ~ 1. The initial manifestation of something. – 2. A thing from which copies are made, especially a prototype. – 3. DIPLOMATICS · The first complete and effective version of a record. – 4. LAW · The thing itself or a duplicate intended to have the same effect by the person creating it.

    Syn: prototype

    RT: copy, duplicate, duplicate original, genuine, record copy, version

    Notes: An original may have preceding versions, which may themselves be considered distinct originals. A written speech may have gone through several drafts, and a photographic print may be made from a negative. Originals are considered to be the most authentic form of a document, based on the assumption that any copy involves some loss of fidelity. That assumption is questionable in the electronic environment, where a sequence of digits may be demonstrated to be identical (although the display of those digits may vary depending on the system used to view them).

    In some instances, copies are designated as originals by law. In particular, microfilmed records are legally equivalent to the originals.

    †70 *(Duranti 1998, p. 165):* An original is the first complete and effective document, that is, an original must present the qualities of primitiveness, completeness and effectiveness. With facsimile transmission, the first two qualities belong in the document transmitted while the latter belongs in the document received.

    †84 *(Fed. R. Evid., 1001 (3)):* An 'original'[3] of a writing or recording is the writing or recording itself or any counterpart intended to have the same effect by a person executing or issuing it. An 'original' of a photograph includes the negative or any print there from. If data are stored in a computer or similar device, any printout or other output readable by sight, shown accurately to reflect the data, is an 'original.'

original entry, n. ~ The initial record of a transaction, recorded sequentially, used as a source for posting in other ledgers.

    RT: daybook, shop book

    Notes: Daybooks and shop books are books of original entry. Transactions are recorded as they occur; information about those transactions is later transcribed to other books, such as ledgers organized by account.

original order (also **registry principle, respect for original order,** *l'ordre primitif, respect de l'ordre intérieur*), n. ~ The organization and sequence of records established by the creator of the records.

    RT: aggregated records, arrangement, context, provenance, restoration of original order

    Notes: Original order is a fundamental principle of archives. Maintaining records in original order serves two purposes. First, it preserves existing relationships and evidential significance that can be inferred from the context of the records. Second, it exploits the record creator's mechanisms to access the records, saving the archives the work of creating new access tools.

Original order is not the same as the order in which materials were received. Items that were clearly misfiled may be refiled in their proper location. Materials may have had their original order disturbed, often during inactive use, before transfer to the archives; see **restoration of original order.**

A collection may not have meaningful order if the creator stored items in a haphazard fashion. In such instances, archivists often impose order on the materials to facilitate arrangement and description. The principle of respect for original order does not extend to respect for original chaos.

†109 (Guercio 2001, p. 249): Since files and series reflect the aggregation of records in relation to the activity undertaken, this order should be maintained not only during the phase when the records are current, but also in the phase of preservation, whether through the identification of records selected for preservation or for purposes of research, in order to guarantee the possibility of meaningful future use.

originating office (also **originating agency**) ~ *see:* office of origin

orthochromatic, adj. ~ PHOTOGRAPHY · Sensitive to blue and green light.

> *RT:* monochrome, panchromatic
>
> *Notes:* Orthochromatic describes the spectral sensitivity of monochromatic (black-and-white) photographic materials, which are not sensitive to red light. As a result, reds and oranges in the original appear much darker relative to blues and greens of equal brightness. Early photographic materials, especially film and plates used in the camera, were orthochromatic. Most black-and-white photographic papers continue to use orthochromatic emulsions, allowing the materials to be handled in the darkroom under red light.

OS ~ *see:* operating system

OSI ~ *see:* Open Source Initiative, Open Systems Interconnection Reference Model

other title information, n. ~ DESCRIPTION · Information that appears in conjunction with, but is distinct from, the title proper, a parallel title, or statement of responsibility.

> *BT:* descriptive element
>
> *RT:* parallel title, subtitle, title, title proper
>
> *†120 (APPM2 1989, 1.1E):* Any title information, other than title proper or parallel titles, appearing on material. This may include subtitles and phrases appearing in conjunction with the title proper or parallel titles indicating the character, contents, etc., of the material or the occasion and/or motive for its production. For single items this may also include place of writing or delivery, addressee, and place to which written.

out letter, n. ~ Correspondence sent from an individual or organization to another individual or organization.

> *RT:* correspondence, in letter
>
> *Notes:* Out letters are sometimes maintained as a separate record series.

outgassing (also **off gassing**), n. ~ The release of material in the form of a vapor as a result of deterioration.

> *Notes:* Vinegar syndrome outgassing products, resulting from the decomposition of triacetate film, include acetic acid.

Syn: Synonym · *†:* see Bibliography · *Superscript:* Definition number

output, n. ~ 1. COMPUTING · Information that is the result of data processing activity and that is made available externally. – 2. COMPUTING · The processes that allow information to be extracted from a system.

RT: hard copy, input

Notes: Output may be in human-readable form, such as a display or printout. It may also be in machine-readable form, such as a bitstream passed from one function to another, or on a recorded medium such as tape or disk.

outreach, n. ~ The process of identifying and providing services to constituencies with needs relevant to the repository's mission, especially underserved groups, and tailoring services to meet those needs.

Notes: Outreach activities may include exhibits, workshops, publications, and educational programs.

†223 *(Personal communication, V Chapman Smith (7 June 2004)):* Effective outreach is more than an event or a series of activities. It is the process of assessing and developing institutional capacity to meet the needs of under served audiences. This process may lead an institution to reframe its mission, vision and goals to the contemporary situation. Successful outreach requires an environmental assessment of community (potential constituent) needs, potential partners and resources, and potential impact. This type of assessment will also help an institution develop an effective marketing plan and strategies for whatever programming is developed. Why are you doing any programming or collecting? What's the benefit/value? Who are you trying to reach? How do you know they will come? Who will use the collection? What's your institution's brand or how are you perceived? How are you differentiated from others? On the collections side, some institutions are reassessing the cataloguing of their collections based on their outreach. They are finding new stories documented in collections that align better with current community needs. Others have changed their acquisition priorities based on outreach.

†232 *(SAA, "Institutional Evaluation"):* The archives should identify its various constituencies in terms of its purpose, plan and implement methods to assess the needs of these groups in relation to the resources of the institution, and devise outreach programs that will fit their needs. These program may include workshops, conferences, training programs, courses, festivals, exhibits, publications, and similar activities, aimed at such groups as students, faculty members, scholars, administrators, researchers, donors, records creators, or the general community.

outtake, n. ~ Moving image material created during production but not included in the final version.

RT: moving image

Notes: 'Outtake' frequently describes takes that had to be reshot because of some mistake, such as a blooper.

overexposure, n. ~ PHOTOGRAPHY · A condition in which too much light reaches the light-sensitive material during image formation.

Notes: With negative film, overexposure results in highlights being forced onto the shoulder of the characteristic curve, compressing the tones (blocking up). With print materials, highlights are not light and detail in the shadows is lost in black. In color transparencies, colors are washed out (desaturated) and highlights are a blank white.

overlay, n. ~ 1. A transparent or translucent sheet that, when placed over another sheet, adds additional information to form a composite. – 2. COMPUTING · Graphic information that can be layered on other information.

Notes: An overlay[1,2] can mask (remove) or add information to that on the underlying sheet.

oversize, adj. ~ Larger than normal.

Notes: 'Oversize' often describes materials that cannot be stored in standard-sized housings. What is standard varies from repository to repository, although many consider anything too large to fit in a document box to be oversize. Oversize materials are often stored flat or rolled on a supporting tube. 'Oversized' is sometimes used as a noun to represent the class of larger-than-normal materials.

P

pack (also **reel pack**), n. ~ The smoothness and tension of the wind of film or tape on a hub.

> *RT:* buckle, cinching
>
> *Notes:* A good pack is free from buckling, cinching, and other wind irregularities.
>
> †*103 (UNESCO A/V Glossary 2001):* Tape packs are wound under a considerable amount of tension. This is necessary to maintain the shape of the tape pack. A reel of tape can be permanently damaged if the tape pack tension is too high or too low. If the tension is too high, the tape backing can stretch. If the tension gets too low, tape layers can slip past each other, resulting in pack slip, cinching, or popped strands on playback.

packet, n. ~ A group of bits transmitted over a network.

> *Notes:* Packets typically contain information about routing, the type of information contained, and some sort of error detection code. Messages are broken up into packets to be transmitted over the network, then reassembled on the receiving end.

page, n. ~ 1. A sheet of paper, especially one bound in a publication; a leaf. – 2. DESCRIPTION · One side of a leaf.

> *RT:* leaf
>
> †*11 (AACR2, 2.5B1):* Give the number of pages or leaves in a publication in accordance with the terminology suggested by the volume. That is, describe a volume with leaves printed on both sides in terms of pages; describe a volume with leaves printed on only one side in terms of leaves; and describe a volume that has more than one column to a page and is numbered in columns in terms of columns.

pagination, n. ~ 1. The act of numbering each side of a leaf (page²) in a manuscript or volume. – 2. The nature in which a work is numbered.

> *RT:* foliation
>
> *Notes:* Pagination is distinguished from foliation, in which each leaf is numbered separately.

Paige Box, trademark ~ A cardboard container designed to store records.

> *BT:* box
>
> *Notes:* While the Paige Company makes boxes in a variety of sizes and for specialized formats, in common parlance 'Paige box' usually refers to a box 9 × 15 × 12 inches with a detachable lid.

PAL, n. ~ An analog television broadcast standard using 625 scanning lines.

> *RT:* video
>
> *Notes:* PAL is an acronym for **Phased Alternation by Line**. PAL is used throughout most of Europe, except for France, which uses SECAM.

paleography, n. ~ 1. The study and analysis of ancient writing, including the identification of origin, period, and the formation of individual characters. – 2. The study of handwriting.

> *Notes:* Paleography includes the study of writing in both inscriptions and manuscripts.
>
> †*70 (Duranti 1998, p. 37–38):* The publication of [Dom Jean Mabillon's *De Re Diplomatic Libri VI* in 1681] marks the birth date of diplomatics and paleography. . . .

However, the science which studies ancient scripts[3] did not yet have a name; the term paleography was coined by another Benedictine, Dom Bernardo de Monffauçon, who published *Palaeographia graeca, sive de ortu et progressu literarum* in 1708, but the systematic study of types of script was initiated by Mabillon.

palimpsest, n. ~ 1. A manuscript made on material, usually parchment, that has been previously used, then cleaned for reuse. – 2. A web server hosting Conservation OnLine, maintained by the Preservation Department at Stanford University under the oversight of Walter Henry.

Notes: In a palimpsest[1], portions of the previous writing are frequently visible. A double palimpsest has been cleaned and reused twice. – For palimpsest[2], see http://palimpsest.stanford.edu/.

†248 (Roberts and Etherington 1982): The extent to which the earlier writing could be removed depended to a great degree on the ink used. Early carbon inks, which merely lay on the surface of the parchment, could be removed more or less completely simply by sponging, but the later iron gall inks were much more difficult to remove because of the interaction with the fibers of the tannin present in the ink. They had to be scraped and then treated with a weak acid, such as the citric acid of an orange. Even then traces of the original writing remained. Wetting the parchment in this manner softened it to such an extent that it was necessary to treat the skin with dry lime to make it dry and white once again. The word 'palimpsest' derives from the Greek roots meaning 'rub away again.' Also called 'rescript.'

pamphlet, n. ~ A short, nonserial, bound work of more than one sheet, usually with a soft cover; a booklet.

Syn: booklet

RT: brochure, leaflet, publication

Notes: Pamphlets are larger than a leaflet, but smaller than a book.

†88 (Fowler 1965, p. 66): The introduction of the word *brochure* in the 19th century was probably due to misconception of the French uses. In French *brochure* is used where the French *pamphlet* (chiefly applied to scurrilous or libelous or violently controversial pamphlets) is inappropriate. The sense 'a few leaves of printed matter stitched together' has always belonged in English to pamphlet, though it has by the side of this general sense the special one (different from the French) 'pamphlet bearing on some question of current interest (especially in politics or theology)'.

pamphlet box, n. ~ A container designed to hold flimsy materials, such as newsletters or pamphlets.

BT: box

NT: Princeton file

Notes: A pamphlet box may be open or closed. It is distinguished from a Princeton file, which is open on the top, back, and part of the front. A cut-corner pamphlet box is open on the top and upper half of the back.

pancake, n. ~ A roll of film or tape on a flangeless hub.

RT: hub

panchromatic, adj. ~ Sensitive to all visible colors of light.

RT: monochrome, orthochromatic

Notes: 'Panchromatic' is used to describe monochromatic (black-and-white) photographic emulsions that accurately reproduce different colors in terms of their relative brightness. Panchromatic emulsions are distinguished from monochromatic or orthochromatic emulsions, which are not sensitive to all portions of the spectrum.

panorama, n. ~ 1. A picture with 360° view, especially a landscape. – 2. A picture that depicts a wide, horizontal view. – 3. PHOTOGRAPHY · An image that is significantly longer in the horizontal dimension.

> *RT:* perspective, view

> *Notes:* The panorama[1] originates in the late 17th century. A panorama was often painted on a cylindrical wall or on a long scroll. – Panorama[2] is now used in a more general sense to refer to images that give a broad view of the landscape. – In photography, panorama[3] refers to a variety of formats. Wide-field and banquet panoramas consist of a single frame with correct perspective. **Cirkut panoramas** are made using a specialized camera that sweeps through an angle during exposure while scrolling the film to track against the camera motion. Cirkut panoramas have distorted perspectives. **Mosaic panoramas** are made by piecing together separate photographs, usually a standard-sized format; mosaic panoramas also have a distorted perspective.

Panorama reader, trademark ~ A software application used to view Standard Generalized Markup Language (SGML) documents.

> *Notes:* Panorama was a browser plug-in, no longer available, that was distributed by Interleaf. It was commonly used to view early Encoded Archival Description finding aids before that standard was adapted to support XML.

paper, n. ~ 1. Sheets made by extracting fibers from a suspension through a fine screen, where they are combined through matting or felting, then dried. – 2. A newspaper. – 3. A scholarly essay or lecture read at a conference or presented for publication. – 4. A student essay. – 5. Negotiable instrument, especially one that is evidence of debt.

> *DF:* papers, papyrus, parchment, vellum

> *NT:* acid-free paper, alkaline-reserve paper, bond paper, chemical wood pulp, contact paper, cover paper , durable paper, fanfold, glassine, kraft paper, mechanical wood pulp, permanent paper , rag paper, resin-coated paper

> *Notes:* Paper[1] is most commonly made from plant fibers, including cotton, wood, linen, or grass. However, it may also be made from animal fibers, such as wool or silk, or from synthetics, such as spun polyester. Paper may have a smooth, laid, or woven texture. It may be coated with clay to give it a sheen and to prevent inks from being absorbed into the paper fibers. Paper comes in varying thicknesses (weights); paper thicker than twelve points is generally called board.

paper sizes ~ *see:* A4, foolscap, legal size, letter size

> *RT:* sheet

> *Notes:* In the United States the most common sizes are letter (8½ × 11 inches) and legal (8½ × 14 inches); manufacturers specify other sizes in inches. British standards include foolscap (13½ × 17 inches), post (15½ × 19 inches), Demy (17½ × 22½ inches), up to Double Imperial (30 × 44 inches). The German DIN A standard includes sizes ranging from A10 (26 × 37 mm) to 4A0 (1682 × 2378 mm), with A4 (210 × 297 mm) being the closest to letter size. The B sizes are intended for posters, and C sizes for envelopes. The German A and B sizes have been adopted as ISO standards and are now widely used throughout Europe.

paper tape (also **punched paper tape, punched tape**), n. ~ COMPUTING · A continuous ribbon of paper with parallel rows of holes punched across the short dimension to encode binary data for Teletypes and computers.

RT: tape

Notes: Paper tape was used with Teletype and Telex machines to create messages. After a connection to another device was established, the tape was read and transmitted at the maximum rate to reduce connection time. It was also used by early computers to create, enter, and store information in a reliable, machine-readable format. Early tapes used a five-bit Baudot code, while later tapes used seven-bit ASCII with an eighth bit for parity checking.

paperless office, n. ~ A place of work that uses electronic documents, rather than paper, to create, store, and use information.

   †263 *(Sellen and Harper 2002, p. 2):* Let's first take a look at the origins of the concept of the paperless office – the expectation that electronic technologies would make paper in the office a thing of the past. . . . The understanding was that it came from Xerox PARC. . . . In the mid-1970s, when PARC was new, a *Business Week* article featured the then head of PARC, George Pake, making a series of predictions about the office of the future. This article implies as much about the demise of the typewriter as it does about paper. . . . Paperlessness was not an issue for most of the researchers anyway and it was only 'outsiders' who made the claim that that was what PARC was about.

papers, ~ n. ~ 1. A collection. – 2. A collection of personal or family documents; personal papers. – 3. Government · Records indicating an individual's identity or status.

   DF: paper

   RT: document, manuscript, manuscript collection, record

   Notes: Papers[1] is used generically to encompass materials in a variety of formats, including manuscripts, typescripts, clippings, photographs. 'Papers' connotes materials in sheets. It is sometimes used in the title of a collection, even though that collection includes bound works such as scrapbooks or diaries, and may even contain even three-dimensional artifacts. – Papers[2] can be equally as encompassing in format but connotes materials associated with an individual or family, apart from official records of a business or organization.

paperwork management ~ *see:* records management

papyrus, n. ~ Sheets of writing material made by weaving strips of pith taken from the plant *Cyperus papyrus.*

   DF: paper

   Notes: Papyrus is a forerunner of paper, and was used by ancient Egyptians, Greeks, and Romans between the 4th century B.C. and the 4th century A.D.

   †248 *(Roberts and Etherington 1982):* One common characteristic of papyrus, regardless of quality, is the difference between the two sides of the sheet, which stems from the strips being at right angles to each other. The recto side, on which the strips run horizontally, was the side generally preferred for writing, while the verso, which had vertical strips, was less frequently used. A material as pliable as papyrus was well suited to be rolled, and when this was done the recto became the inner side and the verso, with no writing, the outer side.

parallel title, n. ~ Description · A title, appearing in conjunction with the title proper, in another language or script.

   BT: descriptive element

   RT: other title information, title

parchment, n. ~ 1. Sheets of writing material made from polished sheepskin or goatskin. – 2. High-quality, translucent paper with an appearance that imitates such writing materials. – 3. A manuscript on parchment.

    DF: paper

    RT: vellum

    Notes: Parchment[1] is often used interchangeably with vellum, although vellum is made from calfskin.

    †15 *(AAT 2000):* For finer quality calf parchment, use 'vellum.' The terms parchment and vellum sometimes have been and still are both confused and used interchangeably.

Paris Principles, n. ~ The *Statement of Principles* adopted by the International Conference on Cataloguing Principles (ICCP), organized by the International Federation of Library Associations and Institutions (IFLA) in Paris, October 1961.

    RT: description

    †272 *(ICCP Principles 1961):* The principles here stated apply only to the choice and form of headings and entry words – i.e. to the principal elements determining the order of entries – in catalogues of printed books [and library materials having similar characteristics] in which entries under authors' names and, where these are inappropriate or insufficient, under the titles of works are combined in one alphabetical sequence. They are framed with special reference to catalogues enumerating the contents of large general libraries: but their application to the catalogues of other libraries and to other alphabetical lists of books is also recommended, with such modifications as may be required by the purposes of these catalogues and lists.

part, n. ~ 1. DESCRIPTION · A portion of a larger work established by the author, publisher, or manufacturer that is complete in itself. – 2. ARCHIVES · A division within the hierarchy of a collection. – 3. MUSIC · A piece written for one voice or instrument in a musical composition.

    DF: fascicle

    RT: episode, volume

    Notes: For monographic works, a part[1] is usually synonymous with volume. However, it may refer to a bibliographic unit intended to be bound, with other parts, into a volume. A part is distinguished from a fascicle, the latter being a temporary division that is not necessarily congruent with an intellectual division. – Part[2] can refer to a series within a record group or collection, a folder within a series, or an item within a folder.

password, n. ~ 1. A word or phrase used to identify an individual or gain access to some place. – 2. COMPUTING · A string of characters, used in combination with a unique account ID when logging in, to authenticate a user to a system.

    Notes: Depending on the system, passwords[2] may be formed from letters, numbers, or other characters.

pasteup, n. (**paste up**, v.) ~ GRAPHICS · The process of arranging on a board the copy and images that will make up a printed page in preparation for reproduction.

    Notes: Pasteup is now largely obsolete due to the widespread use of computerized publishing and printing software.

PAT ~ *see:* Photographic Activity Test

patent, n. ~ 1. A privilege, property, or authority granted to an individual by a gov-

ernment or sovereign. – 2. INTELLECTUAL PROPERTY · The exclusive right to make,
use, or sell an invention that is novel, useful, and not obvious. – 3. The record of
such a grant or right.

> *BT:* intellectual property
>
> *RT:* land grant
>
> *Notes:* The Constitution grants the United States Congress the authority to
> issues patents[3]. Patents are codified in 35 USC 101–103.

patron, n. ~ An individual who uses the collections and services of a repository; a
customer, a researcher.

> *Syn:* reader, researcher, user
>
> *Notes:* 'Patron' connotes an individual who is not a member of the repository
> staff.

PDF (also PDF-A) ~ *see:* Portable Document Format

peeling, n. ~ The separation of the surface layer from the base of a laminated material.

> *RT:* flaking
>
> *Notes:* Peeling is nearly synonymous with flaking, although it connotes limited
> or local deterioration.

PEM ~ *see:* Preservation Environment Monitor

pending file, n. ~ A group of documents filed chronologically under some future date
when they require further attention or action.

> *Syn:* follow-up file, suspense file, tickler file

perfecting order ~ *see:* restoration of original order

perforation, n. ~ 1. A hole punched in a surface. – 2. A series of small holes in a sheet
to make it possible to tear the sheet neatly. – 3. Holes along the side of motion picture film used to transport the film through a camera, projector, or other equipment.

performance rights, n. ~ A copyright owner's exclusive right to control the public
presentation or a work, either live, through broadcast, or in moving image or
sound recordings.

> *DF:* mechanical rights
>
> *BT:* intellectual property
>
> *RT:* copyright
>
> *†281 (USC, 17 USC 101):* COPYRIGHT · To 'perform' a work means to recite,
> render, play, dance, or act it, either directly or by means of any device or process or,
> in the case of a motion picture or other audiovisual work, to show its images in
> any sequence or to make the sounds accompanying it audible.

permanence, n. ~ The inherent stability of material that allows it to resist degradation over time.

> *RT:* archival quality

Permanence of Paper for Publications and Documents in Libraries and Archives,
n. ~ A standard (NISO Z39.48, ISO 9706) that "establishes criteria for coated and
uncoated paper that will last several hundred years without significant deterioration under normal use and storage conditions in libraries and archives."

> *RT:* archival bond, permanent paper
>
> *†222 (Z39.48, 1992):* This standard [Z39.48] identifies the specific properties
> of such paper and specifies the tests required to demonstrate these properties.

permanent paper, n. ~ Paper manufactured with minimal inherent vice and the ability to resist degradation over time.

   BT: paper

   RT: archival bond, durable paper, Permanence of Paper for Publications and Documents in Libraries and Archives

   Notes: Permanent paper is made using materials and techniques, such as those specified in the standard *Permanence of Paper for Publications and Documents in Libraries and Archives*, to minimize the introduction of chemical impurities and to resist the effects of chemical impurities in the environment. 'Permanent paper' is also called **durable paper**, although the latter implies the additional ability to withstand heavy use.

   †248 *(Roberts and Etherington 1982):* [Within the limits of present-day technology, the highest] quality of paper would be manufactured from 100% rag (new linen), flax, cotton, or hemp, undyed and unbleached, and produced by hand or machine. It would contain no loading or color additives, and beating and drying would be controlled so as to obtain maximum folding and tearing strengths.

permanent records, n. ~ Materials created or received by a person, family, or organization, public or private, in the conduct of their affairs intended to be preserved because of the enduring value contained in the information they contain or as evidence of the functions and responsibilities of their creator.

   Syn: archival records

   BT: record

   RT: archives

   Notes: Some archivists may distinguish permanent records from archives, the former representing records still in the hands of the records creators before transfer to the archives. In the vernacular, 'archives' is often used to refer to any collection of documents that are old or of historical interest, regardless of how they are organized; in this sense, the term is synonymous with permanent records.

permanent value, n. ~ The ongoing usefulness or significance of records, based on the administrative, legal, fiscal, evidential, or historical information they contain, that justifies their continued preservation.

   Syn: archival value

   BT: value

   RT: continuing value, enduring value

   Notes: Many archivists do not describe archival collections as having permanent value; changing circumstances may make it reasonable to deaccession a collection. Rather, collections are retained only as long as they have continuing or enduring value.

permanent withdrawal ~ *see:* deaccessioning

permission, ~ n. ~ 1. An authorization to do something. – 2. COMPUTING · Rights to access certain systems, programs, or files associated with a user ID. – **permissions,** pl. n. ~ 3. Control over the use of materials based on a variety of rights.

   Notes: Permissions³ includes both physical and intellectual property rights. Permissions are often tied to conditions of use, such as the requirement that any reproduction of material include the name of the repository.

permit, n. ~ A record of a permission granted by an authority; a license.

   RT: license

permuted index, n. ~ An index that contains an entry for each nontrivial word in a title, with the entry words alphabetized and centered on the page surrounded by the rest of the title.

> *Syn:* rotated index
> *BT:* index
> *RT:* keyword in context index
> *Notes:* In a permuted index, as much of the title as possible appears on either side of the entry word; long titles may be truncated at the beginning or the end. A stop list may be used to suppress entries for words with no value for retrieval, such as articles and conjunctions, or a go list may be used to generate entries for specific words.

persistent object preservation, n. ~ A technique to ensure electronic records remain accessible by making them self-describing in a way that is independent of specific hardware and software.

> *BT:* conversion
> †132 *(GAO 2002, p. 50):* NARA is investigating an advanced form of conversion combined with encapsulation known as persistent object preservation (POP). Under this approach, records are converted by XML tagging and then encapsulated with metadata.

Persistent Uniform Resource Locator, n. (**PURL**, abbr.) ~ Computing · 1. A stable Uniform Resource Locator (URL) that provides a redirection to a resource's current URL. – 2. A service that offers such redirection.

> *RT:* Uniform Resource Locator
> *Notes:* A PURL service provides a means to link a stable URL to a resource, even if the resource's location changes. A PURL service maintains a simple database of PURLs and the associated, current URLs. A PURL published in different places can continue to point to the resource with a single change to the database, rather than having to change all published versions.

person, n. ~ 1. A human individual. – 2. A legal entity with recognized rights and duties that is treated as a human individual; an artificial person; a legal person; a corporation.

> *RT:* juridical person
> †142 *(InterPARES Terminology):* Persons are the subject of rights and duties; they are entities recognized by the juridical system as capable of or having the potential for acting legally.

personal computer ~ *see:* computer

personal file, n. ~ A file containing duplicates of records kept by an individual for ease of reference.

> *RT:* convenience file, office file
> *Notes:* If personal files contain duplicates of record copies preserved elsewhere, their contents are often considered nonrecords.

personal name, n. ~ Description · The word or phrase by which an individual is known and distinguished from others, especially the form used as a heading.

> *BT:* name
> †11 *(AACR2, 22.1A):* In general, choose, as the basis of the heading for a person, the name by which he or she is commonly known. This may be the person's real name, pseudonym, title of nobility, nickname, initials, or other appellation.

personal papers (also **personal records, private papers**), n. ~ 1. Documents created, acquired, or received by an individual in the course of his or her affairs and preserved in their original order (if such order exists). – 2. Nonofficial documents kept by an individual at a place of work.

RT: collection, family papers, manuscript, nonofficial papers

†119 (Henry 1998, p. 315): The value of archives is cultural and humanistic, not just bureaucratic. Archival programs that collect records or personal papers, which may contain electronic media, find the new definition of record [as evidence of a business transaction] bewildering. Personal papers may never show 'evidence' of 'business transactions,' but such archival sources provide a wealth of information needed for society's memory.

†281 (USC, 44 USC 2201): The term personal records² means all documentary materials, or any reasonably segregable portion thereof, of a purely private or non-public character which do not relate to or have an effect upon the carrying out of the constitutional, statutory, or other official or ceremonial duties of the President. Such term includes - (A) diaries, journals, or other personal notes serving as the functional equivalent of a diary or journal which are not prepared or utilized for, or circulated or communicated in the course of, transacting Government business; (B) materials relating to private political associations, and having no relation to or direct effect upon the carrying out of constitutional, statutory, or other official or ceremonial duties of the President; and (C) materials relating exclusively to the President's own election to the office of the Presidency; and materials directly relating to the election of a particular individual or individuals to Federal, State, or local office, which have no relation to or direct effect upon the carrying out of constitutional, statutory, or other official or ceremonial duties of the President.

perspective, n. ~ 1. Techniques of representing depth, especially on a two-dimensional surface, through the use of vanishing points, foreshortening, and aerial effects. – 2. The position of a camera relative to its subject.

NT: bird's-eye view, worm's-eye view

RT: aerial photograph, elevation, oblique, panorama, projection, view

Notes: Perspective² includes closeups, as well as bird's-eye and worm's-eye views.

pertinence, n. ~ A principle of arranging records based on content, without regard for their provenance or original order.

RT: functional pertinence, territorial pertinence

†98 (Gilliland-Swetland 2000a, p. 12): The French conception of respect des fonds did not include the same stricture to maintain original order (referred to in French as respect de l'ordre intérieure), largely because French archivists had been applying what was known as the principle of pertinence and rearranging records according to their subject content.

petition, n. ~ A written request submitted to an authority.

RT: memorial

†110 (NARA Senate Records): Generally speaking, in the late 18th and 19th centuries a petition, unlike a memorial, included a prayer (e.g., petition of John Smith praying that his claim be granted). Memorials also express opposition to ('remonstrate against') some pending action. In modern usage, there is no apparent difference between a memorial and a petition, and petition has become the

commonly accepted generic term. A similar document transmitted to Congress by a legislative body such as a State legislature takes the form of a resolution and is sometimes termed a memorial.

pH, n. ~ A measure of the acidity or alkalinity of some substance, determined by the concentration of hydrogen ions.

  RT: acid, alkali, buffer

  Notes: pH is measured on a scale from 0 to 14; values below 7.0 are acidic, and values above 7.0 are alkaline. A pH of 7.0 is neutral.

phase box, n. ~ A simple, relatively inexpensive box designed to offer immediate, short-term protection of books, scrapbooks, albums, and other bound items.

  BT: box

  Notes: A phase box is typically constructed from two sheets of board that have been glued at their centers to form a cross. The boards are creased so that they can be wrapped around the book and are held together with string or hook-and-loop fasteners.

Phased Alternation by Line ~ *see:* PAL

phased preservation, n. ~ A preservation management technique that emphasizes actions that have the greatest impact on the preservation of collections as a whole, rather than concentrating on treating individual items.

  Notes: Phased preservation includes surveys to establish priorities, disaster planning, environmental controls, and holdings maintenance.

  †103 *(UNESCO A/V Glossary 2001):* (phased conservation) A concept developed at the Library of Congress, originally conceived to meet the short-term needs of items that would eventually be given full conservation treatment. Surveying is an important aspect of phased treatment; items are categorized by certain characteristics or conservation problems so that they may later be retrieved for treatment.

phonetic index, n. ~ An ordered list of materials organized under codes that represent the sound of names or words.

  BT: index

  RT: Soundex

  Notes: A phonetic index makes it possible to look up something without knowing how it was spelled. Many censuses have a phonetic index to name. Most techniques to create index codes use the first letter of the name followed by digits representing subsequent sounds. For example, Smith, Smythe, and Smyth might all be coded S530. Different techniques, such as Russell's Soundex, Simplified Soundex, American Soundex, and Miracode, use slightly different rules, producing different codes.

phonodisc ~ *see:* phonograph record

phonograph, n. ~ A machine used to play back sound recorded in a groove on a cylinder or disk; a record player.

phonograph record (also **audio disc, phonograph album, recording**), n. ~ A disk or cylinder with a spiral grove in which sound vibrations have been fixed using an analog signal.

  DF: compact disc, record

  BT: sound recording

  NT: long-playing record

  RT: album

Notes: 'Phonograph record' connotes a disk format, although the term include cylinder recordings. Disks were made in a variety of sizes. Larger records, 10 to 12 inches in diameter with playing times of more than five minutes at 33⅓ revolutions per minute are often called **albums** or **long-playing records** (often abbreviated **LPs**). Many early disks were metal plates coated with lacquer; later disks were made of vinyl. Common recording speeds included 16, 33⅓, 45, and 78 revolutions per minute.

†281 (USC, 17 USC 101): Copyright · Material objects in which sounds, other than those accompanying a motion picture or other audiovisual work, are fixed by any method now known or later developed, and from which the sounds can be perceived, reproduced, or otherwise communicated, either directly or with the aid of a machine or device. The term 'phonorecords' includes the material object in which the sounds are first fixed.

phonography ~ *see:* stenography

phonorecord, n. ~ A sound recording in any format.

Syn: sound recording

Notes: 'Phonorecord' is used primarily in the context of copyright law.

phonotape ~ *see:* audiotape

Photo CD, n. ~ A compact disc format introduced in 1992 by Eastman Kodak to store high-quality photographic images in a proprietary format.

BT: compact disc

Notes: Photo CDs are available in two formats. The Photo CD is intended for use with 35 mm film. The Pro Photo CD offers higher resolution and is intended for large format negatives and transparencies.

photocopy, n. ~ 1. A duplicate made using an optical system that quickly and inexpensively reproduces an image of the original without an intermediate negative. – 2. A copy made using an electrostatic process.

BT: copy

RT: electrostatic process, reprint, reproduction

Notes: Photocopy techniques include thermal, wet, and dry processes, although most contemporary machines [2005] use an electrostatic process.

photograph, n. ~ 1. A still picture formed on a light-sensitive surface using an optical system and fixed by a photochemical process. – 2. An image rendered using a camera.

DF: photomechanical, print

BT: document, picture

NT: aerial photograph, albumen photograph, ambrotype, cabinet card, card-mounted photographs, cased photographs, chlorobromide photograph, cyanotype, daguerreotype, digital photograph, gelatin silver photograph, gum print, lantern slide, movie still, negative, photographic print, printing-out paper, slide, stereograph, tintype, transparency

RT: combination printing, electrophotography, film, graphic records, image, microphotography, photomicrography, pigment print, positive, rephotography, separation, snapshot, stock shot, stop-motion photography, telephotography, visual materials

Notes: Most traditional photographic processes use a silver halide as the light-sensitive material, although light-sensitive salts of copper, iron, and uranium have been used as well. The silver halide is reduced to metallic silver in black-and-white photographs and is used to form a dye in color photographs. In the 19th century, collodion was commonly used as a binder for negatives, prints, ambrotypes, and tintypes, and albumen was the most common binder for prints. Most modern photographic processes use gelatin to bind the silver halide to a film, paper, or glass support.

Technically, a photograph[1] is distinguished from a print[1], in which the image is formed mechanically rather than photochemically. However, print[3] is commonly used to describe images originally made with a camera but reproduced using a photomechanical process, such as a halftone or a Woodburytype. Such images were, at some point, a photograph before reproduction. However, digital photographs now capture and record images that are printed using a nonphotographic print process.

†130 (Images in Time 2003, p. 166): All images constitute a record, irrespective of the value we may attach to the information they contain. The unique property of photographic records reside in their ability to capture a moment in time and to highlight the inevitable passing of time. Although the setting and depth of vision that are chosen already imply a certain voluntary or arbitrary selection, the photographic lens perceives and records the space in a homogeneous manner and it is this global view that can provide us with useful information, sometimes capturing details not even intended by the photographer himself.

†257 (Sauer 2001, p. 44): While the visual authority of the photograph is now increasingly undermined by the wizardry of digital technology, the 'truthfulness of facts' in a photograph has always been presumed to reside in its verisimilitude.' Ever since Paul Delaroche purportedly exclaimed, 'From today, painting is dead,' the photograph has been perceived as an objective record of reality, the product of a mechanical and therefore neutral means of documentation. . . . Photographs derive the authority of their content from realism and accuracy, what J. B. Harley calls 'talismans' of authority; archival photographs convey their message through function and context. . . . The photograph is neither truth nor reality, but a representation willed into existence for a purpose and mediated by the persons concurring in its formation.

Photographic Activity Test, n. (**PAT,** abbr.) ~ A standard procedure (ISO 14523) to check for potential chemical reactions between materials used to make enclosures and photographs stored in those enclosures.

†225 (IPI): Developed by IPI, this test predicts possible interactions between photographic images and the enclosures in which they are stored. The PAT is also used to test the components of enclosures, such as adhesives, inks, paints, labels, and tapes. The test involves incubating materials in temperature- and humidity-controlled chambers to simulate aging and takes from four to six weeks. After incubation and sample evaluation, a final report is provided. ¶ The PAT was designed to screen enclosures for possible chemical reactions with photographs. There are other tests that can screen for potential physical damage such as blocking and abrasion.

photographic archives, n. ~ 1. A collection of photographs, often with accompanying materials in other formats, made or received by an individual, family, or organization in the conduct of affairs and preserved because of the enduring value of the information contained in those records. – 2. A division within an organization responsible for maintaining such materials.

BT: archives

Syn: Synonym • †: see Bibliography • *Superscript:* Definition number

photographic print, n. ~ An image formed on paper coated with a light-sensitive substance using an optical system and fixed by a photochemical process.

BT: photograph

Notes: Many modern photographic prints are on resin-coated paper to make them easier to process.

photomechanical, n. ~ 1. A process to reproduce photographic images as prints[1] using a matrix[1] and ink. – 2. A print made using such a process.

DF: photograph

RT: Albertype, collotype, dye transfer process, halftone, print, Woodburytype

Notes: Photomechanical processes often use a halftone screen to approximate the continuous tones of the original photograph. Because Woodburytypes and dye transfer prints can accurately reproduce a continuous-tone image with an optical quality of detail, they are often mistaken for photographs.

photomicrography, n. ~ The processes and techniques used to create greatly enlarged photographs of things normally too small to be seen with the unaided eye.

RT: microphotography, photograph

Notes: Photomicrography is distinguished from microphotography, the use of photographic processes and techniques to create highly reduced images.

photomontage, n. ~ 1. The technique of creating an image by combining photographs, sometimes with other materials, to form a unified image. – 2. An image created using such a technique.

DF: collage, combination printing, composite

BT: montage

Notes: In a photomontage, the image is not perfectly unified; the use of different images as parts of the whole is not disguised. Photomontage is distinguished from collage, which is a work in which the pieces do not form a unified picture. Distinguish from combination prints and composites[3], which have unified images that give the appearance of being made with a single negative.

Photostat, trademark (**stat**, abbr.) ~ 1. A photocopying process that makes duplicates with the same polarity as the original. – 2. A copy made by this process.

Notes: Photostat and stat were often used generically for any type of photocopy.

†300 (Yates 1989, p. 54): In 1911, the Taft Commission on Economy and Efficiency evaluated the use and economics of the Photostat, a brand of photocopier, as part of its investigation of efficiency in office methods. At a cost of $500.00, the apparatus was expensive.... While point-of-origin copying was clearly preferable, the commission found the Photostat cost-effective as an alternative to retyping complicated documents (especially tables) or redrawing diagrams.

physical control, n. ~ The function of tracking the storage of records to ensure that they can be located.

RT: administrative control, intellectual control, process control

Notes: Intellectual control provides a means of identifying potentially relevant materials, with a pointer to where those materials are stored. Physical control ensures that the records are, in fact, where that pointer specifies. In some instances, those pointers may be absolute, pointing to a specific box on a specific shelf in a specific room. In other cases, the pointer may be relative, pointing to a collection and box number, which reflect a position within a range of similar numbers.

†265 (Skupsky and Mantaña 1994, p. 154): Careful physical control of records ensures that critical records are available when needed. Even when ineffective recordkeeping practices do not justify sanctions, the organization may still find itself severely disadvantaged by its inability to produce evidence for its own case. Besides reducing the organization's efficiency, poor recordkeeping practices may lead to future litigation because the organization may not know its legal obligations.

physical custody, n. ~ Possession, care, and control, especially for security and preservation.

> *RT:* custody, legal custody
>
> *Notes:* Physical custody may be, but is not always, coupled with legal custody.

physical form, n. ~ The overall appearance, configuration, or shape, derived from material characteristics and independent of intellectual content.

> *BT:* form
>
> *RT:* extrinsic element
>
> *†70 (Duranti 1998, p. 134):* The term *physical form* refers to the external make-up of the document, while the term *intellectual form* refers to its internal articulation. Therefore the elements of the former are defined by diplomatists as external or *extrinsic*, while the elements of the latter are defined as internal or *intrinsic*.

physical record, n. ~ COMPUTING · A contiguous area of storage defined by the characteristics of the storage device and operating system.

> *DF:* logical record
>
> *RT:* block

physical restriction note, n. ~ DESCRIPTION · A note indicating limitations on the handling and use of material because of preservation or security considerations.

> *BT:* note
>
> *RT:* restriction
>
> *Notes:* For example, a physical restriction note may indicate that patrons may have access to the original under exceptional circumstances, but that a copy is available for use.

picture, n. ~ 1. An image, especially on a surface. – 2. The portion of a video signal that forms the image. – 3. SLANG · A motion picture.

> *DF:* motion picture
>
> *NT:* drawing, photograph, print
>
> *RT:* graphic, image, video, visual materials
>
> *Notes:* A picture[1] may be formed using a variety of techniques, including drawing, painting, printing, photography, or video. It may depict something in the real world or the imagination, or it may be entirely nonrepresentational. In general, a picture is a two-dimensional rendering on an opaque surface. Although, a picture is not necessarily on a flat surface; for example, a picture on a ball. 'Picture' may also refer to a virtual representation in three dimensions through the use of computer graphics, or it may give the appearance of three dimensions, as in stereographs.

picture postcard ~ *see:* postcard

picture show ~ *see:* motion picture

piece, n. ~ 1. An item. – 2. A part physically separate from a larger whole.

> *Syn:* item
>
> *Notes:* Piece[1] is more common in the United Kingdom. – Piece[2] is used to describe a portion of something that clearly has separate components, such as the lid of a teapot.

piece count, n. ~ The number of physically discrete items in a collection.
> *BT:* count

PIER ~ *see:* Preservation of the Integrity of Electronic Records

pigeonhole, n. ~ A small compartment used for storing folded document.
> *BT:* file cabinet
> *RT:* flat filing
> *Notes:* Pigeonholes are usually found in groups, ranging from a few on a desk to many in a pigeonhole cabinet.
> *†300 (Yates 1989, p. 28–29):* Through the middle of the [nineteenth] century, the pigeonhole was the primary storage device for [incoming] correspondence, sometimes supplemented by a desk spindle on which papers could be impaled. ¶ When the pigeonholes filled up, letters were often tied up in bundles and stored in a safe place. At low levels of correspondence, such a storage system was satisfactory. The letters of the last year or two could be kept in the pigeonholes, so that by the time letters were retired they were not being actively used. As business – and correspondence – increased in the midcentury period, however, pigeonhole desks and cabinets became less satisfactory storage systems.

pigment print, n. ~ A photographic or photomechanical print in which the image is formed by a pigment rather than silver or a dye.
> *NT:* gum print
> *RT:* photograph, print
> *Notes:* Examples of processes to make pigment prints include gum bichromate, carbon, and bromoil. These processes are often used for fine art photography.

piracy, n. ~ The illicit reproduction or distribution of material that is an infringement of intellectual property law.
> *RT:* bootleg, infringement
> *†165 (Lessig 2004):* If piracy means using the creative property of others without their permission, then the history of the content industry is a history of piracy. Every important sector of big media today – film, music, radio, and cable TV – was born of a kind of piracy. The consistent story is how each generation welcomes the pirates from the last.

Pittsburgh Project ~ *see:* University of Pittsburgh Electronic Records Project

pixel, n. ~ 1. An element in an array that forms an image. – 2. A unit of measure used to describe the size or resolution of an image.
> *RT:* bitmap
> *Notes:* A pixel[1] contains information about the brightness and, for color images, the hue of the element. A pixel may be represented by a single bit, restricting the image to bitonal values. In monochromatic images, a pixel is at least a byte, capable of representing 256 shades. For color images, a one-byte pixel can represent only 256 colors; a three-byte pixel can represent more than 16 million colors. The height and width of an image are often measured in terms of pixels, and the resolution may be measured in terms of pixels per inch or centimeter.

pixel depth, n. ~ The number of bytes used to form a pixel[1] in a graphics array.
> *RT:* bit depth

pixilation, n. ~ 1. The representation of an image through the use of discrete rather than continuous quantities. – 2. The distortion of an image resulting from discrete values failing to adequately represent a continuous value.

Notes: A halftone is an analog equivalent to pixilation[1]. A continuous-tone image is broken up into an array of light or dark elements; variation in the distribution of elements approximates different tones. A bitmap breaks up an image into pixels arranged in a grid. A line running diagonally across a grid made of squares will have a staircase pattern on the edge. The higher the image resolution, the less noticeable the effect. – Coarse pixilation[2] is sometimes used intentionally to obscure portions of an image, such as a face on television news.

pixmap ~ *see:* bitmap

PKI ~ *see:* public key infrastructure

PL, abbr. ~ [United States] public law.

    Notes: Also abbreviated Pub. L., P.L.

placard, n. ~ A notice printed on card or board for public display, especially a poster.

    RT: poster

plaintext, n. ~ Information that can be read without decryption.

    RT: ciphertext, cryptanalysis, cryptography

    Notes: Plaintext is typically used in the context of cryptography and describes information to be coded or that has been decoded.

plan, n. ~ 1. A sequence of steps to accomplish something. – 2. A map of a small region, such as a town or city, drawn with considerable detail. – 3. A diagram showing the structure of something. – 4. ARCHITECTURE · A sketch or drawing, showing the layout of a structure, especially a horizontal section.

    BT: map

planar, adj. ~ Flat; shallow; having no significant thickness.

    Syn: two-dimensional

    RT: sheet

    Notes: As used in this glossary, 'planar' describes materials that are nearly two-dimensional and frequently flexible, as distinguished from three-dimensional objects. Paper, film, and cloth are examples of planar materials.

planetary camera, n. ~ Equipment for production of microfilm that consists of a table to hold the original, an upright to support the film unit (camera) overhead, lights extending above and to the side of the table, and a control unit.

    Syn: flatbed camera

    BT: microfilm camera

    RT: microfilm

    Notes: When filming with a flatbed camera, both the film and document are stationary during exposure.

plat, n. ~ A map, especially one showing property lines.

    BT: map

plate, n. ~ 1. A metal sheet used for printing; a printing plate. – 2. A print pulled from such a metal sheet. – 3. An illustration in a book, printed separately from the text. – 4. PHOTOGRAPHY · A sheet of glass coated with a light-sensitive emulsion.

    DF: film

    RT: print

    Notes: A plate[1] is used in engraving, offset printing, rotogravure, and other processes. – A plate[3] is frequently on different paper from the text and printed using a different process. Plates may be tipped in individually, bound in as a separate signature, or kept in an accompanying portfolio. They are typically not included in the pagination sequence.

platter, n. ~ 1. Slang · A phonograph record. – 2. The disk on a turntable that supports the phonograph record. – 3. A disk.

polarity, n. ~ Photography, Micrographics · The tonal values of an image relative to the original.

> *RT:* negative, positive
>
> *Notes:* Polarity indicates whether an image is a positive or a negative. An image with negative polarity, a negative, has tones that are reversed from those in the original.

policy, n. ~ An official expression of principles that direct an organization's operations.

> *NT:* access policy, acquisition policy
>
> *RT:* procedure, standard
>
> *Notes:* 'Policy' is sometimes used as a plural noun to refer to the whole of an organization's policies. Policies are distinguished from procedures, which detail how policies are implemented at the operational level.

polyester, n. ~ A clear plastic film that is relatively stiff, cannot be stretched, and is hard to tear.

> *NT:* Melinex, Mylar
>
> *Notes:* Polyester film is commonly used to make protective enclosures and is used as the base for some photographic films. Not all polyester films are identical. Different manufacturing processes leave different residual chemicals in the film, some of which may have an adverse effect on archival materials.

polyethylene, n. ~ A thermoplastic material made from polymerized ethylene.

> *NT:* Tyvek
>
> *Notes:* Polyethylene film ranges from sparking clear to hazy and is easy to stretch but hard to tear. Polyethylene film is sometimes used to make enclosures for photographs and phonograph albums.

polypropylene, n. ~ A thermoplastic material similar to polyethylene, but somewhat stiffer and softening at a higher temperature.

> *Notes:* Polypropylene film ranges from sparkling clear to hazy and can be stretched but is hard to tear.

polyvinyl acetate, n. (**PVA**, abbr.) ~ A water-soluble plastic resin used as an adhesive.

polyvinyl chloride, n. (**PVC**, abbr.) ~ A thermoplastic resin produced by the polymerization of vinyl chloride gas.

> *Notes:* PVC film is a clear plastic that can be stretched but is hard to tear. It has been widely used to make pages with pockets to hold photographs, slides, baseball cards, coins, and other small items. However, PVC outgases chemicals that can damage adjacent materials.

Portable Document Format, trademark (**PDF, PDF-A**, abbr.) ~ A file format developed by Adobe Systems that can be used to distribute formatted output, including text and graphics, from a variety of applications to users working on a variety of platforms.

> *RT:* Acrobat, document interchange
>
> *Notes:* The PDF format can be created using a variety of authoring tools, including Acrobat. The format can be read using the freely distributed Adobe Reader (previously called Acrobat Reader), which is both a stand-alone application and a plug-in for browsers. PDF is not perfectly platform-independent as it requires a reader to render the file, although reader software exists for most plat-

forms. PDF-A is an extension of the format intended to be appropriate for the long-term preservation of digital documents. See http://www.aiim.org/standards.asp?ID=25013.

†162 (LeFurgy 2003): A committee of government, business, and academic representatives is exploring a promising approach to long-term preservation of text-based digital documents. Sponsored by The Association for Information and Image Management (AIIM) and The Association for Suppliers of Printing, Publishing and Converting Technologies (NPES), the committee is working to establish an archival standard for Adobe's Portable Document Format (PDF). Known as PDF-A, the potential standard intends to specify a limited, stable subset of PDF for text-based documents that must remain valid for a number of years. The effort has been underway since 2002, and the ultimate aim is to have PDF-A endorsed and owned by the International Organization for Standardization (ISO).

portal, n. ~ An entry point, especially a web page, that provides access to information from a variety of sources and that offers a variety of services.

> *Notes:* Originally, portals principally organized information from other sources but have expanded to include email, chat, shopping, and other services. A portal may be public or restricted to an intranet. Portals can frequently be personalized so that users can tailor the interface based on their preferences.

portfolio, n. ~ 1. A flat case for holding loose documents. – 2. Examples of work, frequently held in such a case. – 3. The responsibilities associated with an office or job, especially a diplomat. – 4. The financial assets of an individual or organization, considered as a whole.

> *BT:* container
>
> *Notes:* A portfolio[1] is frequently two boards hinged together and fastened on the loose sides with a string or a zipper.

portrait, n. ~ A representation of an individual's likeness.

> *Notes:* Portraits may be a drawing, painting, photograph, or other two-dimensional media. Portraits may also be created in relief and sculpture. They may be head-and-shoulders, bust, three-quarters, or full-length.

portrait orientation (also **portrait mode**), n. ~ A layout that is taller than wide.

> *RT:* format, landscape orientation

positive, n. ~ PHOTOGRAPHY · An image in which the tones match those in the original.

> *RT:* negative, photograph, polarity
>
> *Notes:* In a positive, highlights appear light and shadows appear dark. Positives can be on paper, film, glass, or other support.

post, v. ~ 1. To make an entry in an index. – 2. COMPUTING · To upload a file or information to a server; for example, post to the Internet, post to a Listserv.

postcard, n. ~ A card, commonly 4 × 6 inches, used for sending short messages through the mail.

> *Notes:* Postcards made after 1906 often have an illustration on one side. A **real photo postcard** has a photographic image, as opposed to a **picture postcard**, which has a photomechanical or printed image.
>
> †167 (D Levy 2001, p. 87): The invention of the postcard created a form where brevity would be the rule rather than the exception. After a short period of experimentation in the private sector, the first postcards used on a mass scale were created by national governments by Austria in 1869, by Britain in 1870, and by the

United State in 1873. At the international postal congress the following year, it was agreed that cards, although varying in size from country to country, could cross national borders without being restamped.

postcombination indexing ~ *see:* postcoordinate indexing

postcoordinate indexing (also called **postcombination indexing**), n. ~ A method of indexing materials that creates separate entries for each concept in an item, allowing the item to be retrieved using any combination of those concepts in any order.

> *DF:* precoordinate indexing
>
> *BT:* indexing
>
> *Notes:* In postcoordinate indexing, complex subjects are represented by several different headings rather than a single heading. For example, a history of Arizona might be assigned the headings 'Arizona' and 'History'. In precoordinate indexing, the work might be given a single heading, 'Arizona – History'. Searching in a postcoordinate system typically relies on Boolean operators to combine the separate headings, such as "Search (subject = Arizona) and (subject = history)."
>
> †159 (Lancaster 1998, p. 44): The flexibility associated with postcoordinate systems is lost when index terms must be printed out on paper or on conventional catalog cards. Printed indexes and card catalogs are precoordinate; they have the following characteristics: 1. The multidimensionality of the term relationship is difficult to depict. 2. Terms can only be listed in a particular sequence, which implies that the first term is more important than the others. 3. It is not easy (if not completely impossible) to combine terms at the time a search is performed.
>
> †159 (Lancaster 1998, p. 32): Postcoordinate systems emerged in the 1940s, when they were implemented through the use of various types of cards. A modern computer-based system, operated online, can be considered to be a direct descendant of those manual systems.

postcustodial theory of archives, n. ~ The idea that archivists will no longer physically acquire and maintain records, but that they will provide management oversight for records that will remain in the custody of the record creators.

> *RT:* custody, noncustodial records
>
> *Notes:* The postcustodial theory shifts the role of the archivists from a custodian of inactive records in a centralized repository to the role of a manager of records that are distributed in the offices where the records are created and used.
>
> †119 (Henry 1998, p. 319): Supporters of a new paradigm for electronic records promote the notion of 'post-custodialism,' which defines a centralized archives as 'an archives of last resort.' New paradigm supporters urge archivists to 'cease being identified as custodians of records' because, among other things, this role 'is not professional.' An archives with custody is 'an indefensible bastion and a liability.' These writers maintain that creators of records or other institutions, whether they are archives or not, can take care of archival records.

poster, n. ~ 1. A printed illustration on a large sheet. – 2. A large, flexible sheet bearing text, usually illustrated, that is publicly displayed to advertise or promote something. – 3. Computing · An individual who sends (posts) a message to a newsgroup or mailing list.

> *DF:* broadside
>
> *RT:* placard
>
> *Notes:* A poster[1] is usually mass-produced and intended to be hung as decoration.

†278 (LCGTM 1995, p. 540): Single or multi-sheet notices made to attract attention to events, activities, causes, goods, or services; also, purely decorative posters. For posting, usually in a public place; chiefly pictorial. Intended to make an immediate impression from a distance.

posting up, n. ~ Creating an entry in an index that is more general than the subject being indexed.

Notes: Posting up runs against the general principle of indexing under the most specific term possible. Posting up makes it possible, especially in manual systems, to search groups of related concepts.

†159 (Lancaster 1998, p. 29): In the manual retrieval systems . . . it was necessary to post up from specific to generic terms; e.g., the use of the term oranges in indexing an item caused citrus fruits, fruit, and even, perhaps, crops to be assigned also. This was done to allow generic searches. Were it not done, it would be virtually impossible to perform a complete search on, say, all fruit.

powdering (also **chalking**), n. ~ A printing defect in which the ink is not properly fixed on the surface and can be rubbed off.

RT: red rot

†248 (Roberts and Etherington 1982): The vehicle penetrates the paper but the pigment is left lying loosely on the surface. The defect is caused either by an ink that is too mobile, or by a paper that is too absorbent.

practical obscurity, n. ~ The principle that private information in public records is effectively protected from disclosure as the result of practical barriers to access.

RT: privacy

Notes: Practical barriers to access include travel to view the record, the passage of time, and the limits of indexing. When public records are accessible on the Internet, those barriers are diminished.

†223 (Personal communication, Ken Withers, 9 December 2003): The term 'practical obscurity' first appears in *U.S. Dept. of Justice v. Reporters Committee for Freedom of the Press,* 489 U.S. 749 (1989). Considering the application of FOIA exemption 7(c) to a rap sheet, the court held that where the subject of a rap sheet is a private citizen and the information is in the Government's control as a compilation, rather than as a record of what the Government is up to, the privacy interest in maintaining the rap sheet's 'practical obscurity' is always at its apex while the FOIA-based public interest in disclosure is at its nadir. Thus, as a categorical matter, rap sheets are excluded from disclosure by the exemption in such circumstances.

†233 (EPIC 2003): While court files always have been public, they were considered to enjoy 'practical obscurity.' That is, the records were stored in such an inaccessible fashion that only the determined and resourceful could obtain them. To this day, most records probably are stored at the local level on different types of media (paper, magnetic tape) and are indexed with varying degrees of accuracy and usefulness.

preamble, n. ~ A section at the beginning of a document that indicates and explains the motivation underlying the subject of the document.

PRECIS, n. ~ A system of generating complex, coordinated access points for subject indexing.

Notes: PRECIS is a contraction of PREserved Context Information System.

†159 (Lancaster 1998, p. 56): In PRECIS, computer programs generate a com-

plete set of index entries and cross references for an item from a string of terms and instruction codes provided by an indexer. The subject matter of a document is described as a series of terms that are put in a context-dependent sequence. . . . Each term is essentially dependent on the term immediately before it.

precision, n. ~ 1. The extent to which something is measured. – 2. INFORMATION RETRIEVAL · The ratio of relevant items to all items retrieved.

> *RT:* accuracy, benchmark, error, recall, relevant
>
> *Notes:* Precision[1] is often expressed in terms of deviation from an established benchmark. – Precision[2] measures the quality of a search. It is possible to retrieve all relevant items in a database (a 100% recall ratio), but the precision of the search is likely to be low. If a database contains 100 items, and 25 are relevant to a search, a search that returns all items has 100% recall but only 25% precision.
>
> †277 *(Delpi Group 2002, p. 14):* Recall is inversely proportional to precision. The more precise you are about defining what you want to look for, the fewer documents are recalled.

precoordinate indexing, n. ~ A method of indexing materials that combines separate concepts in an item into a single heading.

> *DF:* postcoordinate indexing
>
> *BT:* indexing
>
> *Notes:* In precoordinate indexing, a complex subject is represented by a single heading rather than separate headings for different aspects of the subject heading. For example, a history of Arizona might be assigned the heading 'Arizona – History.' In postcoordinate indexing, the work might be given separate headings 'Arizona' and for 'History'. A precoordinate indexing system can clearly indicate the relationship of concepts used as headings. For example, a work on Alfred Stieglitz's photography and Georgia O'Keefe's paintings might be given the headings 'Stieglitz, Alfred – Photography' and 'O'Keefe, Georgia – Painting'.

preliminary inventory, n. ~ A listing of the contents and condition of a collection made before processing.

> *RT:* inventory
>
> *Notes:* A preliminary inventory is often made on receipt of a collection to provide basic physical and intellectual control over the materials. During processing, the preliminary inventory may be revised to reflect changes in order and weeding of materials, and notes may be added to give more detail or indicate any access restrictions.

preprint, n. ~ 1. An article, usually of an academic nature, distributed before being published or presented at a conference. – 2. An article, usually of an academic nature, that is intended for publication and that has been distributed in preliminary form for comment and review.

> *RT:* EPrints
>
> *Notes:* In some disciplines, preprints are limited to those articles accepted for publication by a peer-reviewed journal. In other fields, preprints may be used to describe research memoranda, working papers, and technical reports.

prescribed source ~ *see:* chief source of information

preservation, n. ~ 1. The professional discipline of protecting materials by minimizing chemical and physical deterioration and damage to minimize the loss of information and to extend the life of cultural property. – 2. The act of keeping from harm, injury, decay, or destruction, especially through noninvasive treatment. – 3. LAW · The obligation to protect records and other materials potentially relevant to litigation and subject to discovery. – **preserve**, v. ~ 4. To keep for some period of time; to set aside for future use. – 5. CONSERVATION · To take action to prevent deterioration or loss. – 6. LAW · To protect from spoliation.

DF: conservation, restoration

RT: alteration, immutability, security

Notes: Preservation[2] is sometimes distinguished from conservation[1], the latter describing treatments to repair damage. However, preservation activities are often considered a subdiscipline within the profession of conservation[2]. – Preservation[3] is used in many public records laws to distinguish records from nonrecords; records are those materials that warrant preservation, that are set aside (usually by being filed). Materials that are not set aside for subsequent use do not fall within the scope of that legal definition. In this context, preservation is roughly synonymous with filing, with no connotation of permanent preservation.

†43 (Conway 2000): In the early years of modern archival agencies – prior to World War II – preservation[2] simply meant collecting. The sheer act of pulling a collection of manuscripts from a barn, a basement, or a parking garage and placing it intact in a dry building with locks on the door fulfilled the fundamental preservation mandate of the institution.

†48 (CJS, Records §32): A public officer, by virtue of his office, is the legal custodian of all papers, books, and records pertaining to his office. It is his duty to preserve[4] the public records, and to ensure that nobody alters or destroys them. He is also responsible for delivery of such documents to his successor. The law presumes that a public officer will properly perform his duty as to the care, management, and control of records, and their preservation, and if a particular paper is not found in a public office where, if in existence, it ought to be, it will be presumed that it never existed.

†160 (Zublake IV 2003, p. 12): The scope of a party's preservation[3] obligation can be described as follows: Once a party reasonably anticipates litigation, it must suspend its routine document retention/destruction policy and put in place a 'litigation hold' to ensure the preservation of relevant documents.

†265 (Skupsky and Mantaña 1994, p. 74): The duty to preserve[6] records during the pendency of litigation overrides any business procedures that may be in place for destruction of records, including otherwise appropriate destruction under a records retention program. Once the duty to preserve is in effect, a duty also arises to notify appropriate organization personnel of the need to preserve relevant records.

preservation copy, n. ~ The version of a thing set aside to protect its informational content from harm, injury, decay, or destruction.

BT: copy

RT: preservation transfer copy

Notes: A preservation copy may be either the original or a preservation transfer copy. It is used only to make other copies for access.

Preservation Environment Monitor, n. (**PEM**, abbr.) ~ Equipment that monitors and records temperature and relative humidity and that can predict the effects of those changing conditions on the longevity of organic materials.

RT: accelerated aging test, preservation index, time-weighted preservation index

Syn: Synonym · †: see Bibliography · Superscript: Definition number

Notes: The monitor was developed by the Image Permanence Institute at the Rochester Institute of Technology.

†230 *(IPI, Preservation Environment 2002):* The PEM calculates and displays, in real time, values that reflect the decay rate of organic materials stored in that location. These values, known as Preservation Index (PI) and Time-Weighted Preservation Index (TWPI), show how temperature and humidity combine to influence the rate of decay processes such as paper discoloration, dye fading, deterioration of plastics, and textile embrittlement. The PEM displays PI and TWPI values alternately with temperature and RH on a 15-second cycle. Thus, no computer is needed to immediately determine the overall quality of storage conditions with respect to the 'natural aging' rate of all types of organic objects in collections.

preservation index, n. ~ A quantitative measure of the quality of a storage environment that is based on the impact of relative humidity and temperature on organic materials.

RT: Preservation Environment Monitor, time-weighted preservation index

Notes: The concept of preservation index was developed by the Image Permanence Institute in 1995.

†291 *(IPI, PI and TWPI):* PI values, expressed in units of years, show the combined effect of temperature and RH on the decay rate of vulnerable organic materials in collections and give a general idea of how long it would take for them to become noticeably deteriorated, assuming that the temperature and RH did not change from the time of measurement onward. PI helps to quantify how good or bad the environmental conditions are at that moment. If conditions change over time, the life expectancy of an object also changes. PI is not meant as a predictor of the useful life of any particular object. It is simply a convenient measure of the effect of current environmental conditions on the overall life expectancy of a collection.

preservation laboratory ~ *see:* conservation laboratory

preservation metadata, n. ~ Information about an object used to protect the object from harm, injury, deterioration, or destruction.

BT: metadata

†210 *(OCLC/RLG Preservation Metadata 2001, p. 4):* Preservation metadata may be used to store technical information supporting preservation decisions and actions; document preservation actions taken, such as migration of emulation policies; record the effects of preservation strategies; ensure the authenticity of digital resources over time; [and] note information about collection management and the management of rights.

†235 *(Puglia, Reed, and Rhodes 2004, p. 11):* Preservation metadata encompasses all information necessary to manage and preserve digital assets over time. . . . ¶ Preservation metadata is information that will assist in preservation decision-making regarding the long-term value of a digital resource and the cost of maintaining access to it, and will help to both facilitate archiving strategies for digital images as well as support and document these strategies over time. Preservation metadata is commonly linked with digital preservation strategies such as migration and emulation, as well as more "routine" system-level actions such as copying, backup, or other automated processes carried out on large numbers of objects.

preservation methods and techniques ~ *see:* conversion, emulation, migration, phased preservation, preservation microfilm, preservation photocopy, reformat

Notes: Paper-based preservation techniques include preservation photocopying, preservation microfilming, and preservation transfer microfilming. These techniques preserve the content of records, but the artifactual and intrinsic value of the originals cannot be captured in the reproduction.

Phased preservation and preservation management look at the preservation needs of a body of materials as a whole, assessing both the physical condition and the value of the materials to determine how to allocate resources to maximize the impact of preservation efforts.

Digital preservation techniques include conversion, migration, and emulation.

preservation microfilm, n. ~ Microfilm made using materials and techniques to ensure continued access to materials that are in poor condition or to protect the originals from repeated handling.

BT: microfilm

Preservation of the Integrity of Electronic Records (also **UBC Project**), n. (**PIER**, abbr.) ~ A research project at the University of British Columbia designed to identify and define the requirements for creating, handling, and preserving reliable and authentic electronic records.

Notes: The project was done, in part, in collaboration with the United State Department of Defense.

†74 (Duranti, Eastwood, and MacNeil, http://www.interpares.org/UBCProject/intro.htm): The objectives of the research project are: to establish what a record is in principle and how it can be recognised in an electronic environment; to determine what kind of electronic systems generate records; to formulate criteria that allow for the appropriate segregation of records from all other types of information in electronic systems generating and/or storing a variety of data aggregations; to define the conceptual requirements for guaranteeing the reliability and authenticity of records in electronic systems; to assess those methods against different administrative, juridical, cultural and disciplinary points of view.

preservation photocopy, n. ~ A photocopy made using materials and techniques to ensure continued access to materials that are in poor condition or to protect the originals from repeated handling.

BT: copy

preservation transfer copy, n. ~ A copy made to ensure continuing access to an item that cannot be preserved because of its ongoing deterioration.

RT: preservation copy

preserver, n. ~ 1. DIPLOMATICS · The juridical person responsible for the long-term preservation of authentic records, such as an archives. – 2. PHOTOGRAPHY · A piece of brass that wraps around the edge of the image in a cased photograph, serving as a simple frame.

Notes: A brass mat between the cover glass and the image is not part of a preserver^2.

presidential library, n. ~ An archival repository within the National Archives and Records Administration that preserves and makes available the papers, records, and other historical materials of individuals elected to the Office of the President of the United States.

Notes: The presidential library system is made up of ten presidential libraries and two presidential materials staffs (for Nixon and Clinton). These are not traditional libraries but rather repositories for preserving and making available the papers, records, and other historical materials of presidents starting with Herbert Hoover. Each presidential library contains a museum and provides an active series of public programs.

Presidential Recordings and Materials Preservation Act, n. (**PRMPA,** abbr.) ~ A federal law (44 USC 2111 note) that required Nixon presidential historical materials relating to "Abuses of Governmental Power" (i.e., Watergate) and to the constitutional and statutory duties of President Nixon and his White House staff to be transferred to the National Archives and Records Administration for retention and processing for public access.

Notes: PRMPA applies only to presidential historical materials from the administration of Richard Nixon. Under the statute and implementing regulations (36 CFR 1275), materials related to 'Abuses of Governmental Power' (as defined) and to the constitutional and statutory duties of the president and his White House staff are retained and processed for public access by NARA, while NARA must segregate and return to the estate of former President Nixon those specific materials identified as personal.

†*281 (USC, 44 USC 2201):* When the Archivist considers it to be in the public interest he may accept for deposit – 1) the papers and other historical materials of a President or former President of the United States, or other official or former official of the Government, and other papers relating to and contemporary with a President or former President of the United States, subject to restrictions agreeable to the Archivist as to their use; and – 2) documents, including motion-picture films, still pictures, and sound recordings, from private sources that are appropriate for preservation by the Government as evidence of its organization, functions, policies, decisions, procedures, and transactions.

presidential records, n. ~ Official records from the office of the President of the United States, as defined in 44 USC 2201 (*see citation*).

BT: record

†*281 (USC, 44 USC 2201):* The term 'Presidential records' means documentary materials, or any reasonably segregable portion thereof, created or received by the President, his immediate staff, or a unit or individual of the Executive Office of the President whose function is to advise and assist the President, in the course of conducting activities which relate to or have an effect upon the carrying out of the constitutional, statutory, or other official or ceremonial duties of the President. Such term includes any documentary materials relating to the political activities of the President or members of his staff, but only if such activities relate to or have a direct effect upon the carrying out of constitutional, statutory, or other official or ceremonial duties of the President; but does not include any documentary materials that are official records of an agency (as defined in section 552(e) [1] of title 5, United States Code); personal records; stocks of publications and stationery; or extra copies of documents produced only for convenience of reference, when such copies are clearly so identified.

Presidential Records Act, n. ~ A federal law (44 USC 2201–2207) passed in 1978 that governs the official records of presidents, vice presidents, and their staffs that were created or received after 20 January 1981.

RT: National Archives and Records Administration

Notes: The act made the public the legal owner of the official records of the president, which were formerly private records, and established a new statutory structure under which presidents must manage their records and the National Archives and Records Administration controls and provides access to the records after the end of each president's term.

press copy ~ *see:* letterpress copybook

pressing, n. ~ All copies of a published work produced by a molding process.

RT: printing

Notes: Examples of materials issued in a pressing include phonograph records, compact discs, and DVDs. A single edition of any of these formats may be released in several pressings, using the same molds. Although produced at different times, the works are essentially identical. A pressing is roughly equivalent to a printing.

preventive care (also **preventive conservation**), n. ~ The mitigation of deterioration and damage through the formulation and implementation of policies and procedures for appropriate environmental conditions; handling and maintenance during storage, exhibition, packing, transport, and use; integrated pest management; emergency preparedness and response; and reformatting and duplication.

primary source, n. ~ Material that contains firsthand accounts of events and that was created contemporaneous to those events or later recalled by an eyewitness.

RT: secondary source

Notes: Primary sources emphasize the lack of intermediaries between the thing or events being studied and reports of those things or events based on the belief that firsthand accounts are more accurate. Examples of primary sources include letters and diaries; government, church, and business records; oral histories; photographs, motion pictures, and videos; maps and land records; and blueprints. Newspaper articles contemporaneous with the events described are traditionally considered primary sources, although the reporter may have compiled the story from witnesses, rather than being an eyewitness. Artifacts and specimens may also be primary evidence if they are the object of study.

†223 *(Personal communication, Leon C. Miller, 27 August 2004):* Whether something is a primary or secondary source depends on how it is used, not some quality of the document or record itself. . . . For example, Sandburg's biography of Lincoln is a primary source for Sandburg researchers but a secondary source for Lincoln researchers.

†249 *(Robyns 2001, p. 368):* Primary sources, we must constantly reiterate, are the subjective interpretations of another person's observation of an event or activity. Not surprisingly, therefore, many professional historians have written that it is their duty to approach primary sources with a healthy skepticism in the research process.

primary value, n. ~ The value of records derived from the original use that caused them to be created.

DF: secondary value

BT: value

RT: administrative value, archival value, fiscal value, legal value

Notes: Primary values include administrative, fiscal, legal, and operational value. These values relate to the usefulness or significance to the creator as regards managing ongoing, day-to-date programmatic and housekeeping activities, tracking finances and budgets, and protecting legal interests. The records that result from these activities can demonstrate accomplishments, accountability, fiscal responsibility, and rights and interests.

†112 *(Ham 1993, p. 7):* Primary values are ephemeral. Though a few records may have long-term or even permanent primary value, most of these values expire when the activity or action that resulted in the record's creation is completed. For example, when a political campaign has run its course, when there is a satisfactory settlement of a will in a probate court, or when the seven years of risk of an IRS audit have passed, the primary value of the records ends. For the archivist, primary values usually are of secondary importance.

†259 *(Schellenberg 1984, p. 58):* The values that inhere in modern public records are of two kinds: primary values for the originating agency itself and secondary value for other agencies and private users. Public records are created to accomplish the purposes for which an agency has been created – administrative, fiscal, legal, and operating. But public records are preserved in an archival institution because they have value that will exist long after they cease to be of current use, and because their values will be for others than the current users.

Princeton file, n. ~ A container with an open top, back, and lower part of the front and that is used to store loose or flimsy materials, such as pamphlets.

BT: pamphlet box

Notes: A Princeton file is distinguished from a cut-corner pamphlet box, which is open on the top and upper half of the back.

principal copy ~ *see:* record copy

print, n. ~ 1. Paper or a similar flat material that bears text or a design that has been transferred or impressed from a plate, block, or screen. – 2. A single copy or version made using such a process. – 3. Paper that bears a photographic image, especially a positive image. – 4. MOTION PICTURES · A copy of a film made from a negative, especially a copy made for distribution.

DF: photograph

BT: picture

NT: blueprint, brownprint, collotype

RT: dye transfer process, electrostatic process, engraving, etching, halftone, image, imbibition process, impression, letterpress, lithography, photomechanical, pigment print, plate, thermography, visual materials

Notes: Print[1] encompasses a wide range of materials produced using different processes. Processes used for images include etching, lithography, engraving, woodcut, and silkscreen. Processes for text include letterpress, offset lithography, and laser printing. Prints are usually ink on paper, although other materials may be used. This sense of print is distinguished from photographic prints (print[4]), which are produced by the photochemical action of light rather than by a mechanical process.

print film, n. ~ 1. MICROGRAPHICS, MOTION PICTURES · A fine-grain, high-resolution film with a characteristic curve designed for making contact copies. – 2. PHOTOGRAPHY · Negative film; film used to make prints rather than slides or transparencies.

BT: film

RT: micrographics

BT: Broader Term • *NT:* Narrower Term • *RT:* Related Term • *DF:* Distinguish From

†301 (Zwaneveld 2000, Eddy Zwaneveld, 17 August 2000): The problem is that the manufacturers of print film use shorter life expectancy criteria for the design of their print film than for film production or film printing elements. A print would typically be worn out by or before the time the color would fade and that moment arrives much sooner if a print is in theatrical circulation. Even when an unused print is stored in the dark though and when stored under the same conditions as a negative or intermediate element, it will fade more quickly.

printed archives ~ *see:* printed records

printed records, n. ~ Copies of published and near-print documents created or received by an individual or organization and preserved because of their enduring value.

> *BT:* record
>
> *Notes:* A collection of printed records is called a **printed archives.**

printer, n. ~ 1. The individual or organization responsible for the printing of a book, as distinct from the publisher. – 2. A computer peripheral used to transform electronic information to a tangible medium, such as text or images on paper.

> *NT:* impact printer, inkjet printer, laser printer
>
> *Notes:* A printer is distinguished from a press, the latter using type or plates to transfer ink to the print medium.

printing, n. ~ 1. PUBLISHING · All the copies of a book printed at one time; an impression². – 2. A style of handwriting in which the characters are formed separately; a disjoined hand.

> *DF:* edition
>
> *Syn:* disjoined hand
>
> *RT:* cursive, impression, pressing
>
> *Notes:* An edition¹ may include several printings¹. However, any change made to the type or plates would result in a different edition. – Printing² is distinguished from cursive.

printing dupe, n. ~ An intermediate that is used exclusively to make copies of an edited master.

> *BT:* intermediate
>
> *RT:* camera microfilm

printing-out paper, n. ~ Photographic paper in which the image is formed through the action of light alone.

> *BT:* photograph
>
> *Notes:* Printing-out papers were prevalent from the invention of photography through most of the 19th century. A negative was sandwiched between glass and a sheet of printing-out paper in a frame, and the whole was then placed in the sun. The light slowly changed the silver halide to metallic silver. The photographer could monitor the printing progress in reduced light by pulling the paper away from the negative; if more exposure was needed, the sandwich was returned to sunlight to continue printing. After exposure, the prints were fixed to halt further development. Printing-out papers produce images that are a purplish brown and were usually toned to a purple black. Unfixed printing-out paper, often used for portrait proof prints, are often rust-colored and show signs of silver mirroring. Eastman Kodak marketed printing-out paper under the name Studio Proof, intended specifically for portrait proofs.

> *†125 (Horrigan 2003, p. 411):* Portrait photographers submitted proofs to cus-

tomers on unfixed printing-out paper that would darken completely in a week or two. This prevented a customer's keeping the proofs as 'good enough,' and not ordering finished prints.

printout, n. ~ Paper output from a computer.

> *Syn:* hard copy
>
> *RT:* fanfold, typescript
>
> †265 *(Skupsky and Mantaña 1994, p. 61):* Although computer records may not be admissible if prepared specifically for trial, courts have generally concluded that printouts made long after the original data entry, including printouts made specifically for trial, are admissible. . . . Another court has concluded that, although printouts made long after the data entry and in the regular course of business are admissible, printouts made specifically in preparation for trial are not made in the regular course of business, and are not admissible.

PRISM, n. ~ A research project at Cornell University exploring preservation of digital information.

> *Notes:* See http://www.library.cornell.edu/preservation/prism.html.
>
> †17 *(InterPARES Authenticity, p. 30):* Cornell University's PRISM Project, which focuses on policy enforcement for ensuring information integrity in the areas of preservation, reliability, interoperability, security, and metadata. PRISM is investigating the long-term survivability of digital information, reliability of information resources and services, interoperability, and security (including the privacy rights of users of information and the intellectual property rights of content creators), and the metadata that make it possible to ensure information integrity in digital libraries.

privacy, n. ~ 1. The quality or state of being free from public scrutiny. – 2. The quality or state of having one's personal information or activities protected from unauthorized use by another.

> *RT:* anonymity, confidential, data protection, disclosure-free extract, practical obscurity, public, publicity rights, sensitive
>
> *Notes:* Under tort law, invasion of privacy includes theft of one's identity, intentionally disturbing one's solitude, disclosing nonpublic information about another, and placing another in a false public light. In some states, publicity rights are covered under privacy laws.
>
> †48 *(CJS, Records §104):* The Freedom of Information Act does not apply to personnel and medical files and similar files the disclosure of which would constitute a clearly unwarranted invasion of personal privacy.
>
> †48 *(CJS, Records §76):* Under the [Privacy Act of 1974 (5 USCA §552a and note)], subject to exceptions, no agency shall disclose any record which is contained in a system of records by any means of communication to any person, or to another agency, except pursuant to a written request by, or with the prior written consent of, the individual to whom the record pertains.

private key, n. ~ In a dual-key encryption system, the sequence of characters that is used to decrypt ciphertext encrypted with the corresponding public key.

> *RT:* public key cryptography

private papers ~ *see:* personal papers

privileged information, n. ~ Information that need not be disclosed in legal proceedings, even though it may be relevant.

Notes: Different privileges grant individuals the right to withhold information in certain circumstances. For example, attorneys and accountants cannot be compelled to disclose information about their clients, and journalists cannot be forced to disclose confidential sources. Some freedom of information laws include a deliberative-process privilege that allows a government agency to restrict access to some draft materials so that government employees can engage in frank and open discussion of ideas.

probative record, n. ~ A record that serves as evidence of an action taken.

> *BT:* record

> *†17 (InterPARES Authenticity, p. 15):* Records whose written form is required by the juridical system as proof that an action has taken place prior to its documentation.

procedure, n. ~ 1. The manner and steps in which some action is taken. – 2. Computing · A group of instructions in a program designed to perform a specific set of operations; a subroutine

> *DF:* function

> *NT:* executive procedure

> *RT:* policy, standard

> *Notes:* A procedure[1] may be written or unwritten. – Procedure[2] is typically associated with high-level programming languages. In some languages a procedure is distinguished from a function[2], the latter performing an operation on some values and returning a result based on those values. In low-level languages, a procedure is typically called a subroutine.

> *†70 (Duranti 1998, p. 131):* It might be observed that in many cases we already know the procedures[1] [that create documentary products] from various sources such as annual reports, procedure manuals, policy files. But do we? These sources tell us how administrative action was supposed to be carried out, rather than how it actually was carried out; they tell us what the procedures ought to be, what management expected to happen, what the system was built for, and finally what the image was that the creating agency wished to reflect. On the contrary, an analysis of the procedures which begins from their final products allows a verification of the discrepancies between rules and actuality and of the continuous mediation taking place between legal-administrative apparatus and society, and makes the reality attainable. This has always been the primary purpose of diplomatic analysis, and its value has not decreased.

> *†70 (Duranti 1998, p. 115–116):* [An analysis of the ideal structure of an integrated procedure[1] that generates a document includes the following phases. 1) Introductory phase or *initiative*, the start of the procedure. 2) Preliminary phase or *inquiry*, the elements necessary to evaluate the situation. 3) *Consultation*, the collection of opinions and advice. 4) *Deliberation*, the final decision making. 5) Controlling phase or *deliberative control*, the control exercised by a physical or juridical person different from the author of the document embodying the transaction, on the substance of the deliberation and/or on its form. 6) *Execution*, all the actions which give formal character to the transaction (i.e., validation, communication, notification, publication).

proceedings, n. ~ 1. A record of business conducted at a meeting, especially the published papers of a conference; transactions[5]. – 2. Law · The actions taken in a court, from commencement to judgment.

DF: minutes

Syn: transaction

process control, n. ~ The management and oversight of actions taken on records in a records center or archives.

RT: intellectual control, physical control

processable document, n. ~ A file format for electronic exchange and representation that allows the content to be modified by the recipient.

RT: document interchange, Open Document Architecture

Notes: A processable document includes information about its logical structure that allows it to be revised.

processed document ~ *see:* near-print document

processing, n. ~ 1. The arrangement, description, and housing of archival materials for storage and use by patrons. – 2. The steps taken to make the latent image on exposed photographic or microfilm materials visible; see archival processing[1]. – 3. COMPUTING · The machine execution of instructions in a computer program.

NT: arrangement, description

RT: archival processing

Notes: Some archives include accessioning as part of processing.

†133 *(Ford):* A collective term used in archival administration that refers to the activity required to gain intellectual control of records, papers, or collections, including accessioning, arrangement, culling, boxing, labeling, description, preservation and conservation.

producer, n. ~ An individual responsible for the overall administration and finances of a motion picture, video, theatrical, or audio program.

RT: publisher

Notes: A producer may also have a role in the artistic and creative aspects of the program.

production, n. ~ 1. The performance of a creative work. – 2. All the steps involved in the preparation and presentation of such a performance. – 3. The process of manufacturing something, especially in mass quantities. – 4. LAW · The process of retrieving documents and making them available for use in a legal proceeding, especially as part of discovery.

RT: discovery

Notes: Production[1] includes, for example, plays, motion pictures, video programs, audio recordings, and similar performances.

production company, n. ~ An organization responsible for the financial, technical, and administrative aspects relating to the preparation and creation of a motion picture, video program, audio recording, or similar work.

production date, n. ~ DESCRIPTION · The date on which a motion picture, video program, sound recording, or similar creative work (a production) was completed.

BT: date

Notes: When expressed as a range, production dates refer to the start and end of production.

production papers, n. ~ Manuscripts and proofs reflecting the different stages of a creative work during its preparation.

Notes: Production papers for motion picture, video, or theatrical productions may include scripts[3], set and costume designs, and reports and schedules. For books, they may include the original manuscript or typescript, editorial notes, and galley proofs. Production papers often have handwritten annotations and changes.

profile, n. ~ 1. A vertical cross-section representing the different layers of a landform. – 2. The outline of a person's face. – 3. A short descriptive article, especially a biography.

  BT: cartographic record

PROFS Case, n. ~ A lawsuit (*Armstrong v. Executive Office of the President*, 1 F.3d 1274 [DC Cir 1993]) filed by Scott Armstrong, American Historical Association, the American Library Association, the Center for National Security, and others, relating to access to and the disposition of email records.

  RT: electronic mail

  Notes: The case takes its name from the IBM PROFS (Professional Office System) email system used in the White House. In a later opinion, the US Court of Appeals also held that National Security Council staff solely advise and assist the president and thus create presidential records not immediately subject to the Freedom of Information Act (see *Armstrong v. Executive Office of the President*, 90 F.3d 553 (D.C. Cir. 1996), cert. denied, 520 U.S. 1239 (1997)).

  †21 (*Baron 1999*): On January 19, 1989, the last day of the Reagan Administration, a federal court in Washington, D.C. granted a temporary restraining order to preserve a collection of PROFS backup tapes from the National Security Council (NSC) and EOP's Office of Administration, in a lawsuit brought by several individuals and nonprofit associations captioned *Armstrong v. Bush* and filed as a Federal Records Act (and Freedom of Information Act) challenge. The PROFS tapes contained, among other things, electronic mail messages of Oliver North concerning the Iran-Contra affair, transmitted over the NSC's internal e-mail system. [Citing *Armstrong v. Bush*, 721 F. Supp. 343, 345 n.1 (D.D.C. 1989).] ... On January 6, 1993, as amended on January 11, Judge Charles R. Richey issued an injunction against the EOP (including the NSC), holding that based on the characteristics of the proprietary e-mail systems in place within the EOP and NSC at the time, the defendants' written records policies directing that hard copies of e-mail messages be printed out as the sole means of preserving e-mail records was arbitrary, capricious and contrary to the U.S. federal records laws. [Note: *Armstrong v. Executive Office of the President*, 810 F. Supp. 335 (D.D.C. 1993).] This holding was affirmed on later appeal to the U.S. Court of Appeals for the District of Columbia. [Note: See *Armstrong v. Executive Office of the President*, 1 F.3d 1274 (D.C. Cir. 1993). On January 15, 1993, the government's emergency motion for a partial stay of the district court's Order was granted by the U.S. Court of Appeals, allowing EOP components to delete e-mail messages from their live operating systems, so long as all record information was preserved in identical form on backup tapes. Order of January 15, 1993, Civ. No. 93-5002 (D.C. Cir.).]

program, n. ~ 1. A function or activity of an organization. – 2. A brochure or leaflet describing a musical or theatrical performance. – 3. A public performance. – 4. A performance broadcast on television or radio. – 5. COMPUTING · A sequence of instructions given to a computer to perform a specific task; a computer application.

  Syn: application, computer program

  RT: code

program records (also **substantive records**), n. ~ Records that relate to the substantive activities an organization undertakes to accomplish its mission or mandate; operational records[2].

    DF: administrative records

    Syn: operational records

    BT: record

    RT: operational value

programming language, n. ~ The semantics and syntax used to write instructions for a computer.

    RT: natural language

    Notes: A programming language can be low- or high-level. Low-level programming languages, such as assembly language, reflect the particular hardware of the machine for which they are written. A high-level language, such as C, Basic, Cobol, Fortran, or Pascal, must be translated to a form that the machine can understand through the use of a compiler.

project file ~ *see:* case file

projection, n. ~ 1. DRAFTING · A technical or architectural drawing, especially one that emphasizes the geometry of the object rather than the appearance of depth. – 2. MAPS · Techniques for representing three-dimensional space on a two-dimensional surface.

    RT: cartography, drawing, perspective

    Notes: Examples of projection[2] include Mercator, cylindrical, sinusoidal, and Goode's.

    †192 *(Monmonier 1996, p. 8):* Map projections, which transform the curved, three-dimensional surface of the planet into a flat, two-dimensional plane, can greatly distort map scale. Although the globe can be a true scale model of the earth, with a constant scale at all points and in all directions, the flat map stretches some distances and shortens others, so that scale varies from point to point.

promptness, n. ~ The quality of being timely.

    RT: reliability

    †48 *(CJS, Records §11):* It is essential to the official character of public registers that entries therein be made promptly or without such long delay as to impair their credibility.

proof print, n. ~ A photographic print, generally supplied with similar images, supplied to a client to aid in the selection of the version that will be used for the final copy.

    Notes: Proof prints are often unfinished in the sense that they may not have been retouched or the exposure may be imperfect. In the 20th century, studio photographers often provided customers with proof prints on unfixed printing-out paper. Over time, the image would degrade, taking on an overall bronze cast, forcing customers to purchase prints they wanted to keep.

protection master, n. ~ A high-quality copy of an edited master that can be used to make printing masters.

    BT: master

    Notes: A protection master is created for use in case the original master is damaged.

    †97 *(Feltenstein 2003):* The fine-grain [master], which is also called a 'protection master,' can be used to make duplicate negatives from which other prints are struck.

Also, if the original negative is damaged – and many of them eventually are – you can copy a segment of the fine-grain and insert a new section of 'dupe' negative into the original. The fine-grain print yields a negative that looks almost like what you would get from a camera negative. There's very little loss of sharpness or detail.

protocol, n. ~ 1. The rules of etiquette and ceremony that govern diplomatic relations between states. – 2. A diplomatic document, especially a treaty or compact, signed by the negotiators but subject to ratification. – 3. An amendment to a treaty or convention. – 4. SCIENCE · Procedures followed during experiments. – 5. COMPUTING · A standard that describes the technical processes used to exchange information, especially across a network. – 6. DIPLOMATICS · The first portion of a document, containing the administrative context of the action (the persons involved, the time and place, and the subject) and the initial formulas.

   BT: intrinsic element

   Notes: Examples of protocols[5] include TCP/IP, SMTP, HTTP, and FTP.

Protocol for Metadata Harvesting ~ *see:* Open Archives Initiative

protocol register, n. ~ A register containing unique, consecutive numbers assigned to records and including additional information about the identity of persons involved and the documentary context of the record.

   †*178 (MacNeil 1995, p. 26):* The purpose of registers [in Italy known as protocol registers] is to control the stages of distribution and transit for every official document that passes through the registry. The protocol register, for example, records the document's protocol number (i.e., a unique identifier), the name and official title of the sender, the protocol number in the office of the sender (if applicable), the nature of the action, and indication of any enclosures and their types, the assigned classification number, and the office handling the matter.

prototype, n. ~ The first manifestation of a thing or process.

   Syn: original

   Notes: A prototype connotes something that is complete, as opposed to a design or sketch. However, a prototype also connotes something that is being demonstrated and subject to being refined.

provenance, n. (**provenancial**, adj.) ~ 1. The origin or source of something. – 2. Information regarding the origins, custody, and ownership of an item or collection.

   RT: arrangement, context, creator, custodial history, entity of origin, fonds, office of origin, original order, provenience

   Notes: Provenance[1] is a fundamental principle of archives, referring to the individual, family, or organization that created or received the items in a collection. The **principle of provenance** or the *respect des fonds* dictates that records of different origins (provenance) be kept separate to preserve their context.

   †*70 (Duranti 1998, p. 177):* The principle of provenance, as applied to appraisal, leads us to evaluate records on the basis of the importance of the creator's mandate and functions, and fosters the use of a hierarchical method, a 'top-down' approach, which has proved to be unsatisfactory because it excludes the 'powerless transactions,' which might throw light on the broader social context, from the permanent record of society.

   †*98 (Gilliland-Swetland 2000a, p. 12):* The principle of provenance has two components: records of the same provenance should not be mixed with those of a different provenance, and the archivist should maintain the original order in which the records were created and kept. The latter is referred to as the principle of

original order in English and *Registraturprinzip* in German. The French conception of *respect des fonds* did not include the same stricture to maintain original order (referred to in French as *respect de l'ordre intérieure*), largely because French archivists had been applying what was known as the principle of pertinence and rearranging records according to their subject content.

†121 (Henson 1993, p. 67): APPM recognizes the primacy of *provenance* in archival description. This principle holds that that significance of archival materials is heavily dependent on the context of their creation, and that the arrangement and description of these materials should be directly related to their original purpose and function.

provenance access, n. ~ A technique of locating relevant materials based on characteristics of the origins of the materials (the provenance).

RT: subject access

Notes: Provenance access complements subject access. For example, reviewing a repository's collections, listed by provenance, can often be a useful means of locating materials relevant to a query. For example, a researcher studying Phoenix in the 19th century might start with the papers of the George Luhrs and Dwight Heard because of their prominence as civic leaders. That researcher might reject the papers of city archaeologist Odd Halseth, because his work related to pre-Columbian cultures.

provenience, n. ~ The site of an archaeological excavation.

RT: provenance

Notes: Provenience and provenance are fundamentally synonyms for source or origin. However, provenance is used in archives and museology, whereas provenience is used in archaeology.

prox. ~ *see:* inst

psychrometer, n. ~ An instrument used to measure relative humidity and to calculate dew point.

RT: hygrometer

Notes: A psychrometer uses two thermometers. The bulb of one is wet, the other is dry. As water evaporates from the wet bulb, its temperature drops. A chart used to compare the two readings indicates the relative humidity. A **sling psychrometer** has its thermometers mounted so that they can be swung to create air flow.

Pub. L., abbr. ~ [United States] public law.

Notes: Also PL and P.L.

public, adj. ~ 1. Available and open to all; not private. – 2. Relating or belonging to the members of a community. – 3. Relating or belonging to the government rather than an individual or organization. – 4. CORPORATIONS · Having shares that are traded on an open market.

RT: confidential, privacy

public hearing, n. ~ A formal proceeding that is, within reasonable limits, open to anyone and that provides members of the audience an opportunity to present comments to the presiding officials.

DF: public meeting law

BT: hearing

public key, n. ~ In a dual-key encryption system, the sequence of characters that is used to encrypt plaintext so that it cannot be read without the corresponding private key.

RT: public key cryptography

public key cryptography, n. ~ A technique to encrypt and decrypt messages using a pair of different keys.

BT: cryptography

RT: private key, public key, public key infrastructure, symmetric-key encryption

Notes: Because the key used to decrypt a message cannot be deduced from the key used to encode a message, the encoding key can be made public. Anyone can use an individual's public key to encrypt a message that only the individual can decrypt using the private key. Public key cryptography was a breakthrough because it was the first technology that not require keys be exchanged in advance. Two individuals, each with their own public and private keys, can send each other messages that are completely confidential. Alice sends Bob messages using Bob's public key; only Bob has the key to decrypt and read her messages. Bob sends Alice messages using Alice's public key; only Alice has the private key to read his messages.

Public key cryptography can be used to authenticate the sender of a message. A message encoded with the private key can be decrypted with the public key. If Alice receives an encrypted message that can be read with Bob's public key and if she has confidence that the public key is Bob's, then she can have equal confidence that the message is from Bob. A certificate authority serves as a trusted third party to give Alice confidence in Bob's public key.

†168 (S Levy 2001, p. 70): Instead of using one single secret key, you could use a key pair. The tried-and-true symmetrical key would be replaced by a dynamic duo. One would be able to do the job of scrambling a plaintext message – performing the task in such a way that outsiders couldn't read it – but a secret trapdoor would be built into the message. The other portion of the key pair was like a latch that could spring open that trapdoor and let its holder read the message. And here was the beauty of the scheme: yes, that second key – the one that flipped open the trapdoor – was of course something that had to be kept under wraps, safe form the prying hand of potential eavesdroppers. But its mate, the key that actually performed the encryption, didn't have to be a secret at all. In fact, you wouldn't want it to be secret. You'd be happy to see it distributed far and wide.

public key infrastructure, n. (**PKI**, abbr.) ~ The underlying systems and processes necessary to support the trustworthiness and wide-scale use of public key encryption to authenticate individuals in a digital environment, especially over the Internet.

RT: certificate authority, digital certificate, Information Technology – Open Systems Interconnection – The Directory: Public-key and Attribute Certificate Frameworks, public key cryptography

Notes: Certificate authorities (CAs) are key components of PKI. They serve as a trusted third party that certifies that someone using a public key is, in fact, the person he or she claims to be. A CA issues an X.509 digital certificate that serves as an identification card, and the CA offers a service to validate its digital certificates.

PKI defines the encryption techniques, identification procedures, and other processes necessary for the system to be trustworthy.

public meeting law, n. ~ A statute requiring a government agency to conduct business in plain view of the public.

DF: public hearing

RT: sunshine law

Notes: Public meeting laws are intended to give citizens the opportunity to observe government so that officials can be held accountable for their actions. Most public meeting laws require advance notice of meetings, including the agenda. The laws often contain provisions as to how and when officials can meet, both to ensure that no agreements are made by circumventing the law and to allow certain types of business to be conducted in private.

public record, n. ~ 1. Data or information in a fixed format that was created or received by a government agency in the course of business and that is preserved for future reference. – 2. Records filed with a government agency to give constructive notice. – 3. Government records that are not restricted and are accessible to the public.

BT: record

RT: constructive notice, local records

Notes: A number of federal laws define public record[1] in different contexts. For example, 44 USC 3301, Public Printing and Documents, defines records (cited below), as does the Freedom of Information Act, and the Family Education Rights and Privacy Act. Public record is also defined in the Federal Rules of Evidence. Many states also have similar definitions of public record in different statutes. In general, the legal definition of public record encompasses almost any information held in a governmental office. However, freedom of information laws, also called open records laws, may restrict the public's right of access to those records. For example, records relating to current procurement processes, pending litigation, or national security are typically restricted to protect government interests.

†10 *(AJS, Records §26):* The question whether raw data collected by public departments or officials constitutes a public record, within the meaning of the rule giving private persons the right of access to, inspection of, or copying of public records, appears to depend largely on the provisions of the statute giving the right of access, inspection, or copying. Some cases take the view that material gathered by way of preliminary investigation does not become a public record before some official action of approval or disapproval. On the other hand, the drawing of a distinction between writings representing tentative action and those memorializing ultimate action has been regarded as objectionable, not only because it is inconsistent with the principle which underlies the statutes making public writings freely available for inspection, but also because it provides a device by which a public official can hinder a citizen's legitimate attempt to obtain writings which are clearly within the strictest definition of a public record.

†48 *(CJS, Records §31):* In the absence of a showing of fraud or unauthorized alteration, a public record imports absolute verity. It is presumed to be correct, and cannot be collaterally attacked. The record is prima facie evidence of the facts therein set forth, and under some circumstances may be regarded as conclusive evidence thereof.

†48 *(CJS, Records §2):* A 'public record' is defined as one required by law to be kept, or necessary to be kept in the discharge of a duty imposed by law, or directed by law to serve as a memorial and evidence of something written, said, or done, or a written memorial made by a public officer authorized to perform that function, or a writing filed in a public office. ¶ The elements essential to constitute a public record are, namely, that it be a written memorial, that it be made by a public officer, and that the officer be authorized by law to make it. . . . The two main requirements

of a public record are that it shall be accurate and durable. . . . A record is intended not only to give an instrument perpetuity, but also publicity, or to give notice.

†84 (Fed. R. Evid., 803 (8)): Public records and reports. Records, reports, statements, or data compilations, in any form, of public offices or agencies, setting forth (A) the activities of the office or agency, or (B) matters observed pursuant to duty imposed by law as to which matters there was a duty to report, excluding, however, in criminal cases matters observed by police officers and other law enforcement personnel, or (C) in civil actions and proceedings and against the Government in criminal cases, factual findings resulting from an investigation made pursuant to authority granted by law, unless the sources of information or other circumstances indicate lack of trustworthiness.

†281 (USC, 44 USC 3301): Records includes all books, papers, maps, photographs, machine readable materials, or other documentary materials, regardless of physical form or characteristics, made or received by an agency of the United States Government under Federal law or in connection with the transaction of public business and preserved or appropriate for preservation by that agency or its legitimate successor as evidence of the organization, functions, policies, decisions, procedures, operations, or other activities of the Government or because of the informational value of data in them. Library and museum material made or acquired and preserved solely for reference or exhibition purposes, extra copies of documents preserved only for convenience of reference, and stocks of publications and of processed documents are not included.

public use file, n. ~ A copy of a record made available for public use in which information has been redacted in accordance with provisions of open records or privacy laws.

Syn: disclosure-free extract

publication, n. ~ 1. A work that expresses some thought in language, signs, or symbols and that is reproduced for distribution. – v. ~ 2. The act of publishing such a work.

NT: microform publication

RT: booklet, brochure, grey literature, leaflet, near-print document, open access publication, pamphlet, quasi-publication, record, report

Notes: Although traditionally associated with books and magazines, publication includes motion pictures, websites, CD-ROMs, videotapes, sound recordings, and other document formats. 'Publication' connotes a work that is widely distributed, especially by a commercial publisher. However, it also includes works of limited distribution, such as those issued by a vanity press. Similarly, a single copy of a dissertation deposited as a public record in a library may be considered published because it is available (distributed) to the public.

Works of limited distribution that have the physical characteristic of a publications, such as a binding and title page, are described as quasi-publications or near-print documents. The rise of on-demand printing using sophisticated desktop publishing software and high-quality printers is blurring the distinction between quasi-publications and publications.

Publication has a preservation function by increasing the chances that at least one copy will be preserved if other copies are damaged or destroyed.

†281 (USC, 17 USC 101): COPYRIGHT · The distribution of copies or phonorecords of a work to the public by sale or other transfer of ownership, or by

rental, lease, or lending. The offering to distribute copies or phonorecords to a group of persons for purposes of further distribution, public performance, or public display, constitutes publication. A public performance or display of a work does not of itself constitute publication.

publicity rights, n. ~ Intellectual property · An individual's exclusive privilege to control the commercial use of their identity and likeness.

> *BT:* intellectual property
>
> *RT:* privacy

publisher, n. ~ 1. An individual or organization that produces and markets creative works for distribution. – 2. The owner of a newspaper.

> *RT:* distributor, producer
>
> *Notes:* Publisher¹ is principally associated with books and periodicals but includes other formats such as music, photographs, and art reproductions.

pulp, n. ~ 1. A slurry of fibrous plant material that has been crushed or broken up, especially for use in making paper. – 2. Publishing · Genre fiction printed on cheap paper.

> *NT:* chemical wood pulp, mechanical wood pulp
>
> *Notes:* Pulp¹ may be prepared chemically or mechanically.

pulping, ~ n. ~ A technique of destroying paper documents by soaking them in water and grinding them into pulp; maceration.

> *Syn:* maceration
>
> *RT:* destruction

pulpit ladder, n. ~ A ladder with a platform at the top and a handrail along the steps and top.

> *Notes:* Pulpit ladders are generally more stable than an A-frame or extension ladder. They are commonly used for retrieving boxes of records from high shelves. A worker can easily and safely stand on the platform.

punched card *see:* Hollerith card (also **punch card, Hollerith card, IBM card, tab card**), n. ~ A card that records data or machine instructions through a pattern of perforations.

punched paper tape (also **punched tape**) ~ *see:* paper tape

purging, n. ~ The process of pulling and disposing of unwanted materials.

> *Syn:* culling, weeding

PURL ~ *see:* Persistent Uniform Resource Locator

PVA ~ *see:* polyvinyl acetate

PVC ~ *see:* polyvinyl chloride

Q

qualification of signature, n. ~ DIPLOMATICS · A reference to the title and capacity of an individual, included with the signature in a document.

qualified Dublin Core ~ *see:* Dublin Core

quality index, n. ~ MICROGRAPHICS · A standard (MS23) to evaluate the subjective relationship between the legibility of printed text and the resolution pattern resolved in a microimage.

†282 *(US Newspaper Project 2002):* First generation microfilm of newspapers shall provide a high resolution quality to allow duplication through as many as four generations. In determining the reduction ratio, the quality index (Q.I.) method as described in ANSI/AIIM MS23-1998 shall be used, with the understanding that other factors – most importantly the condition of the newspapers themselves – will directly influence the choice of both image orientation and reduction. For the master negative (first generation) a quality index of 8.0 or above is generally expected.

quasi-publication, n. ~ A booklike document that is not commercially published and that has limited distribution.

Syn: near-print document

RT: grey literature, publication, report

questioned document, n. ~ A writing of uncertain authenticity because its origin or authorship is in doubt.

R

RAD ~ *see:* Rules for Archival Description

radiograph, n. ~ An image made using high-energy radiation that can pass through an opaque object.

> *RT:* x-ray
>
> *Notes:* Radiographs may be made by x-rays, gamma rays, or atomic particles. They are commonly made using specially sensitized photographic film or, in digital imaging systems, a detector.

rag paper, n. ~ Paper made with cotton or linen fiber, instead of or in addition to pulp.

> *BT:* paper

raking light, n. ~ Illumination using rays of light almost parallel to the surface.

> *Syn:* oblique light
>
> *Notes:* The extreme angle of raking light reveals subtle changes in the shape of a surface, which may result from uneven stretching of a canvas, warping of a support, or cracks in paint or emulsion. It can also indicate how an artist applied or changed paint.

RAMP ~ *see:* Records and Archives Management Programme

random access, n. ~ Computing · A method that allows information to be retrieved from memory or storage in any order.

> *RT:* direct access, sequential access
>
> *Notes:* Random access is distinguished from serial access. Information on a hard drive is randomly accessed by directing the heads to a specific cylinder and sector. Information on a tape cannot be accessed until the heads pass all preceding data in sequence.

range, n. ~ A row of shelves made up from more than one section.

> *Syn:* row, run
>
> *RT:* section, shelving

Rare Book and Manuscript Section, n. (**RBMS,** abbr.) ~ A professional organization that promotes the interests of librarians, curators, and other specialists concerned with the acquisition, organization, security, preservation, administration, and use of special collections, including rare printed books, manuscripts, archives, graphics, music, and ephemera.

> *RT:* American Library Association
>
> *Notes:* RBMS is part of the Association of College & Research Libraries (ACRL), a division of the American Library Association.
>
> †238 *(RBMS):* RBMS works to prepare special collections libraries and librarians to better serve the needs of users by creating opportunities for professional growth in special collections librarianship. In pursuit of its mission, RBMS: defines, develops, and promulgates guidelines; initiates and encourages continuing professional education programs; promotes study, research, and publication relevant to work in special collections; [and] provides its members with a means of communication through its publications, programs, workshops, seminars, and meetings.

raster graphic, n. ~ An image formed from a grid of pixels.

> *DF:* vector graphic

RT: bitmap

Notes: Raster graphics are typically generated by scanning rows sequentially from top to bottom. A television image is an example of a raster graphic.

RBMS ~ *see:* Rare Book and Manuscript Section

RC paper ~ *see:* resin-coated paper

Notes: 'RC' is a trademark of Eastman Kodak that is used to denote its resin-coated papers.

RDF ~ *see:* Resource Description Framework

read, v. ~ 1. To view and comprehend a written language. – 2. Computing · To access data from a storage device or other input medium.

RT: access

read-only memory, n. (**ROM**, abbr.) ~ Computing · Storage containing data that can be read but not changed, especially integrated chips and certain compact discs.

RT: firmware, write once read many

Notes: Some computer chips and compact discs are examples of read-only memory. For example, most computers contain a boot program in a ROM chip, which contains instructions on how to load the operating system into random access memory (RAM). Originally, ROM chips were programmed during manufacture; they could be read but not updated. The data or instructions in programmable (PROM) and erasable programmable (EPROM) chips can be changed, but they are distinguished from RAM because they retain information after power is turned off.

reader, n. ~ 1. An individual who uses the collections and services of a repository; a customer. – 2. Micrographics · Equipment designed to enlarge the highly reduced reproduction on microfilm to make it eye-readable. – 3. Computing · Equipment or software that can transfer data from one device or format to make it available to another device or application.

DF: microform reader

Syn: patron, researcher, user

Notes: Reader[1] usually does not include repository staff.

reader-printer, n. ~ Equipment that enlarges microfilm images so that they can be easily viewed and that has the ability to make hardcopy prints of the images.

DF: enlarger-printer

RT: microfilm, microform reader

Notes: Reader-printers can produce copies in normal room light without a darkroom. Early reader-printers used a photographic process, but most reader-printers now use an electrostatic process. Some modern reader-printers incorporate scanners that create a digital copy.

reader service (also **reader's services**), n. ~ The process of facilitating patron use of a repository's facilities and collections.

RT: reference

Notes: 'Reader service' is sometimes used synonymously with reference service. However, the term is generally broader than helping patrons locate holdings relevant to their search and includes registration, orientation, and copying. In large repositories, reader service may include amenities such as food service or assistance with lodging or parking.

reading file, ~ n. ~ A file containing materials ordered by date or other time sequence that is circulated for reading or reference.

RT: chronological file

Notes: A reading file is generally distinguished from a chronological file (chron file), which is kept by its creator for personal use.

reading room (also **reference room, research room, search room**), n. ~ A secure space area designed for patrons to work with a repository's holdings.

Notes: A reading room usually has finding aids and reference materials for patron use.

real photo postcard ~ *see:* postcard

realia, n. ~ A three-dimensional object.

RT: artifact, object, replica, specimen

Notes: Anglo-American Cataloguing Rules distinguishes realia from replicas.

reappraisal (also **retention review**), n. ~ 1. ARCHIVES · The process of identifying materials that no longer merit preservation and that are candidates for deaccessioning. – 2. RECORDS MANAGEMENT · The process of reviewing materials to reassess their retention value.

RT: appraisal, deaccessioning

Notes: A repository may reappraise[1] holdings because the original appraisal was faulty, the repository's collecting policy has changed, or the perceived value of the material has changed over time.

reborn digital ~ *see:* electronic record

recall, n. ~ 1. A measure of an information system's ability to retrieve items relevant to a search, typically measured as a ratio of relevant items retrieved to all relevant items in the database. – v. ~ 2. LIBRARIES · To request a patron to return a book, especially for use by another patron.

RT: precision, relevant

Notes: It is possible to recall[1] all relevant items in a database (a 100% recall ratio), but the precision of the search is likely to be low. If a database contains 100 items, and 25 are relevant to a search, a search that returns all items has 100% recall but only 25% precision.

receipt data, n. ~ Information in electronic mail systems regarding the date and time of receipt of a message, or an acknowledgment of receipt or access by an addressee.

Notes: Receipt data is defined in 36 CFR §1234.

reciprocating file, n. ~ Equipment that stores materials in containers that rotate much like a Ferris wheel.

Notes: A reciprocating file is intended to increase the number of files per square foot of storage space.

reconditioning, n. ~ MOTION PICTURES · The process of cleaning and lubricating motion picture prints.

RT: conditioning

Notes: Reconditioning also includes removing abrasion and scratches.

record, n. ~ 1. A written or printed work of a legal or official nature that may be used as evidence or proof; a document. – 2. Data or information that has been fixed on some medium; that has content, context, and structure; and that is used as an extension of human memory or to demonstrate accountability. – 3. Data or information in a fixed form that is created or received in the course of individual or institutional activity and set aside (preserved) as evidence of that activity for

†10 (AJS, Records §7): Under direct attach a record does not import verity. No presumptions arise to support it, and it can survive only in the event that it speaks the truth and is free from error.

†10 (AJS, Records §99): He who acts in reliance on the record has behind him not only the natural equities of his position, but also the special equity arising from the protection afforded everyone who trusts the record.

†17 (InterPARES Authenticity, p. 7): A record is assumed to be a representation of a fact or act that is memorialized on a physical carrier – that is, a medium – and preserved by a physical or juridical person in the course of carrying out its activities. It follows that a record cannot exist before its elements have been inscribed or affixed to a medium.

†40 (Chambers 1988, p. 896 ff): v. ~ Probably before 1200 *recorden* to repeat, recite . . . , later to set down in writing . . . ; borrowed from Old French, repeat, recite, report, learned borrowing from Latin, and borrowed directly from Latin *recordari*, remember, call to mind. . . . – n. ~ Probably before 1300, *rekord* testimony; later record state or fact of being recorded . . . and an official written account.

†54 (Dearstyne 1992, p. 1): [Records are] . . . any type of recorded information, regardless of physical form or characteristics, created, received, or maintained by a person, institution, or organization. . . . Records are extensions of the human memory, purposefully created to record information, document transactions, communicate thoughts, substantiate claims, advance explanations, offer justifications, and provide lasting evidence of events. Their creation results from a fundamental human need to create and store information, to retrieve and transmit it, and to establish tangible connections with the past.

†66 (Duff 1996, p. 29): Records, the fundamental instrument of business transactions, are mutating from a concrete, static, structured document to formless, dynamic data that resides in a computer's memory or on a disk. As records migrate from a stable paper reality to an intangible electronic existence, their physical attributes, vital for establishing the authenticity and reliability of the evidence they contain, are threatened. . . . Records are utilitarian in nature, and are created to fulfill a business function and document business processes. . . . They are created in the first instances to control or direct an organization and to help orient staff to a common goal or purpose. They have residual value because they document the outcomes of the directing and controlling activities and because they provide evidence of an organization's rights as well as its obligations to its staff and society.

†130 (Images in Time 2003, p. 166): All images constitute a record, irrespective of the value we may attach to the information they contain.

†164 (Lemieux 2001, p. 91–92): Even within the archival profession, there are many differences among archivists' conceptualization of records. Perhaps the argument is best summed up with the observation that one person's 'management information' is another person's 'record.' . . . More generally, the research offers a warning to archivists to be wary of assuming that archival conceptualizations about records are absolutes when they are only one possible way of understanding recorded information.

†187 (McGovern and Samuels 1997, p. 20): Data become records when the content, context, and structure are tied together to provide both meaning and functionality.

†219 (Park 2001, p. 273): Indiana University's *Electronic Records Project* . . . found that records exist within the structure and context of information systems

as the consequence of a business event, but not as discrete physical objects.

†281 (USC, 5 U.S.C. §552a): The term 'record' means any item, collection, or grouping of information about an individual that is maintained by an agency, including, but not limited to, his education, financial transactions, medical history, and criminal or employment history and that contains his name, or the identifying number, symbol, or other identifying particular assigned to the individual, such as a finger or voice print or a photograph.

†281 (USC, 44 USC 3301): 'Records' includes all books, papers, maps, photographs, machine readable materials, or other documentary materials, regardless of physical form or characteristics, made or received by an agency of the United States Government under Federal law or in connection with the transaction of public business and preserved or appropriate for preservation by that agency or its legitimate successor as evidence of the organization, functions, policies, decisions, procedures, operations, or other activities of the Government or because of the informational value of data in them. Library and museum material made or acquired and preserved solely for reference or exhibition purposes, extra copies of documents preserved only for convenience of reference, and stocks of publications and of processed documents are not included.

†300 (Yates 1989, p. 12): Henry Metcalfe argued 'Now, administration without records is like music without notes – by ear. Good as far as it goes – which is but a little way – it bequeaths [sic] nothing to the future. Except in the very rudest industries, carried on as if from hand to mouth, all recognize that the present must prepare for the demands of the future, and hence records, more or less elaborate, are kept.'

record copy (also **copy of record, official copy, principal copy**), n. ~ The single copy of a document, often the original, that is designated as the official copy for reference and preservation.

    Syn: file copy

    RT: copy, official files, official record, original, record

record group (also **archive group**), n. ~ A collection of records that share the same provenance and are of a convenient size for administration.

    NT: collective record group, general record group

    RT: collection, fonds, manuscript group, subgroup

    Notes: A record group is a hierarchical division that is sometimes equivalent to provenance, representing all the records of an agency and its subordinate divisions. However, the records of a large agency may be broken into several record groups, treating the records of different divisions as separate collections rather than as a series.

†120 (APPM2 1989, p. 1.0A): A body of organizationally related records established on the basis of provenance with particular regard for the administrative history, the complexity, and the volume of records and archives of the institution or organization involved.

†124 (Holmes 1984, p. 166): Before the National Archives began using the term 'record group' the Public Record Office in Great Britain was using the term 'archive group' to designate the records of an entire agency, no matter how large, including the records of entire ministries. The British practice, we believed, if applied in the National Archives, could lead sometimes to groupings too large for

administrative convenience. We thought it better to divide the records of such large 'agencies' as departments into a number of separate record groups, usually reflecting the bureaus within departments and of 'convenient size' for administration. ¶ On the Continent the French term '*fonds d'archives*' – meaning the body or stock of records of a record-creating unit – was widely known in archival literature and accepted as the basis of arrangement work. . . . As applied in practice, the records of any subordinate office that kept records, no matter how small the office, were considered a '*fonds*.' This was going to the other extreme of 'convenient size,' and the 'record group' principle as defined in the National Archives united the records of subordinate offices under their superior offices, usually up to the bureau level. Also the records of small though essentially independent satellite agencies were often included with the records of major agencies to which they were related.

record layout, n. ~ A description of the content, length, and position of each data element of a record in a database or a data file.

> *Notes:* Record layout is independent of the physical structure of a record. For example, the same record layout may be structured using comma- or tab-separated values, or with fixed-length fields.

record series ~ *see:* series

record type, n. ~ 1. A distinctive class of records defined by their function or use. – 2. A class of records defined by their style, subject, physical characteristics, or form[2].

> *RT:* genre

> *Notes:* Examples of record types[1] include baptismal records, deeds, and accounting ledgers. – Examples of record types[2] include moving images, photographs, oral histories.

recordation, n. ~ The act of entering an instrument in a public registry or records office.

> *RT:* file, record

> †10 (AJS, Records §47): Both the necessity and the effect of recordation rest solely on statute. The recording of deeds and other instruments affecting the title to land is purely a system of legal institution, and not of common right or abstract justice. At common law in England, there was no system of registration, and the rule between claimants of the same title was found in the maxim '*prior in tempore potior est in jure.*' At an early date in the country, however, to obviate frauds arising out of secret conveyances, statutes were enacted in the several jurisdictions requiring the registration of conveyances in order to render them valid as against subsequent bona fide purchasers.

recorder, n. ~ 1. Equipment for capturing pictures, sound, or other phenomenon on some medium. – 2. A county or municipal official who is responsible for keeping public records, especially those filed for constructive notice.

> †10 (AJS, Records §195): Recorders are ministerial officers on the faithful performance of whose duties the validity of transfer of land especially depends, and they, and the sureties on their official bonds, are generally held to strict accountability for their acts and omissions in the performance of their official duties.

recording ~ *see:* phonograph record

recordkeeping, n. ~ The systematic creation, use, maintenance, and disposition of records to meet administrative, programmatic, legal, and financial needs and responsibilities.

recordkeeping requirements, n. ~ Statutory or regulatory requirements, or administrative directives, that define obligations for the creation and maintenance of records by an organization.

Notes: Recordkeeping requirements for divisions of the federal government are generally specified in 36 CFR Title XII, Subchapter B. Recordkeeping requirements for specific industries or companies as regulated by federal agencies (for example, the Securities and Exchange Commission or the Food and Drug Administration) are scattered throughout the Code of Federal Regulations.

†82 *(Federal Records Management Glossary 1989):* Since each agency is legally obligated to create and maintain adequate and proper documentation of its organization, functions, and activities, it needs to issue recordkeeping requirements for all activities at all levels and for all media and to distinguish records from nonrecord materials and personal papers.

recordkeeping system, n. ~ Coordinated policies and procedures that enable records to be collected, organized, and categorized to facilitate their management, including preservation³, retrieval, use, and disposition.

RT: filing system

Notes: Recordkeeping systems may be manual or automated.

†132 *(GAO 2002):* An electronic recordkeeping system may be either a distinct system designed specifically to provide recordkeeping functionality or part of another system. A distinct electronic recordkeeping system will comprise an application program which provides recordkeeping functionality, data and metadata needed for management of the records controlled by the system, and any electronic records managed by the system. An electronic recordkeeping system may be part of another system, such as an application system or an electronic document management system, when the design of that system includes recordkeeping functionality.

†265 *(Skupsky and Mantaña 1994, p. 63):* [A] witness who gives foundation testimony should be thoroughly familiar with the recordkeeping system that produced the document. The witness should be prepared to testify concerning the steps that went into preparation of the document, procedures used to ensure accuracy of the systems of records involved, reliance by the organization on records such as the one in question in the conduct of its everyday affairs, and any special foundation requirements that the courts have established for the particular type of record in question.

records administration ~ *see:* records management

records administration program ~ *see:* records management program

records administrator ~ *see:* records manager

records analyst, n. ~ An individual who specializes in the examination and evaluation of systems and procedures related to the creation, processing, storing and disposition of records.

RT: records manager, records officer

Notes: 'Records manager', 'records analyst', and 'records officer' are sometimes used interchangeably, although the titles often indicate different responsibilities in an organization.

Records and Archives Management Programme, n. (**RAMP**, abbr.) ~ A UNESCO program established in 1979 that seeks to make the general public and decision-makers aware of the importance of records and archives, to assist states in the establishment of efficient records and archives management infrastructures, and to participate in international debate on the principal issues facing archives.

records center, n. ~ A facility used for low-cost storage of inactive and semicurrent records before those records are destroyed or transferred to an archives.

> *BT:* repository

> *Notes:* A records center is frequently located in a warehouse facility, where space is cheaper than in prime office space.

records center box, n. ~ A corrugated cardboard box, approximately one cubic foot, designed to hold either legal or letter size files.

> *BT:* box

> *Notes:* A records center box measures approximately 10 × 12 × 16 inches. It is tall enough to hold files vertically, long enough to hold legal folders parallel to the long side, and wide enough to hold letter files parallel to the short side. Frequently, the top is not attached to the body of the box.

records continuum, n. ~ A model of archival science that emphasizes overlapping characteristics of recordkeeping, evidence, transaction, and the identity of the creator.

> *RT:* life continuum, life cycle

> *Notes:* The records continuum model deemphasizes the time-bound stages of the life cycle model.

> *†273 (Steemson):* A records continuum perspective can be contrasted with the life cycle model. The life cycle model argues that there are clearly definable stages in record-keeping and creates a sharp distinction between current and historical record-keeping. The record continuum, on the other hand, has provided Australian records managers and archivists with a way of thinking about the integration of record-keeping and archiving processes. ¶ The life cycle model sees records passing through stages until they eventually 'die', except for the 'chosen ones' that are reincarnated as archives. A continuum-based approach suggests integrated time-space dimensions. Records are 'fixed' in time and space from the moment of their creation, but record-keeping regimes carry them forward and enable their use for multiple purposes by delivering them to people living in different times and spaces. [Citing Sue McKemmish.]

records control schedule ~ *see:* retention schedule

records creation, n. ~ The first stage in the records life cycle, when records are accumulated either through creation or receipt.

> *BT:* life cycle

records custodian ~ *see:* custodian

Records Disposal Act of 1943, n. ~ A federal law (57 Stat 380) defining records and authorizing the National Archives Council to develop procedures to schedule records for disposal, to dispose of the records, and to reproduce records on microfilm so that the originals could be disposed of.

> *RT:* Federal Records Act

> *Notes:* Formally titled "An Act to Provide for the Disposal of Certain Records of the United States Government," the law was introduced as H.R. 2943 and made law on 7 July 1943.

records disposition program ~ *see:* records management program

records inventory ~ *see:* inventory

records maintenance and use, n. ~ The second stage in the records life cycle, involving the storage, retrieval, and handling of records during the course of business in an office.

> *BT:* life cycle

records management, n. ~ The systematic and administrative control of records throughout their life cycle to ensure efficiency and economy in their creation, use, handling, control, maintenance, and disposition.

> *BT:* management
>
> *RT:* content management, document management
>
> †109 *(Guercio 2001, p. 252):* The general purpose of a system of records management is that of providing the creator with the records necessary to support the efficient continuation of its activities, guaranteeing the recorded evidence, whether for internal purposes or for regulatory compliance. The specific objectives concern: the production and acquisition of reliable records for legal and technical purposes; the organization of the creation of records in an orderly and coherent manner linked to the functions performed; the transmission and preservation of authentic records; the speed and efficiency of retrieval in the context of the administrative activity carried out.

records management application, n. (**RMA,** abbr.) ~ Software that aids the management of records, especially electronic records, including the use of a file plan for classifying records and of a records schedule for identifying records that are due for disposition.

> *DF:* document management application, electronic information system
>
> *RT:* Design Criteria for Electronic Records Management Software Applications, electronic recordkeeping system
>
> *Notes:* RMAs may be used for electronic or paper records, but most are implemented to manage electronic records. RMAs are distinguished from document management applications, the latter emphasizing version control and lacking records scheduling and disposition functions. The Department of Defense has issued a performance standard for evaluating and certifying RMAs (DoD 5015.2).
>
> †132 *(GAO 2002, p. 12):* In response to the difficulty of manually managing electronic records, agencies are slowly turning to automated records management applications to help automate electronic records management life-cycle processes. The primary functions of these applications include categorizing and locating records and identifying records that are due for disposition, as well as storing, retrieving, and disposing of electronic records and assigning them to an appropriate records retention and disposition category.

records management program (also **disposition program, records administration program, record disposition program, records retention program**), n. ~ The activities, policies, and procedures within an organization to implement records management.

> *Notes:* The scope of materials that fall within a records management program depends on the context.
>
> †49 *(Cox 1990, p. 74):* To preserve the historical records of local governments, archivists must offer a comprehensive record administration program that promises cost-savings, efficient retrieval of information, and the cultural benefits of the preservation of that government's memory.

†265 *(Skupsky and Mantaña 1994, p. 132):* A records retention program that reflects consistent procedures based on business needs will generally be legally acceptable. Inconsistent procedures may be viewed as attempts to destroy evidence and circumvent justice. Improper destruction of records 'looks bad' and raises judicial concern about possible evil intent or wrongdoing.

records manager (also **records administrator**), n. ~ An individual responsible for the administration of programs for the efficient and economical handling, protecting, and disposing of records throughout their life cycle.

    RT: archivist, records analyst, records officer

    Notes: 'Records manager', 'records analyst', and 'records officer' are sometimes used interchangeably, although the titles often indicate different responsibilities in an organization. Records managers' activities include developing file plans and retention schedules; working with clerks and supervisors to identify ways to improve recordkeeping practices; reviewing appropriate media for records; planning storage facilities for active and inactive records; overseeing microfilm and scanning for space reduction or preservation; and developing and implementing essential records programs.

    †108 *(Greene, et al., 2001):* Anyone who works as a keeper of stuff in a corporate environment cannot afford to worry too much about the fine distinctions between Record Manager, Librarian, Archivist and Document Control Manager. The key is to keep what the corporation needs. Need is difficult to define, but people in corporations know when you have something, or have organized something, in a way they find useful for the task at hand. If you keep stuff no one needs, it is quite likely your collection will be trashed, given away or simply die from lack of use.

records officer, n. ~ An individual in an organization who serves as the liaison between a unit and the records management program.

    RT: records analyst, records manager

    Notes: 'Records manager', 'records analyst', and 'records officer' are sometimes used interchangeably, although the titles often indicate different responsibilities in an organization. A records officer may not be trained as a records manager but is responsible for oversight of the day-to-day records management activities within a unit under the general supervision of the records management program.

records retention program ~ *see:* records management program

records schedule (also **records retention schedule**) ~ *see:* retention schedule

records survey, n. ~ The process of gathering basic information about an organization's records, including their quantity, form, location, physical condition, storage facilities, rate of accumulation, and associated business processes.

    BT: survey

    Notes: Records surveys facilitate planning for records management programs.

recto, n. ~ 1. The front of a printed sheet. – 2. A right-hand page in a bound work that is open.

    RT: obverse, verso

    Notes: In Western tradition, the recto is the right page in a spread and usually bears an odd page number. It is the opposite side from the verso.

red rot (also **red decay**), n. ~ 1. The deterioration of leather into a powder. – 2. The hardening and embrittling of leather.

    RT: powdering

Notes: Leather bindings before 1830 may become hard and brittle. Later leather bindings suffer red rot, which may completely destroy the leather.

red tape, n. ~ Bureaucratic forms and processes that have become an end in themselves and an obstacle to accomplishing some objective.

RT: bureaucracy

Notes: The term is derived from red linen tape (sometimes called red rope) used to bind documents.

†167 *(D Levy 2001, p. 61):* Who among us hasn't felt trapped in a tangle of paperwork and bureaucratic red tape, unable to make a move without a form?

redaction, n. ~ 1. The process of concealing sensitive information in a document before being released to someone not authorized to see that information. – 2. FORMAL · The process of editing or revising a document for publication.

Syn: cleaning

RT: disclosure-free extract

Notes: Redaction[1] may be used to protect an individual's privacy or to ensure classified information is not compromised.

†66 *(Duff 1996, p. 35):* Finally, the record must be redactable, which means that the system must be able to mask part of the record. This last requirement is particularly important for systems that carry personal or proprietary information.

redox, n. ~ A blemish that appears as small, reddish spots on gelatin silver photographs.

Notes: 'Redox' describes the process that forms the blemishes, a localized, cyclic reduction and oxidation of the silver in the image area. Redox appears most commonly on film (including microfilm), but may also appear on prints.

reduction printing, n. ~ The process of duplicating a film onto a format that is smaller than the original.

reduction ratio, n. ~ A linear measure of the proportion of decrease in image size between an original and its reproduction.

RT: magnification

Notes: In an image with a 12:1 reduction ratio, a twelve-inch ruler would measure one inch on the film.

reel, n. ~ A hub with flanges used to store film or tape.

RT: flange, hub, spool

reel pack ~ *see:* pack

reel-to-reel ~ *see:* open reel

reference, n. ~ 1. A note pointing to the source of information cited. – 2. A note pointing to sources for more information. – 3. An entry in a catalog or index directing the user to another heading; a cross-reference. – 4. A service to aid patrons in locating materials relevant to their interests; see reference interview. – 5. Something used for comparison. – 6. Consultation; use.

NT: equivalence relation, name-title reference, upward reference, use reference, used for reference

RT: cross-reference, note, reader service, reference interview

†68 *(Duff and Johnson 2001, p. 47–48):* When making reference[4] requests, either in person or over the telephone, to a reference librarian or archivist, or to an information retrieval system, a user will refine his or her search request several times depending on the feedback from the person or the system.

†96 *(Gartrell 1997, p. 59):* Providing reference service for JWT and other business users quickly showed us some distinctions between our accustomed academic researchers and those in the business world. We found that business inquirers most often need the answer, they need it now, and want it in 'packaged' form. They are not, as a rule, much interested in where the answer came from or in the interesting twists in the process of finding it. Scholars are more likely to enjoy the chase and participate in an exchange of ideas about how to track down an elusive bit of documentation.

reference code, n. ~ A unique combination of letters and numbers used to identify a folder or item to facilitate storage and retrieval.

> *Syn:* call number
>
> *Notes:* Reference codes are often hierarchical, made up of separate numbers for collection, series, folder, and item numbers, or collection, box, and folder numbers. For example, RC 15:56/21 might represent the 21st item in the 56th box in the 15th collection.

reference copy, n. ~ 1. A copy of a record kept for easy access to the information it contains, as opposed to its intrinsic or evidential value. – 2. A copy of a record distributed to make recipients aware of the content but not directing the recipient to take any action on the matter. – 3. A specific copy used as a benchmark for purposes of checking the quality of other copies.

> *BT:* copy
>
> *RT:* information copy

reference interview, n. ~ A conversation between an archivist and a researcher designed to give the researcher an orientation to the use of the materials, to help the researcher identify relevant holdings, and to ensure that research needs are met.

> *RT:* exit interview, reference
>
> *Notes:* Reference interviews are conducted to ascertain the identity of the researcher, as a security measure; to determine the researcher's information needs and purpose; to guide the researcher to appropriate access tools and relevant sources; to inform the researcher of basic procedures and limitations on access, handling of documents, and reproduction; and, after research has been completed, to evaluate the success of the visit and the effectiveness of the reference service offered. The **initial reference interview** is often referred to as an **orientation interview** or the **entrance interview**. The interview at the end of a research visit is often referred to as an **exit interview**.

reference room ~ *see:* reading room

reference value ~ *see:* informational value

refile, v. ~ To return an item to its original storage location after use.

> *RT:* interfile

reformat, v. ~ 1. To create a copy with a format or structure different from the original, especially for preservation or access. – 2. To migrate information from one carrier to another.

> *RT:* copy, format, migration
>
> *Notes:* In principle, an item can be reformatted without any effect on its content. For example, a nitrate negative can be reformatted by making a duplicate on safety film. However, Marshall McLuhan's observation that "The medium is the message" is a reminder that physical characteristics influence meaning. In the case

of a reformatted photograph, some information embedded in the material nature of the original will be lost in the reproduction. For example, a modern copy print of a 19th-century cabinet print will almost certainly use a different process, may not be the same size, and may not reproduce the back; the process, size, and date, which can help date the original, are missing from the reformatted copy.

Data files may be reformatted so that they can be read by different programs or to counter technological obsolescence. For example, a document created in Word 5 must be reformatted before it can be read by Word XP or by any version of WordPerfect. Or, home movies may be reformatted to DVDs. Such reformatting may be imperfect, with a resulting loss of meaning.

register, n. ~ 1. A record containing entries in the form of a list. – 2. A volume recording names or events. – 3. COMPUTING · Hardware used to store a fixed amount of data, often a word, a byte, or a bit.

> *BT:* finding aid

> †52 *(Crabb 1917, p. 590):* (Record, Register, Archive.) *Record* is taken for the thing *recorded*, or the collection in which a thing is *recorded*; *register* either for the thing *registered* or the place in which it is *registered*; *archive*, mostly for the place, and sometimes for the thing: *records* are either historical details or short notices, which serve to preserve the memory of things; *registers* are but short notices of particular and local circumstances; *archives* are always connected with the state: every place of antiquity has its *records* of the different circumstances which have been connected with its rise and progress and the various changes which it has experiences; in public *registers* we find accounts of families and of their various connections and fluctuations; in *archives* we find all legal deeds and instruments which involved the interests of the nation, both in its internal and external economy. In an extended application of these terms, *records* contain whatever is to be remembered at ever so distant a period; *registers*, that which is to serve present purposes; *archives*, that in which any things are stored.

> †178 *(MacNeil 1995, p. 26):* The purpose of the registers [known in Italy as protocol registers] is to control the stages of distribution and transit for every official document that passes through the registry. The protocol register, for example, records the documents protocol number (i.e., a unique identifier), its date, the date when it was received (in the case of documents received), the name and official title of the sender, the protocol number in the office of the sender (if applicable), the nature of the action, an indication of any enclosures and their types, the assigned classification number, and the office handling the matter.

registration, n. ~ 1. The process of formally enrolling with an official body for certain rights or privileges. – 2. The process of entering information in a register. – 3. MUSEUMS · The process of entering information about museum holdings into a recordkeeping system. – 4. PRINTING, PHOTOGRAPHY · The process of aligning of several images, especially color separations, to form a single image.

> *RT:* accession

> *Notes:* Examples of registration[1] include registering a copyright, an automobile license, and land title. When approved, such information is typically entered into a public record, although that record is not always in the form of a register. Archives commonly ask patrons to complete a registration form containing their name and an agreement to follow policies and procedures.

†70 (Duranti 1998, p. 139–140): *Registration* is the action of transcribing a document in a register, carried out by an office different from that issuing the document and specifically entrusted with that function. When registration takes place, the number assigned to the document in the register is included in the document with a formula attesting to that action. The formula and registration number may be added to the document, not by the registration office, but by the notary or lawyer responsible for the compilation of the document, following proper authorization by the registration office.

registry, n. ~ A division within an organization responsible for the recording, control, and maintenance of records.

registry principle ~ *see:* original order

registry system, n. ~ The policies and procedures that govern the recording, control, and maintenance of records within an organization through the use of registers, lists, and indexes.

†109 (Guercio 2001, p. 260–261): The registry system, fully developed in medieval chanceries such as that of the papacy, originally consisted of the entire transcription of definitive – but not all – records. In the course of time – in the face of the growth of the production of records and of specialization of systems of registration – it developed into the extraction and transcript only of the identifying elements of records, with the objective of securely controlling their maintenance within a records system and of furnishing proof of the existence of the record over time.

regulation, n. ~ 1. The process of controlling something through rule or procedure. – 2. A rule that is issued by an authorized government agency and that has the force of law.

> *NT:* administrative regulation
>
> *RT:* law
>
> *Notes:* A regulation[2] issued by a federal agency is published in the *Code of Federal Regulations.*

reintegration, n. ~ The process of refiling materials that were misfiled or missing.

related term, n. ~ A cross-reference pointing to an associated concept of similar specificity in a hierarchy.

> *BT:* cross-reference
>
> *RT:* equivalence relation, Guidelines for the Construction, Format, and Management of Monolingual Thesauri
>
> *Notes:* Related terms are part of the syndetic structure used in a thesaurus, especially one constructed using the ANSI Z39.19 standard, *Guidelines for the Construction, Format, and Management of Monolingual Thesauri.* Related terms are reciprocal to each other. For example, an entry for 'camera' may include a related-term reference to 'photography', in which case the entry for 'photography' would have a related-term reference to the entry for 'camera'.

relational database, n. ~ Information that has been organized, structured, and stored into tables of rows and columns (flat files) so that related data elements from different tables can be manipulated and extracted for various purposes.

> *BT:* database
>
> *RT:* flat file
>
> *Notes:* The relational database model was developed by Edgar Codd about 1970. Each table consists of named columns (attributes). A logical record consists of fields taken from related rows in different tables.

relative humidity, n. ~ The amount of moisture in the air, expressed as a percent of the maximum moisture air can hold at a given temperature.

    RT: humidity

relaxation, n. ~ A conservation treatment to flatten a document by exposing it to humid air.

release date, n. ~ 1. The date when an item, especially an audio or moving image production, is first distributed to the public. – 2. The date on which restricted materials can be made available to the public.

    BT: date

relevant, adj. ~ LAW · Useful to prove or disprove some matter or fact.

    RT: discovery, precision, recall

    †265 *(Skupsky and Mantaña 1994, p. 71):* The duty to preserve records arises from the same sources as the duty to create them: statute, regulation, and contract. When the records relate to litigation or potential litigation an additional duty arises to preserve relevant material. Once records become relevant to a legal dispute, the fact that there was no duty to have created them in the first place becomes irrelevant.

reliability, n. (**reliable**, adj.) ~ 1. The quality of being dependable and worthy of trust. – 2. The quality of being consistent and undeviating. – 3. DIPLOMATICS · Created by a competent authority, according to established processes, and being complete in all formal elements. – **rely**, v. ~ 4. To have confidence in; to believe in.

    RT: accuracy, authenticity, completeness, diplomatics, promptness, sufficiency, trustworthiness, veracity, verification

    Notes: Reliability is a relative concept associated with authenticity, accuracy, sufficiency, completeness, integrity, consistency, and dependability. In general, reliability is synonymous with trustworthiness. It takes on narrower senses in different contexts.

    A system is reliable[2] if it produces consistent results. A calculator that always reports that $2 \times 2 = 4$ is reliable; one that occasionally reports $2 \times 2 = 5$ is not.

    In diplomatics, a record is reliable[3] only if it was created by someone with appropriate authority, if it was made following proper procedures, and if all information and steps were finished. In this sense, reliability does not ensure the accuracy of the content of a record.

    †10 *(AJS, Records §99):* He who acts in reliance on the record has behind him not only the natural equities of his position, but also the special equity arising from the protection afforded everyone who trusts the record.

    †67 *(Duff 1998, p . 88):* The mere existence of a record does not ensure that it will faithfully represent a transaction or an event; its credibility must be ensured through the establishment of reliable methods and procedures for its creation, maintenance, and use over time. A society or culture endorses certain recordkeeping procedures and endows them with the ability to create trustworthy records.

    †100 *(Gilliland-Swetland and Eppard 2000):* The degree to which a record can be considered reliable is dependent upon the level of procedural and technical control exercised during its creation and management in its active life. Authenticity, by contrast, is the responsibility of archival management of inactive records, and is an absolute concept.

    †180 *(MacNeil 2000, p. 39):* A reliable record is one that is capable of standing for the facts to which it attests. Reliability thus refers to the truth-value of the

record as a statement of facts and it is assessed in relation to the proximity of the observer and recorder to the facts recorded.

relief image, n. ~ An image that is formed by minor variations in surface depth.

> *DF:* intaglio
>
> *Notes:* Woodburytypes and carbon prints are examples of relief images. The denser areas of the image are formed by thicker layers of pigment; highlights are formed in areas with little or no pigment, allowing the support to show through. Although three-dimensional, the depth of a relief image is negligible, and the relief is often visible only when the print is viewed with raking light. For sculpture on a surface with a noticeable relief use 'bas relief'. For designs cut or carved into a surface, use 'intaglio'.

remake, n. ~ An audio or moving image production[1] based on an earlier work using a different script[3], cast, and crew.

remote access, n. ~ A means of connecting to computer equipment through a network[2].

> *DF:* direct access
>
> *Notes:* 'Remote access' connotes a computer connection outside an established network, such as a dial up connection or a virtual private network connection.

remote-sensing imagery, n. ~ Images, especially of a planetary surface, that are used to evaluate, measure, or map cultural or physical features, and that are made from an airplane or spacecraft.

> *Notes:* Many remote-sensing images are made using nonphotographic techniques. For example, images may be made by radar to measure surface elevation or by heat-sensing equipment to represent fires as shapes on a map.

remote storage, n. ~ Facilities for housing materials away from where they are used; off-site storage.

> *Syn:* off-site storage
>
> *Notes:* Remote storage may be used to house inactive or low-use materials, reducing the costs of storing records in expensive office areas by moving them to less expensive warehouse facilities. Remote storage may also be used to keep copies of vital (essential) records to increase the chances that at least one copy will survive a disaster.

removable media, n. ~ Material used to store data that can be taken out of a machine.

> *DF:* fixed media
>
> *Notes:* Floppy disks, magnetic tape, and compact discs are examples of removable media.

removed archives (also **captured archives**), n. ~ Archives that have been taken from the country in which they were originally accumulated; migrated archives.

> *Syn:* migrated archives
>
> *BT:* archives
>
> *RT:* alienation, estray, replevin

repair, n. ~ The process of rehabilitating a worn or damaged item, generally more intensive than mending but less so than restoration.

> *RT:* mend, restoration

rephotography (also **repeat photography**), n. ~ A technique of making a photograph that has an image that is, except for the date of exposure, as nearly identical as possible to the image of an earlier photograph.

> *RT:* photograph

Notes: Comparing the original and contemporary photographs makes it possible to see changes over time. Minimally, rephotography places a camera at the same location of the original to recreate the original vantage point. Rephotography may also consider the time of day and time of year to ensure that natural light conditions are the same.

replevin, n. ~ An action to recover property that has been improperly or illegally taken.

    RT: alienation, removed archives

    Notes: Replevin is frequently used to describe efforts to recover public records that are in private hands.

replica, n. ~ A precise copy of an object.

    DF: counterfeit, forgery, reproduction

    RT: copy, facsimile, fake, object, realia, version

    Notes: 'Replica' implies a three-dimensional artifact. 'Replica' carries no connotation of deceit, as does 'forgery' or 'counterfeit'.

report, n. ~ 1. A narrative, summary, or record of events, decisions, or understandings. – 2. A document that contains the results of an investigation or research. – 3. Law · Collections the decisions of a court or group of courts that are published to promote uniform application of laws.

    NT: annual report, committee report, conference committee report, corporate report

    RT: grey literature, narrative record, publication, quasi-publication

    Notes: Reports[1] may be oral or written. They often have a formal structure and prescribed content. They are often produced on a recurring basis to capture changes in information over time. – Reports[1,2] are generally intended for limited distribution but may be formally published for broad distribution. – Reports[3] are frequently called **reporters**.

    †48 (CJS, 77 CJS §2–3): Reports[3] are collections of the authoritative expositions of the law by the regularly constituted judicial tribunals supplemented and arranged by an officer called the court reporter. . . . ¶ A complete report of a decided case usually includes the syllabus or headnote, the names of the respective counsel, the statement of the case, and the opinion of the court.

    †94 (Garner 1995, p. 758): Traditionally, a law *report*[3] is a written account of a proceeding and a judicial decision, and the *reporter* is the person responsible for making and publishing that account. In American English, however, *reporter* has been blurred into *report* – primarily because of West Publishing Company's "National Reporter" system (established in 1879), each *Reporter* being a set of books containing judicial opinions from a geographic area within the country. Formerly, fastidious writers tried to distinguish the senses by capitalizing one but not the other. . . .

    †300 (Yates 1989, p. 77): Reports[1,2] were the major formal mechanism by which managers and executives at all levels acquired information about what went on at lower levels, information on the basis of which they made decisions for the future. Reports were of two basic types: routine or periodic reports, which were issued at regular intervals to provide information on normal operations; and special reports, which analyzed (usually in response to a special request) a specific problem, opportunity, idea, or physical entity.

repository, n. ~ A place where things can be stored and maintained; a storehouse.

    NT: archives, depository, library, records center

    RT: historical society

    Notes: Used throughout this work to refer to any type of organization that holds documents, including business, institutional, and government archives, manuscript collections, libraries, museums, and historical societies, and in any form, including manuscripts, photographs, moving image and sound materials, and their electronic equivalents.

    †201 (Nevada Glossary): A central place in which an aggregation of data is kept and maintained in an organized way, usually in computer storage. Depending on how the term is used, a repository may be directly accessible to users or may be a place from which specific databases, files, or documents are obtained for further relocation or distribution in a network. A repository may be just the aggregation of data itself into some accessible place of storage or it may also imply some ability to selectively extract data. Related terms are data warehouse and data mining.

repository guide ~ *see:* guide

reprint, n. ~ 1. A book that is reissued by the publisher in a new form or one that is issued by another publisher as a photo reproduction. – 2. A single article printed separately from the journal in which it originally appeared; an offprint.

    DF: issue

    RT: facsimile, impression, offprint, photocopy

    Notes: A reprint typically has the same formatting as the version in the journal, including the same page numbering. Authors are frequently given a small number of reprints.

reproduction, n. ~ 1. Something that is made in imitation of an earlier style; a facsimile[1]. – 2. A duplicate made from an original; a copy[1]. – v. ~ 3. To make copies.

    DF: replica

    Syn: copy

    RT: electrostatic process, facsimile, fake, photocopy, version

    Notes: 'Reproduction' includes two- and three-dimensional works, as distinguished from 'replica', which connotes three-dimensional works.

reproduction ratio ~ *see:* magnification

reprographics, n. ~ The techniques and processes used to copy documents.

    RT: copy, imaging, micrographics

    Notes: Reprographics encompasses all processes and techniques, including electrostatic copying, micrographics, and printing.

repurpose, n. ~ Taking information from an existing source and adapting it for use in another format or a different work.

    Notes: Transforming a printed dictionary to a CD-ROM or a website may be described as repurposing.

request, n. ~ 1. An inquiry. – 2. An oral or written expression asking for something.

    Notes: In archives, a request connotes a single reference transaction, although more than one item may be retrieved.

request for comment, n. (**RFC**, abbr.) ~ 1. A formal statement, usually a document, seeking input on some matter. – 2. An official publication for Internet standards documents and other publications of the Internet Engineering Steering Group (IESG), Internet Architecture Board (IAB), and the Internet community.

†28 (Finnish Technology Award Foundation 2004): It is a regrettably well spread misconception that publication as an RFC provides some level of recognition. It does not, or at least not any more than the publication in a regular journal. In fact, each RFC has a status, relative to its relation with the Internet standardization process: Informational, Experimental, or Standards Track (Proposed Standard, Draft Standard, Internet Standard), or Historic. This status is reproduced on the first page of the RFC itself, and is also documented in the periodic 'Internet Official Protocols Standards' RFC (STD 1). But this status is sometimes omitted from quotes and references, which may feed the confusion.

†239 (New Hacker's Dictionary 1994, p. 355): One of a long-established series of numbered Internet standards widely followed by commercial software and freeware in the Internet and Unix communities. . . . The RFCs are unusual in that they are floated by technical experts acting on their own initiative and reviewed by the Internet at large, rather than formally promulgated through an institution such as ANSI. For this reason, they are known as RFCs even once adopted.

request slip, n. ~ A form submitted to retrieve from storage for use, typically in a reading room; a call slip, a research request slip, a reference slip.

Syn: call slip

Requirements for the Management of Electronic Records, n. (**MoReq**, abbr.) ~ Model specifications for electronic records management system requirements.

Notes: MoReq was developed by Cornwell Management Consultants and is used in the European Communities. The document is available online at http://www.cornwell.co.uk/moreq.

†17 (InterPARES Authenticity, p. 29–30): MoReq has been designed to be 'pragmatic' and 'usable,' and its purpose is to ensure that an ERMS will 'manage electronic records with the desired levels of confidence and integrity.' . . . Like DoD 5015.2, MoReq is a software specification, and accordingly it differs from the InterPARES requirements in that it explicitly focuses on system functionality over procedures, and on implementation methods over records management principles.

Research Libraries Group, n. (**RLG**, abbr.) ~ An international cooperative of libraries, archives, museums, and other institutions that maintains a union catalog, provides other information resources, and undertakes research projects of interest to its members.

BT: bibliographic utility

RT: Research Libraries Information Network

Notes: See http://www.rlg.org/.

Research Libraries Information Network, n. (**RLIN**, abbr.) ~ A bibliographic utility that includes the RLG Union Catalog.

BT: bibliographic utility

RT: Research Libraries Group

Notes: RLIN contains catalog records from more than a hundred member libraries, archives, and museums. In 2004 RLIN was renamed RLIN 21 to reflect upgrades to the underlying infrastructure.

research room ~ *see:* reading room

research value ~ *see:* informational value

researcher, n. ~ An individual who uses the collections and services of a repository; a customer; a patron; a reader[1].

Syn: patron, reader, user

residual data (also **ambient data**), n. ~ Information that has been deleted from a computer system but which persists and can be recovered using extraordinary means.

Notes: Residual information may be found in unallocated storage or in file slack space. This information is not normally accessible through the operating system, but generally requires special software to be recovered. This data came from files that have been deleted but not erased; although the pointer to the file in the file system directory has been deleted, the data remains until overwritten. Residual data may also be found in a file that contains information that has been functionally deleted, but which is not normally visible within the application.

residual hypo test, n. ~ A technique to measure the amount of fixer (hypo) the remains in a photographic emulsion after processing[2].

NT: densitometric method (silver), methylene-blue test

RT: archival processing

resin-coated paper, n. (**RC paper**, abbr.) ~ A laminate of plastic and paper used to make photographic prints; also called **water-resistant paper**.

BT: paper

Notes: Resin-coated papers use a base that sandwiches a sheet of paper between two sheets of plastic. The plastic prevents the paper from absorbing processing chemicals, significantly shortening processing time.

resolution, n. ~ 1. Optics · A measure of the sharpness and detail in an image or optical system. – 2. Law · A formal expression of a corporate or public body, expressing an opinion, decision, or action.

NT: concurrent resolution, joint resolution, simple resolution

RT: acutance, sharpness

Notes: Resolution[1] is often determined by photographing a standard target and measuring the lines per millimeter that can be discerned in the developed image. Resolution quality depends on the optical system, the type of film, the manner in which the film is processed, and other factors.

resource, n. ~ 1. An asset available for use. – 2. Computing · A component of a computer system, including processors, memory, and input/output devices. – 3. Computing · Information and services available for use through a network.

RT: material, object, Resource Description Framework, web page

Notes: Resource[1] includes materials, personnel, and money. – Resource[3] is used as a generic term to refer to almost any object that can be addressed through a network; see Resource Description Framework.

Resource Description Framework, n. (**RDF**, abbr.) ~ A XML-based standard designed to facilitate machine processing of metadata describing information and services available online (resources).

RT: resource

Notes: The standard is being developed by the World Wide Web Consortium. See http://www.w3.org/RDF/.

†240 (W3C RDF 2003): The Resource Description Framework (RDF) is a language for representing information about resources in the World Wide Web. It is particularly intended for representing metadata about Web resources, such as the title, author, and modification date of a Web page, copyright and licensing information about a Web document, or the availability schedule for some shared resource. However, by generalizing the concept of a 'Web resource', RDF can also be used to represent information about things that can be identified on the Web,

even when they cannot be directly retrieved on the Web. Examples include information about items available from on-line shopping facilities (e.g., information about specifications, prices, and availability), or the description of a Web user's preferences for information delivery. ¶ RDF is intended for situations in which this information needs to be processed by applications, rather than being only displayed to people. RDF provides a common framework for expressing this information so it can be exchanged between applications without loss of meaning.

respect de l'ordre intérieur ~ *see:* original order

respect des fonds ~ *see:* provenance

respect for archival structure ~ *see:* archival structure

respect for original order ~ *see:* original order

responsibility ~ *see:* statement of responsibility

restoration, n. ~ The process of rehabilitating an item to return it as nearly as possible to its original condition.

> *DF:* conservation, preservation
>
> *RT:* mend, repair, restore
>
> *Notes:* Restoration may include fabrication of missing parts with modern materials, but using processes and techniques that are similar to those originally used to create the item.

restoration of original order (also **perfecting order**), n. ~ The process of returning materials to the organization and sequence established by their creator.

> *RT:* original order

restore, v. ~ 1. COMPUTING · To retrieve a copy of data stored on backup media, typically when the original data has been damaged or become corrupt. – 2. CONSERVATION · To rehabilitate an item, returning it as nearly as possible to its original condition.

> *RT:* backup, restoration

restriction, n. ~ Limitations on an individual access to or use of materials.

> *NT:* administratively controlled information, donor restriction
>
> *RT:* access, classified, closed, closed file, physical restriction note
>
> *Notes:* **Access restrictions** may be defined by a period of time or by a class of individual allowed or denied access. They may be designed to protect national security (classification[3]), personal privacy, or to preserve materials.
>
> **Use restrictions** may limit what can be done with materials, or they may place qualifications on use. For example, an individual may be allowed access to materials but may not have permission or right to copy, quote, or publish those materials, or conditions may be imposed on such use. In addition to legal use restrictions, such as privacy and copyright, donor agreements often contain use restrictions.

retention period (also **disposition standard**), n. ~ The length of time records should be kept in a certain location or form for administrative, legal, fiscal, historical, or other purposes.

> *RT:* contingent records
>
> *Notes:* Retention periods are determined by balancing the potential value of the information to the agency against the costs of storing the records containing that information. Retention periods are set for record series, but specific records within that series may need to be retained longer because they are required for litigation or because circumstances give those records unexpected archival value.

†265 *(Skupsky and Mantaña 1994, p. 135):* Records retention periods generally will be based on several factors. ¶ Operational / Record User Needs – retention periods based upon an organization's need to preserve records to protect the organization's rights, conduct, business, or facilitate research. ¶ Legal Requirements – retention periods stated in statutes, regulations and rules establishing legal minimum periods for maintaining records. These periods can be enforced by government by subjecting the party to fines, penalties and loss of rights. ¶ Legal Considerations – retention periods based on other legal issues such as statutes of limitation or a legal duty to preserve records for future or current litigation, tax or other audit. ¶ Historical – retention periods to preserve records for public historical or research needs or as part of internal organizational archives.

retention review ~ *see:* reappraisal

retention schedule (also **disposal schedule, records schedule, records retention schedule, transfer schedule**), n. ~ A document that identifies and describes an organization's records, usually at the series level, provides instructions for the disposition of records throughout their life cycle.

> *NT:* general records schedule
> *RT:* schedule
> *Notes:* Retention schedules may also include instructions for the disposition of documents and other materials that are not official records.

reticulation, n. ~ 1. An irregular pattern of lines. – 2. PHOTOGRAPHY · An image characterized by an irregular pattern of lines in the emulsion formed during processing.

> *Notes:* Reticulation² is generally considered a defect, usually resulting from immersing film in solutions with different temperatures. The emulsion absorbs an unusual amount of water and does not retain its original, smooth surface after drying. However, reticulation may be used for artistic effect. The collotype process uses a reticulated colloid (gelatin or albumen) to form an image on a printing plate.

retirement, n. ~ The process of transferring records from active files to inactive storage.

> *RT:* disposition

retouching, n. ~ PHOTOGRAPHY · The process of altering an image, especially to remove defects.

> *Notes:* Retouching includes both correction of mechanical problems, such as removing shadows from dust, as well as substantive alterations to the image, such as removing utility wires or covering blemishes or wrinkles in a portrait. In non-digital photography, retouching may be done with pencils, a brush and inks, or with an airbrush. It may be done on a negative, before printing, or on a print. In digital photography, retouching is typically done on a computer before printing.

retrieval, n. ~ The process of locating material or information in storage and returning it for use.

reusable media, n. ~ COMPUTING · Data storage that enables existing data to be overwritten and replaced with new data.

> *DF:* write once read many
> *Notes:* Magnetic tape is an example of reusable media. Reusable media are distinguished from write-once, read-many (WORM) media.

reversal film, n. ~ Photographic film that produces a positive image without need for an intermediary negative.

RT: direct positive

Notes: Reversal films are often used for slides, transparencies, and motion pictures. Kodachrome, Ektachrome, and Fujichrome are examples of reversal films.

reversibility, n. ~ PRESERVATION · The ability to undo a treatment, returning the object to the condition it was in before treatment.

Notes: Sometimes referred to as the **principle of reversibility**. Encapsulation is considered reversible, whereas lamination is not.

†12 *(Appelbaum 1987):* The property of a treatment that allows a knowledgeable conservator to 'turn back the clock' on a treatment. In functional terms, this does not require that the object be identical to what it was, only that we can return it to a state where our treatment choices are as broad as they were before the treatment in question was performed.

†103 *(UNESCO A/V Glossary 2001):* Reversibility is an important goal of conservation treatment, but it must be balanced with other treatment goals and options.

RFC ~ *see:* request for comment

RFC 1630 ~ *see:* Uniform Resource Identifier

RFC 1737 ~ *see:* Uniform Resource Name

RFC 1738 ~ *see:* Uniform Resource Locator

RFC 2045 ~ *see:* Multipurpose Internet Messaging Extensions

RFC 2822 ~ *see:* electronic mail

rights-and-interests records, n. ~ Vital (or essential) records that document the privileges, possessions, and concerns of an organization or individuals with whom it does business.

BT: essential records, vital records

Notes: Vital records[2], also called essential records, include emergency operating records and rights-and-interests records. Emergency records are typically stored in paper format to avoid machine and power dependence. They describe responsibilities, including delegation of authority and line of succession. Examples include the records necessary to mobilize and protect manpower and resources and to ensure health, safety, and order. Government agencies may also include records relating to the mobilization of military, civil defense, and public health operations. Rights-and-interests records include those records necessary after initial recovery to protect the assets and rights of the organization, its employees, and others. Rights-and-interests records may include payroll, leave and insurance records, titles and deeds to real property, contracts, and other similar data.

rights management, n. ~ A system that identifies intellectual property rights relevant to particular works and that can provide individuals with access to those works on the basis of permissions to the individuals.

NT: digital rights management

RT: intellectual property

risk analysis (also **risk assessment**), n. ~ The evaluation of the possibility of incurring loss, damage, or injury and a determination of the amount of risk that is acceptable for a given situation or event.

RT: strategic information management

risk management, n. ~ The systematic control of losses or damages, including the analysis of threats, implementation of measures to minimize such risks, and implementing recovery programs.

RLG ~ *see:* Research Libraries Group

RLIN ~ *see:* Research Libraries Information Network

    Notes: In 2004, RLIN was renamed RLIN21 to reflect upgrades to the database infrastructure.

RMA ~ *see:* records management application

roll, n. ~ 1. A document wound into a cylinder; a scroll. – 2. A length of film or tape wound into a cylinder, frequently on a core or reel. – 3. A list of persons or property made for a special purpose, such as a muster roll, a tax roll. – 4. A record of official proceedings. – 5. MOVING IMAGES ~ A camera rotation along an axis running between the camera and the subject.

    Notes: A roll[1] is frequently made up of several pieces of parchment or paper that attach at the edges to make a long, continuous strip.

roll film, n. ~ PHOTOGRAPHY · A strip of plastic, coated with a light-sensitive emulsion, that is significantly longer than it is wide and that is intended to hold several images side by side in a single row.

    DF: sheet film

    BT: film

    Notes: Roll film is distinguished from sheet film, which usually holds a single image. After processing, roll film often is cut into flat strips for storage. Film generally refers to undeveloped materials; once the images have been developed, they are often called negatives, transparencies, or slides.

ROM ~ *see:* read-only memory

rotary camera, n. ~ Equipment designed to quickly and automatically reproduce large quantities of documents on microfilm.

    Syn: flow camera

    BT: microfilm camera

    RT: microfilm

    Notes: A rotary camera films documents while they are being transported through the device. The device frequently uses a rotating, circular drum as the transport mechanism, hence the name. The film is also in motion during filming; optics ensure that the image of the document is stationary relative to the film. The camera size limits the width of documents to be filmed, but it can accept very long documents.

rotary scanner, n. ~ Equipment designed to quickly and automatically produce a digital image of a document while the document is being transported past a stationary sensor.

    BT: scanner

    Notes: Rotary scanners generally use a drum for a transport mechanism, distinguishing them from flatbed scanners. Rotary scanners are designed for high-speed and may be capable of scanning several hundred documents a minute.

rotated index, n. ~ An index that contains an entry for each nontrivial word in a title, with the entry words alphabetized and centered on the page surrounded by the rest of the title.

    Syn: permuted index

    BT: index

    Notes: As much of the title as possible appears on either side of the entry word; long titles may be truncated at the beginning or the end. A stop list may be used to suppress entries for words with no value for retrieval, such as articles and conjunctions, or a go list may be used to generate entries for specific words.

rough, n. ~ A first draft.

rough cut, n. ~ MOVING IMAGES · An assembly of shots and scenes in sequence, but without detailed attention to the precise point where the final cuts will be made.

 RT: moving image

row, n. ~ 1. Sections of shelves assembled side by side. – 2. COMPUTING · A record in a database table.

 Syn: range, run

 RT: shelving

Rules for Archival Description, n. (**RAD**, abbr.) ~ A standard for the description of archival fonds.

 RT: archival description, descriptive standard

 Notes: Prepared under the direction of the Planning Committee on Descriptive Standards, a committee of the Bureau of Canadian Archivists, representing L'Association des archivistes du Québec, the Association of Canadian Archivists. Published by Bureau of Canadian Archivists, 1990.

 †252 (RAD 1990, p. xv): RAD provides archivists with a set of rules which 'aim to provide a consistent and common foundation for the description of archival material within a fonds, based on traditional archival principles.' [citing Rule 0.1] ¶ It is essential, therefore, that archivists using these rules in their descriptive work remember that they are an extension of AACR2R to cover materials in archives that are part of a fonds. In some cases RAD modified or augments an AACR2R rule; in other cases the rules are equivalent to AACR2.

run, n. ~ 1. Sections of shelves assembled side by side. – v. ~ 2. COMPUTING · To carry out a process or program.

 Syn: range, row

 RT: shelving

rushes, n. ~ MOVING IMAGES · Prints[4] of takes shot during one day, intended to be viewed before shooting continues the next day.

 RT: moving image, work print

S

s.l., abbr. ~ 1. *Sine loco*; without place. – 2. Session law. – 3. Statute law.

    Syn: n.p.

    Notes: S.l.[1] was typically used in bibliographic citations to indicate that no city of publication was listed. Contemporary practice is to use 'n.p.' for no place.

s.n., abbr. ~ *Sine nomine*; without name.

    Notes: S.n. is typically used in bibliographic citations to indicate that the name of the publisher or distributor is unknown.

SAA ~ *see:* Society of American Archivists

Sabattier effect, n. ~ PHOTOGRAPHY · A partial reversal of tones in a photograph due to exposure to light during development, resulting in an image with a combination of normal and reversed polarity.

    DF: solarization

    Notes: The effect, described by French scientist Armand Sabattier in 1862, has an appearance similar to solarization. Photographers sometimes use it intentionally for aesthetic value.

safety film, n. ~ Photographic or motion picture film made using a cellulose acetate or polyester base.

    RT: cellulose acetate

    Notes: Safety film is slow burning, as distinguished from highly flammable nitrate film.

salvage plan, n. ~ The procedures necessary for the rescue of materials after fire, flood, or other disaster.

    BT: disaster plan

sampling, n. ~ 1. STATISTICS · The process of selecting items from a collection to stand for the collection as a whole. – 2. SOUND RECORDINGS · The frequency and precision with which an analog signal is measured when converted to digital format.

    NT: exceptional sampling, exemplary sampling, illustrative sampling, systematic sampling

    RT: census, fat file method

    Notes: A variety of techniques may be used to select a sample[1] from a larger group. In appraisal, sampling may be used to select a representative portion of records for preservation from a large series that will not be preserved in its entirety. In litigation, a large records series may be sampled to determine if that series is likely to contain relevant materials. – Sampling[2] determines the quality of the digital recording; the higher the frequency of the sampling rate and the greater the range of values that can be captured, the closer the digital version approximates the original performance being recorded.

    †262 (*Sedona Principles 2003, p. 43*): Sampling[1] usually (but not always) refers to the process of statistically testing a database for the likelihood of relevant information. It can be a useful technique in addressing a number of issues relating to litigation, including decisions what repositories of data are appropriate to search in a particular litigation, and determinations of the validity and effectiveness of

searches or other data extraction procedures. Sampling can be useful in providing information to the court about the relative cost burden versus benefit of requiring a party to review certain electronic records.

Sarbanes-Oxley Act, n. ~ A federal law passed in 2002 (Public Law 107-204) intended to protect investors by improving the accuracy and reliability of corporate disclosures made pursuant to the securities laws, and for other purposes.

Notes: The act was passed in reaction to accounting scandals involving Enron and Arthur Andersen. The act includes a number of requirements for reporting and internal controls, with significant implications for records management to ensure compliance.

scale, n. ~ 1. The ratio between the size of something and its representation. – 2. A graphic illustrating the relative size of something.

RT: cartography, chart, drawing, globe, map

Notes: Maps and architectural, engineering, and technical drawings are often to scale[1], accurately reflecting the proportions of the thing they represent. Scale is often expressed verbally; for example, one inch equals one mile. If the map is reproduced at a different size, that statement of scale is no longer accurate in the reproduction. – A scale is often a thick rule with different units on either side, one for the map or drawing, the other for the thing represented. Such a scale retains its accuracy if reproduced at a different size.

scanner (also **optical scanner**), n. ~ 1. COMPUTING · A device used to transform an analog image into a raster graphic. – 2. A device capable of reading and converting a coded pattern into alphanumeric data.

NT: flatbed scanner, rotary scanner

RT: bar code

Notes: A scanner[1] may be used to capture pictures or text. Scanned text may be parsed using optical character recognition (OCR) software to turn it into character data. – A scanner[2] designed to read bar codes generates character data rather than an image.

scanning, n. ~ The process of a creating raster graphic that reproduces a document or image by converting reflected or transmitted light into a digital signal that can be stored, transmitted, and reconstructed for display as an electronic image.

BT: digitization, electronic imaging

RT: digital photograph

Notes: 'Scanning' connotes a two-dimensional original. Electronic images of three dimensional objects or space are generally described as digital photographs.

scene, n. ~ 1. A physical setting or place, especially as in a photograph, painting, or similar work. – 2. A segment of a dramatic work representing a continuous sequence of actions.

RT: bird's-eye view, cityscape, landscape, moving image, seascape, sequence, shot

Notes: In theatrical works, acts are typically divided into scenes[2]. In moving image productions, a scene[2] (similar to a paragraph in a written work) is made up of shots (sentences), and scenes are combined to form sequences (chapters).

schedule, n. ~ The process of identifying and describing records held by an organization, determining their retention period, and describing disposition actions throughout their life cycle.

RT: retention schedule

schema, n. ~ A formal description of a data structure.

> *Notes:* Shemas are frequently used define a database in terms of tables and columns and the markup language of an extensible markup language (XML) document.

> *†299 (W3C, XML Schema 2000):* XML Schemas express shared vocabularies and allow machines to carry out rules made by people. They provide a means for defining the structure, content and semantics of XML documents.

scope and contents note, n. ~ DESCRIPTION · A narrative statement summarizing the characteristics of the described materials, the functions and activities that produced them, and the types of information contained therein.

> *BT:* descriptive element, finding aid

> *RT:* abstract, archival description, contents note

> *Notes:* Scope and content notes are part of finding aids and catalog records.

> *†120 (APPM2 1989, 1.7B2):* Give information relating to the general contents, nature, and scope of the described materials. For archival collections give (in this order) the specific types and forms of material present, noting the presence of graphic or other nontextual materials such as illustrations, maps, charts, drawings, plans, photographs, sound recordings, or computer files; the dates within which the material bulks largest (if appropriate); when appropriate, the functions or activities resulting in the creation of the records; and the most significant topics, events, persons, places, etc., represented. . . .

scope note, n. ~ 1. A statement indicating the proper use of a heading in a thesaurus, authority file, or classification scheme. – 2. A symbol appearing with a heading that specifies a particular sense.

> *Notes:* A scope note[1] often refers to other headings with related or overlapping meanings to help users determine the most appropriate heading. – In this glossary, superscript numbers are used as scope notes[2] to specify a particular sense in a definition.

scrapbook, n. ~ A blank book, often with a simple string binding, used to store a variety of memorabilia, such as clippings, pictures, and photographs.

> *BT:* album

screening, n. ~ 1. The process of reviewing materials in a collection for classified, confidential, or private information that should be restricted. – 2. The act of showing a moving image production.

> *RT:* moving image, segregation, weeding

> *Notes:* 'Screening' connotes removal of materials at the folder level or higher, while 'weeding' connotes item-level separation. Screening[1] is frequently combined with segregation, to move restricted materials to separate storage, and with weeding, to remove and dispose of duplicates and documents without archival value.

screenplay, n. ~ The script[3] of a moving image production.

> *BT:* moving image

> *Notes:* Screenplays may be little more than an outline or may have detailed acting and scene directions. 'Screenplay' connotes a work for television or film, as distinguished from a script[3], which include programs intended for the theater, television, film, or radio.

script, n. ~ 1. Handwriting. – 2. An original document. – 3. The written text of a dramatic work. – 4. COMPUTING · A file that contains commands normally entered one at a time from the keyboard but that is executed as a batch process.

BT: extrinsic element

†70 *(Duranti 1998, p. 135):* The other extrinsic element which used to have great significance for diplomatists, but progressively lost it, is the *script[1]*. While it is the task of paleography to determine what type of script is proper to an era and an environment, it is the task of diplomatics to examine other characteristics of the script, such as the layout of the writing with respect to the physical form of the document, the presence of different hands or types of writing in the same document, the correspondence between paragraphs and conceptual sections of the text, type of punctuation, abbreviations, initialisms, ink, erasures, corrections, etc. With the invention of the printing press, and later, of the typewriter, some of these characteristics became irrelevant to the purpose of diplomatic criticism. The need for careful examination of these characteristics is arising again, however, thanks to the advent of new technology. Computer software, for example, may be considered as part of the extrinsic 'script,' because it determines the layout and articulation of the discourse, and can provide information about provenance, procedures, processes, uses, modes of transmission and, last but not least, authenticity.

seal, n. ~ 1. A die or stamp with a design used to make an impression in wax or on paper. – 2. A piece of wax, lead, or other material bearing a design from a die or stamp that serves as a sign of authenticity. – 3. A design impressed into paper from a die or stamp that serves as a sign of authenticity. – 4. A substance that must be broken before opening a container, used to detect unauthorized access. – v. ~ 5. To restrict access to, especially of court records. – 6. To authenticate or execute a document by marking with a design (seal[3]).

BT: extrinsic element

NT: electronic seal

RT: sigillography

Notes: The design in a seal[2,3] may be either raised or impressed.

†48 *(CJS, Records §11):* A scroll which the clerk puts on a record to the side of the signatures of the parties to the instrument is a proper representation of a corporate seal[2,3].

†70 *(Duranti 1998, p. 138–139):* The most important extrinsic element of medieval documents, and the least common and relevant in contemporary documents, is the *seal[2]*. Examining seals, diplomatists focus their attention on the material they are made of, their shape, size, typology (as it related to the figure in the impression: heraldic type, equestrian, monumental, hagiographic, majestic, etc.), legend or inscription (which runs clockwise around the central figure along the edge of the seal, starting from the top), and the method of affixing them (seals may be hanging or adherent). The analysis of these components is directed to ascertaining the degree of authority and solemnity of a document, its provenance and function, and its authenticity.

search, n. ~ 1. The process of examining materials to find something. – 2. A set of instructions to a computer program or database to retrieve information that meets specified criteria.

NT: full-text search, keyword and context index, keyword in context index, keyword out of context index, known-item search

RT: browse

search room ~ *see:* reading room

searcher ~ *see:* researcher

seascape, n. ~ An scene in which the ocean or seashore is the predominant subject.

> *RT:* cityscape, landscape, scene

SECAM, n. ~ A standard for an analog, color television signal used in France, Eastern Europe, the former Soviet Union, and French-speaking Africa.

> *RT:* video
>
> *Notes:* The abbreviation is frequently expanded as Séquential Couleur à Mémoire and as Système Electronique pour Couleur avec Mémoire. The image has 625 lines, 50 fields, and 25 frames per second.

secondary source, n. ~ 1. A work that is not based on direct observation of or evidence directly associated with the subject, but instead relies on sources of information. – 2. A work commenting on another work (primary sources), such as reviews, criticism, and commentaries.

> *RT:* primary source

secondary value, n. ~ The usefulness or significance of records based on purposes other than that for which they were originally created.

> *DF:* primary value
>
> *BT:* value
>
> *RT:* archival value, informational value
>
> *Notes:* Secondary value includes informational or evidential value.
>
> †112 (Ham 1993, p. 7): [Secondary values] are values that some records have because of the uses, often unforeseen, to which they can be put by individuals other than those for whom the records were originally created. For instance, the primary value of probate court records is to govern the distribution of a deceased person's property, but these records are also invaluable to historians studying family wealth or tastes and genealogists nourishing a family tree. The secondary values of a record are long lasting and are the main concern of the archival appraiser.
>
> †274 (Stephens and Wallace 2001, p. 6): Research or historical values are generally designated as secondary values. Legal value can be either a primary or a secondary value, depending on the purpose and function of a record.

secretarial notes, n. ~ DIPLOMATICS · A note, usually at the end of business correspondence, indicating clerical aspects and associated materials.

> *Notes:* Secretarial notes usually follow the qualification of signature. They often include the initials of the typist, the presence of attachments, and any individuals who were copied.

section, n. ~ 1. A unit of shelving, single- or double-sided, consisting of horizontal shelves between standards, uprights, or upright frames. – 2. CARTOGRAPHY · A graphic depicting the profile where a surface (usually a plane) intersects the ground and the underlying structures along the plane.

> *Syn:* bay, compartment
>
> *RT:* cartographic record, range, shelving

security, n. ~ Measures taken to protect materials from unauthorized access, change, destruction, or other threats.

> *RT:* authorization, preservation
>
> †223 (Personal communication, Rich Dymalski (email)): Both the logical and physical means that will insure that information is protected. 'Logical Security' is an intangible process that identifies, authenticates, authorizes, protects, and provides access control over programs and data. A password is an example of logical

security for data stored or transmitted. 'Physical Security' refers to material factors (facility, environment, communication wiring, devices, etc.). Anchoring desktop computers with locks is an example of a physical security item.

security classification, n. ~ The process of assigning restrictions to materials, limiting access to specific individuals, especially for purposes of national security.

> *BT:* classification
> *RT:* declassification

security copy, n. ~ A reproduction of a record created and managed to preserve the information in case the original is damaged.

> *BT:* copy
> *RT:* backup, essential records, vital records
> *Notes:* Security copies are typically stored off site. They are distinguished from backups in that security copies typically include only vital (essential) records. A backup may be used as a security copy if it is created and stored in a manner that allows retrieval of a complete set of vital records.

security microfilming, n. ~ The process of duplicating records, especially vital records, on microfilm to protect them against disaster.

> *RT:* microfilm

see also reference, n. ~ A cross-reference from a heading to another, related headings.

> *DF:* see reference
> *BT:* cross-reference

see reference, n. ~ A cross-reference from a nonauthority form of a heading to a preferred form of the heading.

> *DF:* see also reference
> *BT:* cross-reference

segregation, n. ~ The process of separating documents that must be stored separately because of their physical condition or because they contain classified, confidential, or private information.

> *RT:* screening, separation
> *Notes:* Segregation is commonly a part of screening or processing.

select and dispose (also **selection and disposition**), n. ~ An acquisition note that directs the appraisal or processing archivists that the series in question should be heavily weeded, typically at the folder level.

> *RT:* disposition

selection, n. ~ 1. The process of identifying materials to be preserved because of their enduring value, especially those materials to be physically transferred to an archives[1]. – 2. The process of choosing materials for exhibition, publication, reformatting.

> *RT:* appraisal

self-documenting, adj. ~ COMPUTING · Having well-chosen identifiers and comments embedded in a program to make the code readable without external documentation.

> *Notes:* Self-documenting can describe systems, software, records, or documents.

self-indexing files, n. ~ A technique to access items by filing them under subject headings without creating a separate index.

> *RT:* indexing
> *Notes:* Self-indexing files work well when each item has a single, clear subject.

A self-indexing system can include a cross-reference by filing a dummy under a heading that indicates where the item is filed.

semiactive records ~ *see:* semicurrent records

semicurrent records (also **semiactive records**), n. ~ Records that are seldom used in day-to-day operations and that are appropriate for off-site storage.

> *BT:* record
> *RT:* inactive records

sensing mark, n. ~ A mark recorded on roll microfilm outside the image area that can be used to count frames automatically.

> *Syn:* blip code

sensitive, adj. ~ 1. RECORDS · Containing personal or confidential information that should be protected from public scrutiny. – 2. RECORDS · Containing information that is potentially embarrassing and that individuals may expect to be kept private.

> *RT:* classified, confidential, privacy
> *Notes:* Information in records may be sensitive because of legal, financial, or personal considerations.

separation, n. ~ 1. PHOTOGRAPHY, PRINTING · A monochromatic image that contains information about one of the primary colors of a full-color image. – 2. AUDIO RECORDING · The degree to which different channels in a composite signal can be differentiated. – 3. RECORDS · The process of removing materials from a collection for separate storage; segregation.

> *RT:* photograph, segregation
> *Notes:* A separation^1 is generally one of a set. For example, the dye transfer process breaks the color information in the original image into three separations, one for each primary color. Each separation is used to print a different color dye, the images superimposed so that the combination reproduces the full color of the original. Some processes create a fourth separation used to include black for added density. Separations are usually on film to make printing plates or prints. However, individual separation prints are sometimes made as proofs during printing. – An example of separation^2 is stereo recording, which must minimize crossover between left and right channels. – Separation^3 often involves replacing the item with a separation sheet. Examples include pulling nitrate negatives from a collection for transfer to cold storage or removing folded, oversize materials so they can be stored flat.

separation sheet, n. ~ A form filed in the original location of an item, indicating that the item is stored elsewhere.

> *Notes:* A separation sheet preserves the context of items that are stored in a different location by creating a record at the original location. For example, a folded map may be removed from a folder so that it may be stored flat or a nitrate negative may put in cold storage to protect surrounding documents and to retard deterioration. A separation sheet describing the item and indicating its current location is put in the original's place to let people know of its existence.

sequence, n. ~ 1. A series of things arranged in order. – 2. MOVING IMAGES · A portion of a moving image production that contains extended action typically made up of several scenes and often with complex camera movements.

> *RT:* moving image, scene, shot
> *Notes:* In moving image productions, a sequence^2 (a chapter) is made up of scenes (paragraphs) that are made up of shots (sentences).

sequential access, n. ~ 1. Computing · A technique of retrieving and processing information in a file or on storage media by starting at the beginning, then proceeding to each following record in order. – 2. Computing · A method of retrieving and processing information in a file by matching the order of transactions to the order in which the information is stored in the file.

    RT: direct access, random access

    Notes: Some storage media require sequential access. For example, information on tape can only be accessed sequentially.

    †237 *(Ralston 1976, p. 2):* Indirect methods [of access] may be classified 1) as sequential, in which there is some type of search through a sequence of records (but generally not a complete search that starts from the first record and proceeds through the whole file), or 2) as nonsequential, in which the desired record is located without such a search. A common nonsequential method is based on the use of an index and is usually called 'Index Sequential Access Method' (ISAM). Other nonsequential access methods use key transformations and are usually referred to as 'randomizing' or 'hashing' techniques.

serial, n. ~ 1. A continuing publication issued in installments, typically numbered and dated. – 2. Moving images · A program with a storyline that continues through separate episodes released over time.

    DF: series

    RT: issue, magazine

    Notes: Each installment of a serial[1] is typically called an issue. – Serials[2], such as *The Mask of Zorro*, were common in theaters through the 1950s.

    †11 *(AACR2):* [serial[1]] A publication in any medium issued in successive parts bearing numeric or chronological designations and intended to be continued indefinitely. Serials include periodicals; newspapers; annuals (reports, yearbooks, etc.); the journals, memoirs, proceedings, transactions, etc., of societies; and numbered monograph series.

serialized microform, n. ~ A microfilm format that stores images sequentially on a continuous roll.

    BT: microfilm, microform

    Notes: The roll may be an open reel, cassette, or cartridge.

series, n. ~ 1. A group of similar records that are arranged according to a filing system and that are related as the result of being created, received, or used in the same activity; a **file group**; a **record series**. – 2. Bibliography · A group of items, each with its own title, also bearing a collective title for the group as a whole.

    DF: batch, serial

    RT: class, manuscript group, subseries

    †120 *(APPM2 1989, 1.0A):* [Series[1]] File units or documents arranged in accordance with a filing system or maintained as a unit because they relate to a particular subject or function, result from the same activity, have a particular form, or because of some other relationship arising out of their creation, receipt, or use. Also known as record series. In archival practice, the series is the usual unit of cataloging or description.

series description, n. ~ A description of a series[1], including the title, scope and content note, size or volume, dates of the material, and arrangement.

BT: Broader Term · *NT:* Narrower Term · *RT:* Related Term · *DF:* Distinguish From

series descriptive system, n. ~ A technique of creating finding aids using the series[1] as the primary level of control, rather than the record group or fonds.

> *RT:* archival description, hierarchical description
> *Notes:* The series descriptive system is intended to maintain control of series over time. It was first widely adopted in Australia in response to frequent administrative changes and the consequent existence of multiprovenance series.

SGML ~ *see:* Standard Generalized Markup Language

SGML Open ~ *see:* Organization for the Advancement of Structured Information Standards

shadow, n. ~ PHOTOGRAPHY · Areas of low density in negatives or areas of high density in positives.

> *RT:* highlight
> *Notes:* Shadows appear dark or opaque in positives and light or transparent in negatives.

sharpness, n. ~ A subjective impression of clarity of detail in an image.

> *DF:* acutance
> *RT:* focus, resolution
> *Notes:* Sharpness is distinguished from acutance, which is an objective measure edge between two areas. Sharpness is influenced by acutance, resolution, contrast, color[1,2], and subject.

sheet, n. ~ 1. A broad, relatively thin material that often is rectangular. – 2. PRINTING · A large sheet of paper on which a number of pages have been printed, to be folded and trimmed to form consecutive pages for a publication. – 3. A map or drawing, often one in a series. – adj. ~ 4. Broad, relatively thin, and flat.

> *RT:* paper sizes, planar, two-dimensional
> *Notes:* Sheet[1,4] is roughly synonymous with 'two-dimensional', in that the depth is much less than the length and width. A sheet may be pliable; when distorted it forms a curved or angular surface in three dimensions. – The pages on a sheet[2] often are folded and trimmed to make a section, but a sheet may contain pages from more than one section.

sheet film, n. ~ PHOTOGRAPHY · Flat, thin plastic coated with a photographic emulsion.

> *DF:* roll film
> *BT:* film
> *RT:* notch code
> *Notes:* Sheet film typically contains one image, although microfiche is sheet film containing many images. Sheet film is distinguished from roll film, which is much longer than wide and which typically contains several images in a single row side by side. 'Film' generally refers to undeveloped materials; once the images have been developed, they are often called negatives, transparencies, or slides.

shelf, n. ~ A flat sheet of metal, wood, or other rigid material that has been mounted horizontally and that is used to store materials.

> *RT:* shelving
> *Notes:* Shelves are commonly set into a frame or mounted using brackets.

shelf list, n. ~ A description of a repository's holdings that is organized in the same order that the materials are stored.

> *Notes:* An example of a shelf list is a set of catalog cards for books that are ordered by call number. Shelf lists are generally used by staff for collection control

rather than as an access tool. However, if the materials are classified according to a subject scheme, browsing the list provides access similar to browsing the shelves.

shelving, n. ~ Furniture made of shelves for storing materials.

>*NT:* back-to-back shelving, compact shelving, open shelf filing

>*RT:* bay, compartment, double shelving, honeycombing, range, row, run, section, shelf, stacks, standard

>*Notes:* A group of rows of shelving is often referred to as 'stacks'. A group of shelves, one above the other and supported by the same uprights or standards, may be called a bay or a section. A group of bays or sections may be called a row or range. Different types of shelving include adjustable, bracket, cantilever, compact, and roller.

shop book, n. ~ A volume, usually a ledger, containing a record of original entries of a transactions made in the usual course of business by a shopkeeper, trader, or other business person.

>*DF:* daybook

>*RT:* account book, ledger, original entry

short, n. ~ A motion picture that generally runs less than an hour, often for only a few minutes.

>*RT:* feature

>*Notes:* Shorts are distinguished from feature¹ length films, which usually run for more than an hour. No standard definition sets time limits for either shorts or features.

shorthand ~ *see:* stenography

shot, n. ~ 1. PHOTOGRAPHY, MOVING IMAGES · The scene captured from a camera's point of view. – 2. PHOTOGRAPHY · An image made using a camera; an exposure³. – 3. MOVING IMAGES · An uninterrupted run of the camera, recording a continuous segment of time on film.

>*RT:* exposure, moving image, scene, sequence

>*Notes:* In moving image productions, shots² (similar to sentences in a written work) are combined to form scenes (paragraphs), which are combined to form sequences (chapters).

show case, n. ~ A cabinet with a transparent top or sides, typically made from glass or Plexiglas, that protects materials while on exhibit.

>*Syn:* display case, exhibition case

SHRAB ~ *see:* State Historical Records Advisory Board

shredding, n. ~ The process of cutting or tearing into strips.

>*RT:* destruction

>*Notes:* Shredding is a common technique to destroy paper documents. A shredder may cut in a single direction, producing thin strips the length of the document. Some shredders cut in a second direction, turning those strips into very small pieces.

shrink-wrap license, n. ~ An agreement granting conditions and terms of use that are acknowledged and agreed to by breaking a thermoplastic seal.

>*BT:* license

>*RT:* click-wrap license

>*Notes:* Shrink-wrap licenses are frequently used with software.

sig., abbr. ~ Signed.

sigillography, n. ~ The study of seals.

> *RT:* seal

signature, n. ~ 1. A name, initials, or other distinctive mark made by an individual. – 2. PRINTING · An identifying mark on the first page of a section of a book. – 3. PRINTING · Sets of printed pages that, when folded, make up a section of a book.

> *NT:* electronic signature
>
> *Notes:* A signature[1] is often used to indicate a signatory's agreement to the terms of a document. As such, a signature may indicate that a record is complete. – Technically, a signature[2], is just the identifying mark on the section, but the term has come to mean the section itself.
>
> †276 *(CTG 1997, p. 1):* Historically, the legal concept of signature[1] is very broad and can be defined as any mark that is made with the intention of authenticating a marked document or record. Signatures serve to give evidence or authenticate a record by identifying the signer with the signed record. In some contexts, a signature records the signer's approval or authorization of the signed record and the signer's intention to give it legal effect. A signature also has some ceremonial significance, and can impart a sense of clarity and finality to a record or transaction. For purposes of evidence, a signature must provide for 1) signer authentication i.e., the signature must indicate who signed a record and should be difficult for another person to (re)produce without authorization, and 2) record authentication.

silking, n. ~ The process of applying thin, nearly transparent silk cloth to one or both sides of a leaf to strengthen or repair it.

> *RT:* encapsulation, lamination

silver gelatin photograph ~ *see:* gelatin silver photograph

silver halide, n. ~ Light-sensitive crystalline salts formed from the combination of silver and bromine, chlorine, or iodine.

> *Notes:* Silver halides are used in photographic film and paper.

silver mirroring (often **mirroring**), n. ~ A metallic sheen in high-density areas of photographs caused by the migration of silver to the surface.

> *RT:* bronzing, tarnish

simple act, n. ~ DIPLOMATICS · Something done toward a single purpose by a physical or juridical person.

> *BT:* act
>
> †70 *(Duranti 1998, p. 110):* The examination of documents issued by public authorities reveals the existence of two distinct types of actions, or act: those which were undertaken by the authority on its own direct initiative, of its own will, in the context of its political-sovereign capacity; and those which were initiated by other juridical or physical persons, public or private. In the former case, the moment of the action comprises one *simple act* consisting of the order given by the authority to its chancery to compile the document expressing its will. In the latter case, we have a *compound act* or *procedure*, consisting of well-defined stages or phases.

simple copy, n. ~ A copy that reproduces the content, but not the format, of the original.

> *BT:* copy
>
> *RT:* imitative copy

simple object access protocol, n. (**SOAP**, abbr.) ~ An XML-based protocol for accessing services over the Internet using Hypertext Transfer Protocol (http).

RT: Extensible Markup Language

†267 (SOAP 2003): SOAP Version 1.2 (SOAP) is a lightweight protocol intended for exchanging structured information in a decentralized, distributed environment. It uses XML technologies to define an extensible messaging framework providing a message construct that can be exchanged over a variety of underlying protocols. The framework has been designed to be independent of any particular programming model and other implementation specific semantics.

simple resolution, n. ~ A measure that deals with matters entirely within the prerogatives of one chamber of the United States Congress, that does not contain legislation, and that does not require concurrence of the other chamber or presidential approval.

> *BT:* resolution

sink mat, n. ~ A mount with additional space between the cover and the backing.

> *BT:* mat
>
> *Notes:* Sink mats are used for flat objects with significant depth, such as a seal, a magazine, or a glass plate. They are often used for warped items. Material between the cover and the backing, often layers of mat board, form a space (sink) that surrounds the item.

sizing, n. ~ 1. A substance used to fill the pores in fibrous materials. – 2. The process of treating materials with such a substance.

> *Notes:* Sizing is commonly added to paper, either by adding it to the pulp during manufacture or by coating the surface during finishing. Sizing gives paper a smooth surface that prevents ink from bleeding into the fibers. In some photographic processes, the paper is sized to keep light-sensitive salts on the surface in order to increase image sharpness. Sizing is commonly made from starch, gelatin, alum, albumen, or rosin.

skew, n. ~ 1. IMAGING · A condition in which the axis of the original is improperly aligned in the reproduction. – 2. IMAGING · A condition in which angles in an original are distorted in a reproduction. – 3. COMPUTING · A misalignment of a tape system, resulting in data being written to or read from the wrong location.

> *Notes:* Skew[1] causes a reproduction to appear to be at an angle. – Skew[2] may be caused by rotary imaging equipment.

skippet, n. ~ A small box, usually wood or metal, used to protect a seal that is attached to a document.

slide, n. ~ 1. PHOTOGRAPHY · A positive photographic image on transparent film that has been mounted to facilitate projection. – 2. SCIENCE · A piece of glass used to hold a specimen for viewing under a microscope.

> *DF:* transparency
>
> *BT:* photograph
>
> *RT:* lantern slide
>
> *Notes:* Slide[1] connotes a 35 mm transparency in a 2 × 2 inch mount designed for use in a projector, although the term is used to describe similar formats in other sizes. A super slide is made from a larger size film, also mounted in a 2 × 2 inch mount, but with greater ratio of image-to-mount area.

sling psychrometer ~ *see:* psychrometer

slip law, n. ~ The first official publication, issued before being included in general laws, of a bill that has been made law.

BT: law

Notes: A slip law may be a single sheet or a small pamphlet.

slip sheet, n. ~ 1. A thin, smooth paper or other material inserted under a window mat to protect the mounted work. – 2. Printing · A leaf inserted between printed works to prevent the transfer of the image from the surface of one work to the back of an adjacent work. – 3. Printing · The process of inserting dummy pages in a work to indicate where separately printed illustrations are to be inserted.

RT: barrier sheet

Notes: Slip sheets³ often have figure numbers, titles, and other notes that aid in proper placement of the illustrations.

slipcase, n. ~ A cover, open on one side, designed to slide over and protect an item.

BT: container

Notes: Slipcases made from two pieces of heavy board were often used for individual phonograph records. For books and albums, the slipcase usually has five sides of board; the spine is usually visible through the open side.

SMD ~ *see:* specific material designation

SMPTE ~ *see:* Society of Motion Picture and Television Engineers

snapshot, n. ~ 1. Photography · A photograph, often made quickly, with little or no attention to formal composition. – 2. Computing · A copy of a database, website, or other dynamic document at a specific moment in time.

RT: photograph

Notes: Sir John Herschel coined snapshot¹ in 1860, by analogy to the hunter's term for a quick shot made without careful aim. Snapshots became common after the introduction of point-and-shoot cameras, such as Kodak's, in 1888. Starting in the 1960s, some fine art photographers adopted an aesthetic that mimicked the common visual characteristics of the snapshot.

SOAP ~ *see:* simple object access protocol

Society of American Archivists, n. (**SAA**, abbr.) ~ An organization of professional archivists based in the United States, with members from around the world.

Notes: Founded in 1936, the Society is North America's oldest and largest national archival professional association. It serves the educational and informational needs of its members and promotes the identification, preservation, and use of records of historical value. See http://www.archivists.org/.

Society of Motion Picture and Television Engineers, n. (**SMPTE**, abbr.) ~ An organization of engineers, technical directors, cameramen, editors, technicians, manufacturers, educators, and consultants in the moving image industry.

Notes: SMPTE develops standards, provides education, shares information about developments in moving image technology, and promotes networking. See http://www.smpte.org/.

sodium thiosulfate ~ *see:* fixer

soft copy, n. ~ Computing · Information stored or displayed in a computer system.

DF: hard copy

RT: copy

Notes: Soft copy includes information displayed on a screen or stored on disk. It is distinguished from hard copy, which has been printed to paper.

soft focus, n. ~ Photography · Having an image that is not sharp as the result of optical imperfections.

RT: focus

Notes: True soft focus results when light from a subject is focused in different planes. Soft focus can be produced by lenses with spherical aberration or by diffusion in the optics. Portrait photographers often use lenses that are intentionally designed to introduce soft focus or use a diffusion screen in front of the lens to hide blemishes or glamorize the subject. Images that are not sharp are often described as soft, although 'soft focus' is not exactly synonymous with 'out of focus'.

software, n. ~ COMPUTING · The instructions that direct the operation of computer hardware.

RT: application, computer program, firmware, hardware

Notes: 'Software' includes both system software, which governs the operation of specific hardware, and application software, which is designed to perform a specific task on the system.

software dependent, adj. ~ COMPUTING · Requiring specific programs to be able to create, store, transmit, or access data.

RT: hardware dependent, open system

Notes: Generally used to describe applications that use closed, proprietary programs and data formats that are difficult to migrate to other hardware or software systems.

Solander box, n. ~ A wooden case with the lid hinged to the base and with clasps on the fore-edge.

BT: box

RT: clamshell case, document case

Notes: The exterior of a Solander box is often covered with fabric and the interior lined with heavy paper. A Solander box may be constructed like a clamshell case. Three of the sides of the lid and the base are roughly the same size and designed to nest, while the fourth side of the lid and base is shared and serves as a hinge. In some designs, the top is relatively shallow. The box was invented by botanist Daniel Charles Solander when working at the British Museum (1773–1782).

solarization, n. ~ PHOTOGRAPHY · The reversal of tones due to extreme overexposure.

DF: Sabattier effect

Notes: A very bright object may appear dark in a photograph as the result of solarization. For example, the sun may appear dark in an otherwise normal image. Solarization is distinguished from the Sabattier effect, which results in a reversal of tones due to exposure to light during development.

solvent lamination ~ *see:* lamination

sort, n. ~ 1. A particular order or sequence. – 2. Things that have been put in a particular order. – 3. PRINTING · A particular character in a font. – v. ~ 4. The process of organizing things into different classes or a particular order.

Notes: A special sort³ is a character not usually included in a font, such as fractions, symbols, and superior and inferior letters and figures.

sound recording (also **audio recording**), n. ~ Any medium capable of capturing and reproducing an audible signal.

Syn: phonorecord

NT: phonograph record

Notes: 'Sound recording' is a generic term used to encompass a wide range of formats, including phonograph records, magnetic tape, compact discs, and computer files. The term does not include multimedia recordings that include sound, such as the soundtrack on a motion picture.

†281 (USC, 17 USC 101): Copyright · Works that result from the fixation of a series of musical, spoken, or other sounds, but not including the sounds accompanying a motion picture or other audiovisual work, regardless of the nature of the material objects, such as disks, tapes, or other phonorecords, in which they are embodied.

Soundex, n. ~ A technique to create a phonetic index, making it possible to look up a name or word using a coded form of its sound rather than spelling.

RT: phonetic index

Notes: The Soundex system was initially patented by Robert C. Russell in April 1918 (US patent 1,261,167). Soundex is sometimes used generically to mean any phonetic index.

soundtrack, n. ~ 1. Moving images · The portion of a film or moving image recording that is reserved for the audio signal. – 2. Moving images · A commercial recording of the music from a motion picture.

Notes: In motion pictures on film, the soundtrack[1] is a physically separate area in which the audio signal is recorded. The soundtrack is commonly an analog signal recorded as patterns of light and dark running parallel to the frames that make up the picture. The signal may also be recorded on a magnetized strip that is coated along the length of the film. In digital and magnetic recordings, the soundtrack is usually a separate channel from the visual signal. – A soundtrack[2] is not a complete transcription of the audio portion of a film. It excludes most or all dialog and includes only the music.

source document, n. ~ 1. Reprographics · The original from which a copy is made. – 2. Computing · A document containing information entered into a computer during data entry; an input record.

space-saving microfilm ~ see: disposal microfilming

span dates ~ see: inclusive dates

special diplomatics, n. ~ Diplomatics · The application of diplomatic theory (general diplomatics) to a particular records creator, including an analysis of the particular characteristics of the creator's recordkeeping procedures and resulting documents.

BT: diplomatics

special list, n. ~ A finding aid that describes series, folders, or items from different collections that relate to the same topic.

BT: finding aid

Notes: A special list typically goes into greater detail than a standard finding aid.

special records, n. ~ Materials stored separately from other records because their physical form or characteristics require unusual care or because they have nonstandard sizes.

BT: record

RT: nonprint materials, nontextual records, visual materials

Notes: Examples of special records include electronic, audiovisual, microform, cartographic and remote-sensing imagery, architectural and engineering, printed, and card records.

special sign, n. ~ Diplomatics · A mark that identifies individuals involved in the compilation, receipt, or execution of a record.

BT: extrinsic element

†70 (Duranti 1998, p. 138): Among the extrinsic elements, the diplomatists of medieval documents used to include the *special signs*, which should be regarded rather as intrinsic elements because of their function of identifying the persons involved in the documentation activity. The special signs can be divided into two categories: the signs of the writer and the subscribers, and the signs of the chancery or the records office. The first category includes the symbols used by notaries as personal marks in the medieval period, corresponding to the modern notarial stamp, and the crosses used by some subscribers in place of their name. The second category includes the *rota* and *bene valete* used by the paper chancery; the monogram of the sovereign's personal name used in imperial and royal chanceries; the initials *m.p.r.* for *manu proprio*; the double s for *s(ub) scripsi*; and all the various office stamps.

specific material designation, n. (**SMD**, abbr.) ~ A term indicating the special class of material (usually the class of physical object) to which the descriptive unit belongs (e.g., sound disc). [AACR2]

RT: general material designation

specificity of indexing ~ *see:* depth indexing

RT: indexing

specimen, n. ~ 1. An item of natural origin. – 2. An item that is a representative example of class.

DF: artifact

BT: material

RT: object, realia

Notes: Specimen[1] is often used to distinguish biological, botanical, and geological materials from man-made artifacts.

spider ~ *see:* harvester

SPINDEX (also **SPINDEX II, SPINDEX III**), n. ~ An early computer application to assist in the production and indexing of finding aids for records and manuscript collections.

Notes: SPINDEX is derived from Selective Permutation INDEXing.

†22 (Barth 1997): [Beginning in 1964] LC developed two separate systems, the Master Record of Manuscript Collections (MRMC) to provide administrative control over holdings, and SPINDEX (emerging out of the previous punch card project) to provide automated forms of access to archival materials. The National Archives joined the automation effort in 1967, and developed a derivative system from SPINDEX geared more specifically for archival collections at NARA called SPINDEX II. ¶ SPINDEX II focused on providing access to archival collections by automating previously prepared and published finding aids. ¶ The National Archives used SPINDEX II extensively throughout the 1970s, producing among other guides, the first comprehensive index to the Papers of the Continental Congress in conjunction with the American Bicentennial. NARA also used the system to prepare up-to-date collection guides (subject-based, and format-based) as well as the National Historical Publications and Records Commission's Directory of Archives and Manuscript Repositories. NARA did make the SPINDEX II system available to other organizations, and the system was used widely both as an archival control program, but also in a records management capacity for many corporations in the United States, Canada, and Australia.

†122 (Hickerson 1981, p. 29): The basic SPINDEX II programs provide for the printing of a register (a formatted, narrative collection description or abstract) and an index. The index provides for a primary sort of keywords, alphabetically or chronologically, and a secondary sort by either title or date. . . . After the staff of the NHPRC decided to use SPINDEX in the creation of a national data base of information on archives and manuscripts in the United States, they requested that NARS make significant changes in the SPINDEX II software package. Carrying out these modifications resulted in the creation of SPINDEX III.

spindle, n. ~ A sharp metal spike mounted vertically on a base, on which documents are impaled.

spirit process, n. ~ A technique to make multiple copies of a document from a master.

> *DF:* stencil process
>
> *Notes:* Spirit process and **ditto** are often used as synonyms. The master is a heavy piece of paper, which is placed in front of a sheet with a coating of wax and carbon. Writing or typing on the front of the master transfers the wax to the back of the master. During printing, alcohol is used to dissolve a thin layer of the wax on the back of the master, which is then transferred to a sheet of paper.

splice, n. ~ A joint between two separate pieces of roll film or tape to create a continuous strip.

> *Notes:* A splice may use cement, tape, ultrasonic welding, or other means to connect the two pieces.

split screen, n. ~ MOVING IMAGES · Two or more separate images presented simultaneously within the same frame.

> *BT:* format
>
> *RT:* moving image
>
> *†147 (James 2004):* On the real-time television series '24,' split screens put us in two places at once, watching the counterterrorist heroes and the villains they're chasing.

spoliation, n. ~ The intentional destruction, alteration, or concealment of evidence, especially documents.

> *Notes:* In general, courts have found that the routine destruction of records after reasonable, scheduled retention periods is not spoliation. However, if there is a reasonable likelihood of litigation or audit, destruction of relevant records may be considered spoliation, even if the retention period has passed.
>
> *†265 (Skupsky and Mantaña 1994, p. 105):* Additionally, the spoliation, or attempt to suppress material evidence by a party to the suit, favorable to an adversary, is sufficient foundation for an inference of his guilt or negligence.

spool, n. ~ 1. A hub, usually with flanges, on which film or tape is wound for storage. – v. ~ 2. COMPUTING · To transfer data to a queue for temporary storage pending further action.

> *RT:* reel
>
> *†239 (New Hacker's Dictionary 1994, p. 392):* [Spool[2]] From early IBM 'Simultaneous Peripheral Operation On-Line,' but is widely thought to have been contrived for the effect. To send files to some device or program (a spooler) that queues them up and does something useful with them later. Without qualification, the spooler is the print spooler controlling output of jobs to a printer; but the term has been used in connection with other peripherals (especially plotters and graphics devices) and occasionally even for input devices.

spreadsheet, n. ~ A computer program that provides accounting worksheets, each sheet containing rows and columns.

Notes: In a spreadsheet, a cell may contain a formula that displays a value that has been calculated from values in other cells. Changing the value in one cell affects the values in other cells that refer to the changed value. VisiCalc was the first spreadsheet program for personal computers. Other examples include Excel, Lotus 1-2-3, and Quattro Pro.

stability, n. ~ The quality of resisting change or deterioration.

RT: fixity

†215 *(O'Toole 1998, p. 272):* Here were the oral and literate side by side, but writing has some advantages. In written form, information achieved a stability and durability it would not have so long as it remained only in the mind or in spoken words. What is more, writing was in itself coming to be recognized as an effective way for gathering and sharing information: some people would now learn things only from books, Bede realized.

stacks, n. ~ Repositories · An area where materials are stored, especially an area furnished principally with shelving.

RT: shelving

†224 *(Petroski 1999, p. 167):* In the nineteenth century the idea arose of keeping a library's collection of books in a space separate from the reading room, and this led to the development of the bookstack as we know it today.

staging, n. ~ Preservation · The process of preparing materials for storage or use; conditioning[1].

Syn: conditioning

RT: acclimation

Notes: Staging is commonly used to describe steps necessary to acclimatize materials in cold storage for use at normal temperatures and relative humidities, or to acclimatize materials at normal temperatures and humidities for cold storage.

staging area, n. ~ 1. An area set aside to allow materials to be stabilized before being placed in or removed from storage. – 2. A holding area.

RT: archival storage conditions

Notes: Staging areas are commonly used to allow time for materials that are stored in cold storage vaults to come to room temperature before being used by patrons. They are also used to store new accessions so that the materials can be reviewed for insects, vermin, mold, and other contaminants prior to accessioning, and to hold materials prior to destruction.

stamp, n. ~ 1. A device used to print, impress, perforate or emboss a design or letters on an item, especially paper. – 2. A mark made by such a device. – 3. A small piece of printed paper attached to a letter or container to indicate the payment of duties, taxes, or postage. – v. ~ 4. To mark with a stamp.

RT: emboss, time stamp

Notes: Stamps[1] are usually small and intended for hand use. The letters or design are typically raised. Stamps are commonly inked or used to transfer a pigment or metal from foil. A blind stamp uses no such ink or pigment, and leaves only an impression of the design.

stamping, n. ~ The act of placing a mark (a stamp[2]) on materials to indicate ownership, legal custody, review, or approval.

RT: marking

BT: Broader Term · NT: Narrower Term · RT: Related Term · DF: Distinguish From

Notes: A reference number may be placed within the stamp.

stand-alone system, n. ~ Hardware or software that is capable of starting and completing a function independently.

    BT: system

    RT: turnkey system

standard, n. ~ 1. A benchmark or reference used to measure some quality or practice. – 2. An international, national, or industry agreement that establishes qualities or practices in order to achieve common goals. – 3. SHELVING · A vertical beam or pole used to hold shelves; an upright.

    Syn: upright

    NT: content standard, convention, data structure standard, data value standard, de facto standard, de jure standard, descriptive standard, guideline, technical standard

    RT: benchmark, best practices, policy, procedure, shelving

    Notes: In this glossary, specific standards are entered under the full name, with cross-references under their standard number. For example, the Department of Defense's records management standard is entered under its title, *Design Criteria for Electronic Records Management Software Applications*, with a cross-reference from DoD 5015.2.

    †66 *(Duff 1996, p. 347):* De jure standards emanate from legislative bodies and are regulatory in nature, while de facto standards derive from particular products that dominate the market. Voluntary consensus standards emerge from cooperative ventures and usually reflect consensus building and compromise. Almost all archival standards are voluntary consensus standards.

    †260 *(Schmelzer 2003):* A standard is simply an agreement on common practices among multiple parties. Standards have been around for a long time – electric current, railroad gauges, the metric system, and even musical notation are examples of standards. However, the processes that interested parties follow to establish standards can differ dramatically. Standards can either be de facto (occurring as a result of natural market movement and adoption) or prescribed (established by formal agreement). De facto standards often result when one vendor dominates a market, while prescribed standards develop in competitive environments where market participants realize that agreement upon a standard will benefit all of the participants. De facto standards incite little argument, because the market as a whole decides them. However, prescribed standards cause much consternation, because of the often contentious processes that lead to their establishment.

Standard Generalized Markup Language, n. (**SGML**, abbr.) ~ An international standard (ISO 8879) metalanguage used to define sets of tags to identify the relationship between document content and structure for use by information processing applications.

    NT: Extensible Markup Language

    RT: document interchange, document type definition, Encoded Archival Description, markup

    Notes: Developed by Charles F. Goldfarb in 1974 and published as a standard in 1986. Extensible markup language (XML) is a simplified version of SGML intended for use on the web. Hypertext Markup Language (HTML) is an example of a markup language defined in SGML.

stat ~ *see:* Photostat

State Historical Records Advisory Board, n. (**SHRAB**, abbr.) ~ A central advisory board within each state for historical records planning and for projects funded by the National Historical Records and Publications Commission.

> *RT:* National Historical Publications and Records Commission

> *†37 (Burke 2000, p. 37):* The [SHRAB] serves as a coordinating body to facilitate cooperation among historical records repositories and other information agencies within the state and as a state-level review body for grant proposals as defined in the Commission's guidelines. Specifically, the board may perform such duties as sponsoring and publishing surveys of the conditions and needs of historical records in the State; soliciting or developing proposals for projects to be carried out in the State with NHPRC grants; reviewing proposals by institutions in the State and making recommendations about these to the Commission; developing, revising, and submitting to the Commission State priorities for historical records projects . . . ; promoting an understanding of the role and value of historical records; acting in an advisory capacity to the state archives and other statewide archival or records agencies; and reviewing, through reports and otherwise, the operation and progress of projects in the State financed by NHPRC grants. [Citing 36 CFR §1206.38(a–b).]

statement of responsibility, n. ~ CATALOGING · A word or phrase indicating the individuals who participated in the creation or production of a work, often including information about their role.

> *BT:* descriptive element

> *†11 (AACR2):* A statement, transcribed from the item being described, relating to persons responsible for the intellectual or artistic content of the item, to corporate bodies from which the content emanates, or to persons or corporate bodies responsible for the performance of the content of the item.

static website, n. ~ A website that uses Uniform Resource Locators (URLs) to point to fixed content.

> *DF:* dynamic website

> *BT:* website

> *Notes:* The content of a web page on a static website may – and usually does – change over time as the referenced files are edited and updated. A static website is distinguished from a dynamic website, which draws content from a database to produce different content, sometimes changing each time it is viewed, using the same URL.

stationery binding, n. ~ The branch of bookbinding associated with books intended to be written in.

> *BT:* binding

> *Notes:* Stationery binding is distinguished from letterpress binding, which refers to that branch of bookbinding associated with books intended to be read. Stationery binding includes ledger, record, and account books; manifold and duplicate books, receipt books, checkbooks, passports, bankbooks, and loose-leaf volumes. It includes a variety of forms of mechanical binding, as well as punching, perforating, padding, ruling, and other miscellaneous binding operations. 'Stationery binding' is sometimes referred to as **vellum binding** because at one time the books were generally covered in vellum.

> *†248 (Roberts and Etherington 1982):* The style of binding applied to books

used for written records, e.g., blankbooks, is by necessity much different from that for books meant to be read. Their shape, size, and durability depend on the purpose for which they are intended; consequently, stationery bindings vary greatly in style, complexity, and quantity. Blankbooks, including court record books, which are generally required for permanent records, are bound in a different style from letterpress work because not only must the binding withstand heavy use, it must also open very flat for writing purposes.

statute, n. ~ A law, especially one established by legislation.

> *Syn:* law

stemming, n. ~ SEARCHING · The process of extracting and searching the root form of a word to find all variants.

> *Notes:* The use of a wild-card search is a simple approximation of stemming. Stemming the word archives as such as 'archiv*' would ideally find archive, archives, archival, archivist, archivists, and other words beginning with 'archiv'.

stencil process, n. ~ A technique to make multiple copies of a document by pressing ink through holes in a master onto paper.

> *DF:* spirit process
> *RT:* mimeograph

stenography (also **phonography**, **shorthand**), n. ~ 1. The process of using shorthand script[1] to transcribe speech. – 2. The process of transcribing speech using a specialized typewriter.

> †*300 (Yates 1989, p. 37):* Stenography[1], or phonography (as it was often called) – taking dictation by shorthand and later transcribing it – seems to have played only a limited role in business before the typewriter.

step-and-repeat camera, n. ~ A microfilm camera that produces a series of separate images according to a predetermined sequence of rows and columns.

> *BT:* microfilm camera
> *RT:* microfiche, microfilm
> *Notes:* Step-and-repeat cameras typically use 105 mm microfilm, which is cut after processing to create microfiche.

step wedge, n. ~ A standard piece of film consisting of areas with discrete tones progressing from opaque to transparent that is used to calibrate and test photographic films and papers.

> *RT:* benchmark, densitometer, gray scale
> *Notes:* When photographic materials are contact printed with a step wedge, the resulting image is a gray scale. A densitometer is used to measure the reflection or transmission of light from each discrete tone. Those measurements are then compared to measurements made from the step wedge.

stereo photography ~ *see:* stereoscopic photography

stereograph (often **stereo**), n. ~ Two photographs mounted together which, when viewed together, give the illusion of three dimensions.

> *DF:* stereopticon
> *BT:* photograph
> *RT:* card-mounted photographs, stereoscopic photography
> *Notes:* Stereographs were very common from the 1850s through the 1910s. The earliest stereographs were made from daguerreotypes. Most 19th-century stereographs were albumen prints on cards measuring 3⅜ × 7 inches, although

stereographs were made using other formats. Most 20th century stereographs used gelatin silver prints on cards the same size. Stereographs are commonly viewed in a special viewer that displays the left image to the left eye and the right image to the right eye.

stereopticon, n. ~ 1. A projector that can show two images on a screen, allowing one image to dissolve into the other. – 2. A magic lantern.

> *DF:* stereograph
>
> *Syn:* magic lantern
>
> *RT:* lantern slide

stereoscopic photography (often **stereo photography**), n. ~ A technique for using two photographs to produce an image with the appearance of three dimensions.

> *RT:* stereograph
>
> *Notes:* The two photographs in a stereoscopic photograph are made simultaneously using two cameras (or a specialized camera with two lenses) roughly 2½ inches apart. This separation is roughly the distance between the human eyes. The images are typically viewed using a device that displays the left image to the left eye, and the right image to the right eye. Stereoscopic photographs made using daguerreotypes date to the beginning of photography; pairs of stereoscopic prints on cards (stereographs) were popular from the 1850s through the 1910s; and stereoscopic transparencies made using 35 mm film were made as early as the 1920s and popularized with Kodak's Stereo Realist camera in the 1940s.

sticktion ~ *see:* sticky shed syndrome

sticky shed syndrome (also **sticktion**), n. ~ A condition resulting from the deterioration of the binder in magnetic tape that results in gummy residues on tape heads during playback.

> *Notes:* Sticky shed appears primarily in audio, computer, and video tapes manufactured in the United States between the mid-1970s and mid-1980s. The binder used to hold the metallic particles on the base can absorb water and weaken. When the tape is played back, the oxide particles rub off the tape and build up on the equipment.

still picture (also **still image**) ~ *see:* movie still, photograph

stock shot, n. ~ Moving images, Photography · Images kept on file in a library for later use or sale.

> *RT:* photograph
>
> *Notes:* Stock shots may be moving or still images. They are collected to meet a variety of possible uses. For example, a photographer may keep stock shots of landscapes or street scenes for use in advertisements. The images may be older and used in period works.

stop list, n. ~ A list of words to be ignored in full-text indexing.

> *RT:* go list
>
> *Notes:* A stop list typically contains common words that add little meaning to the work being indexed, such as prepositions and conjunctions.

stop-motion photography, n. ~ Moving images · A technique in which each frame is shot separately so that the objects photographed can be adjusted to give the appearance of live motion.

> *RT:* photograph
>
> *Notes:* The television programs "Gumby" and "Wallace and Grommit" are examples of stop-motion photography.

strategic information management, n. ~ The skills that enable professionals and organizations to make well-informed decisions that result in a competitive advantage in the business world.

> *BT:* management
> *RT:* cost-avoidance justification, cost-benefit analysis, risk analysis
> *Notes:* Strategic information draws on principles of records and information management, information technology, and strategic management.

stripping, n. ~ 1. The process of pulling and disposing of unwanted materials in a series. – 2. Removing one layer of a laminate from another. – 3. REPROGRAPHICS · Positioning film containing images of text and illustrations on a carrier sheet (a goldenrod) to create a printing plate.

> *Syn:* culling, weeding
> *Notes:* Weeding and culling connote item-level separation, where purging, stripping[1], and screening connote removal of materials at the folder level or higher.

structural metadata, n. ~ Information about the relationship between the parts that make up a compound object.

> *BT:* metadata
> †90 *(IMLS Framework 2001):* Structural metadata can be thought of as the glue that binds compound objects together, relating, for example, articles, issues and volumes of serial publications, or the pages and chapters of a book.
> †235 *(Puglia, Reed, and Rhodes 2004, p. 10):* Structural metadata might include whether the resource is simple or complex (multi-page, multi-volume, has discrete parts, contains multiple views); what the major intellectual divisions of a resource are (table of contents, chapter, musical movement); identification of different views (double-page spread, cover, detail); the extent (in files, pages, or views) of a resource and the proper sequence of files, pages and views; as well as different technical (file formats, size), visual (pre- or post-conservation treatment), intellectual (part of a larger collection or work), and use (all instances of a resource in different formats – TIFF files for display, PDF files for printing, OCR files for full text searching) versions.

structure, n. ~ The manner in which elements are organized, interrelated, and displayed.

> *BT:* record
> *RT:* content, context, format
> *Notes:* Along with content and context, structure is one of the three fundamental aspects of a record. Internal structure includes the relationship of content within a record, while external structure places a record in the context of an order, a series, and a collection. Structure also refers to the appearance of a document, including the fonts and formatting of the text and any associated graphics.
> †187 *(McGovern and Samuels 1997, p. 19): Structure* is the format of the document, such as a purchase order, registration form, or memorandum. ¶ For paper records, all of the characteristics are embedded in each physical artifact, or document. In electronic form, while the content of the message may be somewhat familiar, the context and structure are embedded in hardware and software.
> †231 *(Digital Preservation Testbed 2003, p. 16):* The structure of a digital record refers to the structure as it was originally made and reproduced on the screen. This is the logical hierarchy of, and the relationships between, the parts of the record. The structural elements of email are, for example, the headers, the message text

and any attachments. The structural elements of a report (a text document) on the other hand can be formed by a cover sheet, a table of contents, chapters (divided into sections and paragraphs) and a bibliography and/or appendices. ¶ It is important that these structural elements are correctly identified and that sections of the email or report are reproduced in the right order. It is also important to know whether there are other essential structural characteristics, for example the presence of footnotes or endnotes in a text document. If this structure is lost as the result of a migration, the record may be reproduced wrongly.

subbing, n. ~ PHOTOGRAPHY · A thin layer of material that helps an emulsion adhere to the base.

Notes: A thin layer of cellulose nitrate was often used as a subbing layer between the gelating emulsion and cellulose acetate base of early 20th-century photographic film.

subfield code, n. ~ DESCRIPTION · A delimiter followed by a data element identifier to mark the beginning of different types of information within a field.

Notes: For example, in the MARC format field 245, Title and statement of responsibility, subfield code a indicates the title proper; subfield code b, other title information; and subfield c, the statement of responsibility. Because the delimiter is a nondisplaying control character (ASCII 31), different systems use different characters to display it. The dollar sign ($) or pipe (|) is often used to represent the delimiter. For example, $aAlice in Wonderland / $cLewis Carroll.

†285 *(LC USMARC 1994, p. 7):* Subfield codes identify the individual data elements within the field, and precede the data elements they identify. Each data fields contains at least one subfield code. The subfield code consists of a delimiter [$1F_{16}$, 8-bit] followed by a data element identifier. Data element identifiers defined in USMARC may be any ASCII lowercase alphabetic or numeric character. In general, numeric identifiers are defined for data used to process the field, or coded data needed to interpret the field. Alphabetic identifiers are defined for the separate elements which constitute the data content of the field.

subgroup, n. ~ A body of related records within a record group or collection, each corresponding to an administrative subdivision in the originating organization.

RT: record group

Notes: In some instances, subgroups are based on geographical, chronological, functional, or similar types of the material itself. If the organization has a complex hierarchical structure, each subgroup may be further divided into subordinate subgroups to reflect the levels of the hierarchical structure.

subheading, n. ~ 1. CATALOGING, INDEXING · A word or phrase added to a heading to further distinguish categories under the heading. – 2. A word or phrase added to a heading used to distinguish the heading from similar headings.

RT: heading

Notes: A subheading[1] is usually separated from the heading with a mark of punctuation. A dash is often used to separate subheadings for different classes within a heading. For example, 'Arizona–Pictorial works'. – Various schemes may be used for subheadings[2] used to distinguish one heading for another. For example, birth and death dates added to a personal name are distinguished using a comma, while fuller forms of a name are in parentheses. For example, Miller, Mrs. J. (Anna), b. 1825 is distinguished from Miller, Mrs. J. (Wanda), b. 1954.

subject, n. ~ 1. A principal theme or topic of a work. – 2. VISUAL ARTS · The content described or depicted in a work.

> *DF:* genre
> *Syn:* topic
> *Notes:* A subject[1] may be a person, corporation, place, topic, or period of time. It may be real or fantastic. A work may have more than one subject. – The subject[2] of an artwork may be both what the work is *of* (what is depicted) and what the work is *about* (the symbolic meaning of what is depicted). For example, a photograph *of* a young boy working hawking newspapers on the street may be *about* the exploitation of child labor.

subject access, n. ~ A technique of locating relevant materials based on topical (subject) content of the materials.

> *RT:* provenance access

subject analysis ~ *see:* analysis

Subject Cataloging Manual: Subject Headings, n. ~ A standard for the use of headings found in the Library of Congress Subject Headings (LCSH), including directions for adding subheadings to form precoordinated headings for more specific retrieval.

> *RT:* Anglo-American Cataloguing Rules, Library of Congress Subject Headings
> *Notes:* Published by the Library of Congress and available from the Cataloging Distribution Service.

subject classification, n. ~ The organization of materials into categories according to a scheme that identifies, distinguishes, and relates the concepts or topics of the materials.

> *BT:* classification
> *RT:* subject-numeric filing system
> *Notes:* Subject classification systems may use words or phrases to represent the subjects, or they may use codes, such as alpha-numeric, alphabetic-subject, decimal, duplex-numeric, mnemonic, or subject-numeric.

subject entry, n. ~ CATALOGING · A description of a work (an entry) in a catalog, register, or list that is filed under a heading that represents a concept or topic in the work.

> *BT:* entry

subject file, n. ~ A collection of documents (a file[1]) relating to some topic.

> *RT:* case file
> *Notes:* Subject files can relate to any type of topic, such as a action, event, person, place, project, or other subject. They are distinguished from case files, which relate to a situation affecting or relating to some particular investigation or administrative action. Where the documents in case files typically capture the same categories of information about each investigation or action, the content and format of documents in subject files is often varied.

subject guide ~ *see:* guide

subject-numeric filing system, n. ~ A technique of organizing materials alphabetically under a word used as the principal topic, then under a number for any subdivision of that topic.

> *BT:* filing system
> *RT:* subject classification
> *Notes:* An example of a subject-numeric heading is Accounting 6, where 6 represents purchase orders.

subscription, n. ~ 1. An agreement to pay for a something or a service to be delivered over time. – 2. A signature on a document.

subseries, n. ~ A body of documents within a series readily distinguished from the whole by filing arrangement, type, form, or content.

> *RT:* series

substantive records ~ *see:* program records

substitution microfilming ~ *see:* disposal microfilming

subtitle, n. ~ 1. An extension of the principal title (the title proper), usually distinguished from the principal title by design or a different typeface. – 2. MOVING IMAGES, THEATER · Dialog that is displayed as text, usually at the bottom of the frame or above or below the stage.

> *DF:* closed captioning
>
> *RT:* caption, inner title, other title information, title
>
> *Notes:* In cataloging, a subtitle[1] is called other title information. – Subtitles[2] are commonly used in foreign language films and operas to supply a translation of the dialog. In silent films, inner titles displayed full-screen between shots are sometimes called subtitles.

successor, n. ~ 1. An individual or organization that assumed the position, role, or functions of a predecessor. – 2. An organization that assumed the mission or program areas of a predecessor organization.

sufficiency, n. (**sufficient,** adj.) ~ Having enough information to meet the needs of the user.

> *RT:* adequacy of documentation, completeness, reliability
>
> *Notes:* A record may be complete, but insufficient, if it contains all the required information but not the information that is needed. When determining the elements necessary to be captured in the record of a process, it is essential that enough elements are included to ensure that the process is sufficiently documented.

summary guide (also **summary of records**), n. ~ A terse description of a repository's holdings, typically the provenance, title, series, dates, and extent of each collection.

> *BT:* guide

summary inventory ~ *see:* inventory

summary of records ~ *see:* summary guide

sunshine law, n. ~ A statute requiring public access to meetings and records of a governmental body.

> *RT:* Freedom of Information Act, open records law, public meeting law

supercomputer ~ *see:* computer

superscription, n. ~ DIPLOMATICS · An indication of the name of the author of a document or of its action that appears in the protocol.

> †70 *(Duranti 1998, p. 143):* Today, the superscription tends to take the form of an entitling; sometimes, however, it coexists with the entitling. It still appears by itself in all contractual documents (the superscription includes the mention of the first party), in declarative documents (those beginning with the pronoun 'I,' followed by the name of the subscriber), and in holographic documents, such as will (e.g., 'This is the last will and testament (title) of John Smith of Vancouver' (superscription)).

supplied title, n. ~ CATALOGING · A word or phrase naming a work that is supplied by a cataloger and used in the absence of a title proper on the chief source of information.

> *BT:* descriptive element

RT: title

Notes: A supplied title may be taken from a nonprescribed source of information in the item or from a reference source, or it may be composed by the cataloger.

supporting records, n. ~ Records that are not required to be made but are created to document and explain some action.

BT: record

surface cleaning, n. ~ PRESERVATION · The process of cleaning undesirable, superficial dirt or grime from a document without liquids.

Notes: Surface cleaning typically begins with a soft brush. In some instances, dry-cleaning bags and plastic erasers might be used. Documents made with pastels, charcoal, graphite pencil, or watercolors, or documents that are fragile, cannot be easily cleaned using these techniques as the pigments may be removed along with the dirt and the support may be damaged.

survey, n. ~ 1. A broad, general overview. – 2. The process of measuring the boundaries and contents of a piece of land. – 3. A map that records the boundaries and contents of a piece of land. – 4. A measure of some attitude or quality of a sample population made using a poll or questionnaire.

NT: records survey

suspense file, n. ~ A group of documents filed chronologically under some future date when they require further attention or action.

Syn: follow-up file, pending file, tickler file

BT: file

suspension ~ *see:* destruction suspension

symmetric-key encryption, n. ~ A technique of using a single key for translating information into ciphertext and subsequently decoding the ciphertext back to plaintext.

DF: dual-key encryption

BT: key

RT: cryptography, public key cryptography

Notes: Symmetric-key encryption is distinguished from dual-key encryption, which uses different keys for encryption and decoding.

syndetic relationships, n. ~ The conceptual connections between terms, including genus (broader than), species (narrower than), nonpreferred equivalence (use, see), preferred equivalent term (used for), and associated term (related term).

RT: cross-reference

Notes: The relationships and the manner in which those relationships are organized is described as the syndetic structure.

synthetic classification, n. ~ A technique to construct faceted codes to identify, distinguish, and relate categories.

BT: classification

RT: faceted classification

Notes: Faceted classification is an example of synthetic classification.

system, n. ~ 1. Any collection of related components and procedures treated as a whole. – 2. COMPUTING · Software that controls the basic functionality of a computer; an operating system.

NT: computer system, distributed system, experiential system, stand-alone system, turnkey system, utility system

RT: business activity structure classification system, database management system, decision support system, digital assets management system, document retrieval system, electronic document management system, electronic information system, electronic recordkeeping system, executive information system, executive support system, expert system, filing system, geographic information system, information system, interactive media, juridical system, legacy system, management information system, Open Archival Information System, open system, operating system, transaction processing system

Notes: In computing, system[1] can refer to diverse combinations of hardware, software, information, and procedures and may also include human activities.

systematic management, n. ~ The organization, supervision, and oversight of the conduct of a business or activity based on rational processes and procedures.

RT: business process

Notes: Systematic management is distinguished from work directed by an individual's idiosyncratic and personal style.

†*300 (Yates 1989, p. 1):* The philosophy of management that evolved in response to new needs, later to be labeled systematic management, promoted rational and impersonal systems in preference to personal and idiosyncratic leadership for maintaining efficiency in a firm's operation.

†*300 (Yates 1989, p. xvii):* The managerial philosophy that emerged, first in the railroads and later in manufacturing firms, sought to achieve better control of business processes and outcomes by imposing *system*, in great part through formal communication. According to this philosophy or theory, which has been designated by Joseph Litterer as 'systematic management,' efficiency was to be gained by substituting managerially mandated systems for ad hoc decisions by individuals, whether owners, foremen, or workers. These systems were established, operated, evaluated, and adjusted – that is to say, managed or controlled – all on the basis of flows of information and orders. ¶ Systematic management was built on the assumption that individuals were less important than the systems they functioned within.

systematic sampling, n. ~ A technique of selecting items from a group based on some formal characteristic, without regard to the content of the items.

BT: sampling

RT: fat file method

Notes: Examples of systematic sampling include pulling all files of a given size (see fat file method) and pulling all files in which the surname begins with a given letter. Although relatively easy to implement, it is not statistically valid.

systems development, n. ~ COMPUTING · The process of managing a system throughout its life cycle, including requirements definition, specification, programming, implementation, maintenance, and modification.

T

tab, n. ~ 1. A small protrusion used to grasp or for a label. – 2. A part of a file guide or folder that extends from the body and is used for a label. – 3. COMPUTING · A control character used to lay out data or as a delimiter between fields.

> *Notes:* Tab[3] typically connotes key on a keyboard or computer control character (ASCII 9) used to organize information into columns and is often used to indent the first line of a paragraph. The same character is sometimes used as a delimiter between fields in data files. The vertical tab character (ASCII 11) controls vertical spacing.

tab card ~ *see:* punched card

tag, n. ~ 1. A label containing information that is attached, sometimes with string, to something. – **field tag**, n. ~ 2. A short string of characters used to label the class of a data element in a record.

> *RT:* label

> *Notes:* A MARC tag[2], for example, is formed from three digits, such as 245 for the title field and 651 for a Geographical Added Entry. Encoded Archival Description (EAD) uses a short string enclosed in angle brackets to indicate the beginning and end of a specific type of data, such as <bioghist> for biographical/historical notes or <physdesc> for statements of extent. Hypertext Markup Language (HTML) and extensible markup language (XML) use pairs of tags to indicate the beginning and end of data elements embedded in text; for example <H1> and </H1> surround a first-level heading.

Tagged Image File Format, n. (**TIFF**, abbr.) ~ COMPUTING · A standard (ISO 12234-2) for storing a raster graphic and metadata that describes the image content and characteristics.

> *Notes:* TIFF is a proprietary format and trademark owned by Adobe, although the specifications are published and freely available. It is platform independent and widely supported.

tape, n. ~ 1. A long, thin, flat strip of material. – 2. A format that uses a long, thin strip of material wound on a hub and sometimes housed in a cartridge or cassette.

> *NT:* audiotape, digital audio tape, magnetic tape, videotape

> *RT:* paper tape

> *Notes:* Tape[1] may be made from paper, plastic, or cloth. It is often coated with adhesive on one or both sides and is used to seal materials or repair tears. – Tape[2] is used for audio, video, and data formats.

target, n. ~ 1. A benchmark used for testing and calibrating optical and reproduction systems. – 2. MICROFILMING, IMAGING · A document, added to materials before being imaged, that provides information about the materials.

> *Notes:* Targets[1] often contain graphic patterns, such as a series of progressively closer parallel lines, used to test for resolution and astigmatism. A gray scale or color tablet may be used to match the tonal range and colors in the reproduction with the original. – Targets[2] often contain information that describe the materials, problems with the originals, missing materials, or the filming process.

tarnish, n. ~ 1. A discoloration or dullness on metal, especially the result of silver oxidation. – 2. PHOTOGRAPHY · A discoloration of photographic images resulting from metallic silver in the image combining with oxygen or sulfur compounds.

> *RT:* bronzing, silver mirroring

taxonomy, n. ~ A structure used for classifying materials into a hierarchy of categories and subcategories.

> *RT:* classification, classification scheme, ontology

> †*295 (Whatis.com website):* In theory, the development of a good taxonomy takes into account the importance of separating elements of a group (taxon) into subgroups (taxa) that are mutually exclusive, unambiguous, and taken together, include all possibilities. In practice, a good taxonomy should be simple, easy to remember, and easy to use.

TDS, abbr. ~ Typed document signed.

technical access requirements note, n. ~ DESCRIPTION · Information about any special equipment needed to use materials.

> *BT:* descriptive element

> *Notes:* For example, a note might indicate that a light table is needed to view negatives, or that special hardware or software is necessary to access electronic records.

technical drawing, n. ~ A graphic using lines and symbols that follows precise conventions of scale and projection, typically used in architecture, construction, engineering, or mapping.

> *BT:* drawing

> *RT:* architectural drawing, cartography, engineering drawing

technical reference model, n. ~ A structured vocabulary used to ensure that technical terms in an enterprise architecture are carefully defined, related, and used consistently.

> *BT:* enterprise architecture

technical standard, n. ~ A standard[1,2] with precise, formal specifications that, when properly followed, will produce consistent results.

> *BT:* standard

TEI ~ *see:* Text Encoding Initiative

telecommunications, n. ~ A system to convey information using an electromagnetic system.

> *Notes:* 'Telecommunications' connotes communication over a distance, such as telephony, television, radio, or computer network. Telecommunications may be used for text, speech, or images, or it may be used for transmission of control information to mechanical systems.

telegram, n. ~ A text message that is transmitted using a sequence of electrical pulses and then recorded on paper.

> *Notes:* Telegraphy describes systems invented in the mid-19th century, especially a system that uses a series of pulses to represent letters, such as Morse code. The message may be handwritten by a telegraph operator listening to a message as a series of long and short tones. Later development recorded the message mechanically. Originally transmitted over wires, telegrams were later sent over the radio.

telematics, n. ~ The integration of computers and communications to support data communications.

telephotography, n. ~ 1. PHOTOGRAPHY · Techniques and equipment used to make photographs of distant objects. – 2. COMMUNICATIONS · The transmission of a photographic image over communication lines.

    RT: photograph

television, n. ~ 1. The techniques, equipment, and practices used to send and receive moving images with accompanying sound transmitted by means of an electrical signals; video. – 2. A receiver used to view and listen to such a program.

    RT: kinescope, video

    Notes: Although 'video' refers specifically to the visual aspects of a television signal, it is often used interchangeably with 'television'.

Telex, n. ~ A low bandwidth network connecting teletypewriters around the world.

temporary record (also **disposable records**), n. ~ A record of ephemeral value that can be destroyed immediately or after a specified time period.

    Syn: transitory record

    BT: record

    Notes: Temporary records are distinguished from permanent records, which must be kept indefinitely.

terminal, n. ~ COMPUTING · An input[1] or output[1] device that operates independently of the system to which it is linked.

    NT: dumb terminal

terminal digit filing, n. ~ A technique of organizing files under the last few digits of an identifying number, and then sequentially by any preceding numbers.

    Notes: Terminal digit filing has the advantage of distributing files evenly throughout the system, making it easier to allocate space for expansion. Use of terminal digital filing for the social security number 123-45-6789 would sort it first under 9, then under 12345678.

territorial pertinence, n. ~ The practice of placing documents with content relevant to a region in a repository within the region.

    RT: pertinence

    Notes: Territorial pertinence is distinguished from territorial provenance. For example, under territorial pertinence, records relating to a newly formed county would be transferred to the new county; under territorial provenance, the records would remain with the agency that created them.

test pattern, n. ~ A graphic pattern used as a benchmark to test and calibrate video equipment.

    Notes: Originally developed for use in television, test patterns are also used with computer monitors. Test patterns commonly include color bars, and resolution and alignment targets. Test patterns may be generated from an electrical signal or may be a printed or digital graphic transmitted as an image.

text, n. ~ 1. Written words. – 2. The principal portion of a printed work, as distinguished from front and back matter, notes, marginalia, or illustrations. – 3. A book intended for use in instruction; a textbook.

    BT: intrinsic element

    RT: copy, document, writing

    Notes: Text[1] encompasses all forms of writing, including printing, and typing. The words carved on a tombstone are an example of text, as are the representation and record of words in electronic format, such as a word processing document. Text includes numerals, punctuation, and symbols, but is distinguished from illustrations.

    †44 *(Cook 2001, p. 25):* No text is an innocent by-product of administrative or personal action, but rather a constructed product – although that conscious con-

struction may be so transformed into unconscious patters of social behaviour, language conventions, organization processes, technological imperatives, and information templates that links to its constructed nature have become quite hidden.

Text Encoding Initiative, n. (**TEI**, abbr.) ~ Guidelines for encoding in Standard Generalized Markup Language (SGML) or Extensible Markup Language (XML) machine-readable texts of interest to the humanities and social sciences.

RT: markup

Notes: The TEI is sponsored by the Association for Computers and the Humanities (ACH), the Association for Computational Linguistics (ACL), and the Association for Literary and Linguistic Computing (ALLC). See http://www.tei-c.org/.

text processing, n. ~ The use of a computer to create, edit, manipulate, analyze, store, display, or print written words.

RT: word processing

Notes: Text processing includes more than word processing, which is focused on documents. Text processing includes, for example, optical character recognition (OCR), formatting, and creation of concordances. Text processing packages are often specialized for one particular function, such as parsing noun phrases, where word processing connotes packages that integrate many different functions.

textual bibliography, n. ~ The study of different printings and editions of a printed work.

BT: bibliography

Notes: A textual bibliography seeks to identify variations in a text and whether the author, editor, compositor, printer, or another is responsible for those variations.

textual criticism, n. ~ Techniques that use varying copies to determine the authentic content of the original work.

RT: critical apparatus

Notes: When the original of a work no longer survives, textual criticism offers a means to infer the contents of the original. For example, different printings of a novel may have incorporated errors; different editions of *Moby Dick* might describe the rope in Ahab's boat as either a 'soiled snake' or a 'coiled snake'. If Melville's manuscript is not available, comparison of different printings can help determine the correct version.

Textual criticism includes recension, the identification of the earliest forms of the text, and emendation, the construction of a revised text that incorporates the most reliable variant.

textual records, n. ~ A general classification of records with content that is principally written words.

BT: record

RT: nontextual records

Notes: Textual records are distinguished from nontextual records, which include audiovisual, cartographic, and machine-readable records.

TGM ~ *see:* Thesaurus for Graphic Materials

TGN ~ *see:* Thesaurus for Geographic Names

thematic guide ~ *see:* guide

thermography, n. ~ 1. A printing or duplicating process that uses heat without liquids. – 2. Techniques to create images that represent variations in temperatures in an object.

RT: electrostatic process, print

Notes: Thermography[1] often uses an ink, pigment, or toner that is fixed on the paper (or other support) using heat. Many electrostatic processes are examples of thermography because they use heat to fuse the toner.

thermohygrometer, n. ~ A device that measures temperature and humidity but does not create a record of the measurement.

RT: hygrometer, hygrothermograph

thermoplastic lamination ~ *see:* lamination

thesaurus, n. (**thesauruses, thesauri,** pl.) ~ 1. A list of words with related meanings, including synonyms and antonyms. – 2. A specialized vocabulary of words and phrases, commonly used for indexing, that indicates a preferred term among synonyms and shows relationships between terms.

RT: authority file, controlled vocabulary, cross-reference, Guidelines for the Construction, Format, and Management of Monolingual Thesauri

Notes: A thesaurus is distinguished from dictionaries and glossaries, the latter not establishing a preferred term among synonymous terms. A thesaurus often contains nothing more than headings and their relationships, where dictionaries and glossaries usually contain definitions and annotations on word use.

†111 (Z39.19): A thesaurus is a controlled vocabulary arranged in a known order and structured so that equivalence, homographic, hierarchical, and associative relationships among terms are displayed clearly and identified by standardized relationship indicators that are employed reciprocally. The primary purposes of a thesaurus are (a) to facilitate retrieval of documents and (b) to achieve consistency in the indexing of written or otherwise recorded documents and other items, mainly for postcoordinate information storage and retrieval systems.

Thesaurus for Geographic Names, n. (**TGN,** abbr.) ~ A controlled vocabulary of place names intended for use as headings in catalogs and indexes.

RT: controlled vocabulary

Notes: Published by the Getty Research Institute. An online version is available at http://www.getty.edu/research/tools/vocabulary/tgn/.

Thesaurus for Graphic Materials, n. (**TGM,** abbr.) ~ A controlled vocabulary of subjects, forms, and genres relating to visual materials, intended for use as headings in catalogs and indexes.

RT: controlled vocabulary

Notes: Published by the Prints and Photographs Division of the Library of Congress. TGM was originally published as two separate works, *LC Thesaurus for Graphic Materials* (**LCTGM**) and *Descriptive Terms for Graphic Materials* (**GMGPC**). The works were combined in a single volume in 1995 and are now referred to, respectively, as TGM I and TGM II. Available online at http://www.loc.gov/rr/print/tgm1/ and http://www.loc.gov/rr/print/tgm2/.

thymol, n. ~ A toxic, carcinogenic, crystalline compound once used as a preservative and fungicide.

tickler file, n. ~ A group of documents filed chronologically under some future date when they require further attention or action.

Syn: follow-up file, pending file, suspense file

TIFF ~ *see:* Tagged Image File Format

time lapse photography (also **timelapse photography**), n. ~ Moving images · A technique of filming slow movements and then showing them at an accelerated rate.

Syn: Synonym · †: see Bibliography · *Superscript:* Definition number

RT: moving image

Notes: In time lapse photography, a frame may be exposed once every minute, hour, or other interval. When the film is shown at normal speed, usually around 24 frames per second, the exposure time is compressed. Time lapse photography makes it easy for humans to perceive change that takes place very slowly over time.

time stamp, n. ~ A notation made on a record indicating the time, and sometimes the date, that some action occurred.

BT: extrinsic element

RT: chronological file, stamp

Notes: 'Time stamp' connotes some sort of mechanical mark (see stamp). The mark may be added to a record, such as a stamp indicating the time a letter was received. In electronic records, the time stamp may be an entry in a log that is linked as associated metadata.

time-weighted preservation index, n. (**TWPI**, abbr.) ~ A measure of organic material's life expectancy (preservation index) based on the cumulative effects of changes in environment.

RT: Preservation Environment Monitor, preservation index

Notes: The concept of time-weighted preservation index was developed by the Image Permanence Institute.

†291 (IPI, PI and TWPI): Nearly every storage environment is dynamic, changing with the weather, with the seasons, or by conscious actions taken to save money or to be more comfortable. It is difficult enough to know the effect of any given static condition on the decay rate of a collection; the total effect of changing conditions over time was impossible to obtain at all, until the conception of the Time-Weighted Preservation Index (TWPI).

timeliness, n. ~ The quality of punctuality and proximity to an event.

Notes: Timeliness affects the reliability of records, as records produced contemporaneously with an event are generally considered to be more accurate than records produced later. However, the reliability of untimely records can be improved by a showing that the delay has no effect on the contents of a record.

tintype, n. ~ A direct-positive photograph made using the wet-collodion process, using a base of iron coated with black varnish.

Syn: ferrotype

BT: collodion photographs, photograph

RT: ambrotype, wet collodion

Notes: Tintype is a misnomer, as they are almost always made on iron, not tin.

tipping in, n. ~ The process of inserting a leaf into a bound work using a narrow strip of adhesive on the edge nearest the binding.

Notes: Tipping in is commonly used to insert illustrations, errata slips, or other materials that are printed separately.

title, n. ~ 1. A word or phrase indicating profession, office, social rank, or other distinction. – 2. The rights and privileges to control and dispose of property. – 3. Legal evidence of ownership; a deed. – 4. A word or phrase that identifies a work. – 5. CATALOGING · The word or phrase, taken from a prescribed source, by which a work is known. – 6. LAW · A portion of a body of statutes or code.

BT: descriptive element, intrinsic element

NT: title proper

RT: alternative title, collective title, deed, inner title, key title, other title information, parallel title, subtitle, supplied title, uniform title

> *Notes:* Examples of title[1] include Dr., chief financial officer, and king. – A title[2] is the right of ownership, as distinguished from a deed, which is an instrument that serves as evidence of that right. – While title[3] is often used synonymously with deed, deed is generally used only in the narrower sense of the instrument. – In its fullest sense, title[5] includes both the title proper, as well as subtitles and other title information, but it generally does not include information about responsibility, edition, or imprint.

title block, n. ~ An area on maps or technical drawings used for identifying and descriptive information.

title entry, n. ~ CATALOGING · A description of a work (an entry) in a catalog, register, or list that is filed under a heading for the word or phrase by which the work is known (the title[5]).

> *BT:* entry

title inventory ~ *see:* inventory

title proper, n. ~ CATALOGING · The chief name of a work, including any alternative title but excluding parallel titles and other title information.

> *BT:* title

> *RT:* other title information, uniform title

TLS, abbr. ~ Typed letter signed.

tonal range, n. ~ PHOTOGRAPHY · The number of shades between the lightest and darkest areas of an image.

> *Notes:* Tonal range is often measured in stops, or factors or two. If the darkest part of a print reflects 3% of light and the brightest portion reflects 98%, the tonal range is approximately five stops (3, 6, 12, 24, 48, 96). Even though the tonal range is only five stops, the print may have a near infinite number of shades between the lightest and darkest portions of the print.

topic, n. ~ 1. A theme. – 2. The subject of a work.

> *Syn:* subject

topic map, n. ~ A standard (ISO/IEC 13250) that uses Standard Generalized Markup Language (SGML) or Extensible Markup Language (XML) to describe knowledge structures, including topics, their relationships, and their sources.

topical date, n. ~ The location where a document was created or compiled.

> *BT:* date

> *RT:* chronological date

> *Notes:* This phrase is a nonidiomatic translation of the Latin concept *topos datum* and Italian term *data topica*.

> †70 *(Duranti 1998, p. 143):* In contemporary documents, the entitling is usually followed by the *date*, indicating the place *(topical* date) and/or the time *(chronological* date) of the compilation of the document and/or the action which the document concerns. In medieval and early modern documents, the date is in the eschatocol. In very solemn documents, the date is present in both the protocol[6] and the eschatocol.

toponymy, n. ~ The study of place names.

> *BT:* onomastics

Toronto Tenets, n. ~ Principles and criteria for designing, developing, and maintaining a representational scheme and communication structure for archival context information.

RT: Encoded Archival Context

Notes: The tenets were developed at the Toronto Archival Context Meeting, March 2001 and serve as the foundation of Encoded Archival Context (EAC).

total archives, n. ~ A strategy to document the historical development and all segments of a community by acquiring both official administrative records as well as related personal papers and corporate records.

RT: archives

Notes: Total archives was developed in Canada. It emphasizes collecting a wide range of materials, including architectural drawings, maps, microfilm, and other documentary forms.

†*116 (Hayworth 1993, p. 56):* The concept is articulated as an 'attempt to document all aspects of historical development, seeking the records not just of officialdom or of a governing elite but of all segments of a community,' and 'combining official administrative records and related private files, architectural drawings, maps, microfilm, and other documentary forms all touching on the development of the organization or region. . . ." [Citing *Canadian Archives, Report to the Social Sciences and Humanities Research Council of Canada* (Ottawa, 1980), pp. 63–64.]

TR01 ~ *see:* cold storage

track, n. ~ 1. The path on which information is recorded. – 2. A discrete segment of content in a sound recording; a cut; a band.

Notes: In phonograph records, the track[1] is a continuous spiral groove cut in the disk, and different tracks[2] are typically separated by a thin, visually distinct area. In compact discs, the track[1] is laid out in a continuous spiral. In magnetic tape, several tracks[1] are often laid down parallel to the length of the tape; they may be read or written simultaneously (parallel recording), one after another (serial recording), or in alternate directions (serpentine recording). Some magnetic tape formats use a helical scan with tracks[1] running diagonal to the length of the tape.

trademark, n. (**TM**, abbr.) ~ A word, phrase, or design used to distinguish a manufacturer's or seller's product.

BT: intellectual property

Notes: To receive protection under federal law, a trademark must be distinctive rather than descriptive, affixed to products in the marketplace, and registered with the U.S. Patent and Trademark Office.

trailer, n. ~ 1. AUDIO-VIDEO, MICROGRAPHICS · A blank section at the end of a film or tape. – 2. MOVING IMAGES · A short film, intended to be shown in theaters, that promotes an upcoming feature; a preview.

DF: leader

RT: moving image

Notes: A trailer[1] protects the recorded information at the end of the tape or film. – Trailers[2] usually include excerpts from the feature.

transaction, n. ~ 1. An exchange between two or more entities (individuals or agencies). – 2. The commercial exchange (sale and purchase) of goods. – 3. DIPLOMATICS · An act or several interconnected acts in which more than one person is involved and by which the relations of those persons are altered. – 4.

Computing · Data and operations related to a specific task that must be processed completely or rejected. – **transactions**, pl. n. ~ 5. A record of business conducted at a meeting, especially the published papers of a conference; proceedings.

> *Syn:* proceedings
>
> *BT:* action
>
> †70 *(Duranti 1998, p. 169):* To have a transaction³ it is not sufficient to have a communication, but it is necessary that such a communication creates, modifies, maintains, or extinguishes a relationship with other persons.
>
> †167 *(D Levy 2001, p. 15):* Although we can't tell just by looking at it, this receipt was probably produced using a digital cash register, a computer incorporating a printer and a cash drawer. If so, a digital record of my tuna-fish-chips-and-water transaction² was being created as the sales clerk punched the cash register keys; and from this the paper version we see before us was printed.

transaction processing system, n. ~ A computer system that performs and logs routine business activities.

> *BT:* information system
>
> *RT:* system
>
> †19 *(Bantin 2002):* The most basic business system and the heart of most organizations is the Transaction Processing System (TPS). . . . The primary goal of these systems is to automate computing intensive business transactions, such as those undertaken in the financial and human resource functional areas. The emphasis is on processing data (sorting, listing, updating, merging), on reducing clerical costs, and on outputting documents required to do business, such as bills, paychecks and orders. The guiding principles of these systems are to create data that is current, accurate, and consistent.

transactional file, n. ~ Principally Canadian · A collection of documents (a file¹) relating to a specific action, event, person, place, project, or other subject.

> *Syn:* case file

transcript, n. ~ 1. A written record that is a verbatim account of something spoken. – 2. Law · A written record of testimony given at trial, especially one made by the court reporter. – 3. A handwritten or typed copy of a document. – 4. A record of a student's coursework, final grades, and other accomplishments in school.

> *RT:* copy

transfer, n. ~ Records · The process of moving records as part of their scheduled disposition, especially from an office to a records center, or from a records center to an archives.

> *RT:* disposal
>
> *Notes:* Transfer may involve a change in custody without a change in title.

transfer file (also **transfer case, transfer box, trans file**), n. ~ A container roughly 10 × 13 × 24 inches designed to hold the contents of a file cabinet drawer.

> *BT:* box

transfer list, n. ~ A list of files being moved from one area to another, especially from an office to a records center or archives.

> *Syn:* transmittal list

transfer schedule ~ *see:* retention schedule

transitory record, n. ~ A record that has little or no documentary or evidential value and that need not be set aside for future use.

Syn: temporary record

BT: record

RT: ephemeral value

Notes: Examples of transitory records include correspondence that requires no administrative action, policy decision, or special handling; and nonrecord copies of quasi-official notices, such as memoranda, that are not used as the basis of an administrative or program action or decision.

transmission, n. ~ 1. The process of sending messages. – 2. A message that has been sent, especially one sent via broadcast. – 3. DIPLOMATICS · The transfer of a record from one party to another.

RT: draft

†179 (*MacNeil 2002*): Whereas reliability is connected to the process of documentary creation, authenticity is connected to its transmission and involves verifying or establishing the document's authorship, its place and date of origin, its status as an original or copy, and the history of its transmission, maintenance, and custody over time and space.

transmission form, n. ~ DIPLOMATICS · The overall appearance, configuration, or shape of a record, independent of its intellectual content, when received (after transmission).

RT: form

transmittal list, n. ~ A list of files being transferred from one area to another, especially from an office to a records center.

Syn: transfer list

transparency, n. ~ PHOTOGRAPHY · A positive photographic image on a transparent base.

DF: slide

BT: photograph

Notes: 'Transparency' is often used to describe an unmounted, large-format image, especially those on 4×5 inch film, as distinguished from a slide, which connotes a 35 mm transparency in a mount.

triacetate ~ *see:* cellulose acetate

trim, n. ~ MOVING IMAGES · Portions of film cut from a shot when editing a motion picture.

Notes: Trims are saved in case they need to be reincorporated in the process of working from a rough cut to the finished film.

true copy, n. ~ LAW · A reproduction that is not an exact copy of the original, but which is sufficiently close to be understandable.

BT: copy

trustworthiness, n. (**trustworthy**, adj.) ~ The quality of being dependable and reliable[1].

NT: adequacy of documentation, authenticity, credibility, veracity

RT: accountability, diplomatics, reliability, trustworthy information system, valid

Notes: In general, trustworthiness is synonymous with reliable. In archival literature and records, trustworthiness is often defined in terms of reliability and authenticity. This definition loses its apparent circularity when the reliability of records is understood in the diplomatic sense, 'created with appropriate authority, according to established processes, and being complete in all its formal elements.'

BT: Broader Term · *NT:* Narrower Term · *RT:* Related Term · *DF:* Distinguish From

In the context of electronic records, trustworthiness often implies that the system is dependable and produces consistent results based on well-established procedures.

†66 (Duff 1996, p. 34): The environment in which records reside can either increase or decrease their reliability and trustworthiness. The courts bestow a high degree of trust in records that are 'kept in the regular course of business activity ... as shown by the testimony of the custodian or other qualified witness, unless the source of information or the method or circumstances of preparation indicate lack of trustworthiness.' [Citing Federal Rules of Evidence, Rule 803].

†72 (Duranti 1995, p. 8): It is generally accepted by all literate civilizations that documents are trustworthy (that is, *reliable*) because of their completeness and controlled procedure of creation, and which are guaranteed to be intact and what they purport to be (that is, *authentic*) by controlled procedures of transmission and preservation, can be *presumed* to be truthful (that is, *genuine*) as to their content.

†179 (MacNeil 2002): The archival notion of document trustworthiness borrows from a number of traditions, the most influential of which are the rationalist tradition of legal evidence scholarship, specifically the rules governing the admissibility of documents, the modernist tradition of historical criticism, specifically the procedures governing the treatment of historical sources and the diplomatic tradition of documentary criticism. In all these traditions, the concepts of reliability and authenticity are posited on a direct connection between the word and the world and are rooted, both literally and metaphorically, in observational principles.

trustworthy information system, n. ~ A computer application designed to create, store, and retrieve data according to well-documented processes that ensure records based on those data are authentic and reliable[4].

RT: trustworthiness

Notes: Design of a trustworthy information system for electronic recordkeeping involves documenting the rationale, implementation, and application of decisions relating to systems documentation, security measures, audit trails, disaster recovery plans, and record metadata. See, Minnesota Historical Society, State Archives Department, *Trustworthy Information Systems Handbook* (March 2000), available at http://www.mnhs.org/preserve/records/tis.html.

tub file, n. ~ A small container that is open at the top and that is normally used for storing high-activity records at their point of use.

BT: container

turnkey system, n. ~ A computer system, including hardware and software, that is delivered ready to complete a specific function without further programming.

BT: system

RT: stand-alone system

Notes: The phrase is derived from the sense that all that is necessary to use the system is to 'turn the key.'

two-dimensional, adj. ~ 1. GEOMETRY · Having length and width, but no depth. – 2. VERNACULAR· Planar; flat; shallow; sheet[4].

Syn: planar

RT: sheet

Notes: In this glossary, 'two-dimensional' is used in the vernacular sense to describe materials that have little depth relative to their height and width. Two-dimensional items may be pliable; they can be distorted so that they are no longer flat but define a curved surface in three dimensions. Although they have some thickness, paper, film, and cloth are examples of two-dimensional materials.

TWPI ~ *see:* time-weighted preservation index

typescript, n. ~ A document produced using a typewriter.

> *DF:* manuscript
>
> *RT:* printout
>
> *Notes:* Typewritten documents are generally classified as manuscripts but are more accurately described as typescripts.

Tyvek, trademark ~ A spun polyethylene film manufactured by DuPont that is available in soft and hard forms.

> *BT:* polyethylene
>
> *Notes:* Soft-structure Tyvek has many of the qualities of cloth and may be used where the material needs to drape, such as protective apparel. Hard-structure Tyvek has qualities of paper and plastic film; it is strong and hard to tear.

U

UBC Project ~ *see:* Preservation of the Integrity of Electronic Records

UDDI ~ *see:* Universal Description, Discovery and Integration

ULAN ~ *see:* Union List of Artist Names

ult. ~ *see:* inst

ultrafiche, n. ~ Microfiche containing reproductions with a reproduction ratio of 90× or greater.

> *BT:* ultrafiche
>
> *NT:* ultrafiche
>
> *Notes:* Ultrafiche can contain many more images than standard microfiche.

ultraviolet light filter, n. ~ A device used to block ultraviolet light.

> *Notes:* Common forms of ultraviolet filters include film placed on windows or plastic shields placed around fluorescent bulbs.

U-matic, trademark ~ A proprietary standard for broadcast-quality video equipment using ¾-inch tape in cassettes.

> *BT:* videocassette
>
> *Notes:* U-matic is a trademark of Sony.

unclaimed property law ~ *see:* abandoned property law

underexposure, n. ~ Photography · A defect in a photographic image resulting from an insufficient amount of light (or other radiant energy).

> *RT:* exposure
>
> *Notes:* Underexposed negatives have little image density, even in the highlights, and are sometimes described as 'thin'. Underexposed transparencies are dark overall. Underexposed prints typically have little image density.

Unicode, n. ~ A standard (ISO/IEC 10646) for encoding characters and symbols from virtually all languages in computer systems.

> *BT:* character set
>
> *Notes:* Unicode has the potential of representing more than a million characters, and several thousand are currently defined. It includes alphabetic systems, such as those based on the Latin, Cyrillic, and Greek characters, as well as ideographic systems, such as Chinese, Japanese, and Korean. Unicode also defines special graphics, including characters for math, currency, and ornamental dingbats.

Uniform Resource Identifier, n. (**URI**, abbr.) ~ A standard (RFC 1630) string of characters that identifies an object or service using registered protocols and name spaces.

> *DF:* Uniform Resource Locator
>
> *NT:* Uniform Resource Locator, Uniform Resource Name
>
> *†284 (W3C/IETF URI Planning 2001):* There is some confusion in the web community over the partitioning of URI space, specifically, the relationship among the concepts of URL, URN, and URI. The confusion owes to the incompatibility between two different views of URI partitioning, which we call the 'classical' and 'contemporary' views. ¶¶ 1.1 Classical View ¶ During the early years of discussion of web identifiers (early to mid 90s), people assumed that an identifier type would be cast into one of two (or possibly more) classes. An identifier might

specify the location of a resource (a URL) or its name (a URN) independent of location. Thus a URI was either a URL or a URN. There was discussion about generalizing this by addition of a discrete number of additional classes; for example, a URI might point to metadata rather than the resource itself, in which case the URI would be a URC (citation). URI space was thus viewed as partitioned into subspaces: URL and URN, and additional subspaces, to be defined. The only such additional space ever proposed was URC and there never was any buy-in; so without loss of generality it's reasonable to say that URI space was thought to be partitioned into two classes: URL and URN. Thus for example, 'http:' was a URL scheme, and 'isbn:' would (someday) be a URN scheme. Any new scheme would be cast into one or the other of these two classes. ¶¶ 1.2 Contemporary View ¶ Over time, the importance of this additional level of hierarchy seemed to lessen; the view became that an individual scheme does not need to be cast into one of a discrete set of URI types such as 'URL', 'URN', 'URC', etc. Web-identifier schemes are in general URI schemes; a given URI scheme may define subspaces. Thus 'http:' is a URI scheme. 'urn:' is also a URI scheme; it defines subspaces, called 'namespaces'. For example, the set of URNs of the form 'urn:isbn:n-nn-nnnnnn-n' is a URN namespace. ('isbn' is an URN namespace identifier. It is not a 'URN scheme' nor a 'URI scheme'). ¶ Further according to the contemporary view, the term 'URL' does not refer to a formal partition of URI space; rather, URL is a useful but informal concept: a URL is a type of URI that identifies a resource via a representation of its primary access mechanism (e.g., its network 'location'), rather than by some other attributes it may have. Thus as we noted, 'http:' is a URI scheme. An http URI is a URL. The phrase 'URL scheme' is now used infrequently, usually to refer to some subclass of URI schemes which exclude URNs.

Uniform Resource Locator, n. (**URL,** abbr.) ~ A standard (RFC 1738) string of characters that identifies an object or service on the basis of where it is stored on a network (especially the web) and the protocol necessary to access it.

> *DF:* Uniform Resource Identifier
>
> *BT:* Uniform Resource Identifier
>
> *RT:* Persistent Uniform Resource Locator
>
> *Notes:* URL and Uniform Resource Identifiers (URI) are often used synonymously. See citation under Uniform Resource Identifier.
>
> †245 *(RFC 2396, 1998):* The term 'Uniform Resource Locator' (URL) refers to the subset of URI that identify resources via a representation of their primary access mechanism (e.g., their network 'location'), rather than identifying the resource by name or by some other attribute(s) of that resource.

Uniform Resource Name, n. (**URN,** abbr.) ~ A standard (RFC 1737) string of characters that allows an object or a service to be accessed over a network.

> *BT:* Uniform Resource Identifier
>
> *Notes:* The standard notes the intention "that the lifetime of a URN be permanent. That is, the URN will be globally unique forever, and may well be used as a reference to a resource well beyond the lifetime of the resource it identifies or of any naming authority involved in the assignment of its name." If the location of an object or service changes, it should be possible to locate the object or service through its URN.

†245 (RFC 2396, 1998): The term 'Uniform Resource Name' (URN) refers to the subset of URI that are required to remain globally unique and persistent even when the resource ceases to exist or becomes unavailable.

uniform title, n. ~ A word or phrase used as a heading to consistently identify variant forms of a work that appear with a different title.

> *RT:* title, title proper
>
> *†11 (AACR2, 25.1):* A uniform title provides the means for bringing together all catalogue entries of a work when various manifestations (e.g., editions, translations) of it have appeared under various titles. A uniform title also provides identification for a work when the title by which is known differs from the title proper of the item being cataloged.

union case, n. ~ A booklike enclosure made used to house daguerreotypes and ambrotypes.

> *RT:* cased photographs
>
> *Notes:* Union cases were patented by Samuel Peck in 1854. They were made from sawdust and shellac using a thermoplastic molding process. They often had ornate designs on the outside.

union catalog, n. ~ Descriptions of several repositories' holdings integrated into a single catalog.

> *BT:* catalog
>
> *RT:* general index

Union List of Artist Names, n. (**ULAN**, abbr.) ~ A controlled vocabulary that contains standard headings that identify artists, with additional information about the artist.

> *RT:* authority file
>
> *Notes:* See http://www.getty.edu/research/tools/vocabulary/ulan/.
>
> *†5 (ULAN 2000):* The ULAN is a structured vocabulary that contains around 250,000 names and other information about artists. The coverage of the ULAN is from Antiquity to the present and the geographic scope is global. The scope of the ULAN includes any identified individual or corporate body (i.e., a group of people working together) involved in the design or creation of art and architecture. ¶ The focus of each ULAN record is the artist. Linked to each record are names, relationships (including student-teacher relationships), locations (for birth, death, and activity), important dates (such as for birth and death), notes, and sources for the data. Names for any artist can include the vernacular, English, other languages, natural order, inverted order, nicknames, and pseudonyms. Among these names, one is flagged as the preferred name, or descriptor. ¶ The ULAN includes names and associated information about artists. Artists may be either individuals (persons) or groups of individuals working together (corporate bodies). Artists in the ULAN generally represent creators involved in the conception or production of visual arts and architecture. Some performance artists are included (but typically not actors, dancers, or other performing artists).

uniqueness ~ *see:* archival nature

unit of description ~ *see:* descriptive unit

unitized microform, n. ~ Individual frames or strips of microfilm that have been inserted into a jacket or aperture card, especially to allow direct access to individual documents in isolation from other documents.

BT: microfilm, microform

Notes: Unitized microforms may be single-page documents, typically mounted on aperture cards, or they may be groups of images of a multipage document, often on roll film that has been cut and inserted into jackets.

Universal Description, Discovery and Integration, n. (**UDDI,** abbr.) ~ A specification for publishing and discovering information about online businesses through the web, including their name, products, services, and locations.

Notes: UDDI is often compared to a telephone book's white, yellow, and green pages. It operates within the Organization for the Advancement of Structured Information Standards (OASIS). See http://www.uddi.org/.

Universal Preservation Format, n. ~ A standard being developed for the long-term preservation of digital video.

Notes: See http://info.wgbh.org/upf/.

†283 (UPF Glossary): The Universal Preservation Format is a file format that utilizes a container or wrapper structure. Its framework incorporates metadata that identifies its contents within a registry of standard data types and serves as the source code for mapping or translating binary composition into accessible or useable forms. The UPF is designed to be independent of the computer applications that created them, independent of the operating system from which these applications originated, and independent of the physical media upon which it is stored. The UPF is characterised as 'self-described' because it includes within its metadata all the technical specifications required to build and rebuild appropriate media browsers to access its contained material throughout time.

Universal Resource Locator ~ *see:* Uniform Resource Locator

University of British Columbia Project ~ *see:* Preservation of the Integrity of Electronic Records

University of Pittsburgh Electronic Records Project, n. ~ A research project that identified requirements for preserving evidence in electronic form.

Notes: The requirements, published as *Functional Requirements for Evidence in Recordkeeping* and frequently referred to as the Pittsburgh Project, were based on law, customs, standards and professional best practices accepted by society and codified in the literature of the legal, auditing, records management, information technology, management, and medical professions. Because they focus on the preservation of evidence, rather than application requirements for archival or recordkeeping systems, they can be applied to manual, electronic, or hybrid systems.

†91 (Functional Requirements 1996): Supported by the National Historical Publications and Records Commission, the University of Pittsburgh School of Information Sciences has conducted a research project to examine variables that affect the integration of recordkeeping requirements in electronic information systems. This project was intended to examine one means to rectify such problems. The major objectives of this research project were to develop a set of well-defined recordkeeping functional requirements – satisfying all the various legal, administrative, and other needs of a particular organization – which can be used in the design and implementation of electronic information systems. The project also proceeded to consider how the recordkeeping functions are affected by organizational policies, culture, and use of information technology standards, systems design, and implementation.

unqualified Dublin Core ~ *see:* Dublin Core

upload, v. ~ COMPUTING · To transfer data, especially a file, from a workstation to a network server.

    RT: download

upright, n. ~ SHELVING · A vertical beam or pole used to support shelves; a standard.

    Syn: standard

upward reference, n. ~ A cross-reference from a specific concept to a more general concept; a direction to a broader term.

    BT: cross-reference, reference

    RT: broader term, downward reference

    Notes: Upward references are part of the syndetic structure used in a thesaurus. Upward references are reciprocal to downward references. For example, separate entries for beds, chairs, and chests may include upward references to furniture. The entry for furniture would include each of those terms as a downward reference.

URI ~ *see:* Uniform Resource Identifier

URL ~ *see:* Uniform Resource Locator

URN ~ *see:* Uniform Resource Name

USC, abbr. ~ United States Code.

use analysis, n. ~ A methodology to assess the worth of records based on the potential for future consultation.

    BT: appraisal

    Notes: Use analysis requires archivists to be familiar with the needs of their patrons and their past patterns of records use, as well as considering physical, legal, and intellectual impediments to access.

    †107 (Greene 1998a, p. 157): At least three things are glaringly obvious about the utilitarian approach to records appraisal. The first is that it is not perfect. Of course, if no archival theory or practice could be allowed unless it was 'perfect,' we would have not theory or practice. Ultimately, the question becomes whether appraisal based on [use analysis], granted its many imperfections, is better or worse than the proposed practical alternatives. The second is that its practicality and broad applicability depends upon a growing number of use studies. Because every repository serves a somewhat different clientele, has a different mandate from its resource allocators, and must deploy different resources, in an ideal world, every repository would do it own detailed use studies for every segment of its collections. These could be as simple as the MHS call-slip analysis, as complex as a process of user interviews, or as intensive as a citation analysis. The world not being ideal, most repositories will have to extrapolate from studies done by similar institutions regarding similar records. The third is that this is not a Magic Bullet. Utilitarian appraisal does not equal 'easy' appraisal. Unless we abandon appraisal as an archival responsibility, we will never make appraisal easy because we can never make it scientific or mechanistic. If it were otherwise, I am convinced, there would be absolutely no reason for archivists to exist. But a utilitarian method will provide a better rigor and rationale for appraisal decisions.

use copy, n. ~ A reproduction of a document created for use by patrons, protecting the original from wear or theft; an access copy[1].

    Syn: access copy

BT: copy

Notes: Use copies[1] may be made in a variety of formats. Photocopying was often used to make inexpensive use copies of textual documents and, usually with limited success, photographs. Use copies are now likely to be digital scans of the original.

use reference, n. ~ A cross-reference from a nonpreferred heading to a preferred heading; a direction to a prescribed heading.

BT: reference

RT: Guidelines for the Construction, Format, and Management of Monolingual Thesauri

Notes: Use references are part of the syndetic structure used in a thesaurus, especially one constructed using the ANSI Z39.19 standard, *Guidelines for the Construction, Format, and Management of Monolingual Thesauri*. They provide links from headings with similar meanings to the one heading to be used for indexing and cataloging. They are reciprocal to used for references. For example, in the *Library of Congress Subject Headings* the now obsolete subject heading Afro-Americans has a use reference to African Americans.

use restriction ~ *see:* restriction

used for reference, n. ~ A cross-reference under a preferred heading from nonpreferred headings; a direction from a nonpreferred heading.

BT: reference

RT: Guidelines for the Construction, Format, and Management of Monolingual Thesauri

Notes: Used for references are part of the syndetic structure used in a thesaurus, especially one constructed using the ANSI Z39.19 standard, *Guidelines for the Construction, Format, and Management of Monolingual Thesauri*. They provide links from headings with similar meanings to the one heading to be used for indexing and cataloging. They are reciprocal to use references. For example, in the *Library of Congress Subject Headings* the heading African Americans lists a used for reference from the now obsolete subject heading Afro-Americans.

user, n. ~ 1. An individual who uses the collections and services of a repository; a patron; a reader; a researcher; a searcher. – 2. COMPUTING · An individual with an account on a system. – 3. COMPUTING · An individual who is the consumer of an application, utilizing it to perform some function, as distinguished from the programmer who created the application.

Syn: patron, reader, researcher

Notes: Patron, reader, researcher, and searcher typically connote a user[1] who is not a member of the repository staff. Different words may be used to describe a user, especially one using nontextual formats; for example, listener or viewer.

user interface, n. ~ The means by which a human communicates with hardware or a software application.

Notes: 'User interface' emphasizes design, rather than specific input/output devices. For example, a keyboard, mouse, and monitor may be parts of a user interface, but not an interface themselves. The command-line interface (CLI) is an example of a user interface, which often uses a character-based prompt displayed on a monitor, with information entered from a keyboard. The graphical user interface (GUI) may use icons displayed on a monitor, with actions performed by a mouse click.

BT: Broader Term · NT: Narrower Term · RT: Related Term · DF: Distinguish From

user study (also **use study**), n. ~ Research conducted to understand patrons, their needs, and how they make use of collections and finding aids.

Notes: User studies may be qualitative or quantitative. They may focus on patron demographics, on their information needs, or their ease of locating materials relevant to their interests.

USMARC ~ *see:* MARC

USMARC Format for Archival and Manuscripts Control ~ *see:* MARC Format for Archival and Manuscripts Control

utility system, n. ~ A program, hardware, or combination to perform basic, routine operations in support of a larger system.

BT: system

Notes: Examples of utility systems include tape loaders, print spoolers, and sorting algorithms.

V

v. ~ *see:* volume

vacuum drying ~ *see:* freeze drying

valid, adj. ~ 1. Based on sound and reasonable principles. – 2. Law · Acceptable or binding under law. – 3. XML · Well-formed and compliant with a document type definition (DTD).

   RT: trustworthiness, validation, well formed

   †48 *(CJS, Records §17):* In order to constitute a valid[2] record it must be made by an officer having the authority to do so, or, as stated otherwise, it is essential that it be made by the person whose duty it is to make the record, or the transcription of an instrument into the record books must be made by or under the superintendence of the officer therefor. An entry made in a record book by an unauthorized person is void, and cannot be validated by subsequent curative statute.

validation, n. ~ 1. The process of establishing truth or soundness (validity); see authentication. – 2. The process of declaring or rendering something to make it legally binding or to indicate it is in proper legal form. – 3. The process of ensuring something is suitable in a particular environment. – 4. A mark indicating that something is legally acceptable; see certification.

   RT: authentication, certification, valid, verification

   †57 *(Dictionary of Computing 1996, p. 527):* Verification and validation[3] [is] a general term for the complete range of checks that are performed on a system in order to increase confidence that the system is suitable for its intended purpose. This range might include a rigorous set of functional tests, performance testing, reliability testing, and so on, in which case the term verification, validation and testing is more appropraite. Although a precise distinction is not always drawn, the verification aspects normally refers to completely objective checking of conforming to some well-defined specification, while the validation aspect normally refers to a somewhat objective assessment of likely suitability in the intended environment.

valuation, n. ~ The process of determining a cash amount that materials would likely sell for and that is acceptable to both the seller and the buyer.

   Syn: monetary appraisal

   RT: appraisal, evaluation

value, n. ~ 1. The amount something might bring if offered for sale; market value; monetary value; fiscal value. – 2. Records · The usefulness, significance, or worth of something to an individual or organization. – 3. Computing, Mathematics · The information assigned to a record, field, or variable; data value. – 4. The relative brightness of an image; tonal value; see tonal range.

   NT: administrative value, archival value, artifactual value, associational value, continuing value, enduring value, ephemeral value, evidential value, fair market value, fiscal value, historical value, informational value, intrinsic value, legal value, monetary value, operational value, permanent value, primary value, secondary value

   RT: appraisal, evaluation

   †274 *(Stephens and Wallace 2001, p. 6):* The records appraisal concept holds that the retention value[2] of business records must be established based on identi-

fying the primary and secondary values the records possess, and then making judgments as to when, if ever, these values expire or decline to the point where disposal of the information can be contemplated. Primary values are those reflecting the basic business purpose(s) served by the records, the reason they were created. Secondary values reflect other uses to which the information may be put during the course of their life cycle, uses that may justify continuing retention after the expiration of primary values. Administrative or operational values are usually identified as primary values. Research or historical values are generally designated as secondary values. Legal value can be either a primary or a secondary value, depending on the purpose and function of a record. A records series can (and usually does) possess several of these values simultaneously, and they may change during a record's life cycle.

Vandyke process, n. ~ A photographic process using light-sensitive iron salts producing brown lines on a tan background (positives) or tan lines on a brown background (negatives) that is commonly used to reproduce architectural drawings.

> *RT:* brownline

vapor phase deacidification ~ *see:* deacidification

variable-length field, n. ~ COMPUTING · An area in a file or record that changes size based on the length of data being stored.

> *DF:* fixed-length field
>
> *BT:* field
>
> *Notes:* Variable-length fields are distinguished from fixed-length fields, which always allocate the same amount of space. Variable-length fields often have defined minimum and maximum sizes.

variable-occurrence field, n. ~ A unit of computer storage (a field) that does not appear in every record.

> *BT:* field
>
> *Notes:* A note field in a MARC record is an example of a variable occurrence field.

variant, n. ~ A particular instance of a work with differences from other manifestations of the same work.

> *RT:* variorum edition, work
>
> *Notes:* Used primarily for printed works, 'variant' can apply to any work in any medium. Two photographic prints made from the same negative may be variants because differences in cropping, exposure, and development.
>
> †114 *(Harrod 1978, p. 862):* [Variants] are frequent in hand-printed books and are accounted for by the fact that mistakes were noticed and the type altered during printing, the sheets already printed remaining untouched.

variant name, n. ~ CATALOGING · A form of the word or phrase by which an individual, family, or organization is known that differs from the official or preferred form.

> *BT:* name
>
> *Notes:* Variant names include nicknames, pen names, acronyms, and names used before being changed.

variorum edition, n. ~ A work that includes a version of a text established by the editor, as well as the editor's notes, and the commentary of critics.

> *RT:* definitive edition, variant
>
> †177 *(J Lynch 1999):* Variorum is Latin for 'of the various'; it comes from the longer phrase, *editio cum notis variorum editorum,* 'an edition with the notes of

various editors.' ¶ A variorum edition gives not only the text the editor established, or the editor's own notes, but those of earlier critics as well. The Johns Hopkins Variorum Edition of Edmund Spenser, for instance, includes notes not only by that edition's editors, but by dozens of earlier critics, going back to the eighteenth century: for any passage in Spenser, the reader can see what earlier commentators have had to say about it. ¶ Other variorum editions reproduce not critical commentary but textual variants and conjectural emendations proposed by many other editors. The Arden Shakespeare, for example, gives the readings in all the important early witnesses (the sixteenth- and seventeenth-century quartos and folios), and, when they're relevant, the readings proposed by editors from the eighteenth, nineteenth, and twentieth centuries.

vault, n. ~ 1. A specially secured room or cabinet. – 2. A safe.

> *Notes:* In archival repositories, 'vault' connotes a room for storing particularly valuable holdings. Ideally, vaults are fire-resistant and structurally separate from the rest of the building.

VCR ~ *see:* videocassette recorder

vector graphic (also **object-oriented graphic**), n. ~ COMPUTING · Algorithms that use shapes and lines to create images.

> *DF:* raster graphic

vellum, n. ~ 1. Sheets made from unsplit calfskin, treated with alum and polished. – 2. High-quality paper with a rough surface that imitates the appearance of such writing materials.

> *DF:* paper
>
> *RT:* parchment
>
> *Notes:* Vellum is distinguished from leather, which is tanned. Vellum is often used interchangeably with parchment[1], although parchment may also be made from goat or lamb skin.

vellum binding ~ *see:* stationery binding

veracity, n. ~ The degree to which something is correct, accurate, and free of error or distortion, whether by omission or commission.

> *BT:* trustworthiness
>
> *RT:* accuracy, reliability

verification, n. ~ 1. The process of determining truth or accuracy. – 2. A formal declaration, made before an authority such as a notary public, that statements in a document are true. – 3. COMPUTING · The process of ensuring that data in backups, copies, or excerpts are identical to the data in the original files, that the data was not corrupted or lost during transfer.

> *RT:* certification, reliability, validation
>
> †57 (*Dictionary of Computing 1996, p. 527*): Verification[3] and validation [is] a general term for the complete range of checks that are performed on a system in order to increase confidence that the system is suitable for its intended purpose. This range might include a rigorous set of functional tests, performance testing, reliability testing, and so on, in which case the term verification, validation and testing is more appropraite. Although a precise distinction is not always drawn, the verification aspects normally ¶ refers to completely objective checking of conforming to some well-defined specification, while the validation aspect normally refers to a somewhat objective assessment of likely suitability in the intended environment.

†78 (Eco 1998, p. 19): There exists a process of verification[1] that is based on slow, collective, public performance by what Charles Sanders Pierce called 'the Community.' It is thanks to human faith in the work of this community that we can say, with some serenity, that the Donation of Constantine was false, that the earth turns around the sun, and that Saint Thomas at least knew the planet is round.

versal, n. ~ Large illuminated letters at the beginning of a page or a section of text.

> *RT:* historiated, illumination

version, n. ~ A variant with, usually slight, differences from an earlier form.

> *RT:* copy, edition, original, replica, reproduction

> *Notes:* A version is often a particular instance of something made during development. For example, the subsequent revisions of a document are different versions. However, a version may indicate a different form, such as an abridged version, a translation, or an adaptation.

version control, n. ~ Techniques, especially in an automated environment, to control access to and modification of documents and to track versions of a document when it is revised.

> *RT:* document management application

> *Notes:* Version control is usually implemented as software, such as a document management application. The software allows people to use the documents in a library at the same time. A check-in and check-out function ensures that different people cannot attempt to make simultaneous revisions to a document. The software can be configured to keep previous drafts (versions) of a document. In computer programming, version control provides similar functions, but often operates on portions of code within a single application.

verso, n. ~ 1. The side of a page intended to be read second. – 2. The side of a sheet that is printed second.

> *RT:* recto

> *Notes:* In Western tradition, the verso is the left page in a spread, usually having an even page number. It is the opposite side of a recto.

vertical aerial, n. ~ A photograph made from the air with the axis of the lens pointing directly down.

> *BT:* aerial photograph

> *RT:* oblique aerial

vertical cut recording, n. ~ A technique of recording sound on an analog disc by cutting the signal into the bottom of the groove, causing the pickup stylus to move up and down.

> *RT:* lateral cut recording

> *Notes:* Edison's Diamond Disc and Pathé discs use this technique. Because of the up-and-down movement of the stylus, it is sometimes called hill and dale.

vertical file, n. ~ 1. Furniture used to hold folders containing documents and designed to provide access from the short side. – 2. Materials, often of an ephemeral nature, collected and arranged for ready reference.

> *DF:* lateral file

> *BT:* file cabinet

> *RT:* artificial collection

> *Notes:* Vertical files[1] commonly have two, four, or five drawers. They may be designed to hold letter or legal size folders. – A vertical file[2] is an example of an artificial collection.

†167 (D Levy 2001, p. 68–69): Melvil Dewey, the inventor of the Dewey Decimal System, adapted the idea of the library card catalog . . . to produce the vertical filing system we still use today. In this system, consisting of hanging file folders and stored in file cabinets, it was much easier to add documents to folders, to add new folders, and to move folders around. Vertical files also took up considerably less space than flat files. . . . The new vertical filing system was much acclaimed; it won a gold prize in the 1893 Chicago World's Fair.

vertical mode, n. ~ 1. The arrangement of images on roll film with frames (portrait or landscape) oriented parallel to the long axis of the film; synonymous with motion picture mode. – 2. The arrangement of images on microfiche with frames filling the rows in a column before preceding to the next column.

> *DF:* comic mode, horizontal mode
>
> *Syn:* ciné mode

vesicular film, n. ~ MICROGRAPHICS · A duplicating film made with light-sensitive diazonium salts suspended in a thermoplastic base and developed with heat.

> *Notes:* When the film is exposed, the diazonium salts release nitrogen. When exposed to heat, the nitrogen expands to form bubbles (vesicles) in the film. Vesicular film usually creates a negative image.

VHS ~ *see:* Video Home System

video, n. ~ 1. Moving images, with sound, recorded electronically. – 2. A television program that has been recorded on tape, DVD, or other medium; a video recording.

> *DF:* motion picture, movie
>
> *Syn:* video recording
>
> *BT:* moving image
>
> *RT:* composite, image, laserdisc, MII, National Television Systems Committee, PAL, picture, SECAM, television, videodisc, visual materials
>
> *Notes:* Although video refers specifically to the visual aspects of a television signal, 'video' and 'television' are often used interchangeably.

Video Home System, n. (usually **VHS,** abbr.) ~ A half-inch videocassette format developed by JVC for home use.

> *BT:* videocassette
>
> *Notes:* VHS became a de facto standard, replacing Betamax.

video recording (often shortened to **video**), n. ~ A television program that has been recorded on tape, DVD, or other medium.

> *Syn:* video

videocassette, n. ~ Magnetic tape stored on two hubs in a shell used to store moving images, usually with sound.

> *NT:* U-matic, Video Home System
>
> *Notes:* Common formats include U-matic, Beta, VHS, and Hi-8.

videocassette recorder, n. (**VCR,** abbr.) ~ Equipment designed to record and play back television signals on magnetic tape housed in a cassette.

> *Notes:* Home VCR formats include the Betamax, VHS, and Hi-8. Commercial formats include U-matic and BetaSP.

videodisc, n. ~ An optical disk used to store moving image productions.

> *RT:* LaserDisc, optical disk, video
>
> *Notes:* Videodiscs are approximately twelve inches in diameter and hold up to sixty minutes of programming. The video component is an analog signal; the audio component may be analog or digital. The format does not support home

recording. They were intended for commercial distribution of motion pictures or television programs and have been largely superseded by DVDs. Tradenames include LaserDisc and SelectaVision.

videotape, n. ~ Magnetic tape used to record video and audio signals.

>*BT:* tape

>*Notes:* Research on recording television programs on tape began in 1951 but was not practical for use in broadcasting until the mid–1950s. Common broadcast formats include 2-inch open reels, 1-inch open reel, ¾-inch U-matic cassettes, and ¾-inch cassettes. Consumer formats include ¾-inch Betamax and VHS cassettes, and Hi-8 cassettes.

view, n. ~ 1. An area that can be seen from a particular perspective. – 2. COMPUTING · That portion of a database that a user is allowed to access (view). – 3. DESCRIPTION · A cartographic perspective that represents the landscape as though details are projected on an oblique plane.

>*RT:* panorama, perspective

>*Notes:* View^1 is commonly used generically for graphic works to distinguish them from diagrams, charts, and verbal descriptions. – Examples of view^3 include bird's-eye views, panorama, and worm's-eye view.

vinegar syndrome, n. ~ PRESERVATION · Conditions that result from the deterioration of cellulose acetate, especially photographic film, and that include the release of acetic acid.

>*RT:* cellulose acetate

>*Notes:* The effects of vinegar syndrome include brittleness, shrinking, and a harsh, acidic odor; channeling may also be visible.

vintage print, n. ~ PHOTOGRAPHY · A print made by the photographer at nearly the same time as the original image.

>*Notes:* 'Vintage print' is used to distinguish prints that were made long after the picture was taken and sometimes by an individual other than the photographer.

virtual, adj. ~ The conceptual representation (of a thing) apart from its physical implementation; logical.

>*Syn:* logical

virtual record, n. ~ COMPUTING · A collection of related fields that are treated as a unit but assembled from various sources.

>*Notes:* A virtual record is not a single object, but drawn from many sources. The virtual record of an invoice may draw information about the purchaser, merchandise, and prices from many different tables. To be reliable as a record, it must be possible to reconstruct a virtual record over time without change. For instance, if the price of an item changes, its price on a previously issued invoice must remain the same.

Visual Artists Rights Act, n. ~ A federal law passed in 1990 (17 USC 1 §106A), which provides for the 'rights of certain authors to attribution and integrity.'

>*BT:* intellectual property

>*RT:* copyright, moral rights

>*Notes:* The act grants individuals the right to claim authorship of their work; to prevent the use of their names as the authors of works that they did not create; to prevent the use of their names as the authors of the work in the event of a dis-

tortion, mutilation, or other modification of the work that would be prejudicial to their honor or reputation; to prevent any intentional distortion, mutilation, or other modification of that work that would be prejudicial to their honor or reputation; and to prevent the intentional or grossly negligent destruction of a work of recognized stature.

visual literacy, n. ~ The ability to decipher cultural and technological systems that express meaning using graphic images, icons, or symbols.

> *RT:* iconography

> *Notes:* Visual literacy is the ability to 'read' an image and connotes the ability to understand an image as more than the appearance of things. Visual literacy understands images as creative constructs that communicate a subject and exist in a context that contributes to the understanding of that subject.

> †215 (O'Toole 1998, p. 283): We hear increasingly of 'visual literacy,' the ability to 'read' pictorial images – still and moving photographs, for example – to answer the surprisingly difficult question of what they are 'about.'

> †258 (Schwartz 1995, p. 55): At the same time that the rigour of diplomatic criticism is undermined by the inherent ambiguity of the photograph, diplomatics is a useful conceptual tool by which archivists may come to achieve a greater degree of visual literacy, and by that I mean the ability to 'read' the message of the photograph, to comprehend its evidential value, and understand it as an archival document. . . . By studying the photograph, not as a more or less accurate transcription of the material world, but in terms of its relationships with the persons concurring in its formation, diplomatic principles and concepts may help to break the presumed link between the photographic image and visual 'truth' by revealing the photograph to be the mediated representation of reality; the product of a series of decisions; created by a will, for a purpose, to convey a message to an audience.

visual materials, n. ~ A generic term used to collectively describe items of a pictorial nature, including prints, paintings, photographs, motion pictures, and video.

> *RT:* audiovisual, drawing, graphic, iconography, image, motion picture, moving image, nonprint materials, nontextual records, photograph, picture, print, special records, video

Visual Resources Association, n. (**VRA**, abbr.) ~ A nonprofit organization for professionals working in the field of visual information that seeks to further knowledge, research, and education, and to promote cooperation with related disciplines.

> *Notes:* See http://www.vraweb.org/.

> †169 (T Levy 2002): Our international membership includes information specialists; digital image specialists; art, architecture, film, and video librarians; museum curators; slide, photograph, microfilm, and digital archivists; architectural firms; galleries; publishers; image system vendors; rights and reproductions officials; photographers; art historians; artists; and scientists.

vital records, n. ~ 1. Records that document significant life events, including births, deaths, marriages, divorces, and public health matters; vital statistics. – 2. Emergency operation records immediately necessary to begin recovery of business after a disaster, as well as rights-and-interests records necessary to protect the assets, obligations, and resources of the organization, as well as its employees and customers or citizens; essential records.

> *DF:* essential records

Syn: vital statistics
BT: record
NT: rights-and-interests records
RT: emergency-operating records, important records, security copy
Notes: Vital records[2] typically document delegation of authority and lines of succession and include legal documents and contracts, financial records, and other documents that establish the rights and obligations of the organization, its employees and customers, stockholders, and citizens.

vital statistics, n. ~ Public records required by law that document significant life events, such as births, deaths, marriages, divorces, and public health events, and that are kept by city, county, state, or other governmental body.
Syn: vital records
RT: civil register

vocabulary, n. ~ 1. The set of terms used in an index or in the headings of a catalog. – 2. Computing · The set of labels used in an Extensible Markup Language (XML) document.
RT: controlled vocabulary
†270 (St. Laurent 2000, p. 3): A set of [XML] labels is often called a vocabulary. When large groups of people can accept a common vocabulary, or even declare it a standard of some sort, applications of many different kinds on many different kinds of computers and networks can share an understanding of the contents of XML documents using that vocabulary.

voice mail, n. ~ 1. Spoken messages recorded using telephone equipment. – 2. A system for recording, playback, and management of telephone messages. – 3. Spoken messages recorded and delivered as attachments to electronic mail.
Notes: Voice mail[1] is an aural equivalent to email. The system is usually a computer application that can respond to simple commands entered using the keypad of a touch-tone phone.

vol. ~ *see:* volume

volume, n. (**v.**, **vol.**, abbr.) ~ 1. A collection of pages bound together. – 2. Cataloging · A major division of a published work, distinguished from similar divisions of the same work by a title page, half-title, cover title, or portfolio title, and usually having separate pagination, foliation, or signatures[3]. – 3. A group of issues of a periodical, usually for a single year. – 4. Computing · A removable unit of storage. – 5. Audio · The relative loudness of a sound recording or program.
RT: part
Notes: A volume[1] in the physical sense may not coincide with a volume[2] in the bibliographic sense.

voucher, n. ~ 1. A record that confirms payment or discharge of debt. – 2. A written or printed authorization to disburse funds.

VRA ~ *see:* Visual Resources Association

W

warrant, n. ~ A writ that authorizes or directs an act.

    DF: literary warrant

    Notes: 'Warrant' commonly refers to a writ issued to a law enforcement officer for a specific action, such as search, arrest, or extradition.

waste book (also **blotter**), n. ~ A bookkeeping record, typically a bound volume, detailing in rough form each day's receipts and expenditures in order of their occurrence.

    DF: daybook

    RT: account book, journal, ledger

    †55 *(Densmore 2000, p. 79):* The terms 'waste book', 'daybook', and 'journal' were sometimes used interchangeably. A waste book is simply the rough form of a daybook; 'journal' usually refers to the book used in double entry bookkeeping to separate transactions into debits and credits.

watermark, n. ~ A design in paper, formed by a difference in amount of fiber, that is visible when viewed by transmitted light.

    RT: digital watermark

    Notes: Watermarks may be either lighter or darker than the surrounding area, depending on the manner in which they are made.

    †248 *(Roberts and Etherington 1982):* Forms of the watermark are generally divided into four very broad classes: 1) the very earliest, generally consisting of simple circles, crosses, knots, ovals, three-hill symbols, triangles, and the like, which were easy to construct simply by twisting and bending soft wires. (These early marks also included many pomme crosses, based on the Greek cross with balls or circles at the ends of the cross bars. A similar watermark, found on Italian paper of the 14th century, consists of a circle above which is a patriarchal or papal cross. These earliest marks were prevalent from about 1282 to 1425); 2) watermarks emphasizing man and his works. (Thousands of designs of this nature have been noted, a large number of them featuring human hands in various forms); 3) watermarks consisting of flowers, fruit, grains, trees and other plants, etc.; and 4) watermarks consisting of wild, domesticated, and legendary animals.

web ~ *see:* World Wide Web

    †173 *(Long 2004):* Effective with this sentence, Wired News will no longer capitalize the "I" in internet. ¶ At the same time, Web becomes web and Net becomes net. . . . the decision wasn't made lightly. Style changes are rarely capricious, since change plays havoc with the editor's sacred cow, consistency. ¶ A change in our house style was necessary to put into perspective what the internet is: another medium for delivering and receiving information. That it transformed human communication is beyond dispute. But no more so than moveable type did in its day. Or the radio. Or television.

web page, n. ~ A resource accessed using the Hypertext Transfer Protocol (HTTP) and rendered by a browser for display or printing.

    RT: home page, resource

    Notes: In its simplest form the resource is a file, typically containing text formatted for display using Hypertext Markup Language (HTML). 'Web page' connotes a base file of MIME type text/html, which may incorporate other files, such as graphics, text included from other files, or Cascading Style Sheets (CSS). It may be a composite of several files assembled using frames. Web pages commonly use the extension .html or .htm, although the extensions .asp, .cfm, .cgi, .php, and .jsp may indicate server-side processing of files that are ultimately delivered and rendered as text/html. A web page may be static, with fixed content, or dynamic, with changing content derived from a database.

website, n. ~ A collection of web pages related by content or domain.

  NT: dynamic website, static website

  Notes: In its simplest form, a website is the collection of all files on a single server identified by a single domain. In some instances, a single server may host several sites; for example, an Internet service provider may host many subscriber websites on a single server. A large, complex website may span several servers and potentially several domains but is unified by its content; for example, a corporation may host its static and dynamic web pages on different servers, each with a different domain.

  †32 *(Boudrez and Eynde 2002, p. 24):* If a website of a local department of a political party is part of the general website of that party, it is easier to archive the complete website. Otherwise the danger exists that files, frames or frame sets are missing and that the archives and online version differ thoroughly.

weeding, n. ~ The process of identifying and removing unwanted materials from a larger body of materials.

  Syn: culling, purging, stripping

  RT: screening

  Notes: Weeding and culling connote item-level separation, where purging, stripping, and screening connote removal of materials at the folder level or higher.

well formed, adj. ~ XML · A document that complies with the XML specification rules for structure and syntax.

  RT: valid

wet collodion, n. ~ A photographic process that uses collodion as the binder and silver salts as the light-sensitive agent.

  BT: collodion photographs

  RT: ambrotype, ferrotype, tintype

  Notes: The wet collodion process was used primarily to make glass negatives and tintypes. It was in common use from 1851 through the 1870s, when it was replaced by processes that used a gelatin binder. The plate must be coated, exposed, and developed before the collodion dries. Negatives made using the wet collodion process are sometimes called **wet plate negatives**.

wet mount, n. ~ The process of attaching a flat object, such as a drawing, text, or photograph, to a board or other support using liquid adhesives.

  RT: dry mount, mount

wet plate negative ~ *see:* wet collodion

widescreen, n. ~ Moving images · An image format with an aspect ratio greater than 1:1.65.

  BT: format

  RT: Academy format, aspect ratio

  Notes: Widescreen ratios may be as high as 1:2.5. Cinemascope, Panavision, and Vistavision are examples of widescreen formats.

will, n. ~ Law · A document giving instructions on how an individual's property is to be disposed of after the individual's death.

wire recording ~ *see:* magnetic wire recording

withdrawal, n. ~ The removal of holdings from a repository's collections.

> *RT:* deaccessioning
>
> *Notes:* Withdrawal sometimes connotes the permanent removal of materials as the result of weeding or reappraisal. It is sometimes used with the sense of a temporary loan, usually to the office of origin.

witness, n. ~ 1. Someone who has personal knowledge of something, especially a crime, an accident, or a newsworthy event. – 2. An individual who is present when a document is signed and adds her or his own signature to the document as evidence of the transaction. – 3. LAW · An individual who gives testimony as part of a hearing or other legal proceeding, in person or by deposition or affidavit.

> †48 (CJS, 97 CJS Witnesses §1): The term witness, in its strict legal sense, means one who gives evidence in a cause before a court; and in its general sense includes all persons from whose lips testimony is extracted to be used in any judicial proceeding, and so includes deponents and affiants as well as persons delivering oral testimony before a court or jury.

Woodburytype, n. ~ A photomechanical process that produces continuous-tone images on paper using carbon pigment in a gelatin binder.

> *RT:* photomechanical
>
> *Notes:* The process was used in fine publications in the last third of the 19th century.

word-by-word arrangement, n. ~ A sorting technique that orders entries based on each word or phrase in a heading, including spaces and some punctuation, as a filing element.

> *DF:* letter-by-letter arrangement
>
> *Notes:* Word-by-word arrangement is distinguished from letter-by-letter arrangement, the latter ignoring spaces and punctuation between words.

word-by-word	*letter-by-letter*
access copy	access copy
access restriction	accessibility
accessibility	accession
accession	access restriction

word processing, n. ~ The process of creating, formatting, and editing documents with the assistance of computers.

> *RT:* text processing
>
> *Notes:* Modern word processing applications have sophisticated text formatting functions, including the ability to incorporate graphics. Examples of word processing programs include WordStar, EMACS, Word, and Word Perfect.

work, n. ~ 1. The material manifestation of individual or group activities or efforts, especially items of a creative nature. – 2. The body of an artist's or writer's creative output. – 3. CATALOGING · In Seymour Lubetsky's model, a bibliographic entity that is realized in different expressions and manifestations.

> *RT:* edition, variant

work print, n. ~ MOVING IMAGES · A print made quickly and often without correction that is used for rushes and assembling the rough cut so that the original is preserved.

> *RT:* moving image, rushes

Notes: Work prints are used for visuals or soundtracks. They provide the director, editor, and others a copy that can be used for trial cuttings. Once the cutting points have been established, the undamaged original can be edited.

working files, n. ~ 1. Documents, such as notes, drafts, and calculations, created and acquired in the process of assembling another document. – 2. COMPUTING · Temporary files created in the process of some operation.

Notes: Temporary files[1] may include materials by the author of the final document, as well as documents and reports created by others by relied on as sources for the final document. – Temporary files[2] are often deleted by the process that creates them. Some operating systems have a specific directory that applications may use to store temporary files; a utility program routinely cleans out the temporary directory to eliminate files that, for some reason, were not properly deleted by the creating process.

workstation ~ *see:* computer

World Wide Web, n. (**web, WWW**, abbr.) ~ 1. The massive collection of information and services accessible over the Internet through the Hypertext Transfer Protocol (HTTP). – 2. The servers and network infrastructure used to store and deliver web-based information and services.

RT: Internet

Notes: World Wide Web is often used interchangeably with Internet. However, the Internet is the larger network on which the web resides. The web is commonly associated with browsers, such as Firefox, Internet Explorer, Netscape, and Opera. Because browsers often provide the ability to access information and services using other protocols, such as File Transfer Protocol (FTP) and Gopher, non-HTTP services are often considered to be part of the web.

†28 (Finnish Technology Award Foundation 2004): [Tim] Berners-Lee, with a background in system design in real-time communications and text-processing software development, invented the Web while working at CERN, world's largest particle physics laboratory in Geneva, Switzerland. ¶ The web was first made available to the public in 1991. Berners-Lee created the first server, browser, and protocols central to the operation of the Web: the URL address, HTTP transmission protocol and HTML code.

WORM ~ *see:* write once read many

worm's-eye view, n. ~ An image that depicts its subject from a low elevation, especially from ground level.

BT: perspective
RT: bird's-eye view

wow, n. ~ A distortion in the reproduction of an image or sound recording, usually resulting from a slow, repetitive variation in the speed of a playback device.

RT: flutter

writ, n. ~ A written order issued by a court in the name of a state or other competent authority, ordering the addressee to do or refrain from doing some specified act.

write, v. ~ 1. To affix letters, numbers, symbols, or other characters on a surface using a pen, pencil, stylus, or similar device. – 2. To fix ideas on a medium. – 3. COMPUTING · To record data on a medium.

RT: cursive, writing

Notes: Write[1,2] is distinguished from 'draw', the former connoting words and language, and the latter connoting images. – Writing[2] is distinguished from print[1], the latter connoting the mass production on a printing press. Writing² encompasses the use of mechanical devices, such as word processors or typewriters.

write once read many, n. (**WORM**, abbr.) ~ COMPUTING · A data storage format, usually an optical disk, that allows information to be read, but not modified, after it has been recorded.

> *DF:* reusable media
> *BT:* optical disk
> *RT:* read-only memory
> *Notes:* Some WORM technologies allow information to be erased by overwriting the data, obliterating the information with a solid bit pattern.

writer, n. ~ 1. The author of a text. – 2. DIPLOMATICS · The individual responsible for the intellectual content of a document.

> *RT:* addressee, author
> †70 *(Duranti 1998, p. 86):* The writer is not a clerk or a secretary, because these individuals are not 'persons' with regard to the documents they compile: they are not competent for the articulation of the discourse within the documents, unless they have delegated authority for it (a clerk may be competent for writing the entries in a register, but usually the responsibility belongs to an officer . . .).

writing, n. ~ Any written or printed work; a document¹.

> *Syn:* document
> *RT:* text, write
> †215 *(O'Toole 1998, p. 272):* Here were the oral and literate side by side, but writing has some advantages. In written form, information achieved a stability and durability it would not have so long as it remained only in the mind or in spoken words. What is more, writing was in itself coming to be recognized as an effective way for gathering and sharing information: some people would now learn things only from books, Bede realized.

WWW, *see:* World Wide Web

X

X3.4 ~ *see:* ASCII

X12 ~ *see:* Electronic Data Interchange

X.509 ~ *see:* Information Technology – Open Systems Interconnection – The Directory: Public-key and Attribute Certificate Frameworks

x-ray, n. ~ 1. High-energy electromagnetic radiation with a wavelength in the approximate range from 0.01 to 10 nanometers. – 2. An image formed by such radiation that records varying density within an opaque object.

    RT: radiograph

Xanadu, n. ~ A technology proposed by Theodore Holm Nelson to use computers to provide interrelated content with bidirectional links and rights management.

    Notes: See http://www.xanadu.com.

    †200 (Nelson 2000): Project Xanadu, the original hypertext project, is often misunderstood as an attempt to create the World Wide Web. ¶ It has always been much more ambitious, proposing an entire form of literature where links do not break as versions change; where documents may be closely compared side by side and closely annotated; where it is possible to see the origins of every quotation; and in which there is a valid copyright system – a literary, legal and business arrangement – for frictionless, non-negotiated quotation at any time and in any amount. The Web trivialized this original Xanadu model, vastly but incorrectly simplifying these problems to a world of fragile ever-breaking one-way links, with no recognition of change or copyright, and no support for multiple versions or principled re-use. Fonts and glitz, rather than content connective structure, prevail. ¶ Serious electronic literature (for scholarship, detailed controversy and detailed collaboration) must support bidirectional and profuse links, which cannot be embedded; and must offer facilities for easily tracking re-use on a principled basis among versions and quotations. ¶ Xanalogical literary structure is a unique symmetrical connective system for text (and other separable media elements), with two complementary forms of connection that achieve these functions – survivable deep linkage (content links) and recognizable, visible re-use (transclusion). Both of these are easily implemented by a document model using content lists which reference stabilized media.

xerography ~ *see:* electrostatic process

XHTML ~ *see:* Extensible Hypertext Markup Language

XML ~ *see:* Extensible Markup Language

XSL ~ *see:* Extensible Stylesheet Language

XSLT ~ *see:* Extensible Stylesheet Language Transforms

Y

yellowing, n. ~ A condition in which material is discolored, turning from a neutral white shade to shades of cream, ivory, or beige.

Notes: Yellowing affects certain papers, especially those made from unbleached or ground wood pulp. It may also appear in photographs as the result of stains from residual sulfur and other contaminants.

†223 *(Personal communication, Jill Teasley, 11 March 2004):* If stored in a warm and humid environment, the cellulose content of paper may begin to deteriorate. One sign of such deterioration is that the edges of the paper may begin yellowing.

Z

Z39.2 ~ *see:* MARC

Z39.9 ~ *see:* International Standard Serial Number

Z39.19 ~ *see:* Guidelines for the Construction, Format, and Management of Monolingual Thesauri

Z39.48 ~ *see:* Permanence of Paper for Publications and Documents in Libraries and Archives

Z39.50 ~ *see:* Information Retrieval Application Service Definition and Protocol Specification for Open Systems Interconnection

Z39.84 ~ *see:* Digital Object Identifier

Z39.85 ~ *see:* Dublin Core

zoom, v. ~ 1. To show greater detail. – 2. To move in closer to a subject.

Notes: Zoom[1] is used in some computer applications to mean magnifying an image without changing the frame size to see greater detail. – Zoom[2] is used in moving image productions to mean either the process of moving the camera closer to a subject so that the subject fills the frame or to use a variable focal length lens (a zoom lens) for the same effect.

Bibliography

This bibliography includes descriptions of the sources of the citations in the body of the glossary. The entries are arranged in standard bibliographic order, by author and title, or by title if the author is unknown. Initial articles (a, an, and the) are disregarded, with entries alphabetized under the next word.

Each citation in the body of the glossary includes a bibliography number following a dagger sign (†) to facilitate locating its entry here. Following the bibliography number, the citation includes a short, mnemonic word or phrase based on author names, key words in the title, or the organization that is responsible for the work. For example, many will recognize the abbreviation USC as the *United States Code* and CJS as the *Corpus Juris Secundum*. In some instances, the mnemonic will provide readers with enough context to avoid having to check this bibliography for the full description of the source. For example, a reader may find the mnemonics Duranti, SAA, AACR2, NISO, and CFR sufficient information about the source for their needs, even though it does not indicate the particular document. The mnemonic is followed by the year of publication, if known, and by details locating the citation in the work.

URLs were checked shortly before the glossary went to press. Active links are identified as 'available,' and resources no longer available are identified as 'formerly available.' While web resources are notoriously unstable, those used in this work are surprisingly persistent. Even when a URL changes, the resource can often be found by searching a key phrase in a search engine or the Internet Archive Wayback Machine.

†1 "About CENSA" [web page]. Collaborative Electronic Notebook Systems Association, n.d. Formerly online at http://www.censa.org/html/f_aboutcensa.html.

†2 "About NISO" [web page]. National Information Standards Organization, 2003. Available online at http://www.niso.org/about/l.

†3 "About OCLC" [web page]. OCLC, 2004. Available online at http://www.oclc.org/about/.

†4 "About the National Archives and Records Service of South Africa" [web page]. The Service, n.d. Available online at http://www.national.archives.gov.za/aboutnasa_content.html.

†5 "About the ULAN" [web page]. John Paul Getty Trust, 2000. Available online at http://www.getty.edu/research/conducting_research/vocabularies/ulan/about.html.

†6 Abraham, Terry. "Archives and Entropy: The Closed System" [web page]. February 1999. Available online at http://www.uidaho.edu/special-collections/papers/entropy.htm. "The concept behind this paper was first presented in the course of a talk on 'Assembling and Organizing a Collection' given at a Local Records Workshop for the Washington State Historical Records Inventory Project, Bellingham, Washington, August 17, 1977. It was subsequently reworked into a publication entitled 'Entropy and archival disorder.' *Provenance* 11:1(Spring 1984) 94–99. Further contemplation and reconsideration of the topic produced the following."

†7 *The Academy of Certified Archivists* [website]. The Academy, 18 March 2004. Available online at http://www.certifiedarchivists.org/.

†8 Adkins, Elizabeth W. "The Development of Business Archives in the United States: An Overview and a Personal Perspective." *American Archivist* 60:1 (Winter 1997), p. 8–33.

†9 *American Association for State and Local History* [website]. The Association, 2003. Available online at http://www.aaslh.org.

†10 *American Jurisprudence: A Modern Comprehensive Text Statement of American Law, State and Federal* – 2nd ed. West Group, 1962– .

†11 *Anglo-American Cataloguing Rules [AACR2]* – 2nd ed., revised. American Library Association, Canadian Library Association, Library Association Publishing Limited, 1988.

†12 Appelbaum, Barbara. "Criteria for Treatment: Reversibility." *Journal of the American Institute for Conservation* 26:2 (1987). Available online at http://aic.stanford.edu/jaic/articles/jaic26-02-001_1.html.

†13 "Appraisal Methodology." Library and Archives Canada, Information Management Services, Summer 2000. Available online at http://www.collectionscanada.ca/information-management/061101_e.html.

†14 *Archival Research Catalog Glossary.* National Archives and Records Administration, n.d. Available online at http://arcweb.archives.gov/.

†15 *Art and Architecture Thesaurus.* John Paul Getty Trust, 2000. Available online at http://www.getty.edu/research/tools/vocabulary/aat/.

†16 *Association of Canadian Archivists* [website]. The Association, 1995–2003. Available online at http://archivists.ca.

†17 "Authenticity Task Force Report." *The Long-term Preservation of Authentic Electronic Records: Findings of the InterPARES Project* [web page]. The Project, n.d. Available online at http://www.interpares.org/book/interpares_book_d_part1.pdf.

†18 Ayto, John. *Twentieth Century Words*. Oxford University Press, 1999.

†19 Bantin, Philip C. "Electronic Records Management: A Review of the Work of a Decade and a Reflection on Future Directions." *Encyclopedia of Library and Information Science* 71:34 (2002).

†20 Bantin, Philip C. "Strategies for Managing Electronic Records: A New Archival Paradigm? An Affirmation of Our Archival Traditions?" *Archival Issues* 23:1 (1998), p. 17–34. Citations from online version, available at http://www.indiana.edu/~libarch/ER/macpaper12.pdf.

†21 Baron, Jason R. "E-mail Metadata in a Post-Armstrong World." *Proceedings of the Third IEEE META-DATA Conference*, 6–7 April, 1999. Formerly online at http://www.computer.org/proceedings/meta/1999/papers/83/jbaron.html.

†22 Barth, Christopher D. "Archivists, Genealogists, Access, and Automation: Past and Present Trends in Archival Access Technologies and their Implications for the Future of Genealogical Research in Archives" [webpage]. 1997. Formerly online at http://www.arcticwind.com/cdb/writings/archives1.shtml.

†23 "Basic Concepts for Discussion." Unpublished manuscript for InterPARES2, 2003.

†24 Bastian, Jeannette Allis. "A Question of Custody: The Colonial Archives of the United States Virgin Islands." *American Archivist* 64:1 (Spring/Summer 2001), p. 96–114.

†25 Bearman, David, and Jennifer Trant. "Authenticity of Digital Resources: Towards a Statement of Requirements in the Research Process." *D-Lib Magazine* June 1998. Available online at http://www.dlib.org/dlib/june98/06bearman.html.

†26 Bergeron, Bryan. *Dark Ages II: When the Digital Data Die*. Prentice Hall PTR, 2002.

†27 Berner, Richard C. *Archival Theory and Practice in the United States: A Historical Analysis*. University of Washington Press, 1983.

†28 "Berners-Lee Wins Inaugural Millennium Technology Prize" [web page]. Finnish Technology Award Foundation, 15 April 2004. Available online at http://www.technologyawards.org/index.php?article_id=3932.

†29 "Bethesda Statement on Open Access Publishing" [web page]. 20 June 2003. Available online at http://www.earlham.edu/~peters/fos/bethesda.htm.

†30 *Black's Law Dictionary* – 7th ed. West, 1999. Bryan A. Garner, ed.

†31 Boles, Frank, and Mark A. Greene. "Et tu Schellenberg? Thoughts on the Dagger of American Appraisal Theory." *American Archivist* 59:3 (Summer 1996), p. 298–310.

†32 Boudrez, Filip, and Sofie Van den Eynde. *DAVID: Archiving Websites*. Stadarchief Stad Antwerpen, July 2002. Available online at http://www.antwerpen.be/david/website/teksten/Rapporten/Report5.pdf.

†33 Bouissac, Paul, editor in chief. *Encyclopedia of Semiotics*. Oxford University Press, 1998.

†34 Bradsher, James Gregory. "The FBI Records Appraisal." *Midwestern Archivist* 13:2 (1988), p. 51–66. Republished in *Archival Issues* 25:1–2 (2000), p. 100–118.

†35 Brichford, Maynard J. *Archives and Manuscripts: Appraisal and Accessioning.* Society of American Archivists, 1977.

†36 Briston, Heather. "Digital Rights Management and Archivists." *Archival Outlook* July/August 2003, p. 14.

†37 Burke, Frank. "The Beginning of the NHPRC Records Program." *American Archivist* 63:1 (Spring/Summer 2000), p. 18–42.

†38 Bush, Vannevar. "As We May Think." *The Atlantic Monthly* July 1945. Citations from online version available at http://www.theatlantic.com/unbound/ flashbks/computer/bushf.htm.

†39 "Center for Integrated Pest Management" [website]. The Center, n.d. Available online at http://cipm.ncsu.edu/.

†40 *Chamber's Dictionary of Etymology.* Chambers, 1988. Robert K. Barnhart, ed.; Sol Steinmetz, managing ed.

†41 Ciardi, John. *A Browser's Dictionary: and Native's Guide to the Unknown American Language.* Harper & Row, 1980.

†42 Clanchy, M. T. *From Memory to Written Record: England 1066–1307.* Blackwell, 1993.

†43 Conway, Paul. "Overview: Rationale for Digitization and Preservation." *Handbook for Digital Projects: A Management Tool for Preservation and Access.* Northeast Document Conservation Center, 2000. Available online at http://www.nedcc.org/digital/dighome.htm.

†44 Cook, Terry. "Postmodernism and the Practice of Archives." *Archivaria* 51 (Spring 2001), p. 14–35.

†45 Cook, Terry. *The Archival Appraisal of Records Containing Personal Information: A RAMP Study with Guidelines.* UNESCO, 1991. Available online at http:// www.unesco.org/webworld/ramp/html/r9103e/r9103e00.htm#Contents.

†46 Cook, Terry. "The Concept of Archival Fonds and the Post-Custodial Era: Theory, Problems and Solutions." *Archivaria* 35 (Spring 1993), p. 24–37.

†47 *Copyright Issues in Digital Media.* United States, Congressional Budget Office, August 2004. Available online at http://www.cbo.gov/ftpdocs/57xx/doc5738/ 08-09-Copyright.pdf.

†48 *Corpus Juris Secundum: A Contemporary Statement of American Law as Derived from Reported Cases and Legislation.* West, 1994.

†49 Cox, Richard. *American Archival Analysis: The Recent Development of the Archival Profession in the United States.* Scarecrow, 1990.

†50 Cox, Richard. "Messrs. Washington, Jefferson, and Gates: Quarrelling About the Preservation of the Documentary Heritage of the United States." *First Monday* 2:8 (4 August 1997). Available online at http://www.firstmonday.dk/issues/ issue2_8/cox/.

†51 Cox, Richard. "The Record: Is it Evolving?" *The Records and Retrieval Report: The Newsletter for Professional Information Managers* 10:3 (March 1994), p. 1–16.

†52 Crabb, George M. *Crabb's English Synonymes.* Grosset & Dunlap, 1917. With an introduction by John H. Finley.

†53 Craig, Barbara L., and James M. O'Toole. "Looking at Archives in Art." *American Archivist* 63:1 (Spring/Summer 2000), p. 97–123.

†54 Dearstyne, Bruce W. *The Archival Enterprise: Modern Archival Principles, Practices, and Techniques.* American Library Association, 1992.

†55 Densmore, Christopher. "Understanding and Using Early Nineteenth Century Account Books." *Archival Issues* 25:1-2 (2000), p. 77–89. Originally published in *Midwestern Archivists* 5:1 (1980), p. 5–19.

†56 *Describing Archives: A Content Standard.* Society of American Archivists, 2004.

†57 *Dictionary of Computing.* Oxford University Press, 1996.

†58 "Digimarc Comments to USPTO Regarding Technological Protection Systems for Digitized Copyrighted Works Technology, Education, and Copyright Harmonization (TEACH) Act of 2002." United States, Patent and Trademark Office, 14 January 2003. Available online at http://www.uspto.gov/web/offices/dcom/olia/teachcomments/digimarc.pdf.

†59 *Digital Object Standard: Metadata, Content and Encoding* [web page]. California Digital Library, 18 May 2001. Available online at http://www.cdlib.org/about/publications/CDLObjectStd-2001.pdf.

†60 "Digital Signature Guidelines: Tutorial" [web page]. Information Security Committee, Science and Technology Section, American Bar Association, n.d. Available online at http://www.abanet.org/scitech/ec/isc/dsg-tutorial.html.

†61 "DIRKS Manual for Commonwealth Agencies." *Archives Advice* 50 (April 2001). Published by the National Archives of Australia. Available online at http://www.naa.gov.au/recordkeeping/rkpubs/advices/advice50.html.

†62 Dollar, Charles. "Archivists and Records Managers in the Information Age." *Archivaria* 36 (Autumn 1993), p. 37–52.

†63 Dow, Elizabeth H.; with David R. Chestnutt, William E. Underwood, Helen R. Tibbo, Mary-Jo Kline, and Charlene N. Bickford. "The Burlington Agenda: Research Issues in Intellectual Access to Electronically Published Historical Documents." *American Archivist* 54:2 (Fall/Winter 2001), p. 292–307.

†64 Doyle, Michael. "Experiments in Deaccessioning: Archives and On-line Auctions." *American Archivist* 54:2 (Fall/Winter 2001), p. 350–362.

†65 *Dublin Core Metadata Initiative* [website]. The Initiative, 1995– . Available online at http://dublincore.org.

†66 Duff, Wendy. "Ensuring the Preservation of Reliable Evidence: A Research Project Funded by the NHPRC." *Archivaria* 42 (Fall 1996), p. 28–45.

†67 Duff, Wendy. "Harnessing the Power of Warrant." *American Archivist* 61:1 (Spring 1998), p. 88–105.

†68 Duff, Wendy, and Catherine A. Johnson. "A Virtual Expression of Need: An Analysis of E-Mail Reference Questions." *American Archivist* 54:1 (Spring/Summer 2001), p. 43–60.

†69 Duhon, Bryant. "Enterprise Content Management: What Is It? Why Should You Care?" *AIIM E-Doc Magazine* 17:6 (November/December 2003).

†70 Duranti, Luciana. *Diplomatics: New Uses for an Old Science.* Society of American Archivists and Association of Canadian Archivists in association with Scarecrow Press, 1998.

†71 Duranti, Luciana. "Origin and Development of the Concept of Archival Description." *Archivaria* 35 (Spring 1993), p. 47–54.

†72 Duranti, Luciana. "Reliability and Authenticity: The Concepts and Their Implications." *Archivaria* 39 (Spring 1995), p. 5–10.

†73 Duranti, Luciana, and Heather MacNeil. "The Protection of the Integrity of Electronic Records: An Overview of the UBC-MAS Research Project." *Archivaria* 42 (Fall 1996), p. 46–67.

†74 Duranti, Luciana, Terry Eastwood, and Heather MacNeil. *The Preservation of the Integrity of Electronic Records.* University of British Columbia, n.d. Available online at http://www.interpares.org/UBCProject/index.htm.

†75 Durrance, Cynthia J. "Authority Control: Beyond a Bowl of Alphabet Soup." *Archivaria* 35 (Spring 1993), p. 38–46.

†76 Eastwood, Terry. "Jenkinson's Writings on Some Enduring Archival Themes." *American Archivist* 67:1 (Spring/Summer 2004), p. 31–45.

†77 Eastwood, Terry. "Nailing a Little Jelly to the Wall of Archival Studies." *Archivaria* 35 (Spring 1993), p. 232–252.

†78 Eco, Umberto. *Serendipities: Language and Lunacy.* Columbia University Press, 1998.

†79 *Electronic Signatures: A Review of the Exceptions to the Electronic Signatures in Global and National Commerce Act.* National Telecommunications and Information Administration, June 2003. Available online at http://www.ntia.doc.gov/ntiahome/frnotices/2002/esign/report2003/coverack.htm.

†80 "Establishment of an ICA Section on Notarial Records: Statement of Objectives" [web page]. International Council on Archives, 2003. Available online at http://www.ica.org/biblio/SAN_ObjectivesEN.pdf.

†81 Eusman, Elmer. "Iron Gall Ink." *The Iron Corrosion Website.* European Commission on Preservation and Access, n.d. Available online at http://www.knaw.nl/ecpa/ink/ink.html.

†82 *A Federal Records Management Glossary.* National Archives and Records Administration, 1989.

†83 *Federal Register.* United States, Government Printing Office. Available online at http://www.gpoaccess.gov/fr/search.html.

†84 *Federal Rules of Evidence.* United States, Government Printing Office. Available online through the Cornell Legal Information Institute at http://www.law.cornell.edu/rules/fre/overview.html.

†85 Feeney, Kathleen. "Retrieval of Archival Finding Aids Using World-Wide-Web Search Engines." *American Archivist* 62:2 (Fall 1999), p. 206–228.

†86 "File Transfer Protocol: RFC 959" [web page]. W3C Network Working Group, 1985, 1994. Available online at http://www.w3.org/Protocols/rfc959/.

†87 "Filing Systems." [web page]. Texas State Library and Archives Commission, 1998. Available online at http://www.tsl.state.tx.us/slrm/recordspubs/fs.html.

†88 Fowler, H. W. *Fowler's Modern English Usage.* – 2nd ed. Oxford University Press, 1965. Revised and edited by Sir Ernest Gowers.

†89 Fox, Michael J., and Peter L. Wilkerson. *Introduction to Archival Organization and Description.* Getty Information Institute, 1998.

†90 *A Framework of Guidance for Building Good Digital Collections.* Institute for Museum and Library Services, 2001. Available on the web at http://www. imls.gov/scripts/text.cgi?/pubs/forumframework.htm.

†91 *Functional Requirements for Evidence in Recordkeeping.* School of Information Sciences, University of Pittsburgh; 1996. Available online at http://www. archimuse.com/papers/nhprc/.

†92 "The Future of Anglo-American Cataloguing Rules." Art Libraries Society of North America 27th Annual Conference, Vancouver, BC, 27 March 1999. Sherman Clarke, panel moderator. Available online at http://www.arlisna.org/ news/conferences/1999/proceedings/aacr2.htm.

†93 Garlick, Karen. "Archives Preservation Update: Holdings Maintenance: An Overview." *The Book and Paper Group Annual* 11 (1992). Available online at http://aic.stanford.edu/conspec/bpg/annual/v11/bp11-36.html.

†94 Garner, Bryan A. *A Dictionary of Modern Legal Usage.* Oxford, 1995.

†95 Garner, Bryan A. *Garner's Modern American Usage.* Oxford, 2003.

†96 Gartrell, Ellen G. "Some Things We Have Learned . . . : Managing Advertising Archives for Business and Non-Business Users." *American Archivist* 60:1 (Winter 1997), p. 56–70.

†97 "George Feltenstein and Ned Price of Warner Bros. on Making Truly Classic DVDs." *Barnes & Noble.com* [website]. BN.com, August 2003. Available online at http://video.barnesandnoble.com/search/interview.asp?cds2Pid=1939&ctr=186 912.

†98 Gilliland-Swetland, Anne J. *Enduring Paradigm, New Opportunities: The Value of the Archival Perspective in the Digital Environment.* CLIR, February 2000. Available online at http://www.clir.org/pubs/abstract/pub89abst.html.

†99 Gilliland-Swetland, Anne J. "Maintaining and Providing Access to Electronic Evidence: The US Experience." Presented at the Preservation of Digital Records in the Information Society, the Information Society Commission and the National Archives, Dublin Castle, 28 August 2000.

†100 Gilliland-Swetland, Anne J., and Philip B. Eppard. "Preserving the Authenticity of Contingent Digital Objects: The InterPARES Project." *D-Lib Magazine* 6:7/8 (July/August 2000). Available online at http://www.dlib.org/dlib/july00/ eppard/07eppard.html.

†101 "GILS: Global Information Locator Service." [website]. Available online at http://www.gils.net/.

†102 *Glossary of Document Technologies: ANSI/AIIM TR2-1998.* AIIM, 1998.

†103 *Glossary of Terms Related to the Archiving of Audiovisual Materials.* UNESCO, 2001. Prepared by a working group from the Round Table on Audiovisual Records. Gerald Gibson, General Compiler and Editor. Sven Allerstrand, Translator Coordinator.

†104 Goerler, Raimund E. "Archives in Controversy: The Press, the Documentaries, and the Byrd Archives." *American Archivist* 62:2 (Fall 1999), p. 307–324.

†105 "The Government Paperwork Elimination Act" [web page]. National Oceanic and Atmospheric Administration, 24 February 2003. Available online at http://www.cio.noaa.gov/itmanagement/gpea.htm.

†106 Greene, Mark A. "A Brief and Opinionated History of Archival Appraisal Theory." Unpublished manuscipt, 1998.

†107 Greene, Mark A. "'The Surest Proof': The Use of Business Records and Implications for Appraisal." *Archivaria* 45 (Spring 1998), p. 157.

†108 Greene, Mark A., Frank Boles, Bruce Bruemmer, Todd J. Daniels-Howell. "The Archivist's New Clothes; or, the Naked Truth about Evidence, Transactions, and Recordness." *University of Michigan Sawyer Seminar* (Winter 2001). Available online at http://hdl.handle.net/1805/42.

†109 Guercio, Maria. "Principles, Methods, and Instruments for the Creation, Preservation, and Use of Archival Records in the Digital Environment." *American Archivist* 64:2 (Fall/Winter 2001), p. 238–269.

†110 *Guide to the Records of the United States Senate: Appendix E, Glossary of Legislative and Archival Terms*. National Archives and Records Administration, 1989. Available online at http://www.nara.gov/nara/legislative/senate_guide/sgtoc.html. Based on Robert W. Coren, Mary Rephlo, David Kepley, and Charles South, *Guide to the Records of the United States Senate at the National Archives, 1789–1989: Bicentennial Edition* (Doct. No. 100–42), (National Archives and Records Administration, 1989).

†111 *Guidelines for the Construction, Format, and Maintenance of Monolingual Thesauri*. ANSI/NISO, 1993. Available online at http://www.niso.org/standards/resources/Z39-19.html.

†112 Ham, F. Gerald. *Selecting and Appraising Archives and Manuscripts*. Society of American Archivists, 1993.

†113 Harris, Kenneth E., and Chandru J. Shahani. "Mass Deacidification: An Initiative to Refine the Diethyl Zinc Process." Library of Congress, 1994. Available online at http://palimpsest.stanford.edu/byorg/lc/massdeac/dez.html.

†114 Harrod, Leonard Montague. *The Librarians' Glossary of Terms Used in Librarianship, Documentation, and the Book Crafts and Reference Book*. Westview, 1978.

†115 Harvey, Miles. *The Island of Lost Maps: A True Story of Geographic Crime*. Random House, 2000.

†116 Hayworth, Kent M. "The Voyage of RAD: From the Old World to the New." *Archivaria* 35 (Spring 1993), p. 55–63.

†117 Hazard, Gerald C., Jr., and Michele Taruffo. *American Civil Procedure: An Introduction*. Yale University Press, 1993. Cited in *Black's Law Dictionary* – 7th ed. West, 1999.

†118 Hengemihle, Frank H., Norman Weberg, and Chandru J. Shahani. *Desorption of Residual Ethylene Oxide from Fumigated Library Materials*. Library of Congress, November 1995. Preservation Research and Testing Series No. 9502. Available online at http://www.loc.gov/preserv/rt/fumigate/fume.html.

†119 Henry, Linda J. "Schellenberg in Cyberspace." *American Archivist* 61:2 (Fall 1998), p. 309–327.

†120 Hensen, Steven L. *Archives, Personal Papers, and Manuscripts: A Cataloging Manual for Archival Repositories, Historical Societies, and Manuscript Libraries* – 2nd ed. (Society of American Archivists, 1989).

†121 Henson, Steven L. "The First Shall Be First: APPM and Its Impacts on American Archival Description." *Archivaria* 35 (Spring 1993), p. 64–70.

†122 Hickerson, H. Thomas. *Archives & Manuscripts: An Introduction to Automated Access.* Society of American Archivists, 1981. Part of the *SAA Basic Manual Series.*

†123 Hirtle, Peter B. "Archival Authenticity in a Digital Age." *Authenticity in a Digital Environment.* Council on Library and Information Resources, 2000, p. 8–23. Available online at http://www.clir.org/pubs/abstract/pub92abst.html.

†124 Holmes, Oliver W. "Archival Arrangement – Five Different Operations at Five Different Levels." *Modern Archives Reader: Basic Readings on Archival Theory and Practice.* National Archives and Records Service, 1984, p. 162–180. Edited by Maygene F. Daniels and Timothy Walch.

†125 Horrigan, David. "Court Documents: Will They Age Well?" [web page] Law.com, 17 February 2003. Available online at http://www.law.com/jsp/article.jsp?id=1044059447630.

†126 Hunter, David, et al. *Beginning XML.* Wrox Press, 2000.

†127 "HyperText Markup Language (HTML) Homepage" [web page]. World Wide Web Consortium, 1995–2003. Available online at http://www.w3.org/MarkUp/.

†128 "ICA in Brief" [web page]. International Council on Archives, n.d. Available online at http://www.ica.org/static.php?ptextid=bref&plangue=eng.

†129 "Identity & Access Management: Transforming e-Security into a Catalyst for Competitive Advantage" [website]. RSA Security, 2003. Formerly online at http://www.rsasecurity.com/solutions/idmgt/.

†130 *Images in Time: A Century of Photography at the Alhambra, 1840–1940.* Patronato de la Alhambra y Generalife, 2003.

†131 *In Answer to Your Query: Fair Use.* Copyright Office, Library of Congress, 1999. FL 102. Available online at http://www.copyright.gov/fls/fl102.pdf.

†132 *Information Management: Challenges in Managing and Preserving Electronic Records: GAO-02-586.* United States, Government Accounting Office, 2002. Available online at http://www.gao.gov/cgi-bin/getrpt?GAO-02-586.

†133 *Information Management Terminology.* Unpublished manuscript from Ford Motor Company.

†134 "Information Technology – Computer Graphics – Metafile for the Storage and Transfer of Picture Description Information : ISO/IEC 8632" [web page]. ISO, 1999. Available online at http://www.iso.ch/iso/en/ittf/PubliclyAvailable Standards/c032378_ISO_IEC_8632-1_1999(E).zip.

†135 "Institute of Certified Records Managers" [website]. The Institute, 2003. Available online at http://www.icrm.org/.

†136 *International Center of Photography Encyclopedia of Photography.* The Center, 1984.

†137 "International Conference of the Round Table on Archives (CITRA)" [web page]. International Council on Archives, n.d. Available online at http://www.ica.org/citra/english/index_eng.html.

†138 *Internet Security Glossary: RFC 2828* [web page]. Faqs.org, 2000. Available online at http://www.faqs.org/rfcs/rfc2828.html.

†139 "[InterPARES 2 Project Description.]" Received via personal communication.

†140 *The InterPARES Glossary: A Controlled Vocabulary of Terms Used in the InterPARES Project* No. 2, Vol. 1. University of British Columbia, 2002. Available online at http://www.interpares.org/documents/InterPARES%20Glossary%202002-1.pdf.

†141 *InterPARES: International Research on Permanent Authentic Records in Electronic Systems* [website]. The Project, 2002. Available online at http://www.interpares.org.

†142 "InterPARES Terminology Cross." Unpublished manuscript.

†143 "Intrinsic Value in Historical Material." National Archives and Records Administration, 1982. Staff Information Paper Number 21. Available online at http://www.archives.gov/research_room/alic/reference_desk/archives_resources/archival_material_intrinsic_value.html.

†144 *ISAD(G): General International Standard Archival Description.* International Council on Archives, 2000. Available online at http://www.ica.org/biblio/cds/isad_g_2e.pdf.

†145 "ISSN and the Key Title" [web page]. ISSN, n.d. Available online at http://www.issn.org:8080/English/pub/faqs/principle/.

†146 "ITU Announces New Edition of X.509 Recommendation . . ." [web page]. International Telecommunications Union, 31 March 2000. Available online at http://www.itu.int/ITU-T/news/sg7-x509.html.

†147 James, Caryn. "Split-screen images grabbing attention." *ContraCosta Times.com* 12 January 2004. Formerly online at http://www.contracostatimes.com/mld/cctimes/entertainment/movies/7690108.htm.

†148 Jansen, Eric. *NetLingo: The Internet Dictionary.* NetLingo, 2002.

†149 Jenkinson, Hilary. *A Manual of Archive Administration.* Percy Lund, Humphries, 1966.

†150 Jimerson, Rand. "Review of James M. O'Toole *Records of American Business.*" *Economic History Services Book Reviews.* EH.net, 11 May 1998. Available online at http://www.eh.net/bookreviews/library/0091.shtml.

†151 Johnson, Gary. "Forbidden Fruit: The Golden Age of the Exploitation Film [book review]." *Images: A Journal of Film and Popular Culture* Issue 8 (1999). Available online http://www.imagesjournal.com/issue08/reviews/forbiddenfruit/book.htm.

†152 Johnston, Pete, and Bridget Robinson. "Collections and Collection Description." *Collection Description Focus Briefing Paper 1.* UKOLN, January 2002. Available online at http://www.ukoln.ac.uk/cd-focus/briefings/bp1/bp1.pdf.

†153 Jones, Bernard E., ed. *Encyclopedia of Photography.* Arno, 1974. Reprint of the 1911 ed. published as *Cassell's Cyclopedia of Photography.*

†154 Kaplan, Elisabeth. "We Are What We Collect, We Collect What We Are: Archives and the Construction of Identity." *American Archivist* 63:1 (Spring/Summer 2000), p. 125–151.

†155 Kline, Mary-Jo. *A Guide to Documentary Editing.* – 2nd ed. Johns Hopkins University Press, 1998.

†156 Klopfer, Lisa. "Oral History and Archives in New South Africa: Methodological Issues." *Archivaria* 52 (Fall 2001), p. 100-125.

†157 Knowles, Elizabeth, with Julia Elliot. *The Oxford Dictionary of New Words.* Oxford University Press, 1997.

†158 Krizack, Joan D. *Documentation Planning for the U.S. Health Care System.* Johns Hopkins University Press, 1994.

†159 Lancaster, F. W. *Indexing and Abstracting in Theory and Practice* – 2nd ed. University of Illinois Graduate School of Library and Information Science, 1998.

†160 *Laura Zublake v. UBS Warburg LLC, UBS Warburg, UBS AG: Opinion and Order 02 Civ. 1243 (SAS).* U.S. District Court, Southern District of New York, 22 October 2003. Opinion of Justice Shira A. Scheindlin. Available online at http://www.nysd.uscourts.gov/courtweb/pdf/D02NYSC/03-08785.PDF.

†161 "The Laws on Openness" [web page]. Iowa Freedom of Information Council, n.d. Available online at http://www.drake.edu/journalism/foi/frameopenness_laws.html.

†162 LeFurgy, William G. "PDF-A: A New Digital Preservation Format." *Government Record News: The Newsletter of the Government Records Section of the Society of American Archivists* May–June 2003. Available online at http://www.archivists.org/saagroups/gov/newsletters/May2003.asp#digital.

†163 Leggio, Angeletta, Hilary Berthon, and Colin Webb. "A National Cellulose Acetate Search?" Presented to the First National Symposium, Book and Paper Group, AICCM, Canberra, March 2000. Available online at http://www.nla.gov.au/nla/staffpaper/2000/webb3.html.

†164 Lemieux, Victoria L. "Let the Ghosts Speak: An Empirical Exploration of the 'Nature' of the Record." *Archivaria* 51 (Spring 2001), p. 81–111.

†165 Lessig, Lawrence. "Some Like It Hot." *Wired* 12:3 (March 2004), p. 102–103. Available online at http://www.wired.com/wired/archive/12.03/lessig.html.

†166 Levy, David M. "Digital Libraries and the Problem of Purpose." *D-Lib* 6:1 (January 2000). Available online at http://www.dlib.org/dlib/january00/01levy.html.

†167 Levy, David M. *Scrolling Forward: Making Sense of Documents in the Digital Age.* Arcade, 2001.

†168 Levy, Steven. *Crypto: How the Code Rebels Beat the Government – Saving Privacy in the Digital Age.* Viking, 2001.

†169 Levy, Trudy. "Visual Resources Association – The Resource for Visual Information." *D-Lib Magazine* 8:2 (February 2002) Available online at http://www.dlib.org/dlib/february02/02inbrief.html#LEVY.

†170 Library of Congress. Network Development and MARC Standards Office. "MARC 21: Harmonized USMARC and CAN/MARC" [web page]. Library of Congress, 1998. Available online at http://www.loc.gov/marc/annmarc21.html.

†171 Linard, Laura, and Brent M. Sverdloff. "Not Just Business as Usual: Evolving Trends in Historical Research at Baker Library." *American Archivist* 60:1 (Winter 1997), p. 88–98.

†172 "LOCKSS" [website]. Stanford University, n.d. Available online at http://lockss.stanford.edu/.

†173 Long, Tony. "It's Just the 'internet' Now." *Wired News* 16 August 2004. Available online at http://www.wired.com/news/culture/0,1284,64596,00.html.

†174 Lubar, Steven. "Information Culture and the Archival Record." *American Archivist* 62:1 (Spring 1999), p. 10–22.

†175 Lynch, Clifford A. "Authenticity and Integrity in the Digital Environment: An Exploratory Analysis of the Central Role of Trust." *Authenticity in a Digital Environment* Council on Library and Information Resources, 2000. Available at http://www.clir.org/pubs/reports/pub92/contents.html.

†176 Lynch, Clifford A. "Institutional Repositories: Essential Infrastructure for Scholarship in the Digital Age." *ARL Bimonthly Report* 226 (February 2003). Available online at http://www.arl.org/newsltr/226/ir.html.

†177 Lynch, Jack. *Guide to Literary and Rhetorical Terms* [website]. The author, 1999. Available online at http://www.andromeda.rutgers.edu/~jlynch/Terms/.

†178 MacNeil, Heather. "Metadata Strategies and Archival Description: Comparing Apples to Oranges." *Archivaria* 39 (Spring 1995), p. 22–32.

†179 MacNeil, Heather. "Trusting Records in a Post-Modern World" [web page]. Institute for Advanced Technology in the Humanities, May 2002. Presentation at the University of Virginia. Available online at http://www.iath.virginia.edu/sds/macneil_text.htm.

†180 MacNeil, Heather. *Trusting Records: Legal, Historical, and Diplomatic Perspectives.* Kluwer, 2000. Quoted in Richard Cox. "Rediscovering the Document: Three Recent Views." *Records & Information Management Report* 18:3 (March 2002), p. 1–13.

†181 Maher, William J. "Archives, Archivists, and Society." *American Archivist* 61:2 (Fall 1998), p. 252–265. Incoming presidential address delivered 30 August 1997.

†182 *Management of Electronic Records: Issues and Guidelines.* Advisory Committee for the Co-ordination of Information Systems, United Nations, 1990.

†183 *A Manual for Small Archives.* Archives Association of British Columbia, 1999. Available online at http://aabc.bc.ca/aabc/msa/.

†184 "Manuscript Division Publications" [web page]. Manuscripts Division, Library of Congress, 1997. Text from *Library of Congress Acquisitions: Manuscripts, 1994–95* (the Library, 1997). Available online at http://www.loc.gov/rr/mss/msspubs.html.

†185 McCrank, Lawrence J. *Historical Information Science: An Emerging Unidiscipline.* Information Today, 2002.

†186 McCullagh, Adrian, and William Caelli. "Non-Repudiation in the Digital Environment." *First Monday* 5:8 (August 2000). Available online at http://www.firstmonday.dk/issues/issue5_8/mccullagh/

†187 McGovern, Timothy J., and Helen W. Samuels. "Our Institutional Memory at Risk." *Cause/Effect* 20:3 (Fall 1997), p. 19 ff.

†188 *McIntyre v. Ohio Elections Commission 514 US 334.* United States, Supreme Court, 19 April 1995. Available online at http://caselaw.lp.findlaw.com/scripts/getcase.pl?court=us&vol=514&invol=334.

†189 McRanor, Shauna. "A Critical Analysis of Intrinsic Value." *American Archivist* 59:4 (Fall 1996), p. 400–411.

†190 "METS: An Overview & Tutorial" [web page]. Library of Congress, 18 July 2003. Available online at http://www.loc.gov/standards/mets/METSOverview. v2.html.

†191 Miller, Frederic M. *Arranging and Describing Archives and Manuscripts.* Society of American Archivists, 1990.

†192 Monmonier, Mark. *How to Lie with Maps* – 2nd ed. University of Chicago Press, 1996.

†193 Moody, Glyn. "The Greatest OS That (N)ever Was (continued)." *Wired* 5:8 (August 1997). Available online at http://www.wired.com/wired/archive/ 5.08/linux.html.

†194 Moore, Reagan W. "Workshop on Research Challenges in Digital Archiving" [web page]. San Diego Super Computing Center, 2003. Available online at http://www.sdsc.edu/NARA/Publications/Web/NSF-preservation-4-03.ppt.

†195 "More about IFLA" [web page]. International Federation of Library Associations and Institutions, 23 April 2004. Available online at http://www. ifla.org/III/intro00.htm.

†196 Nadeau, Luis. *Encyclopedia of Printing, Photographic, and Photomechan-ical Processes.* Atelier Luis Nadeau, 1990.

†197 "NASCIO" [website]. National Association of State Chief Information Officers, n.d. Available online at https://www.nascio.org/.

†198 *National Archives and Records Administration* [website]. The agency, n.d. Available online a http://www.archives.gov/.

†199 *National Association of Government Archives and Records Administra-tors* [website]. The Association, n.d. Available online at http://www.nagara.org/.

†200 Nelson, Theodore Holm. "Xanalogical Structure, Needed Now More than Ever: Parallel Documents, Deep Links to Content, Deep Versioning and Deep Re-Use" [web page]. Xanadu.com, [23 May 2000?]. Available online at http://www.xanadu.com.au/ted/XUsurvey/xuDation.html.

†201 *Nevada Information Management Community Glossary.* Nevada State Library and Archives, 29 August 2001. Available online at http://dmla.clan.lib.nv.us/ docs/nsla/nerc/guidance/AcroGloss.htm.

†202 "New Orleans Notarial Archives" [web page]. New Orleans Notarial Archives, 2000–2004. Available online at http://www.notarialarchives.org/.

†203 Newhall, Beaumont. *The History of Photography: From 1839 to the Present* – revised and enlarged ed. Museum of Modern Art, 1982.

†204 *NFACE Project Overview: Purpose, Goals, and Activities: Final Report.* COSHRC and AASLH, July 2002. Available online at http://www.coshrc.org/ reports/NFACE/FinalReport/NFACEfinal.pdf.

†205 "NHPRC Strategic Plan" [web page]. National Archives and Records Administration, 19 June 1997. Available online at http://www.archives.gov/ grants/about_nhprc/strategic_plan.html.

†206 "19th Century American Landscape Painting." *Cosmopolis* 12 (December 2000). Available online at http://www.cosmopolis.ch/english/cosmo12/ americanlandscape.htm.

†207 "NTSC (National Television Systems Committee)" *Dictionary* @ *AudioVideo101* [web page]. AudioVideo101.com, n.d. Available online at http://www.audiovideo101.com/dictionary/dictionary.asp?dictionaryid=320.

†208 "NUCMC Frequently Asked Questions" [website]. Library of Congress, 23 September 2002. Available online at http://lcweb.loc.gov/coll/nucmc/newfaqs.html.

†209 *OASIS* [website]. Organization for the Advancements of Structured Information Standards, n.d. Available online at http://www.oasis-open.org/.

†210 OCLC/RLG Working Group on Preservation Metadata. *Preservation Metadata for Digital Objects: A Review of the State of the Art*. OCLC/RLG, 31 January 2001. A White Paper by the OCLC/RLG Working Group on Preservation Metadata. Available online at http://www.oclc.org/research/projects/pmwg/presmeta_wp.pdf.

†211 Olsen, Stefanie. "Yahoo crawls deep into the Web" [webpage]. CNET News.com, 2 March 2004. Available online at http://news.com.com/2100-1024-5167931.html.

†212 "An Online Guide to Information Technologies and Tools for Transportation Planning." Department of Urban Studies and Planning, Massachusetts Institute of Technology, 1996. Formerly online at http://yerkes.mit.edu/NARC/home.html.

†213 *Open Archives Initiative* [website]. The Initiative, n.d. Website available at http://www.openarchives.org/.

†214 *Open Source* [website]. Open Source Initiative, 2003. Available online at http://www.opensource.org/.

†215 O'Toole, James M. "'Commendatory Letters': An Archival Reading of the Venerable Bede." *American Archivist* 61:2 (Fall 1998), p. 266–286.

†216 *Our Culture, Our Future: Indigenous Cultural and Intellectual Property Rights.* Michael Frankel & Company and Terri Janke, 1998. Formerly online at http://www.icip.lawnet.com.au/index.html.

†217 "Papers / Files / Records / Archives: Advice for Clerks, and for Custodians of Record" [web page]. Library Committee of Quaker Life, March 2003.

†218 Parezo, Nancy. "Preserving Anthropology's Heritage: CoPAR, Anthropological Records, and the Archival Community." *American Archivist* 62:2 (Fall 1999), p. 271–306.

†219 Park, Eun G. "Understanding 'Authenticity' in Records and Information Management: Analyzing Practitioner Constructs." *American Archivist* 64:2 (Fall/Winter 2001), p. 270–291.

†220 Pederson, Ann, ed. *Keeping Archives*. Australian Society of Archivists, 1987.

†221 *Performance Guideline for the Legal Acceptance of Records Produced by Information Technology Systems*. Association for Information and Image Management, 1992.

†222 *Permanence of Paper for Publications and Documents in Libraries and Archives.* NISO, 1992.

†223 Personal communication with the author.

†224 Petroski, Henry. *The Book on the Bookshelf.* Alfred A. Knopf, 1999.

†225 "The Photographic Activity Test" [web page]. Image Permanence Institute, n.d. Available online at http://www.rit.edu/~661www1/sub_pages/8page8.htm.

†226 Pitti, Daniel V. "Creator Description: Encoded Archival Context." *Authority Control: Definition and International Experiences*. Florence, Italy; 10–12 February 2003. Available online at http://www.unifi.it/universita/biblioteche/ac/relazioni/pitti_eng.pdf.

†227 Pitti, Daniel V. "Encoded Archival Description: An Introduction and Overview." *D-Lib Magazine* 5:11 (November 1999). Available online at http://www.dlib.org/dlib/november99/11pitti.html.

†228 Pork, Henk J. *Rate of Paper Degradation: The Predictive Value of Artificial Aging Tests*. European Commission on Preservation and Access, 2000. Available online at http://www.knaw.nl/ecpa/publ/porck2.pdf.

†229 "Position Statement on Diversity" [web page]. Society of American Archivists, 1999. Available online at http://www.archivists.org/statements/diversity statement.asp.

†230 "The Preservation Environment and Climate Notebook: Information Sheet." Image Permanence Institute, Rochester Institute of Technology, 2002. Available online at http://www.rit.edu/~661www1/sub_pages/specsheetpr.pdf.

†231 *Preserving Email*. Digital Preservation Testbed, The Hague 2003. Part of the series *From Digital Volatility to Digital Permanence*. Available online at http://www.digitaleduurzaamheid.nl/bibliotheek/docs/volatility-permanence-email-en.pdf. The Digital Preservation Testbed is an initiative of the Dutch National Archives and the Dutch Ministry of the Interior and Kingdom Relations.

†232 "Principles of Institutional Evaluation" Society of American Archivists, n.d.

†233 "Privacy and Public Records" [web page]. Electronic Privacy Information Center, 28 April 2003. Available online at http://www.epic.org/privacy/publicrecords/.

†234 Puglia, Steven. "Reformatting and Copying Architectural Records." *Architectural Records Conference Report*. Conservation Center for Art and Historic Artifacts, 2000. Available online at http://www.ccaha.org/arch_rec/Puglia_lecture.htm.

†235 Puglia, Steven, Jeffrey Reed, and Erin Rhodes. *Technical Guidelines for Digitizing Archival Materials for Electronic Access: Creation of Production Master Files – Raster Images*. National Archives and Records Administration, 2004. Available online at http://www.archives.gov/research_room/arc/arc_info/techguide_raster_june2004.pdf.

†236 Quass, Annemarie. "Data warehousing principles for the strategic management of information: A synthesis of contemporary practices, theories and principles." *South African Business Review* December 2000.

†237 Ralston, Anthony, ed. *Encyclopedia of Computer Science* – 1st ed. Van Nostrand Reinhold, 1976.

†238 "Rare Books and Manuscript Section" [website]. Association of College and Research Libraries. Available online at http://www.rbms.nd.edu/.

†239 Raymond, Eric S., comp. *The New Hacker's Dictionary* – 2nd ed. MIT Press, 1994. Based on the *Jargon File*, first begun in 1975 by Raphael Finkel and maintained by an informal community and first published by Guy Steele as *The Hacker's Dictionary* (Harper and Row). Various versions are available on the web.

†240 *RDF Primer* [web page]. W3C, 2003. Available online at http://www.w3c.org/TR/rdf-primer/.

†241 *Records Management Standards and Procedures : Related Programs : Section 2.6.* British Columbia Ministry of Forests, 1997. Available online at http://www.for.gov.bc.ca/tasb/manuals/recman/rm2-6.htm.

†242 Reimer, Stephen R. "Manuscript Studies: Medieval and Early Modern" [website]. The author, 1998. Available online at http://www.ualberta.ca/~sreimer/ms-course/course/branchs.htm.

†243 *Report on Current Recordkeeping Practices within the Federal Government, prepared for the National Archives and Records Administration, prepared by SRA International.* National Archives and Records Administration, 10 December 2001. Prepared by SRA. Available online at http://www.archives.gov/records_management/initiatives/report_on_recordkeeping_practices.html.

†244 "Revised OSHA Records Management Program: ADM 12-0.4A" [web page]. Occupational Safety and Health Administration, 3 August 1998. Available online at http://www.osha.gov/pls/oshaweb/owadisp.show_document?p_table=DIREC TIVES &p_id=1474&p_search_str=&p_search_type= &p_status=CURRENT &p_text_version=FALSE.

†245 "RFC 2396 : Uniform Resource Identifiers (URI) : Generic Syntax." The Internet Society, 1998. Available online at http://www.ietf.org/rfc/rfc 2396.txt.

†246 Rivlin, Gary. "Leader of the Free World: How Linus Torvalds Became Benevolent Dictator of Planet Linux, the Biggest Collaborative Project in History." *Wired* 11:11 (November 2003). Available online at http://www.wired.com/wired/archive/11.11/linus.html.

†247 Robek, Mary F., Gerald F. Brown, and David O. Stephens. *Information and Records Management: Document-Based Information Systems.* McGraw-Hill, 1996.

†248 Roberts, Matt T., and Don Etherington. *Bookbinding and the Conservation of Books: A Dictionary of Descriptive Terminology.* United States, Government Printing Office, 1982. Citations in this glossary are taken from an online version prepared in 1994 by Walter Henry, available at http://palimpsest.stanford.edu/don/don.html.

†249 Robyns, Marcus C. "The Archivist as Educator: Integrating Critical Thinking Skills into Historical Research Methods Instruction." *American Archivist* 64:2 (Fall/Winter 2001), p. 363–394.

†250 Rosenblatt, Betsy. "Moral Rights Basics" [website]. Harvard Law School, 1998. Available online at http://cyber.law.harvard.edu/property/library/moral primer.html.

†251 Ross, Seamus, Martin Donnelly, and Milena Dobreva. *New Technologies for the Cultural and Scientific Heritage Sector: DigiCULT Technology Watch Report 1.* European Commission, 2003. Available online at http://www.digicult.info/downloads/twr2003_01_high.pdf.

†252 *Rules for Archival Description [RAD].* Bureau of Canadian Archivists, 1990. Prepared under the direction of the Planning Committee on Descriptive Standards.

†253 Russell, Beth M., and Robin L. Brandt Hutchinson. "Official Publications at Texas A&M University: A Case Study in Cataloging Archival Material." *American Archivist* 63:1 (Spring/Summer 2000), p. 175–184.

†254 "SAA and Others Question Constitutionality of Copyright Term Extension" [web page]. Society of American Archivists, n.d. Available online at http://www.archivists.org/news/copyright_amicus.asp.

†255 Samuels, Helen Willa. "Who Controls the Past?" *American Archivist* 49:2 (Spring 1986), p. 109–124).

†256 Santosus, Megan, and Jon Surmacz. "The ABCs of Knowledge Management" [website]. CIO.com, 23 May 2001. Available online at http://www.cio.com/research/knowledge/edit/kmabcs.html.

†257 Sauer, Cynthia K. "Doing the Best We Can? The Use of Collection Development Policies and Cooperative Collecting Activities at Manuscript Repositories." *American Archivist* 64:2 (Fall/Winter 2001), p. 308–349.

†258 Schwartz, Joan M. "'We make our tools and our tools make use': Lessons from Photographs for the Practice, Politics, and Poetics of Diplomacy." *Archivaria* 40 (Fall 1995), p. 40–74.

†259 Schellenberg, Theodore. "The Appraisal of Modern Public Records" *Modern Archives Reader: Basic Readings on Archival Theory and Practice.* National Archives and Records Service, 1984, p. 57–70. Edited by Maygene F. Daniels and Timothy Walch.

†260 Schmelzer, Ronald. "'Open' is a Four-Letter Word." *SearchWebServices* [website]. ZapThink, 1 April 2003. Available online at http://searchweb services.techtarget.com/originalContent/0,289142,sid26_gci 890730,00.html.

†261 Sebera, Donald K. *Isoperms: An Environmental Management Tool.* Commission on Preservation and Access, 1994. Available online at http://www.clir.org/pubs/reports/isoperm/isoperm.html.

†262 *Sedona Principles: Best Practices Recommendations & Principles for Addressing Electronic Document Production.* Sedona Conference, 2003. Available online at http://www.thesedonaconference.org/miscFiles/SedonaPrinciples 200303.

†263 Sellen, Abigail J., and Richard H. R. Harper. *Myth of the Paperless Office.* MIT Press, 2002.

†264 Sickinger, James. "Literacy, Documents, and Archives in the Ancient Athenian Democracy." *American Archivist* 62:2 (Fall 1999), p. 229–246.

†265 Skupsky, Donald S., and John C. Montaña. *Law, Records and Information Management: The Court Cases.* Information Requirements Clearinghouse, 1994. The authors' extensive references to case law have been omitted from the citations.

†266 Smith, Abby. "Authenticity in Perspective." *Authenticity in a Digital Environment.* Council on Library and Information Resources, May 2000. p. 69–75. Available online at http://www.clir.org/pubs/abstract/pub92abst.html.

†267 "SOAP Version 1.2 Part 1: Messaging Framework" [web page]. World Wide Web Consortium, June 2003. Available online at http://www.w3.org/TR/SOAP/.

†268 Söderberg, Johan. "Copyleft vs. Copyright: A Marxist Critique." *First Monday* 7:3 (4 March 2002). Available online at http://firstmonday.org/issues/issue7_3/soderberg/index.html.

†269 Spingarn-Koff, Jason. "Look Ma, I'm a Multimedia Artist." *Wired* 8:6 (19 June 2000). Available online at http://www.wired.com/news/culture/0,1284,37054,00.html.

†270 St. Laurent, Simon. *XML Elements of Style.* McGraw-Hill, 2000.

†271 "Standard Administrative Procedure: 61.99.01.M0.01–Records Management." Texas A&M University, revised 26 February 2002. Available online at http://rules.tamu.edu/saps/619901M001.htm.

†272 *Statement of Principles.* International Conference on Cataloguing Principles, October 1961. Commonly known as the *Paris Principles.* Available online at http://www.ddb.de/news/pdf/paris_principles_1961.pdf.

†273 Steemson, Michael. "Confident Australian Records Managers Pick Up the Challenge of the Future" [web page]. Caldeson Consultancy, n.d. Available online at http://www.caldeson.com/confidnt.html.

†274 Stephens, David O., and Roderick C. Wallace. "Electronic Records Retention: Fourteen Basic Principles." *ARMAil Central New York* 10:4 (March 2001). Available online at http://archives.syr.edu/cnyarma/ARMAil0301.pdf.

†275 Suderman, Jim. "Context, Structure and Content: New Criteria for Appraising Electronic Records" [webpage]. 2 November 2001. Available online at http://www.rbarry.com/suderman-wholepaper7_postscript011102.htm.

†276 *A Survey of Key Concepts and Issues for Electronic Recordkeeping: CTG.MFA-001.* Center for Technology in Government, State University of New York at Albany/SUNY, August 1997. Available online at http://www.ctg.albany.edu/publications/reports/key_concepts/key_concepts.pdf.

†277 *Taxonomy and Content Classification: Market Milestone Report: Featuring a Delphi Group Assessment of Verity.* Delphi Group, 2002.

†278 *Thesaurus for Graphic Materials.* Cataloging and Distribution Service, Library of Congress, 1995. Compiled and edited by the Prints and Photographs Division, Library of Congress.

†279 *Thomas: Legislative Information on the Internet* [website]. Library of Congress, n.d. Available online a http://thomas.loc.gov.

†280 "The 12 Rules of OLAP." *Byte.* June 1994 Special Report. Available online at http://www.byte.com/art/9406/sec8/art11.htm.

†281 *United States Code.* United States, Government Printing Office. Available online through the Legal Information Institute of the Cornell University Law School at http://straylight.law.cornell.edu/uscode/.

†282 "USNP Preservation Microfilming Guidelines" [web page]. Library of Congress, 19 July 2002. Available online at http://www.loc.gov/preserv/usnpspecs.html.

†283 "Universal Preservation Format Glossary" [web page]. WGBH, n.d. Available online at http://info.wgbh.org/upf/glossary.html.

†284 "URIs, URLs, and URNs: Clarifications and Recommendations 1.0" [web page]. World Wide Web Consortium/IETF URI Planning Interest Group, 21 September 2001. Available online at http://www.w3.org/TR/uri-clarification/.

†285 *USMARC Specifications for Record Structure, Character Sets, and Exchange Media.* Network Development and MARC Standards Office, Library of Congress, 1994.

†286 Walne, Peter, ed. *Dictionary of Archival Terminology: English and French with Equivalents in Dutch, German, Italian, Russian and Spanish* – 2nd ed. K. G. Saur, 1988. ICA Handbook Series, Volume 7.

†287 Weber, Lisa B. "Archival Description Standards: Concepts, Principles, and Methodologies." *American Archivist* 52:4 (Fall 1989), p. 504–513.

†288 Weber, Lisa B. "Record Formatting: MARC AMC." *Describing Archival Materials: The Use of the MARC AMC Format.* Hayworth Press, 1990. Richard P. Smiraglia, ed. Issued separately and as a special issue of *Cataloging and Classification Quarterly* 11:3–4.

†289 *Webopedia* [website]. Internet.com, n.d. Available online at http://www.webopedia.com/.

†290 "Welcome to the School of Informatics Homepage" [website]. The School, Edinburgh University, n.d. Available online at http://www.inf.ed.ac.uk/.

†291 "What are PI and TWPI?" [web page]. Image Permanence Institute, n.d. Available online at http://www.rit.edu/~661www1/sub_pages/8page17a1.htm.

†292 "What is an 'Agency Record?'" *FOIA Update* 2:1 (Fall 1980). Available online at http://www.usdoj.gov/oip/foia_updates/Vol_II_1/page3.htm.

†293 "What is Grey Literature?" [web page]. New York Academy of Medicine Library, 2002. Available online at http://www.nyam.org/library/greywhat. shtml.

†294 "What We Collect: Manuscripts" [web page]. National Library of Australia, n.d. Available online at http://www.nla.gov.au/ms/mscoll.html.

†295 *Whatis.Com: Look It Up: Definitions for Thousands of the Most Current IT-Related Words* [website]. TechTarget, 2000– . Available online at http://whatis.com/.

†296 "What's New: Electronic Commerce Forms: Requirements, Issues, and Solutions." Cohasset Associates, n.d. Formerly online at http://www.cohasset. com/main/library/coh_articles/whatnew_body_ecforms.htm.

†297 Williams, Don. "Debunking of Specmanship." *RLG DigiNews* 7:1 (15 February 2003). Available online at http://www.rlg.org/preserv/diginews/v7_v1_ feature1.html.

†298 Wynar, Bohdan S.; Arlene G. Taylor, ed. *Introduction to Cataloging and Classification* – 8th ed. Libraries Unlimited, 1992.

†299 "XML Schema" [web page]. World Wide Web Consortium, 2000. Available online at http://www.w3.org/XML/Schema.

†300 Yates, JoAnne. *Control Through Communication: The Rise of System in American Management.* Johns Hopkins University Press, 1989.

†301 Zwaneveld, Eddy. "Message, 17 August 2000" *AMIA-L* [Listserv archives]. Association of Moving Image Archivists, 1999– . Available online at http://lsv.uky.edu/archives/amia-l.html.

About the Author

Richard Pearce-Moses has worked as an archivist for more than 20 years and has been a Certified Archivist since 1989. A specialist in photographic archives, he authored a statewide catalog of photographic collections in Texas and has regularly taught workshops on the administration of photographic archives for the Society of American Archivists (SAA).

Pearce-Moses also has worked with local and state government records and collections of historical and personal papers at the University of Texas, the Texas State Library and Archives, Arizona State University, and the Heard Museum, Phoenix. Currently he is working at the Arizona State Library and Archives to establish programs to manage electronic records and digital government information.

His service to the archival profession includes membership on the SAA Committee on Archival Information Exchange, SAA liaison to the USMARC Advisory Board, chair of SAA's Visual Materials Section, member of Council, and 2005-2006 SAA president. He also has served on numerous national and international archival research projects.

Pearce-Moses has a bachelor's degree in photojournalism and a master's degree in American Studies from the University of Texas at Austin, and a master's degree in library and information science from the University of Illinois at Urbana-Champaign.